Handbook of Justice Research in Law

Handbook of Justice Research in Law

Edited by

Joseph Sanders

University of Houston Law Center
University of Houston
Houston, Texas

and

V. Lee Hamilton

Department of Sociology
University of Maryland
College Park, Maryland

Kluwer Academic / Plenum Publishers

New York, Boston, Dordrecht, London, Moscow

Library of Congress Cataloging-in-Publication Data

Handbook of justice research in law/edited by Joseph Sanders and V. Lee Hamilton.
p. cm.
Includes bibliographical references and index.
ISBN 0-306-46340-7
1. Justice. 2. Sociological jurisprudence. I. Sanders, Joseph. II. Hamilton, V. Lee.

K240 .H36 2001
340'.11—dc21

00-049774

ISBN 0-306-46340-7

233 Spring Street, New York, N.Y. 10013

http://www.wkap.nl/

10 9 8 7 6 5 4 3 2 1

A C.I.P. record for this book is available from the Library of Congress

Printed in the United States of America

Contributors

William P. Bridges, *Department of Sociology, University of Illinois at Chicago, Chicago, Illinois 60607*

Karen S. Cook, *Department of Sociology, Stanford University, Stanford, California 94305*

Barry C. Feld, *University of Minnesota Law School, Minneapolis, Minnesota 55455*

William L. F. Felstiner, *Cardiff University Law School, Cardiff, United Kingdom, and Law and Society Program, University of California, Santa Barbara, Santa Barbara, California 93106*

V. Lee Hamilton, *Department of Sociology, University of Maryland, College Park, Maryland 20742*

Valerie P. Hans, *Department of Psychology, University of Delaware, Wilmington, Delaware 19802*

Karen A. Hegtvedt, *Department of Sociology, Emory University, Atlanta, Georgia 30322*

Deborah R. Hensler, *Stanford University Law School, Stanford, California 94305*

Robert Howard, *Department of Political Science, Georgia State University, Atlanta, Georgia 30303*

Kwok Leung, *Department of Management, City University of Hong Kong, Hong Kong, China*

E. Allen Lind, *Fuqua School of Business, Duke University, Durham, North Carolina 27708*

Jill McCorkel, *Department of Sociology, Northern Illinois University, De Kalb, Illinois 60115*

Michael W. Morris, *Graduate School of Business, Stanford University, Stanford, California 94305*

Robert L. Nelson, *Department of Sociology, Northwestern University, Evanston, Illinois 60208*

Ben Pettit, *Department of Political Science, University of California, Santa Barbara, Santa Barbara, California 93106*

Joseph Sanders, *University of Houston Law Center, Houston, Texas 77204*

Frederika E. Schmitt, *Department of Sociology and Anthropology, Millersville University, Millersville, Pennsylvania 17551*

John Scholz, *Department of Political Science, State University of New York at Stony Brook, Stony Brook, New York 11794*

Tom R. Tyler, *Department of Psychology, New York University, New York, New York 10003*

Neil Vidmar, *Duke University Law School, Durham, North Carolina 27706*

Preface

Justice—a word of great simplicity and almost frightening scope. When we were invited to edit a volume on justice in law, we joked about the small topic we had been assigned. Often humor masks fear, and this was certainly one of those times. Throughout the project, we found daunting the task of covering even a fraction of the topics that usually fall under the umbrella of justice research in law.

Ultimately, the organization of the book emerged from the writing of it. Our introductory chapter provides a road map to how the topics weave together, but as is so often the case it was written last, not first. It was only when we had chapters in hand that we began to see how the many strands of justice research might be woven together. Chapters 2–4 on the basic forms of justice—procedural, retributive, and distributive—are the lynchpin of the volume; they provide the building blocks that permit us to think and write about each of the other substantive and applied chapters in terms of how they relate to the fundamental forms of justice. In the large central section of the volume (Chapters 5–9), the contributors address many ways in which the justice dimensions relate to one another. Most important for law is the relationship of perceptions of procedural justice and the two types of substantive justice—retributive and distributive. The final section of the book (Chapters 10 and 11) turns to the larger question of whether conceptions of justice in the legal context differ depending on one's gender or culture.

Our first and greatest debt is to the authors of the individual chapters who provided us with so much wonderful material and whose messages seem to us to weave together to create a whole larger than the sum of the parts. It is nevertheless true that, although the contributions here are substantial, they are not all that could have been said on the topic. We sought coverage of several other topics without success: in some cases, such as race, we were unable to find anyone to agree to contribute; in several others, we received initial agreements but the authors were for one or another reason unable to complete their chapters. This is almost always true of edited volumes and we mention it only with the goal of freeing up the readers' imaginations. If you can imagine a topic related to justice, it probably could have appeared here. It may even be one we sought to have do so. Most important, we believe that any of a dozen or more other topics—had they resulted in chapters to this volume—could have been organized under the same umbrella as the one that appears in the finished work. We believe that the essays that are included provide the reader with a good sense of where research on justice in law stands today as well as fruitful ideas about how to extend our knowledge in the future.

Aside from our fundamental debt to the authors of the chapters that appear here, we are indebted to Bruce Sales and Felice Levine, and to the personnel at Kluwer Academic / Plenum

Publishers, especially our editor, Eliot Werner, and production editor, Tuan Hoang. They each helped to inspire the work and, in their own ways, gave it its final shape.

Beverly Ward at the University of Houston devoted many hours organizing the materials making certain that the chapters conformed to a uniform style. Her efforts are very much appreciated.

Completing this project would have been more difficult without the support of our respective universities. We would like to thank Dean Irwin Goldstein at the University of Maryland and the University of Houston Law Foundation.

The work that went into soliciting and editing the chapters was indirectly supported in part by the National Science Foundation (grants SES-9113914 and SES-913967). Those grants, which supported work on conceptions of responsibility in organizations across cultures, provided us the breathing space to think about justice at the same time.

In the last analysis, trying to encompass justice in its manifold forms—in such a way as to enlighten ourselves about its reach through and around the law—has been a humbling experience as well as an exciting one. We feel that we have learned much more than we have taught. In that spirit, we invite you to join us in the search for justice.

Joseph Sanders
V. Lee Hamilton

Contents

I

Introduction

1

Justice and Legal Institutions

Joseph Sanders and V. Lee Hamilton

All virtue is summed up in dealing justly.
Aristotle (1953:141)

A. INTRODUCTION

Justice is a fundamental concept in social life. Often we speak of justice or injustice when discussing the great events of the day, but a sense of injustice also frequently results from the quotidian events in our life. Consider, for example, the following, all-too-common experience of those of us who commute to work by automobile. At some point along the route cars must queue up in one lane to exit onto another road. The queue stretches for several hundred yards, with traffic moving forward in fits and starts. Inevitably, some cars cut in line far ahead of those who have lined up at the back of the exit queue. The near-universal reaction to such behavior is anger at the interloper and a sense that what we have witnessed is an occasion of injustice.

Justice concerns do not end with our commute. Eventually, we arrive at work and begin our daily tasks. Around 10 a.m. a co-worker comes by and says he has just been told he was not getting an expected promotion. According to the co-worker, the boss never liked him and gave him no opportunity to make an argument as to why he, rather than someone else, should get the new position. That evening, sitting at the dinner table, we tell our spouse about the co-worker and also about a recent new employee who, it is alleged, was hired only because he is a nephew of the boss. Again a sense of injustice arises.

As these examples indicate, justice is a yardstick against which we measure everything from the world economic and social order to the events of everyday life. Indeed, our dinner table conversation may range over a variety of topics: the appropriateness of the death penalty for a recently convicted killer, impeachment proceedings against the President, the denouement in Clint Eastwood's film *The Unforgiven* (Miller, 1998). In each case, questions of justice are never far from the surface.

Joseph Sanders • University of Houston Law Center, Houston, Texas 77204. V. Lee Hamilton • Department of Sociology, University of Maryland, College Park, Maryland 20742.

Handbook of Justice Research in Law, edited by Sanders and Hamilton. Kluwer Academic / Plenum Publishers, New York, 2000.

Obviously only a small slice of a topic as broad as justice could ever be captured in one book. Much of what is important must be left in the background. In this volume two factors narrow the scope of our discussion. First, the book focuses on law and legal institutions. Some of the essays in the book deal with justice considerations in specific legal areas such as lawyer–client relations. All of the chapters explicitly address the question of how justice considerations affect legal arrangements. Second, the essays are empirical. They focus on what social science research can tell us about perceptions of justice and how those perceptions affect our attitudes and behaviors.

B. JUSTICE AND LAW

Nowhere are justice concerns closer to the surface than in law. In part, this is because law's normative validity is tied to a sense of justice. Absent a belief that legal arrangements are just, the line between the tax man and the thief, between a court and a kangaroo court are blurred if not erased. A law's legitimacy, its "rightness" depends in part on a perception that it is just. When Solomon cleverly discovered the true mother of a child by threatening to have it cut in half he accomplished more than resolve a dispute in a particular case. Then and now, the report of the trial served the greater purpose of demonstrating that he was a leader who would produce just outcomes and who, therefore, deserved to have his commands obeyed. As Solomon and others in authority positions quickly realize, naked power is rarely sufficient in itself to command compliance. Without a sense that decision makers and arrangements are just, compliance is an instrumental decision, one made within the calculus of gain and loss, apprehension versus successful avoidance. A sense of justice, however, engenders normative obedience. Laws may be obeyed and judicial outcomes honored because people perceive them to be legitimate. They ought to be followed because people come to believe one should voluntarily obey commands of authorities even when to do so is contrary to one's self-interest and one's individual morality (Tyler, 1990). Justice research helps us to understand why some laws and some legal regimes are felt to be legitimate while others are not.

There is a second reason why justice is particularly important in legal contexts. As Holmes said, "law is the witness and external deposit of our moral life" (Holmes, 1897). We look to law to assess the direction of our moral compass. Groups often fight over the content of law for symbolic as well as instrumental reasons. For example, Joseph Gusfield explains the movement to enshrine Prohibition in the Constitution as a "symbolic crusade" led by nativist groups wishing to affirm their control of the moral contours of the society (Gusfield, 1963). Today, both those who oppose the death penalty and those who oppose the decriminalization of abortion find fault with the law because they believe it is an external marker of an unjust society.

However, if the idea of justice is central to legal discourse, its existence is frequently controversial. In part, this is because law is not a perfect witness of our moral life. Law is at least partially autonomous from the society around it and, therefore, the application of legal rules does not perfectly reflect the "just" outcome that might be achieved in a nonlegal setting, frequently because of a commitment to some uniquely legal principle. Rules of evidence routinely deviate from everyday means of persuasion (O'Barr, 1982; Conley and O'Barr, 1990). Even decision rules have unique legal components. An example might be the common law's commitment to the doctrine of *stare decisis*.[1]

The controversy surrounding legal outcomes also reflects the different expectations and goals people may bring to disputes. If a hope of justice propels litigants to the courtroom and interest groups to the legislature, a sense of injustice sometimes drives people to riot following unacceptable legal outcomes. Trials by definition pit two parties, and sometimes two communities against each other; communities who have different views of what constitutes justice. The different responses of the white and black communities to the outcomes in the O. J. Simpson criminal and civil trials are a high-profile example. In sum, many justice norms come from outside the law itself and are not uniformly distributed in the society. If we are to understand justice norms within the legal context we must first look outside the law to perceptions of justice in the society at large.

C. EMPIRICAL STUDY OF JUSTICE

Debates about justice routinely make appeals to normative judgments. At the societal level, normative arguments undergird various theories of social justice (Habermas, 1996; Rawls, 1971; Nozick, 1974; Barry, 1989). Normative arguments also play an important role in discussions about particular areas of law. Within the area of criminal law, for example, people debate the types of conduct that are the appropriate occasions for the application of criminal sanction (Packer, 1968; Feinberg, 1970). Once individuals are convicted, people debate whether we ought to pursue rehabilitative or just-desert models of criminal sanctioning (Braithwaite and Pettit, 1990).

Normative though they may be, these justice arguments often are premised on empirical assumptions. For example, within the criminal law the movement away from rehabilitative models and indeterminate sentencing and toward just-desert models and determinate sentencing in the 1980s was premised in large part on research findings that rehabilitative programs did little to reduce recidivism (Greenberg, 1977; Allen, 1981; Spader, 1986). Even at the societal level, normative arguments often have empirical underpinnings. John Rawls's argument for his well-known "difference principle" for the distribution of goods and benefits in society appears to be based in part on a theory of social envy which suggests that increasing inequality can produce strains that are difficult for a stable society to endure (Rawls, 1971). Social science research on this point may inform the normative debate about just distributions.

Moreover, justice concepts themselves have become the focus of empirical research. Researchers may ask individuals their opinion as to whether a proposed law or a court outcome is just. For example, we might inquire as to whether U.S. immigration policy is just, whether employees of the Immigration and Naturalization Service (INS) treat people fairly, or whether an individual's expulsion from the country was a just result. Justice research permits us to map the nature and scope of between-group differences (and similarities) on immigration questions as well as a large number of other topics such as the justness of the welfare system or the tax code.[2] Simple questions such as these are but the tip of the iceberg when it comes to justice research today. In the last two or three decades empirical research on justice has grown enormously in both volume and sophistication. This book surveys these research findings.

D. THE DIMENSIONS OF JUSTICE

Thus far we have spoken of justice as if it were a unitary concept. This is not true. As the examples at the beginning of this introduction suggest, the sense of injustice may occur for a variety of reasons. We may experience a lack of justice along several different dimensions. The first three essays are organized around three core justice dimensions: retributive justice, procedural justice, and distributive justice. These dimensions may be thought of as three basic building blocks. When any of these are violated we are often left with a sense of injustice as the examples that began this chapter indicate. Were one set to the task of constructing a set of legal institutions that would enjoy the legitimacy and support of citizens in a society, one would wish to create decision making apparatuses that address all three dimensions. We begin with retributive justice.

1. Retributive (Corrective) Justice

Retribution is a passionate reaction to the violation of a rule, norm, or law that evokes a desire for punishment of the violator (Durkheim, 1893/1964: 85–96). Consider again the commuting experience. When drivers cut in front of the line our anger is, at least in part, a reaction to the fact that we know that they will "get away with it." Nothing will happen although we sorely wish that it would. It is this impulse that served as the inspiration for a wacky episode in the 1932 W. C. Fields film *If I Had a Million*. Fields inherits a million dollars from an eccentric stranger. With part of his newfound wealth he buys a fleet of secondhand cars and hires people to drive them. Fields then lines everyone up in a parade and takes to the road. Whenever he observes a roadhog, Fields signals the car immediately behind him and the driver peels out of line to crash into the offender. Fields, like us in the exit queue, wants retribution and at least while we are driving to work we are likely to think that he spent his inheritance wisely. He has, after all, restored balance to the moral order. He has given us hope that maybe it is a "just world" after all (Lerner, 1980).

Neil Vidmar's opening essay on retributive justice explores the desire for retribution and revenge. He notes that retribution may be the oldest, most basic, and most pervasive justice reaction associated with human social life. Here we should note that the concept of retributive justice is a very close relative of the concept of corrective justice. It might be said that retributive justice focuses somewhat more on the subjective psychological reaction of the victim while corrective justice concerns itself with a more objective analysis of what is needed to restore the status quo ante. As a consequence, retributive justice is more emotive and less cognitive. Jules Coleman suggests that retributive justice is concerned with punishment whereas corrective justice is concerned with compensation (Coleman, 1992:348–354). To the degree this is the case, retributive justice is more concerned with what happens to a wrongdoer whereas corrective justice is more concerned with what happens to the wrongdoer's victim. These differences, however, should not obscure the substantial degree to which the terms are synonyms (Aristotle, 1953:148–153). Both are concerned with our perceptions of what is required to "set things right" after some untoward event. In this sense, both are backward looking. They attempt to adjust the current state of affairs to compensate for something that happened in the past. But, as Vidmar notes, both are also forward looking. A social psychological analysis of retributive and corrective justice must recognize the future impact of punishment on things such as restoring both the self-worth of the victim and the group norms and values that are cast in doubt by the offense (Vidmar, this volume, p. 39).

From one point of view, retributive justice is the more fundamental concept. Insofar as the legal right to pursue a corrective justice remedy (e.g., tort damages for an injury) is given to the aggrieved or injured party, it is sometimes thought of as a civilized transformation of a more basic instinct that one is entitled to "settle a score" or to "get even" with one who has wronged me. The fact that it is the injured party, and not others, who is given "standing" to pursue a legal remedy reveals the quasi-retributive nature of recourse (Zipursky, 1998). It is not essential, however, to resolve the issue of primacy. What is important is to recognize that the retributive/corrective justice dimension concerns *both* the wrongdoer and the wronged.

Most research on retribution has taken place within the context of formal legal processes, especially those involving criminal justice issues. The anger felt by victims of crime frequently translates into an urge to punish, to set things right. In response, societies everywhere have institutionalized mechanisms for dealing with violations of social prohibitions. These mechanisms serve to assuage the victim and at the same time to define the boundaries and social values of groups. The mechanisms also put constraints of proportionality and impersonality around an otherwise potentially unbridled desire for revenge.

Within court and correctional systems, proportionality is concerned with factors such as the severity of the wrong, the wrongdoer's responsibility and remorse, equity across wrongdoers, and, sometimes, the needs of the wrongdoer. Vidmar reminds us that while formal legal systems may normatively specify the conditions of proportionality of punishment, a social psychological analysis must treat proportionality as an empirical issue. Do victims or third parties apply a cognitive formula of proportionality or do they respond without regard to proportionality? If they do employ a proportionality formula, how similar is it to that of the legal system? When legal regimes reflect individual and societal proportionality norms they are more likely to achieve retributive justice. There is some evidence that criminal sanctions generally do conform to societal norms (Rossi and Berk, 1997) but this does not mean they conform to those of the victim or the victim's family.

Vidmar notes that outside criminal justice issues relatively little research has been directed at revenge as a psychological and social phenomenon. His essay attempts to correct this situation by indicating how the research should include other areas and by drawing attention to the close nexus between retribution and research on anger, aggression, and violence. Understanding this relationship is a stepping stone toward a larger issue that dominates the last pages of Vidmar's essay. What set of institutional mechanisms are most likely to restore homeostasis for the victim while at the same time avoiding a cycle of revenge and retribution that sometimes consumes families, communities, and even whole societies (Miller, 1990)? For example, to what extent does the impersonality of legal procedures persuade individuals to accept outcomes that fall short of their particular sense of retributive and corrective justice? This question directs our attention to the second justice dimension: procedural justice.

2. Procedural Justice

As **Tom Tyler** and **Allan Lind** note in their essay, procedural justice research is concerned with people's "reactions to decisions of legal authorities, their acceptance of legal rules, and their assessment of the fairness of the procedures through which decisions are made and rules applied." Issues of procedural justice reach beyond the courtroom, however. They may arise whenever a third party makes a decision about an individual's responsibility or entitlements.

A central finding in the early procedural justice research conducted by Thibaut and Walker (Thibaut and Walker, 1975) was that when compared with individuals who experienced nonadversary procedures, individuals who experienced adversary trial procedures rated them as fairer and the verdict as more satisfactory. This outcome was extended to a more general result that an opportunity for "voice," for a chance to tell one's story, generally increased the perceived fairness of the procedure and of the outcome. Early interpretations of this result were largely instrumental. The procedures are fairer because they increase the individual's control over the process and thereby increase one's influence on the ultimate decision. Newer theories of procedural justice recognize the noninstrumental dimension of procedural justice. For example, Tyler and Lind developed a "group-value" theory of procedural justice that emphasizes "the symbolic and psychological implications of procedures for feelings of inclusion in society and for the belief that the institution using the procedure holds the person in high regard" (Tyler and Lind, this volume, p. 75). The theory points to three factors that are important to the belief that procedures are fair: neutrality (the authority engages in evenhanded treatment), trust (the authority tries to be fair), and status recognition (the authority treats one politely, with dignity, and with respect for one's rights and opinions). Their chapter discusses this and later theoretical variations premised on the idea that the real sting of procedural unfairness is its diminution of one's social self-identity.

The failure of our co-worker mentioned at the beginning of this chapter to get the promotion involves questions of procedural justice. The "procedure" he experienced seems objectionable in several ways. He was given no chance to make an appeal for the job and he believed that the "judge" (his boss) was not impartial. In such a situation it is quite unlikely that the co-worker will accept this result. If, however, the co-worker had been given an opportunity to make an argument as to why he should get the promotion, if he believed that his argument was fairly considered, and if he felt that his boss was neutral and impartial, the research reviewed by Tyler and Lind indicates he would have more readily accepted the decision. This is so even if the co-worker believes the outcome itself was unfair. Indeed, under many circumstances overall impressions of fairness are more strongly influenced by procedural factors than by outcomes.

This does not mean procedure universally trumps distributive and retributive considerations. An individual's assessment of the distributive justice of a decision has a greater impact on behavior than it does on attitudes. One is less likely to comply with a decision that is perceived to be distributively unjust (Tyler, 1990:103). Moreover, the ability of procedural justice perceptions to dampen disappointment from perceived retributive or distributive injustices depends in part on the primacy of procedural justice information. If we come to believe the procedure is fair this judgment anchors our overall assessment to such an extent that subsequent outcome information has relatively little effect. When we are presented with distributive justice information first, however, subsequent procedural justice assessment has a much smaller impact. According to Tyler and Lind this suggests that "procedural justice judgments and distributive judgments may be less distinct cognitively than has been thought to be the case—one type of justice judgment can apparently be substituted for another as people generate overall impressions of how they are being treated" (Tyler and Lind, this volume, p. 78). This leads us to the third justice dimension: distributive justice.

3. Distributive Justice

If it were up to us, how would we allocate such things as rights, wealth, income, and love? These are questions of distributive justice. As **Karen Hegtvedt** and **Karen Cook** note in their chapter on distributive justice, much of the social science work in this area has examined the conditions under which allocations will be defined as just or equitable. Almost everyone now agrees that there are multiple distributive justice principles, not one. When individuals are instructed to pursue fairness, they apply different allocation rules depending on the situation. "Generally, people specify equitable or contributions-based rules in work situations where productivity is a central concern, an equal division where group harmony is paramount, and a needs-based distribution rule in contexts focusing on social welfare" (Hegtvedt and Cook, this volume, p. 96).

When our company hired the boss's nephew earlier in this chapter, it raised a distributive justice concern. Desert-like equitable rules tend to dominate workplace allocations. Among a set of applicants, the most qualified, i.e., those who will make the greatest contribution to the organization, should be hired. Because the new employee is the boss's nephew, we are uncertain that this distributive justice principle has been applied and the allegation that he was hired *only* because he was related to the boss implies that the hire was unjust because it was not based on contribution-based rules.

Consider how we would feel, however, if we had heard that the boss had redrafted his will, that the boss had no spouse and no children, and that he had named his nephew and two nieces as the equal beneficiaries of his estate solely because of their biological relationship to him. The fact that for most people this outcome seems less unjust than the boss's decision to employ his nephew tells us, among other things, that the contribution principle does not define just distributions in every exchange.

The will drafting example allows us to make one additional point. Consider how we would react on discovering that the boss had summarily excluded us from his will. Very few would consider this an occasion of an injustice. In this context we do not believe that the boss had an obligation to extend his justice concern universally to all fellow humans. Generally, the scope of justice concerns will vary depending on the allocation being made (or the retribution being sought) and the relationship of the parties. The importance of justice considerations varies depending on the closeness of social, economic, cultural, and family ties. Some people and groups may be so far outside the pale that we do not believe that justice concerns inform our dealings with them. Occasions of ethnic cleansing remind us that sometimes certain groups are thought to be entitled to nothing.

It would be a mistake to conclude that a single distributive justice principle applies to each situation. For example, conflicting goals of competition and cooperation in the workplace may cause us to put some emphasis on both equity and equality norms when distributing benefits. In part this reflects the fact that we may have multiple goals in a given situation. In the workplace, management may have instrumental goals that allocate rewards to the most productive but also group maintenance goals that argue for greater equality in allocations.

Here it is worth noting the parallels between distributive and retributive justice judgments. First, there are similarities between retributive and distributive justice principles. With respect to distributive justice, several decades of research has confirmed that desert (i.e., equitable distributions), equality, and need are the basic building blocks from which just distributions are constructed. While there has been far less research in the retributive justice tradition, similar principles appear to play a crucial role. Desert, of course, is central to retributive justice judgments. In Vidmar's terms, the level of perceived wrongdoing has the greatest effect on victim arousal. When one knowingly causes harm this increases victim arousal and the severity of punishment. Factors that mitigate actor culpability reduce a desire for retribution. Equality also plays a role in retributive justice judgments in the sense that people who commit similar wrongful acts produce similar responses, both from their victims and from a legal system that adjudicates them for their wrongs. Need may play an important role in several ways. Need as a reason for wrongdoing may lessen our desire for retributive justice. Moreover, need affects sanctions. For example, Vidmar notes that exhibitions of remorse and apology reduce a desire for retribution. Remorse produces this result in part because it may cause us to alter our judgments about the level of intentionality of the act but it also may have an effect because we think the individual is in less need of sanctions to minimize the likelihood of future wrongdoing. And, as with distributive justice judgments, retributive judgments also involve multiple goals and therefore the use of more than one justice principle. In general, when retributive justice questions arise within the context of formal legal processes, because the state may wish simultaneously to punish and to rehabilitate, need-based principles frequently compete with desert-based principles.

Hegtvedt and Cook's chapter discusses other factors that influence distributive justice decisions, including: an individual's age and gender, and personal values; and interpersonal factors such as the existence of affective ties between the allocator and the recipients. Their chapter also discusses how people react to perceived injustice. Under various circumstances we may, for example, alter our own inputs, change the objects of our comparisons, or leave the situation. Consider again the boss's nephew. If we see that he is getting ahead even though he is less competent that his co-workers we may decide to stop working so hard ourselves, or we might even decide to seek employment elsewhere. It may be, however, that we do not make any behavioral change. Rather, we just mark him as a "special case" and stop including him when comparing our efforts to those of our fellow workers. Hegtvedt and Cook discuss the various factors that cause us to have these and other reactions to perceived distributive injustices. They also discuss justice research in specific settings such as close relations and organizations.[3]

E. THE RELATIONSHIP AMONG THE JUSTICE DIMENSIONS

Retributive, procedural, and distributive justice do not exist independently of each other. In the past most justice research focused on one or another justice dimension, but more and more frequently research examines the ways in which the dimensions interact. There is no single best way to discuss the relationship among justice dimensions. Because this is a volume about justice in legal settings and because a key component of justice within legal institutions is procedure, we have chosen to highlight the relationship between procedural justice and substantive (retributive and distributive) justice. We begin with two observations about the relationship between procedural and substantive justice.

First, the term *procedure* can mislead if not used carefully. This is so because procedure, especially legal procedure, plays a dual role in the resolution of retributive justice and distributive justice issues (Hart, 1961). As the procedural justice literature clearly points out, procedures that are perceived to be fair (e.g., the authority exhibits neutrality, trust, and status recognition) may generate acquiescence even in the face of perceived outcome injustice. The purpose of many procedures is simply to achieve procedural justice.

Procedure also has a second purpose, to produce "correct" outcomes. Some outcomes do not involve questions of distributive or retributive justice. However, with respect to legal procedures we are very often interested in their ability to produce distributively just and retributively just outcomes. People are less likely to comply with outcomes perceived to be distributively or retributively unjust. Moreover, institutions that routinely fail to achieve distributive and/or retributive justice are likely to lose political and social support even if they are perceived to be procedurally just. The purpose of just procedures is not solely a way to "cool out" the losers in retributive and distributive disputes. It is also to arrange things so as to come as close as possible to achieving what people perceive to be retributive and distributive justice.

From this point flows another which is even more important. Procedures designed to maximize the likelihood that an outcome will be distributively or retributively just may conflict with procedures that are designed to maximize the perception of procedural justice. A fuller understanding of how people integrate their assessment of these different dimensions will assist us in designing procedures that optimize overall justice judgments.

Second, procedural justice questions arise in a fundamentally different context from distributive and retributive justice questions because they always involve a "judge." Both retributive and distributive justice judgments involve at least two people. This point is obvious with respect to distributive justice. If there is only one person, questions of distributive justice cannot arise (setting aside such questions as justice between species). As to retributive justice, at a minimum there must be an (alleged) wrongdoer and a victim. Distributive and retributive justice outcomes involve the relative situation of two or more individuals. Like responsibility, justice is a relationship between or among individuals. Neither retributive nor distributive justice is an issue for the proverbial person alone on a desert island. Justice is a relative, not an absolute, thing.

If distributive and retributive justice judgments require at least two individuals, procedural justice requires an additional element. Procedural justice questions cannot arise unless someone plays the role of the judge who allocates benefits or sanctions. Sometimes this role is played by one of the individuals involved in a distributive or retributive justice allocation. This occurs when a victim exacts personal revenge against a wrongdoer or when one contributor to a joint project is able to impose his preferred allocation on other participants. Within legal contexts this role is more frequently played by a third party who may have a greater or lesser direct interest in the underlying controversy. As the research on procedural justice makes clear, the nature and extent of judicial independence is a key variable affecting the parties' justice perceptions. Justice perceptions may also be affected by the way the third party interacts with the disputants.

In his book *Bureaucratic Justice*, Jerry Mashaw distinguishes three models of justice: bureaucratic rationality, professional treatment, and moral judgment (Mashaw, 1983). Each of these describes a different way the third-party judge may approach a dispute. Bureaucratic rationality involves the adoption of an accurate, cost-effective method of achieving an administrative goal such as the payment of disability benefits to eligible persons. Its output is the implementation of decisions "in essentially factual and technocratic terms" (Mashaw, 1983:25). Professional treatment is in some ways the opposite of bureaucratic rationality. The goal is to serve the client, constrained by cost. "The professional must at least tailor advice or treatment to his or her own resources: some clients must be rejected or given less in order that others, who are needier, may be helped more.... Justice lies in having the appropriate professional judgment applied to one's particular situation *in the context of a service relationship*" (Mashaw, 1983:27, 29). The moral judgment model sees decision making as value defining. This model is particularly appropriate within the context of adjudication, which Mashaw defines as a procedure to determine who *deserves* what. As we shall see, the choice of justice models has an effect on perceptions of procedural and substantive justice.

The five essays in the middle section of the book illustrate ways in which procedures and the dimensions of justice interact. We begin with the chapter by William Felstiner and Ben Pettit.

1. Engaging the Legal System

In their seminal article on how disputes develop and ripen into legal controversies, Felstiner, Abel, and Sarat describe a process of "Naming, Blaming, and Claiming" (Felstiner, Abel, and Sarat, 1980–81). In the naming stage an individual comes to understand that an experience was injurious. Following this step an individual may link injury to a perceived wrong caused by some individual, organization, or other entity. The claiming stage involves asking someone for a remedy, to obtain retributive justice, distributive justice, or both. Claims may be brought directly to the attention of the alleged wrongdoer and if that entity agrees with the claim the dispute comes to an end. Often, however, people turn to law to seek a remedy. Sometimes this is done because the other party will not accept responsibility but on other occasions people may seek out lawyers even prior to confronting the other side, or they may obtain a lawyer because without engaging the law they cannot achieve their objective (e.g., obtain a divorce).[4]

Engaging the legal system to assist with a claim means that one crosses a fundamental threshold. In order to engage the law claimants are forced to surrender their ordinary understandings and experiences. Actions and actors brought into the legal system are dealt with only after they and their dispute are translated into a set of legal categories (e.g., debtor–unsecured creditor, lessor–lessee, suit for negligent entrustment). Western courts tend to treat as irrelevant and inappropriate those accounts that attempt to introduce the details of litigants' social lives (Conley and O'Barr, 1990). Sometimes this process begins in court. Even small-claims courts that are open to litigants without lawyers engage in this transforming work. For most, however, the reshaping of a claim into legal form is a process that begins in the lawyer's office. It is here, as well, that the interaction between procedural justice and substantive outcomes first occurs.

In their essay on lawyer–client relations, **W. L. F. Felstiner** and **Ben Pettit** focus on the problems of paternalism and power. Within Mashaw's terminology, the relationship between lawyer and client is best described as one of professional treatment; the lawyer's job is to serve the client. As Felstiner and Pettit note, the service has both substantive and procedural components and it is in the clash of these two elements that complications arise. Substantively, lawyers possess the skills necessary to transform controversies into their appropriate legal form. Procedurally, the concern is with how lawyers treat clients interpersonally. According to Felstiner and Pettit, a healthy lawyer–client relationship envisions the lawyer being accessible, responsive, empathetic, promptly attentive, and motivated primarily by professional values, not financial gain. Lawyer paternalism may be reflected in lawyer attitude, but the more difficult justice problems arise when lawyers make decisions for clients.

There are many inappropriate motives for paternalistic behavior. However, substantive justice concerns also push lawyers in this direction. The lawyer possesses the power inherent in the ability to translate disputes into legal language and in the process of doing so may subtly influence the client's interests and decisions. Sarat and Felstiner (1995:32) offer the following useful example of this process. The interaction is between a woman and her lawyer. In this exchange the lawyer offers unsupportive responses to the client's rhetoric about blame and then changes the subject as a way of redirecting the conversation.

> CLIENT: There was a harassment and verbal degradation. No interest at all in my furthering my education. None whatsoever. Sexual harassment ...
> LAWYER: Mmn-uh.
> CLIENT: Then he undertook to lecturing me, and I'd say, "I don't want to hear this. I don't have time right now." I would lock myself in the bathroom and he would break in. And I was just to listen, whether I wanted to or not.... The man was not well.
> LAWYER: Okay. Now how about any courses you took?

In this exchange the lawyer is deflecting the client away from the objective of retributive justice, something the no-fault divorce regimes now in place in the United States are unwilling to provide, and directing the client toward distributive justice issues (the division of marital property), something with which the legal rules surrounding divorce are prepared to deal. Whatever else might be said of this exchange, it is worth noting that in this instance it is the law itself that is being paternalistic and the lawyer is only a messenger.

In other situations lawyers act paternalistically, attempting to persuade clients to take a certain course of action because the client preference is not in accord with the substantive outcome preferred by the law. Again, divorce cases offer a good example. A client may, at the time of the divorce, express a desire to allow the spouse to have whatever he or she wants. The lawyer's impulse is to create a distribution that obtains as much as possible for the client. In this situation lawyers may imagine that they are acting in the longer-term interest of their clients. The danger is that in pursuing this goal the attorney may jeopardize other values. Most fundamentally, as Stewart Macaulay's businessmen noted long ago, pursuing all one is entitled to under existing legal rules may harm the ability of the parties to maintain a long-term relationship (Macaulay, 1966). Even when lawyers do correctly anticipate clients' long-term and best interest there may still be a procedural justice price to pay for paternalistic behavior. The substantive–procedural conflict is summed up by Felstiner and Pettit in the following way: "if clients perceive paternalistic representation to limit their participation, they will experience it as less 'fair.' Thus, regardless of substantive result, paternalism may lead to less-satisfied clients" (Felstiner and Pettit, this volume, p. 139).

2. Procedures in a Retributive Context

Today, few societies permit blood feuds and the ability to use self-help to resolve perceived acts of wrongdoing is greatly limited. Instead, most societies have created institutions that put a third party between the wrongdoer and the victim. Most frequently, the state interposes itself and stands as a surrogate for one or both of the parties involved in the underlying dispute. In criminal cases the state, not the victim, conducts the prosecution. The state, representing the community, seeks retribution and simultaneously seeks to reaffirm the social values of the society.

Moreover, the state provides a third-party authority, the judge, whose job it is to determine the appropriate retributive (corrective) response. The presence of a judge makes each trial an occasion that gives rise to both retributive justice and procedural justice concerns. Under these circumstances, it is not surprising that a complex set of legal procedures define acceptable court behavior. Some of these procedures speak to procedural justice issues. Many of the constitutional due process rights that exist in U.S. constitutional law are of this variety. The right to confront witnesses and the right to a representative and impartial jury each speak to issues of neutrality, trust, and status recognition. Other procedures, such as a right to appellate review and sentencing guidelines, speak to issues of retributive justice. Still other procedures speak to both procedural justice and retributive justice issues. The right to counsel is such a procedure. From a procedural justice perspective it may increase a sense of trust and status recognition. From a retributive justice perspective, it may increase the likelihood that retribution will be visited only on those who have in fact violated community norms.

It is important to note the focus of many of these procedures. If a general purpose of the criminal law is to address the desires of victims for retribution, in its particulars the criminal law's procedural safeguards more often address the retributive and procedural justice concerns of the wrongdoer. It is true, as some critics complain, that the criminal procedure is more concerned with the rights of the accused than those of the victim. Why would this be the case? One answer is that when confronted with retributive justice cases the most successful third-party resolutions are those that provide retribution for the victim (and the society) and at the same time minimize the perception on the part of the wrongdoer that he now has been wronged. A central objective of procedures in the retributive justice setting is to break the cycle of retribution by causing the wrongdoer to accept and comply with the third-party resolution.

The preceding discussion has used criminal law examples, but the criminal justice system is not the only and certainly not the most successful example of how legal institutions work to achieve multiple procedural and retributive justice goals. The next two essays in this section examine these issues in two different contexts: the juvenile court and regulatory agencies. In both essays we may look for ways in which the formal procedures succeed in responding to wrongdoing without unleashing a cycle of revenge and retribution.

Barry Feld's essay on the juvenile court reviews one of the most fascinating and complex U.S. efforts to search for the correct balance between retributive and procedural justice. He begins with a valuable overview of the emergence of the modern juvenile court in the early part of the twentieth century. A number of developments caused the progressive "child savers" who began the court to reject many of the goals of retributive justice. Positive criminology rejected "free will" and claimed that deviant behavior was "determined." These positions undermined the idea that juveniles were morally responsible for their conduct and led to an effort to "change" offenders rather than punish them. All of this was accompanied by a sanctioning regime designed to "treat" delinquents based on a rehabilitative ideal. Here the state stands as a surrogate not only for victims of wrongdoing, but also for the child's family. The state becomes *parens patriae*, the father of the child.

For the purposes of this essay, it is especially important to note that a court based on treatment norms developed an entirely different set of procedures from those used for adults. One did not have to commit a criminal act (i.e., an act defined as criminal in a statute) in order to come within the aegis of the court. The court's "status jurisdiction" permitted it to respond to such behaviors as smoking, idleness, and sexual activity. Procedures designed to achieve retributive justice—if that is even an appropriate word in this context—did not focus on assuaging the anger of victims or on adjusting sanctions to be proportionate to wrongdoing. Instead, they focused on the "needs" of the juvenile as viewed through the lens of the medical, treatment model. Thus, procedures designed to assure a correct outcome did not include a right to counsel in part because one did not have to determine if the child "deserved" to be treated by the court. As Feld notes, "Because a youth's offense provided only a symptom of his or her 'real' needs, indeterminate and nonproportional dispositions potentially could continue for the duration of minority" (Feld, this volume, p. 159).

Given this different focus on need, it was inevitable that the procedures designed to achieve procedural justice were also altered. The original juvenile court's most ardent admirers might in fact have argued that the court posed few if any procedural justice issues because a court hearing did not involve a conflict of interest. What the court did was in the child's "best interest." The court imposed "dispositions," not sentences. It would be a mistake, however, to conclude that the juvenile court was totally insensitive to procedural justice concerns. Efforts were made to lend a sense of caring and trust to the proceedings and the system "envisioned a specialized judge trained in social sciences and child development whose empathetic qualities and insight would aid in making individualized dispositions" (Feld, this volume, p. 158). Ideally, such a hearing might well be perceived as fair because of the sense of trust and status recognition it offered. Unfortunately, the ideal was seldom achieved (Platt, 1977).

Feld next discusses what he calls the "constitutional domestication of the juvenile court," a pair of U.S. Supreme Court opinions that reintroduced some traditional criminal law due process requirements such as assistance of counsel, a right to confront and cross-examine witnesses, and proof of delinquency "beyond a reasonable doubt." As Feld notes, by providing delinquents with some procedures traditionally reserved for criminal trials, they also legitimated greater punitiveness. In essence, it legitimated more traditional retributive justice notions. The Supreme Court refused, however, to give juveniles all of the procedures that accompany adult criminal trials. For example, there is no right to trial by jury. Thus, the juvenile court still occupies an uncertain middle ground.

In the remainder of his essay, Feld examines the results of this compromise, some of which are clearly unhappy. For example, it appears from a number of studies that greater procedural formality, as indicated by the presence of counsel, results in more severe sentences. Justice research suggests why this may be so. Counsel and a reasonable doubt standard may give the judge greater confidence that the child is in fact a fitting object for retribution—that the child deserves sanction. Moreover, counsel may impede the ability of the child to exhibit remorse or express apology, factors that are known to ameliorate retributive impulses. More generally, procedures designed to increase substantive accuracy may, by excluding legally irrelevant testimony, reduce the ability of the individual to participate in a way that maximizes voice.

In the concluding pages of his essay, Feld addresses a number of additional topics, including the ongoing tension between treatment versus punishment reflected in the increasing tendency to waive serious juvenile offenders to adult courts, the actual treatment juveniles receive in correctional facilities, and the fact that minority youth are treated more harshly by the juvenile corrections system. The latter topic brings to the forefront the fact that even within retributive justice, questions of equality of treatment are important. A system of retribution, like a system of distribution, will be perceived to be less just when equals are treated unequally and in some situations equality may trump equity and need as the dominant justice dimension.

The next chapter in this section is by **Robert Howard** and **John Scholz**. The essay is particularly valuable because it examines justice questions in regulatory agencies that enforce rules (the IRS) and also in administrative agencies that primarily distribute benefits (Medicaid). Thus, the chapter examines agency procedures both when they are attempting to achieve retributive (corrective) justice and when they are attempting to achieve distributive justice.

The essay pushes to the forefront an issue that thus far has remained in the background of our discussion. Ideally, decision makers should "correctly" decide every case. Unavoidably, however, some cases will be wrongly decided. Agencies must adopt some set of procedures that attempt to achieve retributive or distributive justice in the individual case. Howard and Scholz ask, should these procedures be more *lenient* or more *stringent*? They define "a mistake in denying a right [to a benefit] or improperly enforcing an obligation where none exists," as an error of excessive stringency. On the other hand, " a mistake in granting a right [to a benefit] where none exists, or failing to enforce an obligation that does exist" is an error of excessive leniency. The question of leniency is hardly unique to administrative decision making. The due process revolution in juvenile courts can be understood in part as an effort to reduce the frequency with which juvenile courts sanctioned children who did not "deserve" this treatment. An example of this is the Supreme Court's requirement that the state employ a "beyond a reasonable doubt" standard in delinquency adjudications. By this step, Howard and Scholz would say the Court made juvenile court administration more lenient.

The question of leniency or stringency is particularly salient in an administrative agency context. The ideal of individualized justice that defines criminal and civil litigation is impossible in many agency settings where a small number of bureaucrats are confronted with very large caseloads and there is relatively little time to decide each case. Here, as elsewhere, the problem is exacerbated by the fact that some individuals exploit procedures to get undeserved benefits or to avoid duties, and thus the procedures must guard against opportunism.

The middle part of Howard and Scholz's paper discusses the causes and consequences of agency errors and presents the case for stringency and the case for leniency. They pose the fundamental agency dilemma as follows: "If all citizens were opportunistic, the costs of maintaining an enforcement system capable of detecting and deterring all noncompliance would be prohibitive, but if the agencies do not discover and discourage cheating, then scarce resources are squandered, and the large middle group might lose its incentive to comply" (Howard and Scholz, this volume, p. 211). Agencies must try to find a balance of stringency and leniency that maximizes "justice as perceived by those who voluntarily comply."

The dilemma is reflected in an agency's choice to use a less formal, case-by-case approach versus a more formal, rule-bound approach to resolving cases. The adoption of the federal Administrative Procedures Act in 1946 ushered in a period where agencies became more and more rule-oriented. Howard and Scholz discuss the backlash against this trend among scholars such as Nonet and Selznick (1978) and Bardach and Kagan (1981). These critics argue against undue reliance on formal procedures when the procedures themselves become reified at the expense of achieving substantive (i.e., distributive and retributive) justice.

Ultimately, then, the Howard and Scholz essay again demonstrates the potential tension between the goals of procedural justice on the one hand and retributive or distributive justice on the other. Steps we might take to increase an individual's perception of fair procedure can, in the context of administrative decision making, lessen the probability that the agency will arrive at the substantively correct decision. Unfortunately, the most inadequate administrative procedures have the potential of producing an even worse result. They may increase the probability of substantive errors while at the same time leaving the individual with no sense of procedural justice.

Agency procedure is particularly prone to this unfortunate outcome. At the outset of their essay Howard and Scholz quote one commentator who describes administrative agencies as a "headless, fourth branch of government." Most fundamentally, proceedings before an agency occur without an independent third-party decision maker. Of course, even in criminal cases the independence of the decision maker is suspect insofar as the judge is employed by the state. An independent judiciary is an attempt to increase the likelihood that the judge will be neutral and impartial. Administrative agency rulings do not work this way. At least until the citizen exhausts all administrative remedies, agency officials are often both party and judge. In this situation administrative decisions already put at risk one component of procedural justice, the perception that the decision maker is neutral.

This neutrality component may be particularly important in the administrative agency context. In Mashaw's terms, administrative decision making is most frequently a type of Bureaucratic Rationality. Recall, bureaucratic rationality involves the adoption of an accurate, cost-effective method of achieving an administrative goal such as the payment of disability benefits to eligible persons. Its output is the implementation of decisions "in essentially factual and technocratic terms" (Mashaw, 1983:25). Mashaw notes that at the core of this method of decision making is the requirement of impartiality, i.e., the neutral application of rules. It is not that voice is irrelevant. Bureaucratic procedures that treat people summarily and that offer people little chance to give their story or to defend their actions minimize the trust and status recognition that form the other two legs of Tyler and Lind's "group-value" theory of procedural justice. But in the context of bureaucratic decision making, the absence of neutrality and impartiality, even more than a lack of voice, may create a particularly strong sense of procedural injustice.

3. Procedures in a Distributive Context

As we noted earlier, disputes brought to law are translated into a legal form before they are processed. Once they are transformed a specific set of procedural and evidentiary rules narrow the scope of permissible evidence. The evidence that is permitted is introduced in a very stylized fashion. The rituals of courtroom evidentiary presentations—such as examination, cross-examination, objections—are the stuff of countless film and television dramas. Dissatisfaction with the central elements of traditional legal dispute resolution—a focus on a narrow set of legal issues and a tendency to reach binary outcomes in which one party prevailed and the other lost—led to the growth of the alternative dispute resolution (ADR) movement. ADR describes a variety of noncourt dispute resolution mechanisms but the primary alternatives are arbitration and mediation.

Deborah Hensler's essay focuses on mediation which, as she notes, is at the core of the ADR movement because it promises to empower disputants to resolve disputes on their own with the assistance of a nonauthoritative neutral party who is not empowered to find facts or assign fault. Because mediation comes relatively close to a simple bilateral settlement between the parties to a dispute, one might conclude that questions of distributive justice would dominate any discussion. From this perspective, mediation is best when it accomplishes two things: it leads to a settlement and the settlement reached is optimal in the sense that the parties converge on an outcome that reflects how the case would be resolved were it to be litigated. The mediator assists a bargain "in the shadow of the law" (Mnookin and Kornhauser, 1979).

The nature of this assistance has itself become controversial. Hensler's essay addresses the question of what constitutes "good" mediation. She outlines two competing paradigms. In one the mediator is an evaluator who helps the parties exchange information about the strengths and weaknesses of their legal and factual claims and offers a neutral estimate of the monetary value of the case. The second paradigm offers a different vision in which the purpose of mediation is to get parties to focus on the different interests that underlie their dispute and to shape a mutually beneficial "win–win" solution. Rather than narrowing issues, parties are advised to put more issues on the table so as to create more opportunities for trade-offs. Importantly, the role of the mediator is to help parties focus on interests, rather than positions, and to assist them in generating options for resolving their dispute that will provide joint gains. An effective mediator facilitates this value-creating process, rather than pressing parties to put a compromise dollar value on their dispute; hence, this process is often called *facilitative mediation*.

Facilitative mediation places more weight on the parties' role. As noted by one practice manual adopting this approach, mediators are not there to make a decision or to pronounce on who is right or wrong. Rather, they are there to promote the disputants' use of constructive problem solving skills (Bennett and Hermann, 1996:11).

The evaluative paradigm is clearly focused on distributional considerations. The facilitative paradigm is more complex. From one point of view a facilitative mediator is also concerned with distributive justice and in fact supporters of this type of mediation may claim that a facilitative procedure maximizes distributive justice. Because the parties may differentially value things, by placing a wider range of things on the table the facilitator makes it possible to get more of what each wants. However, the proponents of a facilitative model do not rest their argument solely on this ground. In part they prefer this paradigm for procedural justice reasons. Theoretically the facilitative model does more to empower the parties to the dispute, give them greater voice, and provide a greater sense of inclusion. Moreover, a facilitative mediator is less likely to depart from neutrality by revealing a preference for one party's position. Facilitative mediation produces a greater sense of procedural justice and thus greater satisfaction.

Hensler's essay reviews the empirical research by RAND and other investigators concerning the relative frequency of evaluative versus facilitative mediation and whether either alternative produces better procedural or distributive justice outcomes. With the limited data now available, she is unable to find a substantial distributional effect associated with the choice of paradigm. Moreover, there is little evidence that facilitative mediation has more positive effects than evaluative mediation on party relationships, on disputants' ability to manage disputes, or on their understanding of themselves and others. As Hensler notes, given the relatively poor quality of research data to date these results must be considered provisional. Much of the work is based on interviews with the disputants' attorneys, not the disputants themselves. Perhaps future research will indicate that disputants in facilitative settings express greater satisfaction than those in evaluative settings.

Hensler's essay makes two other points that are worth noting. First, there is a feminist and minority critique of facilitative mediation that objects to its subjective, informal approach and its requirement that the parties engage one another and search for a wide-ranging settlement of their dispute. In part, this critique is premised on the concern that in its effort to provide voice and procedural justice for the parties, facilitative mediation may give less powerful disputants less of what they sought, less distributive justice.

Second, both attorneys and judges tend to prefer evaluative mediation. Hensler surmises that this reflects a belief that most civil legal disputes are distributional in nature and a disinterest or disinclination for broader party (client) participation in dispute resolution. This result echoes the Felstiner and Pettit point that many lawyers emphasize the distributional aspects of their client's case as it is defined by the law. They do not wish to "waste" much time on discussions that do not further this vision of distributive justice.

The last chapter in this section addresses the question of how to determine whether an arrangement is distributively just. The essay by **Robert Nelson** and **William Bridges** explores the issue of pay inequality between jobs held by men and women. They do not focus on the question of whether men and women holding the same job are paid the same. Rather they examine what is commonly called the issue of comparable worth: wage difference between different jobs that are held predominantly by men or women. In the 1980s a series of lawsuits questioned the legality and the justness of wage differentials in different but similar jobs. For example, in *County of Washington v. Gunther*, the first Supreme Court case to deal with this question, the jobs involved were male prison "guards" and female prison "matrons" (*County of Washington v. Gunther*, 1981).

The *Gunther* court held that Title VII's prohibition against pay discrimination could include comparable worth claims. However, in the following years the courts routinely rejected these claims. They did so by accepting a market explanation for observed differences. Wage differences between different jobs simply reflect the supply of and demand for labor in these jobs. Because employers cannot individually alter these factors, they face and respond to an inflexible cost of labor for each job. Nelson and Bridges systematically examine the evidence underlying the market explanation and find it wanting in several regards. It is clear, however, that when accepted, the market explanation is a legitimating justification for wage inequalities.

The success of the market explanation tells us a good deal about the relationship of the courts to questions of distributive justice. As Nelson and Bridges note, the market explanation externalizes responsibility for wage inequalities outside the organization. It deflects the distributive justice decision from the firm to society at large and the firm itself does not appear to be making a distributively unjust allocation. Neither does the organization appear to be intentionally discriminating; it is not acting in a way that calls for retributive justice. The market explanation makes employer decisions appear procedurally just as well. Decisions are impartial and neutral, governed by external forces over which the employer has no control. When we adopt a market explanation, differences in wages fall outside the scope of justice discourse, at least as it applies to the organization.[5]

Nelson and Bridges examine the appeal of this view to the judiciary. Were the courts to adopt a comparable worth approach to between-job discrimination they feel they would be drawn into the very difficult and subjective task of evaluating the relative value of different jobs and the degree to which organizational practices rather than market forces created wage differences. There is a frequently noted reluctance of the judiciary to become involved in multifaceted disputes in part because they have relatively little faith that their procedures will be able to produce the substantively just outcome. It is not surprising that they would be very willing to accept market explanations that permit them to avoid this step. In the process the courts themselves are about the business of constructing the social reality of what constitutes distributive justice and distributive injustice. The power of the courts to do this is reflected in the response Nelson and Bridges report they often get when discussing their research with colleagues: "Isn't that a dead issue now?" (Nelson and Bridges, this volume, p. 293).

Nelson and Bridges describe the market explanation for between-job gender inequality as the dominant discourse. In our culture markets explain and justify this type of inequality. To date the plaintiffs in this litigation have been unable to unsettle this dominant explanation, but by their efforts they indicate that it is not universally accepted. This raises a larger set of questions about the relationship between justice and culture. Within cultures, how widely shared are justice perceptions? And across cultures, how much variance do we observe in perceptions of justice? The last two chapters in the volume address these issues.

F. JUSTICE AND CULTURE

Some have argued that a concern for justice is an inherent human characteristic (Lerner, 1981). People make a considerable effort to justify their actions even in situations such as a war where one might think this would be unnecessary (Kelman and Hamilton, 1989). As the contents of this entire volume indicate, justice concerns influence people's thoughts and actions and inform the way they construct and judge institutions. Even if the concern for justice is universal, it could be the case that people have widely different understandings of what is just. This is not the case (Tyler, Boeckmann, Smith, and Huo, 1997). As the first three essays in this volume indicate, there is wide consensus about the criteria for making justice judgments. Demographic characteristics—age, education, gender, race—do not produce differences as to how to define justice. This is true for procedural (Tyler, 1988), distributive (Lane, 1986), and retributive justice (Rossi and Berk, 1997). Given the widespread agreement on the attributes of retributive justice, it is not surprising that there also tends to be a consensus on the attribution of responsibility for wrongdoing (Sanders and Hamilton, 1987). Moreover, within the United States most people tend to agree that different justice principles apply in different situations: equity in work settings, equality in legal settings, and need in the family (Deutsch, 1985). This does not mean that all people agree as to the proper criteria for each situation. It does indicate, however, that disagreements do not break along standard demographic lines. The variance is not socially segmented.

Agreement is greatest when people are asked about the proper criteria for making justice judgments, what may be called abstract principles of justice such as the equity rule. When we move away from this level in either direction consensus lessens. At the micro level, people are less likely to agree about the justice of a particular outcome. At the macro level, people are more likely to disagree about things such as the level of inequality in society (Kluegel and Matějů, 1995). Relatively disadvantaged groups tend to favor equality while better off groups favor equity principles typically based on merit, even if this leads to greater inequality (Hegtvedt and Cook, this volume, p. 123). Importantly, however, many individuals simultaneously hold both egalitarian and inegalitarian views about macroeconomic justice (Kluegel and Matějů, 1995). Conflict exists both between and within individuals.

Against this backdrop **Jill McCorkel**, **Frederika Schmitt**, and **Valerie Hans**'s essay on "Gender, Law, and Justice" is particularly helpful. They survey the many facets of feminist jurisprudence at the end of the century. Separate sections discuss the similarities and differences among the liberal, radical, difference, postmodern legal, and critical strands of feminism. Not infrequently these feminisms lead in opposing directions, e.g., declaiming or exalting gender differences. The different strands reflect the conflicts that exist among a group that shares much in common.

A fair amount of energy has been expended looking for differences between men and women in their orientations toward law and justice. The best-known statement about gender differences is that of Carol Gilligan in her book *In a Different Voice*. She described two different "ethics." An ethic of *rights*, which she associates with men, responds to moral problems in terms of logic and moral reasoning. An ethic of *care*, which she associates with women, responds to moral problems in terms of communication and reciprocity in relationships. This distinction resonates with the distinction between evaluative and facilitative mediation in Hensler's essay and also underlies the degree to which formal court-based adjudication, with its focus on individualism, formal rights, and responsibility rules that do not attend to the specifics of relationships, more nearly approximates the ethic of rights. In turn this approach to adjudication can shape our sense of what constitutes retributive and distributive justice. If legal rules define people narrowly as juridical persons with only a few attributes (e.g., the reasonable person of tort law) other attributes they possess may be excluded when examining whether the outcome they received at the hands of the legal system was just.

The strength of Gilligan's work is that it opens our eyes to possibilities about how institutions may be organized. Its weakness is that its assertion that the preference for the ethic of care versus the ethic of rights strongly breaks on gender lines is factually wrong. Empirical work testing whether or not women speak in a distinctive voice has produced little support for the hypothesis (McCorkel, Schmitt, and Hans, this volume, pp. 310–311; Hegtvedt and Cook, this volume, p. 99; Leung and Morris, this volume, p. 351). As yet, strong differences in the way the genders think about the moral and ethical issues that underpin perceptions of justice have failed to emerge. But this does not mean there are not important differences in certain areas.

McCorkel, Schmitt, and Hans review the differences between men and women concerning crimes such as rape and spouse abuse. For example, men and women tend to disagree about the relevance of victim behavior in assessing the correct retributive response to rapists. They also review legal changes in both areas that tend to reflect women's position, e.g., rape shield laws and rules of evidence permitting women to introduce battered woman syndrome evidence in cases where women have murdered their abusive husbands. Within the categories set out above, the gender differences we do observe tend to exist at a more micro level (whether justice was done in a particular case) and a more macro level (what evidence should be used in making a justice judgment) rather than at the middle level of justice criteria themselves. Future researchers may well wish to examine in greater detail the interaction of these different levels. Here, McCorkel, Schmitt, and Hans echo a point made by Nelson and Bridges. The political power to define a situation and to implement laws reflecting that definition has a strong impact on justice judgments even when individuals employ similar justice criteria.

The final essay in this reader brings us full circle. **Kwok Leung** and **Michael Morris** discuss justice through the lens of culture and ethnicity. The cross-cultural study of justice is theoretically interesting because it permits us to uncover variations that may not exist in any single culture. The research has increasing practical importance as well. Migration and economic globalization create societies and organizations comprised of people who identify with different cultures. With increasing contact among cultures, differences in perceptions of justice may have large consequences.

Leung and Morris pick up on the point made earlier that even when people agree about abstract principles of justice, specific beliefs that determine how the principle applies may vary. For example, an equity principle may be shared across Asian villages but people in one village may believe that the primary contribution is work productivity and people in another village may believe the primary contribution is years lived in the village. Knowing about the abstract principles may not permit one to predict an individual's judgment about particular cases (Shweder, Mahapatra, and Miller, 1987).

More importantly, there is substantial evidence of between-society differences at the abstract level as well. Although subsequent research has not confirmed Gilligan's hypothesis that the ethic of care and the ethic of rights break on gender lines in the United States, there is now a body of research suggesting that cultures differ along a similar line. For example, when American and Indian students are confronted with a situation in which justice is in conflict with interpersonal responsibilities, Americans are more likely to yield to justice concerns and Indians to interpersonal responsibilities. When asked to justify their choice, Americans more frequently mention fairness and rights. These and similar results are most frequently understood as a reflection of the fact that Western societies are relatively more individualistic and place personal autonomy above role obligations. In contextual or collectivist societies such as India and Japan "following role expectations in a given situation is the means to realize one's true nature" (Leung and Morris, this volume, p. 351). This line of research indicates that the moral basis of justice principles varies across cultures. These differences are in turn reflected in justice judgments.

With respect to distributive justice judgments, for instance, among members of collectivist societies the equity rule is more frequently replaced by equality or need rules. When equity rules are used, what counts as an input is also influenced by culture. Because attachment and loyalty to groups is emphasized in collectivist societies, it is not surprising that seniority becomes a relatively more important consideration in equity judgments than is true in individualist cultures. Parallel differences exist with respect to procedural and retributive justice judgments as well.

Overall, there is increasing evidence that the group-value model of procedural justice applies across cultures and that procedural fairness is a more important predictor than perceived favorability of outcome in predicting satisfaction with a disputing process. However, researchers have also observed consistent cultural differences. In collectivist cultures where maintaining ongoing stable relationships is particularly important, people express weaker support for adversarial processes and stronger support for alternative dispute mechanisms such as mediation.

In addition to the individualist–collectivist distinction, another dimension along which cultures differ is "power distance." Power distance refers to the acceptance of hierarchy in a society. In societies high on power distance those at the top are accorded relatively more privilege and deference; some research now suggests that members of these societies are less upset when a superior treats them in a way that violates the relational model of procedural justice.

Cross-cultural differences exist in the realm of retributive justice as well. Proportionality, making the punishment fit the crime, is important in all cultures. However, cultures vary in the importance their members attach to different factors in assessing responsibility and prescribing sanctions. When judging responsibility members of individualistic cultures are more sensitive to information about the actor such as the degree of intentionality and the nature of past behavior. Members of collectivist cultures are more sensitive to the actor's social role and the influence of others. Differences also appear in sanctioning behavior. Research comparing Japan and the United States indicates that Americans—members of a more individualistic society—are more likely to propose sanctions that isolate the individual wrongdoer. Japanese respondents are more likely to propose sanctions that restore relationships among the actor, the victim, and society. Criminal justice practices reflect this orientation. Foote describes these practices as a type of benevolent paternalism designed to compel wrongdoers to confess the error of their ways and, in return, to expend considerable resources attempting to reintegrate them into society (Foote, 1992).

Although we have focused on cultural differences, Leung and Morris emphasize that these differences exist against a backdrop of substantial cross-cultural agreement about the dimensions of justice. Across societies the concepts of equity, need, and equality-based allocations are well understood. For example, Indians understand what equity allocations would look like even in situations where they would not choose to use them; Westerners may be less likely to apply equality principles in workplace allocations, but they are very likely to do so in family matters. Moreover, all the dimensions are used in each society, albeit with different frequency. There is even substantial overlap with respect to what counts as an input. Americans may not give as much weight to seniority as Japanese when making workplace equity allocations, but this factor does play a role.

G. CONCLUSION

The essays in this volume provide a broad survey of the rich empirical research on justice judgments. Together, they address three broad issues that we believe should be the focus of future research. One about which we have been explicit is the relationship among justice dimensions; the other two, the study of justice across disciplines, and cultural–structural interactions, flow from this discussion. In conclusion we wish to say a few words about each of these issues.

1. The Relationship among Justice Dimensions

In their essay on procedural justice Tyler and Lind hold out the enticing possibility that "global theories of justice judgment, which explain not only procedural justice phenomena, but also distributive and retributive justice phenomena, might well be within our reach" (Tyler and Lind, this volume, p. 78). A goal of this volume is to advance this effort. Much of our discussion has been directed at the relationship between procedure and substantive justice. As we have noted throughout, within legal contexts procedures play a dual role of achieving substantive justice and providing the disputants with a sense of procedural justice. This is the case in situations where the primary focus is on either distribution or retribution.

When disputes come to law the procedure–substance interaction involves several steps. First, as we have seen in the Felstiner and Pettit; Howard and Scholz; and Hensler essays, law transforms disputes by determining which justice principles are to be considered and how the principles are to be applied in each case. The choice of justice principles is an issue of substantive law. The application of principles involves the law of evidence. One purpose of evidentiary rules is to increase the probability that the substantive principles will be applied accurately. Rules against the admissibility of hearsay evidence are an example. In order to achieve this goal, however, hearsay rules may impede the ability of people to "tell their story." Within the group-value theory of procedural justice, an inability to tell one's story can in turn undermine a sense of procedural justice. We must emphasize "can." For it may be the case that disputants can be persuaded that the competing goals of a dispute settlement forum require substantive and procedural justice trade-offs. Indeed, some of the interactions between lawyers and clients in advance of trial can be understood in this light. We will benefit from future research that continues to move beyond examining the relative importance of perceptions of procedural and substantive justice and explores how people respond to procedures that make different trade-offs between substantive and procedural justice goals.

2. The Study of Justice across Disciplines

The first three essays in this volume review the voluminous psychological literature on subjective justice judgments, as does the final chapter by Leung and Morris. Among the social sciences, the psychological study of justice judgments is far and away the most mature. It is also relatively closed. The literature in this field only occasionally incorporates literature outside of psychology and when it does it is often philosophical and jurisprudential writing on the objective criteria of justice.

The remaining essays in this reader are not in the mainstream of psychological justice studies. They are authored by people from criminology, political science, law, and sociology as well as psychology.[6] They vary in their use of the psychological research. Some chapters frequently refer to psychological findings but most rarely mention them. This state of affairs raises the question of what the various disciplines offer each other. In this essay we have offered some of our thoughts on this issue.

The psychological findings provide a foundation on which other disciplines can and should build. We can better understand what is at stake in styles of mediation, the way regulatory agencies enforce rules, and the way we handle juvenile (and adult) offenders if we are attuned to how these relate to perceptions of procedural and substantive justice. For example, the heated debate within the ADR movement over facilitative versus evaluative mediation discussed by Deborah Hensler is easier to appreciate when we understand that the choice entails a decision as to whether procedural justice or substantive justice considerations should be primary.

In turn, other disciplines have the potential to enrich psychological research. They suggest a number of hypotheses about relationships between styles of judging and the disputants' perceptions of procedural justice. For example, if Mashaw is correct, then perceptions of impartiality are particularly important when the decision maker employs a bureaucratic justice style of decision making. By suggesting relationships between styles of dispute resolution and perceptions of procedural justice, legal scholars turn our attention back toward earlier procedural justice work in the tradition of Thibaut and Walker.

Research on actual courts suggests a number of other issues that are worth exploring. For example, sociological research on disputing frequently distinguishes one-shot litigators from repeat players (Galanter, 1974). Are repeat players equally satisfied with trials in which they receive procedural but not distributive justice? Another example arises from the fact that when people do find themselves in a dispute we observe a good deal of forum shopping. Increasingly, businesses attempt to avoid the public courts entirely by arranging for arbitration in their contracts. Forum shopping also occurs when people choose mediation over litigation. There is now considerable evidence that in many circumstances people are more satisfied with mediation (Tyler, 1997). Still another type of forum shopping occurs when people avoid courts altogether. Research in the United States and elsewhere suggests that individualism–collectivism affects the extent to which a legal procedure is regarded as fair (Greenhouse, 1986; Bierbrauer, 1992). What mix of procedures and substantive orientations causes litigants to choose one forum over the other, and what does this choice of fora tell us about how people trade off between procedural and substantive justice? The answers to such speculations are most likely to emerge from research work that integrates knowledge across disciplines.

3. Cultural–Structural Interactions

A multidisciplinary approach to questions of justice should advance our understanding of another important relationship, that between cultural values and structural relationships. As the closing essay by Leung and Morris indicates, an important strength of psychological research is its ability to assess the role of culture in justice judgments. In recent years, this research has begun to pay more attention to the role of social and legal structures. Many of the essays in this volume have indicated the critical importance of these factors.

The essays by Nelson and Bridges; McCorkel, Schmitt, and Hans; and Hensler discuss the importance of one's position in the social structure on perceptions of justice.[7] The feminist and minority critiques of mediation are particularly revealing. They argue that the informality of mediation may produce a sense of procedural justice but may also make it easier for the more powerful to prevail substantively. Although there is limited evidence for the proposition that minority group members and women are disadvantaged by mediation the critique itself reflects a relationship between one's position in the society and justice judgments.

Parties with less power tend to identify less with their community and to be less committed to their society. This, in turn, has effects on justice judgments. People who identify with their community evaluate authorities more positively in terms of the fairness of their treatment. Moreover, individuals who are committed to the society rely more heavily on procedural judgments and less heavily on instrumental judgments when forming judgments about a policy or a decision. For example, a study of employee reactions to how their supervisors dealt with a work conflict found that those who identified more with the organization assessed the supervisor's conduct in terms of how fairly they were treated (procedural justice) while those who identified less with the organization assessed the conduct in terms of whether they received a favorable outcome (distributive justice) (Huo, Smith, Tyler, and Lind, 1996).

Legal structures also play an important role in justice judgments. The essays by Feld; Hensler; and Howard and Scholz indicate ways in which the organization of a dispute settlement forum affects both procedural and substantive justice. The "constitutional domestication" of the juvenile court is a case in point. The due process revolution altered the court's structure by introducing lawyers and a more adversarial posture. Of equal importance, it changed the court's focus from what was wrong with the child to what the child had done wrong. In turn, these changes in turn altered the nature of both procedural and retributive justice. Procedurally, the introduction of lawyers and the narrowing of the evidence that should be considered when adjudicating a delinquent gave less room for the delinquents to participate. Substantively, by causing the juvenile courts to focus more on what the child did and less on what the child needs, the revolution altered the definition of retributive justice.

McCorkel, Schmitt, and Hans describe similar if less dramatic changes in the prosecution of sexual assault and domestic violence cases. Nelson and Bridges describe a set of cases where the plaintiffs were unable to alter the courts' view of substantive justice in gender play inequality. Each of these examples indicates the crucial role the legal system plays in justice judgments.

4. Summing Up

As the examples at the beginning of this chapter indicate, justice concerns are pervasive. Every day we encounter numerous situations about which we make retributive and distributive justice judgments. Collectively, these judgments are an important part of our culture. Because many of these judgments are incorporated into the rules and procedures of courts and administrative agencies, the law is an embodiment of culture. Simultaneously, legal structures shape and direct our cultural beliefs about what constitutes a just outcome. This is most obvious with respect to questions of substantive justice. For example, the introduction of battered woman syndrome evidence in spouse abuse cases fundamentally alters the retributive justice equation in some cases. More subtle are the law's effects on procedural justice judgments. By emphasizing adversarial adjudication, by holding themselves open to a wide variety of aggrieved parties, and by offering an individualized trial to each litigant, U.S. courts reinforce the individualism that is the hallmark of our culture. In other societies the legal system is structured to support a more communal culture (Hamilton and Sanders, 1992). In turn, these cultural orientations shape perceptions of justice in the everyday affairs of life. At the last, the study of justice, like the study of society in general, is the investigation of how culture and structure are woven together to create and sustain a social order.

H. ENDNOTES

1. On the question of the ways in which law may or may not be autonomous see Bourdieu (1987), Lempert (1987), and Kornhauser (1998).
2. For a discussion of the scope of justice concerns see Tyler, Boeckmann, Smith, and Huo (1997).
3. We had hoped to include a chapter devoted entirely to justice in organizations. The Hegtvedt and Cook discussion provides an introduction to this growing field.
4. As Conley and O'Barr note, in practice the three stages are much more complex, reactive, and unstable than this brief description suggests. For example, one may go to a lawyer with a claim and the lawyer may help one determine who to blame (Conley and O'Barr, 1998:78).
5. For a discussion of the scope of justice concerns see Tom R. Tyler, Robert J. Boeckmann, Heather J. Smith, and Yuen J. Huo, 1997, *Social Justice in a Diverse Society*, p. 210, Boulder, CO: Westview Press.
6. Unfortunately, our plans for a chapter by an economist were unrealized. Questions of justice, especially distributive justice, have been at the core of economic analyses at least since Smith, Ricardo, and Marx. The absence of an economic analysis of justice is a serious shortcoming of this volume.

7. Conspicuous by its absence is a chapter specifically on race and ethnicity. Again, our original plans to include such a chapter were unrealized.

REFERENCES

Allen, F. A. (1981). *The Decline of the Rehabilitative Ideal: Penal Policy and Social Purpose*. New Haven, CT: Yale University Press.

Aristotle. (1953). *The Nicomachean Ethics* (J. A. K. Thompson, Trans.). Baltimore: Penguin Books.

Bardach, E., and Kagan, R. (1981). *Going by the Book: The Problem of Regulatory Unreasonableness*. Philadelphia: Temple University Press.

Barry, B. (1989). *Theories of Justice*. Berkeley: University of California Press.

Bennett, M. D., and Hermann, M. (1996). *The Art of Mediation*. Notre Dame, IN: National Institute for Trial Advocacy.

Bierbrauer, G. (1992). Toward an Understanding of Legal Culture: Variations in Individualism and Collectivism Between Kurds, Lebanese, and Germans. *Law and Society Review, 28*, 243–264.

Bourdieu, P. (1987). The Force of Law: Toward a Sociology of the Juridical Field. *Hastings Law Journal, 38*, 805–853.

Braithwaite, J., and Pettit, P. (1990). *Not Just Deserts: A Republican Theory of Criminal Justice*. London: Oxford University Press.

Coleman, J. L. (1992). *Risks and Wrongs*. London: Cambridge University Press.

Conley, J. M., and O'Barr, W. M. (1990). *Rules Versus Relationships: The Ethnography of Legal Discourse*. Chicago: University of Chicago Press.

Conley, J., and O'Barr, W. (1998). *Just Words: Law, Language and Power*. Chicago: University of Chicago Press.

County of Washington v. Gunther, 452 U.S. 161, 101 S.Ct. 2242 (1981).

Deutsch, M. (1985). *Distributive Justice: A Social Psychological Perspective*. New Haven, CT: Yale University Press.

Durkheim, E. (1964). *The Division of Labor in Society* (G. Simpson, Trans.). Toronto: Collier–Macmillan Canada Ltd. (Original work published 1893).

Feinberg, J. (1970). *Doing and Deserving: Essays in the Theory of Responsibility*. Princeton, NJ: Princeton University Press.

Felstiner, W., Abel, R., and Sarat, A. (1980–81). The Emergence and Transformation of Disputes: Naming, Blaming, and Claiming. *Law and Society Review, 15*, 631–654.

Foote, D. (1992). The Benevolent Paternalism of Japanese Criminal Justice. *California Law Review, 80*, 330.

Galanter, M. (1974). Why the "Haves" Come Out Ahead, Speculations on the Limits of Legal Change. *Law and Society Review, 9*, 95–160.

Greenberg, D. F. (1977). The Correctional Effects of Corrections: A Survey of Evaluations. In D. F. Greenberg (Ed.), *Corrections and Punishment, 8*, 111–148.

Greenhouse, C. J. (1986). *Praying for Justice*. Ithaca, NY: Cornell University Press.

Gusfield, J. (1963). *Symbolic Crusade: Status Politics and the American Temperance Movement*. Urbana: University of Illinois Press.

Habermas, J. (1996). *Between Facts and Norms: Contributions to a Discourse Theory of Law and Democracy*. (W. Rehg, Trans.). Cambridge, MA: MIT Press.

Hamilton, V. L., and Sanders, J. (1992). *Everyday Justice: Responsibility and the Individual in Japan and the United States*. New Haven, CT: Yale University Press.

Hart, H. L. A. (1961). *The Concept of Law*. London: Oxford University Press.

Holmes, O. W. (1897). The Path of the Law. *Harvard Law Review, 10*, 459.

Huo, Y. J., Smith, H. J., Tyler, T. R., and Lind, E. A. (1996). Superordinate Identification, Subgroup Identification, and Justice Concerns: Is Separatism the Problem, is Assimilation the Answer? *Psychological Science, 7*, 40–45.

Kelman, H., and Hamilton, V. L. (1989). *Crimes of Obedience*. New Haven, CT: Yale University Press.

Kluegel, J. R., and Matějů, P. (1995). Egalitarian vs. Inegalitarian Principles of Distributive Justice. In J. R. Kluegel, D. S. Mason, and B. Wegener (Eds.), *Social Justice and Political Change: Public Opinion in Capitalist and Post-Communist States*. New York: Aldine de Gruyter, 209–238.

Kornhauser, L. (1998). A World Apart? An Essay on the Autonomy of the Law. *Boston University Law Review, 78*, 747.

Lane, R. E. (1986). Market Justice, Political Justice. *American Political Science Review, 80*, 383–402.

Lempert, R. (1987). The Autonomy of Law: Two Visions Compared. In G. Teubner (Ed.), *Autopoietic Law: A New Approach to Law and Society*. Berlin: de Gruyter.

Lerner, M. J. (1980). *The Belief in a Just World*. New York: Plenum Press.

Lerner, M. J. (1981). The Justice Motive in Human Relations: Some Thoughts on What We Know and Need to Know About Justice. In M. J. Lerner and S. C. Lerner (Eds.), *The Justice Motive in Social Behavior*. New York: Plenum Press, 11–35.

Macaulay, S. (1966). Non-contractual relations in business: A preliminary study. *American Sociological Review, 28*, 55–67.

Mashaw, J. L. (1983). *Bureaucratic Justice: Managing Social Security Disability Claims*. New Haven, CT: Yale University Press.

Miller, W. I. (1990). *Bloodtaking and Peace Making: Feud, Law and Society in Saga Iceland*. Chicago: University of Chicago Press.

Miller, W. I. (1998). Clint Eastwood and Equity: The Virtues of Revenge and the Shortcomings of Law in Popular Culture. In A. Sarat and T. Kearns (Eds.), *Law and the Domains of Culture*. Ann Arbor: University of Michigan Press, 161–202.

Mnookin, R., and Kornhauser, L. (1979). Bargaining in the Shadow of the Law: The Case of Divorce. *Yale Law Journal, 88*, 950.

Nonet, P., and Selznick, P. (1978). *Law and Society in Transition: Toward Responsive Law*. New York: Harper & Row.

Nozick, R. (1974). *Anarchy, State, and Utopia*. New York: Basic Books.

O'Barr, W. M. (1982). *Linguistic Evidence: Language, Power and Strategy in the Courtroom*. New York: Academic Press.

Packer, H. (1968). *The Limits of the Criminal Sanction*. Stanford, CA: Stanford University Press.

Platt, A. (1977). *The Child Savers* (2nd ed.). Chicago: University of Chicago Press.

Rawls, J. (1971). *A Theory of Justice*. Cambridge, MA: Harvard University Press.

Rossi, P., and Berk, R. (1997). *Just Punishment: Federal Guidelines and Public Views Compared*. New York: Aldine de Gruyter.

Sanders, J., and Hamilton, V. L. (1987). Is There a 'Common Law' of Responsibility? *Law and Human Behavior, 11*, 277–297.

Sarat, A., and Felstiner, W. (1995). *Divorce Lawyers and Their Clients*. London: Oxford University Press.

Shweder, R. A., Mahapatra, M., and Miller, J. G. (1987). Cultural and Moral Development in India and the United States. In J. Kagan and S. Lamb (Eds.), *The Emergence of Morality in Young Children*. Chicago: University of Chicago Press, 1–83.

Spader, D. J. (1986). Megatrends in Criminal Justice Theory. *American Journal of Criminal Law, 13*, 157.

Thibaut, J., and Walker, L. (1975). *Procedural Justice: A Psychological Analysis*. New York: Wiley.

Tyler, T. R. (1988). What is Procedural Justice? Criteria Used by Citizens to Assess the Fairness of Legal Procedures. *Law and Society Review, 22*, 301–335.

Tyler, T. R. (1990). *Why People Obey the Law*. New Haven, CT: Yale University Press.

Tyler, T. R. (1997). Citizen Discontent with Legal Procedures: A Social Science Perspective on Civil Procedure Reform. *American Journal of Comparative Law, 45*, 871.

Tyler, T. R., Boeckmann, R. J., Smith, H. J., and Huo, Y. J. (1997). *Social Justice in a Diverse Society*. Boulder, CO: Westview Press.

Zipursky, B. C. (1998). Rights, Wrongs, and Recourse in the Law of Torts. *Vanderbilt Law Review, 51*, 1.

II

The Dimensions of Justice

2

Retribution and Revenge

Neil Vidmar

A. HEINOUS CRIMES AND THE MINUTIAE OF EVERYDAY LIFE

Retribution and revenge continue to play a central role in modern systems of criminal law and move jurists and philosophers to write volumes on the subject. Commenting on Dostoevsky's theme of retribution in *Crime and Punishment*, H. L. A. Hart wrote:

> Perhaps some of us would wish to hasten the disappearance of these ideas not only from public policy and the criminal law, but from human consciousness altogether. Nonetheless, we still need to understand the moral and psychological appeal which these ideas have, for they have not disappeared yet nor have they been relegated wholly to the sphere of private moral censure. (*Punishment and Responsibility*, 1968:158)

In response to Justice Marshall's assertions in *Furman v. Georgia* (1972) that capital punishment has its roots in private vengeance that was transformed into violent retaliation by members of a group or tribe against persons committing hostile acts toward other group members and is thus an outmoded rationale for punishment in civilized societies, Justice Stewart wrote:

> The instinct for retribution is part of the nature of man, and channeling that instinct in the administration of criminal justice serves an important purpose in promoting the stability of a society of government by law. When people begin to believe that organized society is unwilling to impose upon criminal offenders the punishment they "deserve," then are sown the seeds of anarchy—of self-help, vigilante justice and lynch law. (at 2761)

Retribution and revenge, two highly related concepts, are arguably the oldest, most basic, and most pervasive justice reactions associated with human social life. Anthropologists have argued that they are the principal means of social control in "prelaw" societies as diverse as the precolonial tribes of New Guinea, the Dafla hill people of India, African Bushmen, and American Indians (e.g., DuBois, 1961; Furer-Haimendorf, 1967; Hoebel, 1954). Retribution and revenge are primary themes in the Homeric tales, Icelandic sagas, and the Old Testament

Neil Vidmar • Duke University Law School, Durham, North Carolina 27706.

Handbook of Justice Research in Law, edited by Sanders and Hamilton. Kluwer Academic / Plenum Publishers, New York, 2000.

(Miller, 1990, 1996, 1998). The themes of retribution and revenge are played out not only in our classical literature like *Crime and Punishment* but they also drive box office receipts in movies like *Death Wish*, *The Godfather*, and *Thelma and Louise*. Victims of crime (see Halleck, 1980) and those who hear about crime (see Ellsworth and Gross, 1994) seek retribution. Retribution lies at the core of the victims rights movement (Fletcher, 1995; Henderson, 1985) and shapes developments in the law of evidence with respect to the admissibility of "abuse excuses" (Mosteller, 1996). Retribution is an important concept in the development of meanings of criminal responsibility (Umphrey, 1999) and in the willingness to forgive very serious crimes such as apartheid crimes in South Africa (Gibson and Gouws, 1999).

While scholarship about retribution and revenge has tended to focus on criminal justice, empirical evidence also indicates the importance of retribution in other matters related to law. Medical malpractice (Sloan *et al.* 1994), discrimination (e.g., Crowe, 1978), and, indeed, a panoply of civil lawsuits (Keeva, 1999; Merry and Silbey, 1984; Shuman, 2000) can be primarily fueled by a desire for retribution. Retribution also figures in doctrinal analyses of tort law regarding the relative weights and merits of punishment versus compensation (Coleman, 1992). The perceived outrageousness of the defendant's actions in civil lawsuits may be correlated with judgments about the appropriate severity of punishment and the amounts awarded for punitive damages (Kahneman, Schkade, and Sunstein, 1998). Retributive motives appear at the core of intractable business disputes and affect the chances that they can be resolved by nonlitigation (see Kim and Smith, 1993; McEwen and Milburn, 1993).

A focus on law and legally related topics, however, ignores broader contexts in which retribution motives are relevant. Fritz Heider's classic work, *The Psychology of Interpersonal Relations* (1958), showed that retribution and revenge are omnipresent in all the interstices of ordinary social relations. Retributive reasoning appears early in the development of the child (Piaget, 1948) and affects young children's explanations of peer and family violence (e.g., Astor, 1994). Parents confronted with the sudden death of a child experience retributive feelings (Drenovsky, 1994). Children who articulate goals of revenge in response to conflict with friends are more likely to have fewer and poorer quality friendships (Rose and Asher, 1999). Remorse and apology affect retributive responses in numerous settings, but these tendencies differ between cultures, and they vary according to whether the offender is a member of one's own group or an outsider (Hamilton and Sanders, 1992; Leung and Morris, this volume; Ohbuchi, Agarie, and Kameda, 1989).

In this chapter I develop a conceptual framework to study retribution as a psychological and social phenomenon. The approach differs distinctly with most writings in law and philosophy that are devoted to developing a jurisprudential rationale. Section B explores a number of crucial conceptual issues, including how a social science approach differs from legal and philosophical approaches. My discussion explores the sociological and psychological functions that punishment serves. This discussion suggests that at a functional level retribution is forward looking as well as backward looking, an insight that has broad import, including formal justification for punishment. The discussion in Section B also helps to provide a perspective on "disinterested" punishment responses, that is, responses of persons apparently not directly affected by the rule violation, and the closely related phenomenon of "victimless" crimes. While much of empirical research has been concerned with criminal justice issues, the research paradigm applies to many other areas of social relations. Section C discusses the cognitive dynamics of retribution. Section D turns to the emotional and behavioral aspects of retribution. The analysis draws attention to the close nexus between retribution and research on aggression and violence (see also Felson and Tedeschi, 1995; Tedeschi, Smith, and Brown, 1974). Surprisingly, the obvious conceptual tie between these two areas has been almost ignored. The latter is deeply concerned with behavior, but research on the former has neglected the behavioral consequences of arousal of retributive justice emotions. By making this linkage explicit we quickly see that arousal of retributive feelings can have serious social and psychological consequences. The review indicates that most empirical research on retribution has used a "cold" cognitive model to explain retributive feelings but that a "hot" model that considers emotional factors is essential to study retribution. Finally, the research paradigms have typically stopped at the point of investigating the antecedents of emotions without following up on the sequelae of arousal. This last insight raises implications for legal and other settings in which punishment is administered.

A qualification is important before turning to Section B. Given the pervasiveness of retribution and revenge as justice motives, it is remarkable that so little empirical research has been devoted to these topics. More than 15 years ago, Hogan and Emler (1981) and Dale Miller and I (Vidmar and Miller, 1980) attempted to draw attention to the paucity of work on the subject by psychologists and other social scientists. Hogan and Emler persuasively argued that social psychology has been too concerned with questions of distributive justice and, in consequence, has neglected the more pervasive phenomenon of retributive justice. A review of the research literature that has been produced in the intervening decades indicates that volumes of material bearing on distributive justice (e.g., Gaertner and Klemish-Ahlert, 1991; Mellers and Baron, 1993) and procedural justice (e.g., Lind and Tyler, 1988; Tyler, 1990) have been produced, but new empirical research on retribution is relatively sparse. To be sure there are individual studies and even recognition of its importance more generally in justice research (e.g., Feather, 1996, 1998; Tyler, Boeckmann, Smith, and Huo, 1997), but the subject still has received much less systematic attention by social scientists than it deserves.

To set the stage for issues that arise in this essay, consider a simple hypothetical incident and a series of questions that arise from it. A professor is lecturing to his class. Near the end of the period a student raises his hand and asks a question. The professor responds by calling the student stupid for asking that question, draws attention to the fact that he has already flunked two tests, and asserts that perhaps his IQ is too low for adequate university performance. In addition, he makes an unflattering remark about the student's facial birthmark. The professor walks out of the room leaving the student and his classmates in stunned silence. The next morning the student and his classmates learn that within hours after the incident, the professor was accidentally sideswiped by a bus and suffered a broken arm and multiple bruises.

Even though the bus incident was totally unconnected to the professor's violation of professional and interpersonal codes of behavior, it is likely that the target of the professor's attack, the other members of the class, and even some students who had already heard about the incident would feel a sense of satisfaction. In fact, each reader of the above scenario will probably assert that the professor suffered condign punishment.

Robert Hogan and Nicholas Emler (1981:133) argued that

> insofar as philosophers and social scientists have considered retribution at all, it has been in the context of formal legal processes. Retribution is also and perhaps more frequently an issue in the minutiae of our everyday informal dealings with one another. Even in the most trivial details of their encounters, people cannot ignore the claims of retributive justice.

Hogan and Emler slightly overstate their case about past neglect—but only slightly. Emile Durkheim (1893/1964:85–96) argued that the urge to punish is a "passionate reaction" to violations of socially constructed rules that are held informally among members of groups as well as formally. As noted above, Fritz Heider's (1958) classic theory of interpersonal relations recognized the pervasiveness of retributive reactions in simple dyadic relationships. In fact, both Heider and Hans Kelsen (1943), to name two social scientists, drew attention to the fact that even outside events—such as the hypothetical professor's bus encounter—are viewed as signs that the recipient of harm has done something against the "ought forces, the objective order" (Heider, 1958:264). Heider's analysis suggests that even if we learned only that the professor had been hit by a bus, there is a tendency to interpret his suffering as a judgment for harm done. Melvin Lerner's (1971, 1977; Lerner and Miller, 1978) "Just World" hypothesis is rooted in similar psychological dynamics.

We can think of many alternative endings to the hypothetical scenario involving the professor's violation of common rules of social conduct and raise questions about different qualitative and quantitative reactions to those endings. The student's classmates immediately speak out with indignation against the professor. After class the recipient of the abuse slaps the professor in the hallway in front of other students, or perhaps pushes him causing a fall that breaks the professors arm. Or perhaps the student or his classmates file a protest with the dean who sanctions the professor; perhaps the sanctioning occurs within a couple of weeks or, alternatively, it occurs a year later after a formal hearing. Or perhaps the professor is never sanctioned and the student never retaliates. Perhaps the professor expresses remorse for the behavior or, instead, remains unrepentant. The gender or race of the professor or the student could differ. Instead of a professor–student relationship the scenario could involve a similar norm violation involving two professors or two students.

Criminal violations, especially those involving death or serious injury, are likely to evoke more intense emotional responses than this contrived example of the rude professor. However, the example makes the point, argued by Heider and by Hogan and Emler, that retributive justice emotions arise in many human encounters outside of legal contexts. The alternative scenarios about outcomes from the classroom incident raise important other questions about retribution. Are reactions different if the justice is dispensed by the victim, by neutral authorities, or by "acts of fate" (or God)? What are the consequences when nothing happens to the perpetrator? When are reactions confined to affect and cognitions alone and when do they result in behavioral responses? Do retributive feelings dissipate over time? Under which circumstances do they persist? How does excessive punishment of the offender or offender remorse affect retributive reactions? To what degree is the intensity of a retributive reaction influenced by the context, or by personality variables, or by the nature of the relationship of the parties?

Before turning to these empirical questions we need to sort out some conceptual issues.

B. CONCEPTUAL ISSUES

1. Retribution as a Moral Reaction

Retribution is a slippery concept that has eluded attempts at a parsimonious definition, although many philosophers, legal scholars, and social scientists have tried. As noted, Durkheim (1893/1964:85–96) asserted that retribution is a passionate reaction to the violations of a rule, norm, or law that evokes a desire for punishment of the violator. Heider (1958:264; see also Miller, 1993:Chapter 1) contrasted reactions to benefits bestowed with harms caused by another. The former evokes gratitude whereas the latter is a violation of "ought" forces calling for punishment of the offender.

A focus on the violation of norms and rules is particularly important to avoid confusion.

Psychologists have often used the term *punishment* to refer to aversive stimulation used to condition the behavior of rats in a Skinner box or to deter a child from touching an electric outlet (see Vidmar and Miller, 1980:568). Indeed, the term *retribution* has also been used to describe allocation rules for the distribution of outcomes within groups (e.g., Törnblom and Jonsson, 1985, 1987). These uses of the term *punishment* are misleading for my present purposes and specifically ignored in the rest of this chapter.

However, even in the context of a rule violation it is important to conceptually separate motives for punishment. Vidmar and Miller (1980) classified punishment reactions according to two main types: behavior control and retribution. They further distinguished whether the primary goal of the punishment was to change behavior or assert power over the actual offender or whether the goal was directed toward others in the social environment. This classification scheme, slightly revised from the original, is reproduced as Table 1.

Behavior control motives are similar to what are commonly labeled utilitarian motives. When a rule, norm, or law is violated the punishment reaction may be simply the elimination of present or future violations or restoration of the status quo. As the top half of Table 1 indicates, the reaction may be directed against the offender or intended as a message to others. In criminal law these goals are usually called "specific" and "general" deterrence. Thus, punishment may be sought to deter the actual offender, isolate him, reeducate him, or force him to give restitution to the victim. Alternatively, punishing the offender may serve, by example, to deter others from committing the rule violation, to prevent vengeance by the victim, or to disavow the act. Behavior control is not concerned with the moral character of the offender or even his or her intention. The amoral application of pain was clearly captured in Anthony Burgess's novel *A Clockwork Orange* (1962): Alex, the main character, was subjected to highly aversive procedures of behavior modification to suppress his capability to carry out violence but was released as soon as suppression was accomplished. Consider that behavior control motives are relevant to family and informal group settings as well. A child may be deprived of her allowance, given a "time out," or forced to repay her sister in order to deter future rule violations. At the same time the punishment also conveys a message to her siblings about behavior and may prevent retaliation by the victimized sibling.

In contrast, retributive justice is concerned with the moral nature of the offense. In the film version of *A Clockwork Orange* this concern was expressed in the voice of the prison guard who muttered, with apparent Kantian logic, that behavior modification was not right, that Alex *deserved* to be punished. Heider (1958:263–276) observed that when one person is

TABLE 1. A Classification of Purposes Underlying Punishment Reactions

	Target	
	Offender	Social group
Behavior control	Deterrence; isolation elimination; reeducation of offender; restitution to victim	General deterrence or threat; prevention of vengeance by victim or others, upholding morale of conformers; disavowal of act
Retribution	Change in offender's belief system vis-à-vis victim or societal rule; reaffirmation of private self-image of victim or surrogates; status degradation and differentiation of offender; assertion of power over offender	Vindication of societal rule; reestablish social consensus about validity of rule; diffuse release of psychological tension through social comparison processes; restore group cohesion and legitimacy

judged to have intentionally harmed another, far more is involved than the social, physical, or material hurt. The offender is perceived as demonstrating contempt for the person harmed, as asserting power over the victim, or as declaring the superiority of the offender's beliefs or value systems over those of the victim. The anger felt by the victim translates into an urge to punish to reestablish the psychological equilibrium. Punishment helps to nullify the offender's contempt for the victim by establishing the moral inferiority of the offender and the superiority of the victim and the rules that guide interpersonal relations. In his discussion of "vengeance" for perceived serious wrongs, Robert Solomon (1990:40–41) has argued

> to seek vengeance for a grievous wrong, to revenge oneself against evil: that seems to lie at the very foundation of our sense of justice, indeed, at the heart of ourselves, our dignity and our sense of right and wrong.... Vengeance is the "undoing of evil", "getting even" for wrong.
>
> It is not just punishment, no matter how harsh. It presupposes personal, emotional intensity, not just an abstract sense of obligation or rationality. yet, it is not just aggression and self-assertion either but, in a deep philosophical sense, getting even, putting the world back in balance, supplying the retribution or retaliation that will put things right and pay back the offender. It is not first of all a thought ... but rather a feeling, a primal sense of the moral self and its boundaries.

However, these emotional reactions to moral wrongs extend beyond the victim, his kin, and extended social relationships (e.g., Peristiany, 1966). William Miller (1996:5) argues that "a desire for justice and the capacity for experiencing something like indignation at injustice is a near universal feature of adult affective life." Miller explores this theme in the psychological appeal of tales in Icelandic sagas, *The Iliad*, *Hamlet*, and modern films like *Death Wish*, *Dirty Harry*, and *Unforgiven*. He argues that "the modern [Clint] Eastwood style revenge narrative takes us from indignation and outrage at a wrong, via fear and loathing of a wrongdoer, to a sense of satisfaction of having the wrong righted on the body of the wrongdoer." A similar point was made by the Israeli court that sentenced Adolph Eichmann: "punishment is necessary to defend the honor or the authority of him who was hurt by the offense so that failure to punish may not cause his degradation" (see Arendt, 1976:287).

While Miller, Solomon, and the Israeli court have focused on extreme wrongs, the basic dynamics would appear to easily apply to more mundane interpersonal relations. Why is it that the reader of this chapter feels a sense of injustice at the behavior of the hypothetical rude professor and, perhaps, a sense of satisfaction when he subsequently suffers? Heider (1958:273) as well as others (Mäkelä, 1966; Ranulf, 1964; Scheler, 1961; Westermarck, 1932) also took cognizance of third-party reactions to a rule violation in their discussion of "disinterested" retributive emotions. Drawing on the earlier work of Westermarck (1932), Heider argued that we feel strong emotions about an injustice because we sympathize with the person who was harmed or with his reactions to the harm.

Durkheim (1893/1964), however, had earlier drawn attention to the *social* implications of rule violations. Rules, norms, and laws help to define the boundaries and social values of groups. Violations of these prescriptions and proscriptions are a threat to the values of the group and its social cohesion. Durkheim's insight helps explain retributive reactions to "victimless" crimes such as prostitution or gambling in which a reactor to the offense perceives a threat to the value system of the group. Mead (1918) and Malinowski (1926) also drew attention to the group motives involved in punishment. Indeed, pigs, rats, and even inanimate objects were formally prosecuted for crimes by the early Greeks and citizens of the Middle Ages (see Berman, 1994). The likely function of such prosecutions was to reestablish social consensus about group norms. Kai Erikson (1966) explored the boundary-maintaining dynamics of threats to group values in his study of the Salem witch trials, and Gusfield (1963) examined the phenomenon in the context of the Temperance Movement that led to Prohibition. Contemporary controversy about homosexuality also involves concern about societal values (see Herek, 1986, 1988). Fletcher's (1995) proposed victim-oriented criminal justice reforms take into account the fact that punishment of offenders serves as a symbol for political groups that identify with victims, although he does not explore the dynamics for the groups themselves.

Punishment of rule offenders, therefore, may serve group maintenance functions. In their classic study of Polish peasant society in Europe and the United States, Thomas and Znaniecki (1902/1943) argued that the primary purpose of punishment was renewal of group values, the effects on the offender being only a secondary consideration. George Hebert Mead (1918:587) made the same point: The offense threatens social structure; punishment serves to identify the offender as an enemy and "to awaken in law abiding members of society the inhibitions which make rebellion impossible to them" (see also Ranulf, 1964).

Unlike the passage cited from the Israeli court's decision on Eichmann, which focused on the victims, Garfinkel (1956) saw punishment as a status degradation ceremony that serves maintenance functions for group values. Punishment, in his view, asserts group values by lowering the status of the offender. Punishment disavows the offensive act because the status degradation that accompanies punishment defines the offender as outside the group. A corollary of the above theorizing is that when an offender recants or shows remorse for an offense, group values are even more strongly affirmed. Recall that in George Orwell's *1984* (1971), the ultimate purpose of Room 101 was to foster love of Big Brother's rules. Garland (1991:195) has argued that the criminal penalty

> communicates meaning not just about crime and punishment but also about power, authority, legitimacy, normality, morality, personhood, social relations and a host of other tangential matters. Penal signs and symbols are one part of a complex array of institutional discourses that seek to organize our moral and political understanding and to educate our sentiments and sensibilities. They provide a continuous, repetitive set of instructions as to how we should think about good and evil, normal and pathological, legitimate and illegitimate, order and disorder. Through their judgments, condemnations and classifications they teach us how to judge, what to condemn and how to classify.

Although, as noted previously, much sociological and social psychological theorizing has centered on serious crimes, a moment's reflection will suggest that the same dynamics apply to violations of rules in primary and secondary groups. Members of work (or student) groups, social or religious groups, and families can experience retributive emotions when group norms are threatened; and they often respond to those feelings with gossip, ostracism, or other sanctions.

The lower half of Table 1 summarizes the above discussion. Retributive reactions may arise from dynamics associated with the harm to the specific victim. The accompanying punitive responses seek to reaffirm the self-image of the victim or those who identify with her, to change the offender's belief system, or to assert power over the offender. At the same time the offense threatens group solidarity. Punishment of offenders attempts to restore solidarity by degrading the offender, vindicating the rule, and reestablishing group consensus about the morality of the rule.

2. Retribution, Revenge, and Vengeance

There is considerable debate and conceptual confusion about the terms *retribution*, *revenge*, and *vengeance* in everyday usage and in scholarly and legal writings. The dictionary says *retribution* is recompense or reward; the dispensing or receiving reward or punishment. *Revenge* and *vengeance* are roughly synonymous terms referring to retaliation in kind or degree: the infliction of injury in return for an insult, injury, or offense. *Retribution* can have a more neutral connotation than *vengeance* or *revenge*, which are personal and always connote negative affect and actions. However, the use of the term *retribution* in criminal law is always on punishment and the negative emotions. This chapter also focuses on punitive responses, but views retribution and revenge as having similar underlying dynamics.

3. Retribution in Criminal Law

As observed at the beginning of this chapter, in *Furman v. Georgia* (1972) Justice Stewart took issue with Justice Marshall's view that retribution was outdated, arguing that the desire for the death penalty involves retribution, channeling an instinct that is psychologically necessary for a stable society.

The Marshall–Stewart disagreement reflects a problem that has troubled criminal law and philosophical analysis, namely, how to distinguish legal from extralegal (or nonlegal) retaliation against offenders and to justify formal punishment schemes (Feinberg, 1970; Golding, 1975). Robert Nozik (1981:366–368), for example, listed five dimensions that separate retribution and revenge:

1. Retribution is done for a wrong while revenge may be done for an injury or harm or slight and need not be for a wrong.
2. Retribution sets an internal limit to the amount of the punishment, according to the seriousness of the wrong, whereas revenge internally need set no limit.
3. Revenge is personal ... whereas the agent of retribution need have no special or personal tie to the victim of the wrong for which he extracts retribution.
4. Revenge involves a particular emotional tone, pleasure in the suffering of another, while retribution either involves no emotional tone, or involves another one, namely pleasure at justice being done. Therefore, the thirster after revenge will often want to experience (see, be present at) the situation in which the revengee is suffering, whereas with retribution there is no special point in witnessing its infliction.
5. There need be no generality in revenge ... whether [the person] seeks vengeance, or thinks it appropriate to do so, will depend on how he feels at the time about the act of injury. Whereas the imposer of retribution ... is committed to ... general principles ... mandating punishment in other similar circumstances.

The themes of wrongs, proportionality, and impersonality dominate discussions of legal punishment (see Golding, 1975; Hart, 1963; Packer, 1968; Radin, 1980; Van den Haag, 1975). Cottingham (1979), for example, identified nine forms of retribution theories set forth by philosophers: repayment, desert, penalty, minimalism, satisfaction, placation, annulment, and denunciation. But while formal theories of punishment have high utility in the development of a rational jurisprudence, they may lead social scientists too far astray from the social psychological dynamics of retributive emotions and behaviors. William Miller (1996; see also Jacoby, 1983; Solomon, 1990), for example, persuasively argues that it is impossible to determine what retribution, as elaborated by Nozik, would look like without the accompaniment of emotions like indignation, disapproval, or outrage, or the desire to see an offender suffer.

There are at least four ways that a social psychological analysis of retribution needs to differ from most legal/philosophical analyses of formal punishment rationales. First, as already elaborated, the analysis should not separate revenge and retribution, except insofar as the retaliatory impulse is evoked in the victim or in third parties. The core underlying social and psychological mechanisms that evoke the response are the same, although they may differ in the degree of intensity, ego involvement, and social focus.

Second, legal/philosophical rationales tend to emphasize that while utilitarian goals of punishment are forward looking, retributive impulses are backward looking, that is, they focus on a wrong that has already been committed. In contrast, while a social psychological analysis must indeed consider the wrong that occurred, it must also recognize the present and future implications of punishment for such things as restoring the self-worth of the victim or solidifying group norms and values that are jeopardized by the offense.

Third, while formal legal rationales attempt to normatively specify the conditions of proportionality of punishment, a social psychological analysis must treat proportionality as an empirical issue. The question is whether victims or third parties apply a cognitive formula of proportionality or respond without regard to proportionality. Consider responses to an insult. One victim's justice needs may be satisfied by a reply insult, another's by gossip about the offender, another's by killing the offender, and still another's by killing not only the offender but also the offender's clansmen. Notions of proportionality are time bound, culturally bound, and subject to individual differences. For instance, among the Netsilik Inuit the permissible scope of retribution for a murder differed, depending on whether the murderer was a member of the victim's extended kinship group or a member of an out group. In the former instance retaliatory action was limited to the offender, but in the latter instance it extended to all members of the offender's kinship group (see Balikci, 1970).

In *Coker v. Georgia* (1977) the U.S. Supreme Court, reflecting changes in social attitudes, decided that capital punishment for the crime of rape was excessive, thus overturning laws that had been in existence from the beginning of the country. In short, social psychological analysis needs to measure retributive justice impulses along empirical continua. Legal punishment schemes may attempt to specify proportionality according to an ordered consistent rationale, but the psychological and social responses may be quite independent of such schemes. Indeed, *Fowler* indicates that even formal proportionality schemes may change in response to altered social and cultural values.

Fourth, formal legal and philosophical analyses are based on cognitive models of reasoning whereas emotions, most centrally anger, are central in understanding psychological processes. Psychological models need to combine cognitive, emotional, and behavioral components. Legal models may be very useful in understanding the cognitive mechanisms (e.g., Schultz and Darley, 1991), but they have little to say about the human emotions that accompany them or the behavioral impulses that result.

4. Retribution, Benefit, and Distributive Justice

Heider (1958:Chapter 10) contrasted reactions to benefits and harms. He thus took cognizance of the dictionary definition of *retribution* as a justice reaction involving positive as well as negative emotions, reward as well as punishment. Nevertheless, he noted an asymmetry in the effects of benefit and harms. An actor bestowing a benefit on another does usually evoke positive reactions. Heider observed that the act of benefiting may also convey power and status of the giver over the recipient. Nevertheless, he noted that a harm is far more likely to demonstrate power over the recipient than benefit. A harm is usually interpreted as an expression of contempt and evokes anger, the strongest of the negative emotions (Ellsworth,

1994; Ellsworth and Smith, 1988; Lazarus, 1991). The insight of Heider is that while benefits and harms may fall along opposite sides of a continuum, harms invoke stronger emotional responses and may also invoke different cognitive structures.

Hogan and Emler (1981) similarly considered benefits and harms together. They noted that most research and theorizing in psychology has focused on distributive justice in a positive sense, that is, the bestowing of rewards for contribution. They criticized the heavy research emphasis on distributive forms of justice to the neglect of harms, asserting that the underlying assumption of this approach is that "human relations are largely about how pools of goods and resources are to be distributed" rather than about the moral rules and their proscriptions that guide human interaction. Hogan and Emler (1981:131) offered four reasons for considering retribution the more central justice reaction. First, although people may be rewarded for conforming to social rules, rewards for conformity are unreliable and not typically part of moral expectations: We obey rules because they are right, not because we will be rewarded. At the least, violations of rules are more salient than conformity to those rules. Second, societies everywhere appear to have socially institutionalized mechanisms for dealing with violations of social prohibitions. Third, in administering justice, communities tend far more to punish culprits rather than compensate victims (see also Miller, 1996:3). Fourth, while it may be assumed that members of a community have the desire to break the rules from time to time, they are deterred because of the social costs involved.

The discussions of Heider and Hogan and Emler (see also Miller, 1993) recognize that principles of reciprocity (e.g., equity) are common to retributive and distributive justice reactions. Notions of intention of the actor and amounts of harm (e.g., the *lex talionis*) guide retributive emotions and punishment responses. This observation does not contradict the argument that proportionality is an empirical, as opposed to a normative, issue since people may respond with different cognitive structures and notions about proportionality as well as about when rules have been violated.

5. Levels of Analysis

An essential problem for social psychological research on retributive justice motives is to determine how they are represented in psychological structures. An empirical study requires that they be amenable to operationalization. Consequently, some levels of analysis will prove more fruitful than others in achieving this goal.

A number of biologically oriented writers (e.g., Alexander, 1987; Boyd and Richerson, 1992; Chagnon and Irons, 1979; Trivers, 1971) have argued that retribution has a biological basis. However, Boyd and Richerson argue that in large social groups norms of reciprocity are unlikely to evolve as a result of natural selection; rather, moralistic behavior evolves out of punishment directed toward noncooperators. The models used for this approach are primarily theoretical and provide no direct information on how retributive reactions exist in the person's psychological makeup.

Sociological writers such as Durkheim (1893/1964) and Thomas and Znaniecki (1902/1943), as already discussed, provide rich sources of insight from which to develop hypotheses. At the same time, these authors' main interest was with the objective consequences of retribution for the sociological characteristics of groups. Their focus was on latent functions (Merton, 1957) rather than explicit cognitive or emotional mechanisms, and their levels of analysis did not extensively explore specific group behavior.

Psychoanalytic writers (e.g., Alexander and Staub, 1956; Menninger, 1966; Pincoffs,

1966) stressed unconscious fears and other drives, like sadism, that generate reactions to criminals or other rule offenders. Psychoanalytic theory is not empirically testable, but research such as the study of the authoritarian personality (Adorno, Frenkel-Brunswick, Levinson, and Sanford, 1950), which has roots in the psychoanalytic tradition, is amenable to empirical testing, but that work does not directly address the issues of the representation of retributive components in psychological structures.

Svend Ranulf's (1964) theorizing about "disinterested punishment" shows how a partial bridge can be developed between social structure and psychological mechanisms. Ranulf hypothesized that the "middle class" will be most morally punitive in their orientation toward crime. He hypothesized that the middle class demands a high degree of self-restraint of its members and a commitment to rules as ends in themselves. Consequently, the associated psychological frustration of individual desires and needs results in greater punitiveness toward those who do not follow the rules. Ranulf relied on a historical analysis of Greek and Puritan societies to bolster his hypothesis, but his reasoning suggests that different personality and attitudinal manifestations of retribution will result from structural variations within a given society and between societies.

C. PSYCHOLOGICAL MECHANISMS IN RETRIBUTIVE JUSTICE

Heider's (1958:265–276) analysis of retribution in interpersonal relations provides a starting point for the present model of the psychological dynamics of retributive justice. His analysis included cognitive and affective components, homeostatic tendencies, the concept of the self, the moral "oughtness" associated with rules, and "disinterested" responses.

Consider, first, the responses of the victim of an intentional harm. Whether the harm is a physical injury, an economic injury, or a social insult, if the victim subjectively perceives the act as undeserved, she will perceive the injury as an expression of contempt by the offender for her self-worth and the values associated with that self. The act of harming is also an expression of power over the victim and induces disharmony in the victim's cognitive structures of the world and its "oughtness." The emotional response is anger. Quoting Bacon (1597), Heider (1958:263) observed that "contempt is that which putteth an edge upon anger, as much or more than the harm itself."

Following the arousal of anger, the consequent desire for punishment of the offender may serve several purposes. It may be an attempt to change the offender's belief structures to be consistent with those of the victim. It may also serve the function of reasserting the power and moral status of the victim that was lowered by the harmful act. Hence, the most satisfying form of revenge occurs when the offender is aware of why and who is administering the retaliatory punishment. Heider observed that in Homer's *Odyssey*, Odysseus would not consider himself avenged if Polyphemus were ignorant of who had blinded him and for what offense, a theme repeated untold times in classic literature, pulp novels, and modern movies. Third, to the extent that others are aware of the offender's contemptuous act, punishment helps to reestablish the victim's moral standing in the eyes of the relevant social community. The arousal of the emotion of anger, therefore, is a key component to retributive responses, but it arises in the context of cognitive mechanisms.

The arousal of anger is mediated by cognitions involving the nature of the harm and the perceived intention of the offender. Interpretation of the harm and its magnitude always has a social component. For example, even a physical or economic harm will be interpreted differently, depending on social and cultural expectations. The meaning will also be mediated by status factors between the harmdoer and the victim. In some cultural settings, for example, a higher status person may bestow injuries as a right of status differential whereas in other settings an injury committed by a higher status person would be seen as worse because the action violates the role obligations of higher status persons (e.g., Hamilton and Sanders, 1992). A physician who sexually assaults a patient under his care is likely to evoke greater sanctions than a physician who assaults someone not under his care (see Skolnick and Shaw, 1994).

Social injuries may evoke stronger reactions than physical or economic injuries. Social injuries, that is, insults to oneself or one's family or membership group, speak to the very core of selfhood (see Bond and Venus, 1991; Felson, 1978, 1982; Mikula, Petri, and Tanzer, 1990). There is an extensive literature on cultures of honor (e.g., Nisbett and Cohen, 1996; Peristiany, 1965) wherein an insult is inextricably bound up with a person's self and social standing. Nisbett and Cohen's recent research, which will be discussed below, demonstrates that the "culture of honor" dynamics are not confined to Mediterranean or tribal societies (Peristiany, 1965) but are at play in subcultures within the United States.

Third-party observers of a harm may also feel retributive emotions that are directed toward the harmdoer. Social scientists and philosophers alike have struggled with the problem of how to explain third-party, or "disinterested," reactions. That is, why do people respond so strongly to a perceived harm to a person or group that have no immediate connection to them? Psychological explanations have tended to fall into two categories. The first is based on identification with the victim. Simply, the observer of the harm places herself in the position of the victim and reacts as a surrogate victim. The psychoanalytic theories (Alexander and Staub, 1956; Menninger, 1966) emphasize this dynamic, but a similar notion is contained in Robert Solomon's (1990) argument that compassion for victims is a "natural justice" reaction that may have its origins in our sociobiological nature.

The second view conceptualizes the reactions of third parties in terms of violation of a social contract. Justice feelings arise out of the socialization process wherein we internalize the rules that make cooperation in groups possible. Violation of those rules threatens the perceived fabric by which society works and this engenders hostility toward the rule violator. From this point reactions to the offender follow the same path as the identification interpretations. Solomon (1990:Chapter 3) has critiqued the social contract position. He argues that the social contract is an artificial construct that ignores natural emotions like empathy and it implies that all human actions are based on self-interest. Jackson's critique is powerful but the identification/empathy model and the social contract model should be viewed as complementary models, rather than as antagonistic.

There is evidence that threats to internalized beliefs about justice do cause disharmony and motivate adjustments in belief structures (e.g., Lerner and Miller, 1978). Similarly, Ranulf's (1964) notion that the higher commitment to rules that restrain behavior causes greater punitive reactions to offenders is consistent with a social contract hypothesis. Research on the presence of repression in persons scoring high on measures of authoritarianism (Adorno *et al.*, 1950) is also consistent with this hypothesis.

Both the "identification" and "social contract" hypotheses fall quite short of a complete explanation because they ignore an important component of human life, namely, our nature as creatures of social groups. Durkheim (1893/1964), Thomas and Znaniecki (1902/1943), and more recently Garland (1991), as described earlier, drew attention to the fact that rule violations also have social consequences. An offense is a threat to community consensus about the correctness—that is, the moral nature—of the rule and hence the values that bind social groups together. In this sense the offense makes the social group or community a victim. Hostility toward the offender can thus arise from "belongingness" in the group independent of empathy toward the specific victim or of internalized feelings about a social contract. Indeed, this perspective helps us to understand hostility involving "victimless" crimes. It also helps us understand particular vitriol directed against apostates (see Toch, 1965:175–178; Vidmar and Miller, 1980). Persons who subscribe to group values and then reject them evoke greater outrage than persons who were never group members. For instance, it is highly unlikely that the *fatwa* and reward for killing Salman Rushdie as author of *The Satanic Verses* would have resulted if he had been raised as a Christian rather than as a Muslim (see Lewis, 1991; Pipes, 1990).

This perspective about the threat of an offense to group or community values also draws attention to the fact that punishment can serve the goal not only of attempting to change the beliefs or status of the offender but also of reestablishing consensus about the moral nature of the rule among members of the relevant social community. This was the point made by Garfinkel (1956) in his analysis of punishment as a status degradation ceremony. In short, as discussed by Vidmar and Miller (1980), retributive justice motives may arise from the perceived harm to the group or social community's shared values. The consequent desire for punishment of the offender serves the purpose of attempting to confirm or reestablish social consensus about the moral or "ought" nature of the rule that was violated. The offender, per se, may be a secondary target of the retributive response. Viewed from this perspective "disinterested" retributive justice is not disinterested at all: The response of the individual is based on identification with her or his group and the threat to values held by that group.

Retributive responses, whether from the direct victim of harm or from third parties, involve disturbances in cognitions about self, group values and "oughtness" which cause a negative affective reaction (anger) and a consequent desire to reestablish homeostasis by seeing the offender suffer loss of status and power. Under many conditions retributive arousal will have behavioral consequences in the form of aggression or other punitive responses toward the offender. This leads us to consider major variables that mediate the genesis and strength of retributive responses, both affective and behavioral. It also leads to consideration of the effect of punishment of the offender on the restoration of homeostasis, reduction of negative affect, and lessening of punishment responses.

D. AROUSAL OF RETRIBUTIVE MOTIVES AND THEIR CONSEQUENCES

The psychological, sociological, and philosophical writings about retribution and revenge, therefore, point to a six-stage model of their psychological dynamics: (1) there is a perceived rule or norm violation; (2) the rule violator's intention is perceived as blameworthy; (3) the combination of (1) and (2) threatens or actually harms values related to the perceiver's personal self, status, or internalized group values; (4) the negative emotion of anger is aroused; (5) the cognitions and aroused emotions foster reactions against the violator; (6) during or following punishment the anger dissipates, cognitions return toward homeostasis, and the rule or norm is perceived to be vindicated.

Several observations can be offered about this model. First, while ordinarily the stages will follow in sequence, this need not inevitably be the case. For instance, a person who is frustrated through some impersonal cause may adjust her cognitions to ascribe blame after the fact of anger arousal.

The second point is that the third stage involving the threat to values involving the reactor's personal status or her values as a member of a group will, most typically, be articulated in the form of violated justice principles. Heider's reference to "oughtness" is the abstract way of attempting to conceptualize this phenomenon. But whether the reaction is to a personal insult or to a harm bestowed to a third party, people usually respond with articulation of some form of the phrase "justice demands." The execution or imprisonment of a convicted murderer evokes statements that "justice is done." In noncriminal contexts the notion of retribution is similarly articulated as "desert" "justice," "righting a wrong," and the like. In short, the psychological nature of "oughtness" is typically a subjective phenomenon composed of an inchoate combination of cognitions and emotions whose separate elements cannot be isolated beyond words like *justice* and *injustice*. This component of the retribution reaction can probably only be studied through operationalizations that allow indirect observations of its effects.

The third point concerns the last stage and is especially important. Both theoretical and empirical perspectives must be amenable to the possibility that, rather than dissipating arousal and anger, punishment of the offender might actually increase anger and cognitions of harm. The act of punishment might validate the perception of harm or remove any ambiguity about the motivation or character of the offender. It is quite reasonable to hypothesize that in some instances punishment of an offender could move the social psychological field further from homeostasis. This latter possibility was not considered in Heider's formulation or in other scholars' discussions of the subject. To take a single example, do relatives of a murder victim who view the execution of the perpetrator find peace in their cognitive and emotional selves or does viewing the execution increase psychological disturbances? While there appears to be no systematic research on this question, it is clearly a question worth asking.

Finally, each of the stages will be mediated by cultural, social, and individual factors. Thus, for example, the importance of the specific rules or norms may vary across cultures. The status of the violator or the violator–victim relationship may differ across cultures or settings and affect perceptions, cognitions, and behavioral responses against the violator.

Most of the empirical literature that has explicitly focused on retribution has not traced these states or their consequences. Rather, retributive motives have simply been assessed without exploration of their psycho- and sociodynamic consequences. For example, a number of studies of attitudes toward the death penalty have shown that retribution rather than deterrence of crime is a principal reason for favoring the death penalty (e.g., Vidmar and Ellsworth, 1974). But the empirical explorations have stopped at this point. What has not been explored in retribution research are the behavioral consequences of the arousal of retribution motives. How are they expressed? What happens if the "urge to punish" is suppressed? What happens to individual and group responses when the killer is executed?

There is a literature that begins to shed light on these questions; but, surprisingly, it has not been linked to the retribution literature. That literature is research on aggression and violence. And, it should be added, research on aggression and violence frequently fails to mention or give sufficient attention to retribution. For instance, as will be discussed immediately below, the recent work of Nisbett and Cohen (1996) on honor and violence can be cast as a study of retribution even though the term *retribution* is mentioned only twice (on p. 38) and *vengeance* and *revenge* not at all. Other research on aggression does not even come close although, as will be shown, the research paradigms used in many of the studies implicitly begin with a violation of norms or rules.

1. Insult and Action: A Cultural Perspective

Peristiany's (1966/1974) volume on the dynamics of honor and shame in Mediterranean societies emphasized the close relationship between the concept of self-worth, group belongingness, and the need to act on a perceived insult to honor in order to maintain self-worth and social standing. Peristiany (1966/1974:11) argued that

> Honor and shame are the constant preoccupations of individuals in small scale, exclusive societies where face to face personal, as opposed to anonymous, relations are of paramount importance and where the social personality of the actor is as significant as his office.... when the individual is encapsulated in a social group an aspersion on his honor is an aspersion on the honor of his group. In this type of situation the behavior of the individual reflects that of this group to such an extent that, in his relations with other groups, the individual is forcibly cast in the role of his group's protagonist. When the individual emerges with a full social personality of his own, his honor is his sole keeping.

Peristiany's contrast between Mediterranean and Western societies and their sociostructural differences can be placed in a still broader context by reference to Triandis's (1996) distinction between cultures of individualism and collectivism. Triandis (1996:94), for example, has empirically demonstrated differences between Greek and American cultures with respect to attitudes toward punishment as well as conceptions of proper behavior. Clearly, group membership influences psychological perspectives and conditions what is viewed as a moral offense. Furthermore, group membership also conditions cognitive and emotional reactions and responses to them (see also Leung and Morris, this volume; Semin and Rubini, 1990). It is here that Nisbett and Cohen's (1996) research on the psychology of honor provides important empirical insights bearing on the mechanisms of retribution (see also Cohen, 1996; Cohen and Vandello, 1998).

Based on historical and sociological evidence and field research, Nisbett and Cohen (1996) hypothesized that male college students socialized in the southern United States would be more prone to express aggression in response to an insult than male students raised in northern states. Their reasoning was that socialization of males in the southern United States causes them to have attitudes making them hypersensitive to violations of rules of behavior that can be interpreted as a threat to their image of manliness. In a series of ingenious experiments, Nisbett and Cohen showed that, relative to students raised in the North, males raised in the South had stronger cognitive, emotional, and physiological reactions when they were insulted by another male. Moreover, the arousal caused by the insult resulted in southern males subsequently exhibiting aggressive behaviors toward a third-party male who had no direct connection to the male who had insulted him. (However, these reactions of the Southerners were not enhanced when the insult occurred in front of others as opposed to privately.)

The Nisbett and Cohen studies are highly relevant to the understanding of retributive emotions for several reasons. First, they demonstrate that reactions to rule violations involving the concept of self are socially conditioned and not limited to persons raised in Mediterranean societies. Second, they provide empirical data supporting the empirical linkages hypothesized by Heider and other theorists: that is, perception of a harm to oneself caused by another person leads to cognitions about intentions, expressed negative mood states, and heightened physiological arousal. Third, they demonstrate some behavioral consequences of these attitudinal and emotional changes. In the experimental paradigm used by Nisbett and Cohen the aggressive behavior was directed toward a third party but it is quite reasonable to hypothesize that if the subjects had had the opportunity to express aggression against the person who actually insulted them, the behavioral response would have been even stronger. Indeed, other studies in the Nisbett and Cohen volume are consistent with this interpretation. Fourth, the experimental paradigm used in the research demonstrates how psychological mechanisms related to retribution can be experimentally mapped.

A fifth and final point involves the potential generalizability of the Nisbett and Cohen findings beyond the culture of the South. In fact, Peristiany (1966/1974:11) anticipated such generalizability when he noted the similarity between Mediterranean men's reactions to perceived insults and those of school gangs and street corner societies. Similarly, at the end of their volume Nisbett and Cohen observe the similarity of southern males' responses to urban gang members' codes of the streets. Physical acts of retribution often occur when a person perceives him- or herself as being "dissed" (i.e., shown disrespect).

These findings are consistent with more general bodies of research on cross-cultural differences in psychological reactions. In an essay on cross-cultural differences in emotions, Ellsworth (1994:25–26) observed that

> It makes sense that there should be differences [in the dynamics of emotions] across cultures. Cultures differ in their definitions of novelty, hazard, opportunity, attack, gratifications, and loss, and in their definitions of appropriate responses. They differ in their definitions of significant events and in their beliefs about the causes of significant events, and these differences affect their emotional responses.... Finally, cultures differ in their beliefs about the meaning of emotional experiences, expressions, and behaviors.

Zajonc (1998) has reviewed other research showing cross-cultural differences in emotions.

Markus and Kitayama (1991) have shown how the self-concept is influenced by culture and society which in turn influences cognitions, emotions, and behaviors. Leung and Morris (this volume) have reviewed other literature relevant to retributive reactions and concluded that anger responses to injustice vary across cultures as a result of differences in the degree to which the culture endorses individualism versus collectivism, the extent to which authority roles are endorsed, the extent to which responses to conflict emphasize self-control and harmony, and the degree to which it is emphasized that personality is malleable.

This literature, therefore, suggests how psychological dynamics intimately associated with retribution and revenge are influenced by the socialization process and by cultural contexts.

2. Retribution in Studies of Anger and Aggression

While the Nisbett and Cohen studies focused on the cultural factors that lead to arousal and consequent generalized aggressiveness toward a third party, the extensive literatures on the psychology of anger and aggression contain studies with experimental paradigm roughly similar to that of Nisbett and Cohen demonstrating direct retaliation against the offender.

Although making no reference to Heider, Lazarus's (1991) theorizing about the arousal of anger is, with certain limitations, quite consistent with this view. Departing from psychologists, such as Berkowitz (1989), who suggest that anger can arise from any frustration, Lazarus insists that insult is the primary component in the arousal of anger. His "cognitive–motivational–relational theory" posits that anger arises solely from threats to self-esteem, or ego identity. Anger, in Lazarus's view, arises from an appraisal pattern that involves attribution of blame to a person, including the self, or entity that reflects negatively on self-identity and an evaluation that the perceived demeaning offense is "best ameliorated by attack" (1991:224–225). Lazarus attempted to explain the arousal of anger toward an offender in response to perceived harms bestowed on third parties—what Heider and others refer to as *disinterested* responses—through the mechanism of vicarious identification with the victim. While generally consistent with Heider and the position taken in this chapter, Lazarus's theory can be seen to be more of a psychological than a social psychological theory insofar as it does not give sufficient attention to the broader social and group maintenance functions that insults and harms convey.

In responding to the type of criticism that Lazarus identified, Berkowitz (1993) distinguished between *instrumental* aggression and *hostile* aggression. While the former is intended to achieve some goal other than harm, the latter is in response to the violation of social rules. Hostile aggression also involves ascriptions of intentions to the perpetrator of the harm. This formulation too is not inconsistent with the view set forth in this chapter, but at the core Berkowitz's theorizing sees rule violations as a moderator of negative affect caused by frustration. Like Lazarus's theorizing it also ignores, or at least downplays, the social causes and consequences of rule violations that were identified by Heider, Durkheim, and others.

In contrast to Lazarus and Berkowitz, Averill's (1982) theory of anger and aggression suggests that social norms define and dictate how anger arises. Averill posits that anger arises from a perception of an offense and of a blameworthy offender. Social norms also channel when and how the anger will be expressed, if at all. There is considerable similarity in Averill's stages that lead to anger and the stages that lead to retributive responses. However, his work, too, remains focused on the individual as opposed to the individual as a creature of the groups to which he or she belongs.

A selective review of some leading studies of aggression shows that insult or other rule violations evoke what can easily be characterized as retributive responses, though few of these studies attempted to directly analyze the cognitive mechanisms that moderated the responses. Nevertheless, they are extremely useful in considering the emotional and behavioral consequences of rule violations.

Ohbuchi and Ogura (1984, 1985; see also Borden *et al.*, 1971; Dengerink and Myers, 1977: Dengerink *et al.*, 1978) conducted laboratory experiments in which subjects received electric shocks from a stranger and then had the opportunity to retaliate. Their subjects retaliated with an approximate level of proportionality. Green (1968) demonstrated that an insult by a confederate, as well as generalized frustration, provoked higher levels of aggression against a confederate.

Other research has demonstrated that attributions of intent mediate aggressive responses. Johnson and Rule (1986), for example, conducted an experiment in which a subject was or was not insulted by a co-worker and then had an opportunity to deliver an aversive noise to the co-worker. Prior to the insult some of the subjects were provided with information intended to mitigate the co-worker's insult. Physiological measures of arousal were taken before the subject had the opportunity to retaliate. Insulted subjects exposed to mitigation information exhibited smaller increases in physiological arousal in response to the insult, reported less annoyance about the insult, and subsequently retaliated at lower levels than subjects who had not been informed of the mitigating factors.

3. "Disinterested" Retributive Responses

An insult involves direct psychological, social, or physical harm to the reactor but as Durkheim, Mead, Thomas and Znaniecki, Ranulf, and Heider, among others, have observed, retributive responses must also be understood in terms of the indirect harm to the social group and the values that its members have internalized. Ranulf's theory and psychoanalytic writers (e.g., Menninger, 1966; Weihofen, 1951) have centered on the frustration of individual desires that causes punitive reactions against those who violate rules. Heider, in contrast, was content to simply emphasize the notion of the "oughtness" of rules without concerning himself with how the feeling of "oughtness" came about. The sociological writers such as Durkheim and Mead were concerned about identification with social groups and the rules that are internalized through membership in those groups. Each of these levels of analysis has merit—and may be a rich source of theorizing.

Recent work by Fiske and Haslam (1996), drawing on Heider's cognitive theory of interpersonal relations, has begun to demonstrate that a great deal of human social thinking involves concerns about social relationships. Tyler and Lind (1992) have similarly emphasized the importance of group membership and feeling of belonging on justice reactions, albeit their emphasis has been on procedural justice. An extension of these theoretical perspectives leads to hypotheses about the degree of cognitive and affective response to an offender being directly associated with the degree of relational proximity of the reactor to the victim: the closer the cognitive relationship, the greater the likelihood of a retributive reaction.

However, it is also clear that retributive reactions occur in response to offenses where there is no direct connection between reactor and victim. Instead, the offense threatens deeply held moral values. Murder, for example, is an offense against a rule that is deeply internalized in almost all members of all societies. Although studies of death penalty attitudes find that beliefs about deterrence or the cost of keeping someone in prison for life are associated with support for capital punishment (e.g., Steiner, Bowers, and Sarat, 1999), retributive motives appear to be the most basic cause for its support (Bohm, 1992; Sarat and Vidmar, 1976; Vidmar and Ellsworth, 1974a).

Ellsworth and Ross (1983) concluded that for most people attitudes toward capital punishment are basically emotional. Reasons given for supporting the death penalty are determined by the affective reaction to the crime; the rationalization of beliefs about it comes afterward. In a comprehensive review of research on death penalty attitudes, Ellsworth and Gross (1994) concluded that factual information about such things as deterrence or discrimination is generally irrelevant to people's attitudes and in fact, people are aware that this is so. Those authors concluded that fear of murder is not the driving emotion behind support of the death penalty. Rather, it is likely that frustration and anger about crime drive support. Ellsworth and Gross (1994) observed that research indicates that anger is an empowering emotion (e.g., Ellsworth and Smith, 1988). Thus, the expression of anger may serve the role of helping to restore homeostasis in response to the cognitive and emotional upset evoked by the crime. Ellsworth and Gross observed that few attempts have been made to explore emotions underlying capital punishment attitudes.

Ogloff and Vidmar (1994) exposed samples of respondents to graphic testimony by former male child victims of homosexual assaults by members of a religious order. A video and a combined video and newsprint presentation of the testimony evoked stronger negative emotional responses that control and newsprint-only conditions. Persons in the former conditions recommended significantly longer sentences for the perpetrators, suggesting that degree of emotional arousal is a mediator of punishment responses.

Using data from four surveys, Warr, Meier, and Erickson (1983) explored public attitudes toward 19 offenses. They found that seriousness of offense, and societal frequency, are the central criteria people use to judge appropriate punishment. Consequently, they concluded that retributive and not utilitarian motives underlie attitudes toward crime.

Tyler and Boeckmann (1997) examined attitudes associated with public support for California's "three strikes" law that mandates life in prison for repeat felons. Like the research on death penalty attitudes, Tyler and Boeckmann's findings strongly suggest that support for the law is not solely related to perceptions of risk of victimization or dangerousness. Rather, support is associated with the evaluation of perceived changes in social conditions, including perceptions of a decline of morality in society, the decline of discipline within the family, and increases in the diversity of society. In short, punitiveness and retribution are associated with concerns about moral cohesion in society. If the Tyler and Boeckmann hypothesis is correct, those authors have shown that the phenomenon that Thomas and Znaniecki (1902/1943) uncovered among Polish peasants generalizes to mass urban societies. Concern with the rule breaker is often subordinate to more general concerns about threats to group values.

Gusfield's (1963) analysis of the Women's Christian Temperance Union movement revealed that a law supported by practical arguments against the evil of alcohol was actually motivated by status threats against the morals and value systems of WCTU members. Similarly, the argument that AIDS is God's punishment for persons who engage in homosexual acts or who engage in hard drug use may be seen as responses to threats to the moral fabric that these activities are perceived to entail (e.g., Herek and Glunt, 1993).

Vidmar and Miller (1980:583–584) hypothesized that while the strength of retributive responses may often be positively associated with the perceived degree of social consensus about a rule, diminishing consensus can increase retributive responses among group members who still subscribe to the rule and consequently view the erosion of support for the rule as a direct threat to moral codes, beliefs, and social status. Kai Erikson's (1966) study of the Salem witch trials interpreted the trials as an attempt to reestablish social consensus as Puritan society was besieged by outside influences. Similarly, apostates provoke more extreme retributive responses than outsiders because their rejection of rules and beliefs is a more serious threat to the values of the group (see Vidmar and Miller, 1980). Erikson (1966) observed that those Puritans who admitted to witchcraft and recanted were not hanged.

Thus, from a social and psychological perspective "disinterested" retribution differs from "interested" retribution primarily in the fact that in the former the harm perpetrated by the transgressor involves the internalized rules that bind the self to the group whereas the latter involves a more direct attack on the self that bears on the victim's standing within the group or in relation to internalized group rules.

4. Rule and Offense Characteristics

Heider (1958) hypothesized that the more important the rule is to the belief or value system of the individual reactor or the social group in which the reactor is enmeshed, the more likely a retributive reaction is to occur and the stronger it will be. The moral disapprobation associated with a rule violation may parallel the physical or material harm caused by the act, but, as previously described, offenses against moral values may also evoke strong retributive reactions. Cattle rustling in the American West was considered *malum in se* but, has Nader (1975) has described, among the Sards the act is only a *malum prohibitum*.

Viney, Parker-Martin, and Dotten (1987) compared punishment reactions of college students to four premediated crimes: murder, robbery, arson, and manslaughter. Retributive reactions predominated in response to murder but utilitarian reactions, such as deterrence, predominated in response to the other crimes. In a review of public opinion research, Roberts (1996:496) concluded that for low or moderately serious crimes, people are willing to abandon the retributive principle that punishment should be proportional to the gravity of the crime.

Hamilton and Sanders (1992) compared responses of Americans and Japanese to offenses occurring in family and work settings as well as to offenses involving strangers, the latter being automobile accidents and robbery. With respect to family and work settings, Americans were more likely to advocate retribution (as well as incapacitation and general deterrence) whereas the Japanese were more likely to favor rehabilitation, specific deterrence, and denunciation. Hamilton and Sanders (1992:138) ascribed these differences to American views of the offenses as originating in the individual whereas the Japanese were more sensitive to the role and social context. In consequence, American reactions were toward isolating the individual or extracting retribution but Japanese reactions were more concerned with restoring relationships. However, with respect to offenses involving strangers—the automobile injury and robbery cases—the Japanese assigned more responsibility than Americans and were stricter in their punishment responses. Other findings in the Hamilton and Sanders study indicate that differences are also mediated by role relationships. Leung and Morris (this volume) suggests that cultural responses that moderate retributive responses toward other group members may not apply when the violator is a member of an out-group.

Experimental studies conducted in the United States indicate that retributive responses are influenced by the degree of harm caused by the offense (Shaver, 1970; Shaw, 1967; Shaw and Reitan, 1969; Shaw and Sulzer, 1964; Taylor and Kleinke, 1992; see also Schultz and Darley, 1991). In a series of two studies Vidmar (1977, 1978) presented respondents with vignettes of murder cases in which the offender's intent to shoot and kill the victim was clear and unequivocal, but the result differed: in one condition the bullet was deflected and caused only a minor injury to the victim; in another it caused a serious injury; and in a third condition the victim was killed. The respondents rated the offender's intention to kill equally in all three conditions, but the magnitude of the punishment given by the respondents varied directly with the magnitude of the harm. Hills and Thomson (1999) presented a sample of Australian respondents with offense vignettes. Harsh sentences were imposed for offenses resulting in severe consequences, but there was a tendency toward relatively light sentences when the consequences of the offense were minor. In a noncriminal context, Ohbuchi *et al.* (1989) found that Japanese undergraduates who were actual victims of a psychological harm or who read vignettes about a harm situation expressed more anger and aggression when the magnitude of the harm was substantial rather than minor.

5. Offender Characteristics

Three main classes of offender variables are related to retributive responses: intentionally; role responsibility; and the offender's response to the rule violation.

a. Responsibility Ascription

Legal scholars (e.g., Hart, 1968), philosophers (e.g., Feinberg, 1970), and social psychologists (e.g., Heider, 1958; Piaget, 1948) have emphasized the role that ascribed responsibility plays in punishment responses. Building on the conceptual work of Piaget (1948) and Heider (1958), Shaw and Sulzer (1964) distinguished five levels of responsibility: responsibility through association, simple commission, foreseeability, intent, and justification. Although adults in modern Western cultures do not tend to ascribe responsibility by association, the other levels correspond roughly to the legal concepts of strict liability, negligence, willfulness or premediation, and various forms of mitigating excuses. Ordinarily we would expect that the degree of willfulness and premediation ascribed to the offender will be positively associated with the degree of retributive emotion evoked by the rule violation.

Shultz and Darley (1991) as well as a number of other authors (Darley and Zanna, 1982;

Feather, 1996, 1998; Jaspars, Finham, and Hewstone, 1983; Shaver, 1985) have developed cognitive information processing models, derived in part from judicial and philosophical writings, that connect moral reasoning about levels of responsibilities, or blameworthiness, and punishment responses as applied to nonlegal as well as legal settings. These models consider that judgments of blame are conditioned by developmental and social experience. The cognitive responses, moreover, interact with rule and offense characteristics, perceived role responsibility, and the post-offense behaviors of rule violators.

In samples of American and Japanese respondents, Hamilton and Sanders (1992:143, 163) found positive correlations between ascribed responsibility and willingness to punish wrongdoers in vignettes involving offenses in family and work settings and in situations involving crimes by a stranger. Itoi, Ohbuchi, and Fukuno (1996) similarly found differences between Americans and Japanese in responses to scenarios in which an actor unintentionally harmed someone. Because of their collectivist orientation (Triandis, 1995) Japanese were more sensitive to apologies whereas the more individualistic Americans were, relatively speaking, more likely to accept justifications that denied blameworthiness.

Feather (1996) conducted path analyses on variables purported to be linked to affective reactions to penalties. The offenses judged by his Australian subjects involved domestic violence, plagiarism, shoplifting, and resisting a police order. The path analyses showed that an offender's perceived responsibility influenced the perceptions of seriousness of the offense. Perceived responsibility and seriousness both influenced the degree to which the offender was seen to deserve the penalty. Furthermore, perceived deservingness also was related to judgments about and affective responses to the penalty's harshness. Alicke (1992), studying responses to accidents, found that negative affective responses to the offender's motives, reckless behavior, and the degree of harm produced an "active desire to place a 'stain' on the character of the offender." Both the Feather and Alicke studies demonstrate complex causal reasoning in affective reactions to harms and to consequent sanctioning.

Graham, Weiner, and Zucker (1997) further extended attribution theory in a study of public reactions to the arrest of O.J. Simpson the week following the murder of his ex-wife. Their samples of African-American and white subjects showed that persons who interpreted Simpson's actions as a stable personality disposition, who expressed anger about the crime, and who endorsed retributive as opposed to utilitarian purposes of punishment held more punitive attitudes toward Simpson. African-Americans, relative to whites, tended to view Simpson's actions as more situational, to feel less anger, and to endorse utilitarian goals of punishment. A follow-up experiment involving a hypothetical murder vignette supported the field survey. Graham *et al.* concluded that "[p]unishment decisions following criminal transgressions can be accounted for by individuals' beliefs about the goals of punishment, attributions about the cause of crime, and emotional reactions to the transgressor." This conclusion is generally consistent with the Alicke and Feather conclusions about the complex relationship between attributional tendencies, emotions, and punishment philosophies.

b. Role Responsibility

Hamilton and Sanders (1992) found that while both Japanese and Americans were concerned with the offender's mental state in judging responsibility, Americans were relatively more sensitive to this kind of information than the Japanese. This difference is probably related in large part to the greater emphasis the Japanese place on the social role context of offenses. The Japanese view role hierarchies and the normative responsibilities associated with those roles as very important. These beliefs, in turn, affect how responsibility is ascribed to different actors and consequent punishment responses. Hamilton and Sanders (1996) have extended these insights to study cross-cultural differences between Russians, Japanese, and Americans with respect to corporate wrongdoing. Russians assigned less responsibility to corporate wrongdoers than did Japanese and Americans. Those authors suggested that Russian attitudes are still affected by socialist ideas that do not invest corporate actors with "personhood" to the same degree as the Japanese and American capitalist systems.

Skolnick and Shaw (1994) explored role status effects in a different context. Those authors tested a hypothesis drawn from Wiggins and colleagues' (1965) status liability theory, namely, that a higher-status defendant would be judged more harshly than a lower-status defendant when the crime was serious and related to responsibility associated with the status. Skolnick and Shaw conducted an experiment in which the offender was described as high or low status (a licensed psychotherapist or a graduate student). The crime was associated with professional responsibility (occurring or not occurring in the context of therapy) and was either "serious" or "not serious" (rape versus insurance fraud). The high-status offender was sanctioned more severely than the lower-status offender when the crime was professionally related, but the low-status offender was sanctioned more severely when the crime was not professionally related. Shaw and Skolnick (1996) replicated the basic findings of the earlier experiment in the context of a civil lawsuit. Neither of these two experiments examined whether the basis of the sanctioning was related to retributive or to utilitarian reasons such as specific or general deterrence. Nevertheless, the results provide important information about the impact of role status and responsibility, and they raise intriguing questions about emotional reactions to offenses that have a direct bearing on our understanding of the psychology of retribution.

c. *Remorse and Apology*

Even when an offender is perceived as having knowingly caused a harm, the impact of this perceived intention on punishment responses may be reduced or offset by evidence that the offender experiences remorse. Historical evidence (see Hay, 1975) indicates that at public hangings in England the crowd expected the condemned person to make a confession of his or her bad character and misdeeds from the scaffold. While such confessions may have had entertainment value, they also served the function of affirming moral values of the community. Recall again that during the Salem witch trials, those persons who confessed to witchcraft and showed remorse were not hanged (Erikson, 1966). Hamilton and Sanders (1992) have documented the greater tendency of the Japanese, in contrast to Americans, to seek apologies from miscreants. Apologies serve the dual purpose of helping to integrate the offender back into the group and to reaffirm the moral basis of the value that was violated. Alexander and Staub (1956) observed that people generally respond much more warmly to a "penitent sinner" than to a "righteous man." At a psychological level we can ask what happens to retributive emotions in response to remorse.

Gibson and Gouws (1999) conducted a study of South Africans to determine public responses to the assumption underlying the Truth and Reconciliation Commission's recommendation that persons who confessed nefarious crimes under the apartheid regime should be granted amnesty. They found that leaders were judged more responsible for their acts than followers, that claims to have committed violence for noble purposes did little to exonerate perpetrators, and that actors were judged by the severity of the consequences of their actions. Although the survey involved individual respondents, the political and social context in which the survey took place raises serious questions about the effects of amnesty on social morale and cohesion.

Schwartz, Kane, Joseph, and Tedeschi (1978) explored reactions to a scenario in which two boys used a rope to trip a little girl who suffered with a slight or severe injury as a result. In some conditions one of the boys subsequently expressed remorse or pleasure about the incident while the other boy remained silent. In the remorse condition the female college students exposed to the various conditions perceived the boy as less aggressive, attributed less intent to the act, saw him as less likely to repeat the action, and reduced the recommended amount of punishment he should receive. The study did not clearly separate retributive from utilitarian reactions, but the subjects did perceive the boy expressing pleasure as more "deserving" of punishment. When the consequence of the act was severe rather than slight injury, respondents were more likely to indicate that the boy deserved punishment.

In one of a number of studies assessing public perceptions of liability for criminal offenses, Robinson and Darley (1995:13–28) presented respondents with a series of 11 scenarios involving a locksmith who considered stealing coins from a customer or actually completed the theft. In some conditions the locksmith was remorseful and returned or attempted to return the coins to the safe from which he had stolen them. In the remorse conditions respondents tended to believe the locksmith should not be held liable or, if liable, should receive no punishment.

Several other studies have also assessed the effects of remorse on attitudes toward criminal punishment. Kleinke, Wallis, and Stalder (1992) conducted two studies that examined the effects of denied intent and remorse on the evaluation of a convicted rapist. Multiple regression analysis indicated that recommended prison sentences were predicted by attribution of cause, intent, and remorse. Taylor and Kleinke (1992) examined expressions of remorse in the responses of men and women to a drunk driving accident in which the consequence was either death or monetary damage, and the driver either had a history of drunk driving or did not. Severity of outcome was positively related to sanctions. But, while expressions of remorse affected judgments about the offender's character, remorse had no effect on recommended sanctions. However, Robinson, Smith-Lovin, and Tsoudis (1994) did find evidence that displays of remorse had an indirect effect on severity of sentence recommendations in response to a manslaughter case involving drunk driving. The expression of remorse affected perceptions of the offender's identity, which in turn affected perceptions of the heinousness of the crime. Rumsey (1976) also found that a defendant's expression of remorse lessened the severity of punishment among students responding to a scenario of a negligent homicide. While suggestive, none of these four studies clearly separated retributive from utilitarian motives. Changes in perceptions of the offender's character could have been related to judgments of future recidivism rather than condign punishment.

Ohbuchi and colleagues' (1989) research examined the effects of an apology—an expressed form of remorse—on anger and aggression in a noncriminal context. In one study the victim of a psychological harm received an apology from the harmdoer. In a second experiment subjects played the role of a victim in a hypothetical harm situation. In some conditions restitution accompanied the apology, but in others it did not. Dependent variables involved impressions of the harmdoer's personality, the affective state of the victim, and aggression toward the harmdoer (evaluation of the harmdoer in the first experiment and verbal expressions of aggression in the second study). In both studies, an apology affected the victim's degree of negative affect, desire for further apology, and negative impression of the harmdoer. However, when the harm was severe rather than modest the effects of the apology on aggression toward the offender were attenuated. Moreover, in the final study, the apology was effective in reducing aggression only when it was accompanied by restitution.

No experimental test has been made of Alexander and Staub's (1956) "confessed sinner" hypothesis with respect to its importance for group cohesion. We can hypothesize, however, that under some conditions deviation and remorse strengthens group ties and cohesion more than high rates of group conformity for the simple fact that the deviation helps to define the group's boundaries (see Durkheim, 1964; Thibaut and Kelley, 1958).

6. Individual Differences

The research on cross-cultural differences suggests the way that socialization plays a part in the antecedents and consequents of retributive responses (see generally, Buss and Kendrick, 1998; Fiske, Kitayama, Markus, and Nisbett, 1998). Hence, we should also expect socialization differences within individual cultures. And it is also possible that biological differences between individuals could contribute to individual differences in retributive responses.

A number of studies (e.g., Segerstedt, 1949; Sharp and Otto, 1910; Shaw, 1967) reviewed by Vidmar and Miller (1980) found differences in the strength and nature of retribution and punishment responses between individuals. In the mid-1960s and 1970s a number of studies investigating attitudes toward capital punishment uncovered differences in the rate at which people endorsed retribution as a reason for favoring the death penalty (e.g., Hamilton, 1976, 1978; Sarat and Vidmar, 1976; Vidmar, 1974a). A number of studies also found correlations between the personality measure of authoritarianism (Adorno *et al.*, 1950) and retributive punishment reactions (e.g., Boehm, 1968; Dustin and Davis, 1967; Feather, 1996; Jurow, 1971; Mitchell and Byrne, 1973; Sherwood, 1966; Vidmar, 1974a). Stuckless and Goranson (1992) have in fact developed a "Vengeance Scale" to measure attitudes toward revenge that appears to have criterion and construct validity (see also Holbrook, White, and Hutt, 1995). However, to date these scales have not been tested against behavioral criteria.

Several studies have explored cognitive factors giving rise to retributive tendencies. Astor (1994) explored differences in groups of "violent" and nonviolent children's moral reasoning about provoked and unprovoked violence in family and peer settings. Both groups of children used moral reasoning to condemn unprovoked violence, but the violent group of children focused on the immorality of the acts in the provocation settings and sanctioned hitting back as a form of reciprocal justice. In contrast, the nonviolent group perceived hitting back to be worse than the psychological harm of the provocation. In another study, Graham and Hudley (1994) randomly assigned aggressive and nonaggressive African-American male adolescents to conditions that primed the perception of a physical altercation as intentionally or unintentionally caused. In the unintentional condition and a control condition the adolescents who were classified as aggressive made more extreme judgments of intentionally and preferred physical retaliation than did nonaggressive adolescents. Graham and Hudley proposed that aggressive children had higher construct accessibility for perceiving aggressive intentions.

Viney *et al.* (1987) found no differences in preferences for retributive versus utilitarian punishment for a felony as a function of their respective degrees of beliefs in free will or determinism as a cause of human action. However, there are other findings that appear inconsistent with this conclusion. Berg and Vidmar (1975), Boehm (1968), Centers *et al.* (1970), and Jurow (1971) found that persons scoring high on measures of authoritarianism tended to place more emphasis on the personal characteristics of a criminal offender than persons who had lower authoritarianism scores. The Centers *et al.* research suggests that this may result from the fact that high authoritarians tend to view offenders as personally responsible for their actions, whereas low authoritarians place a greater emphasis on environmental factors as a cause of human behavior. Other researchers, however, have hypothesized that the high and low authoritarians may differ in their susceptibility to affective emotions or conditions of status and authority (Berg and Vidmar, 1975; Mitchell, 1973; Mitchell and Byrne, 1973).

General tendencies toward retribution notwithstanding, the particular rules and circumstances of an offense may interact with these dispositions. For instance, Vidmar (1977, 1978) constructed accounts of criminal offenses where the rule that was violated involved a murder attempt in which one civilian tried to kill another civilian or involved a "crime of obedience" (Hamilton, 1976, 1978) in which a soldier attempted to kill an unarmed prisoner of war under influence of a superior officer. The attempt in both cases resulted in one of three possible outcomes: the victim incurred minor injury, suffered major injury, or was killed. It was predicted that high authoritarians would be more punitive toward the conventional murder attempt and that, relative to low authoritarians, punitiveness would increase with seriousness of outcome. However, because low authoritarians tend to evaluate crimes of obedience more severely that high authoritarians, it was predicted that low authoritarians would not only be more punitive than highs in response to this latter crime but punitiveness would increase in direct relation to severity of harm to the victim. Both predictions were confirmed. Mitchell (1973) also found an interaction between authoritarianism and punitiveness when the defendant in a tavern brawl involved either a draftsman (who shot an off-duty policeman) or an off-duty policeman (who shot a draftsman). Mitchell hypothesized that high authoritarians would defer to the policeman because of his status, whereas low authoritarians would hold him to a higher standard of conduct for the same reason. Recent research by Feather (1998) essentially replicates these earlier findings. In short, these studies, while affirming the importance of individual differences, also indicate the importance of the norm or law that was violated.

7. Punishment and the Restoration of Homeostasis

The psychological model developed in this chapter implies that the violation of the norm or rule, modified by cognitive factors, produces negative emotions and cognitions that punishment of the offender is intended to reduce, that is, to restore homeostasis. Thus, the effects of punishment on restoring homeostasis are theoretically interesting for this reason, but they also have practical applications for theories of legal punishment. Unfortunately there is very little research bearing on this aspect of retribution, and the research that does exist is only tangential to the direct issues.

Recall that Johnson and Rule (1986) found that insulted subjects exhibited smaller increases in physiological arousal if they learned of mitigating circumstances that could be a cause of an insult before the insult occurred rather than learning about the circumstances after it occurred. Moreover, the subjects exhibited less aggression toward the insulting person in the light of mitigating circumstances.

A study by Craig *et al.* (1993) involved a paradigm in which subjects were given an opportunity to retaliate against a person who had given them unduly harsh evaluations. After retaliating in kind the subjects learned that the person had recently suffered a mild or serious misfortune and that they had carelessly overlooked this mitigating information. In conditions where they would subsequently have an opportunity to do the person a favor they were less negative in their evaluation of the person than subjects without an opportunity to provide a favor. The findings provide support for the hypothesis that perceived overretaliation for the harm can be psychologically upsetting. This suggests that principles of equity may be associated with retributive reactions. The previously discussed research by Ohbuchi (Ohbuchi and Izutsu, 1984; Ohbuchi and Kambara, 1985) also indicated a proportionality principle.

Roberts (1996) has reviewed studies of public opinion about sentencing of offenders that point to a proportionality principle as well. Roberts concluded that the studies show that for low and moderately serious crimes, the public endorses the principle that punishment should be proportional to the crime.

The Nisbett and Cohen (1996) research suggests—but only suggests—that if the original offender who delivered the insult is not available for retaliation, the arousal could result in aggression directed toward others. However, no research has directly investigated this hypothesis. Similarly, no research has investigated the degree of dissipation of retributive impulses over time or the effects of punishment of offenders on these impulses. No research has examined the effects of failure to punish offenders on individuals or group cohesion and morale. Yet, this is a psychologically interesting phenomenon that also relates to public policy issues involving the role of punishment in society (Hart, 1968).

If, as this chapter has theorized from the writings of Durkheim and others, threats to group values are an important source of retributive responses, it follows that punishment of a rule violator should help to restore any group cohesion and morale that was damaged as a result of the offense. Similarly, when offenders escape punishment, the consequences for group cohesion and legitimacy should be negative. These are not only interesting hypotheses from a social psychological perspective; they also have direct implications for public policy issues, as exemplified by Hart's (1968) concerns and with Justice Stewart's position in *Furman v. Georgia* (1972) that retributive responses are a normal and necessary component of criminal justice. The basic principles may apply to organizational and other group settings as well. Unfortunately, existing empirical research on these issues is, to say the least, sparse.

E. AGGRESSION, COHESION, AND LEGITIMACY: CONCLUDING THOUGHTS ON RETRIBUTIVE JUSTICE

Philosophers, legal scholars, and social science theorists have recognized that the retribution motive is a central factor in human affairs, large and small. Yet, as this essay and its selective literature review demonstrates, we are a long way from understanding even basic social psychological dynamics of retribution and its behavioral consequences.

In attempting to lay the groundwork for a more intensive study of this phenomenon, this chapter has made a number of arguments bearing on how retribution should be conceptualized. Legal and philosophical writings attempt to distinguish retribution from revenge in order to construct a rational system of punishment, but that distinction has been purposefully jettisoned. This is not to imply that the distinction is unimportant for penal philosophy. However, it distracts us from understanding the "moral and psychological appeal" of retribution that concerned H. L. A. Hart and that was central to the theorizing of Durkheim, Heider, Kelsen, and many others. Consequently, I have argued that revenge and retribution arise out of the same basic psychological dynamics and structures. Additionally, attention has been drawn to the fact that "disinterested" punishment responses that have concerned a number of theorists are not essentially different from those of the immediate victims of a harm, nor are their origins mysterious. The common threads are the moral values that arise out of socialization and group membership, broadly conceived. At the psychological level retributive motives arising among persons who are the direct targets of a harm are different from "disinterested" observers primarily in the personalization of the harm. In fact, disinterested persons may have stronger responses than direct victims. For example, there are numerous instances where the family of a murder victim opposes the death penalty for the killer while the public cries for blood.

I have also tried to make more explicit the psychological stages involved in the arousal of retribution motives that are inherent in Heider's theorizing and to expand on them. To reiterate these stages, there is a perceived harm resulting from a rule or norm violation; the violator's act is perceived as intentional; the combination of these two cognitions threatens the perceiver's personal self, her social status, or internalized group values; the emotion of anger is aroused; the cognitions and anger evoke a punitive response toward the offender in order to lower the status of the offender or vindicate the rule with the homeostatic goal of restoring the world to its preharm condition; anger and social cognitions move toward their preoffense level. A qualifying codicil has been added to this model by suggesting that under some circumstances punishment of the offender could increase retributive justice reactions by validating the perceived harm of the offense or the negative character of the offender. No research bearing directly on this hypothesis was uncovered, but it is worth observing that it is reflected in the common adages bearing on violence begetting more violence in an increasing cycle. For instance, opponents of the death penalty have argued that it increases the climate of violence: "Why do we kill people who kill people to show people that killing people is wrong?" Similar dynamics of psychological justification of victim deservingness may be involved in the minds of perpetrators of domestic violence. Research on Lerner's "Just World" hypothesis (Lerner and Miller, 1978) that bears on the derogation of victims would appear to be consistent with the codicil. This hypothesizing, of course, is consistent with the broader proposition that the interplay of anger and cognitions may be complex and these, in turn, can be affected by a host of cultural, social, personality, and situational variables.

Making these stages explicit has the benefit of drawing attention to the behavioral consequences of retributive justice motives. The linking of the social psychological research on retribution and the literature on aggression may be one of the most important contributions of this essay. The linkage connects retribution with a research paradigm that allows exploration of the relationships between the cognitive, affective, and behavioral facets of retribution. At the same time it draws attention to the fact that most of the empirical research specifically addressing the subject of retribution has tended to stop short of a satisfactory inquiry. For instance, consider the finding that many people favor the death penalty for retribution rather than deterrence (e.g., Sarat and Vidmar, 1976; Vidmar, 1974a). This stops far short of the questions that we ultimately want to have answers for. To wit, does giving vent to punishment impulses increase cohesion in social groups or in the legitimacy accorded the legal system? Or does the failure to allow an outlet for these impulses cause more aggression, lessen group cohesion, or cause people to devalue legal and political institutions? The linking of these literatures works the other direction as well. Aggression on the school playground or in the home or the organizational or business dispute are frequently rooted in retributive justice impulses.

By studying retributive justice in the minutiae of everyday life we will also learn about philosophers' and legal theorists' concerns with the macrosocial questions that have absorbed so much of their scholarly attention. This chapter has attempted to lay the groundwork for such inquiry.

ACKNOWLEDGMENTS. I am deeply indebted to Mary R. Rose for many incisive comments on an earlier draft of this chapter.

REFERENCES

Adorno, T., Frenkel-Brunswick, E., Levinson, D., and Sanford, N. (1950). *The Authoritarian Personality*. New York: Harper.

Alexander, F., and Staub, H. (1956). *The Criminal, the Judge and the Public*. Glencoe, IL: Free Press.

Alexander, P. (1987). *The Biology of Moral Systems*. New York: Aldine DeGruyter.

Alicke, M. D. (1992). Culpable Causation. *Journal of Personality and Social Psychology*, *63*, 368–378.

Arendt, H. (1976). *Eichmann in Jerusalem*. New York: Penguin Books.

Astor, R. (1994). Children's Moral Reasoning About Family and Peer Violence: The Role of Provocation and Retribution. *Child Development*, *65*, 1054–1067.

Averill, James R. (1982). *Anger and Aggression, An Essay on Emotion*: Springer Series in Social Psychology.

Balikci, A. (1970), *The Netsilik Eskimo*. Garden City, NY: The Natural History Press.

Berg, K. S., and Vidmar, N. (1975). Authoritarianism and Recall of Evidence about Criminal Behavior. *Journal of Research in Personality*, *9*, 147–157.

Berkowitz, L. (1989). Frustration–Aggression Hypothesis: Examination and Reformulation. *Psychological Bulletin*, *106*, 59–73.

Berkowitz, L. (1993). *Aggression: Its Causes, Consequences, and Control*. New York: McGraw–Hill.

Berman, P. (1994). Rats, Pigs, and Statues on Trial: The Creation of Cultural Narratives in the Prosecution of Animals and Inanimate Objects. *New York University Law Review*, *69*, 288–326.

Boehm, V. (1968). Mr. Prejudice, Miss Sympathy, and the Authoritarian Personality: An Application of Psychological Measuring Techniques to the Problem of Jury Bias. *Wisconsin Law Review*, *1968*, 734.

Bohm, R. (1992). Retribution and Capital Punishment: Toward a Better Understanding of Death Penalty Opinion. *Journal of Criminal Justice*, *20*, 227–236.

Bond, M., and Venus, C. (1991), Resistance to Group or Personal Insults in an Ingroup or Outgroup Context. *International Journal of Psychology*, *26*, 83–94.

Borden, R., Bowen, R., and Taylor, S. (1971). Shock-setting Behavior as a Function of Physical Attack and Entrinsic Reward. *Perceptual and Motor Skills*, *33*, 563–568.

Boyd, R., and Richerson, P. (1992). Punishment Allows the Evolution of Cooperation (or anything else) in Sizeable Groups. *Ethology and Sociobiology*, *13*, 171–195.

Burgess, A. (1962). *A Clockwork Orange*. New York: Academic Press.

Buss, D., and Kendrick, D. (1988). Evolutionary Social Psychology. In D. Gilbert, S. Fiske, and G. Lindzey (Eds.), *The Handbook of Social Psychology* (4th ed.). New York: McGraw–Hill.

Centers, Richard, Robert Shomer and Arnoldo Rodrigues (1970). A Field Experiment in Interpersonal Persuasion Using Authoritative Influence. *Journal of Personality*, *38*, 392–401.

Chagnon, N., and Irons, W. (1979). *Evolutionary Biology and Human Social Behavior*. North Scituate, MA: Duxbury.

Cohen, D. (1996). Law, Social Policy, and Violence: The Impact of Regional Cultures. *Journal of Personality and Social Psychology*, *70*, 961–978.

Cohen, D., and Vandello, J. (1998). Meanings of Violence. *Journal of Legal Studies*, *27*, 567–584.

Coleman (1992). *Risks and Wrongs*. Cambridge: Cambridge University Press.

Coker v. Georgia, 433 U.S. 485 (1977).

Cottingham, J. (1979). Varieties of Retributivism. *Philosophy Quarterly*, *29*, 238–246.

Craig, K. M., O'Neal, E. C., Taylor, S. L., Yost, E. A., Langley, T., Rainbow, R., Allgower, A., and Folger, R. (1993). Equity and Derogation Against Whom We Have Aggressed. *Aggressive Behavior*, *19*, 355–360.

Crowe, P. (1978). Complaint Reactions to the Massachusetts Commission Against Discrimination. *Law & Society Review*, *12*, 217–236.

Darley, J. M., and Zanna, M. P. (1982). Making moral judgments. *American Scientist*, *70*, 515–521.

Dengerink, H., and Myers, J. (1977). The Effects of Failure and Depression on Subsequent Aggression. *Journal of Personality and Social Psychology*, *35*, 88–96.

Drenovsky, C. K. (1994). Anger and the Desire for Retribution Among Bereaved Parents. *Omega*, *29*, 303–312.

DuBois, C. (1961). *The Peoples of Alor*. New York: Harper & Row.

Durkheim, E. (1964). *The Division of Labor in Society* (G. Simpson, Trans). Toronto: Collier–Macmillan Canada Ltd. (Original work published 1893)

Dustin, D., and Davis, H. (1967). Authoritarianism and Sanctioning Behavior. *Journal of Personality and Social Psychology*, *6*, 222–235.

Ellsworth, P. (1994). Sense, Culture and Sensibility. In S. Kitayama and H. Markus (Eds.), *Emotion and Culture*. Washington, DC: American Psychological Association. 23–50.

Ellsworth, P., & Ross, L. (1983). Public Opinion and Capital Punishment: A close examination of the Views of Abolitionists and Retentionists, *Crime and Delinquency*, *29*, 116–168.

Ellsworth, P., and Gross, S. (1994). Hardening of the Attitudes: American's Views on the Death Penalty. *Journal of Social Issues*, *50*, 19–52.

Ellsworth, P. C., and Smith, C. (1988). From Appraisal to Emotion: Differences among Unpleasant Feelings. *Motivation and Emotion*, *12*, 271–302.

Erikson, K. (1966). *Wayward Puritans: A Study in the Sociology of Deviance*. New York: Wiley.

Feather, N. T. (1996). Reactions to Penalties for an Offense in Relation to Authoritarianism, Values, Perceived Responsibility, Perceived Seriousness, and Deservingness. *Journal of Personality and Social Psychology*, *71*, 571–587.

Feather, N. (1998). Reactions to Penalties for Offenses Committed by the Police and Public Citizens: Testing a Social–Cognitive Process Model of Retributive Justice. *Journal of Personality and Social Psychology*, *75*, 528–544.

Feinberg, J. (1970). *Doing and Deserving: Essays in the Theory of Responsibility*. Princeton, NJ: Princeton University Press.

Felson, R. (1978). Aggression as Impression Management. *Social Psychology Quarterly*, *41*, 205–213.

Felson, R. (1982). Impression Management and the Escalation of Aggression and Violence. *Social Psychology Quarterly*, *45*, 245–254.

Felson, R. B., and Ribner, S. A. (1981). An Attributional Approach to Accounts and Sanctions for Criminal Violence. *Social Psychology Quarterly*, *44*, 137–142.

Felson, R. B., and Tedeschi, J. T., *A Social Interactionist Approach to Violence: Cross-Cultural Applications*. New York: Springer Publishing Company.

Fiske, A., and Haslam, N. (1996). Social Cognition is Thinking About Relationships. *Current Directions in Psychological Science*, *5*, 143–148.

Fiske, A., Kitayama, S., Markus, H., and Nisbett, R. (1998). The Cultural Matrix of Social Psychology. In D. Gilbert, S. Fiske, and G. Lindzey (Eds.), *The Handbook of Social Psychology* (4th ed.). New York: McGraw–Hill. 915–981.

Fletcher, G. (1995). *With Justice for Some: Victim's Rights in Criminal Trials*. Reading, MA: Addison–Wesley.

Furer-Haimendorf, C. (1967). *Moral and Merit: A Study of Values and Social Controls in South Asian Societies*. Chicago: University of Chicago Press.

Furman v. Georgia, 408 U.S. 238 (1972).

Gaertner, W., and Klemish-Ahlert, M. (1991). *Social Choice and Bargaining Perspectives in Distributive Justice*. Berlin: Springer-Verlag.

Garfinkel, H. (1956). Conditions of Successful Degradation Ceremonies. *American Journal of Sociology*, *61*, 420–456.

Garland, D. (1991). Punishment and Culture: The Symbolic Dimension of Criminal Justice. *Studies in Law, Politics and Society*, *11*, 191–222.

Gibson, J., and Gouws, A. (1999). Truth and Reconciliation in South Africa: Attribution and Blame and the Struggle over Apartheid. *American Political Science Review*, *93*, 501–517.

Golding, M. (1975). Punishment: Retributivism (Chapter 5). *Philosophy of Law*. Englewood Cliffs, NJ: Prentice–Hall.

Golding, M. (1975). *Philosophy of Law*. Englewood Cliffs, NJ: Prentice–Hall.

Graham, S., and Hudley, C. (1994). Attributions of Aggressive and Nonaggressive African-American Male Early Adolescents. *Developmental Psychology*, *30*, 365–373.

Graham, S., Weiner, B., and Zucker, G. (1997). An Attributional Analysis of Punishment Goals and Public Reactions to O. J. Simpson. *Personality and Social Psychology Bulletin*, *23*, 331–346.

Gusfield, J. (1963). *Symbolic Crusade: Status Politics and the American Temperance Movement*. Urbana: University of Illinois Press.

Green, R. (1968). Effects of Frustration, Attack and Prior Training in Aggressiveness upon Aggressive Behavior. *Journal of Personality and Social Psychology*, *9*, 316–321.

Halleck, S. (1980). Vengeance and Victimization. *Victimiology* *5*(2–4, 99–109.

Hamilton, V. L. (1976). Individual Differences in Ascriptions of Responsibility, Guilt, and Appropriate Punishment. In G. Bermant, C. Nemeth, and N. Vidmar (Eds.), *Psychology and the Law*. Lexington, MA: Lexington Books. 239–264.

Hamilton, V. L. (1978). Who is Responsible? Toward a Social Psychology of Responsibility Attribution. *Social Psychology*, *41*, 316.

Hamilton, V. L., and Sanders, J. (1992). *Everyday Justice: Responsibility and the Individual in Japan and the United States*. New Haven, CT: Yale University Press.

Hamilton, V. L. and Sanders, J. (1996). Corporate Crime Through Citizen's Eyes: Stratification and Responsibility in United States, Russia, and Japan. *Law and Society Review. 30*, 513–548.

Hart, H. L. A. (1968). *Punishment and Responsibility*. London: Oxford University Press.

Hay, D. (1975). *Albion's Fatal Tree: Crime and Society in Eighteenth-Century England*. New York: Pantheon Books.

Heider, F. (1958). *The Psychology of Interpersonal Relations*. New York: Wiley.

Henderson, L. (1985). The Wrongs of Victim's Rights. *Stanford Law Review, 37*, 937–1021.

Herek, G. (1986). On Heterosexual Masculinity. *American Behavioral Scientist, 29*, 563–577.

Herek, G. (1988). Heterosexuals' Attitudes Toward Lesbians and Gay Men: Correlates and Gender Differences. *Journal of Sex Research, 25*, 451–477.

Herek, G., and Glunt, E. (1993). Public Attitudes Towards AIDS-Related Issues in the United States. In J. R. Pryor and G. D. Reeder (Eds.), *The Social Psychology of HIV Infection*. Hillsdale, NJ: Erlbaum.

Hills, A., and Thomson, D. (1999). Should Victim Impact Influence Sentences? Understanding the Community's Justice Reasoning. *Behavioral Sciences and Law, 17*, 661–671.

Hoebel, E. A. (1954). *The Law of Primitive Man: A Study in Comparative Legal Dynamics*. Cambridge, MA: Harvard University Press.

Hogan, R., and Emler, N. (1981). Retributive Justice. In M. Lerner (Ed.), *The Justice Motive in Social Behavior*. New York: Plenum Press. 125–143.

Holbrook, M. I., White, M., and Hutt, M. (1995). The Vengeance Scale: Comparison of Groups and an Assessment of External Validity. *Psychological Reports, 77*, 224–226.

Itoi, R., Ohbuchi, K., and Fukuno, M. (1996). A Cross-Cultural Study of Preference of Accounts: Relationship Closeness, Harm Severity, and Motives of Account Making. *Journal of Applied Social Psychology, 26*, 913–934.

Jacoby, S. (1983). *Wild Justice: The Evolution of Revenge*. New York: Harper & Row.

Jaspars, J., Fincham, F. D., and Hewstone, M. (1983). *Attribution Theory and Research: Conceptual Developmental and Social Dimensions*. New York: Academic Press.

Johnson, T. E., and Rule, B. G. (1986). Mitigating Circumstances Information, Censure and Aggression. *Journal of Personality and Social Psychology, 50*, 537–542,

Jurow, G. (1971). New Data on the Effect of a 'Death-Qualified' Jury on the Guilt Determination Process. *Harvard Law Review, 84*, 567.

Kahneman, D., Schkade, D., and Sunstein, C. (1998). Shared Outrage and Erratic Awards: The Psychology of Punitive Damages. *Journal of Risk and Uncertainty, 16*, 49–86.

Keeva, S. (1999). Does Law Mean Never Having to Say You Are Sorry? *ABA Journal, 85*, 64–68.

Kelsen, H. (1943). *Society and Nature*. Chicago: University of Chicago Press.

Keltner, D., Young, R., and Buswell, B. (1997). Appeasement in Human Emotion, Social Practice and Personality. *Aggressive Behavior, 23*, 359–374.

Kim, S. H., and Smith, R. H. (1993). Revenge and Conflict Escalation. *Negotiation Journal, 9*, 37–43.

Kleinke, C. L., Wallis, R., and Stalder, K. (1992). Evaluation of a Rapist as a Function of Expressed Intent and Remorse. *The Journal of Social Psychology, 132*, 525–537.

Lazarus, R. (1991). *Emotion and Adaption*. London: Oxford University Press.

Lerner, M. J. (1971). Justified Self-Interest and the Responsibility for Suffering: A Replication and Extension. *Journal of Human Relations, 19*, 550–559.

Lerner, M. J. (1977). The Justice Motive: Some Hypotheses as to its Origins and Form. *Journal of Personality, 45*, 1–52.

Lerner, M., and Miller, D. (1978). Just World Research and the Attribution Process: Looking Back and Ahead. *Psychological Bulletin, 85*, 1030.

Lewis, B. (1991). Behind the Rushdie Affair. *American Scholar, 60*, 185–196.

Lind, E. A., and Tyler, T. (1988). *The Social Psychology of Procedural Justice*. New York: Plenum Press.

Mäkelä, K. (1966). Public Sense of Justice and Judicial Practice. *Acta Sociologica, 10*, 42–61.

Malinowski, B. (1972). *Crime and Custom in Savage Society*. Totowa, New Jersey: Littlefield, Adams and Company.

Markus, H., and Kitayama, S. (1991). Culture and the Self: Implications for Cognition, Emotion, and Motivation. *Psychological Review, 98*, 224–253.

McEwen, C. A., and Milburn, T. W. (1993). Explaining a Paradox of Mediation. *Negotiation Journal, 9*, 23–36.

Mead, G. (1918). The Psychology of Punitive Justice. *American Journal of Sociology, 23*, 577.

Mellers, B., and Baron, J. (Eds.). (1993). *Perspectives on Justice: Theory and Applications*. London: Cambridge University Press.

Menninger, K. (1966). *The Crime of Punishment*. New York: Viking Press.

Merry, S. E., and Silbey, S. S. (1984). What do plaintiffs want? Reexamining the concept of dispute. *The Justice System Journal, 9*, 151–178.

Merton, R. (1957). *Social Theory and Social Structure*. Glencoe, IL: Free Press.
Mikula, G., Petri, B., and Tanzer, N. (1990). What People Regard as Unjust: Types and Structures of Everyday Experiences of Injustice. *European Journal of Social Psychology*, *20*, 133–149.
Miller, W. I. (1990). *Bloodtaking and Peace Making: Feud, Law, and Society in Saga Iceland*. Chicago: University of Chicago Press.
Miller, W. I. (1993). *Humiliation and Other Essays on Honor, Social Discomfort, and Violence*. Ithaca, NY: Cornell University Press.
Miller, W. I. (1996, May). *Remember Me: Revenge and the Making of the Person*. Annual Meeting of the Law and Society Association, Glasgow, Scotland.
Miller, W. I. (1998). Clint Eastwood and Equity: The Virtues of Revenge and the Shortcomings of Law in Popular Culture. In A. Sarat and T. Kearns (Eds.), *Law in the Domains of Culture*. Ann Arbor: University of Michigan Press. 161–202.
Mitchell, H., and Byrne, D. (1973). The Defendant's Dilemma: Effects of Jurors' Attitudes and Authoritarianism on Judicial Decisions. *Journal of Personality and Social Psychology*, *25*, 123.
Mitchell, H. (1973). *Authoritarian Punitiveness in Simulated Juror Decision-making: The Good Guys Don't Always Wear White Hats*. Presented at the Annual Meeting of the Midwestern Psychological Association, Chicago.
Mosteller, R. (1996). Syndromes and Politics in Criminal Trials and Evidence Law. *Duke Law Journal*, *46*, 461–515.
Nader, L. (1975). Forums for Justice: A Cross-cultural Perspective. *Journal of Social Issues*, *31*, 151–173.
Nisbett, R. E., and Cohen, D. (1996). *Culture of Honor: The Psychology of Violence in the South*. Boulder, CO: Westview Press.
Nozik, R. (1981). *Philosophical Explanations*. Cambridge, MA: Harvard University Press.
Ogloff, J. R. P., and Vidmar, N. (1994). The Impact of Pretrial Publicity on Jurors. *Law and Human Behavior*, *18*, 507–526.
Ohbuchi, K., and Izutsu, T. (1984). Retaliation by Male Victims: Effects of Physical Attractiveness and Intensity of Attack of Female Attackers. *Personality and Social Psychology Bulletin*, *10*, 216–224.
Ohbuchi, K., and Ogura, S. (1984). The Experience of Anger: I. The Survey for Adults and University Students with Averill's Questionnaire. *Japanese Journal of Criminal Psychology*, *22*, 15–35.
Ohbucki, K., and Kambara, T. (1985). Attacker's Intent and Awareness of Outcome, Impression Management, and Retaliation. *Journal of Experimental Social Psychology*, *21*, 321–330.
Ohbuchi, K., Agarie, N., and Kameda, M. (1989). Apology as Aggression Control: Its Role in Mediating Appraisal of and Response to Harm. *Journal of Personality and Social Psychology*, *56*, 219–227.
Orwell, G. (1971). *1984*. New York: Harcourt Brace Javanovich.
Packer, H. L. (1968). *The Limits of the Criminal Sanction*. Staford: Stanford University Press.
Peristiany, Jean (Ed.). (1967/1974). *Honor and Shame*, Midway Reprint (1974). Chicago: University of Chicago press.
Peristiany, J. (Ed.). (1996). *Honor and Shame*. Chicago: University of Chicago Press.
Piaget, J. (1948). *The Moral Judgment of the Child*. New York: Macmillan.
Pincoffs, E. (1966). *The Rationale of Legal Punishment*. New York: Humanities Press.
Pipes, D. (1990). *The Rushdie Affair: The Novel, The Ayatollah, and the West*. London: Birch Lane Press.
Radin, M. (1980). Cruel Punishment and Respect for Persons. Super Due Process for Death. *Southern California Law Review*, *53*, 1143–1185.
Ranulf, S. (1964). *Moral Indignation and Middle Class Psychology*. New York: Schocken Books.
Roberts, J. V. (1996). Public Opinion, Criminal Record, and the Sentencing Process. *American Behavioral Scientist*, *39*, 488–499.
Robinson, D. T., Smith-Lovin, L., and Tsoudis, O. (1994). Heinous Crime or Unfortunate Accident? The Effects of Remorse on Responses to Mock Criminal Confessions. *Social Forces*, *73*, 175–190.
Robinson, P. H., and Darley, J. M. (1995). Justice, Liability and Blame. *Community Views and the Criminal Law*. Boulder, CO: Westview Press.
Rose, A., and Asher, S. (1999). Children's Goals and Strategies in Response to Conflicts Within a Friendship. *Developmental Psychology*, *35*, 69–79.
Rumsey, M. G. (1976). Effects of Defendant Background and Remorse on Sentencing Judgments. *Journal of Applied Social Psychology*, *6*(1), 64–68.
Sarat, A., and Vidmar, N. (1976). Public Opinion, the Death Penalty, and the Eighth Amendment: Testing the Marshall Hypothesis. *Wisconsin Law Review*, *1976*, 171–206.
Scheler, M. (1961). *Ressentiment*. New York: Free Press.
Schwartz, G. S., Kane, T., Joseph, J., and Tedeschi, J. T. (1978). The Effects of Post-Transgression Remorse on Perceived Aggression, Attributions of Intents and Level of Punishment. *Journal of Social and Clinical Psychology*, *17*, 293–297.

Segerstedt, T. (1949). Research into the General Sense of Justice. *Theoria, 15*, 323.

Semin, G. R., and Rubini, M. (1990). Unfolding the concept of person by verbal abuse. *European Journal of Social Psychology, 20*, 463–474.

Sharp, F., and Otto, M. (1910). A Study of the Popular Attitude toward Retributive Punishment. *International Journal of Ethics, 20*, 341.

Shaver, K. (1970). Defensive Attribution: Effects of Severity and Relevance on the Responsibility Assigned for an Accident. *Journal of Personality and Social Psychology, 14*, 101–113.

Shaver, K. (1985). *The Attribution of Blame, Causality, Responsibility, and Blameworthiness*. Berlin: Springer-Verlag.

Shaw, M. (1967). Some Cultural Differences in Sanctioning Behavior. *Psychonomic Science, 8*, 45–48.

Shaw, M., and Reitan, H. (1969). Attribution of Responsibility as a Basis for Sanctioning Behavior. *British Journal of Social and Clinical Psychology, 8*, 217–226.

Shaw, J., and Skolnick, P. (1996). When is Defendant Status a Shield or a Liability? Clarification and Extension. *Law and Human Behavior, 20*, 431–442.

Shaw, M., and Sulzer, J. (1964). An Empirical Test of Heider's Levels in Attribution of Responsibility. *Journal of Abnormal and Social Psychology, 69*, 39–54.

Sherwood, J. (1966). Authoritarianism, Moral Realism and President Kennedy's Death. *British Journal of Social and Clinical Psychology, 5*, 264.

Shultz, T. R., and Darley, J. M. (1991). An Information Processing Model of Retributive Justice Based on "Legal Reasoning." In W. M. Kurtiness and J. L. Gewirtz (Eds.), *Handbook of Moral Behavior and Development*, 2. Hillsdale, NJ: Erlbaum. 247–278.

Shuman, D. (2000). The Role of Apology in Tort Law. *Judicature, 83*, 180–189.

Skolnick, P., and Shaw, J. (1994). Is Defendant Status a Liability or a Shield? Crime Severity and Professional Relatedness. *Journal of Applied Social Psychology, 24*, 1827–1836.

Sloan, F., Githens, P., Clayton, E., Hickson, G., Gentile, D., and Partlett, D. (1993). *Suing for Medical Malpractice*. Chicago: University of Chicago Press.

Solomon, R.C. (1990). *A Passion for Justice: Emotions and the Origins of Social Contract*. Reading, MA: Addison–Wesley.

Steiner, B., Bowers, W., and Sarat, A. (1999). Folk Knowledge as Legal Action: Death Penalty Judgments and the Tenet of Early Release in a Culture of Mistrust and Punitiveness. *Law and Society Review, 33*, 461–506.

Stuckless, N., and Goranson, R. (1992). The Vengeance Scale: Development of a Measure of Attitudes Toward Revenge. *Journal of Social Behavior and Personality, 7*, 25–42.

Taylor, C., and Kleinke, C. L. (1992). Effects of Severity of Accident, History of Drunk Driving, Intent, and Remorse on Judgments of a Drunk Driver. *Journal of Applied Social Psychology, 22*, 1641–1655.

Tedeschi, J., Smith, R., and Brown, R. (1974). A Reinterpretation of Research on Aggression. *Psychological Bulletin, 81*, 540–562.

Thibaut, J., and Kelley, H. (1958). *The Social Psychology of Groups*. New York: Wiley.

Thomas, W., and Znaniecki, F. (1943). *The Polish Peasant in Europe and America*. Chicago: University of Chicago Press. (Original work published 1902)

Toch, H. (1965). *The Social Psychology of Social Movements*. Indianapolis: Bobbs-Merrill.

Törnblom, K., and Jonsson, D. (1985). Suburbs of the Equality and Contribution Principles: Their Perceived Fairness in Distribution and Retribution. *Social Psychology Quarterly, 48*, 249–261.

Törnblom, K., and Jonsson, D. (1987). Distribution vs. Retribution: The Perceived Justice of the Contribution and Equality Principles for Cooperative and Competitive Relationships. *Acta Sociologica, 1*, 25–52.

Triandis, H. C. (1995). *Individualism and Collectivism*. Boulder, CO: Westview Press.

Trivers, R. (1971). The Evolution of Reciprocal Altruism. *Quarterly Review of Biology, 46*, 35.

Tyler, T. (1990). *Why People Obey the Law: Procedural Justice, Legitimacy and Compliance*. New Haven: Yale University Press.

Tyler, T., and Lind, E. A. (1992). A Relational Model of Authority in Groups. In M. Zanna (Ed.), *Advances in Experimental Social Psychology*. New York: Academic Press. 115–191.

Tyler, T., and Boeckmann, R. (1997). Three Strikes and You Are Out, But Why? The Psychology of Public Support for Punishing Rule Breakers. *Law & Society Review, 31*, 237–266.

Tyler, T. R., Boeckmann, R. J., Smith, H. J., and Huo,Y.. J. (1997). *Social Justice in a Diverse Society*. Boulder, CO: Westview Press.

Umphrey, M. (1999). The Dialogics of Legal Meaning: Spectacular Trials, the Unwritten Law, and Narratives of Criminal Responsibility. *Law and Society Review, 33*, 393–424.

Van den Haag, E. (1991). For Capital Punishment. *Israel Law Review, 25*, 460–480.

Van den Haag, E. (1975). *Punishing Criminals: Concerning a Very Old and Painful Question*. New York: Basic Books.
Vidmar, N. (1974a). Retributive and Utilitarian Motives and Other Correlates of Canadian Attitudes toward the Death Penalty. *Canadian Psychologist, 15*, 337–356.
Vidmar, N. (1977, June). *Effects of Degree of Harm and Retribution Motives on Punishment Reactions*. Presented at the Canadian Psychological Association, Vancouver, BC.
Vidmar, N. (1978, April). *Outcome, Offense Type, and Retribution as Factors in Punishment Reactions*. Presented at the Eastern Psychological Association, Washington, DC.
Vidmar, N., and Ellsworth, P. (1974). Public Opinion and the Death Penalty. *Stanford Law Review, 26*, 1245–1270.
Vidmar, N., and Miller, D. T. (1980). Social Psychological Processes Underlying Attitudes Toward Legal Punishment. *Law & Society, 14*(3), 565–602.
Viney, W., Parker-Martin, P., and Dotten, S. (1987). Beliefs in Free Will and Determinism and Lack of Relation to Punishment Rationale and Magnitude. *Journal of General Psychology, 115*, 15–23.
Warr, M., Meier, R. F., and Erickson, M. L. (1983). Norms, Theories of Punishment, and Publicly Preferred Penalties for Crimes. *The Sociological Quarterly, 24*, 275–291.
Weihofen, Henry. (1968). *The Urge to Punish*. London: Golloncz.
Westermarck, E. (1932). *Ethical Relativity*. New York: Harcourt Brace.
Wiggins, J., Dill, F., and Schwartz, R. (1965). On "Status Liability." *Sociometry, 28*, 197–209.
Zajonc, R. (1998). Emotions. In D. Gilbert, S. Fiske, and G. Lindzey (Eds.), *The Handbook of Social Psychology* (4th ed.). New York: McGraw–Hill. 591–632.

3

Procedural Justice

Tom R. Tyler and E. Allan Lind

A. INTRODUCTION

We are psychologists and, as a consequence, our focus is on the individual person—on personal judgments and feelings, and on individual actions. The work we will present is based for the most part on interviews with people who have had encounters of one sort or another with legal authorities and on data from experiments that examine in the laboratory artificially created experiences relevant to judgments of fairness.[1] Our central concern is with the psychology of authority and with the very important place of fairness judgments in reactions to authority. We will rely on the group-value model of procedural justice (Lind and Tyler, 1988), which we extended to authority relations in the relational model of authority (Tyler and Lind, 1992), to provide a framework for our analysis.

A large body of research now exists linking people's acceptance of the decisions of legal authorities, as well as their acceptance of legal rules and their endorsement of the legal system in general, to assessments of the fairness of the procedures and social process through which decisions are made and rules applied.[2] This procedural justice effect is widespread and dramatic (for an analysis of early work, see Lind and Tyler, 1988; for a summary of recent work, see Tyler, Boeckmann, Smith, and Huo, 1997; Tyler and Smith, 1997). It occurs in a variety of studies differing widely in their methodologies and in the legal procedures that they examine. We will argue that these procedural justice effects offer important clues about how the legal system can effectively manage disputes. Further, an examination of why people focus on procedural fairness issues offers insights into the nature of the psychological connections between individuals, authorities, and rules by telling us something important about how people *think* about law and legal institutions. Understanding why people place so much importance on procedural fairness helps us to understand why people are often willing to voluntarily accept decisions that they do not agree with and, indeed, why they sometimes accept decisions that they feel are unfair. The psychology of fairness also has much to tell us

Tom R. Tyler • Department of Psychology, New York Unversity, New York, New York 10003. E. Allan Lind • Fuqua School of Business, Duke University, Durham, North Carolina 27708.

Handbook of Justice Research in Law, edited by Sanders and Hamilton. Kluwer Academic / Plenum Publishers, New York, 2000.

about why people obey rules that restrict their behavior in ways that they would otherwise find unacceptable (see Tyler, 1999; Tyler and Blader, 2000, for a general discussion of the antecedents of voluntary cooperation).

B. PSYCHOLOGY AND THE LEGAL CONTEXT

Why should we care about the disputant's judgments and feelings? One reason is that for law to be effective, people must obey it (Tyler, 1990). The legal system is heavily dependent on voluntary compliance. Although the law always involves elements of coercion, in practical terms the legal system has, at best, a limited ability to compel people to obey the law (Tyler, 1990, 1997a,b,c,d). There is a tendency in the general population, and even in other social sciences concerned with law, to think of legal authorities as being so powerful as to be able to compel citizen behavior. In reality, at least in democracies, the power of legal institutions is limited and the effectiveness of law and legal decisions is heavily dependent on widespread voluntary compliance with their directives by those who are affected by those decrees.

Instances of widespread disobedience with court orders abound. In the United States the courts have had great difficulty securing compliance with child-support or domestic restraining orders through threat or punishment (Kressel, 1985). Similarly, in the cases handled in small-claims courts—cases involving landlord–tenant disputes, conflicts among neighbors, nonpayment of bills to businesses for products or services, consumer dissatisfaction with products or services, and other minor disputes—noncompliance with court orders is common (McEwen and Maiman, 1981; Singer, 1994). In larger civil cases the enforcement devices available to a winning party, or to the state, are often so cumbersome and difficult to carry to completion that even here a recalcitrant loser can often avoid payment of an award or effective enforcement of a mandated action.

Criminal laws are similarly difficult to enforce using only threats of punishment. In a review of deterrence research on drug use, for example, MacCoun (1993) suggests that at best 5% of the variance in law-related behavior can be explained by variations in the perceived certainty and severity of punishment. This estimate is consistent with the findings of recent panel studies on law-related behaviors, which show that deterrence considerations have, at best, a minor influence on behavior (see Paternoster, Saltzman, Waldo, and Chiricos, 1983; Paternoster, 1987; Tyler, 1990). Decreases in the use of illegal drugs appear to be more a function of demographics than of increasing penalties and enhanced enforcement efforts. In the case of drunk driving laws, Ross (1982) points out that the level of police enforcement needed to bring the probability of punishment to the level required to deter offenders is prohibitively high.

Thus, because of practical and constitutional limits of coercive power, legal authorities must depend on voluntary deference to their decisions by most of the population most of the time. Authorities need for people to take upon themselves the obligation to obey the law and to voluntarily act on that obligation. Even when authorities possess the power to reward or punish, they benefit from the willingness of people to voluntarily accept their decisions. Voluntary acceptance minimizes the need of authorities to explain and justify each decision, and reduces the need to monitor implementation, and to use collective resources to facilitate compliance. Thus, efforts to understand the effective exercise of legal authority inevitably lead to a concern with attitudes toward authorities in the general population.

Securing voluntary deference to judicial decisions is especially difficult since disputants typically take to legal authorities only those conflicts that have proven to be too difficult for them to resolve themselves through bilateral discussion and negotiation (Rubin, 1980; Thibaut and Walker, 1975). Hence, the legal system is usually presented with conflicts in which the parties are in great disagreement. This makes it especially difficult to give either or both parties what they want and feel they deserve. Further, conflicts typically come to the court after the conflict has a long history of escalating tension, with negative feelings running high (Rubin, 1980). Thus, the courts are faced with the problem of effectively resolving the most difficult conflicts.

These considerations set the stage for the investigation of attitudes that influence the voluntary acceptance of judicial decisions and legal rules. One such attitude is the perceived legitimacy of the judge, mediator, or other legal authority. Legitimacy is the judgment that legal authorities are competent and honest (termed "support" or "personal" legitimacy in the terminology of political psychology) and the judgment that their professional role entitles them to make decisions that ought to be deferred to and obeyed (termed "institutional legitimacy"). Research suggests that both types of legitimacy can combine with feelings of obligation to obey rules and laws to produce compliance with legal orders (Tyler, 1990, 1997b).

Of course, we are not concerned with people's attitudes about legal authorities and their decisions only because those attitudes influence voluntary compliance behavior. People's attitudes are also important in their own right, because a central tenet of democratic government is that, to the extent possible, legal decisions should be based on a consensus of the parties to the dispute about what is just. A central assumption of the democratic ideal is that people should be able to accept the solutions reached by those in power. They should want to accept those solutions. In other words, justice does not come only from the interpretation of legal doctrines by legal scholars, judges, and philosophers, who tell people what is normatively a "just" solution to their problems. Justice also develops from the concerns, needs, and values of the people who bring their problems to the legal system. As Sarat notes: "It would be strange, indeed, to call a legal system democratic if its procedures and operations were greatly at odds with the values, preferences, or desires of the citizens over a long period of time" (1977:430).

Two models exist concerning the ability of procedures to enhance acceptance of decisions. The first is what might be termed a "discourse and consensus" perspective. A consensus about the appropriate resolution for a dispute may emerge from the discussions and presentations of views that occur during the processes of dispute resolution. For example, the recent Japanese third wave movement recognizes this possibility and emphasizes the importance of empowering participants through allowing discourse about the legal norms that should be applied to resolve particular disputes. This position is consistent with Habermas's discourse theory, which seeks to identify the conditions under which discussions among the parties to a conflict can lead to a true "consensus" about the appropriate norms to use in resolving the conflict (see Tyler, 1996). These conditions include allowing open communication and giving the parties involved opportunities to express their views. The consensus perspective emphasizes the convergence of the attitudes of the parties toward a common feeling that a particular solution is fair, a convergence thought to occur through discussion and consideration of the views and needs of others in a conflict. Having reached an agreement people willingly embrace this decision and voluntarily obey it. This perspective is intriguing, but to date there is little empirical support for or against it. Interestingly, however, it is consistent with the emergence of mediation as an increasingly popular form of dispute resolution within the United States. In mediation authorities lack the ability to impose settlements. Hence, they must rely on persuading the parties to the dispute that the dispute is a reasonable solution to the problem they are facing.

In contrast, the other model of process and acceptance, which we term the "legitimacy and deference" perspective, focuses on people's feeling of obligation to obey the decisions of third-party legal authorities. Irrespective of their judgments about a decision, people obey it if they regard the authority who made the decision as entitled to be obeyed. For example, Tyler and Mitchell (1994) found that people deferred to the abortion decisions of the United States Supreme Court if they thought the Court followed fair procedures, even when they felt the decisions were immoral. This approach to dispute resolution focuses not on developing decisions that the parties to a dispute embrace, but on building up feelings of obligation to defer to whatever decisions an authority makes.

Despite differences in their emphasis, both perspectives are united by their attention to the views of those involved in disputes. But, as noted, they are very different in their conception of which types of views ought to be the focus of our concern. We present below our own variant of the legitimacy and deference approach to explaining acceptance of laws and legal decisions, and we discuss some of the research evidence supporting it.

1. The Influence of Experience with Legal Authorities

The work we will present develops from the legitimacy model. It explores how experiences with legal authorities influence: (1) views about the legitimacy of judges, mediators, and courts; (2) willingness to accept their decisions; and (3) willingness to obey legal rules. The overall psychological process we advance is outlined in Figure 1.

Consider three aspects of experience that people might consider as they evaluate what has happened: first, whether they benefit or lose from the experience (outcome favorability); second, whether what they receive seems fair to them, i.e., whether substantive justice exists in the outcome (outcome fairness); and finally, whether the decisions made were made in ways that they regard as fair (procedural fairness).

Some time ago (Tyler and Lind, 1992) we reviewed the existing literature on the influence of the three judgments outlined and found that judgments about legal authorities, legal decisions, and legal rules are most strongly affected by the procedural justice of the experiences. While lawyers and judges often think that people's reactions to their experiences are driven by whether or not they "win" their case, that position is not supported by empirical research on disputing.

This does not mean, of course, that self-interested judgments have no effect. The favorability of the outcome is important in evaluations of satisfaction or dissatisfaction—people are generally not as happy if they lose as they are if they win. But the research shows that they do not extend those negative feelings to their views about law, the judge, or the legal system—as long as they believe that the procedures involved were fair. Further, the research literature shows that people more readily accept and obey decisions made in ways they evaluate as fair, regardless of the favorability of the outcome.

Although they may seem to be so at first glance, the findings of procedural justice studies are not really at odds with the findings of other research suggesting that people's choices among dispute resolution forums are often driven by instrumental, outcome-oriented concerns (Felstiner, Abel, and Sarat, 1980–81). Most procedural justice studies have examined people's *post*-experience evaluations of procedures and authorities, not their *pre*-experience choices. In a direct comparison of these two situations Tyler, Huo, and Lind (1994) found that people are instrumentally focused in making choices among possible procedures for resolving a dispute. In the Tyler *et al.* studies, disputants choose procedures based on what they expect to gain from those procedures, i.e., whether they think those procedures facilitate their likelihood of winning. However, when making evaluations of their experience after the dispute has been resolved, disputants were found to evaluate their experience in noninstrumental terms, i.e., by

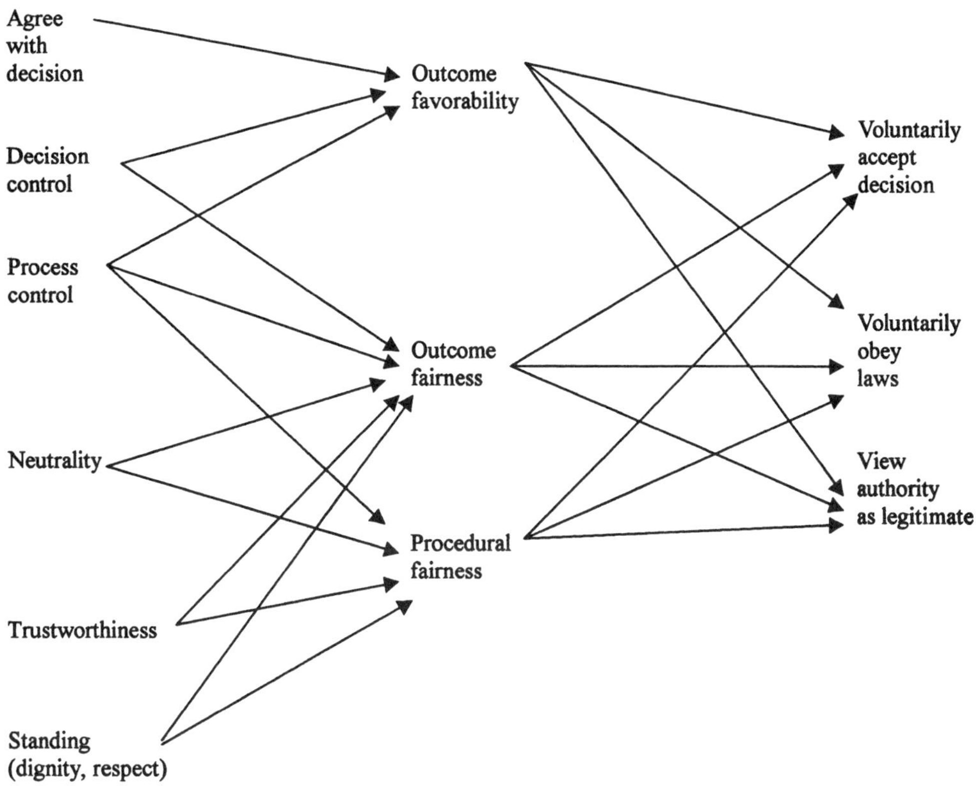

Figure 1. Conceptual model for dispute resolution.

considering issues of procedural justice. Ironically, forums chosen on the basis of instrumental concerns are evaluated in terms of procedural justice, often with the consequence that the very qualities that prompt the choice of procedures will result in low postexperience evaluations. For example, a defendant in a civil lawsuit might choose a particularly contentious litigation option based on his or her belief that that option will lead to less exposure to unfavorable decisions in the case, but then evaluate the experience unfavorably based on elements of the process he or she encountered (and chose!). The irony is all the more striking because, as we noted above, the ultimate acceptance of the outcome will be more closely linked to the experience of procedural fairness than to satisfaction with the outcome.

While recognizing that both choice and postexperience evaluation are important issues, our discussion will focus on postexperience evaluation. We do so because the issue of gaining the acceptance of and/or deference to decisions is a concern about postexperience feelings and behaviors. We will leave aside a discussion of choices among procedures.

2. The Procedural Justice Research of John Thibaut and Laurens Walker

The importance of procedure as a psychological variable was first made prominent through the research of John Thibaut, a psychologist, and Laurens Walker, a law professor (1975). Thibaut and Walker hypothesized, and in their laboratory studies demonstrated, that the use of fair decision-making procedures is one mechanism through which both the winner and the loser can be reconciled to the outcome mandated by a third party, such as a judge. Thibaut and Walker focused much of their work on the psychological consequences of the use of adversary and nonadversary legal procedures. In one of their first studies (Walker, LaTour, Lind, and Thibaut, 1974), undergraduate psychology students experienced adversary or non-adversary procedure trials in the course of an elaborate laboratory simulation of business disputes. Those who experienced adversary trial procedures rated the procedure as fairer and the verdict as more satisfactory than did the students exposed to a simulated nonadversary trial. This effect was seen whether the student won or lost at trial (in the experiment the outcome of the case was controlled and varied as a factor in the experiment).

The study was important to the subsequent development of our understanding of the psychology of procedural justice because it was the first definitive empirical demonstration that differences in procedures produced different judgments of fairness regardless of the outcome of the trial, and because it was the first study to show procedural justice effects resulting from differences in control over the presentation of evidence and arguments (a difference in opportunities for "voice," to use a more current term). The Walker *et al.* study also varied the subjects' knowledge of their side's guilt or innocence independently of the procedural fairness manipulation. The procedure effect emerged regardless of which level of the outcome or belief in innocence manipulations had been experienced by the subject.

The Walker *et al.* study is also important because it was the first study to show the capacity of procedure to increase acceptance of a decision—the subjects rated the *verdict* as more satisfactory in the adversary conditions than in the nonadversary conditions—although this aspect of the Thibaut and Walker project did not come into its own until later researchers began emphasizing the relationship between procedural justice judgments and obedience to authority (e.g., Tyler, 1989, 1990). Throughout the first decade of procedural justice research, researchers focused almost exclusively on the conditions under which the voice effect did and did not occur (see, e.g., Folger, 1977; Folger, Rosenfield, Grove, and Corkran, 1979; Lind, Kurtz, Musante, Walker, and Thibaut, 1980; Lind, Lissak, and Conlon, 1983; Tyler, Rasinski, and Spodick, 1985).

Subsequent studies by the Thibaut and Walker group confirmed that the extent to which a procedure guaranteed the disputants voice in hearings and trials did indeed have strong effects on the perceived fairness of the procedure, with high levels of disputant voice leading to greater perceived fairness (see, generally, Thibaut and Walker, 1975). Thibaut and Walker (1978) offered a theory of procedural justice that focused on the role of disputant voice in producing fair outcomes. They argued that in most legal disputes the key desideratum of the dispute resolution process should be a fair division of goods and harms, building on the work of Stacy Adams (1965), a social psychologist who had argued that people seek to establish psychological "equity" in their interpersonal relations. (Adams defined equity as the apportionment of outcomes in proportion to each individual's contributions to those outcomes.) Thibaut and Walker argued that in disputes about the allocation of outcomes, including most civil justice disputes, allowing the disputants voice in the process, as is done in adversary legal procedures, serves the cause of equity because it gathers information directly from the parties to the dispute. According to the Thibaut and Walker formulation, the parties know best who contributed what to the disputed outcomes.

3. Later Research on Procedural Justice

The Thibaut and Walker research was limited to laboratory studies, but subsequent field studies support their findings. Field studies showed that people involved in real-world trials and hearings are more satisfied with the outcomes they receive when they feel that court procedures are fair (Adler, Hensler, and Nelson, 1983; Casper, Tyler, and Fisher, 1988; Houlden, 1980–81; Lind *et al.*, 1990b; MacCoun, Lind, Hensler, Bryant, and Ebener, 1988). The field studies also confirmed that people are more likely to voluntarily accept and obey decisions when they feel the procedure is fair (Lind *et al.*, 1993; MacCoun *et al.*, 1988; Pruitt, Pierce, McGillicuddy, Welton, and Castrianno, 1993). Further, studies suggest that evaluations of the legitimacy of legal authorities, as well as more general rule-following behavior, are largely based on judgments of the fairness of the procedures through which the authorities make decisions (Friedland, Thibaut, and Walker, 1973; Tyler, 1984, 1990; Tyler, Casper, and Fisher, 1989).

Overall, research in the late 1980s and 1990s revealed that procedural justice judgments have profound effects on legal attitudes and behaviors. For example, Tyler's research (1989, 1990) showed that obedience to laws is affected by whether a person's encounters with legal authorities have involved procedures that the person thought were fair. Other research by Tyler (e.g., Tyler, 1994; Tyler and Mitchell, 1994) has demonstrated that attitudes about such fundamental and important legal issues as abortion laws and affirmative action requirements are affected by the perceived fairness of the judicial and legislative procedures that produced the laws. Lind (1990) showed that the acceptance of changes in legal process is linked closely to the belief that the innovative procedure was fair. Lind, Kulik, Ambrose, and Park (1993) showed that acceptance of non-binding legal decisions, such as those arising in court-sponsored alternative dispute resolution programs, depends to a substantial extent on whether the procedure is seen as fair (see also Pruitt *et al.*, 1993).

These findings suggest a strategy for legal authorities faced with difficult conflicts. By using procedures that people see as fair, authorities can gain greater acceptance for their decisions. The procedural justice literature suggests that judges have substantially more ability than might be thought to gain acceptance for decisions that do not give people what they want or what feel they deserve. The key is to make decisions in ways people will view as fair.

This brings us back to the question of the role of self-interested judgments. As already suggested by the model in Figure 1, where decisions fall relative to expectations and perceptions of deservingness influences satisfaction and dissatisfaction. Further, to some extent outcome favorability influences judgments about fairness. People are more likely to view a procedure as fair when they win. However, the influence of outcomes on the acceptance of decisions is relatively small compared with the direct and indirect effects of procedures.

How reliable are procedural justice effects on the acceptance of decisions? In particular, do they occur even when the issues involved are important? The initial reaction of the legal community to the findings of Thibaut and Walker (1975) was skeptical, perhaps because the original findings were based on laboratory experiments. However, subsequent studies of real disputes in real settings have confirmed the Thibaut and Walker findings in virtually every respect. In fact, comparisons of the magnitude of procedural justice effects observed in laboratory and field settings suggest that procedural justice effects are generally stronger in the field than in the laboratory (Tyler and Caine, 1981).

There is evidence of strong procedural justice effects in both criminal justice and civil justice settings. Tyler and Casper (Casper *et al.*, 1988; Tyler *et al.*, 1989) studied defendants charged with felonies. The defendants studied were interviewed both prior to and following the disposition of their cases. The findings suggest that defendants were less influenced by the outcome of their case (although outcomes ranged from a minimal sentence to 20 years in prison) than by the procedures used by legal authorities. Similar findings are seen in a test of procedural justice effects in a civil justice setting, i.e., a study of court-mandated non-binding arbitration in federal courts. Lind *et al.* (1993) examined the decisions of corporate executives to accept arbitration awards or to move to a formal trial. The amount of money at issue ranged from $10,000 to more than $5,000,000. The findings indicated that decisions about whether to accept arbitration awards were affected much more strongly by assessments of the procedural justice of the arbitration session, than by the magnitude of the arbitration award. As in the criminal setting, procedural concerns did not become less important as the outcomes at stake became more important.

Finally we note that procedural justice effects do not occur only when people are reacting to authorities with whom they have direct personal experiences, like a police officer or mediator, but also occur in reactions to more distant authorities. When people are reacting to national-level legal authorities like the U.S. Supreme Court, they are also influenced by procedural justice beliefs (Tyler, 1993; Tyler and Mitchell, 1994). Tyler studied people's willingness to defer to the *Roe v. Wade* (1973) abortion decision made by the Supreme Court, the decision in which the Court ruled that women have a legal right to personally decide whether or not to have an abortion. The study found that people's judgments about the legitimacy of the Court and their willingness to empower the Court to make future abortion decisions were more strongly influenced by their evaluations of the fairness of Court decision-making procedures than by their agreement with either past Court decisions about abortion or Court decisions in general.

The Tyler study also illustrates an important distinction between the concerns of the legitimacy model and of the consensus perspective which has previously been discussed. The Supreme Court's decision was not found to influence private attitudes about what the law should be. In other words, no consensus building dialogue occurred and the court did not change people's personal views about what is right and what is wrong. However, people felt obligated to defer to the Court because they viewed it as a legitimate institution of the U.S. government. Hence, their public behavior was changed. Kelman and Hamilton (1989) refer to this process as "authorization" and point to the ability of legitimate authorities to gain deference through people's willingness to suspend their own moral judgments.

Tyler (1994; see also Tyler and Belliveau, 1996) also examined the role of procedural justice in the empowerment of national-level political policymaking authorities. He did so in three studies—two scenario experiments and one survey—focused on the legitimacy of Congress. In contrast to the Supreme Court, which is concerned with conflicts of rights, the Congress is concerned with conflicts of interests. The studies examined national policies concerning federal funding of abortions and federal support for training programs for the disadvantaged. In all three studies judgments about the legitimacy of government authorities were independently influenced by evaluations of the fairness of the procedures through which the authorities made policies. As with the Supreme Court, the legitimacy of Congress was influenced by procedural concerns.

One final dimension across which justice concerns might vary is national, ethnic, and/or cultural background. The increasingly diverse nature of U.S. society makes it more and more likely that the conflicts that arise in social interaction will occur among people of different national, cultural, and ethnic backgrounds. Further, the U.S. work force has become more diverse in terms of gender, and more and more U.S. households are headed by women. These factors increase the gender diversity of disputes. Discussions of the future of the U.S. legal system have often raised the possibility that accommodations must be made for this increasing diversity. U.S. legal procedures, developed for the most part through the judgments and actions of white men, may be ill-fitted to the needs of African-Americans, Chicano/Latinos, and/or Asian-Americans, as well as to the needs of women.

The chapter by Leung and Morris in this volume summarizes the literature on culture and justice, and we refer the reader to their excellent review and analysis. Our evaluation of the overall implications of the literature on procedural justice and culture mirrors theirs: Procedural justice phenomena, and especially the "deep structure" of the psychology of procedural justice, seem remarkably invariant across cultures. While there are occasional differences across cultures in either the antecedents or effects of procedural justice judgments, the differences are minor in comparison to the commonality of processes, and those differences that occur are generally differences in degree, rather than differences in kind. A few recent studies illustrate this point.

Recent research on disputing among ethnic subgroups within U.S. society (African-Americans, Chicano/Latinos, Asian-Americans, and whites) suggests broad similarities in an emphasis on the importance of procedural justice among the members of all groups, both for disputes within and disputes across ethnic group boundaries (Lind, Huo, and Tyler, 1994). Research reported by Tyler (1994) shows similarly that the effect of procedural justice judgments on the legitimacy of a national-level institution—Congress—does not vary across ethnicity, gender, income, or education. All of the groups in that study viewed procedural justice as an important basis for evaluating the legitimacy of Congress.

The growth of international economic and political alliances (the North American Free Trade Alliance; the European Union), advances in communications technology, and the increasingly global nature of economic and cultural exchanges all suggest that future disputes are increasingly likely to occur among individuals who differ in their national, cultural, and ethnic backgrounds. As national and international legal institutions attempt to resolve such conflicts, they must find ways that are acceptable to all the parties to disputes. Several studies, dating back more than 20 years, have looked at whether procedural justice phenomena generalize across national and cultural boundaries. Lind, Erickson, Friedland, and Dickenberger (1978) replicated one of the original Thibaut and Walker studies in England, France, and Germany. They found that the voice-to-procedural justice effect that Thibaut and Walker had discovered among Americans generalized across these three Western societies. Leung and Lind (1986) showed that procedural justice effects generalized to Hong Kong Chinese disputants, and Lind, Tyler, and Huo (1997) further demonstrated that similar procedural concerns influenced reactions to the third-party procedures involving judges, mediators, and managers in the United States, Germany, and Hong Kong.

Other recent research findings have confirmed that procedural justice effects generalize more broadly. Sugawara and Huo (1994) conducted a study of Japanese students at Fukushima University to explore their views about how legal disputes should be resolved. They found that, like Americans, Japanese students rated procedural fairness to be the most important characteristic of a desirable dispute resolution procedure, judging it to be more important than outcome fairness, effectiveness, or the ability to facilitate a quick solution (Sugawara and Huo, 1994:135). This finding replicates previous similar findings demonstrating the importance of procedural justice in the Japanese political arena (Takenishi and Takenishi, 1990, 1992).

These findings and others testify to the ubiquity of procedural justice effects. Barrett-Howard and Tyler (1986) tested the generality of procedural justice across conflicts ranging over the four situational dimensions identified by Deutsch. Deutsch (1982) characterized the underlying structure of interdependence among the parties to an interaction along four dimensions: whether they have a cooperative or a competitive relationship; whether they have equal or unequal power; whether their relationship is based on work (task) or friendship (socioemotional); and whether their relationship is formal or informal in nature. Barrett-Howard and Tyler (1986) found that procedural justice was rated overall as the most important dispute resolution characteristic, and was important across a broad variety of types of social settings.

However, there may be some limits to procedural justice effects. Deutsch (1985) has argued that there is a "scope" of justice concerns, with those outside that scope no longer considered entitled to treatment with justice. Deutsch (1985) argued that the scope of justice concerns would be defined by economic concerns, with people extending justice to others with whom they have productive exchange relationships. Huo (1994) tested this notion of "exclusionary justice" for various modalities of justice and found that people were most easily excluded from just access to resources, then from just access to procedural rights, and least easily excluded from just treatment as equal human beings.

The pattern of exclusion seen in Huo's study is consistent with a "relational" perspective on justice. Tyler and Lind (1992) argue that people's justice concerns are defined by their social identifications. In the Huo study, people may have found it easier to deny disliked groups resources, because they did not see resources as key factors in any universal scheme of justice, but difficult to deny the groups respect as human beings because respect goes to the heart of relational notions of justice.

4. Summary

The image of the person that has dominated much recent law and social science discourse is of a self-interested and self-serving "rational" actor whose attitudes and behaviors are shaped by the desire to maximize personal gain from the legal system. As the research reviewed here makes clear, this image fails to recognize all of the factors that matter to people. When dealing with legal authorities, people are primarily concerned with having their grievances handled through procedures that they regard as fair. When fair procedures are utilized by legal authorities, people remain supportive of those authorities irrespective of their actions.

This procedural image of the person is much more optimistic in its implications than is a rational actor model of human behavior. The procedural model suggests that people are willing to accept outcomes that they view as undesirable and even unfair without losing support for social authorities. Hence, authorities have considerable ability to function under conditions of conflict and during periods of scarcity. The key to successful functioning is to make decisions in ways that are viewed by those affected as fair.

C. WHAT MAKES A PROCEDURE FAIR?

Procedural justice researchers have devoted considerable attention not only to demonstrating the importance of procedural justice, but also to discovering the criteria that people use to evaluate the legal procedures they experience. One set of factors that might influence the perceived fairness of procedures are instrumental, the extent to which people receive, or might expect to receive, their desired outcomes. Instrumental factors include judgments reflecting agreement with the decision, or of the degree to which the person had power or control over the decision. Process control or voice, the ability to present evidence and arguments, is arguably at least partially instrumental, since one reason to present evidence is to influence the outcome of the process.

Thibaut and Walker's original theorizing on the psychological antecedents of procedural justice argued that disputants define procedural justice in control terms (Thibaut and Walker, 1975). Thibaut and Walker argued that people want to maintain control over decisions that affect them. In the face of intractable conflicts, where solutions cannot be reached through bilateral negotiation, people reluctantly turn to third parties (mediators or judges) to resolve their conflicts. Because it is the only way to resolve the dispute, the disputants give up some control over decisions. However, disputants want to retain control over the process of evidence presentation, to retain some indirect influence over the judge's decisions. According to Thibaut and Walker, fair procedures, in the eyes of a disputant, are procedures that allow the disputant to maintain an optimal level of control over what happens to him or her. Extending this line of theorizing, disputants should value voice only if they feel that the exercise of voice enhances their influence over the judge's decision.

As studies accumulated, however, it became clear that the Thibaut and Walker explanation of the voice effect would need some modification. Particularly troubling, in light of research that emerged in the latter half of the 1980s, was the close connection between control over outcomes and procedures that is implicit in the Thibaut and Walker theory. As noted above, Thibaut and Walker thought that adversary procedures were seen as fair because the high level of voice mandated by these procedures appears to the disputants to allow them a way to secure fair outcomes. Later theorists, ourselves included (Lind and Tyler, 1988), questioned how this assertion could be reconciled with laboratory research (e.g., Lind *et al.*, 1983) showing that voice effects occur even when disputants have more direct means to ensure the fairness of outcomes (as is the case in mediation procedures, where the disputants can reject outcomes that they feel are unfair) or with survey research (e.g., Tyler *et al.*, 1985) that suggested that voice enhances judgments of procedural fairness because it provides an opportunity for the expression of values, rather than for any instrumental value it might have.

Later research showed other procedural justice effects that were difficult to reconcile with the notion that procedures are judged in terms of the outcomes they produce or in terms of control. For example, studies of disputants' reactions to court procedures found that procedural justice judgments correlated as highly with feelings that one had been treated in a dignified and polite fashion as with evaluations of the outcome of the procedure or its favorability to the disputant's case (Lind *et al.*, 1989, 1990; Tyler, 1989; Tyler and Folger, 1980). One laboratory study showed that voice effects occur even in situations where the exercise of voice could not conceivably affect the outcome of the procedure (Lind, Kanfer, and Earley, 1990).

1. New Theories of Procedural Justice

We reviewed procedural justice research through the mid-1980s and concluded that many procedural justice processes appear to be relatively unaffected by the outcome or the expected outcome of the procedure (Lind and Tyler, 1988). To explain these aspects of the justice judgment process, we proposed a "group-value" theory of procedural justice judgments that emphasized the symbolic and psychological implications of procedures for feelings of inclusion in society and for the belief that the institution using the procedure holds the person in high regard. Tyler (1990) extended group-value theory by identifying three factors that seem to be especially important to the feeling that one is secure within society and thus to the belief that procedures are fair. Tyler posited that feelings that authorities are trustworthy and benevolently disposed toward the person making the justice judgment (a factor that he termed "trust"), feelings that one is viewed by authorities as a full-fledged member of society (termed "standing"), and the belief that one is accorded evenhanded, nondiscriminatory treatment (termed "neutrality") are crucial to judgments of procedural fairness.

Neutrality reflects the degree to which people feel that authorities are creating a "level playing field," by engaging in evenhanded treatment of all. Neutrality involves honesty, unbiased treatment, consistency, and factual decision-making. Prejudice, the idea of discrimination based on group membership, is perhaps the strongest evidence of a lack of neutrality, since people are not given an equal opportunity to have access to social resources.

People are also affected by the degree to which they feel that the authorities with whom they deal are motivated to *try* to be fair to them and to others in the group—a factor Tyler called "trust." The perception of a motivation to be fair is crucial to people's feelings about authorities, since it both reflects the character of the individual authority and is the basis for predicting his or her future behavior. Inferences such as whether a person is sincere and whether or not he or she is considering the opinions of others are linked to judgments about the basic motives of the decision-maker.

Information about standing is most directly linked to people's judgments about their status within a social group, as reflected in their interpersonal treatment by group authorities. When one is treated politely and with dignity and when respect is shown for one's rights and opinions, feelings of positive standing are enhanced (Tyler and Bies, 1990). On the other hand, undignified, disrespectful, or impolite treatment by an authority carries the implications that one is not a full member of the group.

In a later work (Tyler and Lind, 1992), we noted that all three of these factors are easily seen as judgments concerning one's relationship with authorities, so we advanced a "relational model of authority" as an elaboration of group-value theory to specific questions about the acceptance of authority. We argued that the belief that an authority is legitimate and subsequent obedience to the authority's orders and decisions are profoundly affected by procedural justice judgments. We argued further that these justice judgments in turn are based largely on the relational factors of perceived trust, standing, and neutrality. Relational factors influence procedural justice judgments, we suggested, because they reflect the implications of an authority experience for people's sense of their relationship to the authority and the larger society.

Tyler and Lind (1992; Lind and Tyler, 1988) suggest that when people deal with third-party authorities they focus on judgments about the nature of their social relationship with society and social authorities. These judgments dominate their evaluations of their experiences. Such concerns are of two types. First, people are concerned about their long-term relationship to the social group and the interplay of autonomy and control implied by any such relationship. Individuals give up substantial control over their life as a member of society. But they want to feel that they are an equal member of society, and are not disadvantaged relative to others (Tyler and Dawes, 1993). If procedures are fair, then, over the long term, people can feel secure about the long-term gains from group membership. An even more important aspect of relational concerns, we argue, arises from the fact that people also derive much of their social identity from their standing as full-fledged members of their group or society. That standing is communicated to them via treatment by group authorities. Fair procedures communicate positive standing whereas unfair procedures raise questions about one's standing as a group member.[3]

The Lind and Tyler theories have focused the attention of justice researchers on the social psychological dynamics of justice judgments. In recent years, even the investigation of the original structural variable in the procedural justice literature—provision or denial of voice—has taken on a rather psychological tone. Shapiro and Brett (1993) and Tyler (1987) have found that occurrence of the voice effect itself depends on whether the legal authority in question appears to be giving adequate consideration to the views presented in disputant voice conditions. The structural provision of opportunities for voice has no impact on perceived fairness unless the information given to the decision maker is *believed* to have been given adequate consideration (see also Conlon, Lind, and Lissak, 1989). Another example of the importance of psychological factors is seen in a study of procedural justice judgments in response to experiences with court-sponsored arbitration, mediation, trial, and bilateral negotiation (Lind *et al.*, 1990b). In that study the key to explaining differences in the judged fairness of the procedures was not some structural element, but instead disputants' feelings that one procedure was more dignified than another, another very psychological finding.

2. Fairness Heuristic Theory

The psychological focus in procedural justice research and theory in recent years has yielded a much more detailed understanding of justice judgments. But we still lack a coherent explanation of exactly why procedural justice judgments should matter so much in determining how people react to law and legal experiences. Lind (1994; Lind *et al.*, 1993) has attempted to solve some of these problems in an analysis of why procedural justice judgments are so important to behavior in a variety of social contexts, including authoritative contexts such as law. According to Lind's "fairness heuristic theory," the key to understanding procedural justice phenomena lies in appreciating that concern with procedural justice is a response to the core element of virtually all social structures: the inequality of power between the individual on the one hand and the group, organization, or society on the other.

A starting point for fairness heuristic theory, as applied to the connection between fairness and legal behavior, is recognition of a fundamental apprehension that people feel when confronted with the power of the state as manifested by law. Individuals facing legal authority are confronted with what Lind terms the "fundamental social dilemma." The dilemma arises from the fact that social life offers substantially better outcomes than does life without others, but at the same time society can impose severe negative outcomes. In addition, because we obtain at least part of our social identity from our national and regional citizenships, being a part of a particular legal structure is often an important part of how we see ourselves. Thus, there are substantial reasons, both in terms of outcomes and in terms of identity, to belong to and to invest one's resources and identity in an ordered society. On the other hand, when society imbues some people with the power and authority to act as agents of the law, a serious possibility of exploitation and abuse of power arises. One must have authorities for the state to function, but empowering authorities means that members of society must worry about being exploited by them. The basic dilemma is not a conscious analysis, according to Lind, but rather an intuition about social life founded on each individual's experiences with exploitation and rejection on the one hand, and the positive consequences of social relations on the other.

Lind argues that this fundamental social dilemma underlies the decisions that people make with respect to obeying laws and accepting legal authority. At each decision point the dilemma can be resolved either with a cooperative, compliant action or with a self-oriented, disobedient action. But how do people decide, in any given decision context, whether they will comply or disobey? The most common psychological response to the dilemma posed by authority is, Lind argues, to use impressions of fairness, especially impressions of procedural fairness as a heuristic or mental shortcut to guide one to compliance or resistance. If authorities seem to be making decisions in fair ways, people assume that they can obey orders and follow rules without worrying too much about exploitation. If, on the other hand, authorities seem to be acting unfairly, exploitation becomes a real possibility and obedience is seen as a less attractive option. Again it is important to stress that the use of fairness as a heuristic is not a reasoned, conscious action, but instead a cognitive device that people adopt to conserve cognitive and social resources and to guide behavior (such as obedience or disobedience to laws or the acceptance or rejection of a legal decision) that is part and parcel of social life.

The formulation to this point does not diverge much from traditional theories of procedural and distributive justice, but there are some features of the new model that make it quite distinct from traditional justice theories. First, according to the line of theorizing that we have been developing, the real sting of unfairness and feared exploitation lies in the diminution of one's social self-identity (Lind and Tyler, 1988:Chapter 10; Tyler, Degoey, Smith, 1996). Outcome-oriented theories of justice judgments fail to recognize that people are generally quite ready to accept that they must often accept outcomes that are less than all they had hoped for; what people really worry about is rejection or the implication of rejection by society. To lose any specific hoped-for outcome is a normal part of social life, but rejection by authorities carries the implication that one is less of a person than others.

A second point of deviation from traditional theories of justice judgments is to be found in the account of how justice judgments are developed. Because people use justice judgments as a rough index of their security within a social situation, it is reasonable to suppose that a person begins looking for justice-relevant information as soon as he or she enters a social situation. People tend to view their treatment by authorities as especially diagnostic of how they are seen by society, because they view authorities as a personification of society. When they first encounter an authority, people are therefore especially sensitive to any information on which they can build a justice judgment. Because in most real-world situations information about social process and procedure is generally available from the outset of any interaction with authority, while outcome information is not available until later, people form their original justice judgment on the basis of procedures and social process and then later incorporate outcome information into their overall impressions of the fairness of the encounter. That is, overall fairness judgments show what psychologists call "primacy effects" (early information is more potent than later information), and because procedural information is available early, prior to the procedure, while outcome information is usually available after the procedure, procedural information is an especially powerful determinant of overall fairness judgments. In the terms of art used in modern social cognition theory, process information anchors the fairness judgment to such an extent that outcome information can only make relatively minor adjustments.

This explains why so many studies have found that overall impressions of fairness are more strongly influenced by procedural factors than by outcomes, but it also leaves room for outcome fairness judgments to take precedence in some particular situations. Van den Bos, Lind, Vermunt, and Wilke (1997) noted that fairness heuristic theory predicts that the first-received fairness information, whether it is procedural fairness information or distributive fairness information, should have greater impact that later fairness information. In a laboratory experiment they showed that when distributive justice information precedes procedural justice information, the effect of the distributive justice information is greater. One implication of this line of work is that procedural justice judgments and distributive judgments may be less distinct cognitively than has been thought to be the case—one type of justice judgment can apparently be substituted for another as people generate overall impressions of how they are being treated. This in turn suggests that global theories of justice judgment, which explain not only procedural justice phenomena, but also distributive and retributive justice phenomena (see the chapters on these topics in this volume), might well be within our reach.

Fairness heuristic theory also explains why, when they generate judgments of procedural fairness, people focus on the three relational factors that Tyler (1988, 1990) identified. The answer lies in the twin worries of exploitation and exclusion that are posed by the fundamental social dilemma. We would argue that the three factors of standing, trust, and neutrality are central to justice judgments because they serve as ready sources of information about the likelihood that one will be exploited or excluded. Standing is especially relevant to the exclusion possibility, trust is especially relevant to the exploitation possibility, and neutrality serves as a general guarantee that one will not be relegated to secondary status or that one will be the target of discrimination.

A final point of deviation from traditional notions of justice has to do with the way that justice judgments are thought to affect the acceptance of authority and procedures. Lind (1994) argues that justice judgments serve as a social decision heuristic that leads people to shift from one mode of interaction with groups, organizations, and society to another mode of interaction. Specifically, if in the course of interacting with a social unit or authority one feels fairly treated, the fairness heuristic induces people to shift into what Lind calls "group mode," an approach to social relations that is generally cooperative and that patterns later behavior not on expected outcomes but on impressions of fairness. If, on the other hand, early treatment seems unfair, people will adopt what Lind calls "individual mode" ways of responding: They will focus on short-term outcomes and pattern their behavior in ways that maximize those outcomes.

This line of theorizing implies, in terms used in the analysis of causal relationships, that people use justice judgments as both mediators and moderators of the decision to accept legal decisions and procedures. Justice judgments mediate between impressions of process and expected outcomes on the one hand and the acceptance of legal decisions and procedures on the other. In addition, justice judgments moderate the direct effect of outcomes on acceptance because the outcome effect is reduced when justice judgments are positive and enhanced when justice judgments are negative.

This account of the origins and consequences of procedural justice judgments is quite compatible with modern social psychological theorizing about how people form social attitudes and beliefs and make social decisions—something that could not be said for the original Thibaut and Walker theory nor, for that matter, much of the psychologizing seen in traditional law and society scholarship. The image of people as careful utility-maximizers, accumulating all available information and using it to guide their decisions and attitudes, is rather out-of-date. We now know that people use a variety of shortcuts and heuristics as they try to deal with the great flow of social information that confronts them, and that they are far from optimal information processors. Many apparently irrational or maladaptive cognitive biases have been discovered and verified empirically in other realms of social life, and it now seems rather naive to think that people make mistakes in patterning their law-related attitudes and behavior only because of ignorance or deceit.

Many of these points can be illustrated with reference to the analyses of procedural justice judgments described above. Social exchange and other quasi-economic models of legal behavior suppose that people routinely conduct an analysis of the benefits and costs associated with a given procedure or with obeying or disobeying a given authority, but both the thrust of social cognition research and a closer look at the psychological questions involved in legal behavior make this seem unlikely. All but the most experienced legal actors would have trouble arriving at firm conclusions about how much they would benefit or lose from a given procedure or from interacting with a given authority. In fact, there is some evidence that even those who are experienced players in the system do not use outcome information as efficiently as traditional theorists would expect (see, e.g., Lind, Kulik Ambrose, and de Vera Park, 1993). It seems likely that the processes posited by the new theory are so deeply ingrained that even those with substantial personal experience have trouble "deactivating" the intuitive, process-oriented system.

Lind also argues that there are serious psychological difficulties with exchange and economic theories of behavior. The problem with using outcomes to guide one's legal behavior is that outcomes, when they become available (and as argued above, that may be rather late to help with the decision of whether to accept a procedure or obey an authority), are difficult to interpret. If one's outcomes fall short of expectations, is this due to some temporary aberration? Is there some good reason for the poor outcomes? Is the disappointment due to having too high expectations? These are difficult issues to resolve, and they make using outcomes to guide one's reactions a very iffy business indeed. To gather all the relevant information for the sort of analyses social exchange theorists suggest would require constant monitoring of the outcomes others receive, all of the factors that might explain why one received the outcomes one did and why others received the outcomes they did, as well as constant adjustment of expectations through rather complex analyses of past and future outcome contingencies. Fairness heuristic theory suggests that if people did indeed engaged routinely in these sorts of analyses they would become so overburdened cognitively as they tried to sort out these complex issues that they would not have the necessary cognitive capacity left to structure and enact the legal behavior that is the object of the analysis.

A far more likely state of affairs psychologically, according to the theory, is that people make a rough and ready judgment early in the course of an interaction with a legal authority or early in their experience with a legal procedure and then use that judgment to guide them as they get on with the experience. Arriving quickly at a judgment of the likely fairness of the authority or procedure gives reassurance of generally good consequences if the judgment is positive or alerts one to be extra careful (perhaps even to fall back on the type of outcome-oriented analysis posited by the social exchange and economic theorists, however effortful it is) if the judgment is negative. In situations where one is very badly treated by authorities, the fairness heuristic can sometimes manifest itself as a "vendetta response" (Lind, Greenberg, Scott, and Welhans) in which costs are ignored as one tries to harm those who have treated one unfairly.

Of course, *perceived* fairness of treatment in past experiences can be a poor indicator of future exploitation or exclusion in any given instance. It has been reported, for example, that the African-American men enrolled in the infamous Tuskegee syphilis study were treated rather well (for the era), but in the long run they were of course badly used by any standards. Perceptions of fair treatment can even be deliberately manipulated, if someone has the skill to fool people about how they are being viewed or valued. But these are inescapable costs of the use of any heuristic. In fact, the existing research in procedural justice suggests that people are not insensitive to these abuses of their use of fairness as a decision-making criterion.[4] There are studies that show that people pay particular attention to even the slightest evidence of unfair treatment (e.g., Lind and Lissak, 1983) and that they respond to false representations of fair treatment with extremely negative reactions (e.g., Folger, 1977; Folger *et al.*, 1979).

Fairness heuristic theory argues that people use the factors they do to arrive at impressions of fairness because questions like respect, consideration, and neutrality are the sorts of things that people feel most comfortable in making judgments about. However irrational it might seem, at first glance, to use judgments of an authority's politeness or of a procedure's dignity to arrive at judgments of whether one is being treated fairly, these are social signs and symbols that people are comfortable interpreting. Most people are, we would argue, in fact, much better at perceiving whether they are being treated impolitely than they are at interpreting whether the fine they received or the judgment handed down in their lawsuit is fair.

In summary, the central idea of fairness heuristic theory is that people do the best they can, given cognitive limitations, to arrive at judgments about whether they are being treated fairly, and that they then use these fairness judgments to guide their decisions so that they can get on with the legal interactions they are involved in and with life in general. If the solution seems a bit rough, it may well be so, but the fairness heuristic is used, and continues to be used because it works "well enough" and, perhaps most importantly, because it is a workable solution to some difficult problems.

The theoretical account just offered makes a number of predictions that have been tested and confirmed in recent studies. We noted above that Van den Bos *et al.* (1997) found that distributive justice information received before much is known about the procedure can exert a strong effect on the evaluation of later process information, just as fairness heuristic theory predicts. Lind, Kray, and Thompson (1998) conducted an even more direct test of the theory's prediction that fairness judgments are formed early and then are resistant to change, exposing experimental participants to unfair practices in one of three trials of a relatively brief experimental task. They found substantial differences across the trials, with early unfair treatment resulting in much lower overall fairness evaluations than later unfair treatment. Lind, Kray, and Thompson found, as the theory predicted, that the primacy effect is stronger when there is substantial involvement with the group in which the unfairness occurs.

Additional support for the theory comes from some of the data generated by the Lind *et al.* (1998) study of the correlates of wrongful termination claims. One prediction of fairness heuristic theory is that once a person shifts into "group mode" and adopts fairness as the principal guide for behavior, subsequent experience of very unfair treatment will trigger a "vendetta response" that will prompt a person to undertake retaliatory actions even when those actions have substantial cost. Lind *et al.* found that those workers who felt they were dismissed without dignity or lied to about the true reason for their dismissal showed rates of claiming far above what would have been predicted from the behavior of workers who reported less unfair experiences—in statistical terms, there was a substantial discontinuity in the regression between fairness of treatment at termination and claiming behavior.

Additional support for fairness heuristic theory, and for other manifestations of the original Lind and Tyler group-value theory (see Lind and Tyler, 1988; Tyler and Lind, 1992), comes from a number of studies that show a strong causal link between unfair treatment and the diminution of self-esteem. We noted earlier that fairness heuristic theory, like other relational theories of justice, assumes that part of the reason justice is so important is that fair or unfair treatment has implications for one's standing as a full member of society. Unfair treatment is seen as unfair, according to these theories, precisely because it calls into question one's identity as a full-fledged member of society. If membership in one's society is a part of one's social identity, and this would be the case among all but the most disaffected of persons, then unfair treatment should damage self-esteem, by undermining the social identity component of self-esteem. Several recent studies (Tyler, Degoey, and Smith, 1996) have shown, in both laboratory and field settings, that unfair treatment can lower self-esteem.

3. Diversity and Procedural Consensus

The emphasis on psychological issues—on issues like relational judgments and the interpretation of events as reflecting dignity, consideration, and objectivity—raises the possibility that people will arrive at different conclusions about the fairness of a given procedure. When differences in the perceived fairness of a given procedure exist between the disputants in a conflict, the problem of how to specify which procedure is "best" in procedural justice terms becomes especially problematic. Unless all parties define procedural fairness similarly, it will be difficult to find a single procedure that all will regard as just. While there are many factors that might contribute to divergent opinions about what is fair, cultural and gender diversity are among the most mentioned. For example, the Commission on the Future of the California Courts has asserted that "an important element in determining the appropriate process [for resolving disputes] is the cultural experience of the disputants" and that "dispute resolution procedures should foster respect and appreciation for cultural differences" (Dockson, 1993:78).

We mentioned above some findings with respect to cultural differences in procedural justice judgments (and the lack of such differences), and we noted that the Leung and Morris chapter in this volume gives much more detail than we can here about this issue. Nonetheless, in light of statements like that of the Commission, it is worth taking a little more time to consider whether there is widespread difference of opinion about what is fair. As we noted earlier, recent studies suggest that cultural and gender differences in preferences for methods of dispute resolution may, in fact, be quite small (Lind *et al.*, 1994). With respect to the existence of culture- and gender-based differences in the antecedents of procedural fairness, Tyler (1988) found very little evidence of such differences in the psychology of postexperience reactions to dealings with the legal system, and Tyler (1994) did not find either racial or gender-based differences in the psychology underlying people's evaluations of the procedural fairness of national policymaking by Congress. We need to consider some of the issues that these "nondifferences" raise.

There are two ways that the lack of ethnic differences in definitions of the fairness of legal procedures can be viewed. First, these findings may reflect a similarity in the social conditions or values of all members of U.S. society. On the other hand, the lack of differences may also reflect the ability of social structure to override differences in people's objective conditions and experiences. People may have objectively different experiences, but interpret them as similar after they filter their experiences through cultural frameworks.

As we noted earlier, the basic phenomena that make up the psychology of procedural justice are not confined to U.S. society or even to Western cultures. For example, in the Sugawara and Huo study of procedural justice in Japan, the Japanese students considered the opportunity to present evidence important to procedural fairness ($\beta = 0.18, p < 0.05$), but did not place much weight on decision control (the opportunity to reject the decision, $\beta = -0.04$, n.s.; p. 136). These data mirror those seen in many studies conducted in the United States, and they replicate the general implications of a much earlier study by Leung and Lind (1986).

Although the findings of Sugawara and Huo suggest substantial similarities in the psychology of American and Japanese disputants, they also provide some suggestion that the psychology of procedural justice may not be completely the same in all countries. Sugawara and Huo found that the most important component of procedural justice to Japanese respondents was clarity, an element missing in current Western theories of procedural justice (Leventhal, 1976; Thibaut and Walker, 1975). (It should be noted, however, that U.S. researchers have seldom looked at clarity of procedure as an antecedent of procedural justice.) Other authors have suggested that there are important differences between Japanese and U.S. legal consciousness (Hamilton and Sanders, 1992; Smith, 1986; Wagatsuma and Rosett, 1986).

An important task for future studies is to differentiate views about distributive justice (appropriate settlements) or retributive justice (appropriate punishments) from differences in views about appropriate criteria for evaluating procedures for resolving disputes. Legal authorities themselves seem to be less willing to advocate cultural relativism in procedure than in substantive justice. For example, notwithstanding their concerns about cultural differences and their impact on legal *decisions*, the Commission on the Future of the California Courts "is adamant that different legal standards and different legal norms for different cultures are unacceptable" and that "standards and the application of the law should be uniform" (Dockson, 1993:78). Interestingly, the research literature is not inconsistent with this distinction, in that it suggests that cross-cultural differences in views about distributive and retributive justice may be greater than differences in views about procedural justice (Tyler *et al.*, 1997; Tyler and Smith, 1997; see also Leung and Morris, this volume).

4. Summary

Our argument is that empirical research on disputing reveals an image of the psychology of reactions to their experiences with legal authorities substantially different from the image of the self-interested, "rational" actor that dominates much current legal discourse. Instead, empirical studies suggest that people react to their experiences in primarily moral and ethical terms, judging the actions of the authorities with whom they deal against justice criteria, not in terms of what they "win" or "lose" through third-party decisions. In particular, people evaluate the fairness of decision-making procedures and rely on these evaluations to guide their behavior. These findings provide a new perspective on the antecedents of public willingness to defer to legal authorities.

Although self-interest models of the person are widely articulated with the writings of legal scholars, those models have typically not been subjected to empirical tests. Hence, there is no way for those models to be confirmed or disconfirmed. Instead, the rational actor models have relied on the fact the assumptions of self-interested action accord with people's stereotypes about their own and others' behavior. Studies of real legal behavior subject these assumptions to empirical test, and the results suggest that people do not behave in the ways predicted by rational choice models.[5]

These findings demonstrate the value of empirical studies based on interviews with the litigants involved in disputes. Such studies reveal an image of the concerns of those individuals that differs from that presented within much of the rational choice literature. It is only through *empirical* studies that it has been possible to disconfirm the widely held view that people evaluate their experiences with the legal system by assessing how much they win or lose.

D. SOME IMPLICATIONS OF THE RESEARCH

1. Formal and Informal Justice

The model of litigant psychology outlined in this chapter helps to explain the discrepancy between the expected and the observed reactions to formal and informal justice in studies of litigants in the U.S. legal system. In the United States the formal legal system accords those with disputes a variety of types of protection for their rights, including the opportunity to have their dispute resolved by a judge acting on neutral, factual, universalistic interpretations of the law. Considerations of power, wealth, or connections with the judge or a particular social group are not supposed to influence legal decisions.

Whatever the objective merits of formal trials, studies of litigants do not find that such formal justice leads to greater satisfaction, more perceived justice, or greater acceptance of decisions. On the contrary, in civil cases, disputants often express equally positive feelings about arbitration as about trials; and criminal defendants are more favorable toward plea bargaining than trials. Why is informal justice found to be popular? We would argue that, if properly enacted, informal justice procedures are more in accord with the psychology of fairness than are formal justice procedures. For one thing, informal procedures often allow people greater opportunities to participate in some real sense in the process. Further, informal procedures allows third parties the flexibility to display concern and caring—two elements that are likely to exert strong effects on the disputants' feelings of consideration and dignity, as well as on their willingness to trust the authority.

These conflicts over the appropriate form of legal authority are connected to a larger crisis in legitimacy within U.S. society. The development of the modern capitalist economy has changed the nature of interactions among people. Instead of long-term community-based associations in which people know those with whom they deal, and have extensive histories of interaction with those people and with their families, people now have more abbreviated interactions with people who are relative strangers (Kramer and Tyler, 1996; Shapiro, 1987; Zucker, 1986).

Max Weber argued that formal laws and legal authorities evolved to make such non-personalized interactions possible (Arts and van der Veen, 1992). Judges apply a known set of principles uniformly, without invoking personal values or biases. Even the principles themselves are uniform, rather than being influenced by local community norms. As a consequence, legal decisions are predictable and can be made with minimal knowledge of the disputants or their past relationship. There is an "economic value" to the "calculability or foreseeability of rights and duties without which the rational operation of capital enterprise would be seriously endangered" (Kawashima, 1963:58). Thus, calculability and universality are created through the neutrality of the formal trial (Tyler and Degoey, 1995).

However, neutrality captures only part of what makes authority legitimate to the disputants whose problems they are trying to handle. People are also interested in the benevolence of the motives of the authorities with whom they deal—the authorities' *trustworthiness*—and in the symbolic message the process used to handle their problem communicates about their standing as full participants in the society. People want to believe that third parties care about their concerns, consider their arguments, and try to be fair to them—symbols of particularistic attention. This is true both in the United States and in other societies. For example, Kawashima (1963) says of the Japanese legal system: "The notion that a justice measured by universal standards can exist independent of the wills of the disputants is apparently alien to the traditional habit of the Japanese people. Consequently, distrust of judges and a lack of respect for the authority of judicial decisions is widespread through the nation" (p. 50). Similarly, Smith (1986) argues that a tension between law and compassion dominates Western legal consciousness, where only "justice," and not "mercy" (compassion), can occur within the legal system. According to Smith this tension is not found in Japanese legal culture, where there is a "dislike for the rigid application of rules and the desire to achieve social harmony through warm human relations" (p. 369). Hence, in Japan "compassion can be consistent with the rule of law" (p. 343). In Western law, on the contrary, it is difficult for people's need for compassion and caring to be responded to within the framework of the formal law.

In an analysis of authority, Lane (1988) similarly argues that feelings about the benevolence of authorities are important, because feelings of self-respect and self-worth are influenced by people's relationships with group authorities. One way that such information is communicated is through benevolent, caring relationships with authorities. Lane suggests that "big business is considered impartially fair in its hiring, but that [quality] does not satisfy gemeinschaft [fellowship] justice, for large majorities believe that big business doesn't care whether I live or die, only that someone buys what they have to sell" (p. 185). Similarly, Lane argues that the public prefers the warmth of a sympathetic, caring jury to the "cold" rationality of a judge. Sennett makes a similar argument about managerial authority (Sennett, 1980). In fact, recent research within management settings makes clear that trust is central to authority relations in work organizations (Kramer and Tyler, 1996).

Ironically, the formal structures of the legal system make it more difficult for judges to communicate qualities of trustworthiness to disputants. This is the case because people do not infer trustworthy motives from behavior that they think simply reflects the enactment of formal rules as much as they do from informal discretionary actions. Informal justice, such as mediation, seems to provide greater opportunities for the communication of trust than does formal justice, because authorities have more freedom to engage in discretionary actions. Hence its popularity. People want to feel that those who wield authority over them are fundamentally concerned about their welfare. They infer this from knowledge that those individuals are behaving in benevolent ways. Hence, the authorities benefit when they are in an arena that allow them freedom and flexibility of behavior through which to communicate their benevolent motives and caring attitudes to those with whom they are dealing.

2. The Legitimacy of Legal Authority

One of the major social trends within U.S. society is the decline in the legitimacy of legal and political authority (Lipset and Schneider, 1983; Tyler, 1998). As authority becomes less legitimate, the question of why people will obey legal authorities becomes more important. In the future, why will people obey the law? Within the legal community, the development of critical legal studies has undermined the credibility of traditional notions of legal authority by pointing out inconsistencies and incoherence within legal doctrine. The law is consequently receiving less legitimation from formal authorities. Hence, it seems likely that popular feelings about law will become increasingly central to the effectiveness of legal authorities in the future. Yet, as noted, there are signs that popular views about the legitimacy of law are also declining (however, see Tyler, 1998, for a critique of these studies).

To accommodate these widely noted declines in legitimacy, the exercise of legal authority is likely to change in the future. Instead of a top-down application of substantive principles by legal authorities, more emphasis will be placed on the development of consensus among the parties to conflicts. Such a change is already evident in the move toward mediation in dispute resolution. Increasingly, legal authorities are adopting a facilitative role in which greater attention is placed on the concerns of the public. These changes move the exercise of legal authority in the direction of developing a consensus among the parties to a dispute about a solution that they are willing to embrace and accept, instead of imposing a decision derived from abstract legal rules and principles.

Similar changes in the exercise of authority have been observed in Japan. For example, public administration in Japan has taken on an increasingly mediational role in dealing with citizens (Tyler, 1996). Instead of applying legal rules, he finds that administrative agencies are trying to balance among the interests of citizen groups using "guidelines." As a consequence, the policy adopted to solve a similar problem may differ across situations. Policy has lost the universality that is characteristic of legal rules, making it more difficult to predict in advance what the criteria used in any given conflict will be. Instead, a unique settlement is formed within each specific case by balancing the interests of the parties. Social justice is "discovered through ad hoc balancing in each case, rather than appealing to justice as some ultimate rule."

A key question is whether or not this change in the exercise of authority changes the power of the law in society. One possibility is that authorities will still exercise power, but will do so in ways that are more masked. For example, authorities may use their facilitative role to manipulate the agenda so as to create desired social policies. However, they increasingly do not create these policies by promulgating legal rules, i.e., by directly controlling decisions. Instead, they exercise indirect or hidden control through their role as the authorities who structure the agenda of meetings and communicate among the various parties to disputes.

3. Procedural Concerns and Relationship Maintenance

In their original discussion of the psychology of dispute processing, Thibaut and Walker (1975) presented a very positive view of the value of procedural mechanisms. They viewed dealing with the destructive effects of conflict as one of the most important challenges of any society. From this perspective everyone in society benefits from norms and procedures that regulate conflict. Thibaut and Walker sought ways that disputes could be more consensually resolved, even when the disputants could not themselves agree on any particular outcome. Thibaut and Walker sought a consensus about procedures that might substitute for the unobtainable consensus about outcomes. Their concern fits well with the traditional interest of the legal system in finding ways to make decisions that will be acceptable to disputants. As we have already noted, research has strongly supported the effectiveness of procedural justice as a bridging mechanism of the type envisioned by Thibaut and Walker.

There are many indications in studies of disputing within U.S. society that disputes often take on an unnecessarily destructive character, in which those who are a party to disputes not only miss opportunities for mutual gain within interactions (Fisher and Ury, 1981), but also engage in behaviors that have destructive consequences for their ongoing relationships with others (Lempert and Sanders, 1986). In fact, for these reasons, businesses appear to avoid the formal conflict procedures of the legal system (Macauley, 1963). The Thibaut and Walker framework also fits well with systems theories, which view all groups within society as having a common interest in relationship and system maintenance (Easton, 1965: Parsons, 1963, 1967).

Legal and social theorists have recently been more critical of the neutrality of legal authorities, of law, and of the society whose interests those authorities and institutions serve (Kelman, 1987; Scheingold, 1974). These scholars point out that society in fact consists of classes of varying power. Dominant groups have an interest in maintaining an unequal distribution of social resources and use their control over the norms and procedures of society, including the legal system, to do so. These critical analyses of law have argued that there are potential dangers in a procedural focus in assessing the wisdom of any given policy, procedure, or decision. By focusing on procedures, not outcomes, people may be diverting their attention from the failure of the courts to deliver substantive justice. People may be misled or beguiled, substituting fair process for just outcomes. Viewed from this perspective, procedural justice may contribute to "false consciousness"—a discrepancy between people's true interests and their psychological judgments of reality.

On a policy level, there is reason to think that procedural justice *research* can serve as a basis for empowering the disadvantaged in two ways. First, procedural justice findings emphasize the importance of the type of open discussion and expression of views that are central to the Habermas model of discourse. Such public participation is key to developing a consensus about the nature of substantive law. Hence, procedural justice research suggests the potential value of allowing participation into the development and implementation of the law.

Second, by alerting the disadvantaged to the psychological tendency to substitute process for substance, procedural justice research helps people to recognize the mechanisms through which subordination occurs. For example, if people recognize their tendency to accept symbolic justice over real justice, this awareness can influence their later reactions to legal procedures.

We noted this problem above in our discussion of possible errors arising from the use of the fairness heuristic. As we noted there, the research literature suggests that people are, on some level at least, sensitive to and on guard against the possibility that their procedural fairness judgments will be used to trick them. This does not, of course, mean that no such trickery occurs. However, it does mean that people are concerned about the issue raised by critical theorists and sensitive to the possibility of being exploited by others.

Ultimately the way that procedural justice findings are viewed is linked to our image of the major problems facing our society. In the United States two images of liberal democracy are in conflict. One image is that society is dominated by stable and dominating institutions. In this image, law is strong and pervasive in its influence on the thoughts and actions of citizens. From the perspective of this critical framework, the goal of law and society research and writing should be to raise critical questions about those institutions.

The second image is of a more frail democratic social order. This view focuses on concerns about social mechanisms that can hold both individuals and society together in the face of conflicting interests and values. Instead of seeking to undermine existing authoritative institutions, this perspective seeks ways to maintain and enhance the ability of those institutions to govern effectively. From this latter perspective the key problem is stability, i.e., of facilitating the acceptance of authorities that is necessary for society to function. This vision focuses on the risks of a society disintegrating into contending groups, as has occurred in Yugoslavia and the former Soviet Union.

Of course, as is often the case with such debates in political philosophy, the truth for any particular state and time lies in a balance of the two views, and the proper balance in this debate varies depending on whether revolution or hegemony is the stronger force. In the context of stable societies such as the United States or Japan, which have longstanding legal and political frameworks, the need to create a questioning critical consciousness among citizens is a natural preoccupation. From this perspective the most striking aspect of legal authority is the strength of its hold on citizens. In the United States, for example, a large proportion of citizens feel obligated to obey laws and accept legal decisions (Tyler, 1990). Even in controversial cases, such as abortion policy, citizens feel obligated to defer to court decisions (Tyler and Mitchell, 1994). In the United States, many have argued, the general tendency is to regard as legitimate and defer to legal authority (see, e.g., Kelman and Hamilton, 1989). Further, it is not clear that this sense of obligation is declining (Tyler, 1998). The key role of legal scholars is to promote questioning of such authority.

On the other hand, societies in the midst of conflict and turmoil, such as the former Soviet Union or the former Yugoslavia, are searching for potential sources of stability and for mechanisms that can bridge differences in interests and values—for ways to create legitimacy for institutions and authorities. In South Africa, for example, the question is how a new social order can create effectively functioning legal and political institutions. Similarly, the societies of Europe are preoccupied with efforts to develop legitimacy for an overarching political and legal authority—the European Union. Societies in turmoil or transition are seeking mechanisms such as procedural justice for creating an authoritative system of legal authority.

There are increasing indications that the United States is becoming a less stable society, in which concerns over maintaining the effectiveness of the legal order may be of increasing importance (Tyler, 1994, 1998; Tyler and Mitchell, 1994). We may find that, in the future, the question of central importance in legal studies is less a philosophical analysis of why people *ought* to obey the law and more a social science analysis of when people *actually* will obey the law.

One problem in particular is the increasing economic polarization of our nation, the increasing divergence between a small well-off elite, a large middle class with fairly stable incomes but little prospect of real economic progress, and a more or less permanent economic underclass, composed largely of minority group members (Tyler *et al.*, 1997). In the face of this trend, it may well be the case that governments will have increasing difficulty bridging differences and helping disputing groups to reach solutions that are accepted by all sides to a conflict. Hence, identifying effective mechanisms for containing social conflict is likely to emerge as a crucial question in the development of new legal forms, and discovering or designing these mechanisms may emerge as a central role for legal scholars and social scientists alike. If procedural justice can be part of the mechanism for accomplishing this, and especially if it can be a mechanism for making those who "have" more willing to do what is right for those who "have not," we will count our work, and the work of other procedural justice scholars, to be of great value.

E. ENDNOTES

1. In fact, most of the points made in this chapter apply to other authority contexts, as well as to the psychology of legal authority. Indeed, there is good reason to believe (see, e.g., Lind, Tyler, and Huo, 1997) that fairness plays as strong a role in the psychology of nonauthoritative relations as in the psychology of authority relations.
2. We use the term "procedural justice" to refer to the perceived fairness of both informal elements of social process and formal rules and procedures. Some scholars (e.g., Bies and Moag, 1986) draw a distinction between procedural justice and what they term "interactional justice," linking the former to the fairness of formal procedures and the latter to the fairness of the social process. As we have argued before (Lind and Tyler, 1988) we see little point in this distinction, since there seems to be little difference in reactions to procedural and interactional injustices.
3. As we note in more detail below, we do not mean to imply that either of these concerns is mollified by a *conscious* social contract between the individual and society. Rather, people learn that they are safer from exploitation and exclusion when they are treated with respect, when authorities seem to be trying to be fair, and when decisions are made on a factual basis.
4. We must emphasize in the strongest possible terms that we are not saying it is in any sense "good" that people use fallible fairness judgments as a heuristic, only that it appears to be the case that they do so.
5. Interestingly, some very recent work by Miller and Ratner (1996, 1998) suggests that there is a "myth of self-interest" in most lay accounts of the reasons for behavior. That is, most people think that self-interest accounts for much more of human behavior than it actually does.

REFERENCES

Adams, J. S. (1965). Inequity in Social Exchange. In L. Berkowitz (Ed.), *Advances in Experimental Social Psychology*. New York: Academic Press, 2, 267–299.

Adler, P., Hensler, D., and Nelson, C. E. (1983). *Simple Justice: How Litigants Fare in the Pittsburgh Court Arbitration Program*. Santa Monica, CA: RAND.

Arts, W., and van der Veen, R. (1992). Sociological Approaches to Distributive and Procedural Justice. In K. Scherer (Ed.), *Justice: Interdisciplinary Perspectives*. London: Cambridge University Press.

Barrett-Howard, E., and Tyler, T. R. (1986). Procedural Justice as a Criterion in Allocation Decisions. *Journal of Personality and Social Psychology*, *50*, 296–304.

Bies, R. J., and Moag, J. S. (1986) Interactional Justice: Communication Criteria of Fairness. In R. Lewicki, M. Bazerman, and B. Sheppard (Eds.), *Research on Negotiation in Organizations* (vol. 1, pp. 43–55). Greenwich, CT: JAI.

Casper, J., Tyler, T. R., and Fisher, B. (1988). Procedural Justice in Felony Cases. *Law and Society Review*, *22*, 483–507.

Conlon, D. E., Lind, E. A., and Lissak, R. I. (1989). Nonlinear and nonmonotomic effects of outcome on procedural and distributive fairness judgments. University of Illinois, Champaign (unpublished).

Deutsch, M. (1982). Interdependence and Psychological Orientation. In V. J. Derlega and J. Grzelak (Eds.), *Cooperation and Helping Behavior: Theories and Research* (pp. 15–42). New York: Academic Press.

Deutsch, M. (1985). *Distributive Justice*. New Haven: Yale.

Dockson, R. R. (1993). *Justice in the Balance: Report of the Commission on the Future of the California Courts*. San Francisco: Supreme Court of California.

Easton, D. (1965). *A Systems Analysis of Political Life*. Chicago: University of Chicago Press.

Felstiner, W. L. F., Abel, R. L., and Sarat, A. (1980–81). The Emergence and Transformation of Disputes. *Law and Society Review*, *15*, 631–654.

Fisher, R., and Ury, W. (1981). *Getting to Yes*. New York: Penguin.

Folger, R. (1977). Distributive and Procedural Justice: Combined Impact of "Voice" and Improvement on Experienced Inequity. *Journal of Personality and Social Psychology*, *35*, 108–119.

Folger, R., Rosenfield, D., Grove, J., and Corkran, L. (1979). Effects of "Voice" and Peer Opinions on Responses to Inequity. *Journal of Personality and Social Psychology*, *37*, 2253–2261.

Friedland, N., Thibaut, J., and Walker, L. (1973). Some Determinants of the Violation of Rules. *Journal of Applied Social Psychology*, *3*, 103–118.

Hamilton, V. L., and Sanders, J. (1992). *Everyday Justice: Responsibility and the Individual in Japan and the United States*. New Haven: Yale University Press.

Houlden, P. (1980–81). The Impact of Procedural Modifications on Evaluations of Plea Bargaining. *Law and Society Review*, *15*, 267–292.

Huo, Y. J. (1994). *Are There Limits to Justice?: Exclusionary Effects on Justice Attitudes*. Unpublished master's thesis, Department of Psychology, University of California, Berkeley.

Kawashima, T. (1963). Dispute Resolution in Contemporary Japan. In A. T. von Mehren (Ed.), *Law in Japan* (pp. 41–72). Cambridge, MA: Harvard University Press.

Kelman, H. C., and Hamilton, V. L. (1989). *Crimes of Obedience*. New Haven: Yale.

Kelman, M. (1987). *A Guide to Critical Legal Studies*. Cambridge, MA: Harvard University Press.

Kramer, R., and Tyler, T. R. (1996). *Trust in Organizations*. Thousand Oaks, CA: Sage.

Kressel, K. (1985). *The Process of Divorce*. New York: Basic Books.

Lane, R. E. (1988). Procedural Goods in a Democracy: How One Is Treated vs. What One Gets. *Social Justice Research*, *2*, 177–192.

Lempert, R., and Sanders, J. (1986). *An Invitation to Law and Social Science*. New York: Longman.

Leung, K., and Lind, E. A. (1986). Procedural Justice and Culture: Effects of Culture, Gender, and Investigator Status on Procedural Preferences. *Journal of Personality and Social Psychology*, *50*, 1134–1140.

Leventhal, G. S. (1976). Fairness in Social Relationships. In J. Thibaut, J. Spence, and R. Carson (Eds.), *Contemporary Topics in Social Psychology*. Morristown, NJ: General Learning Press. 211–240.

Lind, E. A. (1990). *Arbitrating High-Stakes Cases: An Evaluation of Court-Annexed Arbitration in a United States District Court*. Santa Monica, CA: RAND.

Lind, E. A. (1994). Procedural Justice and Culture: Evidence for Ubiquitous Process Concerns. *Zeitschrift für Rechtssoziologie*, *15*, 24–36.

Lind, E. A., and Tyler, T. R. (1988). *The Social Psychology of Procedural Justice*. New York: Plenum Press.

Lind, E. A., Erickson, B. E., Friedland, N., and Dickenberger, M. (1978). Reactions to Procedural Models for Adjudicative Conflict Situations: A Cross-National Study. *Journal of Conflict Resolution*, *22*, 318–341.

Lind, E. A., Greenberg, J., Scott, K. S., and Welchans, T. D. The Winding Road from Employee to Complainant. *Administrative Science Quarterly* (in press).

Lind, E. A., Kurtz, S., Musante, L., Walker, L., and Thibaut, J. W. (1980). Procedure and Outcome Effects on Reactions to Adjudicated Resolution of Conflicts of Interests. *Journal of Personality and Social Psychology*, *39*, 643–653.

Lind, E. A., Lissak, R. I., and Conlon, D. E. (1983). Decision Control and Process Control Effects on Procedural Fairness Judgments. *Journal of Applied Social Psychology*, *4*, 338–350.

Lind, E. A., and Lissak, R. I. (1985). Apparent Impropriety and Procedural Fairness Judgments. *Journal of Experimental Social Psychology*, *21*, 19–29.

Lind, E. A., MacCoun, R. J., Ebener, P. A., Felstiner, W. L. F., Hensler, D. R., Resnick, J., and Tyler, T. R. (1989). *The Perception of Justice: Tort Litigants' Views of Trials, Court-Annexed Arbitration, and Judicial Settlement Conferences*. Santa Monica, CA: RAND.

Lind, E. A., Kanfer, R., and Early, C. (1990a). Voice, Control, and Procedural Justice. *Journal of Personality and Social Psychology, 59*, 952–959.

Lind, E. A., Kray, L., and Thompson, L. (1998). Primacy Effects in Justice Judgments. Duke Univeristy (unpublished).

Lind, E. A., MacCoun, R., Ebener, P. A., Felstiner, W. L. F., Hensler, D. R., Resnick, J., and Tyler, T. R. (1990b). In the Eye of the Beholder. Tort Litigants' Evaluations of Their Experiences in the Civil Justice System. *Law and Society Review, 24*, 953–996.

Lind, E. A., Kulik, C. T., Ambrose, M., and de Vera Park, M. (1993). Individual and Corporate Dispute Resolution: Using Procedural Fairness as a Decision Heuristic. *Administrative Science Quarterly, 38*, 224–251.

Lind, E. A., Huo, Y., and Tyler, T. R. (1994). ... And Justice for All: Ethnicity, Gender, and Preferences for Dispute Resolution Procedures. *Law and Human Behavior, 18*, 269–290.

Lind, E. A., Tyler, T. R., and Huo, Y. (1994). Procedural Context and Culture: Variation in the Antecedents of Procedural Justice Judgments. *Journal of Personality and Social Psychology, 73*, 767–780.

Lipset, S. M., and Schneider, W. (1983). *The Confidence Gap*. New York: Free Press.

Macauley, S. (1963). Noncontractual Relations in Business. *American Sociological Review, 28*, 55–67.

MacCoun, R. J. (1993). Drugs and the Law: A Psychological Analysis of Drug Prohibition. *Psychological Bulletin, 113*, 497–512.

MacCoun, R. J., Lind, E. A., Hensler, D. R., Bryant, D. L., and Ebener, P. A. (1988). *Alternative Adjudication: An Evaluation of the New Jersey Automobile Arbitration Program*. Santa Monica, CA: RAND.

McCarthy, T. (1978). *The Critical Theory of Jurgen Habermas*. Cambridge, MA: MIT Press.

McEwen, C. A., and Maiman, R. J. (1981). Small Claims Mediation in Main: An Empirical Assessment. *Maine Law Review, 33*, 237–268.

Miller, D. T., and Ratner, R. K. (1996). The Power of the Myth of Self-Interest. In L. Montada and M. J. Lerner (Eds.), *Current Societal Concerns about Justice*. New York: Plenum Press.

Miller, D. T., and Ratner, R. K. (1998). The Disparity between the Actual and Assumed Power of Self-Interest. *Journal of Personality and Social Psychology, 74*, 53–62.

Parsons, T. (1963). On the Concept of Influence. *Public Opinion Quarterly, 27*, 63–82.

Parsons, T. (1967). Some Reflections on the Place of Force in Social Process. In T. Parsons (Ed.), *Sociological Theory and Modern Society*. New York: Free Press.

Paternoster, R. (1987). The Deterrent Effect of the Perceived Certainty and Severity of Punishment: A Review of the Evidence and Issues. *Justice Quarterly, 4*, 173–217.

Paternoster, R., Saltzman, L. E., Waldo, G. P., and Chiricos, T. G. (1983). Perceived Risk and Social Control: Do Sanctions Really Deter? *Law and Society Review, 17*, 457–479.

Pruitt, D. G., Pierce, R. S., McGillicuddy, N. B., Welton, G. L., and Castrianno, L. M. (1993). Long-term Success in Mediation. *Law and Human Behavior, 17*, 313–330.

Ross, H. L. (1982). *Deterring the Drinking Driver*. Lexington, MA: Heath.

Rubin, J. Z. (1980). Experimental Research on Third-Party Intervention in Conflict: Toward Some Generalizations. *Psychological Bulletin, 87*, 379–391.

Sarat, A. (1977). Studying American Legal Culture: An Assessment of Survey Evidence. *Law and Society Review, 11*, 427–488.

Scheingold, S. A. (1974). *The Politics of Rights*. New Haven: Yale University Press.

Sennett, R. (1980). *Authority*. New York: Vintage Books.

Shapiro, D. L., and Brett, J. M. (1993). Comparing Three Processes underlying Judgments of Procedural Justice. *Journal of Personality and Social Psychology, 14*, 101–113.

Shapiro, S. P. (1987). The Social Control of Impersonal Trust. *American Journal of Sociology, 93*, 623–658.

Singer, L. R. (1994). *Settling Disputes: Conflict Resolution in Business, Families, and the Legal System*. Boulder, CO: Westview Press.

Smith, J. C. (1986). Ajase and Oedipus: Ideas of the Self in Japanese and Western Legal Consciousness. *University of British Columbia Law Review, 20*, 341–377.

Sugawara, I., and Huo, Y. J. (1994). Disputes in Japan: A Cross-Cultural Test of the Procedural Justice Model. *Social Justice Research, 7*, 129–144.

Takenishi, A., and Takenishi, M. (1992). Does Commitment Affect the Meaning of Fairness?: Commonality and Stability of Fairness Criteria in a Political Setting. *Social Justice Research, 5*, 415–429.

Takenishi, M., and Takenishi, A. (1990). Why Japanese Citizens Evaluate the New Indirect Tax as Unfair: Fairness Criteria and Their Relative Importance. *Social Justice Research, 4*, 251–264.

Thibaut, J., and Walker, L. (1975). *Procedural Justice*. Hillsdale, NJ: Erlbaum.

Thibaut, J., and Walker, L. (1978). A Theory of Procedure. *California Law Review, 66*, 541–566.

Tyler, T. R. (1984). The Role of Perceived Injustice in Defendant's Evaluations of Their Courtroom Experience. *Law and Society Review*, *18*, 51–74.

Tyler, T. R. (1987). Conditions Leading to Value Expressive Effects in Judgments of Procedural Justice. *Journal of Personality and Social Psychology*, *52*, 333–344.

Tyler, T. R. (1988). What Is Procedural Justice? Criteria Used by Citizens to Assess the Fairness of Legal Procedures. *Law and Society Review*, *22*, 301–355.

Tyler, T. R. (1989). The Psychology of Procedural Justice. *Journal of Personality and Social Psychology*, *57*, 333–355.

Tyler, T. R. (1990). *Why People Obey the Law*. New Haven: Yale University Press.

Tyler, T. R. (1993). Legitimizing Unpopular Public Policies: Does Procedure Matter? *Zeitschrift fuer Rechtssoziologie*, *14*, 47–54.

Tyler, T. R. (1994). Governing Amid Diversity: Can Fair Decision-Making Procedures Bridge Competing Public Interests and Values? *Law and Society Review*, *28*, 701–722.

Tyler, T. R. (1996). The psychology of disputing. In T. Tanese (Ed.), *Law and Society*. Kyoto, Japan: Minerva.

Tyler, T. R. (1997a). Justice and Power in Civil Dispute Processing. In A. Sarat and B. Garth (Eds.), *Sociolegal Studies*. Evanston, IL: Northwestern University Press. 309–346.

Tyler, T. R. (1997b). Compliance with Intellectual Property Laws: A Psychological Perspective. *Journal of International Law and Politics*, *28*, 101–115.

Tyler, T. R. (1997c). Citizen Discontent with Legal Procedures. *American Journal of Comparative Law*, *45*, 869–902.

Tyler, T. R. (1997d). Procedural Fairness and Compliance with the Law. *Swiss Journal of Economics and Statistics*, *133*, 219–240.

Tyler, T. R. (1998). Public Mistrust of the Law: A Political Perspective. *University of Cincinnati Law Review*, *66*, 1–29.

Tyler, T. R. (1999). Why People Cooperate with Organizations: An Identity-Based Perspective. In B. Staw and R. Sutton (Eds.), *Research on Organizational Behavior*. Greenwich, CT: JAI Press, 21, 201–246.

Tyler, T. R., and Belliveau, M. (1996). Managing Workforce Diversity: Ethical Concerns and Intergroup Relations. In D. Messick and A. E. Tenbrunsel (Eds.), *Behavioral Research and Business Ethnics*. New York: Russell Sage Foundation. 171–186.

Tyler, T. R., and Bies, R. (1990). Interpersonal Aspects of Procedural Justice. In J. S. Carroll (Ed.), *Applied Social Psychology in Business Settings*. Hillsdale, NJ: Erlbaum. 77–98.

Tyler, T. R., and Blader, S. L. (2000). *Cooperation in Groups*. Philadelphia, PA: Psychology Press.

Tyler, T. R., and Caine, A. (1981). The Influence of Outcomes and Procedures on Satisfaction with Formal Leaders. *Journal of Personality and Social Psychology*, *41*, 642–655.

Tyler, T. R., and Dawes, R. (1993). Fairness in Groups: Comparing the Self-Interest and Social Identity Perspectives. In B. A. Mellers and J. Baron (Eds.), *Psychological Perspectives on Justice*. London: Cambridge University Press. 87–108.

Tyler, T. R., and Degoey, P. (1995). Collective restraint in a social dilemma situation. *Journal of Personality and Social Psychology*, *69*, 482–497.

Tyler, T. R., and Degoey, P. (1996). Trust in Organizational Authorities: The Influence of Motive Attributions on Willingness to Accept Decisions. In R. Kramer and T. R. Tyler (Eds.), *Trust in Organizations*. Thousand Oaks, CA: Sage. 331–356.

Tyler, T. R., and Folger, R. (1980). Distributional and Procedural Aspects of Satisfaction with Citizen–Police Encounters. *Basic and Applied Social Psychology*, *1*, 281–292.

Tyler, T. R., and Kerstetter, W. (1994). Moral Authority in Law and Criminal Justice: Some Reflections on Wilson's *The Moral Sense*. *Criminal Justice Ethics*, *13*, 44–53.

Tyler, T. R., and Lind, E. A. (1992). A relational Model of Authority in Groups. In M. Zanna (Ed.), *Advances in Experimental Social Psychology* (Vol. 25). New York: Academic Press.

Tyler, T. R., and Mitchell, G. (1994). Legitimacy and the Empowerment of Discretionary Legal Authority. *Duke Law Journal*, *43*, 703–815.

Tyler, T. R., Degoey, P., and Smith, H. J. (1996). Understanding Why the Justice of Group Procedures Matters: A Test of the Psychological Dynamics of the Group-value Model. *Journal of Personality and Social Psychology*, *70*, 913–930.

Tyler, T. R., and Smith, H. J. (1997). Social Justice and Social Movements. In D. Gilbert, S. Fiske, and G. Lindzey (Eds.), *Handbook of Social Psychology* (4th ed., Vol. 2, pp. 595–629). New York: McGraw–Hill.

Tyler, T. R., Rasinski, K., and Spodick, N. (1985). The Influence of Voice on Satisfaction with Leaders: Exploring the Meaning of Process Control. *Journal of Personality and Social Psychology*, *48*, 72–81.

Tyler, T. R., Casper, J. D., and Fisher, B. (1989). Maintaining Allegiance toward Political Authorities: The Role of Prior Attitudes and the Use of Fair Procedures. *American Journal of Political Science*, *33*, 629–652.

Tyler, T. R., Boeckmann, R. J., Smith, H. J., and Huo, Y. J. (1997). *Social Justice in a Diverse Society*. Boulder, CO: Westview Press.

Tyler, T. R., Huo, Y. J., and Lind, E. A. (1999). The Two Psychologies of Conflict Resolution: Differing Antecedents of Pre-experience Choices and Post-experience Evaluations. *Group Processes and Intergroup Relations*, *2*, 99–118.

Wagatsuma, H., and Rosett, A. (1986). The Implications of Apology: Law and Culture in Japan and the United States. *Law and Society Review*, *20*, 461–498.

Walker, L., LaTour, S., Lind, E. A., and Thibaut, J. (1974). Reactions of Participants and Observers to Modes of Adjudication. *Journal of Applied Social Psychology*, *4*, 295–310.

Zucker, L. G. (1986). Production of Trust: Institutional Sources of Economic Structure, 1840–1920. In *Research in Organizational Behavior* (Vol. 8, pp. 53–111). Greenwich, CT: JAI Press.

4

Distributive Justice

Recent Theoretical Developments and Applications

Karen A. Hegtvedt and Karen S. Cook

A. DISTRIBUTIVE JUSTICE: AN OVERVIEW

Theories of justice have developed within the social sciences based on the earlier work of social philosophers and political theorists who for decades have debated issues of inequality and justice within the polity and the meaning of citizenship. One of the most influential works in the twentieth century is the book by John Rawls (1971) entitled *A Theory of Justice*, in which he attempts to specify the appropriate principles of justice in various circumstances. His primary assumption is that the fairest principles of allocative justice are those we would choose if we were not to know our own station in life (i.e., from behind a "veil of ignorance"). In such a case the principles we would select would focus on improving the overall welfare of all in the society, subject to ensuring equal rights to liberties and opportunities and fostering support for distribution principles that arrange inequalities to the greatest benefit of those who are disadvantaged in the society. A related approach to distributive justice has been developed by Brian Barry (1989, 1995) in his recent volumes on justice in which he proposes the concept of "justice as impartiality." According to Barry (1995:7), "a theory of justice which makes it turn on the terms of reasonable agreement" is a theory of justice as impartiality. In game theoretic terms this conception of justice approximates an "assurance game." Barry (1995:51) argues that individuals motivated to behave fairly will follow the rules based on justice as impartiality if they see that enough other people are also following such rules. Barry's conception of justice as impartiality with his emphasis on neutrality provides a framework that is compatible with some of the current work in social psychology on procedural justice. Lind and Tyler (1988), for example, argue that citizens are concerned about being "treated fairly" as much as they are with the outcomes they receive.

While much of the current research in social psychology deals with procedural justice and

Karen A. Hegtvedt • Department of Sociology, Emory University, Atlanta, Georgia 30322. Karen S. Cook • Department of Sociology, Stanford University, Stanford, California 94305.

Handbook of Justice Research in Law, edited by Sanders and Hamilton. Kluwer Academic / Plenum Publishers, New York, 2000.

the relationship between this form of justice and distributive justice, most of the work prior to the mid-1980s focused on various principles of distributive justice and the conditions under which they applied. The general theoretical perspectives on problems of distributive justice within the fields of sociology and psychology derived from cognitive theories of dissonance (e.g., Adams's early work on equity theory in the 1960s) or from exchange notions (e.g., Homans's work on social behavior as exchange and distributive justice as a principle of dyadic exchange). Walster's work (e.g., Walster, Walster, and Berscheid, 1978) combines exchange and dissonance arguments to propose a set of principles that specify when situations are perceived as equitable (e.g., an equality of exchange ratios). It also predicts that in situations defined as inequitable, individuals will act in ways to reduce the dissonance associated with inequity. Cognitive or behavioral responses may range from altering one's perceptions of entitlement to changing the object of social comparison or leaving the situation or the relationship altogether. Subsequent theoretical work (e.g., Berger, Zelditch, Anderson, and Cohen, 1972; Jasso, 1980, 1983, 1990) critiques the exchange approach to distributive justice as too focused on contributions and the consummatory value of rewards, ignoring the status significance of rewards. These authors offer alternative formulations that take into account more fully the role of status distinctions and the nature of more complex social comparisons that result in sentiments of inequity as well as collective reactions to injustice. This work also poses more general "laws" concerning the distribution of justice sentiments in a population and the determinants of reactions to injustice. Recently, Jasso and Wegener (1997) have offered an argument that attempts to integrate under one theoretical umbrella issues of what is just, how people make justice assessments, and how they respond to injustice.

While the Jasso and Wegener perspective awaits empirical scrutiny and the earlier perspectives remain the subject of continued debate, critique, and refinement, the work of Homans, Walster and others still form the basis for predictions concerning the conditions under which allocations will be defined as just or equitable. It is now widely accepted that there are multiple justice principles, not one.[1] They include allocation on the basis of need (see Lerner, 1975), equality, and the standard contributions rule, derived from exchange theory. Moreover, different allocative principles are defined as just under different circumstances (Leventhal, 1976). This insight has mitigated some of the earlier debate over the "one just way" of making allocations or of distributing valued goods. The research on allocation principles is reviewed in more detail in the first major section of this chapter, followed by a review of the research on reactions to situations defined as unjust and recent work on justice in personal relationships. Much of this research uses experimental methods, especially the early work on inequity.

Experimental methods have been critiqued in a variety of texts (e.g., Winer, 1971; Meeker and Leik, 1995) and journals (e.g., Orne, 1962; Bonacich and Light, 1978), including the best known discussion of experimental and quasi-experimental methods by Campbell and Stanley (1963). Experimentation in any field is used primarily as a technique for testing causal claims by creating specific conditions of theoretical interest, controlling factors that might make inference difficult and by creating comparisons that inform the key theoretical hypotheses. In well-designed studies this control allows investigators to rule out spurious causation. As Meeker and Leik (1995:646) note in their comprehensive review chapter: "issues of internal validity concern eliminating spurious effects in an experiment," while "issues of external validity concern the generalizability of results to other settings." Both sets of issues hinge importantly on the careful design of studies to maximize internal validity (and the quality of inferences that can be drawn from the data obtained) and to allow for theoretical generalizability of the results to other settings of interest (maximizing external validity, see

Zelditch, 1969). As they argue, the latter is enhanced when experimental studies are conducted as part of a larger program of research, where replication and extension of the theories being tested can be best accomplished by systematic experimental work, rather than one-shot laboratory or field studies. The trend over time in social psychology has been away from the latter in order to maximize the utility of the information obtained from experiments conducted both inside and outside the laboratory.

Generally, experimental research on allocation, as well as on reactions to injustice, has primarily focused on testing "basic" principles of justice theory. Such research is often referred to as "basic" research, a term that is meant to be contrasted with "applied" research, in which the focus of the inquiry is with the application of the theory. As discussed further below, many experimental studies examine individual preferences for equal or equitable distributions as a way to examine basic theoretical ideas. But in addition, research on actual distributions, for example of health care resources in a society, is viewed as applied research. While this terminology has been used in the social sciences for some time, it is clear that the boundary between these two general classes of research is often blurred. Applied research often allows for tests of the underlying theories of justice and so-called basic research (theory-testing) is often conducted in the context of "real-world" instances of the phenomenon of theoretical interest (e.g., as in the allocation of scarce resources like gasoline during an energy crisis, or of livers and kidneys for organ transplantation). It is our general view that this distinction is less useful in social psychology now than it might have been several decades ago. We will, however, use the term "applied" to call attention to work that directly applies insights from justice theories to phenomena of interest to social scientists in various fields, such as social stratification, social movements, organizations, and criminology, and to social policy analysts. In the next section, we review both basic and applied research relevant to the fairness of allocation decisions.

B. ALLOCATION DECISIONS: EQUITY, EQUALITY, AND NEED

Allocation research typically focuses on the distribution of rewards (or costs) to a circle of recipients by a corecipient (first-party allocation) or an outsider (third-party allocation). Researchers classify the resulting distributions in terms of the extent to which they approximate equal, equitable (contributions-based), or needs-based distributions. Most of the early allocation studies concentrated on the choice between equity and equality in productivity situations. The intent of such studies was to determine how individual characteristics, relationship factors, and situational conditions influenced the choice (see Cook and Hegtvedt, 1983). This traditional approach remains evident in more recent studies, although current trends reflect greater emphasis on cognitive dimensions and group-level factors. In addition, a "resource sharing" paradigm has been developed in which allocations of unearned, public goods are distributed to a pool of recipients (e.g., Messick and Allison, 1987; Samuelson and Allison, 1994). Despite the large number of allocation studies, this work is still characterized by the lack of a cogent theoretical paradigm. One integrative attempt, Leventhal's expectancy value theory of allocation (Leventhal, Karuza, and Fry, 1980), seems to have had little impact on allocation research (see Skitka and Tetlock, 1992, as a possible exception). Some of the themes inherent in his theory, however, emerge in the current work on goals and the motivations underlying allocation decisions.

First we examine the various factors that affect allocation decisions. How individuals "want" to distribute rewards (or costs) may not constitute the fairest distribution (in the eyes of others), but it does provide a starting point for investigating how those individuals will evaluate distributions. We begin with a discussion of the goals and motivations that shape allocation decisions. Then we examine individual-level characteristics and cognitive factors that shape how individuals assess whether a particular distribution rule will fulfill their goals. A discussion of relationship and situational factors, many of which interact with individual-level factors, follows. We note briefly the importance of cross-cultural factors (see also Leung and Morris, this volume) and close with a brief summary of the issues raised by basic allocation research and how these same issues arise in applied settings.

1. Goals and Motivations: In Pursuit of Distributive Justice

Leventhal *et al.* (1980) assume that individuals hold expectancies concerning how particular distribution rules will fulfill specific goals and that people hold multiple goals of varying importance. In addition to fairness, these goals include self-interest, efficiency, obedience to authority, and others. They argue that preferences for the way in which rewards are to be allocated are determined by the combination of expectancies and the value of each goal. Although allocation preference theory has not spurred much empirical work, a number of studies have examined how the pursuit of various goals, each constituting a form of motivation, results in different types of distributions.

When instructed to pursue fairness, individuals specify different allocation rules depending on the situation (see Leventhal, 1976; Leung and Park, 1986; Prentice and Crosby, 1987). Generally, people specify equitable or contributions-based rules in work situations where productivity is a central concern, an equal division where group harmony is paramount, and a needs-based distribution rule in contexts focusing on social welfare. The sometimes conflicting motives of competition and cooperation in work situations parallel dual emphasis on productivity and group harmony. When task structures are competitive, workers are likely to prefer equity, whereas cooperative task structures enhance the preference for equal distributions (Griffith and Sell, 1988). Also, it appears that people favor need-based rules for allocating costs as well as rewards among family members (Wagstaff, Huggins, and Perfect, 1993). Other results, however, demonstrate a more complex pattern. Messick and Sentis (1979) show that individuals in a work situation specify as fair a larger amount to self than to other, even with equivalent contributions. Individuals tend to evaluate their own inputs more favorably than those of others in order to justify receipt of a greater share and still maintain perceived equity. Thus, self-interest may combine with fairness goals in allocation situations.

Despite the general emphasis on equity as the basis for fair division in productivity situations, three issues arise. First, while fairness and self-interest may dominate in allocations in the workplace under normal circumstances, when the situation demands expediency, individuals may opt for other distribution rules. Multiple motives may combine to produce complex allocation choices. Second, individual motives alone are insufficient to understand some types of distribution. Social identity and intergroup relations also influence choices. Finally, the potential conflict between individual-level and group-level interests (i.e., self-interest versus group welfare) raises new concerns about fundamental assumptions in distributive justice research (Tyler and Dawes, 1993; Tyler, Boeckmann, Smith, and Huo, 1997).

Messick (1993) suggests that in situations in which allocations have to be made, equality may be a useful heuristic. Use of an equality rule when the goods or bads being distributed are divisible requires little additional knowledge about recipients other than the number in the pool.[2] An equal distribution may not inhibit conflict over an allocation, but it at least provides a ready anchor from which to adjust the distribution, depending on other factors. Although equality may be a more expedient approach under certain conditions, it is not always the most efficient.

Mitchell, Tetlock, Mellers, and Ordóñez (1993) examine the trade-offs between equality (as fairness) and efficiency (as the goods and services that result from a given input) in allocation decisions. Using a hypothetical society paradigm in which subjects were unaware of their material interests, those who were more concerned with equality tended to allocate in a manner that maximized the incomes of the poorest citizens (maximin) whereas those who focused more on efficiency opted for a compromise between ensuring a floor (to satisfy basic needs) and distributing rewards based on merit. Researchers noted that subjects generally avoided distributions that increase the number below the poverty line. In a follow-up study also involving hypothetical societies. Ordóñez and Mellers (1993) demonstrate that although people make trade-offs between equality and efficiency, trade-offs tend to occur more frequently between emphasis on a minimum salary and the work–salary correlation (i.e., a contributions-based rule). Furthermore, they note that the latter two goals predict fairness and preference judgments better than a basic equality–equity rule. Interestingly, concern for a minimum standard was a stronger predictor of preference rankings than fairness rankings.

In addition to instrumental goals, socioemotional and group maintenance goals may motivate managers in work organizations. Rusbult and her colleagues (Rusbult, Lowery, Hubbard, Maravankin, and Neises, 1988) argue that allocation decisions stemming from the combination of these goals depend also on the mobility of the employees and availability of both labor and rewards. Results show that subjects generally prefer to allocate salary based on workers' competence and dedication. Deviations from equity per se, in the service of maintaining group membership, occur when managers are willing to pay more to highly competent employees with high mobility than those similarly skilled workers with low mobility. The authors' term for this strategy is *rational selective exploitation.* The consequences of this strategy for the morale of the low-mobility, competent employees remain unknown. In addition, some evidence suggests this strategy is particularly pronounced under conditions of low reward availability and low labor availability. Thus, structural conditions often affect how individuals fulfill their multiple goals in an allocation situation.

Embeddedness in groups likewise constitutes a structural factor that may influence goals. A series of studies examines the dual pressures of fairness and intergroup bias when the goal is enhancing group rewards. In some situations individuals may be motivated by both their concern for fairness, manifested in the use of an equity rule to distribute rewards in a work situation, and their concerns for how well their own group members fare in the distribution, possibly requiring deviation from the use of an equity rule. Ng (1984) demonstrates that when in-group members perform well, subjects accentuate the importance of an equitable distribution. Takenishi (1988) notes that even when subjects were told to use an equity rule, they gave a greater than proportional amount to an in-group member who performed well and leveled the reward when an in-group member performed poorly. Other studies suggest that the salience of status differences (Ng, 1986) and emphasis on competition between groups (Towson, Lerner, and DeCarufel, 1981) enhance this effect.

While situational conditions account for some of the propensity to pursue in-group enhancement at the expense of fairness, another study indicates that social value orientations may be equally important. Platow, McClintock, and Liebrand (1990) find that although subjects typically evaluate in-group members more favorably, their allocations do not always correspond to these evaluations. Rather, subjects with a prosocial value orientation tend to make fair allocations and those with a competitive orientation favor allocations reflecting in-group bias.

Although seemingly at odds, a prosocial value orientation and an in-group bias indicate goals or motivations beyond simply egoistic ones. Tyler and Dawes (1993) argue that evidence from the social dilemmas literature (Dawes and Thaler, 1988) and especially from the procedural justice literature (Lind and Tyler, 1988) indicates that when individuals develop a sense of group identity, they are likely to waiver from self-interested goals. Moreover, to the extent that people create rules to maintain relationships, their distributions are less likely to reflect egoistic concerns. Thus, the strength of social bonds affects the motives individuals pursue in allocation situations as well as the resulting distributions.

2. Individual-Level Factors in Allocation Decisions

The nature of goals or motivations in the allocation situation may stem from individual-level characteristics or factors, relational concerns, or features of the situation. Although it is likely that these factors interact, here we attempt to examine them separately.[3] At the individual level, influences include status characteristics (age and gender), personal values and attitudes, and cognitive elements.

a. *Status Characteristics*

Age. Studies of the effects of age on allocation preferences typically frame the question in terms of cognitive development. How does the cognitive maturation of the child, as outlined in the works of Jean Piaget, correspond to changes in preferences for equity, equality, or need-based distributions? Preschoolers are generally more egocentric in their distributions than older children, perhaps because they are cognitively unable to role-take (see Hook and Cook, 1979). Five to seven year olds, in contrast, tend to be more egalitarian regardless of performance levels, whereas older school-age children begin to take into account task performance levels and to understand proportionality (Smith and Krantz, 1981; Hook, 1982; Zinser, Starnes, and Wild, 1991).

More recent work indicates that situational factors are more likely to influence older children's allocation decisions than those of younger children. For example, Keil (1986) demonstrates that sixth graders matched their co-workers' allocations behavior (i.e., acted selfishly or equitably depending on their partner's behavior); second graders, in contrast, tended to act selfishly, though understanding equality, regardless of their co-workers' behavior. Likewise, Sigelman and Waitzman (1991) show that kindergartners allocate equally whereas older children tailor their decisions to fit the context. Those decisions, sometimes, are relatively complex. In a study by McGuillicuddy-DeLisi, Watlang, and Vincher (1994), kindergartners allocated the same to all parties, but third and sixth graders differentiated between friends and strangers. The older children gave more to needy friends than needy strangers, but provided higher rewards for the greater productivity of strangers than friends. It is this use of contextual information that leads Moore, Hembree, and Enright (1993) to argue that there is no unidimensional developmental ordering of stages of reward allocation. Although something developmental is occurring, the process is more complex than simple age and distribution correlations suggest. The role of contextual information in allocation decisions remains important for adults as well, as discussed further below.

Gender. Early work on allocation preferences noted that female allocators take less for themselves than male allocators, regardless of their input levels (see Major and Deaux, 1982). Through the 1980s researchers have questioned whether this pattern of findings reflects inherent personality differences between males and females. Subsequent studies have examined the influence of underlying orientations, which may be stereotypically linked to each sex, and the effect of situational factors.

Watts, Messé, and Vallacher (1982) argue that males tend to be more agency oriented, emphasizing achievement and success, while females are more communally oriented, valuing interpersonal relations. As a consequence, males pay themselves more than females. The potency of these orientations, however, is tenuous. Kahn, Nelson, and Gaeddert (1980) document differences in the interpersonal orientation of males and females that produces the typical gender differences in distribution patterns, but the effect emerges only when situational demands are weak or ambiguous. When situational cues are obvious, such as in the sex-linked nature of the task, gender differences fail to emerge. On what are culturally defined as sex-appropriate tasks (e.g., lawn mowing or sewing), males and females both prefer equity (Reis and Jackson, 1981). Such a pattern is particularly true of traditional women, whereas androgynous females tend to be more generous in their allocations (Jackson, 1989). Thus, orientation may interact with other situational factors.

Major and Adams (1983, 1984) show that increasing accountability by making allocations public or emphasizing future interaction between the allocator and the recipients alters the pattern of male and female allocation preferences. Interpersonal orientation has the expected gender effect on distributions only under conditions of privacy. With public allocations and the expectation of future interaction, allocations tend to be equal. Asdigian, Cohn, and Blum (1994), however, find males allocating more equitably in public than females, especially to strangers who produce low effort. What appears to be the case in examination of gender effects on allocation is that situational factors may arouse gender-role-specific self-presentational concerns (Major and Adams, 1984). For example, in a study of third-party allocations, Stake (1985) shows that although fair norms were similar for both sexes, when told to improve worker relationships (a traditionally female domain), females opted for equal distributions more than did males. Similarly, when increases in productivity (a traditionally male domain) constituted the situational goal, males were more likely to advocate equitable distributions than were females.

b. Personal Values and Attitudes

Relatively few studies examine individual differences in allocation preferences based on personal values and attitudes. A major exception is the work of Norman Feather (1994). In addition to his work, one study follows up on early research focusing on the influence of belief in the Protestant ethic, which emphasizes that if one works hard, one will be rewarded. Stake (1983) finds that subjects who adhere to the Protestant ethic are likely to award greater amounts, based on worker-controlled inputs, than those who do not express such a philosophy. Other studies examine different sets of values.

For example, several researchers (Vecchio and Terborg, 1987; Meindl, 1989) suggest that, although managers are likely to favor merit-based pay systems, their personal philosophies about management, or more generally their own value systems, induce flexibility in the use of various rules. Individual differences in values thus are likely to complicate allocation decisions in a variety of ways. Similarly, Tetlock and Mitchell (1993) dissect liberal and conservative philosophies in terms of their cognitive and motivational assumptions and then draw implications of these assumptions for allocation decisions. They note, however, that despite the effect of philosophical differences, justice judgments remain sensitive to contextual factors and even the methods of study.

How individuals value themselves may also influence their allocation decisions. Brockner, O'Malley, Hite, and Davies (9187) examine the extent to which self-esteem moderates the effects of performance level and partner's allocation pattern (i.e., selfish, equitable, egalitarian, or generous). Results indicate that subjects with low self-esteem are more likely to imitate their partners' reward allocations than are subjects with high self-esteem. For those with high self-esteem, relative performance exerts a strong influence on their allocation decisions.

c. *Cognitive Elements in Allocation Decisions*

Cohen (1982) argues that to understand distribution preferences, it is necessary to examine allocator's perceptions of the situation. In particular, he highlights the importance of attributions. Whether or not allocators perceive recipients as causally responsible for their contributions affects resulting distribution decisions. Cohen thoroughly explores the possible implications not only of different types of attributions (e.g., internal versus external, stable versus unstable, controllable versus uncontrollable), but also the implications of various attribution biases. Some relatively recent empirical work has addressed the former, but little has been done to examine the latter directly.

Generally, in order for individuals to consider invoking an equitable distribution, they must perceive that compensable inputs are under the control of the recipients and are internally caused. Wittig, Marks, and Jones (1981) illustrate the importance of internal causality in a study in which they manipulated possible attributions. When subjects attributed their performance to their own effort (internal, unstable, controllable cause), they made greater allocations to themselves than when their performance seemed related to luck (external, unstable, uncontrollable cause). Elliot and Meeker (1984) likewise confirm the importance of attributions. Subjects allocated more to target recipients who had greater ability, effort, and faced a more difficult task. Some research indicates the greater importance of effort in allocations than ability (an internal, stable cause over which individuals may have little immediate control). Third-party allocators distributed greater rewards to more diligent group members than to the more talented ones (Lamm, Kayser, and Schanz, 1983), even if doing so created inequality between friends (Kayser and Lamm, 1981). Although these studies are limited to comparisons between a few simple attributions, they confirm Cohen's general argument.

Other work examines a greater variety of attributions but does so indirectly by asking subjects what they believe accounts for the differences in performance levels. Presumably such accounts indicate the underlying reasoning that people use to determine whether to allocate equally or equitably. For example, researchers have suggested that women may attribute their inputs to external factors and then take less for themselves, whereas males accentuate their inputs by attributing them to internal factors. Major and Adams (1983), however, fail to find evidence for this reasoning in a study of first-person allocations. In contrast, Stake (1985) does obtain gender differences in third party allocations and attributions. She speculates on how such reasoning affects distribution preferences. In her study, females were more likely to attribute lower productivity rates to internal constraints emphasizing quality workmanship and thus allocated equally while males attributed low performance to lower motivation (i.e., lack of effort) and invoked equitable allocations. Given these mixed results, it is unclear whether attributions mediate between this particular individual-level characteristic and allocation.

Inferred attributions may account for the results in two resource sharing studies. Messick and Allison (1987) examined how knowledge of the size of the resource pool to be shared would affect contributions to the pool by individuals. Given that the resources could only be shared if all six group members' requests for resources were equal or less than the total pool, it was incumbent on the sixth person to request an amount less than the remainder to ensure resources for all of the group members. Although most subjects accepted the unfair amounts, those who did not were more likely to refuse when they believed the others knew the total amount. Such results suggest that the sixth group member believed that the others intentionally shortchanged him/her. Such an internal attribution of maliciousness inhibited willingness to ensure other group members their resources. In the absence of knowledge about the size of the resource pool, no such attribution was likely and the subject could justify requesting an amount that would not exceed the size of the pool.

Similarly, implicit attributions seem to mediate contributions in a public goods dilemma investigated by Van Dijk and Wilke (1993). Some subjects were to receive a high proportion of the public good (high-interest subjects), while others were to receive a small proportion (low-interest subjects). These differences either were justified by an asymmetry of inputs or were not justified by the experimenter. Subjects, particularly high-interest ones, tended to minimize differences in final outcomes in the absence of justification. In effect, the justification served to locate the cause of the difference between the subjects internally, thus entitling some to a higher final outcome. The findings from both of these resource sharing studies suggest the possibility that when differences between subjects are internally caused, deviations from equality are likely, and when differences between subjects are externally caused, deviations from equity are likely.

The biases inherent in attribution processes, however, may complicate this picture. There is some evidence that individuals differentially assess their own inputs. People judge more favorably their own or their group's inputs (Messé, Hymes, and MacCoun, 1986) and may weigh more heavily inputs that they rate more highly (Cook and Yamagishi, 1983). Such patterns suggest the operation of an egoistic bias. Whether other biases discussed by Cohen (1982), such as divergent perspectives or the fundamental attribution error, affect allocation decisions remains to be investigated. In addition, whether characteristics of the relationship or situation interact with or are mediated by attributions are questions for future research.

3. Decisions Beyond the Individual: Effects of Relational and Situational Factors on Allocation

a. Relational Factors

Relational influences on allocation preferences include individuals' relative standings on reward-relevant factors as well as the nature of the relationship between the individuals involved. Because it is necessary to differentiate individuals in work situations in order to establish whether rewards are distributed equitably, relative performance is the most frequently examined relational factor. The second major relational factor to receive attention is relative need. Investigators have examined how affective links between the allocator and the recipients (or among recipients in third-party allocation situations) affect the impact of differences in performance and need.

In impersonal situations, high performers are more likely to prefer equitable distributions and low performers are more likely to prefer equal ones (see Cook and Hegtvedt, 1983). Such a pattern of preferences maximizes material gains for each party. In contrast, between friends, or simply with the anticipation of future interaction between the allocator and recipients, individuals express a greater preference for equality regardless of performance level (Austin, 1980; Sagan, Pondel, and Wittig, 1981). Major, Bylsma, and Cozzarelli (1989) demonstrate that in intimate relationships, individuals often prefer benevolent distributions that benefit one's partner. Such preferences may reflect a politeness ritual (Schwinger, 1980) or concerns for social rewards that may be threatened by self-interested allocation preferences (Reis, 1981). Alternatively, as Tyler and Dawes (1993) speculate, the stronger social bond between friends enhances group identity which in turn suppresses egoistic distributions.

Kayser and Lamm (1981), however, show that third-party allocators fail to provide equal amounts to friends whose performance differences stem from lack of effort by one person. Likewise, Marin (1985) finds no effect of acquaintance; third-party allocators consistently preferred equitable distributions. The preference for equity among nonrecipient allocators may reflect the normative emphasis on equity in workplace situations, especially when one's own interests are not at stake. Moreover, it may be the case that when the allocator is not part of the recipient group, no feelings of group identity emerge to counteract impersonal, normative guidelines.

Most studies on the role of needs in allocation preferences only involve third parties. Given workers with equal contributions to a task, allocators deviate from equality to provide greater rewards to the more needy worker, especially if the workers are friends (Lamm and Schwinger, 1980; Schwinger and Lamm, 1981). Thus, friendship bonds seem to differentially affect third-party allocators, depending on whether social welfare concerns or simply productivity are at issue. When instructed to make just allocations, allocators emphasize need, regardless of the attraction level between recipients (Lamm and Schwinger, 1983). Situational factors, however, affect the extent to which individuals emphasize need in their allocations.

Skitka and Tetlock (1992) suggest that in the distribution of public resources (e.g., health care or welfare), allocators appraise the adequacy of the resource pool and the causes of claimants' needs. When resources are inadequate, individuals presumably engage in attributional analysis to assess the source of need (internal versus external, controllable versus uncontrollable) and the effectiveness of the resources in assuaging the need. Results of a third-party allocation study show that with low scarcity, allocators are more likely to deny claims for those who were responsible for their predicament. Claimants whose needs are internally caused and controllable were likely to receive resources only if their need was high and the use of the resources would be efficient. With high scarcity, subjects provided aid to claimants not responsible for their problems and greatly in need but with a high chance of success. In addition, individual attitudes affected responses. Subjects scoring high in conservatism were more likely than those scoring high on liberalism to devalue the deservingness of people with internal-controllable causes of need. In fact, when no scarcity was present, conservative subjects withheld aid from some claimants. This complex study thus indicates the importance of cognitive, affective, and personal-ideological variables in predicting allocation preferences. It also extends beyond other work by attempting to explain how people process the implications of situational factors in making allocation decisions.

b. Situational Factors

Most work on the effects of situational factors on allocation decisions gives little explicit consideration to motivational and cognitive processes that theoretically link the situation to the distribution. As noted already, situational factors often interact with individual characteristics (e.g., gender), thus complicating the underlying links. The situational factors reviewed here pertain mostly to the nature of what is being distributed: rewards (goods) versus costs (bads) and the amount of each at stake.

In 1980, Harris and Joyce noted that individuals tended to allocate outcomes of a group effort equitably whereas they were likely to distribute expenses equally. Similarly, several studies show that individuals preferred equal allocations of losses (Kayser and Lamm, 1980; Lamm *et al.*, 1983; Törnblom and Jonsson, 1985). But contrasting results have also been obtained. Meeker and Elliott (1987) demonstrate a preference for the equitable distribution of negative outcomes. Törnblom (1988) and Griffith (1989) review additional studies, concluding that mixed results are endemic. The inconsistencies may stem from cultural differences, methodological variations, and the confounding effects of information presented to allocators. In comparing allocations of positive and negative outcomes, Griffith (1989:128) concludes that most of the evidence points to the idea that "what's fair for rewarding individuals or groups is also fair for punishing them." Thus, allocation of expenses or losses is likely to be subject to the influence of similar factors as those reviewed for the distribution of rewards. For example, when motivated by competition, individuals are less likely to prefer an equal distribution of negative outcomes (see Griffith, 1989).

Explanations for the effect of resource scarcity on allocations in three-person groups also focus on underlying motivations. Hegtvedt (1987) found that allocators tend to make materially self-interested distributions when resources were abundant enough to exceed the hourly pay expectations for all group members. But when resources were insufficient to meet these pay expectations, individuals allocated more generously to other group members. Hegtvedt suggests that this pattern of results stems from concerns for other group members and the responsibility stemming from the allocator's role in the larger group when faced with resource scarcity. Whether situational factors actually alter underlying motivations from one of self-interest encompassing social rewards as well as material ones or from the development of group identity remains to be investigated. Some cross-cultural studies also rely on assumptions about different motivations for culturally distinct groups.

c. Cross-Cultural Factors

Generally, there is agreement that allocation preferences are culturally relative, bound to socialization practices and societal norms. Identifying these practices and the norms that account for different motivational bases for allocations may prove to be elusive. Three interesting studies, however, make explicit attempts.

Emphasizing cultural variation in collectivistic orientation, Leung and Bond (1984) compare American and Chinese allocation preferences. Results demonstrate the greater desire for maintaining group solidarity in collectivistic China. Chinese subjects preferred an equitable allocation when dealing with an out-group member or when the individuals had low inputs, whereas they opted for equality with in-group members or when their own inputs were high. Such preference patterns, typically not found among Americans, enhance the well-being of other group members.

Drawing on Hofstede's (1984) categorization of countries, Kim, Park, and Suzuki (1990) reason that people in more individualistic and "masculine" countries such as the United States and Japan are more likely to prefer equitable divisions. Their findings for the United States and Japan, in comparison to South Korea, which is not considered as individualistic and masculine, confirm this reasoning.

Similarly, Walker (1989) dissects the political and social attitudes that distinguish Americans and Australians. His study reveals value differences that may influence allocations. Indeed, he reports that American subjects were more liberal and radical than Australians who were more conservative and stronger endorsers of the Protestant ethic. As a consequence of these value orientations, Americans favored equality more strongly while Australians had a greater preference for equity. Other research challenges these findings indicating that Australians prefer equality and have fairly complex views of individual deservingness (e.g., Feather, 1994).

4. General Allocation Issues and Applications

Researchers have investigated the influence of a wide variety of factors on allocation preferences. Perhaps the most fundamental aspect of this body of research is that many factors—individual, relational, and situational—interact to create variation in the pattern of distribution preferences. Unfortunately, in the absence of an integrated theoretical framework from which to derive predictions concerning allocation preferences and, by implication, fairness assessments, it is difficult to draw firm conclusions. We have accumulated many findings but our current knowledge about fairness in allocation is not necessarily cumulative.

Leventhal and colleagues' (1980) underused theoretical perspective draws attention to goals and expectancies as critical variables predicting allocation decisions. While some studies specifically address the influence of goals on allocations, most investigators do not manipulate or explicitly measure goals and motivations. Based on the research reviewed above, however, it seems likely that individual, relational, and situational factors jointly influence the goals that actors attempt to achieve by their allocation preferences as Leventhal's perspective generally implies but does not spell out. Given that existing research gives clear evidence of the effects of value orientations on allocation decisions, one avenue for future research is to determine specifically how situational and relational factors modify the motivations associated with these value orientations. For example, a given value orientation may suggest that individuals will largely be self-interested in their distribution preferences. Yet, contextual factors such as moderate reward scarcity, public pronouncement of preferences, or emphasis on ties among group members may inhibit the extent to which maximizing self-interested gains determines the allocation decision. Rather, such situational factors may enhance the pursuit of collective interests. How various factors combine to create or to modify individual goals and motivations is a central theoretical and empirical issue for future research.

How cognitive processing affects interpretation of the situation, or, in other words, how individuals attempt to achieve their goals through particular distribution principles, also requires further investigation. Do attributions moderate or mediate situational influences on allocation preferences? Do contextual factors that affect motivations likewise affect processing of other information available in the situation? For example, to the extent that group ties are emphasized, are distribution decisions the result of the motivation to enhance group welfare or cognitive biases concerning the cause of relevant inputs? Such questions draw attention to the complicated interplay between motivations and cognitions.

Drawing out the theoretical links between the various elements involved in the allocation process constitutes the next frontier of research. With greater theoretical understanding of these links, it will be possible to tackle questions that have yet to be addressed. For example, we can begin to address the problem of determining the consequences of competing claims given different allocation preferences among individuals. While the bargaining literature (see Lawler and Ford, 1995) examines the resolution of opposing interests, little of it deals with issues of competing conceptions of fairness (see Hegtvedt and Cook, 1987). On the other hand, the research on allocation preferences stops short of analyzing how people work out their disagreements over what is fair. Yet, such disagreements are endemic in many situations in which allocations occur.

While it is difficult to discern empirically when disagreements are merely conflicts of personal interests (as often assumed in bargaining studies) or are fundamental differences in fairness beliefs (beyond simple personal interests), people frequently debate ways of allocating many different classes of resources (e.g., educational programs, water rights, wetlands, tax burdens). A prime example of variation in justice claims is the distribution of health care resources.[4] Issues of equity have long been discussed in the health care arena (see Anderson, 1972). Given spiraling health care costs and increasing numbers of uninsured individuals, greater attention has recently focused on fairness in the provision of health care services.

Several researchers have analyzed the consequences of the application of various distributive justice principles on the allocation of health care resources (e.g., Haayry and Haayry, 1990; Pereira, 1993). Jecker and Berg (1992) specifically contrast the approach to justice expressed by a sample of rural physicians with the justice conception that dominates Western philosophy. Given the difficulties of providing health care in rural areas, these physicians device accounts for their decisions that may seem at odds with typical approaches to justice.

In general, scarcity forces debates about what is fair. Aaron and Schwartz (1984) label the decisions regarding the rationing of health care in the British National Health Service, which often results in denying certain types of care (e.g., renal dialysis) to elderly patients or the creation of long queues for other treatments (e.g., hip replacements) as "painful prescriptions." Likewise, Mechanic (1989) notes how U.S. health care faces such painful choices. For example, debates over expenditures of health care resources for the elderly versus those for neonates raise concerns about the relevance of what might be termed compensable factors. Often arguments tout the remaining years of life as an important factor in deciding how health care dollars should be spent (Kuhse and Singer, 1988).

What people claim as a just distribution of health care resources often reflects their own value orientations, much like the experimental research indicates. Gill, Ingman, and Campbell (1991) compare the provision of geriatric care in the United States and Great Britain. The more dominant individualist orientation in the U.S. health care system results in a greater provision of geriatric care in the United States whereas such care is provided at lower levels in Great Britain. The British collectivist orientation (and concomitant centralized, government-funded National Health Service) leads to concern for ensuring resources to a broader segment of the population given budget constraints.

Space limitations do not allow a more extensive review of the allocation of health care resources as a justice issue. It is clear, however, that issues raised in the experimental work on allocation decisions do pertain to applied concerns. Moreover, by examining actual allocation decisions and debates in the health care arena, basic researchers may gain insights into a wider array of contextual factors and interpersonal dynamics that may affect allocation preferences more broadly.

C. REACTIONS TO INJUSTICE

Adams's (1965) initial statement on equity in interpersonal relations stimulated a decade of research on reactions to inequity. This early formulation assumed that individuals would assess their outcomes/inputs ratios in comparison to that of some other individual. This "local" comparison provided the basis for determining whether one was inequitably underrewarded, equitably rewarded, or inequitably overrewarded. Adams argued that distress from inequity motivated individuals to respond by: (1) changing their inputs, (2) changing their outcomes, (3) altering their perceptions of their own inputs or outcomes or those of their partner, (4) changing the object of their comparison, or (5) withdrawing from the situation. The first two options coincide with what Walster *et al.* (1978a) label *restoring actual equity* whereas the remaining options fit their category of *restoring psychological equity*. Presumably, individuals would select the least costly form of response.

A flurry of research in the decade after 1965 focused on responses to underpay, equitable pay, and overpay (see Cook and Hegtvedt, 1983, for a review). Studies of this genre were of two types: (1) alterations in input levels on subsequent tasks after receipt of inequitable pay or (2) alterations in outcome levels by the reallocation of a bonus or additional pay. Findings typically confirmed that overrewarded subjects increased their productivity, though the explanations for this effect were inconsistent. In contrast, the pattern of results is less systematic for underrewarded subjects. In experiments of the second type, findings typically show that underrewarded subjects take more bonus pay for themselves and overrewarded subjects take less.

Several limitations characterized these early studies. First, most researchers assumed that inequity would produce an observable reaction. This assumption ignored the possibility, though outlined by Adams, of a cognitive response or no response. Second, the structure of the experimental framework most often disallowed investigation of the choice among possible reactions since only one form of response was studied. And third, despite the early observations by Homans (1961) in an organizational setting, researchers have typically investigated reactions to inequity in laboratory settings.

More recent work on reactions to injustice addresses these limitations. A large body of work examines factors mediating responses to inequity—some of which account for the possibility of nonresponse. Here the focus is on emotional and cognitive mediators, and the role of self-evaluation. Other work notes how individual and contextual factors, as well as procedural justice evaluations, moderate the perceived inequity–reactions relationship. In addition, several investigations move beyond a singular focus on one type of behavioral reaction to include multiple behaviors as well as cognitive responses. Finally, an increasing number of researchers are analyzing responses to injustice in applied settings.

1. Factors that Mediate Reactions to Inequity

The earlier theoretical formulations of Adams (1965) and Walster *et al.* (1978a) have two interrelated shortcomings: they ignore the complexities of justice assessments and they fail to address the complex mechanisms that link perceived inequity to specific reactions to it. Theoretically, such mediating factors may affect not only the occurrence of a response, but also the type of response: behavioral or cognitive, individual or collective.

a. Emotional Mediators

Approaches based on equity theory anticipate the role of distress as one factor mediating responses to injustice, but provide little explication of its nature (see Cook and Hegtvedt, 1983). Studies of distress in inequitable relationships typically involve physiological indicators and self-reports of feelings.

Focusing on physiological measures, there is some evidence supporting the inequity–distress relationship. Galvanic skin response measures indicate that underrewarded subjects (Austin and Walster, 1974; Markovsky, 1988) and overrewarded subjects (Markovsky, 1988) experience more distress compared to equitably paid subjects.

The second approach to studying distress relies on self-reports of feelings measured by adjective checklists or scales of the intensity of different types of emotions. A clear pattern of findings emerges from such studies: Equitably rewarded individuals feel more content and less distressed than do those who are inequitably rewarded, regardless of whether the relationship is intimate (Sprecher, 1986) or impersonal (Austin and Walster, 1974; Vecchio, 1984; Hegtvedt, 1990).

Self-report studies focusing more specifically on Homans's (1961, 1974) theoretical predictions that individuals who are underrewarded are likely to feel angry and those who are overrewarded are likely to feel guilty provide more mixed results. While studies repeatedly confirm that underrewarded individuals are likely to feel anger (Gray-Little and Teddlie, 1978; Hassebrauck, 1986; Hegtvedt, 1990), the extent to which overrewarded individuals feel guilty is unclear. There is some evidence that individuals who benefit from inequity experience positive affect (Davidson, 1984; Hegtvedt, 1990). Although overrewarded individuals may feel more guilty than others as Hassebrauck (1986) demonstrates, the actual levels of guilt may actually be quite low (Hegtvedt, 1990). And, sometimes there are no differences in levels of guilt across reward conditions (Gray-Little and Teddlie, 1978).

Thus, with the exception of feelings of guilt, the work on inequity and distress is consistent with theoretical expectations. But does distress mediate between inequity and behavioral or psychological responses? There is no research that specifically addresses this question. Sprecher's (1992) study of individuals' responses to vignettes asking them to imagine themselves in an imbalanced relationship, first involving underbenefit and then later involving overbenefit, comes closest. Subjects expressed how they "expected" to feel in each situation and the behaviors they anticipated in response to the inequity. Sprecher compared the types of emotion and behavior expected for each type of inequity. Results suggest that underbenefited respondents expect to become distressed and anticipate actions to restore equity. Overbenefited respondents indicate no general distress; they admit possible feelings of guilt, however, and also anticipate enacting equity-restoring behaviors.

Other work investigates the moderating effect of various factors on affective responses. Sprecher (1992) qualifies her inequity–distress reactions results in terms of gender and exchange orientation. Women and individuals with a strong exchange orientation are more likely to report feelings of distress and to try to restore justice. Feldman, Barbaresi, and Caiola (1983) show that if an exchange partner is physically handicapped, inequitably rewarded subjects express less distress than when their partner is not handicapped. It seems that interactants' characteristics may moderate the inequity–distress relationship.

Schafer, (1988) investigates the role of self-esteem in the inequity–distress relationship. He assumes that the experience of inequity in a relationship threatens an individual's self-esteem. Data from a sample of students indicate about 40% of the total effect of inequity on distress is indirect, mediated through levels of self-esteem. He argues that this mediating effect of self-esteem supports the reinterpretation of equity-restoring behavior as self-enhancing behavior designed to maintain or to boost self-esteem.

In summary, a great deal of research confirms the theoretical relationship between inequity and feelings of distress. Unfortunately, whether distress or more specific emotions actually mediate reactions to inequity remains unknown. Future investigations that more explicitly examine how affective responses mediate behavioral and psychological reactions might also simultaneously assess factors that enhance or diminish the relationship (e.g., such factors as gender, exchange orientation, self-esteem). Moreover, future investigations might draw on the sociology of emotions to clarify the meaning of distress and other specific emotions (beyond anger and guilt) and how they may affect the nature of responses to inequity.

b. Cognitive Mediators

Equity theory's assumption that individuals will choose the least costly equity-restoring response begs further explication. Although the assumption suggests a rational approach involving the objective processing of information about the situation, early theorists ignored the potential impact of cognitive factors. The explosion of research on social cognition in recent years (see Fiske and Taylor, 1991) draws attention to a number of cognitive elements that may constitute mechanisms linking perceived inequity to cognitive and behavioral reactions.

One of the fundamental issues in the social cognition literature pertains to how people infer the causes of another actor's behavior. Observers may locate causes within the actor (internal) or as external to the actor. These causal attributions, according to Utne and Kidd (1980), are likely to mediate reactions to injustice. Presumably, determination of the causes for the inequity allows individuals to assess more accurately the relative costs of various equity-restoring behaviors. Attributions to uncontrollable or at least unintentional causes, generally external to the actor, are less likely to stimulate active responses to inequity. In contrast, to the extent that individuals perceive another person as responsible for the inequity they suffer, they are more likely to be distressed and to attempt to relieve that distress through action. When situational factors make appeals to the source of the inequity costly, individuals may opt for alternative methods of restoring equity. Only a few studies, however, have attempted to test empirically any part of Utne and Kidd's formulation. Hassebrauck's (1987) test of Utne and Kidd's prediction is indirect. He examines the effects of misattribution on responses to inequity. When subjects misattribute their pay to a neutral source, they are less likely to attempt to restore equity. In essence, such a misattribution locates the cause of the inequity in an external source.

Hegtvedt, Thompson, and Cook (1993) attempt to examine not only how perceived inequity affects various types of attributions, but also how those attributions affect or mediate reactions to inequity. Female subjects involved in a role-play vignette describing an exchange with a male partner could attribute their underpay, equitable pay, or overpay to attributions to self (the subject), to the other actor (the partner), to the situation, or to the interaction. Results for a structural equation model show that actual outcome/input ratios are positively related to perceived equity. Perceived equity, in turn, positively influences attributions to self and to other, and negatively influences attributions to the interaction. Apparently, equitably and overpaid individuals are willing to take credit for their own outcomes and to provide their partner with some credit because, perhaps, of his/her apparent generosity. They were, in contrast, unlikely to attribute the outcomes to the dynamics of the interaction. But only in mixed-sex dyads did attributions affect responses to injustice. Findings indicate a negative relationship between attributions to other and positive reactions to the inequity, as Utne and Kidd (1980) would expect. But given the positive relationship between perceived inequity and "other" attributions, that external attribution can hardly be said to mediate responses. Only attributions to self seem to mediate anticipated behavioral responses. Individuals who attributed their outcomes to their own effort and ability were more likely to respond positively to their partner (e.g., thank him, agree to work for him in the future). The lack of mediation effects in female dyads may reflect the readiness by which similar others respond to each other; similarity may attenuate the need for cognitive processing in the situation.

Likewise, the role of attributions was not as pronounced as expected in a study by Hunt and Kernan (1991). These researchers predicted that consumers who attribute an inequitable exchange with a company to internal factors would be more likely to engage in active behavior to restore equity. Results indicated, however, that subjects provided with information suggesting an external attribution demonstrate a greater propensity to retaliate. To account for the unexpected results, Hunt and Kernan (1991:695) suggest that such subjects "might still hold a company responsible if they believe that it could have taken a more appropriate course of action. Beliefs about what "could have been" underlie the referent cognition approach (Folger, 1986) to understanding responses to inequity.

Folger (1986) argues that it is necessary to understand how reward distributions are made in order to predict responses to injustice. His referent cognition approach focuses on three cognitive elements: (1) the distance between the actual outcome and the level of outcomes imaginable, (2) the perceived likelihood of remedying the inequitable situation, and (3) the extent to which the existing distribution is justifiable. To the extent that individuals have high referent outcomes, perceive a low likelihood of remedy, or find the existing distribution unjustifiable, they are likely to experience severe inequity distress.

Empirical studies demonstrate an interaction between level of referant outcome and the degree of justifiability (Folger and Martin, 1986). With low justification, subjects whose referent outcomes were high express greater resentment than those with the same justification but low referent outcomes. In contrast, high-justification subjects show an equivalent lack of resentment regardless of the level of referent outcomes. Similarly, referent outcome levels and procedures interact to determine fairness evaluations (Cropanzano and Folger, 1989). When subjects chose their own procedures for allocating outcomes, the level of referent outcomes did not affect fairness assessments. But when another person (i.e., the experimenter) dictates those procedures, subjects feel more unfairly treated with high compared to low referent outcomes. Research in the referent cognition tradition highlights the connection between distributive and procedural justice (see Tyler and Lind, this volume). In addition, the theory identifies conditions that differentiate reactions to identical outcome/input disparities.

Indeed, it is the possibility of understanding why two people respond differently to the same level of inequity that has spurred the research on cognitive mediators to responses to injustice. The research to date, however, demonstrates mixed results and leaves some questions unanswered. Although Utne and Kidd (1980) provide a convincing argument about how attributions mediate responses to inequity, there have been few direct tests of their ideas. Hegtvedt *et al.* (1993) come closest, but their results suggest that whether or not attributions mediate responses depends on other situational conditions. The referent cognition approach (Folger, 1986) offers an alternative cognitive emphasis. Even though it appears that questions of "what could have been" intervene between perceptions of injustice and reactions, in fact the empirical studies indicate that referent cognitions about outcome levels and justifiability of the distributions act more as moderating factors than mediating ones. Thus, overall there is little evidence of the chain of reasoning contributing to responses to injustice. In addition, how the reasoning might affect the nature of the response remains unaddressed. Further research is needed.

c. *The Role of Self-Evaluations*

Another approach to understanding people's subjective experiences of underpay or economic disadvantage that may lead to responses to injustice focuses on self-evaluations.

Della Fave (1980) argues that, through comparisons with generalized others, people develop favorable or unfavorable self-evaluations consistent with their position of advantage or disadvantage in the social structure. Individuals' perceptions that they are causally responsible for their rewards reinforce the position–self-evaluation relationship, which in turn affects their responses to inequality. Insofar as the advantaged have positive self-evaluations, they come to see their reward level as just. Concomitantly, the disadvantaged develop negative self-evaluations, and thus expect lower rewards. As a consequence of the self-evaluation process, inequalities become legitimated. Empirical work, however, has challenged some of the tenets of this reasoning.

In an experimental study, Stolte (1983) demonstrated that disadvantaged actors felt the distribution to be more unfair than advantaged actors, despite the fact that perceived competence varied directly with position. And, in a survey study of perceptions of socioeconomic achievement, Sheplak (1987) indicates that family income exerts the strongest direct effect on fairness evaluations, with self-evaluation (and self-explanation) playing at best a modest role.

These results cast doubt on the Della Fave emphasis on self-evaluation as an important mediator of justice assessments and reactions to injustice. In effect, the failure of self-evaluations to intervene between structural position and evaluations of inequality suggests delegitimation of the distribution of outcomes, which might stimulate behaviors to eliminate the injustice. Yet such responses among the disadvantaged are infrequent. Sheplak (1987) suggests that self-efficacy might prove to be a more accurate intervening mechanism than self-evaluation or self-explanation. To the extent that people fail to perceive themselves as having the ability to control the outcomes they receive they may be more likely to accept the distribution. Future research should address this possibility.

2. Factors that Moderate Reactions to Inequity

Whereas mediating factors identify mechanisms through which perceived inequity may activate certain responses, moderating factors work in conjunction with perceived injustice to facilitate or inhibit those reactions. These moderators may pertain to characteristics of the individuals involved or to features of the context in which the inequity occurs. Thus, for example, situational conditions may differentially condition the responses of males and females to perceived injustice. Recently, much attention has been devoted to the conditionalizing effects of assessments of procedural justice. These moderating factors may also exert direct effects on reactions to injustice.

a. Individual Factors as Moderators

Although Mowday (1987) calls for examination of the impact of individual differences on reactions to inequity in the workplace, little research specifically addresses such factors (see review by Major and Deaux, 1982). As already noted, Sprecher (1992) calls attention to the moderating effects of both gender and exchange orientation on inequity distress and inequity reactions. Another study examines the extent to which females are more likely than males to respond to inequity in a self-depriving manner (Nadkarni, Lundgren, and Burlew, 1991). Previous research (see Major and Deaux, 1982) indicates that females may allocate less to themselves than do males, suggesting that gender role might encourage generosity toward others. Thus, Nadkarni, Lundgren, and Burlew expect females to act in a more self-depriving fashion. Results, however, find the opposite. Three times as many male subjects as females decreased their reward share, despite an initial pay disadvantage created by an opposite-sex partner. It may be the case that reliance on gender role stereotyping is an insufficient basis for understanding gender effects on responses to inequity.

It may be necessary to tap into individual characteristics that do not rely on stereotypical images, which may often be misleading. Huseman, Hatfield, and Miles (1987) investigate an individual difference variable, equity sensitivity, or the extent to which individuals show preferences for different levels of equity, which in turn presumably affect how they respond to inequity. The three categories of equity sensitivity are: (1) benevolents, who prefer that their outcome/input ratios are less than others; (2) equity sensitives, who desire equivalence of outcome/input ratios across actors; and (3) entitleds, who prefer their own outcome/input ratios to exceed those of others. Benevolents tend to be the most distinct group. Miles, Hatfield, and Huseman (1989) show that benevolents, in contrast to the other groups, prefer higher inputs—they work harder for their pay than other groups. Thus, it is not surprising to find that benevolents appear to be more tolerant of underreward inequity than either equity sensitives or entitleds (King, Miles, and Day, 1993). In addition, evidence suggest that benevolents are also more tolerant of overreward, perhaps because they feel able to increase their inputs to correspond with the reward level. As a consequence, benevolents are less likely to experience inequity distress and act accordingly. Results from Patrick and Johnson (1991) demonstrate, as expected, that equity sensitives exhibit the strongest reactions to under- and overreward, although all three equity types are likely to seek a raise or to increase productivity in the respective reward conditions. Equity sensitivity may be an important factor to consider in understanding workers' incentives, demands, and grievances.

Similarly, self-esteem may affect how individuals in the workplace respond to inequity. Brockner (1985) finds that high- and medium-level self-esteem subjects increase their productivity when overrewarded. In contrast, low-self-esteem subjects are actually less productive when overrewarded compared to equitably rewarded. Kwon and Cummings (1994) reiterate the importance of self-esteem in moderating the inequity–response relationship, though they note that it may also interact with the structure of the exchange relationship between the parties. Their hypotheses remain to be tested.

It appears that some individual-level characteristics moderate how people are likely to respond to felt inequity. It is likely, however, that these individual-level factors interact with other contextual elements. Such interactions should be the focus of future research.

b. Contextual Factors as Moderators

Contextual factors are of two types. First, they may pertain to aspects of the *relationship* among the parties involved in a situation. Second, they may pertain to individuals' perceptions of and expectations about the *situation*. These perceptions, along with the actual information provided in or characterizing the situation, create the subjective context in which individuals respond to an injustice.

Relationship Factors. Outside the domain of intimate relations, little research examines the influence of the affective and structural characteristics of the relationship on reactions to injustice.[5] Reis and Burns (1982) investigate whether the implied standards of others affect efforts to restore inequity. They assume that people strive to conform to the standards of significant others. Thus, even in the absence of others, these standards increase in importance when an individual is self-focused. Under conditions of such objective self-awareness, individuals should be motivated personally to evaluate their own behavior as fair. Indeed, results show that self-focused female subjects work significantly harder in response to overpayment than do those who are not self-focused. Thus, it appears that even indirect means of highlighting connectedness between the actors affect reactions to inequity.

The extent to which other group members also suffer injustice influences responses to injustice. Markovsky (1985) examines the effects of comparisons across individuals and across groups. Results show that when identification with the group is low, individual-level comparisons stimulate responses to injustice. The frequency of responses tends to vary directly with the extent of injustice, especially underreward. But when group identification is high, emphasis shifts to group comparisons, which in turn stimulate reactions to injustice. For example, autonomous workers are more likely to complain about their pay level in comparison to other individual workers. However, to the extent that workers have a collective identity of some sort, e.g., "office workers," they will compare their pay to other groups, e.g., warehouse workers, as a basis for assessing injustices and responding appropriately. Markovsky's research highlights not only the importance of group bonds, but also the importance of different types of comparisons, as stressed by a number of sociologists (Berger *et al*, 1972; Törnblom, 1977; Jasso, 1980, 1993).

Brockner, Tyler, and Cooper-Schneider (1992) demonstrate another function of group bonds. They examined how employees' perceptions of the fairness of prior layoffs and their prior commitment to their institution affected subsequent commitment, turnover intention, and work effort. Prior commitment and perceived fairness interacted. Those with low prior commitment demonstrate no difference in the various types of reactions. But for those with high prior commitment, perceived fairness produces greater subsequent commitment, lower turnover intention, and slightly greater work effort whereas perceived unfairness produces the opposite. This study emphasizes the importance of group value for understanding differential responses to an organizational event among those who were not directly disadvantaged.

In addition to the value of the group and the different comparisons available, the actual structural relationship between actors affects potential responses to inequity. Zelditch and Ford (1994) show that the sheer existence of a power structure may inhibit responses to inequity. In an experimental study of decisions and nondecisions in a centralized communication network, subjects on the periphery of the network perceived the occupant of the central position to be more powerful. Even though the central agent did not use power tactics or invoke penalties in response to peripheral actors' attempts to change the inequitable situation, occupants of peripheral positions constrained their actions. As a consequence, these power-disadvantaged subjects were unable to address the inequity created by the network structure.

Power-disadvantaged individuals may not perceive that they possess the means to redress inequity behaviorally.[6] In contrast, power-advantaged individuals who perceive injustice may fail to redress it, despite having the resources to do so (Cook, Hegtvedt, and Yamagishi, 1988). An unjust distribution of rewards, of course, is beneficial to power-advantaged actors. If the situational context allows them to perceive their own talents (or other internally caused factors) to be responsible for the inequity, they may conclude that they deserve more. In contrast, if information suggests to power-advantaged actors that they derive their power and concomitant accumulation of rewards from an external source, then they may attempt to redress the injustice. Indeed, results from Cook *et al.* (1988) show that inequalities in the distribution of outcomes in an exchange network narrowed when powerful actors were made aware of the structural source of their power, giving some credence to the attributional argument. Although only a few facets of the relationship between actors have been explored, it appears that enhancement of group bonds, either through invoking the standards of others, group comparisons, or establishment of commitment, increases attempts to redress injustice in the absence of power differences. Not surprisingly, in general, power differences inhibit attempts by disadvantaged actors to redress injustice. The types of situational conditions that may facilitate the efforts of disadvantaged actors to restore justice require further investigation.

Situational Factors. Individuals interpret the actions of power-advantaged actors or leaders using other information available in the situation. Lawler and Thompson (1978) suggest that individuals respond quite differently to leaders whom they perceive to have had either very little or a great deal of responsibility for creating inequity. In an experimental study, the two subordinate subjects in each group indicated whether they would endorse their leader's inequitable allocation and whether or not they would seek to form a coalition against the leader. Findings show that when the leader bears little responsibility for the type of allocation he or she made, subordinates are more likely to endorse the leader and less likely to revolt than when the leader has a great deal of allocation responsibility. Thus, again, it appears that attributions ultimately may mediate these reactions to injustice.

Likewise, the identity of the inequity-causing agent may affect reactions to inequity (Greenberg, 1986). When the agent is an organization, overpaid individuals are less likely to rectify the injustice that when they receive benefits from a named individual. The impersonality of the organization seems to free individuals from feelings of guilt. Perceptions of the source of inequity may be based more generally on legitimacy. Walker, Rogers, and Zelditch (1988) show that perceptions of the legitimacy of the situation decrease attempts to change an inequitable situation. More specifically, to the extent that subjects see a structure as valid, they are more likely to maintain it even if it produces substantial inequity. Martin and Sell (1986) examine collective reactions to the dictates of a legitimate authority. They find that individuals are more likely to reject an authority's use of an equal distribution rule than an equitable one, especially when individual and group interests coincide. When such interests conflict, however, assessment of the level of self-benefit resulting from the application of a particular distribution principle usually determined whether or not a rule would be rejected. Thus, individuals designate certain distribution principles as more legitimate than others, but their responses depend on calculations of their own self-interest.

Information available in the situation may bolster the perceived legitimacy, even of an unfair distribution, which consequently would reduce the probability of any reaction to the injustice. Sharpley (1991) shows that when the experimenter provides a rationale for rewarding one member of a dyad but not the other, neither dyad member alters his or her work behavior. In contrast, without the rationale, the perceived unfairness affects the performance of both members of the dyad. The rationale itself, however, may vary in terms of its perceived legitimacy.

Greenberg (1993) examines how the nature of the information received may affect responses to inequity, in this case theft as a reaction to underpayment. Valid information stemmed directly from an expert source, was revealed in public, and verified by an independent source. Information with low validity was based on unverified heresay, privately delivered from a person of undisclosed expertise. When information about pay had low validity and was delivered in an interpersonally insensitive manner, the degree of stealing was highest. In contrast, valid information about the pay situation provided in a sensitive way inhibited stealing to a large extent.

Thus, available information—whether about individuals, the structure, or the situation—affects subjective interpretations of the situation, which in turn affect reactions to injustice. Information that provides a legitimate account for the actions of an allocator or the nature of an unjust distribution appears to placate individuals. Such results are consistent with research in the referent cognition tradition regarding justifiability. Ironically, knowledge of such effects (in the hands of the powerful) may work against the interests of the disadvantaged. Future research should examine the consequences of the acceptance of inequity. For example, how does acquiescence affect future interactions involving other types of injustice or injustice in other relationships? Additional work might also examine the conditions facilitating delegitimation, an issue raised by the results of Martin and Sell (1986). The role of self and group interests, in conjunction with the opportunity and various means of redress (such as those made available to the subordinates in the Lawler and Thompson study), may be particularly fruitful topics for research. Finally, future investigations might combine the analysis of moderating and mediating factors in order to understand more explicitly what affects individuals' subjective experiences of injustice and their perceptions of the possibility of redressing the problem.

c. *Procedural Justice*

Even when outcome distributions appear unfair, individuals may fail to respond to the injustice because they believe that the procedures used to produce the distribution are fair. As suggested by referent cognition theory, knowledge of the process of creating inequity is integral to understanding reactions to it. Tyler and McGraw (1986) review 12 studies showing that unjust distributions of wealth do not necessarily lead to political actions by the disadvantaged. They argue that socialization to accept the prevailing system of equal opportunity—to see the procedures as fair—inhibits such reactions. Similarly, in experimental work, perceptions of procedural justice condition evaluations of distributive justice. For example, individuals perceive performance evaluations to be fairer when they also perceive the procedures to be fair (e.g., Greenberg, 1986; Alexander and Ruderman, 1987).

Randall and Mueller (1995), however, find no evidence for the moderating effect of procedural justice on reactions to the distribution of qualitative rewards. Instead, their data suggest a chain effect of procedural justice evaluations on distributive justice evaluations, and the latter on subsequent reactions. Perceptions of procedural justice (defined by involvement in decision-making) are positively related to perceptions of distributive justice (defined as the distribution of qualitative workplace rewards), which in turn are positively related to job satisfaction, organizational commitment, and intent to stay.

The relationship between distributive and procedural justice is the focus of a growing body of research (see Tyler and Lind, this volume). Yet with the exception of Randall and Mueller (1995), little research has examined how the two types of justice combine to affect actual reactions to injustice (either distributive or procedural). Emphasis on procedural justice provides an alternative approach to understanding the differential perceptions of distributive justice. Moreover, in contrast to individual-level moderating factors and some contextual factors, inclusion of procedural justice concerns provides a means for incorporating group value (see Lind and Tyler, 1988; Tyler *et al.*, 1997) into our understanding of distributive justice as a phenomenon involving more than simple assessments of individual deserving. Future research might compare the potency of the various moderating factors in predicting the nature of reactions to injustice.

3. Various Types of Reactions to Inequity

Although the research reviewed above indicates a number of factors that mediate or moderate the inequity–reaction relationship, researchers typically constrain the nature of the reaction under study. That is, the research paradigm or empirical method employed most often measures only one type of response at a time. The investigated response is usually behavioral. As a consequence, there are only a few studies on the use of nonbehavioral (e.g., cognitive) reactions, multiple types of reactions, or on the choice among various modes of equity restoration.

Because workers may feel reluctant to threaten their job status by demanding higher salaries or lowering their inputs, they may opt for less obvious ways to cope with perceived inequity. Two studies focus on cognitive reevaluations that restore a sense of equity. Greenberg (1989) examines how workers evaluate non-monetary benefits (e.g., environmental conditions such as amounts of floor and desk space, extent of privacy, number of windows) 6 months after a pay reduction and 6 months after reinstatement of earlier pay levels. Results indicate that workers rated the environmental rewards as more important determinants of fair pay and required greater amounts of them when they were underpaid financially than when they were equitably paid. These cognitive reevaluations, furthermore, seem to maintain levels of job satisfaction. Similarly, in a laboratory experiment, Stepina and Perrewe (1987) note that subjects enhance their evaluation of work itself in order to compensate for an inequitable situation. In addition, inequitably treated individuals report higher levels of motivation than do those who are equitably treated due to task enhancement. Thus, it appears that cognitive strategies designed to cope with injustice provide benefits beyond simply restoring equity.

A shortcoming of the studies of cognitive reevaluations is actually the mirror image of the problem we identified above with traditional equity research: These studies do not allow the possibility of behavioral responses since they only measure cognitions. Hammock, Rosen, Richardson, and Bernstein (1989) attempt to examine all forms of reactions to inequity. Working within the inequity–aggression paradigm, these researchers measured subjects' aggressive responses (i.e, the level of shock) delivered to partners who presumably had shocked them at lower frequency (positive inequity) or higher frequency (negative inequity) than average. Results show that the intensity of aggressive responses was higher for negative inequity than for positive inequity. There were no differences by equity condition in cognitive responses involving evaluating or derogating the partner. The satisfaction of actual equity may have inhibited the need for the restoration of psychological equity.

Four recent studies, reviewed above for other purposes, include measures of multiple responses to injustice. Hegtvedt *et al.* (1993) measured different anticipated reactions, some behavioral and some cognitive, but ultimately created a single index of the extent to which the reactions are negative or positive. Brockner, Tyler, and Cooper-Schneider (1992) examined various reactions including subsequent organizational commitment, turnover intention, and work effort, as did Randall and Mueller (1995) who looked at job satisfaction, organizational commitment, intent to stay, and actual turnover. These researchers treated each type of reaction separately. Thus, the only indication that some reactions differ from others is the strength of their relationship to distributive justice evaluations. For example, work effort in the Brockner, Tyler, and Cooper-Schneider study and turnover in the Randall and Mueller study are not significantly related to distributive justice evaluations.

Sprecher's (1992) study on anticipated reactions to under- and over-benefiting inequity in close relationships provides another means for assessing the likelihood of different responses. Inspection of means shows that respondents are most likely to increase their contributions to the relationship when overbenefited and to ask their partners to increase his or her contributions when under-benefited. Generally, the least likely option was to do nothing. The likelihood of changing their perceptions of the situation was in between the two extremes of doing nothing and of increasing contributions (or requesting an increase from a partner). Analysis of reactions by gender suggests that females are more likely than males to anticipate responding behaviorally as appropriate for each type of inequity, but males are more likely than females to do nothing.

Recent research on the reactions to injustice has included a greater variety of responses than earlier equity research. In particular, cognitive responses and responses related to nonmaterial or qualitative outcomes have garnered recent attention. The study of factors affecting the choice among reactions, however, remains a major topic for future investigations.

D. JUSTICE IN CLOSE RELATIONSHIPS

Although justice concerns exist in many social situations, investigation of such issues within personal, close relationships is relatively recent. As Mikula and Lerner (1994:1) note, "In everyday thought, close relationships are typically characterized by mutual trust, love, and caring rather than by considerations of what one is entitled to and the assessment of justice and fairness." The juxtaposition of love and the impersonal calculations required by the equity formula may seem at best contradictory, at worst blasphemous. Yet increasingly, researchers have turned to justice or equity approaches to understand relationship satisfaction, commitment, and interpersonal dynamics in close relationships. Moreover, this research informs conceptual issues as well as the relationship between justice and other conceptual domains such as power, social comparisons, and gender roles.

The three categories of close relationships typically studied include married couples, cohabitating couples, and dating couples.[7] Following the Walster *et al.* (1978a) equity formulation, researchers have focused primarily on the effects of equity and inequity on relationship satisfaction and commitment. Other studies have explored factors affecting what is perceived as just in a relationship. More recently, research has examined the extent to which equity and other factors can explain the division of household labor. To address this variety of issues, researchers rely on comparisons of the responses of individuals across dyad types as well as within dyads.

1. Equity Considerations in Close Relationships

As summarized in Sprecher and Schwartz (1994), initial research on equity in close relationships tested Walster and colleagues' (1978a) proposition that individuals participating in inequitable relationships will become distressed and that distress will vary directly with the extent of inequity. Although studies focusing primarily on the inequity–distress relationship support this proposition (e.g., Hatfield, Utne, and Traupmann, 1979; Traupmann, Hatfield, and Wexler, (1983), other investigations indicate that reward or outcome level is a more important predictor of relationship satisfaction than equity (Cate, Lloyd, Henton, and Larson, 1982; Michaels, Edwards, and Acock, 1984). Similarly, Sprecher (1988) demonstrates that another social exchange factor—the level of rewards available in alternative relationships (or the comparison level for alternatives)—exerts a stronger influence on relationship commitment than does equity. Despite the greater impact of other variables, equity clearly affects the positive and negative emotions experienced in relationships. Sprecher (1986) indicates that in dating relationships, inequity, especially under-benefiting inequity, predicts negative emotions, even when controlling for exchange factors such as personal and structural dependence. And, as already reviewed, Sprecher (1992) indicates that individuals, especially those with a high exchange orientation, anticipate making attempts to restore equity in response to distress or in response to the guilt resulting from overbenefit.

Evidence for actual rather than emotional responses to inequity in close relationships is more equivocal, however. A few studies suggest that inequitably treated partners in dating relationships are less likely to "go further" sexually than equitably treated partners (e.g., Walster, Walster, and Traupmann, 1978). And, in married couples, inequitably treated individuals (Walster, Traupmann, and Walster, 1978), especially women (Prins, Buunk, and Van-Yperen, 1993) are more likely to engage in extramarital affairs. In effect the former strategy lowers inputs whereas the latter may represent a form of withdrawal from the relationship. Yet research fails to demonstrate a relationship between inequity and actual withdrawal in terms of relationship dissolution (e.g., Lujansky and Mikula, 1983; Berg and McQuinn, 1986; Felmlee, Sprecher, and Bassin, 1990). Sprecher and Scwartz (1994) suggest that the lack of an inequity–dissolution relationship may be due to the timing of the measurement of inequity and to variation in the resources to which inequity might apply (some resources may be more important than others), lack of attention to moderating variables (such as exchange orientation), and failure to explore cognitive processes linking equity assessments to reactions. Some of these additional considerations appear in research examining factors affecting assessments of equity and evaluations of household division of labor.

Although measures of equity (see Sprecher and Schwartz, 1994) capture the perceived imbalance in a relationship either globally (e.g., "I'm getting a much better deal than my partner") or specifically (e.g., rating own inputs and outcomes in various areas of the relationship) and provide a basis for comparing what researchers define as equitable and inequitable relationships, there is more to understanding what individuals take into account in assessing what is fair in their relationships. Whether equity is an appropriate fairness principle for intimate couples may even be questioned. Below we review alternative approaches to justice in close relationships.

2. Perceiving Justice in Close Relationships: Orientations, Situations, and Comparisons

Clark and Chrisman (1994) argue that there is no clear rule governing the giving and receiving of benefits in intimate relationships. They assess the evidence for concerns with equity, equality, needs, and outcome level and conclude that none of it is "inconsistent with the idea that the prevailing norm for such relationships is that each member ought to be responsive to the other's needs to the best of his/her ability" (Clark and Chrisman, 1994:78). They recognize, however, that people do not always follow the ideal of this communal norm (or any norm). Moreover, rule use may depend on the stage of the relationship, with greater emphasis on communal orientation at the beginning of the relationship.

In contrast to communal orientation, VanYperen and Buunk (1994) highlight the existence of another individual-level variable: exchange orientation. As described above, an exchange orientation refers to emphasis on direct reciprocity in an intimate relationship. Individuals who possess an exchange orientation are more likely to be concerned with equity in a relationship than fulfillment of partner's needs. Buunk and VanYperen (1991) show that perceptions of inequity and equity affect marital satisfaction only among individuals who score high on an exchange orientation scale (or low on communal orientation). In addition, individuals low in exchange orientation were, overall, more satisfied with their relationship. The authors conclude that equity principles are of unequal importance to individuals.

The justice motive model (Lerner, 1981; Desmarais and Lerner, 1994) attempts to account for both communal and exchange effects. This model first characterizes the type of interaction and the nature of the relationship between individuals in terms of three prototypes: identity, unit, and nonunit. The identity prototype for relationships stresses a merging of selves through sameness and the corresponding interactional script is one of vicarious dependency. The unit prototype suggests a similarity between actors in the relationship and an interaction script suggesting convergent goals. In contrast, the remaining prototype nonunit indicates differences between individuals that elicit divergent or competitive goals. The justice motive theory specifies that situational cues within a given context stimulate these schematic definitions of the relationship and the interaction, which in turn highlight the appropriateness of a particular distribution or entitlement rule.

For example, insofar as a situation elicits feelings of caring and closeness (identity relationship and interaction), married partners are likely to divide household chores on the basis of fulfilling the needs of each. Yet when the situation highlights distinctiveness of each partner but the convergence of their goals (e.g., to have a clean house and happy children), they may be more likely to develop an equal division of the tasks. Desmarais and Lerner (1989) argue that it is not surprising that both equity and reward level per se affect relationship satisfaction because such effects depend on how individuals define their relationship and interaction. They show that members of couples who define their relationship like the identity prototype are likely to be most satisfied when their partner's outcomes are high. Extending this argument, Desmarais and Lerner (1990) (reported in Desmarais and Lerner, 1994) specify that when perceptions of the nature of the relationship and interaction shift toward more nonunit ideals, conflict is likely. Thus, the justice motive theory addresses factors influencing evaluations of fairness as well as the consequences of those evaluations.

Although individuals may invoke different justice principles depending on situational circumstances or their personal orientations, evaluations of justice also depend on the comparisons invoked (see VanYperen and Buunk, 1994, for a review). From an equity viewpoint, individuals are likely to engage in relational or local comparisons of input/outcome ratios with their partners. In addition, they may also compare their ratio with those of same-sex others, instigating a referential comparison. Buunk and VanYperen (1991) show that married respondents felt their input/outcome ratio was better than most same-sex others but equal to their spouses. Faring well in the referential comparison, moreover, was positively related to marital satisfaction. Other research suggests that referential comparisons are particularly important among those who feel uncertain about how things are going in their marriage (Buunk, VanYperen, Taylor, Collins, 1991). Such uncertainty often characterizes egalitarian gender-role relationships, especially for women (VanYperen and Buunk, 1991). The referential comparison in such cases provides a framework to substitute for the expectations based on the traditional gender-role division of labor.

3. Justice and the Household Division of Labor

Many studies document considerable inequity in the distribution of child-care tasks and the responsibility for chores (e.g., Biernat and Wortman, 1991). Reflecting this inequitable distribution are studies tracking perceptions of equity across the life cycle. Schafer and Keith (1981) show that perceived inequity increased across the life cycle, with females more apt to detect underbenefit and males to perceive favorable inequity. Focusing only on women, Traupmann and Hatfield (1983) find that they begin marriage with a sense of overbenefit and then move to a period of underbenefit during their middle years. By late middle age, their respondents felt equitably treated. More recently, Peterson (1990) documented differences between males and females in equity perceptions over time. While females are less likely to report changes in feelings of equity, males feel greater equity prior to the arrival of children and after their departure. Thus, for males and females alike the arrival of children influences their perceptions of fairness.

Lennon and Rosenfield (1994) note that equity perceptions in a relationship depend not only on relative contributions and outcomes but also on the structure of the relationship. Women who have few alternatives to marriage and fewer economic resources (in exchange terms, they occupy power-disadvantaged positions) are more likely to view a given division of housework as fair than are women with more alternatives. One's gender ideology also influences perceptions of fairness. Greenstein (1996) finds that inequalities in the division of household labor are more strongly related to perceptions of inequity for egalitarian than for traditional wives. In addition, results show that for egalitarian wives perceptions of inequity have a more pronounced effect on the perceived quality of their marital relationship. Thus, of importance for relationships are not observed inequalities per se in the division of labor but rather the perception of equity or inequity.

The experience of an unequal situation as unfair generally results in lower psychological well-being (Lennon and Rosenfield, 1994), as well as greater unhappiness, especially for women (Robinson and Spitze, 1992). Results from Glass and Fujimoto (1994) show that gender affects the beneficial consequences of perceived equity. For males, perceived equity in the performance of paid work inhibits depression and for females perceived equity in the performance of housework does likewise. Complementing these results is Thompson's (1991) argument that to the extent that women are able to justify the low contributions of males to family work, they are more likely to feel equitably treated. In addition, to the extent that marital partners possess comparable perceptions of fairness, they are likely to report higher relationship satisfaction (Dancer and Gilbert, 1993). Thus, in analyzing the role of fairness in the household division of labor, it is necessary to attend to other structural features of the relationship as well as ideological and cognitive factors that shape the meanings of the actual division of labor.

4. Justice among Intimates: Will the Relationship Last?

Although a relatively new area of inquiry, investigation of the role of justice in close relationships is multifaceted and likely to continue. The area offers tests of traditional equity theory predictions and challenges the universality of the theory. These challenges provide the basis for determining conditions under which perceptions of equity are likely to matter in personal relationships. In doing so, the studies highlight what is unique about such relationships but also contribute to the specification of scope conditions for equity theory. For example, equity concerns may be more important for those with a high exchange orientation.

The research that examines traditional equity hypotheses parallels research in impersonal situations by establishing relationships between equity, distress, and reactions. At this stage, however, the personal relationships literature is less advanced than traditional equity research in examining cognitive factors that may mediate responses to perceived injustice. Similarly, except for research on relationship orientations, little work examines the moderating effect of situational factors. This may be because the assessment of equity in close relationships takes a long-term, rather than a short-term, perspective. Focusing on the latter, however, might enhance understanding of specific conflicts in relationships, how they are resolved, and how the cumulative effects of those conflicts affect the general sense of justice in the relationship. In addition, more research is needed on different types of reactions to injustice among intimate couples. In particular, it seems likely that cognitive distortions, or changes in comparisons are likely alternative responses to injustice because they maintain a long-term commitment.

The literature on justice and the household division of labor reinforces a point relevant to all justice research, namely, people differentially interpret the same objective circumstances. Understanding factors relevant to such evaluations of justice in a relationship, such as power structure, type of comparison, and gender ideology, is useful both theoretically and practically. Future research might examine factors affecting the perceived relevance and weighing of different contributions to the household. Focusing on the resolution of disagreements over household tasks might provide a basis for understanding how new conceptualizations of justice—shared ones at that—emerge. Finally, whether factors outside of the relationships, such as work issues or the influence of extended family and friends, influence assessments of justice remains to be investigated.

To date, research on close relationships has focused primarily on distributive justice in intimate relationships. Thus, two major avenues for future research are obvious. First, the nature of close relationships may be expanded to include parent–child relationships, siblings, close friends, and even mentoring relationships. Second, considerations of procedural justice may affect how one interprets the fairness of their relationships and how they respond to perceived injustice. Research on relationships also includes the important arena of work which we discuss briefly in the next section on distributive justice in organizational settings.

E. ORGANIZATIONAL JUSTICE

Early theorists (Homans, 1961; Adams, 1965) examined reactions to injustice in work settings. With the establishment of equity theory, empirical endeavors shifted to the laboratory. However, over the past decade equity theory has been increasingly applied to the study of organizational settings and the issues of procedural and distributive justice that arise in the workplace.

Tyler and Griffin (1991) find that decision-making authorities in organizations who are concerned with maintaining positive interpersonal relations are as concerned with using procedures that are defined as fair as they are with the perceived fairness of their outcome allocations. Given the goal of promoting positive relations, maintaining procedural justice is as important as the pursuit of distributive justice. The general significance of the use of fair procedures for everything from the hiring and firing process and the allocation of jobs to the distribution of pay and job perks has been demonstrated in the early work of Thibaut and Walker (1975) on procedural justice and more recent work by Tyler (1990) on obedience to authority. Various studies of workplace satisfaction indicate that procedural fairness is an important determinant and, in some cases, a stronger component of satisfaction than distributive justice (cf. Gordon and Fryxell, 1989).

Justice concerns in organizations have also been tied to what are called organizational citizenship behaviors or "extrarole behaviors." In a study of two Midwestern firms in the United States, Moorman (1991), for example, finds that procedural justice, not distributive justice, is the best predictor. Four of five major dimensions of organizational citizenship are significantly related to perceptions of procedural justice, in particular, interactional justice (or fair treatment by a supervisor). The types of citizenship behavior positively affected by procedural fairness on the part of management include altruism, courtesy, sportsmanship, and conscientiousness. In addition, in a study of manufacturing plant employees, Folger and Konovsky (1989) find that organizational commitment is related to procedural justice factors, while pay satisfaction is more closely tied to distributive justice concerns.

In addition to the work on procedural justice in organizational settings, there is continued research on distributive justice in relation to occupational incomes (Headley, 1991), pay satisfaction (Miller, 1989; Sweeney, 1990), comparable worth and the gender wage gap (e.g., Jackson, 1987). Despite the recent emphasis on procedural justice within organizations, workers remain concerned about the ways in which decisions are made about the actual distributions of their pay, job tasks, and perks among other things. These concerns are often triggered by the sense of unfairness or of distributive injustice, as much as by the perception of procedural unfairness. Being denied a pay raise when another worker you perceive as less qualified receives one, for example, is an issue of distributive justice even though, in addition, the workers may have concerns about the procedures followed in evaluating job performance and making the decisions regarding pay raises (Folger and Konovsky, 1989).

Greenberg has developed a model of the components of what he terms organizational justice. In his Figure 1 (1990b:405), he presents both procedural justice and distributive justice as separate components of organizational justice (Sheppard and Lewicki, 1987; Greenberg, 1990b). Procedural justice determines system satisfaction and distributive justice determines outcome satisfaction in his model (see Folger and Konovsky, 1989; Fryxell and Gordon, 1989). Similar research has applied this distinction to studies of mangers' and employees' conceptions of workplace justice, including the equitable distribution of work assignments, perks and pay, as well as the procedures that determine these allocations. Fairer procedures include voice, the suppression of individual bias or particularism, and rememdies for mistaken appraisals or for limited information. Folger and Konovsky (1989), for example, report that organizational commitment and trust in management were associated with high levels of perceived procedural fairness (see also Greenberg, 1990b, for a more complete review of these issues).

Earlier work on organizational satisfaction based on equity theory focused on wage rates or salary. In newer work nonmonetary outcomes that reflect status and power within the organization are also subject to justice evaluations. In fact, in the theoretical framework developed by Berger *et al.* (1972), distributive justice evaluations are fundamentally about "status value" or the symbolic value of items and not their consummatory (or monetary) value. Such items include the location of parking spaces, the size of offices and the nature of the furnishings, and job titles, among other things. Greenberg (1988), for example, in a clever study in which workers in an insurance company were temporarily reassigned to the offices of higher-, equal-, or lower-status co-workers, discovered that performance was affected by office assignment such that those who were overrewarded produced more than those who felt underrewarded in terms of the perceived fairness of the assignment of office space. This work along with the work of Berger and his colleagues (e.g., Berger *et al.*, 1972) indicates that organizational managers run the risk of alienating workers when they do not attend to perceptions of fairness in the allocation of perks other than pay even if they are as minor as the square footage of office space and the convenience of parking locations.

In Greenberg's (1988) study, employees who were temporarily situated in higher-status office space raised their performance while those in lower-status space decreased theirs. Such responses correspond with equity predictions for over- and underreward, respectively. Likewise, Greenberg (1990a) found that employees in a manufacturing plant whose pay was temporarily reduced by 15% had higher theft rates than when their full pay was reinstated.

Theft is sometimes viewed by underpaid employees as a legitimate means of compensating for lower financial rewards. In contrast to reactions to underpay, Cowherd and Levine (1992) observed the positive consequences of narrowing the pay differential between lower-level employees and upper-echelon managers. The smaller pay differential, in effect, suggests that the lower-level employees are overpaid. In response, these employees increase their commitment to management goals, their effort, and their cooperation, thereby enhancing the quality of the products they produce.

Equally important is the reaction of workers to layoffs in their organizations. Recent research indicates that both distributive justice and procedural justice come into play as determinants of the reactions of victims and "survivors" to layoffs. Perceptions of the fairness of these decisions are reflected in subsequent job performance and the organizational commitment of those who witnessed the layoff of their co-workers.

Although these studies are relatively straightforward tests of equity theory in nontraditional contexts, research in applied settings is useful for several reasons. First, real-world contexts may alert researchers to issues beyond the scope of current theorizing. Second, some factors may not be easily operationalized in a laboratory setting. Finally, investigations of perceptions of inequity and the corresponding responses to inequity provide important input into the actual management and labor practices of organizations, a topic of central importance in the work on organizational justice. Moving from the organizational level to the societal level we find that distributive justice issues are central to beliefs about income inequality and attitudes toward welfare, the allocation of tax burdens, and other policy issues.

F. JUSTICE AND BELIEFS ABOUT STRATIFICATION: MICRO- AND MACROJUSTICE PRINCIPLES

One of the more prominent stratification research areas since the 1980s has been the examination of beliefs about economic inequality. Evaluations of the distribution of wealth, income, status, and prestige in society as well as of economic opportunity, redistributive policies, and the plight of those who fall below the poverty line have been a major focus of inquiry using survey methodology comparing various countries in the world. Kluegel and Smith (1986) and Kluegel, Mason, and Wegener (1996) argue that greater attention should be paid to social psychological theories in the study of stratification beliefs. Kluegel and Smith (1986) examine not only beliefs about economic inequality, but also the relationship between these beliefs and conceptions individuals hold about class, their class identification, and images of class differences in society. This work moves beyond earlier Marxist formulations of class consciousness developing a more complete conceptualization of the determinants of class identification and the content of the beliefs in society about class.

In a more recent cross-national effort, Kluegel *et al.* (1995) report the results of a large collaborative project in which researchers in 13 countries conducted surveys about social justice beliefs in relation to attitudes about political change. This edited volume is especially interesting because it includes data on justice beliefs in some countries that have changed dramatically as a consequence of the breakdown of the former Soviet Union. The results from studies in Bulgaria, Czechoslovakia, Estonia, Hungary, Slovenia, Russia, Poland, and East Germany are contrasted with findings from Japan, Great Britain, the United States, West Germany, and the Netherlands. Similar interviews were conducted of approximately 1200 respondents in each country covering many dimensions of justice beliefs including current life situation, household justice (e.g., division of labor), and economic realities, like income inequalities. In addition, attitudes toward political involvement were obtained and linked to standard background factors like party identification, occupation, educational level, employment status, and ethnicity. Two key issues are addressed in this research: (1) what do justice beliefs explain? and (2) how do we explain justice beliefs? The project addresses both microjustice issues concerning allocation among individuals and groups and macrojustice issues of distributive justice at the societal level.

The results reported in Kluegel *et al.* (1995) hold some surprises for justice researchers. Individuals from the Eastern European and formerly communist countries often hold simultaneously incompatible beliefs favoring equality and inequality (or what is referred to as "split-consciousness"), a finding that had been documented in previous work only in the West. Perspectives that imply that there is one overarching "dominant ideology" in a society that determines the structure of the justice beliefs oversimplify the complexity of such beliefs. In most countries in the survey it is the disadvantaged (e.g., women, the poor, and those less educated) who favor equality, while those at the top of the income ladder support equity principles, typically based on merit. Comparing the generations in East and West Germany, it is the young in the East who are less favorable to egalitarianism that the old, though the situation is reversed in what was formerly West Germany. Family need is reported by Kluegel *et al.* (1996) to be accepted less frequently in the West than in the East as a determinant of income fairness, reflecting the history of a focus on individual rights, merit, and achievements in contrast to more collectivist orientations in the formerly communist states. These comparative studies provide fascinating glimpses into the linkages between complex social, economic, and political systems and justice beliefs. These factors also determine differential evaluations of the role of the state in the provision of welfare benefits and as an instrument of intervention and redistribution. The future will surely provide even more in-depth work on the links between microjustice beliefs and principles and the macro-level aggregate consequences of political and economic systems.

G. FURTHER APPLICATIONS OF THEORIES OF DISTRIBUTIVE JUSTICE

In addition to the work on justice in organizational settings and the work on income distributions in society, there have been several innovative applications of equity theory. Cowell (1992), for example, couples notions of inequity with tax evasion. Other researchers examine equity issues in the context of sports. Bretz and Thomas (1992) investigate reactions to inequity in terms of winning or losing final-offer salary negotiations in baseball. Losers—individuals who would perceive themselves as underpaid—are more likely to exhibit a decline in performance (i.e., lower their inputs) and are more likely to leave their teams. Also examining equity in baseball, Harder (1991) looks at the performance of players (excluding pitchers) as a reaction to perceived underpayment prior to becoming a free agent and expectations of a higher salary as a free agent. Consistent with equity theory, batting averages decline in the year before free agency.

During the past two decades another area of research has been the application of principles of justice to a variety of institutional settings in which valued resources are allocated. This work ranges from evaluations of the allocation of work load in families and the distribution of decision-making rights to evaluations of the distribution of income (e.g., Alwin, 1987) and tax burdens (e.g., Kinsey, Grasmick, and Smith, 1991) in the society at large. This category includes a growing number of studies on the allocation of scarce resources as in the medical arena when there is limited access to clinical trials, experimental drugs, or even organs and organ transplantation (e.g., Elster, 1992). As we indicated in our discussion of allocation research, the distribution principles that should apply to access to health care itself and to the health services delivery system more broadly are currently being reexamined. Research in the literature on gerontology, long-term care, and medical ethics is also increasingly addressing issues of distributive justice (e.g., Cook and Donnelly, 1996).

Other applications of justice theory include research on dispute resolution or conflict resolution and the role of third parties (Karambayya and Brett, 1989; Conlon and Fasolo, 1990), and grievance procedures and settlements (Gordon and Bowlby, 1988). The outcome of a grievance settlement, for example, is shown by Gordon and Bowlby (1988) to be a significant determinant of the satisfaction of the grievant. Winners were more likely to feel satisfied with both the process and outcome, whereas losers were much less sanguine. This finding fits with other research suggesting that it is the loss of an outcome or the failure to receive an expected reward that triggers concerns over procedural fairness. As conflict resolution and alternative methods of dispute resolution grow in significance in various institutional sectors (e.g., in family settings, in employee–employer relations and other organizational disputes, and in legal and corporate settings) research on the procedural aspects of justice-related processes and their interaction with considerations of distributive justice will become even more important for both theoretical and applied reasons. Subsequent chapters in this volume discuss work relevant to these concerns. We anticipate in the future a closer relationship between basic endeavors in the development of justice theory and more applied work, continued efforts to understand the social and political implications of the distribution of society's most valued resources and the mechanisms for doing so. It is out hope that future research will lead to a more comprehensive theory of distributive justice, one that integrates existing formulations, clarifies the relationship between distributive and procedural justice, and provides insight into the complex distributive issues of an increasingly global interdependent world.

H. ENDNOTES

1. Although these are the primary rules that have been examined, Reis (1986) notes a number of other possible distribution rules.
2. Evidence (Allison, McQueen, and Schaerfl, 1992) suggests that equal distributions are easiest to execute when the good is already partitioned (e.g., bills of $1, $5, $10, $20 compared to a brick of gold) and the group is small (e.g., three or four group members compared to a dozen or more).
3. Most experimental studies of justice processes examine multiple factors simultaneously. To the extent that one factor conditionalizes the effects of another, the two are said to interact statistically. Such a moderating effect occurs, for example, when the effects of gender on allocation preferences depend on whether the task is sex appropriate for the subject (i.e., when females perform cooking tasks) or inappropriate (i.e., when females fix cars). Females, regardless of their performance level, may prefer equal allocations. But when sex appropriateness of the task is taken into consideration, such a pattern may only arise for allocations on sex-inappropriate tasks; on sex-appropriate tasks, their preferences may reflect self-interested preferences stimulated by their performance level (i.e., low performers prefer equality but high performers opt for equitable allocations). In addition to these moderating effects, researchers sometimes examine mediating effects. In such cases, a factor may have no direct effect on the allocation (or reaction to injustice) but may have an indirect effect, through an additional factor (which may represent some mechanism). For example, the information a person has about performance levels may only affect distribution preferences if the actor makes an internal attribution that the performances are based on individual ability, rather than an external attribution to luck. In this case, the nature of the attribution mediates between performance levels and the allocation decision. Regression analyses using multiple equations allow for the assessment of such indirect or mediating effects.
4. Health care resources involve services provided by physicians, hospitals, nursing homes, and so on. The process of

receiving such resources is distinct in some ways from receiving compensation for work, as is the focus of the most of the studies reviewed. An individual typically does not *earn* the use of health care resources and such resources are not allocated as a reward for positive actions or contributions. Rather, individuals receive these positive goods in response to negative events (or to prevent such events, as in the case of preventive health care).

5. As reviewed below, many studies examine justice issues in intimate relationships. But unlike the allocation literature, in which a major thrust is the comparison between personal and impersonal relationships, the study of reactions to injustice rarely contrasts the two types of relationships.
6. At the macro level, as described by some theories of collective action, power-disadvantaged and unfairly treated individuals fail to respond to felt injustice largely because of their inability to mobilize resources (e.g., Tilly, 1977).
7. Nearly all of the work focusing on these types involves heterosexual couples. A major exception, however, is the *American Couples* study by Blumstein and Schwartz (1983). In addition, more recent work is beginning to examine various types of family relationships (e.g., siblings, parent–child) as forms of close relationships.

REFERENCES

Aaron, H. J., and Schwartz, W. B. (1984). *The Painful Prescription: Rationing Hospital Care*. Washington, DC: Brookings.

Adams, J. S. (1965). Inequity in Social Exchange. *Advances in Experimental Social Psychology*, *2*, 267–299.

Alexander, S., and Ruderman, M. (1987). The Role of Procedural Justice in Organizational Behavior. *Social Justice Research*, *1*, 177–198.

Allison, S. T., McQueen, L. R., and Schaerfl, L. M. (1992). Social Decision-making Processes and the Equal Partitionment of Shared Resources. *Journal of Experimental Social Psychology*, *28*, 23–42.

Alwin, D. (1987). Distributive Justice and Satisfaction with Material Well-Being. *American Sociological Review*, *52*, 83–95.

Anderson, O. W. (1972). *Health Care: Can There Be Equity?* New York: Wiley.

Asdigian, N. L., Cohn, E. S., and Blum, M. H. (1994). Gender Differences in Distributive Justice: The Role of Self-presentation Revisited. *Sex Roles*, *30*, 303–318.

Austin, W. (1980). Friendship and Fairness: Effects of Type of Relationship and Task Performance on Choice of Distribution Rules. *Personality and Social Psychology Bulletin*, *6*, 402–408.

Austin, W., and Walster, E. (1974). Reactions to Confirmation and Disconfirmation of Inequity. *Journal of Personality and Social Psychology*, *30*, 208–216.

Barry, B. (1989). *Theories of Justice*. Berkeley: University of California Press.

Barry, B. (1995). *Justice as Impartiality: A Treatise on Social Justice*, Volume II. Oxford: Clarendon Press.

Berg, J. H., and McQuinn, R. D. (1986). Attraction and Exchange in Continuing and Noncontinuing Dating Relationships. *Journal of Personality and Social Psychology*, *50*, 942–952.

Berger, J., Zelditch, M., Jr., Anderson, B., and Cohen, B. P. (1972). Structural Aspects of Distributive Justice: A Status Value Formation. In J. Berger, M. Zelditch, and B. Anderson (Eds.), *Sociological Theories in Progress* (pp. 119–146). Boston: Houghton Mifflin.

Biernat, M., and Wortman, C. B. (1991). Sharing of Home Responsibilities between Professionally Employed Women and their Husbands. *Journal of Personality and Social Psychology*, *60*, 844–860.

Blumstein, P., and Schwartz, P. (1983). *American Couples*. New York: Morrow.

Bonacich, P., and Light, J. (1978). Laboratory Experimentation in Sociology. *Annual Review of Sociology*, *4*, 145–170.

Bretz, R. D., and Thomas, S. L. (1992). Perceived Equity, Motivation, and Final Offer Arbitration in Major League. *Journal of Applied Psychology*, *77*, 280–287.

Brockner, J. (1985). The Relation of Trait Self-esteem and Positive Inequity to Productivity. *Journal of Personality*, *53*, 517–529.

Brockner, J., O'Malley, M. N., Hite, T., and Davies, D. K. (1987). Reward Allocation and Self-esteem: The Roles of Modeling and Equity Restoration. *Journal of Personality and Social Psychology*, *52*, 844–850.

Brockner, J., Tyler, T. R., and Cooper-Schneider, R. (1992). The Influence of Prior Commitment to an Institution on Reactions to Perceived Unfairness: The Higher They Are, the Harder They Fall. *Administrative Science Quarterly*, *37*, 241–261.

Buunk, B. P., and VanYperen, N. W. (1991). Referential Comparisons, Relational Comparisons, and Exchange Orientation: Their Relation to Marital Satisfaction. *Personality and Social Psychology Bulletin*, *17*, 709–717.

Buunk, B. P., VanYperen, N. W., Taylor, S. E., and Collins, R. L. (1991). Social Comparison and the Drive Upward Revisited: Affiliation as a Response to Marital Stress. *European Journal of Social Psychology*, *21*, 529–546.

Campbell, D., and Stanley, J. (1963). *Experimental and Quasi-Experimental Designs for Research.* Chicago: Rand McNally.

Cate, R., Lloyd, S. A., Henton, J. M., and Larson, J. H. (1982). Fairness and Reward Level as Predictors of Relationship Satisfaction. *Social Psychology Quarterly, 45,* 177–181.

Clark, M. S., and Chrisman, K. (1994). Resource Allocation in Intimate Relationships: Trying to Make Sense of a Confusing Literature. In M. J. Lerner and G. Mikula (Eds.), *Entitlement and the Affectional Bond* (pp. 65–88). New York: Plenum Press.

Cohen, R. L. (1982). Perceiving Justice: An Attributional Perspective. In J. Greenberg and R. L. Cohen (Eds.), *Equity and Justice in Social Behavior* (pp. 119–160). New York: Academic Press.

Conlon, D. E., and Fasolo, P. M. (1990). Influence of Speed of Third-Party Intervention and Outcome on Negotiator and Constituent Fairness Judgments. *Academy of Management Journal, 33,* 833–846.

Cook, K. S., and Donnelly, S. (1996). Intergenerational Relations, Inequality, and Social Justice. In L. Montada and M. J. Lerner (Eds.), *Current Societal Concerns about Justice* (pp. 67–84). New York: Plenum Press.

Cook, K. S., and Hegtvedt, K. A. (1983). Distributive Justice, Equity, and Equality. *Annual Review of Sociology, 9,* 217–241.

Cook, K. S., and Yamagashi, T. (1983). Social Determinants of Equity Judgements: The Problem of Multidimensional Input. In D. M. Messick and K. S. Cook (Eds.), *Equity Theory: Psychological and Sociological Perspectives* (pp. 95–126). New York: Praeger.

Cook, K. S., Hegtvedt, K. A., and Yamagashi, T. (1988). Structural Inequality, Legitimation, and Reactions to Inequity in Exchange Networks. In M. Webster, Jr., and M. Foschi (Eds.), *Status Generalization: New Theory and Research* (pp. 291–308). Stanford, CA: Stanford University Press.

Cowell, F. A. (1992). Tax Evasion and Inequity. *Journal of Economic Psychology, 13,* 521–543.

Cowherd, D. M., and Levine, D. I. (1992). Product Quality and Pay Equity Between Lower Level Employees and Top Management: An Investigation of Distributive Justice Theory. *Administrative Science Quarterly, 92,* 302–320.

Cropanzano, R., and Folger, R. (1989). Referent Cognitions and Task Decision Autonomy: Beyond Equity Theory. *Journal of Applied Psychology, 74,* 293–299.

Dancer, L. S., and Gilbert, L. A. (1993). Spouses' Family Work Participation and Its Relation to Wives' Occupational Level. *Sex Roles, 28,* 127–145.

Davidson, B. (1984). A Test of Equity Theory for Marital Adjustment. *Social Psychology Quarterly, 47,* 36–42.

Dawes, R., and Thaler, R. H. (1988). Anomalies: Cooperation. *Journal of Economic Perspectives, 2,* 187–197.

Della Fave, R. (1980). The Meek Shall Not Inherit the Earth. *American Sociological Review, 45,* 955–971.

Desmarais, S., and Lerner, M. J. (1989). A New Look at Equity and Outcomes as Determinants of Satisfaction in Close Personal Relationships. *Social Justice Research, 3,* 105–119.

Desmarais, S., and Lerner, M. J. (1994). Entitlements in Close Relationships: A Justice-Motive Analysis. In M. J. Lerner and G. Mikula (Eds.), *Entitlement and the Affectional Bond* (pp. 43–63). New York: Plenum Press.

Elliot, G. C., and Meeker, B. F. (1984). Modifiers of the Equity Effect: Group Outcome and Causes for Individual Performance. *Journal of Personality and Social Psychology, 46,* 586–597.

Elster, J. (1992). *Local Justice: How Institutions Allocate Scarce Goods and Necessary Burdens.* London: Cambridge University Press.

Feather, N. T. (1994). Human Values and Their Relation to Justice. *Journal of Social Issues, 50,* 129–151.

Feldman, M. D., Barbaresi, W., and Caiola, V. (1983). Physical Stigma as a Variable in Perceptions of Equity. *Representative Research in Social Psychology, 13,* 46–53.

Felmlee, D., Sprecher, S., and Bassin, E. (1990). The Dissolution of Intimate Relationships: A Hazard Model. *Social Psychology Quarterly, 53,* 13–30.

Fiske, S. T., and Taylor, S. E. (1991). *Social Cognition.* New York: McGraw–Hill.

Folger, R. (1986). Rethinking Equity Theory: A Referent Cognition Model. In H. Bierhoff, R. L. Cohen, and J. Greenberg (Eds.),*Justice in Social Relations* (pp. 145–163). New York: Plenum Press.

Folger, R., and Konovsky, M. A. (1989). Effects of Procedural and Distributive Justice on Reactions to Pay Raise Decisions. *Academy of Management Journal, 32,* 115–130.

Folger, R., and Martin, C. (1986). Relative Deprivation and Referent Cognitions: Distributive and Procedural Justice Effects. *Journal of Experimental Social Psychology, 22,* 531–546.

Fryxell, G. E., and Gordon, M. E. (1989). Workplace Justice and Job Satisfaction as Predictors of Satisfaction with Union and Management. *Academy of Management Journal, 32,* 851–866.

Gill, D. G., Ingman, S. R., and Campbell, J. (1991). Health Care Provision and Distributive Justice: End Stage Renal Disease and the Elderly in Britain and America. *Social Science and Medicine, 32,* 565–577.

Glass, J., and Fujimoto, T. (1994). Housework, Paid Work, and Depression among Husbands and Wives. *Journal of Health and Social Behavior, 35,* 179–191.

Gordon, M. E., and Bowlby, R. L. (1988). Propositions about Grievance Settlements: Finally, Consultation with Grievants. *Personnel Psychology, 41*, 107–123.

Gordon, M. E., and Fryxell, G. E. (1989). Voluntariness of Association as a Moderator of the Importance of Procedural and Distributive Justice. *Journal of Applied Social Psychology, 19*, 993–1009.

Gray-Little, B., and Teddlie, C. B. (1978). Racial Differences in Children's Responses to Inequity. *Journal of Applied Social Psychology, 8*, 107–116.

Greenberg, J. (1986). Differential Intolerance for Inequity from Organizational and Individual Agents. *Journal of Applied Social Psychology, 16*, 191–196.

Greenberg, J. (1988). Equity and Workplace Status: A Field Experiment. *Journal of Applied Psychology, 73*, 606–613.

Greenberg, J. (1989). Cognitive Reevaluation of Outcomes in Response to Underpayment Inequity. *Academy of Management Journal, 32*, 174–184.

Greenberg, J. (1990a). Employee Theft as a Reaction to Underpayment Inequity: The Hidden Cost of Pay Cuts. *Journal of Applied Psychology, 75*, 561–568.

Greenberg, J. (1990b). Organizational Justice: Yesterday, Today, and Tomorrow. *Journal of Management, 16*, 399–432.

Greenberg, J. (1993). Stealing in the Name of Justice: Informational and Interpersonal Moderators of Theft Reactions to Underpayment Inequity. *Organizational Behavior and Human Decision Processes, 54*, 81–103.

Greenstein, T. N. (1996). Gender Ideology and Perceptions of the Fairness of the Division of Household Labor: Effects on Marital Quality. *Social Forces, 74*, 1029–1042.

Griffith, W. I. (1989). The Allocation of Negative Outcomes. *Advances in Group Processes, 6*, 107–138.

Griffith, W. I., and Sell, J. (1988). The Effects of Competition on Allocators' Preferences for Contributive and Retributive Justice Rules. *European Journal of Social Psychology, 18*, 443–455.

Haayry, M., and Haayry, H. (1990). Health Care as a Right, Fairness and Medical Resources. *Bioethics, 4*, 1–21.

Hammock, G. S., Rosen, S., Richardson, D. R., and Bernstein, S. (1989). Aggression as Equity Restoration. *Journal of Research in Personality, 23*, 398–409.

Harder, J. W. (1991). Equity Theory Versus Expectancy Theory: The Case of Major League Baseball Free Agents. *Journal of Applied Psychology, 76*, 458–464.

Harris, R. J., and Joyce, M. A. (1980). What's Fair? It Depends on How You Phrase the Question. *Journal of Personality and Social Psychology, 38*, 165–179.

Hassebrauck, M. (1986). Ratings of Distress as a Function of Degree and Kind of Inequity. *Journal of Social Psychology, 126*, 269–270.

Hassebrauck, M. (1987). The Influence of Misattributions on Reactions to Inequity: Towards a Further Understanding of Inequity. *European Journal of Social Psychology, 17*, 295–304.

Hatfield, E., Utne, M. K., and Traupmann, J. (1979). Equity Theory and Intimate Relationships. In R. L. Burgess and T. L. Huston (Eds.), *Social Exchange in Developing Relationships* (pp. 99–133). New York: Academic Press.

Headley, B. (1991). Distributive Justice and Occupational Incomes: Perceptions of Justice Determine Perceptions of Fact. *British Journal of Sociology, 42*, 581–596.

Hegtvedt, K. A. (1987). When Rewards Are Scarce: Equal or Equitable Distributions? *Social Forces, 66*, 183–207.

Hegtvedt, K. A. (1990). The Effects of Relationship Structure on Emotional Responses to Inequity. *Social Psychology Quarterly, 53*, 214–228.

Hegtvedt, K. A., and Cook, K. S. (1987). The Role of Justice in Conflict Situations. In E. J. Lawler and B. Markovsky (Eds.), *Advances in Group Processes* (Vol. 4, pp. 109–136). Greenwich, CT: JAI Press.

Hegtvedt, K. A., Thompson, K. A., and Cook, K. S. (1993). Power and Equity: What Counts in Attributions for Exchange Outcomes? *Social Psychology Quarterly, 56*, 100–119.

Hofstede, G. (1984). *Culture's Consequences: International Differences in Work-Related Values*. Thousand Oaks, CA: Sage.

Homans, G. C. (1961). *Social Behavior: Its Elementary Forms*. New York: Harcourt Brace Javanovich.

Hook, J. G. (1982). Development of Equity and Altruism in Judgement of Reward and Damage Allocation. *Developmental Psychology, 18*, 825–834.

Hook, J. G., and Cook, T. D. (1979). Equity Theory and the Cognitive Ability of Children. *Psychological Bulletin, 86*, 429–445.

Hunt, J. M., and Kernan, J. B. (1991). Consumer Reaction to Inequitable Exchange: The Role of Causal Inferences. *Journal of Social Psychology, 131*, 685–696.

Huseman, R. C., Hatfield, J. D., and Miles, E. W. (1987). A New Perspective on Equity Theory: The Equity Sensitivity Construct. *Academy of Management Review, 12*, 222–234.

Jackson, L. A. (1987). Gender and Distributive Justice: The Influence of Gender-Related Characteristics on Allocations. *Sex Roles, 17*, 73–91.

Jackson, L. A. (1989). Relative Deprivation and the Gender Wage Gap. *Journal of Social Issues, 45*, 117–133.

Jasso, G. (1980). A New Theory of Distributive Justice. *American Sociological Review*, *45*, 3–32.

Jasso, G. (1983). Fairness of Individual Rewards and Fairness of the Reward Distribution: Specifying the Inconsistency between Micro and Macro Principles of Justice. *Social Psychology Quarterly*, *46*, 185–199.

Jasso, G. (1990). Methods for the Theoretical and Empirical Analysis of Comparison Processes. *Sociological Methodology*, *20*, 369–419.

Jasso, G. (1993). Building the Theory of Comparison Processes: Construction of Postulates and Derivation of Predictions. In J. Berger and M. Zelditch, Jr. (Eds.), *Theoretical Research Programs: Studies in the Growth of Theories* (pp. 212–264). Stanford, CA: Stanford University Press.

Jasso, G., and Wegener, B. (1997). Methods for Empirical Justice Analysis: Part 1. Framework, Models, and Quantities. *Social Justice Research*, *4*, 393–430.

Jecker, N. S., and Berg, A. O. (1992). Allocating Medical Resources in Rural America: Alternative Perceptions of Justice. *Social Science and Medicine*, *34*, 467–474.

Kahn, A., Nelson, R. E., and Gaeddert, W. P. (1980). Sex of Subject and Sex Composition of the Group as Determinants of Reward Allocation. *Journal of Personality and Social Psychology*, *38*, 737–750.

Karambayya, R., and Brett, J. M. (1989). Managers Handling Disputes: Third Party Roles and Perceptions of Fairness. *Academy of Management Journal*, *32*, 687–704.

Kayser, E., and Lamm, H. (1980). Input Integration and Input Weighting on Allocations of Gains and Losses. *European Journal of Social Psychology*, *10*, 1–15.

Kayser, E., and Lamm, H. (1981). Causal Explanation of Performance Differences and Allocations Among Friends. *Journal of Social Psychology*, *115*, 73–81.

Keil, L. (1986). Rules, Reciprocity, and Rewards: A Developmental Study of Resource Allocation in Social Interaction. *Journal of Experimental Social Psychology*, *22*, 419–435.

Kim, K. I., Park, H.-J., and Suzuki, N. (1990). Reward Allocations in the United States, Japan, and Korea: A Comparison of Individualistic and Collectivistic Cultures. *Academy of Management Journal*, *33*, 188–198.

King, W. C., Miles, E. W., and Day, D. D. (1993). A Test and Refinement of the Equity Sensitivity Construct. *Journal of Organizational Behavior*, *14*, 301–317.

Kinsey, K. A., Grasmick, H. G., and Smith, K. W. (1991). Framing Justice: Taxpayer Evaluations of Personal Tax Burdens. *Law and Society Review*, *25*, 845–873.

Kluegel, J. R., and Smith, E. R. (1986). *Beliefs about Inequality*. New York: Aldine.

Kluegel, J. R., Mason, D. S., and Wegener, B. (Eds.). (1995). *Social Justice and Political Change: Public Opinion in Capitalist and Post-Communist States*. New York: Aldine.

Kuhse, H., and Singer, P. (1988). Age and the Allocation of Medical Resources. *Journal of Medicine and Philosophy*, *13*, 101–116.

Kwon, S. K., and Cummings, M. L. (1994). Role of Self-esteem in Resolving Inequity. *Psychological Reports*, *75*, 95–111.

Lamm, H., and Schwinger, T. (1980). Norms Concerning Distributive Justice: Are Needs Taken into Consideration in Allocation Decisions? *Social Psychology Quarterly*, *43*, 425–429.

Lamm, H., and Schwinger, T. (1983). Need Consideration in Allocation Decisions: Is It Just? *Journal of Social Psychology*, *119*, 205–209.

Lamm, H., Kayser, E., and Schanz, V. (1983). An Attributional Analysis of Interpersonal Justice: Ability and Effort as Inputs of the Allocation of Gain and Loss. *Journal of Social Psychology*, *119*, 269–281.

Lawler, E. J., and Ford, R. (1995). Bargaining. In K. Cook, G. Fine, and J. House (Eds.), *Sociological Perspectives on Social Psychology* (pp. 236–256). Boston: Allyn & Bacon.

Lawler, E. J., and Thompson, M. E. (1978). Impact of Leader Responsibility for Inequity on Subordinate Revolts. *Social Psychology*, *41*, 265–268.

Lennon, M. C., and Rosenfield, S. (1994). Relative Fairness and the Division of Housework: The Importance of Options. *American Journal of Sociology*, *100*, 506–531.

Lerner, M. J. (1975). The Justice Motive in Social Behavior: An Introduction. *Journal of Social Issues*, *31*, 1–19.

Lerner, M. J. (1981). The Justice Motive in Human Relations: Some Thoughts on What We Know and Need to Know about Justice. In J. Lerner and S. C. Lerner (Eds.), *The Justice Motive in Social Behavior* (pp. 11–35). New York: Plenum Press.

Leung, K., and Bond, M. H. (1984). The Impact of Cultural Collectivism on Reward Allocation. *Journal of Personality and Social Psychology*, *47*, 793–804.

Leung, K., and Park, H. J. (1986). Effects of Interactional Goal on Choice of Allocation Rule: A Cross-National Study. *Organizational Behavior and Human Decision Processes*, *37*, 111–120.

Leventhal, G. S. (1976). Fairness in Social Relation. In J. W. Thibaut, J. T. Spence, and R. C. Carson (Eds.), *Contemporary Topics in Social Psychology* (pp. 211–239). Morristown, NJ: General Learning Press.

Leventhal, G. S., Karuza, J., Jr., and Fry, W. R. (1980). Beyond Fairness: A Theory of Allocation Preferences. In G. Mikula (Ed.), *Justice and Social Interaction* (pp. 167–208). Berlin: Springer-Verlag.

Lind, A., and Tyler, T. R. (1988). *The Social Psychology of Procedural Justice*. New York: Plenum Press.

Lujansky, H., and Mikula, G. (1983). Can Equity Theory Explain the Quality and Stability of Romantic Relationships? *Journal of Social Psychology*, *22*, 101–112.

Major, B., and Adams, J. B. (1983). Role of Gender Interpersonal Orientation and Self Presentation in Distributive Justice Behavior. *Journal of Personality and Social Psychology*, *45*, 598–608.

Major, B., and Adams, J. B. (1984). Situational Moderators of Gender Differences in Reward Allocation. *Sex Roles*, *11*, 869–880.

Major, B., and Deaux, K. (1982). Individual Differences in Justice Behavior. In J. Greenberg and R. L. Cohen (Eds.), *Equity and Justice in Social Behavior* (pp. 43–76). New York: Plenum Press.

Major, B., Bylsma, W. H., and Cozzarelli, C. (1989). Gender Differences in Distributive Justice Preferences: The Impact of Domain. *Sex Roles*, *21*, 487–497.

Marin, G. (1985). The Preference of Equity When Judging the Attractiveness and Fairness of an Allocator: The Role of the Familiarity and Culture. *Journal of Social Psychology*, *125*, 543–549.

Markovsky, B. (1985). Toward a Multilevel Distributive Justice Theory. *American Sociological Review*, *50*, 822–839.

Markovsky, B. (1988). Injustice and Arousal. *Social Justice Research*, *2*, 223–233.

Martin, M. W., and Sell, J. (1986). Rejection of Authority: The Importance of Type of Distribution Rule and Extent of Benefit. *Social Science Quarterly*, *67*, 855–868.

McGullicuddy-DeLisi, A. V., Watlang, C., and Vincher, A. J. (1994). The Effect of Relationship on Children's Distributive Justice Reasoning. *Child Development*, *65*, 1694–1700.

Mechanic, D. (Ed.). (1989). *Painful Choices: Research and Essays on Health Care*. New Brunswick, NJ: Transaction Publishers.

Meeker, B. F., and Elliott, G. C. (1987). Counting the Costs: Equity and the Allocation of Negative Group Products. *Social Psychology Quarterly*, *50*, 7–15.

Meeker, B. F., and Leik, R. K. (1995). Experimentation in Sociological Social Psychology. In K. S. Cook, G. A. Fine, and J. s. House (Eds.), *Sociological Perspectives on Social Psychology* (pp. 630–649). Boston: Allyn & Bacon.

Meindl, J. R. (1989). Managing to Be Fair: An Exploration of Values, Motives, and Leadership. *Administrative Science Quarterly*, *34*, 252–276.

Messé, L. A., Hymes, R. W., and MacCoun, R. J. (1986). Group Categorization and Distributive Justice Decisions. In H. Bierhoff, R. L. Cohen, and J. Greenberg (Eds.), *Social Theory and Social Structure* (pp. 227–248). New York: Plenum Press.

Messick, D. M. (1993). Equality as a Decision Heuristic. In B. A. Mellers and J. Baron (Eds.), *Psychological Perspectives on Justice: Theory and Applications* (pp. 11–31). London: Cambridge University Press.

Messick, D. M., and Allison, S. T. (1987). Accepting Unfairness: Outcomes and Attributions. Special Issue: Procedural Justice. *Representative Research in Social Psychology*, *17*, 39–51.

Messick, D. M., and Sentis, K. P. (1979). Fairness and Preference. *Journal of Experimental Social Psychology*, *15*, 418–434.

Michaels, J., Edwards, J. N., and Acock, A. C. (1984). Satisfaction in Intimate Relationships as a Function of Inequality, Inequity, and Outcomes. *Social Psychology Quarterly*, *47*, 347–357.

Mikula, G., and Lerner, M. J. (1994). Justice in Close Relationships: An Introduction. In M. J. Lerner and G. Mikula (Eds.), *Entitlement and the Affectional Bond* (pp. 1–9). New York: Plenum Press.

Miles, E. W., Hatfield, J. D., and Huseman, R. C. (1989). The Equity Sensitivity Construct: Potential Implications for Worker Performance. *Journal of Management*, *15*, 581–588.

Mitchell, G., Tetlock, P. E., Mellers, B. A., and Ordóñez, L. D. (1993). Judgments of Social Justice: Compromises Between Equality and Efficiency. *Journal of Personality and Social Psychology*, *65*, 629–639.

Moore, C. F., Hembree, S. E., and Enright, R. D. (1993). The Unfolding of Justice: A Developmental Perspective on Reward Allocation. In B. A. Mellers and J. Baron (Eds.), *Psychological Perspectives on Justice: Theory and Applications* (pp. 183–204). London: Cambridge University Press.

Moorman, R. H. (1991). Relationship between Organizational Justice and Organizational Citizenship Behaviors: Do Fairness Perceptions Influence Employee Citizenship? *Journal of Applied Psychology*, *76*, 845–855.

Mowday, R. (1987). Equity Theory Predictions of Behavior in Organizations. In R. M. Steers and L. W. Porter *Motivation and Work Behavior* (pp. 89–110). New York: McGraw–Hill.

Nadkarni, D. V., Lundgren, D., and Burlew, A. K. (1991). Gender Differences in Self-Depriving Behavior as a Reaction to Extreme Inequity. *Journal of Social Behavior and Personality*, *6*, 105–117.

Ng, S. H. (1984). Intergroup Allocation Bias Before and After Group Discussion. *Journal of Social Psychology*, *124*, 95–103.

Ng, S. H. (1986). Equity, Intergroup Bias, and Interpersonal Bias in Reward Allocation. *European Journal of Social Psychology, 16*, 239–255.

Ordóñez, L., and Mellers, B. (1993). Trade-offs in Fairness and Preference Judgments. In B. A. Mellers and J. Baron (Eds.), *Psychological Perspectives on Justice: Theory and Applications* (pp. 138–154). London: Cambridge University Press.

Orne, M. (1962). On the Social Psychology of the Psychological Experiment. *American Psychologist, 17*, 776–783.

Patrick, S. L., and Jackson, J. J. (1991). Further Examination of the Equity Sensitivity Construct. *Perceptual and Motor Skills, 73*, 1091–1106.

Pereira, J. (1993). What Does Equity in Health Mean? *Journal of Social Policy, 22*, 19–48.

Peterson, C. C. (1990). Husbands' and Wives' Perceptions of Marital Fairness across the Family Life Cycle. *International Journal of Aging and Human Development, 31*, 179–188.

Platow, M. J., McClintock, C. G., and Liebrand, W. B. (1990). Predicting Intergroup Fairness and Ingroup Bias in the Minimal Group Paradigm. *European Journal of Social Psychology, 20*, 221–239.

Prentice, D. A., and Crosby, F. (1987). The Importance of Context for Assessing Deserving. In J. C. Masters and W. P. Smith (Eds.), *Social Comparison, Social Justice, and Relative Deprivation* (pp. 165–182). Hillsdale, NJ: Erlbaum.

Prins, K. S., Buunk, B. P., and VanYperen, N. W. (1993). Equity, Normative Disapproval and Extramarital Relationships. *Journal of Social and Personal Relationships, 10*, 39–53.

Randall, C. S., and Mueller, C. W. (1995). Extensions of Justice Theory: Justice Evaluations and Employees' Reactions in a Natural Setting. *Social Psychology Quarterly, 58*, 178–194.

Rawls, J. (1971). *A Theory of Justice*. Cambridge, MA: Harvard University Press.

Reis, H. T. (1981). Self Presentation and Distributive Justice. In J. J. Tedeschi (Ed.), *Impression Management Theory and Social Psychological Theory* (pp. 269–291). New York: Academic Press.

Reis, H. T. (1986). Levels of Interest in the Study of Interpersonal Justice. *Justice in Social Relations*. 187–210.

Reis, H. T., and Burns, L. B. (1982). The Salience of the Self in Responses to Inequity. *Journal of Experimental Social Psychology, 18*, 464–475.

Reis, H. T., and Jackson, L. A. (1981). Sex Differences in Reward Allocation: Subjects, Partners, and Tasks. *Journal of Personality and Social Psychology, 40*, 465–478.

Robinson, J., and Spitze, G. (1992). Whistle While You Work: The Effect of Household Task Performance on Women's and Men's Well-being. *Social Science Quarterly, 73*, 844–861.

Rusbult, C. E., Lowery, D., Hubbard, M. L., Maravankin, O. J., and Neises, M. (1988). The Impact of Employee Mobility and Employee Performance on the Allocation of Rewards Under Conditions of Constraint. *Journal of Personality and Social Psychology, 54*, 605–615.

Sagan, K., Pondel, M., and Wittig, M. A. (1981). The Effect of Anticipated Future Interaction on Reward Allocation in Same and Opposite Sex Dyads. *Journal of Personality, 49*, 438–449.

Samuelson, C. D., and Allison, S. T. (1994). Cognitive Factors Affecting the Use of Social Decision Heuristics in Resource-Sharing Tasks. *Organizational Behavior and Human Decision Processes, 58*, 1–27.

Schafer, R. B. (1988). Equity/Inequity and Self-esteem: A Reassessment. *Psychological Reports, 63*, 637–638.

Schafer, R. B., and Keith, P. M. (1981). Equity in Marital Roles across the Family Life Cycle. *Journal of Marriage and the Family, 43*, 359–367.

Schwinger, T. (1980). Just Allocation of Goods: Decisions Among Three Principles. In G. Mikula (Ed.), *Justice and Social Interaction* (pp. 95–125). Berlin: Springer-Verlag.

Schwinger, T., and Lamm, H. (1981). Justice Norms and Allocation Decisions: Need Consideration as a Function of Resource Adequacy for Complete Need Satisfaction, Recipients' Contributions, and Recipients' Interpersonal Attraction. *Social Behavior and Personality, 9*, 235–241.

Sharpley, C. F. (1991). Giving a Reason for Unfairness: Effects of Rationale on Australian Students' Performances Within an Implicit Reward Situation. *International Journal of Psychology, 26*, 71–81.

Sheplak, N. (1987). The Role of Self-explanations and Self-evaluations in Legitimating Inequality. *American Sociological Review, 52*, 495–503.

Sheppard, B. H., and Lewicki, R. J. (1987). Toward General Principles of Managerial Fairness. *Social Justice Research, 1*, 161–176.

Sigelman, C. K., and Waitzman, K. A. (1991). The Development of Distributive Justice Orientations: Contextual Influences on Children's Resource Allocations. *Child Development, 62*, 1367–1378.

Skitka, L. J., and Tetlock, P. E. (1992). Allocating Scarce Resources: A Contingency Model of Distributive Justice. *Journal of Experimental Social Psychology, 28*, 491–522.

Smith, D., and Krantz, M. (1981). The Effect of Recipients' Relative Age and Productivity on Children's Reward Allocation. *Journal of Genetic Psychology, 139*, 257–265.

Sprecher, S. (1986). The Relationship between Inequity and Emotions in Close Relationships. *Social Psychology Quarterly*, *49*, 309–321.

Sprecher, S. (1988). Investment Model, Equity, and Social Support Determinants of Relationship Commitment. *Social Psychology Quarterly*, *51*, 318–328.

Sprecher, S. (1992). How Men and Women Expect to Feel and Behave in Response to Inequity in Close Relations. *Social Psychology Quarterly*, *55*, 57–69.

Sprecher, S., and Schwartz, P. (1994). Equity and Balance in the Exchange of Contributions in Close Relationships. In M. J. Lerner and G. Mikula (Eds.), *Entitlement and the Affectional Bond* (pp. 11–41). New York: Plenum Press.

Stake, J. E. (1983). Factors in Reward Distribution: Allocator Motive, Gender, and Protestant Ethic Endorsement. *Journal of Personality and Social Psychology*, *44*, 410–418.

Stake, J. E. (1985). Exploring the Basis of Sex Differences in Third-Party Allocations. *Journal of Personality and Social Psychology*, *48*, 1621–1629.

Stepina, L. P., and Perrewe, P. L. (1987). The Impact of Inequity on Task Satisfaction Internal Motivation, and Perceptions of Job Characteristics. *Journal of Social Behavior and Personality*, *2*, 117–125.

Stolte, J. F. (1983). The Legitimation of Structural Inequality: Reformulation and Test of the Self-Evaluation Argument. *American Sociological Review*, *48*, 331–342.

Sweeney, P. D. (1990). Distributive Justice and Pay Satisfaction: A Field Test of an Equity Theory Prediction. *Journal of Business and Psychology*, *4*, 329–341.

Takenishi, M. (1988). Unfair Allocation in a Competitive Setting: A Self-Presentational Perspective. *Japanese Psychological Research*, *30*, 122–131.

Tetlock, P. E., and Mitchell, G. (1993). Liberal and Conservative Approaches to Justice: Conflicting Psychological Portraits. In A. Mellers and J. Baron (Eds.), *Psychological Perspectives on Justice: Theory and Applications* (pp. 234–255). London: Cambridge University Press.

Thibaut, J., and Walker, W. (1975). *Procedural Justice: A Psychological Analysis*. Hillsdale, NJ: Erlbaum.

Thompson, L. (1991). Family Work: Women's Sense of Fairness. *Journal of Family Issues*, *2*, 181–196.

Tilly, C. (1978). *From Mobilization to Revolution*. New York: McGraw–Hill.

Tindale, S. R., and Davis, J. H. (1985). Individual and Group Reward Allocation Decisions in Two Situational Contexts: Effects of Relative Need and Performance. *Journal of Personality and Social Psychology*, *48*, 1148–1161.

Törnblom, K. Y. (1977). Distributive Justice: Typology and Propositions. *Human Relations*, *31*, 1–24.

Törnblom, K. Y. (1988). Positive and Negative Allocations: A Typology and Model of Conflicting Justice Principles. In E. J. Lawler and B. Markovsky (Eds.), *Advances in Group Processes* (Vol. 5, pp. 141–168). Greenwich, CT: JAI Press.

Törnblom, K. Y., and Jonsson, D. R. (1985). Subrules of the Equality and Contributions Principles: Their Perceived Fairness in Contribution and Retribution. *Social Psychology Quarterly*, *48*, 249–269.

Towson, S. M., Lerner, M. J., and DeCarufel, A. (1981). Justice Rules of Ingroup Loyalties: The Effects of Competition on Children's Allocation Behavior. *Personality and Social Psychology Bulletin*, *7*, 697–700.

Traupmann, J., and Hatfield, E. (1983). How Important is Marital Fairness over the Lifespan? *International Journal of Aging and Human Development*, *17*, 89–101.

Traupmann, J., Hatfield, E., and Wexler, P. (1983). Equity and Sexual Satisfaction in Dating Couples. *British Journal of Social Psychology*, *22*, 33–40.

Tyler, T. R. (1990). *Why People Obey the Law*. New Haven, CT: Yale University Press.

Tyler, T., and Dawes, R. M. (1993). Fairness in Groups: Comparing the Self-interest and Social Identity Perspectives. In B. A. Mellers and J. Baron (Eds.), *Psychological Perspectives on Justice: Theory and Applications* (pp. 87–108). London: Cambridge University Press.

Tyler, T. R., and Griffin. (1991). The Influence of Decision Makers' Goals on their Concerns about Procedural Justice. *Journal of Applied Social Psychology*, *21*, 1629–1658.

Tyler, T. R., and McGraw, K. M. (1986). Ideology and the Interpretation of Personal Experience: Procedural Justice and Political Quiescence. *Journal of Social Issues*, *42*, 115–128.

Tyler, T. R., Boeckmann, R. J., Smith, H. J., and Huo, Y. J. (1997). *Social Justice in a Diverse Society*. Boulder, CO: Westview Press.

Utne, M. K., and Kidd, R. F. (1980). Equity and Attribution. In G. Mikula (Ed.), *Justice and Social Interaction* (pp. 63–93). Berlin: Springer-Verlag.

Van Dijk, E., and Wilke, E. A. (1993). Differential Interests, Equity, and Good Provision. *Journal of Experimental Social Psychology*, *29*, 1–16.

VanYperen, N. W., and Buunk, B. P. (1991). Sex-Role Attitudes, Social Comparison and Relationship Satisfaction. *Social Psychology Quarterly*, *54*, 169–180.

VanYperen, N. W., and Buunk, B. P. (1994). Social Comparison and Social Exchange in Marital Relationships. In M. J. Lerner and G. Mikula (Eds.), *Entitlement and the Affectional Bond* (pp. 89–115). New York: Plenum Press.

Vecchio, R. P. (1984). Models of Psychological Inequity. *Organizational Behavior and Human Performance*, *34*, 266–282.

Vecchio, R. P., and Terborg, J. R. (1987). Salary Increment Allocation and Individual Differences. *Journal of Occupational Behavior*, *8*, 37–43.

Wagstaff, G. F., Huggins, J. P., and Perfect, T. J. (1993). Equity, Equality, and Need in the Adult Family. *Journal of Social Psychology*, *133*, 439–443.

Walker, H. A., Rogers, L., and Zelditch, M., Jr. (1988). Legitimacy and Collective Action: A Research Note. *Social Forces*, *67*, 216–228.

Walker, I. (1989). Effects of Sex, Nationality, and Political Beliefs on Allocation Preferences. *Australian Journal of Psychology*, *41*, 49–59.

Walster, E., Walster, G. W., and Berscheid, E. (1978a). *Equity: Theory and Research*. Boston: Allyn & Bacon.

Walster, E., Walster, G. W., and Traupmann, J. (1978b). Equity and Premarital Sex. *Journal of Personality*, *3*, 82–92.

Walster, E., Traupmann, J., and Walster, G. W. (1978c). Equity and Extramarital Sexuality. *Archives of Sexual Behavior*, *7*, 127–141.

Watts, B. L., Messé, L. A., and Vallacher, R. R. (1982). Toward Understanding Sex Differences in Pay Allocation: Agency, Communion, and Reward Distribution Behavior. *Sex Roles*, *8*, 1175–1187.

Winer, B. J. (1971). *Statistical Principles in Experimental Design*. New York: McGraw–Hill.

Wittig, M. A., Marks, G., and Jones, G. A. (1981). Luck versus Effort Attributions: Effects on Reward Allocations to Self and Other. *Personality and Social Psychology Bulletin*, *7*, 71–78.

Zelditch, M., Jr. (1969). Can You Really Study an Army in the Laboratory? In A. Etzioni (Ed.), *Complex Organizations* (pp. 528–539). New York: Holt, Rinehart & Winston.

Zelditch, M., Jr., and Ford, J. B. (1994). Uncertainty, Potential Power, and Nondecisions. *Social Psychology Quarterly*, *57*, 64–73.

Zinser, O., Starnes, D. M., and Wild, H. D. (1991). The Effect of Need on the Allocation Behavior of Children. *Journal of Genetic Psychology*, *152*, 35–46.

III

The Relationship among Justice Dimensions

5

Paternalism, Power, and Respect in Lawyer–Client Relations

William L. F. Felstiner and Ben Pettit

A. INTRODUCTION

Serious academic attention to lawyers has proceeded down two paths. One explores their social origins, practice settings, financial returns, efforts at organizing the profession and defending its territory, and treatment of women and minority colleagues. Almost all the great sociolegal analyses of American lawyers can be found in this strand—Abel (1989), Heinz and Laumann (1982), Nelson (1988), Carlin (1962, 1966), Abbott (1989), Halliday (1987), Powell (1988), Landon (1990), Galanter and Palay (1991), and Hagan and Kay (1995). The other path examines the relationship of lawyers to their clients. This area of research is relatively undeveloped in the sociolegal literature; it is more the domain of legal academics, particularly clinical law teachers, who prefer normative to empirical inquiry.

This chapter seeks in small measure to redress that imbalance by summarizing the research that is centrally concerned with the lawyer–client relationship. It does so by describing work in three problem areas: (1) *paternalism* or the question of what ought to be the contours of that relationship as it affects decision making and agenda setting, (2) *the actuality of power* or who within the relationship appears to be in charge, and (3) *the neglect of clients by lawyers* or the possible consequences of the existing distribution of power.

We can think of lawyer–client relations in both substantive and procedural terms. Substantively, the traditional position is that lawyers should, to some extent, counsel clients to do the right thing. Lawyers are counsel for the situation who transform client objectives into socially acceptable goals. They are statespersons as well as advocates, and mediate between their clients' questionable objectives and the social good. They refuse to do the clients' most destructive and antisocial bidding, even if it is technically legal. The obverse of this traditional

William L. F. Felstiner • Cardiff University Law School, Cardiff, United Kingdom, and Law and Society Program, University of California, Santa Barbara, Santa Barbara, California 93106. Ben Pettit • Department of Political Science, University of California, Santa Barbara, Santa Barbara, California 93106.

Handbook of Justice Research in Law, edited by Sanders and Hamilton. Kluwer Academic / Plenum Publishers, New York, 2000.

position is the conception of the lawyer as the nonjudgmental tool or agent of the client, serving the client's needs and desires—however selfish they may be—without much regard to broader social and moral consequences. Many practitioners and scholars are concerned that lawyers are increasingly adopting this latter approach to substantive representation.

Procedurally, the concern is with how lawyers treat clients interpersonally. The conception of a healthy lawyer–client relationship envisions the lawyer treating the client well, by being accessible, responsive, empathetic, promptly attentive, intelligible, and motivated by professional values rather than by financial gain. The procedurally just lawyer treats her clients with respect. Again, many believe that a substantial proportion of lawyer–client relationships fall short of this vision of procedural well-being; they suspect that too many lawyers treat their clients with disrespect.

Such issues relate to the distribution of power in the lawyer–client relationship. Clearly these concerns are more salient to the extent that the lawyer holds power over the client. Substantively, a lawyer without much power vis-à-vis a client presumably is less able to influence the client to do the right thing (however conceived), and is more likely to be used by the client as an instrument to further the client's uninfluenced goals. Procedurally, lawyers will likely have less freedom to treat powerful clients with disrespect. The next section discusses the literature on paternalism in the lawyer–client relationship and how it relates to the issue of distribution of power.

B. PATERNALISM

Scholars who focus on paternalism in the lawyer–client relationship are concerned about lawyers manipulating or coercing clients into doing the lawyer's wishes. Since this concern is more worrisome if the distribution of power in the lawyer–client relationship favors the lawyer, those concerned with paternalism often assume, explicitly or implicitly, that the lawyer holds the more powerful position in the relationship. This section of the chapter examines work on lawyer paternalism. Later sections scrutinize this assumption about the lawyer's position of relative power more closely.

1. What Is Paternalism?

Paternalism has recently received substantial attention from philosophers. Definitions range from the simple and general to the precise and complex. Scholars of the lawyer–client relationship most often stipulate that paternalism "involves the imposing of constraints on an individual's liberty for the purpose of promoting his or her own good" (Thompson, 1980:246). A similar and oft-cited definition is "interference with a person's liberty of action justified by reasons referring exclusively to the welfare, good, happiness, needs, interests or values of the person being coerced" (Dworkin, 1971:108). Paternalism is, in other words, "intervention in another's life for his benefit without regard to his consent" (Kultgen, 1996:63).

In an article that has been called the "first significant challenge to lawyer paternalism" (Tremblay, 1987:522, n29), Wasserstrom criticizes the tendency of lawyers to respond to their clients "in a patronizing, paternalistic fashion ... as though the client were an individual who needed to be looked after and controlled, and to have decisions made for him or her by the lawyer, with as little interference with the lawyer as possible" (Wasserstrom, 1975:22). Luban echoes Wasserstrom's complaint, commenting that "Wasserstrom is not talking merely about the lawyer's attitude, though that is by no means morally irrelevant. He is talking of a lawyer's making decisions for the client that the client should perhaps have the right to make for himself. In this sense, a lawyer can be paternalistic whether or not he has a paternalistic attitude" (Luban, 1981:458).

Strictly defined, the motive for an act of lawyer paternalism is to serve the client's best interests as the lawyer understands them. Thus, intervention to protect or serve the interests of parties other than the client is disloyalty rather than paternalism (see, e.g., Dworkin, 1971:108; Luban, 1981:462; Ellmann, 1987a:773–774; Tremblay, 1987:533; Spiegel, 1979:87). Ellmann suggests that a lawyer might manipulate a client in order "to serve her own interests, to serve her clients' interests as she understands them, or to serve the interests of third parties or society." Technically, only manipulation driven by the second motive constitutes paternalism (Ellmann, 1987a:761, 773).[1] This parsing of lawyer motives is conceptually possible, but empirically difficult, since motives are difficult to determine, since even the actor may not understand his or her motives and since in practice many acts originate in mixed motives.

Many scholars are concerned with forms of lawyer paternalism more subtle than the obvious cases of a lawyer overriding a client's decision or taking decisions out of a client's hands. These subtler forms of paternalism involve lawyers knowingly or unknowingly influencing clients' interests and decisions. Though a client surely has a right to change his conception of his own best interests, there is a risk of the lawyer paternalistically imposing her conception of those interests on an easily influenced client who then adopts the lawyer's conception as his own. Such imposition involves social and psychological pressures on the client to conform and may be unintentional on the lawyer's part. Indeed, such imposition seems unavoidable to a certain extent in the context of any lawyer–client relationship (Simon, 1994:1099).[2] Simon (1991:217) notes that "even where they think of themselves as merely providing information for clients to integrate into their own decisions, lawyers influence clients by a myriad of judgments, conscious or not, about what information to present, how to order it, what to emphasize, and what style and phrasing to adopt." If such epistemic interference with the client is inevitable, then so is epistemic paternalism. A lawyer has to make choices in filtering for the client the informational din of the legal world. The choices that the lawyer makes are, to some extent, inevitably products of the lawyer's values and world-view and of the lawyer's perception of the client's situation, interests, and personal qualities. Simon states that the "Dark Secret of Progressive Lawyering is that effective lawyers cannot avoid making judgments in terms of their own values and influencing their clients to adopt those judgments" (1994:1102).

Some scholars nevertheless claim that substantial and sufficient neutrality is possible (Ellman, 1987a:733–739; Dinerstein, 1990:517; Grosberg, 1989:724–725). Ellmann (1987a:767) suggests that "Binder and Price [authors of the most widely discussed model of the client-centered approach to lawyering] emphasize the risk that even the shadow of the lawyer's advice may sway the client's decision, and this risk is surely a large one. Yet to call this prospect a 'risk' will sometimes be a mistake, for the lawyer's advice may affect the client not by overpowering, but informing him." Dinerstein sums up the dilemma: "almost any choice that the lawyer makes concerning her counseling method is likely to compromise some aspect of the client's autonomy. But while Binder and Price are most concerned about the lawyer who overpowers her client, Ellmann is most troubled by the lawyer's failure to treat the client as the kind of competent individual able to hear professional advice without capitulating to it" (Dinerstein, 1990:568).[3]

Dinerstein adds that "while a lawyer cannot help but influence a client, it may be helpful to consider advice as being on a continuum that ranges from the lawyer saying nothing to the client to the lawyer telling the client what to do. On such a continuum, advice is more interventionist than suggestion but less so than persuasion" (Dinerstein, 1990:569). "Whether persuasion enhances or detracts from client autonomy will depend on a number of circumstances, including the nature of the relationship between lawyer and client, the power difference between them, their values, and the nature of the legal problem.... But given the propensity of lawyers ... to act paternalistically towards their clients, a client-centered model that establishes a presumption against the lawyer's use of persuasion is preferable to one that presumes persuasion is acceptable behavior" (Dinerstein, 1990:517).[4]

The *theoretics of practice* literature presents a constructivist take on paternalism.[5] This literature holds that lawyers tend to approach clients with inflexible preconceptions, and thus impose personal and legal categories on clients and their narratives. In doing so, the lawyer forces the clients to fit such conceptions in a self-fulfilling prolepsis. Essential to this dynamic are "the dominant–subordinate positions of client–lawyer hierarchy" (Alfieri, 1992a:815). Alfieri provides an example in which he describes disability lawyers discursively portraying, and thus constructing, disabled widows as impotent victims, all in the process of doing what the lawyers feel is in the widows' best interests. Such lawyers use

> the formative ideals of disability law: benevolence and discipline. Benevolence describes the shared paternalism of the lawyer and state towards the artifactually dependent and incompetent disabled widow. Discipline characterizes the joint lawyer and state devaluation of the artifactually deviant disabled widow. Both benevolence and discipline rely on discursive practices of victimization.... Ideals that depict disabled widows as dependent, incompetent, or deviant are structure-preserving. Practices that place disabled widows in dependent roles and relationships are context-preserving.... [I]deals that portray disabled widows as independent and competent are structure-transforming. Structure-transforming ideals emancipate the disabled from benevolent and disciplinary constraints. Similarly, practices that permit disabled widows to embrace independent roles and collaborative relationships are context-transforming. Context-transforming practices redefine client roles and reorganize client–state relations. (Alfieri, 1992a:788–792)

> Formed by the ideals of benevolence and discipline, the [victimization] strategy reproduces images of widow dependence, incompetence, and deviance in daily discourse. That discourse inhibits counter narratives of widow autonomy and community. (Alfieri, 1992a:812)

Alfieri says that disability lawyers rationalize their behavior by disavowing "expressions or acts of paternalism and devaluation, preferring instead to stress the widows' natural state of dependence and incompetence or the necessity of portraying claimants in that guise." They justify this portrayal on efficiency grounds and assert that any client resistance to such portrayals is temporary and aberrational (Alfieri, 1992a:812–815).

Most of the theoretics of practice literature deals with poverty law—a type of practice where lawyers are generally from different socioeconomic and educational backgrounds than their clients and in which, on the face of it, lawyers appear to be able to exercise a great deal of power vis-à-vis their clients. The goals of this approach are to find ways to empower clients with respect to their lawyers and the rest of their social environment. Lawyer paternalism disempowers clients—most clearly by taking decision-making power out of their hands, more abstrusely by conditioning clients to a passivity that may carry over to more clearly political arenas,[6] and "critically" by "constructing" clients as anonymous, powerless victims and by helping to preserve contexts and structures that do the same (Alfieri, 1992a; White, 1990a; Cunningham, 1992; Steward, 1993; Simon, 1984, 1994).

2. Why Is Paternalism Objectionable?

The most common objection to lawyer paternalism is that it violates the client's autonomy. "Few scholars dispute the importance of autonomy as a value," though few believe in autonomy as an absolute right (Dinerstein, 1990:514–515), and some even suggest that a lawyer has a right to professional autonomy that must be balanced against the client's autonomy interests (see, e.g., Spiegel 1979:110–112). Dinerstein sums up the basic proautonomy/antipaternalism argument as follows:

> Autonomy, or self-determination, means that a person can choose and act freely, according to her own life plan. There are many possible definitions of autonomy, but the capacity to make choices is a key component of the concept. Recognizing a person's autonomy is essential to according respect to that person; respect for autonomy is a cornerstone of liberal legal theory and of the American political system. It can be justified for its intrinsic value and on utilitarian grounds.
>
> A person's autonomy can be compromised in a number of ways. One such way is through paternalism, which operates in counterpoint to autonomy.... [Paternalistic acts] are problematic precisely because they deny people their fundamental right to make their own decisions in their own ways, even if those decisions could somehow objectively be shown to be wrong. (Dinerstein, 1990:512–514)
>
> [P]aternalism is the denial of autonomy; autonomy is "the value against which paternalism offends." (Dinerstein, 1990:513, n57; quoting Dworkin, 1972:70)

A closely related objection is rooted in normative beliefs about how individuals should be treated in human relationships. Wasserstrom presents this position as follows:

> This criticism focuses upon the fact that the professional often, if not systematically, interacts with the client in both a manipulative and paternalistic fashion. The point is not that the professional is merely dominant within the relationship. Rather, it is that from the professional's point of view the client is seen and responded to more like an object than a human being, and more like a child than an adult. The professional does not, in short, treat the client like a person; the professional does not accord the client the respect that he or she deserves. And these, it is claimed, are without question genuine moral defects in any meaningful human relationship. (Wasserstrom, 1975:19; see also Grosberg, 1989:719)

Others suggest that the client is likely to be more satisfied with nonpaternalistic representation. Procedural justice studies suggest that client satisfaction with an adjudicative process is related to client perception of procedural fairness (Lind and Tyler, 1988). If clients perceive paternalistic representation to limit their participation, they will experience it as less "fair." Thus, regardless of substantive result, paternalism may lead to less-satisfied clients (Resnik, Curtis, and Hensler, 1996:371–372). Hillary, Johnson, and Johnson (1989) report that client opinion of lawyer competence and client satisfaction with a lawyer is negatively correlated with the lawyer's use of coercive power toward the client. And Rhode's assertion that "authoritarian, paternalistic interactions between lawyers and clients often obscure the needs that prompted professional consultation in the first place," suggests that paternalism is likely to adversely affect both client satisfaction and appropriate resolution of the client's problem (Rhode, 1994:50).

3. When Might Paternalism Be Justified?

Some clients may desire paternalism from attorneys. They may trust the attorney's judgment about what is best for them more than their own. Some suggest that clients often do delegate paternalistic authority to their lawyer, implicitly if not explicitly, by the act of retaining the lawyer (see discussion in Spiegel, 1979:77–85, and Ellmann, 1987a:764). Such clients may, in effect, give consent to their attorney to do whatever the attorney thinks is in their best interests. To disregard such a request on grounds that this kind of delegation is not in the client's best interests (perhaps in pursuit of client empowerment or another of the values inherent in the objections to paternalism) would be a paternalistic act in its own right (Ellmann, 1987a:764). But lawyers acting on the basis of such consent may easily exceed its boundaries, especially if that consent is implicit (Ellman, 1987a:765). A key issue is whether the client's consent was given "freely and knowingly" (Ellmann, 1987a:765). Spiegel suggests that many clients enter into agreements for representation without sufficient information about options on the structure of representation, hemmed in by constraints of custom that favor lawyer intervention and in an unequal bargaining position vis-à-vis the attorney in terms of power and status (Spiegel, 1979:79–80).

These factors raise the issue of a client's competence to make decisions (including the decision of consenting to paternalistic control). Tremblay (1987:516, n71), for instance, insists that the question of client competence is crucial for paternalism, "for it is only if [clients] are incompetent that intervention could possibly be justified." The term *incompetence* "is intended to mean inability to arrive at a reasoned decision. A person may be competent for some matters but incompetent for others; the concept is fluid and dynamic" (Tremblay, 1987:536). As Luban points out, autonomy is valued because we want people to be able to make choices about their lives. If a person is incompetent to make choices, than he is no longer an autonomous individual with regard to those choices (Luban, 1981:464–466).[7] Luban describes a "slippery slope" approach to consent that involves "hypothetical consent," or "consent in the subjunctive mood: 'He would want this if he were fully rational' " (Luban, 1981:462–466).

The difficulty in investigating competence is finding a sufficiently flexible measuring stick. If we judge competence to make a decision by looking at the outcomes of the decision process we end up in a tautology. As Luban puts it, "it would clearly be wrong to say something like 'You don't really want that. You just think you do because your decision-making mechanisms are impaired. How do I know? If they weren't impaired you wouldn't want that!' " (Luban, 1981:466).

Most conceptions of competent decision-making privilege notions of instrumental rationality and thoughtful, informed deliberation. Some scholars criticize such conceptions for being artifacts of class, gender, and/or race and thus contributing to the subordination of individuals and groups that make decisions differently (Steward, 1993; White, 1990a:7). Others recognize this dilemma and concede that methods of decision making in which material goals may be sacrificed for other values may be valid (Ellmann, 1987a:729; Luban, 1981:475), but nevertheless favor a form of limited paternalism because lawyers have the responsibility to sensitize clients to the form of rationality generally preferred in U.S. culture. Spiegel (1979:109, n281), on the other hand, has much less faith in lawyers and opposes such a model because lawyers tend to equate decisions with which they disagree with incapacity.

A related concern is the temporary incompetence of a client who is emotionally upset. Some argue that such a condition justifies limited paternalism on the part of the lawyer "aimed at restoring or at least improving the client[s'] decisionmaking capacities ... to make decisions that are truly their own" (Ellmann, 1987a:768; see Sarat and Felstiner, 1995:70). Such interference might take the form of imposing a structure on decision making (Ellmann, 1987a:768), forcing the client to delay making the decision (Spiegel, 1979:83), or referring the client to a mental health professional (Margulies, 1990:228–229; Ellmann, 1987a:768). Ellmann (1987a:769–770) warns against lawyers using such justification to attempt client therapy, a danger he sees lurking in the client-centered approach, which he considers overly manipulative.

Often a client will lack sufficient information and insight to be able to make an informed and competent decision. One response to this dilemma is for the lawyer to provide the needed information and educate the client (Spiegel, 1979:104–110; Ellmann, 1987a:765–766). While Spiegel (1979:110–112) believes the costs of doing so may well be feasible and justified, Ellmann fears the price to be paid "in systemic efficiency, perhaps in lawyers' pleasure in their work and its rewards (and thus perhaps ultimately in the quality of legal services), and surely in the time and cost of legal services for people who would now face arduous educational endeavors in the process of solving the far from academic problems which brought them to a lawyer's office" (Ellmann, 1987a:765–766). Such costs would likely be highest for just those clients who are considered most vulnerable to paternalistic action by attorneys—the under educated poor. Ellmann (1987a:766–767) argues that such a trade-off justifies paternalistic manipulation.

Other commentators suggest that lawyer paternalism is justifiable because a lawyer will often make better decisions for the client than would the client herself. This argument need not deny the value of autonomy, nor that paternalism restricts autonomy. It simply asserts that the trade-off—a loss of present autonomy for a better outcome—is worthwhile. Spiegel terms this the "better results' argument," and states: "From the client's perspective, if delegation of decisions to lawyers produces better results, the assumption that clients consent to professional control becomes more reasonable. From the lawyer's and society's perspectives, proof of better results introduces the possibility of justifying professional decision-making on paternalistic grounds" (Spiegel, 1979:85–86). Dinerstein interprets this argument as suggesting that "if the lawyer acts paternalistically and exercises more power over her client's choices (and over the manner in which the client considers those choices) the client's autonomy will be enhanced." He recognizes, however, that this means violating autonomy now in order to gain autonomy in the future and raises the problem of whether and to what extent autonomy as an end can justify compromised autonomy as a means (Dinerstein, 1990:516, n69).

Spiegel, however, presents two reasons why paternalism might often lead to worse, rather than better, results. "First, although the professional is better equipped to use the relevant information, one who is not completely loyal to his client might not use that information for the client's benefit. Second, the client has superior knowledge of the facts of his case and of the relation between his values and objectives and those facts." As discussed above, Spiegel's first reason is technically not an objection to paternalism, but it does remind us of the need for the client to monitor a possibly incompetent or rogue attorney. Rhode makes the related objection to paternalism that "attorneys accustomed to dominating clients' decisionmaking for 'their own good' may too readily replicate these patterns when it serves practitioners' own interests" (Rhode, 1994:50; see also Tremblay, 1987:554, 583). Spiegel's second reason goes to the heart of the paternalism debate. He suggests that because of communication problems, changing circumstances, subjective and often indeterminate values, and possible professional–client class value biases, a lawyer will be unable to understand his client's true needs and values to the extent adequate to make decisions requiring subtle balancing of such needs and values—decisions that Spiegel believes often arise during representation (Spiegel, 1979:100–104).

Tremblay (1987:524–525) goes further and turns the better results argument on its head—paternalism will likely lead to worse, not better, results for the client. The belief that paternalism will produce better results "assumes that decisions made in the context of legal representation have correct answers.... But predicting legal results is notoriously imprecise [and] ... because choices must be based on values, risk aversion, social and psychological consequences and the like, and not strictly on legal analysis, the client generally is in a superior position to make the 'correct' choice on those fronts."

A more ominous justification given the totalitarian excesses of the twentieth century suggests that a competent and well-informed client may still be ignorant of his own best interests because of a false consciousness, an inadequate "political or moral understanding of the world" (Ellmann, 1987a:770; Kennedy, 1982:572). What is the extent to which a lawyer can justify interfering with client autonomy in order to bring that client to a realization of his "true" interests? How does even the critical lawyer know that she has judged the client's true interests correctly? Simon proposes that the test is whether or not "the client come[s] to share that judgment under conditions which lawyer and client agree are nonhierarchical" (Simon, 1984:488).

This form of paternalism, allowing a lawyer the opportunity to attempt to impose her political and social views on her client for the client's own good, follows from the "critical" project to "politicize discrete cases and the lawyer–client relationship in general" in order to remedy the "fact" that "law is politics by other means; precedent and principles simply mask the exercise of power, and our true natures have been suppressed and distorted by the facts imposed by the prevailing ... ideology" (Eastman, 1995:763). As Simon puts it: "To some extent, the Critical vision merely acknowledges a basic fact of contemporary law practice—that lawyers commonly make, and have to make, judgments in terms of their own moral and political commitments about what their clients' interests are. Its most basic difference from the professional vision is that it sees this fact, not as something to be regretted and minimized, but as the source of the most rewarding and exhilarating potential of practice" (Simon, 1984:489).

Paternalism might be justified if one is so intimately connected to another as to clearly know the other's best interests. Kennedy states that "the basis of paternalism is intersubjective unity of the actor with the other; it is identification and intimate knowledge" (Kennedy, 1982:647).[8] Luban nods to this by suggesting that paternalistic intervention is justifiable when a person's wants conflict with his values, and that intersubjectivity is the key to the knowledge of a person's values (Luban, 1981:466–474).

Simon asserts that "empathy and rapport are no less important for autonomy than for paternalism" (Simon, 1991:222). He suggests that both the autonomy approach and the paternalist approach at bottom represent a melding of objective constructs about typical clients or reasonable decision-making processes with intimate knowledge of specific clients. In order to provide a client with the information needed to make an autonomous decision, a responsible lawyer must make judgments about that particular client's needs and interests. Similar judgments must be made by a responsible paternalist lawyer. Simon writes, "we have no criteria of autonomy entirely independent of our criteria of best interests" (Simon, 1991:226). All such judgments entail attempting to understand the client intersubjectively in a situation where the lawyer is in a position of power. Simon suggests that the autonomy versus paternalism debate is more about lawyer anxiety about being faced with this situation than about anything more substantive.

4. The Origins of Paternalism?

Is paternalism in the lawyer–client relationship inevitable? Many scholars believe that it is and that the cause is located in the tensions of this particular type of principal–agent relationship, one in which the agent has training, expertise, and experience on which the naive principal must rely even though it is her matter, money, and life that are involved (see Luban, 1981:458–460; Tremblay, 1987).

Wasserstrom (1975:16–18) is the original and most vigorous exponent of this view. He finds paternalism rooted in the role-differentiated aspects of the lawyer as professional. He believes that the lawyer–client relationship is inherently unequal because of: (1) the client's dependence on the lawyer's expert knowledge and skill; (2) the inaccessibility of legal language; (3) the difficulty of assessing lawyer performance and the resulting reduction in lawyer incentives to respond to client needs; (4) the lawyer's perception that the client is too involved to muster the requisite objectivity to pursue her own best interests effectively; and (5) the impression created in law school that lawyers are special and somehow better than their clients.

Wasserstrom's case so far is one about control rather than about paternalism or how that control is exploited. However, he takes the next step and specifies "the forces that make the [lawyer–client] relationship a paternalistic one" (1975:21–22). Lawyers believe they know more than most people because they are members of a prestigious group with highly trained intellects. Lawyers who find they know more than their clients about the legal arena tend to believe they know "generally what is best for the client." And because clients often approach lawyers as individuals made vulnerable by their legal problem, lawyers see them as people requiring paternalistic care rather than as autonomous individuals.[9] But it is well to remember that Wassertrom is a philosopher rather than an empirical researcher and his views of lawyers are based on personal experience and teaching at an elite law school.

Others also blame legal education and workplace socialization for the arrogance that leads to paternalism. Rhode (1994:50), writing about gender roles, suggests that the "problems often start in law school," and that "the patterns of dominance reinforced in legal education are replicated in later workplace relationships, particularly those involving subordinate groups. Authoritarian, paternalistic interactions between lawyers and clients often obscure the needs that prompted professional consultation in the first instance [and] the adverse effects of professional dominance are compounded by other status inequalities such as class, race, ethnicity and gender."

Critical scholars seem to find the source of paternalism in hierarchical power structures in society that infuse and are replicated by the lawyer–client relationship. Simon (1994:1101–1102) makes the interesting observation that while the traditional left concentrated on political-economic macrostructures, the new "crits" are more concerned with the microstructures of everyday life, such as language, rituals, and customs. These microstructures are insidious and can transform a well-meaning lawyer's actions into disempowering paternalism. This perspective then leads to a political project: Lawyers can and should attack these everyday practices in microbattles, using a day-by-day, case-by-case strategy.

All commentators agree that the underlying distribution of power in the lawyer–client relationship is of paramount importance in understanding paternalism. A consistent theme in the literature on paternalism is that lawyers hold the upper hand and often abuse that position, though not always intentionally. The next section examines the empirical research on power in the lawyer–client relationship. We see that it provides a more complicated and contingent picture than that assumed by participants in the paternalism debates.

C. THE ACTUALITY OF POWER

The predominant, but not exclusive, image of the lawyer–client relationship parallels that of the empirically ungrounded literature on paternalism. That is, the relationship derived from field studies often is described as one of professional dominance and lay passivity (see Heinz, 1983:892; Becker, 1970: 96–97; Johnson, 1972:53: Bankowski and Mungham, 1976; Cunningham, 1992; Alfieri, 1991). The lawyer governs the relationship, defines the terms of the interaction, and is responsible for the service provided. This image is bolstered by studies of a wide range of legal situations and types of legal practices. Thus, Hunting and Neuwirth (1962), writing more than 30 years ago, found that the majority of litigants in automobile accident claims in New York City had no idea what their lawyers were doing in their cases and had no say in when to settle or how much to accept. Legal services lawyers of the kind studied by Hosticka (1979:604) rarely even ask their clients what they want them to do. Such lawyers habitually engage in maneuvers that "exploit and reinforce client dependency on the lawyer's specialized knowledge and technical skill" (Alfieri, 1991:2132). Kritzer's (1990:66) review of a national survey of lawyers and clients in litigated cases finds low client involvement in case development and strategy. Both Blumberg (1967) and Macaulay (1979), writing about entirely different fields of practice, describe the ability of lawyers to control case development and strategy as unidirectional. Lawyers exercise power by manipulating their clients' definitions of the situation and of their role. The actions and reactions of clients, and the consequence of their presence, are barely visible. This unequal relationship is accentuated in franchise law firms that today serve tens of thousands of low-income clients (Van Hoy, 1995:705). From these studies one might think that contemporary lawyers fulfill Bakunin's nineteenth-century prediction about scientific intelligence, namely, that it would produce an aristocratic, despotic, arrogant, and elitist regime (Derber, Schwartz, and Magrass, 1990).

Indeed, even when individual clients are involved in the management of their own cases, that involvement often is limited. Thus, Rosenthal's (1974) notion of a high level of client participation in personal injury litigation is confined in its interactive dimensions to expressing special concerns and making follow-up demands for attention. The few clients who take an active role in their cases are considered hostile and problematic rather than helpful and persistent (Hosticka, 1979:607). In the conventional wisdom, people have "problems" and experts have "solutions" (Illich, Zola, McKnight, Caplan, and Shaiken, 1978). This superordinate position of lawyers is alleged to prevail even with progressive lawyers dedicated to producing social change (López, 1992).

Other research emphasizes the context of legal practice as crucial in shaping lawyer–client interaction. Spangler (1986:166–167, 170), for example, reports that private practitioners and corporate counsel are less likely to dictate action for their clients than are legal services lawyers. Heinz and Laumann (1982:108–109) recognize that there is considerable variation by area of law in the practice characteristic they term "freedom of action," a notion reflecting the lawyer's power to decide on strategy and to operate free of close supervision (Heinz and Laumann, 1982:104).

While these scholars see variation in the locus of power by area of practice, others see variation on a case-by-case basis. Cain (1979) notes that the array of power between lawyer and client varies from client to client: The solicitors she observed adopted their clients' goals as the given agenda unless they had a conflict of interest or the clients exhibited unreal expectations. In the same vein, Bottoms and McClean (1976) find that the extent of participation of criminal defendants in their cases varies by culture, personality, and ideology. Still other researchers find power to be differentially distributed between lawyer and client by task. Reminiscent of Johnson's (1972:46–47) distinction between defining needs and the manner of fulfilling them, Nelson's (1988:264, 267) and Spangler's (1986:60–61, 64) work on large law firms indicates that even though corporations set goals and policy independent of lawyer influence, lawyers have a major say in tactical matters.

Other analysts suggest that power in the professional relationship directly reflects control over resources. Thus, Flood (1987:386–390), having observed the life history of two lawsuits as part of his ethnographic study of a large Chicago law firm, suggests that allocation of power between lawyer and client depends on whether or not the clients are likely to produce repeat business or have the ability to pay fees that command attention. Abel is, perhaps, the strongest proponent of this view. He argues that corporate clients are typically the "dominant" actors in the relationship with their lawyers while solo and small-firm practitioners "dominate" their clients (1989:2014).

Sarat and Felstiner (1995; Felstiner and Sarat, 1992) suggest that attempts to identify a single, stable locus of power in the lawyer–client relationship are doomed to fail. They adopt what White (1992b) terms a "Foucaultian," "post-structural" approach that challenges the " 'conventional,' structural understanding of power [as] ... a thing that people have and wield over others." In their approach "power is not a tool. Rather, like an evanescent fluid, it takes unpredictable shapes as it flows into the most subtle spaces in our interpersonal world" (White, 1992b:1501). They find that "lawyer–client interaction reflects the conflict and chaos that typifies the construction of meaning and play of power in those many mundane occasions on which people seek to create meaning and promote their own interests under conditions of stress and uncertainty. By attending to those interactions we see both the fragility of power as it is exercised and the elusiveness of meaning as it is constructed" (Sarat and Felstiner, 1995:153).

Sarat and Felstiner found that while professionals and their clients in divorce typically occupy different and unequal positions and bring different and unequal resources to bear in their relationship, power in the lawyer–client interactions they observed was part of the "dynamic processes [that] characterize the interaction of law with the culture of common sense and the fluidity, negotiability and ever changing qualities of both law and everyday life" (Engel, 1993:126). As a result of this fluidity, both lawyers and clients were sometimes frustrated by feelings of powerlessness in dealing with the other (White, 1990a). Often no one may be in charge: Interactions between lawyers and clients involve as much drift and uncertainty as direction and clarity of purpose. Sarat and Felstiner found it difficult, at any one moment, to determine who, if anyone, was defining objectives, determining strategy, or devising tactics.

Sarat and Felstiner observed divorce lawyers only. Yet they argue (1995:151–152) that the struggles over meaning and power between lawyers and their clients occur as well in other areas of practice. They extend their findings to law practice generally because they believe that negotiations between lawyers and clients are required across the board on issues such as client expectations and goals, the production of a consistent version of events, the timing of actions, and the division of labor between them. Law practice, they allege, rarely involves the straightforward delivery of a technical service to complacent clients: More often the interaction between lawyer and client resembles a complex, shifting, conflicted set of negotiations. Hurder (1996) adopts a position similar to that of Sarat and Felstiner and calls for an approach to lawyering that recognizes the reality of negotiated power: "Decisions affecting the lawyer–client relationship are negotiated, whether consciously or not. An approach to legal interviewing and counseling that allows principled negotiation of all the terms of the lawyer–client relationship, including the ultimate goals of the relationship, is the best way to create a relationship of equality and effective collaboration" (Hurder, 1996:76).

To the extent that Sarat and Felstiner are on the right track in asserting that lawyer–client relationships are contextual and negotiated, the tendency of paternalism studies to locate power in the hands of the lawyer overstates the actuality of the relationship even in the personal services hemisphere of law practice. Alfieri (1992b:1253) has made this same point. He observes that "for Felstiner and Sarat, the variable elements of mutual dependency and suspicion displace the conventional taxonomy of lawyer representation in terms of categories such as autonomy, paternalism and vanguardism. Contrary to this taxonomy, they conjecture that 'no one may be in charge,' either in 'defining the objectives, determining strategy or devising tactics' of representation." Alfieri suggests that Felstiner and Sarat's findings of relational power undermine the very concept of paternalism since "under paternalistic and vanguard accounts of modernist representation, relational power is substantially denied."

D. THE NEGLECT OF CLIENTS BY LAWYERS

Not only does the literature on lawyer–client relations suggest that clients other than large businesses or other powerful entities are often in no position to *dictate* goals and means to their lawyers, but a separate body of work focusing on the interpersonal dimensions of the lawyer–client relationship indicates that lawyers frequently do in fact neglect and show little respect for their clients. There is a tide of studies that depict lawyers sacrificing their clients' interests in favor of their own (Carlin, 1962, 1966), paying more attention to the courtroom workgroups in which they practice than to their clients' interests (Sudnow, 1964; Eisenstein and Jacob, 1977), putting their clients' cases into cold storage to suit their own capacity for work (Hensler, Felstiner, Selvin, and Ebener, 1985), permitting fee arrangements to dictate strategy (Johnson, 1980), describing the legal system in exaggeratedly negative terms to distance themselves from poor case results (Sarat and Felstiner, 1995), subordinating clients' positions to the bureaucratic exigencies of their offices (Hosticka, 1979), not pushing their clients' cases fully for fear of annoying other lawyers or jeopardizing future business (Macaulay, 1979), doing more work than is necessary in order to pad fees (O'Gorman, 1963:146; Bartlett, 1982), and engaging in group settlement practices that enhance fees at the expense of individual clients (Hensler *et al.*, 1985).

Clients frequently experience lawyers as condescending (see Abel, 1989:247). Legally aided clients are particularly prone to being treated as instances of categories of legal problems rather than full-fledged persons (Hosticka, 1979; Cunningham, 1992). Clients become exasperated when lawyers try to overwhelm them with jargon (Levine, 1992:60). Even an ABA Commission chaired by Hillary Rodham Clinton describes lawyers as becoming dehumanized, unable to relate to clients with compassion (Commission on Women in the Profession, 1988:16). The literature is full of assertions about lawyer arrogance [Hengstler, 1993:62; see Menkel-Meadow, 1994:595 (criticizing the MacCrate Report for not paying enough attention to the human aspects of lawyering)]. Public defenders instruct rather than consult with their clients while some private defense counsel are alleged by their clients to be brash, cold, inattentive, and poor communicators (Casper, 1972:109, 116–117).

Clients complain that lawyers lack empathy (Hengstler, 1993:62; compare Seron, 1994.8-273–274, 278, 300) and are uncooperative, uncommunicative (Curran, 1977.230, Harris *et al.*, 1984:68; Abel, 1989:584), rude, unresponsive, evasive (Rosenthal, 1974:52), and tardy in providing services (Levine, 1992:62). Studies of lawyer–client relations often report client files that were forgotten or lost (see Rosenthal, 1974:48; Felstiner and Sarat, 1992:1475–1476). The most common client complaint about lawyers is that they do not respond to phone calls and letters (Seron, 1994:6-216; Stevens, 1994; Sussman, 1993; see Sambom, 1993; Scottsdale II, 1978:13; Abel, 1989:585), even though communications specialists allege, "nothing says as much to people that I don't care about you as unanswered phone calls" (CLE videotape "One Client at a Time"). In criminal defense work, both assigned counsel and public defenders have been found to ration severely the time they spend with clients (see Casper, 1972:102, 106, 108; Mather, 1979:24).

Problems in communications with clients exist despite the high importance training in such skills is accorded by both law students and their prospective employers (see Garth and Martin, 1993). Lawyers fail both to listen (Seron, 1994:8-270) and to explain legal matters adequately in lay terms (Vogel, 1989;23): Both are matters of capacity (Jaquish and Ware, 1993) and of disposition (Gutmann, 1993:1759). Rosenthal (1974:19) quotes advice given to lawyers by the Wisconsin Bar Association: "Get at the client's problem immediately and stick to it. Don't bother to explain the reasoning process by which you arrived at your advice.... This not only prolongs the interview, but generally confuses the client."

In addition, lawyers are frequently indifferent to client's feelings and to the pace of their affairs. The irrelevance, if not contaminating effect, of client feelings is axiomatic in traditional definitions of the lawyer's role (Binder, Bergman, and Price, 1991). Sarat and Felstiner (1995:128–133) provide extensive accounts of lawyers both refusing to engage with their clients' emotions and schooling clients about the need to separate their emotions from their objectives (see also Cunningham, 1992:1300–1301, on literature in poverty and civil rights practice to the effect that lawyers routinely silence their clients even while "purporting to tell their stories"). A refusal to engage with clients' feelings has an effect on the quality of service provided: Clients whose feelings are ignored or discounted have difficulty in responding to the legal counsel that the lawyer provides as well as to the lawyer herself (see Sarat and Felstiner, 1986:123–124). A common complaint of clients is that no action is taken in their cases over long periods of time (see Sarat and Felstiner, 1995:59–62; Mansnerus, 1995:8). Lawyers may or may not have good reason to delay attending to their clients' affairs, but in either case the clients' frustration is exacerbated by the lawyers' frequent failure to explain the sources of delay.

It is not at all clear what proportion of clients are merely annoyed by the bad manners and consultative postures of lawyers and how often these behaviors inflict serious social or psychological traumas. Procedural justice theorists have found in a wide range of contexts that people are remarkably sensitive to the process that they experience in encounters with authority figures like lawyers. This sensitivity to process has been found to outweigh outcome concerns in politics and in organizations as well as in a wide variety of legal settings including those of misdemeanor and felony defendants and citizens in their encounters with the police and when involved with divorce, mediation, and small-claims courts.

Before procedural justice researchers turned their attention to tort litigation (see Lind *et al.*, 1990), litigant satisfaction was assumed to reflect only considerations of outcome, cost, and delay. Economic analyses of procedures, and the proposals for reform that they lead to, assume that litigants are primarily concerned with recoveries and payouts and with how much it costs and how long it takes to bring a case to closure. Lind and his colleagues (Lind, 1994; Tyler and Lind, 1992; Lind *et al.*, 1990), on the other hand, have found that what they call "dignitary process" issues are even more important than objective outcomes because respectful and dignified treatment implies that the recipient is a full-fledged, valued member of society, a belief that goes to the core of the way that we define our self-identity.

When applied to the question of the level of attention that lawyers give to clients, the procedural justice argument goes like this: People learn about how they stand in the world, they search out and learn about their status, from the quality of their treatment by people in positions of authority, by people who have power over them (see Freeman and Weihope, 1972:30). These encounters provide people an opportunity to learn where they stand in society;

they provide an opportunity to test their social identity. When a client, for instance, is treated politely and with dignity and when respect is shown for and attention is paid to her needs and opinions, her feelings of positive social status are enhanced. On the other hand, when a lawyer treats a client disrespectfully or impolitely, when he ignores her needs or her existence, the client's self-definition is affected and her self-respect is threatened.

If this theory of status definition is correct, then we can see that a lot of ordinary behavior in the lawyer–client context is charged with much greater significance than lawyers either realize or intend. Not answering a phone call, or worse, ignoring a string of phone calls, not answering the mail, not sharing plans and developments with clients, not pushing a client's affairs on to closure, are no longer just bad manners or the inescapable social abrasions inflicted by busy people on those who have hired and depend on them. Instead, suggests the theory, such behavior may inflict serious psychological trauma. Thus, lack of respect for clients reflects not only the power of lawyers to behave without considering the effect of that behavior on their clients, but it may involve the power to cause serious injury to those on whose behalf one is supposedly acting.

E. CONCLUSION

One cannot help wonder whether the generally negative picture of lawyer–client relations portrayed in the three bodies of work that we have reviewed—lawyer paternalism, power, and abuse—actually characterizes the general run of encounters in the personal services hemisphere of law practice. Early returns from a national survey of clients by Felstiner and Lind (1998) suggest that it *does not.* Felstiner and Lind conducted telephone interviews with a random sample of 500 people who had used lawyers in a variety of matters within 3 years of the interview. Analysis of the first 350 interviews indicates that a large proportion of clients are quite satisfied with the relationship with their lawyer. For instance, over 80% of the clients would both use the lawyer and recommend her to a friend if presented with a similar problem in the future.

How are we to explain this disparity between focused research and general survey? Much of it may be an artifact of research structures and traditions. In the first place, a good deal of the research on lawyer–client relationships, particularly that portion on paternalism, originates in the self-reflection of former legal aid or poverty lawyers. Both factors, self-reflection and poor clients, contribute to a picture of a relationship in crisis. The self-reflecting lawyer is necessarily self-critical. To be otherwise would be both immodest and uninteresting. Their particular slice of clients—poor, undereducated, and most important, provided with legal services rather than paying for them—are more likely than most clients to be treated in routine and patronizing fashion than those who are more nearly the social equal of their lawyers and who are their paymasters. This latter sector of the client population is much more numerous than legally aided clients, much more likely to be better, even, well-treated by their lawyers, but much less likely to show up in the literature on lawyer–client relations.

In the second place, an artifact of social research generally is a tendency toward negative critique. It is natural to direct studies toward problematic rather than untroubled areas of inquiry; empirical researchers are more often than not cynics accustomed to revealing patterns of danger or inequity beneath formalistic platitudes or unexamined conventional wisdom (Danet, Hoffinan, and Kermish, 1980:908). This tendency is exaggerated in sociolegal studies because of the salient position for many years of studies in the "gap" between rule and behavior tradition.

Even more important, there really has not been a frontal, empirical assault on questions of paternalism, power, or respect. The evidence on the substantive side is not that when presented with a choice lawyers fail to promote the autonomy of their clients, share power, or act respectfully, but that in the circumstances in which they have been studied they are thought to behave paternalistically, put their own interests ahead of those of their clients, and treat their clients shabbily. These are not the same thing particularly because the "circumstances in which they have been studied" have not been randomized, but rather have emphasized legal aid, solo practitioners and personal injury and criminal defense lawyers. Moreover, we have a strong hunch that if researchers were looking at the question of the general run of lawyer behavior rather than who is taking advantage of whom, they would adopt different research strategies, ask different questions, and produce who knows what results.

F. ENDNOTES

1. Thus, manipulation of clients for sexual or financial purposes (e.g., Rhode, 1994; Spiegel, 1979), sacrificing of individual client interests in order to pursue larger social or group goals (e.g., Bell, 1976; Grosberg, 1989; Margulies, 1990; Resnik, Curtis, and Hensler, 1996), or interference with client goals in order to pursue goals of fairness or justice (e.g., Simon, 1988; Luban, 1988) technically would not be considered paternalistic actions—unless one were to argue that the lawyer in question actually intended some paramount long-run, best-interest benefit (such as moral, psychological, or financial) to the client by such action (see Margulies, 1990:219, n21, 227). See also Ellmann (1992:1158) ("In some circumstances ... a gain for the group as a whole *can* justify a paternalistic interference with the autonomy of its members. This is a potentially pernicious argument, susceptible to immense abuse, yet it is hard to deny that sustaining the group can in some circumstances benefit even its more reluctant members.")
2. Kultgen suggests that all professional–client relationships are suspect in this regard. "Indeed, the professional often subtly shapes the values of the client so that she will 'need,' or want, what the professional thinks she ought to have.... Likewise, the professional may shape the ends of the client by the way he presents alternatives and their costs and consequences.... [T]his occurs at the societal as well as individual level. The professions shape the public's conception of its needs by their philosophies of medicine, law, engineering, and so on" (Kultgen, 1995:191).
3. Much has been written about the propriety of a lawyer expressing moral opinions to a client. Dinerstein states: "With powerful lawyers and powerless clients, however, the danger that the client will take the lawyer's moral suggestion as a *diktat* is quite real and, for the most part, unexamined by the critics. One can argue that the client is free to reject the lawyer's moral advice and continue with the goals the client establishes (if the lawyer agrees) or find another lawyer (if the lawyer does not). But such a response to the problem is insufficient. It fails to take account of some lawyers' tendency to dominate their clients. While some may claim that clients would see the lawyer's moral advice as occupying a less secure footing than her legal advice, the very resonance of moral issues calls such an observation into question. And that is the point: the critics do not want the client to ignore the lawyer's moral advice, they want him to follow it. The trick is to accomplish that result without undermining the client's autonomous choice. It is a trick not yet mastered" (Dinerstein, 1990:562). See also Ellmann (1987b:1021) ("Moral or political advice can provide clients opportunities to learn and hence increase their autonomy") and Margulies (1990:250–252) ("Requiring lawyers to provide nonlegal advice and bring up the interests of third parties, though it will increase lawyer influence over clients, will decrease lawyer manipulation by bringing such issues into open discussion and dialogue").
4. "Even the most non-interventionist client-centered lawyer is likely to feel the strong pull of wanting to give advice to his client. That pull may well lead him to manipulate his client to make the decision that he, the lawyer, wants him to make while seeming to insist that it remains the client's decision. One way that this manipulation could occur—and in my experience both as a lawyer and teacher does occur—is for the lawyer to revisit continually the client's decision and the basis for it until the client comes around to the lawyer's point of view" (Dinerstein, 1990:570, n310).
5. See, e.g., Alfieri (1991, 1992a,b), Cunningham (1992), and White (1990a, 1992a), all of which deal with the issue of subtle processes of often unintentional, and to a certain extent unavoidable, lawyer paternalism. See also Steward (1993).

6. Dinerstein (1990:523) presents the argument that "clients empowered in their relationship with their lawyer might carry over that sense of power to their relationship with bureaucracies and other power structures. Furthermore, if client-centered counseling values the client's individual experience by providing an outlet for its expression within the lawyer–client relationship, clients could be expected to assert themselves authentically within whatever system they are challenging."
7. "What justifies our imposition on another's autonomy? The fact that when his decisionmaking capacity is impaired he really is not autonomous at all" (Luban, 1981:465). Luban adopts Thompson's (1980) suggestion that paternalistic action is only justifiable if (1) the decision of the person who is to be constrained is impaired, (2) the restriction is as limited as possible, and (3) the restriction prevents a serious and irreversible harm. The key trigger condition is the first one—a person's autonomy should only be interfered with if that person's choice of action is faulty in some way. This can be because the person's decision processes are impaired or because the person is lacking information (Luban, 1981:465).
8. This seems to be one of the major points of much of the critical literature and the theoretics of practice literature (and related social science literature that concentrates on the concept of the "other"). Differences of class, race, gender, ethnicity, and so on so distance the (usually subordinated) "other" that intersubjective understanding is perhaps unreachable. The dilemma is that we must not stop striving for it even if the process of striving entails "interpretive violence." An example of the missteps involved might be seen in Cunningham's tale of changing the name of a client in an article on the assumption that the client would want his identity kept private, only to have the client insist that his true name be used as a way of asserting identity in the face of the anonymity the client felt in the courtroom. Cunningham's remorseful *mea culpa* is that his thoughtlessly thoughtful action was "a striking example of apparent paternalism operating below the threshold of awareness" (Cunningham, 1992:1384).
9. Wasserstrom suggests that since paternalism is offensive and springs from role-differentiated behavior of professionals, the way to proceed is to "deprofessionalize" the law—to weaken, if not excise, those features of legal professionalism that tend to produce these kinds of interpersonal relationships. He recommends a "sustained effort to simplify legal language and to make the legal processes less mysterious and more directly available to lay persons" combined with an "explicit effort to alter the ways in which lawyers are educated and acculturated to view themselves, their clients, and the relationships that ought to exist between them" (Wasserstrom, 1975:23).

REFERENCES

Abbott, A. (1989). *The System of the Professions*. Chicago: University of Chicago Press.

Abel, R. L. (1989). *American Lawyers*. London: Oxford University Press.

Alfieri, A. (1991). Reconstructive Poverty Law Practice: Learning Lessons of Client Narrative. *Yale Law Journal, 100*, 2107–2147.

Alfieri, A. (1992a). Disabled Clients, Disabling Lawyers. *Hastings Law Journal, 43*, 769–851.

Alfieri, A. (1992b). Stances. *Cornell Law Review, 77*, 1233–1257.

Bankowski, Z., and Mungham, G. (1976). *Images of Law*. London: Routledge & Kegan Paul.

Bartlett, J. W. (1982). *The Law Business a Tired Monopoly*. Littleton, CO: F. B. Rothman.

Bell, D. A., Jr. (1976). Serving Two Masters: Integration Ideals and Client Interests in School Desegregation Litigation. *Yale Law Journal, 85*, 470–516.

Binder, D., Bergman, P., and Price, S. (1991). *Lawyers as Counselors: A Client-Centered Approach*. St. Paul, MN: West Publishing.

Blumberg, A. (1967). The Practice of Law as a Confidence Game. *Law & Society Review, 1*, 15.

Bottoms, A. E., and McClean, J. D. (1976). *Defendants in the Criminal Process*. London: Routledge & Kegan Paul.

Cain, M. (1979). The General Practice Lawyer and Client. *International Journal of the Sociology of Law, 7*, 331–354.

Carlin, J. E. (1962). *Lawyers on Their Own*. New Brunswick: Rutgers University Press.

Carlin, J. E. (1966). *Lawyer's Ethics—A Survey of the New York City Bar*. New York: Russell Sage Foundation.

Casper, J. D. (1972). *American Criminal Justice: The Defendant's Perspective*. Englewood Cliffs, NJ: Prentice–Hall.

Commission on Women in the Profession. (1988). Report. Chicago: ABA.

Cunningham, C. (1992). The Lawyer as Translator, Representation as Text: Towards an Ethnography of Legal Discourse. *Cornell Law Review, 77*, 1298–1387.

Curran, B. (1977). *The Legal Needs of the Public: The Final Report of a National Survey*. Chicago: American Bar Foundation.

Danet, B., Hoffinan, K. B., and Kermish, N. C. (1980). Obstacles to the Study of Lawyer–Client Interaction: The Biography of a Failure. *Law & Society Review, 14*, 905.

Derber, C., Schwartz, W., and Magrass, Y. (1990). *Power in the Highest Degree: Professionals and the Rise in a New Mandarin Order*. London: Oxford University Press.

Dinerstein, R. D. (1990). Client-Centered Counseling: Reappraisal and Refinement. *Arizona Law Review*, *32*, 501–604.

Dworkin, G. (1971). Paternalism. In R. A. Wasserstrom (Ed.), *Morality and the Law*. Belmont, CA: Wadsworth.

Dworkin, G. (1972). Paternalism. *The Monist*, *56*(1), 64–84.

Eastman, H. A. (1995). Speaking Truth to Power: The Language of Civil Rights Litigators. *Yale Law Journal*, *104*, 763–879.

Eisenstein, J. S., and Jacob, H. (1977). *Felony Justice*. Boston: Little, Brown.

Ellmann, S. (1987a). Lawyers and Clients. *UCLA Law Review*, *34*(3), 717–779.

Ellmann, S. (1987b). Manipulation by Client and Context: A Response to Professor Morris. *UCLA Law Review*, *34*(3), 1003–1022.

Ellmann, S. (1992). Client-Centeredness Multiplied: Individual Autonomy and Collective Mobilization in Public Interest Lawyers' Representation of Groups. *Virginia Law Review*, *78*, 1103–1173.

Engel, D. (1993). Law in the Domains of Everyday Life: The Construction of Community and Difference. In A. Sarat and T. R. Kearns (Eds.), *Law in Everyday Life* (pp. 123–170). Ann Arbor: University of Michigan Press.

Felstiner, W. L. F., and Lind, E. A. (1998, July). *The Effect of Gender on Client Perceptions of Lawyer Behavior*. Paper delivered at the 5th Biennial Meeting of the Working Group on Comparative Study of Legal Professions, Onati, Spain.

Felstiner, W. L. F., and Sarat, A. (1992). Enactments of Power: Negotiating Reality and Responsibility in Lawyer–Client Interactions. *Cornell Law Review*, *77*, 7.

Flood, J. (1987). Anatomy of Lawyering: An Ethnography of a Corporate Law Firm. Ph.D. Dissertation. Northwestern University.

Freeman, H., and Weihope, H. (1972). *Clinical Law Training: Interviewing and Counseling*. St. Paul, MN: West Publishing.

Galanter, M., and Palay, T. (1991). *Tournament of Lawyers: The Transformation of the Big Law Firm*. Chicago: Chicago University Press.

Garth, B. G., and Martin, J. (1993). Law Schools and the Construction of Competence. *Journal of Legal Education*, *43*, 469.

Grosberg, L. M. (1989). Class Actions and Client-Centered Decisionmaking. *Syracuse Law Review*, *40*, 709–788.

Gutmann, A. (1993). Can Virtue Be Taught to Lawyers? *Stanford Law Review*, *45*, 1759.

Hagan, J., and Kay, F. (1995). *Gender in Practice: A Study of Lawyers' Lives*. London: Oxford University Press.

Halliday, T. (1987). *Beyond Monopoly: Lawyers, State Crisis, and Professional Empowerment*. Chicago: University of Chicago Press.

Harris, D., Maclean, M., Genn, H., Lloyd-Bostock, S., Fenn, P., Corfield, P., and Brittan, Y. (1984). *Compensation and Support for Illness and Injury*. Oxford: Clarendon Press.

Heinz, J. (1983). The Power of Lawyers. *Georgia Law Review*, *17*, 891.

Heinz, J., and Laumann, E. (1982). *Chicago Lawyers: The Social Structure of the Bar*. New York: Russell Sage Foundation.

Hengstler, G. A. (1993). Vox Populi: The Public Perception of Lawyers. *ABA Journal*, *79*, 60.

Hensler, D. R., Felstiner, W. L. F., Selvin, M., and Ebener, P. A. (1985). *Asbestos in the Courts: The Challenge of Mass Toxic Torts*. Santa Monica, CA: Rand.

Hillary, M., Johnson, J. T., and Johnson, A. (1989). Social Power and Interactional Style in the Divorce Attorney/Client Dyad. *Journal of Divorce*, *12*(4), 89–102.

Hosticka, C. (1979). We Don't Care What Happened, We Only Care What Is Going to Happen. *Social Problems*, *26*, 599.

Hunting, R., and Neuwirth, G. (1962). *Who Sues in New York City: A Study of Automobile Accident Claims*. New York: Columbia University Press.

Hurder, A. J. (1996). Negotiating the Lawyer–Client Relationship: A Search for Equality and Collaboration. *Buffalo Law Review*, *44*, 71–99.

Illich, I., Zola, I., McKnight, J., Caplan, J., and Shaiken, H. (1978). *Disabling Professions*. London: Marion Boyers.

Jaquish, G. A., and Ware, J. (1993). Adopting an Educator Habit of Mind: Modifying What It Means to 'Think Like a Lawyer.' *Stanford Law Review*, *45*, 1713.

Johnson, E. (1980). Lawyers' Choice: A Theoretical Appraisal of Litigation Investment Decision. *Law and Society Review*, *15*, 567–610.

Johnson, T. (1972). *Professions and Power*. London: Macmillan & Co.

Kennedy, D. (1982). Distributive and Paternalist Motives in Contract and Tort Law, with Special Reference to Compulsory Terms and Unequal Bargaining Power. *Maryland Law Review*, *41*, 563–658.

*Kritzer, H. (1990). *The Justice Broker: Lawyers and Ordinary Litigation*. London: Oxford University Press.

Kultgen, J. (1996). *Autonomy and Intervention: Paternalism in the Caring Life*. London: Oxford University Press.

Landon, D. (1990). *Country Lawyers: The Impact of Context in Professional Practice*. New York: Praeger.

Levine, A. P. (1992). Looking for Mr. Goodlawyer. *ABA Journal*, *78*, 60.

Lind, E. A. (1994). Procedural Justice and Culture: Evidence for Ubiquitous Process Concerns. *Zeitschrift fuer Rechtssoziologie*, *15*, 24.

Lind, E. A., and Tyler, T. R. (1988). *The Social Psychology of Procedural Justice*. New York: Plenum Press.

Lind, E. A., MacCoun, R. J., Ebener, P. A., Felstiner, W. L. F., Hensler, D. R., Resnick, J., and Tyler, T. (1990). In the Eye of the Beholder: Tort Litigants' Evaluations of Their Experiences in the Civil Justice System. *Law and Society Review*, *24*, 953.

López, G. (1989). Reconceiving Civil Rights Practice: Seven Weeks in the Life of a Rebellious Collaboration. *Georgetown Law Journal*, *77*, 1603–1717.

López, G. (1992). *Rebellious Lawyering: One Chicano's Vision of Progressive Law Practice*. Boulder, CO: Westview Press.

Luban, D. (1981). Paternalism and the Legal Profession. *Wisconsin Law Review*, *1981*, 454–493.

Luban, D. (1988). *Lawyers and Justice: An Ethical Study*. Princeton, NJ: Princeton University Press.

Macaulay, S. (1979). Lawyers and Consumer Protection Laws. *Law and Society Review*, *14*, 115.

Mansnerus, L. (1995, June 11). Looking for an Attorney? Here's Counsel. *New York Times*, sec. 3, p. 1.

Margulies, P. (1990). Who Are You to Tell Me That?: Attorney–Client Deliberation Regarding Nonlegal Issues and the Interests of Nonclients. *North Carolina Law Review*, *68*, 213–252.

Mather, L. M. (1979). *Plea Bargaining or Trial?* Lexington, MA: Lexington Books.

Menkel-Meadow, C. The Power of Narrative in Empathetic Learning: Post-Modernism and the Stories of Law. *UCLA Women's Law Journal*, *2*, 287.

Menkel-Meadow, C. (1994). Narrowing the Gap by Narrowing the Field: What's Missing from the MacCrate Report-On Skills, Legal Science and Being a Human Being. *Washington Law Review*, *69*, 593.

Nelson, R. (1988). *Partners with Power: The Social Transformation of the Large Law Firm*. Berkeley: University of California Press.

O'Gorman, H. (1963). *Lawyers in Matrimonial Cases*. Glencoe, IL: Free Press.

Powell, M. J. (1988). *From Patrician to Professional Elite*. New York: Russell Sage Foundation.

Resnik, J., Curtis, D. E., and Hensler, D. R. (1996). Individuals Within the Aggregate: Relationships, Representation, and Fees. *New York University Law Review*, *71*(1–2), 296–401.

Rhode, D. L. (1994). Gender and Professional Roles. *Fordham Law Review*, *63*, 39–72.

Rosenthal, D. E. (1974). *Lawyer and Client: Who's in Charge?* New York: Russell Sage Foundation.

Sambom, R. (1993). Anti-Lawyer Attitude Up. *National Law Journal*, *15*(49), 1.

Sarat, A., and Felstiner, W. L. F. (1986). Law and Strategy in the Divorce Lawyer's Office. *Law & Society Review*, *20*, 97.

Sarat, A., and Felstiner, W. L. F. (1995). *Divorce Lawyers and Their Clients: Power and Meaning in the Legal Process*. New York: Oxford University Press.

Scottsdale II, Long Range Planning Committee, Section on Communications and Public Relations. (1978). *An Updated Communications Agenda for the Legal Profession*. Chicago: National Association of Bar Examiners.

Seron, C. (1994). *When Lawyers Go to Market: The Restructuring of Private Legal Practice*. Unpublished manuscript.

Simon, W. H. (1984). Visions of Practice in Legal Thought. *Stanford Law Review*, *36*, 469–507.

Simon, W. H. (1988). Ethical Discretion in Lawyering. *Harvard Law Review*, *101*, 1083–1145.

Simon, W. H. (1991). Lawyer Advice and Client Autonomy: Mrs. Jones's Case. *Maryland Law Review*, *50*, 213–226.

Simon, W. H. (1994). The Dark Secret of Progressive Lawyering: A Comment on Poverty Law Scholarship in the Post-Modern, Post-Reagan Era. *University of Miami Law Review*, *48*, 1099–1114.

Spangler, E. (1986). *Lawyers for Hire: Salaried Professionals at Work*. New Haven, CT: Yale University Press.

Spiegel, M. (1979). Lawyering and Client Decisionmaking: Informed Consent and the Legal Profession. *University of Pennsylvania Law Review*, *128*(1), 41–140.

Stevens, A. (1994, September 9). Lawyers' Annoying Misdeeds Targeted. *Wall Street Journal*, B1(W), B1(E).

Steward, M. (1993). Just Injustice. *National Black Law Journal*, *12*(4), 230–254.

Sudnow, D. (1964). Normal Crimes: Sociological Features of the Penal Code in a Public Defender Office. *Social Problems*, *12*, 255–276.

Sussman, F. S. (1993, November 26). Lawyers Have to Take the Complaints of Clients More Seriously. *New York Times*, A18, col. 3–5.

Tremblay, P. R. (1987). On Persuasion and Paternalism: Lawyer Decisionmaking and the Questionably Competent Client. *Utah Law Review*, 1987:515–584.

Tyler, T., and Lind, E. A. (1992). A Relational Model of Authority in Groups. *Advances in Experimental Social Psychology*, *25*, 115.

Van Hoy, J. (1995). Selling and Processing Law: Legal Work at Franchise Law Firms. *Law & Society Review*, *29*, 703.

Vogel, H. H. (1989). *Report of ABA Task Force on Outreach to the Public*. Chicago: ABA.

Wasserstrom, R. (1975). Lawyers as Professionals: Some Moral Issues. *Human Rights*, *5*, 1–24.

White, L. E. (1990). *Goldberg v. Kelly* On the Paradox of Lawyering for the Poor. *Brooklyn Law Review*, *56*, 861–887.

White, L. E. (1992a). Paradox, Piece-Work, and Patience. *Hastings Law Journal*, *43*, 851–859.

White, L. E. (1992b). Seeking '... The Faces of Otherness ...': A Response to Professors Sarat, Felstiner, and Cahn. *Cornell Law Review*, *77*, 1499–1511.

6

The Juvenile Court

Barry C. Feld

A. INTRODUCTION

Ideological changes in the cultural conception of children and in strategies of social control during the nineteenth century led to the creation of the first juvenile court in Cook County, Illinois, in 1899 (Platt, 1977; Sutton, 1988). Culminating a century-long process differentiating youths from adult offenders, Progressive reformers applied new theories of social control to new ideas about childhood and created the juvenile court as a social welfare alternative to criminal courts to respond to criminal and noncriminal misconduct by youths.

The United States Supreme Court's decision *In re Gault*, 387 U.S. 1 (1967) began to transform the juvenile court into a very different institution than the Progressives contemplated. Progressiveness envisioned an informal, discretionary social welfare agency whose dispositions reflected the "best interests" of the child. In *Gault*, the Supreme Court engrafted formal due process safeguards at trial onto the juvenile court's individualized treatment sentencing schema. Although the Court did not intend to alter the juvenile court's therapeutic mission, in the subsequent decades, judicial and legislative responses to *Gault* have modified juvenile courts' jurisdiction, purpose, and procedures. As a result, juvenile courts now converge procedurally and substantively with adult criminal courts.

Within the past three decades, judicial decisions, legislative amendments, and administrative changes have transformed the juvenile court from a nominally rehabilitative welfare agency into a scaled-down second-class criminal court for young offenders that provides them with neither therapy nor justice (Feld, 1993a, 1997). This transformation has occurred because of the migration of African-Americans from the rural south to the urban north that began three-quarters of a century ago, the macrostructural transformation of U.S. cities and the economy over the past quarter of a century, and the current linkages in the popular and political culture between race and serious youth crime (Feld, 1999). Two competing cultural and legal conceptions of young people have facilitated juvenile courts' transformation. On the one hand, legal culture views young people as innocent, vulnerable, fragile, and dependent *children* whom

---

Barry C. Feld • University of Minnesota Law School, Minneapolis, Minnesota 55455.

Handbook of Justice Research in Law, edited by Sanders and Hamilton. Kluwer Academic / Plenum Publishers, New York, 2000.

their parents and the state should protect and nurture. On the other hand, the legal culture perceives young people as vigorous, autonomous, and responsible almost *adultlike* people from whose criminal behavior the public needs protection.

The ambivalent and conflicted "jurisprudence of youth" enables policymakers selectively to manipulate the competing social constructs of childhood *innocence* and adult *responsibility* to maximize the social control of young people. In so doing, juvenile justice legal reforms over the past three decades have engaged in a process of "criminological triage." At the "soft end" of juvenile court's jurisdiction, reforms have shifted noncriminal status offenders out of the juvenile justice system into a "hidden system" of social control in the private-sector mental health and chemical dependency industries. At the "hard end" of juvenile courts' jurisdiction, states transfer increasing numbers of youths into the criminal justice system for prosecution as adults. For those delinquents who remain within an increasingly criminalized juvenile justice system, juvenile courts' sentencing policies and practices increasingly reflect criminal courts' goals of punishment and incapacitation rather than an exclusive focus on youths' welfare and "real needs." Proportional and determinate sentences based on the present offense and prior record dictate the length, location, and intensity of intervention. Indeed, throughout the juvenile court's history, disjunctions between rehabilitative rhetoric and punitive reality have persisted and sanctions have oscillated between cycles of leniency and severity (Rothman, 1980; Bernard, 1992). As penal social control increasingly supercedes social welfare as the primary purpose of juvenile court sentences, *Gault*'s concerns about procedural justice acquire greater salience. Although in theory juvenile courts' procedural safeguards closely resemble those of criminal courts, in reality, the justice routinely afforded juveniles is far lower than the minimum insisted on for adult offenders.

The substantive and procedural convergence between juvenile and criminal courts eliminates many of the conceptual and operational differences in strategies of social control for youths and adults. With the juvenile court's transformation from an informal rehabilitative agency into a scaled-down criminal court, some question the need for a separate justice system for young offenders whose only distinction is its persisting deficiencies (Ainsworth, 1991; Feld, 1997). In this chapter, I analyze the original creation and subsequent transformation of the juvenile court from a social welfare agency into a deficient criminal court. Second, I contend that the underlying *idea* of the juvenile court embodies a fundamental flaw because it attempts to combine social welfare and penal social control in one agency. Because social welfare and crime control functions embody irreconcilable contradictions, juvenile courts contain inherent conflicts and inevitably pursue both missions badly. If a state separates social welfare goals from criminal social control functions, then no need remains for a separate juvenile court. Rather, a state could try all offenders in one integrated criminal justice system. But, children do not possess the same degree of criminal responsibility as adults. Adolescent developmental psychology, criminal law jurisprudence, and sentencing policy provide rationale to formally recognize youthfulness as a mitigating factor when judges sentence younger offenders. A "youth discount" provides a conceptual rationale for a sliding scale of criminal responsibility for younger offenders who have not quite learned to be responsible and developed fully their capacity for self-control. Combining enhanced procedural safeguards with formal mitigation of sentences provides youths with greater protections and justice than they currently receive in either the juvenile or criminal justice systems.

B. ORIGINS OF THE JUVENILE COURT

Prior to the creation of juvenile courts, the common law's infancy *mens rea* defense provided the only special protections for young offenders charged with crimes. The common law conclusively presumed that children younger than 7 years of age lacked criminal capacity, while those 14 years of age and older possessed full criminal responsibility. Between the ages of 7 and 14 years, the law rebuttably presumed that offenders lacked criminal capacity (Fox, 1970b; McCarthy, 1977a; Weissman, 1983). If found criminally responsible, however, states executed youths as young as 12 years of age (Streib, 1987).

Historically, the criminal justice system faced the stark alternatives of criminal conviction and punishment as an adult, or acquittal or dismissal. Jury or judicial nullification to avoid excessive punishment excluded many youths from any controls, particularly those charged with minor offenses (Fox, 1970a; Bernard, 1992). To avoid these unpalatable alternatives, special institutions and reformatories for young offenders proliferated in the early to mid-nineteenth century (Hawes, 1971; Rothman, 1971), and, by the turn of the century, juvenile courts separated youths from adults in a separate justice system (Platt, 1977; Ryerson, 1978; Rothman, 1980).

1. The Progressive Juvenile Court

Economic modernization at the end of the nineteenth century transformed the United States from a rural agrarian society into an urban industrial one (Wiebe, 1967). Immigrants from southern and eastern Europe and from the rural United States flooded into the burgeoning cities to take advantage of new economic opportunities, and they crowded into ethnic enclaves and urban ghettoes. The "new" immigrants' sheer numbers, as well as their cultural, religious, and linguistic differences hindered their assimilation and acculturation, and posed a significant nation-building challenge for the dominant Anglo-Protestant western Europeans who had arrived a few generations earlier (Hofstadter, 1955; Higham, 1988).

Changes in family structure and functions accompanied the economic transformation. A reduction in the number and spacing of children, a shift of economic functions from the family to other work environments, and a modernizing and privatizing of the family substantially modified the roles of women and children (Kett, 1977; Lasch, 1977; Degler, 1980). The idea of childhood is socially constructed (Ainsworth, 1991; Postman, 1994). During this modernizing era the upper and middle classes promoted a new ideology of children as vulnerable, corruptible innocents who required special attention and preparation for life (Kett, 1977; Hawes and Hiner, 1985).

Modernization and industrialization sparked the Progressive movement which addressed social problems ranging from economic regulation to criminal justice to political reform (Hofstadter, 1955; Wiebe, 1967). Progressives believed that professionals and experts could develop rational and scientific solutions, and that benevolent government officials could intervene to remedy social and economic problems. Progressives attempted to "Americanize" the immigrants and poor through a variety of agencies of assimilation and acculturation to become sober, virtuous, middle-class Americans like themselves (Platt, 1977; Rothman, 1978, 1980). The Progressives coupled their trust of state power with the changing cultural conception of children and entered the realm of "child-saving." Child-centered reforms, such as the juvenile court, child labor, social welfare, and compulsory school attendance laws, both reflected and advanced the changing imagery of childhood (Cremin, 1961; Trattner, 1965; Tiffin, 1982).

Ideological changes in theories of crime causation led Progressives to formulate new criminal justice and social control policies (Rothman, 1980; allen, 1981). Positive criminology rejected "free will," asserted a scientific determinism of deviance, and sought to identify the factors that caused crime and delinquency (Allen, 1964; Matza, 1964). Reformers assumed that criminal behavior was determined rather than chosen, reduced actors' moral responsibility for their behavior, and tried to change offenders rather than punish them for their offenses.

A growing class of social science professionals adopted medical analogies to "treat" offenders and fostered the "Rehabilitative Ideal" in criminal justice policies. A flourishing "Rehabilitative Ideal" requires a belief in the malleability of human behavior and a basic consensus about the appropriate directions of human change (Allen, 1964, 1981). The "rehabilitative" ideology permeated many Progressive criminal justice reforms such as probation and parole, indeterminate sentences, and the juvenile court, and fostered open-ended, informal, and highly flexible policies (Rothman, 1980). The juvenile court combined the new conception of children with new strategies of social control to produce a judicial-welfare alternative to criminal justice, to remove children from the adult process, to enforce the newer conception of children's dependency, and to substitute the state as *parens patriae*. The juvenile court's "Rehabilitative Ideal" rested on several sets of assumptions about positive criminology, children's malleability, and the availability of effective intervention strategies to act in the child's "best interests."

Progressive "child-savers" described juvenile courts as benign, nonpunitive, and therapeutic, although modern writers question whether the movement should be seen as a humanitarian attempt to save poor and immigrant children (Hagan and Leon, 1977; Sutton, 1988), or as an effort to expand state social control over them (Fox, 1970a; Platt, 1977; Schlossman, 1977). The legal doctrine of *parens patriae*, the State as "superparent," legitimated intervention, and supported the view that juvenile court conducted civil rather than criminal proceedings. Characterizing intervention as a civil or welfare proceeding, rather than criminal, fulfilled the reformers' desire to remove children from the adult justice system and allowed greater flexibility to supervise and treat children. Because reformers eschewed punishment, the juvenile court's "status jurisdiction" enabled them to respond to noncriminal behavior such as smoking, sexual activity, truancy, immorality, or living a wayward, idle, and dissolute life (Rosenberg and Rosenberg, 1976; Schlossman and Wallach, 1978). Juvenile courts' status jurisdiction reflected the social construction of childhood and adolescence that emerged during the nineteenth century, and authorized predelinquent intervention to forestall premature adult autonomy and enforce the dependent position of youth.

The juvenile court's "Rehabilitative Ideal" envisioned a specialized judge trained in social sciences and child development whose empathic qualities and insight would aid in making individualized dispositions. Social service personnel, clinicians, and probation officers would assist the judge to decide the "best interests" of the child. Progressives assumed that a rational, scientific analysis of facts would reveal the proper diagnosis and prescribe the cure. The factual inquiry into the child's social circumstances accorded minor significance to the specific crime because the offense indicated little about his or her "real needs." Because the reformers acted benevolently, individualized their solicitude, and intervened scientifically, they saw no reason to circumscribe narrowly the power of the state. Rather, they maximized discretion to diagnose and treat, and focused on the child's character and lifestyle rather than on the crime.

By separating children from adults and providing a rehabilitative alternative to punishment, juvenile courts rejected the criminal law's jurisprudence and procedural safeguards such as juries and lawyers. Court personnel used informal procedures and a euphemistic vocabulary to eliminate any stigma and implication of an adult criminal proceeding (Mack, 1909; President's Crime Commission, 1967b). They provided confidential and private hearings, limited access to court records, "adjudicated" youths as "delinquent" rather than convicted them of crimes, and imposed "dispositions" rather than sentences. Theoretically, a child's "best interests," background, and welfare guided dispositions (Mack, 1909). Because a youth's offense provided only a symptom of his or her "real" needs, indeterminate and nonproportional dispositions potentially could continue for the duration of minority.

Procedure and substance intertwine in the juvenile court. Procedurally, juvenile courts used informal processes, confidential hearings, and a euphemistic vocabulary to obscure and disguise the reality of coercive social control. Substantively, juvenile courts used indeterminate, nonproportional sentences, emphasized treatment and supervision rather than punishment, and purportedly focused on offenders' future welfare rather than past offenses. Despite their benevolent rhetoric, however, the Progressive "child-savers" who created the juvenile court deliberately designed it to discriminate, to "Americanize" immigrants and the poor, and to provide a coercive mechanism to distinguish between their own and "other people's children."

In their pursuit of the "rehabilitative ideal," the Progressives situated the juvenile court on a number of cultural, legal, and criminological fault lines. They created several binary conceptions for the juvenile and criminal justice systems: either child or adult; either determinism or free will; either dependent or responsible; either treatment or punishment; either social welfare or just deserts; either procedural informality or formality; either discretion or rules. The past three decades has witnessed a shift from the former to the latter of each of these binary pairs in response to the structural and racial transformation of cities, the rise in serious youth crime, and the erosion of the rehabilitative assumptions of the juvenile court.

2. The Constitutional Domestication of the Juvenile Court

During the 1960s, the Warren Court's civil rights decisions, criminal due process rulings, and "constitutional domestication" of the juvenile court responded to broader structural and demographic changes taking place in the United States, particularly those associated with race and youth crime (Feld, 1999). In the decades prior to and after World War II, black migration from the rural south to the urban north increased minority concentrations in urban ghettos, made race a national rather than a regional issue, and provided the political and legal impetus for the civil rights movement (Lemann, 1993). The 1960s also witnessed the "baby boom"-generation increases in youth crime that continued until the late 1970s. During the 1960s, the rise in youth crime and urban racial disorders provoked cries for "law and order" and provided the initial political impetus to "get tough." Republicans seized crime control and welfare as wedge issues with which to distinguish themselves from Democrats, and crime policies for the first time became a central issue in national partisan politics (Beckett, 1997). As a result of "sound-bite" politics, symbols and rhetoric have come to shape penal policies more than knowledge or substance. Since the 1960s, politicians' fear of being labeled "soft on crime" has led to a constant ratcheting up of punitiveness and changed juvenile justice ideology and practice.

These macro-structural and demographic changes eroded the rehabilitative premises of the Progressive juvenile court and undermined support for discretionary, coercive socialization in juvenile courts. A flourishing "rehabilitative ideal" assumes human malleability, the existence of effective techniques to change people, and a general agreement about what it means to be rehabilitated (Allen, 1981). Progressives believed that the new social sciences and their medical model of deviance provided them with the tools to reform people and that they properly should socialize and acculturate the children of the poor and immigrants to become middle-class Americans like themselves. By the time of *Gault*, the Progressives' consensus about state benevolence, the legitimacy of imposing certain values on others, and what rehabilitation entailed and when it had occurred all became matters of intense dispute (Rothman, 1978; Allen, 1981). The decline in deference to professionals and the benevolence of experts led to an increased emphasis on procedural formality, administrative regularity, and the rule of law.

During the turbulent 1960s, several forces combined to erode support for the rehabilitative enterprise and caused the Supreme Court to require more procedural safeguards in criminal and juvenile justice administration: Left-wing critics of rehabilitation characterized governmental programs as coercive instruments of social control through which the state oppressed the poor and minorities (American Friends Service Committee, 1971); liberals became disenchanted with the unequal and disparate treatment of similarly situated offenders that resulted from treatment personnel's exercise of clinical discretion (Rothman, 1978); and conservatives advocated a "war on crime" and favored repression over rehabilitation (Graham, 1970; Beckett, 1997). In the 1960s, the issue of race provided the crucial linkage between distrust of governmental benevolence, concern about social service personnel's discretionary decision-making, urban riots and the crisis of "law and order," and the Supreme Court's due process jurisprudence.

The Warren Court's due process decisions responded to the macro-structural and demographic changes, and attempted to guarantee civil rights, to protect minorities from state officials, and to infuse governmental services with greater equality by imposing procedural restraints on official discretion (Graham, 1970; Rothman, 1978). The Supreme Court's *Gault* decision and later juvenile court cases mandated procedural safeguards in delinquency proceedings, focused judicial attention initially on whether the child committed an offense as prerequisite to sentencing, and demonstrated the linkages between procedure and substance in the juvenile court. In shifting the formal focus of juvenile courts from "real needs" to legal guilt, *Gault* identified two crucial disjunctions between juvenile justice rhetoric and reality: the theory versus the practice of "rehabilitation," and the differences between the procedural safeguards afforded adult defendants and those available to juvenile delinquents. The *Gault* Court emphasized that juveniles charged with crimes who faced institutional confinement required elementary procedural safeguards including advance notice of charges, a fair and impartial hearing, assistance of counsel, an opportunity to confront and cross-examine witnesses, and the privilege against self-incrimination (Rosenberg, 1980; McCarthy, 1981).

In *In re Winship*, 397 U.S. 358 (1970), the Court concluded that the risks of factual errors and unwarranted convictions and the need to protect juveniles against government power required states to prove delinquency by the criminal law's standard of proof "beyond a reasonable doubt" rather than by the lower "preponderance of the evidence" civil standard of proof. In *Breed v. Jones*, 421 U.S. 519 (1975), the Court posited a functional equivalence between criminal trials and delinquency proceedings, and held that the constitutional ban on double jeopardy precluded criminal reprosecution of a youth following a delinquency adjudication.

In *McKeiver v. Pennsylvania*, 403 U.S. 528 (1971), however, the Court denied to juveniles the constitutional right to a jury trial and halted the extension of full procedural parity with adult criminal prosecutions. In contrast to its analyses in earlier decisions, the *McKeiver* Court reasoned that "fundamental fairness" in delinquency proceedings required only "accurate fact-finding," a requirement that a juvenile court judge acting alone could satisfy as well as a jury. Unlike *Gault* and *Winship* which recognized that procedural safeguards protect against governmental oppression, the Court in *McKeiver* denied that delinquents required such protection and instead invoked the stereotype of the sympathetic, paternalistic juvenile court judge. Unfortunately, the *McKeiver* Court did not analyze or elaborate on the differences between treatment as a juvenile and punishment as an adult that warranted the procedural differences between the two systems (Feld, 1988b).

Together, *Gault and Winship* precipitated a procedural and substantive revolution in the juvenile court system that unintentionally but inevitably transformed its original Progressive conception. By emphasizing criminal procedural regularity in the determination of delinquency, the Supreme Court shifted the focus of juvenile courts from paternalistic assessments of a youth's "real needs" to proof of commission of criminal acts. By formalizing the connection between criminal conduct and coercive intervention, the Court made explicit a relationship previously implicit and unacknowledged. Providing delinquents with even a modicum of procedural justice in juvenile courts also legitimated greater punitiveness. Thus, *Gault*'s procedural reforms provided the impetus for the substantive convergence between juvenile and criminal courts, so that for most purposes, contemporary juvenile courts constitute a wholly owned subsidiary of the criminal justice system. It is a historical irony that race provided the initial impetus for the Supreme Court to expand procedural rights to protect minority youths' liberty interests, and now juvenile courts' increasingly punitive sanctions fall disproportionately on minority offenders.

Although the constitutional cases provide a generic procedural framework, it is difficult to generalize about the juvenile court as an institution. State statutes, rather than the constitution, create juvenile courts, and states' legislative definitions and processing of young offenders differ. In most states, juvenile court jurisdiction encompasses criminal and noncriminal misconduct by all persons under 18 years of age, although in some states, adult criminal court jurisdiction begins at 16 or 17 years of age (Snyder and Sickmund, 1995). In addition, even when juvenile court jurisdiction extends until 18 years of age, some states may automatically place younger youths charged with serious offenses in adult criminal court. In a few states, juvenile and criminal courts exercise concurrent jurisdiction over young offenders, and the prosecutor's decision to charge a youth as a juvenile or as an adult determines the forum in which the case will be heard (Snyder and Sickmund, 1995). Consequently, juvenile courts in different jurisdictions confront widely different clientele.

Early proponents of the traditional juvenile court painted an idealized portrait of procedural informality as a means to attain its rehabilitative ambitions. Judicial discretion, local diversity, and informal processes fostered many different versions of juvenile courts that differed substantially in philosophy and practice. Contemporary evaluations of juvenile courts continue to emphasize juvenile court judges' discretion and juvenile courts' organizational and operational diversity (Rubin, 1985).

With *Gault*'s imposition of formal procedures and the emergence of punitive as well as therapeutic goals, states' juvenile courts no longer necessarily conform with the traditional, rehabilitative model, and vary on a number of structural, philosophical, and procedural dimensions (Stapleton, Aday, and Ito, 1982; Hasenfeld and Cheung, 1985). Traditional courts intervene in a child's "best interests" on an informal, discretionary basis, while more formal legalistic courts emphasize rule-oriented decision-making and recognize juveniles' legal rights. "Traditional" and "due process" courts range across a continuum from informal to formal procedures with corresponding structural and substantive differences (Stapleton *et al.*, 1982). Traditional, informal, cooperative courts and formal, adversarial courts differ considerably in the presence of counsel, which provides one important indicator of procedural, substantive, and structural variations among juvenile courts (Handler, 1965; Stapleton and Teitelbaum, 1972; Feld, 1993b).

While juvenile courts vary substantially among the states, they vary within a single state as well. Although the same laws—statutes, appellate opinions, and court rules of procedure—typically apply to all juvenile courts within a state, juvenile justice administration varies substantially with social structure and geographic locale (Kempf, Decker, and Bing, 1990; Feld, 1991; Sampson and Laub, 1993). Differences in social structure affect differences both in juvenile crime rates and in juvenile justice administration, the presence of counsel, rates of pretrial detention, and sentencing practices. For example, whether youths live in metropolitan areas with full-time juvenile courts or in rural areas with part-time juvenile judges affects how courts screen, process, and sentence them.

C. PROCEDURAL JUSTICE IN JUVENILE COURTS

Procedure and substance intertwine inextricably in juvenile courts. The Progressives' *parens patriae* ideology coupled substantive decisions in the child's "best interests" with informal discretionary procedures. The Supreme Court in *Gault* emphasized the disjunction between rehabilitative rhetoric and punitive reality and insisted on greater procedural protections for delinquents. Since *Gault* procedural formality has been associated with an increased emphasis on punishment in juvenile courts both in legal theory and in administrative practice (Gardner, 1987; Forst and Blomquist, 1991; Feld, 1998). When the Supreme Court decided *McKeiver* in 1970, states did not use determinate or mandatory minimum sentencing statutes to constrain juvenile court judges' discretion. Beginning in the mid- to late 1970s, states began to adopt "designated felony," serious offender, mandatory minimum, and determinate sentencing laws (Feld, 1988b; Sheffer, 1995). Legislative revisions of juvenile codes' purpose clauses eliminate even rhetorical support for rehabilitation. These changes repudiate many of the juvenile court's original assumptions that states should treat juveniles differently than adults, that juvenile courts operate in a youth's "best interest," and that rehabilitation is an indeterminate process that cannot be limited by fixed-timed punishment. These changes contradict *McKeiver*'s premise that delinquents require fewer procedural safeguards than do adult criminal defendants because of the benign consequences of therapeutic intervention.

The formal procedures of juvenile and criminal courts have converged under *Gault*'s impetus. There remains, however, a substantial gulf between theory and reality, between the "law on the books" and "law in action." Theoretically, delinquents are entitled to formal trials and the assistance of counsel. In actuality, the quality of procedural justice that juvenile courts provide delinquents remains far different. More than three decades ago, the Supreme Court decried that "the child receives the worst of both worlds: he gets neither the protections accorded to adults nor the solicitous care and regenerative treatment postulated for children" [*Kent v. United States*, 383 U.S. 541, 556 (1996)]. Despite the criminalizing of juvenile courts, most states provide neither special procedures to protect juveniles from their own immaturity nor the full panoply of adult procedural safeguards. States manipulate fluid concepts of children and adults or treatment and punishment in order to maximize the social control of young people. On the one hand, states treat juveniles just like adults when formal equality results in practical inequality. For example, most states use the adult standard of "knowing, intelligent, and voluntary under the totality of the circumstances" to gauge juveniles' waivers of *Miranda* rights and counsel (*Fare v. Michael C.*, 1979; Feld, 1984), even though juveniles lack the legal competence of adults. Research on juveniles' waivers of *Miranda* rights (Grisso, 1980) and waivers of their right to counsel provide compelling evidence of the procedural deficiencies of the juvenile court (Feld, 1989, 1993b). On the other hand, even as juvenile courts become more punitive, most states continue to make benevolent and paternalistic claims and deny juveniles access to jury trials or other criminal procedural rights guaranteed to adult defendants (Feld, 1995). Juvenile courts provide a procedural regime in which few adults charged with crimes and facing the prospect of confinement would consent to be tried. Based on depictions of courtroom dramas and publicized criminal trials, young people have a cultural expectation of what a "real" trial should be. The contrast between the ideal-typical jury trial with a vigorous defense lawyer and the "actualized caricature" of a juvenile bench trial fosters a sense of injustice that may delegitimate the legal process (Ainsworth, 1991).

1. Jury Trials in Juvenile Court

The jury provides a critical procedural safeguard when judges impose punitive, rather than therapeutic, sentences. Only about a dozen states grant juveniles the right to jury trials, and the vast majority uncritically follow the Supreme Court's lead in *McKeiver v. Pennsylvania* and deny youths charged with crimes access to juries (Ainsworth, 1991; Feld, 1995). Without citing any empirical evidence, the *McKeiver* Court posited virtual parity between the factual accuracy of juvenile and adult trials to justify denying juveniles a jury trial. But juries provide special protections to assure factual accuracy, use a higher evidentiary threshold when they apply *Winship*'s "proof beyond a reasonable doubt" standard, and acquit more readily than do judges (Kalven and Zeisel, 1966). An analysis of cases prosecuted in California's juvenile and adult courts concluded that "it is easier to win a conviction in the juvenile court that in the criminal court, with comparable types of cases" (Greenwood, Lipson, Abrahamse, and Zimring, 1983:30–31).

Several factors explain why juvenile court judges would convict youths more readily than would juries (Ainsworth, 1991). Fact-finding by judges and juries differs intrinsically because the former try hundreds of cases each year while the latter may hear only one or two. As a result of hearing many cases routinely, judges become less meticulous in considering evidence, evaluate facts more casually, and apply less stringently than do jurors the concepts of reasonable doubt and presumption of innocence. Although judges' personal characteristics differ from those of jurors, defendants are unable to determine how those factors will affect the decision in their case. Through *voir dire*, litigants may examine jurors about their attitudes, beliefs, and experiences as they may bear on the way they will decide the case; no comparable opportunity exists to explore a judge's background to determine the presence of judicial biases. In addition to the novelty of deciding cases, juries and judges evaluate testimony differently. Juvenile court judges hear testimony from the same police and probation officers on a regular basis and develop settled opinions about their credibility. Similarly, as a result of hearing earlier charges against a juvenile, or presiding over a detention hearing or pretrial motion to suppress evidence, a judge already may have a predetermined view of a youth's credibility, background, and character (Feld, 1984; Ainsworth, 1991). Fact-finding by a judge differs from that by a jury because of an individual fact-finder does not have to discuss the evidence with a group before reaching a conclusion. Although a judge instructs jurors explicitly about the law they apply to a case, when the judge presides at a bench trial, he or she is not required to articulate the law, thus rendering it more difficult to determine whether the judge correctly and understood and applied it.

Moreover, *McKeiver* ignored that constitutional criminal procedures also prevent governmental oppression. In *Duncan v. Louisiana*, 391 U.S. 145 (1968), the Supreme Court found a constitutional right to a jury trial in adult criminal proceedings both to assure factual accuracy *and* to protect against governmental oppression. *Duncan* emphasized that juries protect against a weak or biased judge or an overzealous prosecutor, inject the community's values into law, and increase the visibility and accountability of justice administration. These protective functions are especially critical in juvenile courts, which labor behind closed doors immune from public scrutiny. Appellate courts acknowledge that juvenile court cases exhibit many more procedural errors than do criminal cases and suggest that secrecy fosters a judicial casualness toward the law that visibility might restrain [*R.L.R. v. State*, 487 P.2d 27 (Ala. 1971); *In re Dino*, 359 S.2d 586 (La. 1978)].

Juries have symbolic significance for the juvenile court out of all proportion to their practical impact. As a symbol, granting juveniles the right to a jury trial requires honesty about punishment imposed in the name of treatment and the need to protect against even benevolent governmental coercion. In practice, even in states that theoretically grant delinquents the right to a jury trial, juveniles seldom exercise the right (Feld, 1995). One survey reported that the rates of juvenile jury trials ranged between 0.36 and 3.2% of cases (Shaugnessy, 1979); another reported rates between less than 1 and 3% (Feld, 1995), rates lower than those for criminal defendants.

2. The Right to Counsel in Juvenile Court

Procedural justice hinges on access to and the assistance of counsel. When the Supreme Court decided *Gault*, attorneys appeared in perhaps 5% of delinquency proceedings (Note, 1966; President's Commission on Law Enforcement, 1967b). Despite *Gault*'s formal legal changes, however, the actual delivery of legal services to juveniles has lagged behind. In the immediate aftermath of *Gault*, observers in two metropolitan juvenile courts systematically monitored judicial compliance with the decision and reported that judges neither adequately advised juveniles of their right to counsel nor appointed counsel for them (Lefstein, Stapleton, and Teitelbaum, 1969). Even in those rare delinquency cases in which lawyers appeared, they seldom participated in any meaningful way (Ferster and Courtless, 1972).

In the decades since *Gault*, the promise of an attorney remains unrealized; in many states half or fewer juveniles receive the assistance of counsel to which the Constitution entitles them. In the only study that reports statewide data and makes interstate comparisons of the delivery of legal services, in three of the six states surveyed, lawyers represented only 37.5, 47.7, and 52.7% of juveniles charged with delinquent and status offenses in 1984 (Feld, 1988a). An evaluation of legal representation in North Carolina in 1978 found that the juvenile defender project represented only 22.3% of juveniles in Winston-Salem and only 45.8% in Charlotte (Carlke and Koch, 1980). Other studies reported rates of representation of 26.2 and 38.7% in a southeastern jurisdiction (Aday, 1986), of 32% of the juveniles in a large north central city (Walter and Ostrander, 1982), and of only 41.8% of juveniles in a large, midwestern county's juvenile court (Bortner, 1982). In Minnesota, throughout the 1980s and early 1990s, most juveniles appeared in juvenile court without counsel (Feld, 1993b, 1995). Rates of representation within Minnesota varied enormously from county to county, ranging from a high of 100% in one county to a low of less than 5% in several others (Feld, 1989, 1993b). A substantial minority of youths removed from their homes (30.7%) or confined in correctional institutions (26.5%) were unrepresented at their adjudication and disposition (Feld, 1989). Although lawyers represent larger proportions of juveniles charged with serious crimes (Feld, 1988a, 1993b), serious offenders constitute a small part of juvenile court dockets in most states

(Snyder and Sickmund, 1995). As a result, juveniles charged with minor property offenses, like shoplifting constitute the largest group of unrepresented youths and those most likely to be incarcerated without representation.

Several factors explain why so many youths appear without lawyers in juvenile courts. Affluent parents may decline to retain an attorney. Public-defender legal services may be inadequate or nonexistent in nonurban areas. Juvenile court judges may encourage and readily find waivers of the right to counsel in order to ease their administrative burdens. Judges may give cursory and misleading advisories that inadequately convey the importance of the right to counsel and suggest that the waiver litany constitutes simply a formal technicality. Traditional, treatment-oriented judges may resent legal advocates who attempt to limit their discretion. Judges also may predetermine the disposition they likely will impose on a juvenile and decline to appoint counsel when they anticipate a probationary sentence (Bortner, 1982; aday, 1986; Feld, 1989). In many instances, a juvenile pleads guilty and a judge disposes of the case at the same hearing without benefit of counsel. Whatever the reason, many juveniles who face potentially coercive state action never see a lawyer and waive their right to counsel without consulting with an attorney or appreciating the legal consequences of relinquishing counsel.

Juveniles' waiver of counsel is the most common explanation why so many delinquents appear without a lawyer (Stapleton and Teitelbaum, 1972; Bortner, 1982; Feld, 1984, 1993b). Most state courts use the adult legal standard—"knowing, intelligent, and voluntary" under the "totality of the circumstances"—to assess the validity of juveniles' waivers of constitutional rights [*Fare v. Michael C.*, 442 U.S. 707 (1979); Feld, 1993b]. The crucial issue for juveniles, as for adults, is whether a waiver of counsel can be "knowing, intelligent, and voluntary" if a child waives the right alone and without consulting with an attorney. The problem is exacerbated when judges, in closed, confidential proceedings, seeking predetermined results, create an impression that waiver is a meaningless technicality, and interpret the juvenile's ultimate response to their advisories.

Many scholars have criticized extensively the "totality" approach to juveniles' waivers of rights as an example of state legal policies that treat juveniles just like adults when formal equality puts them at a practical disadvantage (Rosenberg, 1980; Grisso, 1980; Melton, 1989). Despite *Fare*'s adherence to the "totality of the circumstances" approach to gauging waivers of constitutional rights, reasons exist to question whether a typical juvenile's waiver decision is, or even can be, "knowing, intelligent, and voluntary." Empirical evaluations of juveniles' comprehension of *Miranda* rights indicate that most juveniles simply do not possess the capacity of adults to waive constitutional rights "knowingly and intelligently." Professor Thomas Grisso (1980, 1981) conducted tests to determine whether juveniles could paraphrase the words in the *Miranda* warning, whether they could define six critical words in the *Miranda* warning such as "attorney," "consult," and "appoint," and whether they could give correct true–false answers to 12 rewordings of the *Miranda* warnings. He administered structured interviews, designed by a panel of psychologists and lawyers, to three samples of juvenile subjects and two samples of adult subjects, and compared the juveniles' performances with the adult norms. Most juveniles who received the warnings did not understand them well enough to waive their constitutional rights "knowingly and intelligently." Only 20.9% of the juveniles, as compared with 42.3% of the adults, demonstrated adequate understanding of the four components of a *Miranda* warning, while 55.3% of juveniles as contrasted with 23.5% of the adults exhibited no comprehension of at least one of the four warnings. Juveniles most frequently misunderstood the *Miranda* advisory that they had the right to consult with an attorney and to have one present during interrogation. Younger juveniles exhibited even greater difficulties understanding their rights. "As a class, juveniles younger than fifteen years of age failed to meet both the absolute and relative (adult norm) standards for comprehension.... The vast majority of these juveniles misunderstood at least one of the four standard *Miranda* statements, and compared with adults, demonstrated significantly poorer comprehension of the nature and significance of the *Miranda* rights" (Grisso, 1980:1160). Although "juveniles younger than fifteen manifest significantly poorer comprehension than adults of comparable intelligence" (Grisso, 1980:1160), the level of comprehension that youths 16 and older exhibited, although comparable to the adults', left much to be desired.

Moreover, research conducted under "ideal" laboratory conditions may fail to capture sufficiently the individual characteristics, social context, and stressful coercive conditions associated with actual legal proceedings. Youths' responses to hypothetical questions in a relaxed research atmosphere do not replicate adequately advisories that "can be gentle or tough, can explain the rights well or poorly, and in many ways can exert varying amounts of pressure to comply" (Abramovitch, Higgins-Biss, and Biss, 1993:319). Typically, delinquents come from lower-income households and may possess less verbal skills or capacity to understand legal abstractions than the youths who participated in these psychological studies. Moreover, children from poorer and ethnic-minority backgrounds often believe that law enforcement officials will punish them if they exercise their legal rights (Melton, 1989). Immaturity, inexperience, and lower verbal competence than adults render youths especially vulnerable. The host of legal disabilities that states impose on children to protect them from their own developmental limitations, for example, to enter contracts, convey property, marry, drink, drive, or even donate blood, recognize that children have different competencies than adults. While states recognize these developmental differences for other purposes, most states allow juveniles to waive constitutional rights such as *Miranda* and the right to counsel without restriction and to confront the power of the State alone and unaided.

Even when attorneys represent juveniles, they may not perform effectively for their clients. Organizational pressures to cooperate, judicial hostility toward adversarial litigants, role ambiguity created by the dual goals of rehabilitation and punishment, reluctance to help juveniles "beat a case," or internalization of a court's treatment philosophy may compromise the role of counsel in juvenile court (Stapleton and Teitelbaum, 1972; Clarke and Koch, 1980; Bortner, 1982). Institutional pressures to maintain stable, cooperative working relations with other personnel in the system may conflict with effective adversarial advocacy.

Several studies report that juveniles who appear with lawyers in juvenile courts may be at a disadvantage when compared with similarly situated unrepresented youths (Stapleton and Teitelbaum, 1972; Clarke and Koch, 1980; Bortner, 1982; Feld, 1988a, 1989, 1991). While the relationships between the factors producing more severe dispositions and the factors influencing the appointment of counsel are complex, the presence of counsel appears to be an aggravating factor in sentencing (Feld, 1993b). Juvenile court judges consistently appear more likely to incarcerate juveniles who appear with lawyers than those who appear without counsel.

Several reasons may explain the apparent relationship between procedural formality, as indicated by the presence of counsel, and more severe sentences. The lawyers who appear in juvenile court simply may be incompetent and prejudice their clients' cases. While we lack systematic qualitative evaluations of the actual performance of counsel in juvenile courts, the available evidence suggests that even in jurisdictions where juvenile courts routinely appoint counsel, they may not be competent or effective (Knitzer and Sobie, 1984). The American Bar Association (1995:24) summarized some of the systemic obstacles to quality defense representation: "many juvenile public defender systems suffer from underfunding, low morale, high turnover, lack of training, low status in 'career ladders,' political pressure, low salaries and huge caseloads. Effective representation in court-appointed counsel programs was impeded by other factors, such as the appointment of unqualified, inexperienced attorneys; inadequate monitoring of performance; and problems of maintaining independence from the judiciary that appoints the lawyers."

On the other hand, a juvenile court judge's familiarity with a case early in a proceeding may alert her to the eventual disposition that she will impose on a youth following a conviction, and she may appoint counsel if she anticipates more severe consequences (Aday, 1986; Feld, 1989). In most jurisdictions, the same judge who presides at a youth's arraignment and detention hearing later decides the case on the merits and then pronounces sentence. Perhaps judges base their initial decisions to appoint counsel on evidence obtained in the preliminary stages which also influence their subsequent sentencing decisions. If so, the court's extensive familiarity with a case prior to the fact-finding hearing raises basic questions about the fairness and objectivity of the adjudicative process (Ainsworth, 1991).

Another explanation for the aggravating effect that lawyers appear to have on delinquents' sentences is that judges simply may feel free to sentence more severely juveniles who appear with counsel than those without. Within statutory limits, judges may sentence a youth who is represented more severely because adherence to the form of due process insulates their sentences from appellate reversal. In short, there may be a price for the use of formal procedures similar to that experienced by adult criminal defendants who insist on a jury trial rather than pleading guilty. While not explicitly punishing represented juveniles because they appear with counsel, judges may sentence more leniently those youths who appear unaided and contritely throw themselves on the mercy of the court.

Since the *Gault* decision, the juvenile court is first and foremost a legal entity engaged in criminal social control and not simply a social welfare agency. As a legal institution exercising substantial coercive powers over young people, delinquents require safeguards to protect against inappropriate state intervention. The Court in *Gault* declined to rely solely on the benevolence of juvenile court judges or social workers to safeguard the interests of young people, and instead adopted the familiar adversarial model that recognized the conflict between the state and a youth charged with a crime. In an adversarial process, only lawyers effectively can invoke other procedural safeguards designed to protect an accused. Juvenile justice policies that recognized that youths differ somewhat from adults would provide younger offenders with additional procedural safeguards, such as mandatory, nonwaivable assistance of counsel, in order to offset the disadvantages of immaturity and inexperience in the justice process. Implementing a true "protectionist" policy would provide juveniles with more procedural protections than adults, rather than fewer. Instead, juvenile courts' "Crime Control" reality of informal, administrative discretion with minimal adversarial challenge, trumps *Gault*'s "Due Process" ideal to maximize the social control of adolescents.

D. CRIMINOLOGICAL TRIAGE

The *Gault* decision represents a procedural revolution that failed *and* that produced unintended negative consequences. Delinquents, then and now, continue to receive the "worst of both worlds," neither solicitous care and regenerative treatment nor the criminal procedural rights of adults. *McKeiver* denied delinquents criminal procedural equality with adults, but the

Court could not compel states to deliver social welfare services. As a result, delinquents experience punishment but without adult procedural justice. Although *McKeiver* endorsed a "rehabilitative" juvenile court, *Gault*'s insistence on some criminal procedural regularity shifted the focus of delinquency hearings from paternalistic assessments of a youth's "real needs" to proof that she committed a crime. Thus, *Gault* formalized the connection between criminal conduct and coercive intervention, "criminalized" juvenile courts, and fostered their procedural and substantive convergence with criminal courts. Although youths lack procedural parity with adult defendants, providing delinquents with any procedural safeguards at all legitimated more punitive sanctions. Once states grant a semblance of procedural justice, however inadequate, it becomes easier for them to depart from a purely "rehabilitative" model of juvenile justice.

Juvenile courts' increased procedural formality also provided the impetus to adopt substantive "criminological triage" policies. The "triage" process entails diverting noncriminal status offenders out of the juvenile system at the "soft" end of the court's clientele, waiving serious offenders for adult criminal prosecution at the "hard" end, and punishing more severely the residual, middle range of ordinary criminal-delinquent offenders.

1. Jurisdiction over Noncriminal Status Offenders

In the post-*Gault* decades, critics questioned extensively the definition and administration of status jurisdiction (Teitelbaum and Gough, 1977; Allinson, 1983). Since the President's Commission on Law Enforcement (1967a,b) recommended narrowing the range of conduct for which states authorized juvenile court intervention, many professional groups have advocated reform or elimination of juvenile courts' status jurisdiction (e.g., National Council on Crime and Delinquency, 1975; American Bar Association, 1982). Critics focused on the status jurisdiction's adverse impact on children, its disabling effects on families, schools, and other agencies that referred noncriminal offenders to court, and the legal and administrative issues it raises for juvenile courts (Andrews and Cohn, 1974; Katz and Teitelbaum, 1978).

Until recent reforms, most states typically treated status offenses as a form of delinquency and detained and incarcerated status delinquents in the same institutions with criminal delinquents even though they had committed no crimes (Handler and Zatz, 1982). Parental referrals overloaded juvenile courts with intractable family disputes, diverted scarce judicial resources from other tasks, and exacerbated rather than ameliorated family conflict (Andrews and Cohn, 1974). Social service agencies and schools used the court as a "dumping ground" to impose solutions rather than to address sources of conflict. Status jurisdiction raised legal issues of "void for vagueness," equal protection, and procedural justice (Katz and Teitelbaum, 1978; Rubin, 1985). Status jurisdiction gave judges broad discretion to intervene to prevent unruliness or immorality from ripening into criminality. Judges' exercise of standardless discretion to regulate noncriminal misconduct and "immorality" often reflected personal values and prejudices, rather than a "rule of law" and disproportionately affected poor, minority, and female juveniles (Sussman, 1977; Chesney-Lind, 1988).

Three post-*Gault* trends—diversion, deinstitutionalization, and decriminalization—represent judicial and legislative responses to these criticisms of the courts' handling of noncriminal youths (Empey, 1973). The Federal Juvenile Justice and Delinquency Prevention Act of 1974, 42 U.S.C. §§ 5601 *et seq.* (1983), required states to begin a process of removing noncriminal offenders from secure detention and correctional facilities. Federal and state restrictions on comingling status and delinquent offenders in institutions provided the impetus to divert some status offenders from juvenile courts and to decarcerate those who remained in the system.

a. *Diversion*

Since *Gault*, diversion programs represent one juvenile justice reform strategy to provide youths with services on an informal basis (Klein, 1979). Just as the original juvenile court diverted youths from adult criminal courts, diversion programs shift away from juvenile court youths eligible to enter that system. Research findings question, however, whether states' juvenile justice systems have implemented diversion programs coherently or effectively (Klein, 1979; Polk, 1984). The juvenile justice ideology of early identification for treatment expands inherently and lends itself to overreaching. Many diversion programs have not restricted themselves to youths who would otherwise have entered the juvenile justice system but also encompassed "young people who are normally counseled and released by the police, if indeed they have any dealings with the police" (Klein, 1979:165). Consequently, diversion, theoretically intended to reduce juvenile courts' client population, may have had the opposite effect of "widening the net of social control" (Klein, 1979; Polk, 1984). The numbers of juveniles referred to court remains relatively constant despite a declining youth population, while juveniles whom the system previously would have released now are subjected to other forms of intervention (Decker, 1985). Moreover, diversion provides a rationale to shift discretion from the juvenile court itself where *Gault* subjects judges' decisions to some degree of procedural formality, to police or intake "gatekeepers" on the periphery of the system who continue to operate on an informal pre-*Gault* basis with no accountability. In his comprehensive study of the status offenders, *Stubborn Children*, John Sutton (1988:215) concludes that diversion "sanctified and encouraged a strategy for circumventing due process, assured that programs would stay in the discretionary hands of local officials, and encouraged the privatization of long-term social control." Similarly, "net-widening" analyses conclude that "because of the vagueness of the statutes defining status-offense conduct, the low visibility of police decisions in such situations, the low probability of judicial review of these decisions, these programs present an even greater opportunity for abuse" (Decker, 1985:215).

b. *Deinstitutionalization*

Federal and state bans on secure confinement of status offenders provided an impetus to deinstitutionalize noncriminal youths. Although the numbers of status offenders in secure detention facilities and institutions declined by the mid-1980s (Handler and Zatz, 1982; Krisberg and Schwartz, 1983; Schneider, 1984), judges only sent a small proportion of status offenders to secure institutions; most remain eligible for commitment to foster or group homes and other places of confinement (Sutton, 1988). Amendments to the Federal Juvenile Justice Act in 1980 weakened the restrictions on placing noncriminal youths in secure facilities; juvenile justice officials may charge status offenders who run away from nonsecure placements or violate court orders with contempt of court, a criminal-delinquent act, and incarcerate them [42 U.S.C. S 5633(a)(12)(A) (1983); Costello and Worthington, 1981; Schwartz, 1980a]. Juvenile court judges' use of their contempt power to "bootstrap" and convert status offenders into criminal-delinquents remains an important continuing source of gender bias in juvenile justice administration (Bishop and Frazier, 1992). Even though subsequent probation violations may result in incarceration, juveniles initially charged with status offenses enjoy fewer procedural rights than do youths charged with delinquency (Smith, 1993).

c. Decrminalization

Until recent reforms, states classified status offenses as a form of delinquency. Beginning with jurisdictional redefinitions in California in 1961 and New York in 1962, almost every state has decriminalized conduct that is illegal only for children—incorrigibility, runaway, truancy—by relabeling it into new nondelinquency classifications such as Persons or Children in Need of Supervision (PINS) [*N.Y. Family Ct. Act* § 712(b) (McKinney Supp. 1983); *Cal. Welf. and Inst. Code* §§ 600–602 (West 1972); Rubin, 1985]. The most recent legislative strategy is to relabel "juvenile nuisances" as dependent, neglected, or as Children in Need of Protection and Services (CHIPS) (Rosenberg, 1983; Bishop and Frazier, 1992). Label changes simply shift youths from one jurisdictional category to another without significantly limiting courts' dispositional authority. By manipulating classifications, the justice system may relabel former status offenders downward as dependent or neglected youths, upward as delinquent offenders (Mahoney and Fenster, 1982), or laterally into private sector mental health or chemical dependency "treatment" facilities (Klein, 1979; Handler and Zatz, 1982; Schneider, 1984).

Diversion, court referrals, and voluntary parental commitments now shift many youths whom the juvenile justice system previously would have handled as status offenders, especially those who are middle-class and female, into private sector mental health or chemical dependency treatment facilities (Schwartz, 1989b). The Supreme Court in *Parham v. J.R.*, 442 U.S. 609 (1979), ruled that the only process juveniles are due when their parents "voluntarily" commit them to secure treatment facilities is a physician's determination that it is medically appropriate (Weithorn, 1988). Most states' civil commitment laws do not provide juveniles with the same procedural safeguards as they do adults. Clearly, some children's psychological dysfunctions or substance abuse require medical attention. However, many commitments result from status-like social or behavioral conflicts, self-serving parental motives, and medical entrepreneurs coping with under utilized hospitals. The "hidden system" of psychiatric and chemical dependency "treatment" facilities provides a readily available and easily accessible institutional system for troublemaking youth funded by third-party insurance payments. The increased rate of juvenile psychiatric commitments coincided directly with the deinstitutionalization of status offenders (Schwartz, Jackson-Beeck, and Anderson, 1984). The combination of psychiatric hospitals seeking profits, health maintenance organizations with funds to reinvest in other care modalities, insurance and Medicaid coverage for inpatient mental health care, and the malleability of diagnostic categories, permits physicians to medicalize deviance and parents to incarcerate their troublesome children without meaningful judicial supervision (Weithorn, 1988; Schwartz, 1989b).

Historically, the child welfare, mental health, and juvenile justice systems have dealt with relatively interchangeable youths who shift from one system to another depending on social attitudes, available funds, and imprecise legal definitions. The private sector mental health industry serves as the juvenile justice system's institutional successor for the care and control of problematic youths; deinstitutionalization has resulted in transinstitutionalization of some noncriminal juveniles from publicly funded facilities to private institutions (Lerman, 1982, 1984).

Whether states or parents incarcerate the juveniles for their "best interests," for "adjustment reactions" symptomatic of adolescence, or for "chemical dependency," these trends revive the imagery of diagnosis and treatment on a discretionary basis without regard to formal due process considerations. The appropriate social and legal response to minor, nuisance, and noncriminal youngsters goes to the heart of the juvenile court's mission and the normative concept of childhood on which it is based. The debate polarizes advocates of authority and control of youth (Arthur, 1977) and those who view intervention too often as discriminatory and a denial of rights (Murray, 1983; Rubin, 1985). Some states have restricted juvenile courts' status jurisdiction or only allow noncriminal intervention in cases of dependency, neglect, or abuse. But, juvenile court judges strongly resist removal of status jurisdiction because any contraction of their authority over children leads to further convergence with criminal courts.

2. Waiver of Jurisdiction over Serious Juvenile Offenders

Public frustration with crime, fear of recent increases in youth violence, homicide and offenses involving guns, and the racial characteristics of many violent young offenders fuel the popular desire to "get tough." Widespread misgivings about the ability of juvenile courts either to rehabilitate chronic and violent young offenders or simultaneously to protect public safety bolster policies to "crack down" on youth crime and provide the impetus to prosecute larger numbers of youths as adults. These initiatives simplify the transfer of young offenders to criminal courts and expose waived youths to substantial sentences as adults. Such strategies deemphasize rehabilitation and individualized consideration of the offender, stress personal and justice system accountability and punishment, and base decisions on the seriousness of the present offense and prior record.

Increasingly, people and politicians view juvenile courts' traditional commitment to rehabilitation as a bias toward leniency often to the detriment of protecting the public of satisfying the victim. For more than two decades, conservatives have denounced juvenile courts for "coddling" young criminals, and more recently, states legislators have adopted more punitive policies toward young offenders in both the juvenile and criminal justice systems (Torbet *et al.*, 1996). These recent, punitive responses represent simply the latest pendulum swing in the "cycle of juvenile justice," the historical oscillation between leniency and severity that characterizes youth crime policies (Bernard, 1992). But, waiver policies in all of their guises implicate the boundary of criminal "adulthood" and responsibility, and the processes by which states determine whether to prosecute youths in juvenile or criminal courts.

As a result of recent "get-tough" laws, judges, prosecutors, and legislators waive increasing numbers of younger offenders to criminal courts for prosecution as adults. The rate of judicial waiver increased 68% between 1988 and 1992 (Snyder and Sickmund, 1995). Prosecutors in Florida alone transfer more juveniles to criminal court than do all of the juvenile court judges in the country combined (Bishop and Frazier, 1991). In an effort to "crack down" on youth crime, legislators exclude various combinations of age and offenses from juvenile courts' jurisdiction, and then further expand the lists of excluded offenses and reduce the age of criminal responsibility (Torbet *et al.*, 1996).

The "get-tough" juvenile justice policies of the early 1990s reflect macrostructural, economic, and racial demographic changes in cities during the 1970s and 1980s, the emergence of the black underclass, and the rise in gun violence and youth homicides (Massey and Denton, 1993; Blumstein, 1995). Between World War II and the early 1970s, semiskilled high school graduates could get good-paying jobs in the automobile, steel, and construction industries. Beginning in the 1970s, the transition from an industrial to an information and service economy reduced employment opportunities in the manufacturing sectors, and produced a bifurcation of economic opportunities based on skills and education. During the post-World War II period, government highway, housing, and mortgage policies encouraged suburban expansion around the urban centers (Massey and Denton, 1993). The migration of whites to the suburbs, the growth of information and service jobs in the suburbs, the bifurcation of the economy, and the deindustrialization of the urban core increased racial segregation and the concentration of poverty among blacks in the major cities (Wilson, 1987, 1996). In the mid-1980s, the emergence of a structural underclass, the introduction of crack cocaine into the inner cities, and the proliferation of guns among youth produced a sharp escalation in black youth homicide rates (Blumstein, 1995). The age-offense-race-specific increase in youth homicide provided further political impetus to "get tough" and to "crack down" on youth crime as politicians perceived young perpetrators as "other people's children." In this context, because of differences in rates of offending by race, "getting tough" on violence meant targeting young black men. As a result of the connection in the public and political minds between race and youth crime, juveniles have become the symbolic "Willie Horton" of the 1990s (Beckett, 1997).

The "get-tough" waiver policies reflect juvenile courts' broader jurisprudential changes from rehabilitation to retribution. The overarching themes of these legislative amendments include a shift from individualized justice to just deserts, from offender to offense, from "amenability to treatment" to public safety, and from immature delinquent to responsible criminal. State legislatures use offense criteria in waiver laws either as dispositional guidelines to structure and limit judicial discretion, to guide prosecutorial charging decisions, or automatically to exclude certain youths from juvenile court jurisdiction (Feld, 1987, 1995; Torbet *et al.*, 1996). These changes in waiver policy also reflect a fundamental cultural and legal reconceptualization of youth from innocent and dependent to responsible and autonomous. Politicians' "sound bites," like "adult crime adult time," reflect typical criminal policies that provide no formal recognition of youthfulness as a mitigating factor in sentencing. Once youths make the transition to the adult system, criminal court judges sentence them as if they are adults, impose the same sentences, send them to the same prisons, and even execute them for the crimes they committed as children (Feld, 1998; *Stanford v. Kentucky*, 1989).

States legislators adopt social control policies within a binary framework—either child or adult, either treatment or punishment, either juvenile court or criminal court. Unfortunately, jurisdictional bifurcation frustrates effective and rational social control and often results in a "punishment gap" when youths make the transition between the two systems. While violent young offenders receive dramatically more severe sentences as adults than they would have received as juveniles, chronic property offenders who constitute the bulk of youths judicially transferred actually receive shorter sentences as adults than they could have obtained as delinquents had they remained within the juvenile system (Podkopacz and Feld, 1995, 1996). Many recent changes in waiver laws represent an effort to improve the fit between waiver criteria and criminal court sentencing practices, to use juvenile prior records more extensively to enhance the sentences of young adult offenders, and to respond to career criminality that begins in early adolescence but continues into adulthood (Feld, 1998). Efforts to integrate juvenile and criminal court sentencing practices and criminal history records attempt to rationalize control of serious and chronic offenders on both sides of the juvenile and criminal court line.

a. Youth Crime

Rates of crime, youth crime, and violence fluctuate markedly over time. Any description or interpretation of crime trends is especially sensitive to the baseline selected for comparison. The Federal Bureau of Investigation annually publishes national data on crimes known or reported to police and arrests made by law enforcement in its *Crime in the United States: Uniform Crime Reports* (FBI, 1996). The overall FBI Crime Index rate peaked around 1980, declined during the middle 1980s, and then rebounded by the early 1990s to overall rates still somewhat lower than those recorded in 1980 (FBI, 1996). By 1995, the serious crime rate had subsided to the levels previously recorded in the mid-1970s. Thus, during the past two decades the overall serious crime rate oscillated within a ±10% range. Although the aggregate rate of serious Index Crimes in the early 1990s remained somewhat below the peak rate recorded in 1980, the rate of Violent Crime—murder, rape, robbery, and assault—increased dramatically. Between 1974 and 1991, the recent peak year, the violence rate rose 64.4%. Between 1986 and 1995, the rate of violence increased by 10.8%. Beginning in 1986, the rate of violent crime surpassed the previous high recorded in 1980, and escalated rapidly thereafter.

The patterns of Index Crimes committed by juveniles generally mirrored the overall national pattern of serious crimes. Juvenile arrest rates for all FBI Index Offenses declined in mid-decade from the peak rates recorded in 1980 and then gradually rebounded to fates that approached the earlier peak. However, between 1980 and 1994, the juvenile arrest rate for Violent Index Crime increased 58% (Snyder, 1997).

Although violent crimes comprise a small component of the overall serious crime index and juveniles comprise a smaller proportion of all arrests for violence, the rates of juvenile violence, especially homicide, surged dramatically between the mid-1980s and early 1990s. The juvenile arrest rate for all violent crimes increased by 67.3% in the decade between 1986 and 1995, and 12.0% just between 1991 and 1995 (FBI, 1996). Over the past decade, the rate of increase for juvenile homicide arrests was the greatest for any offense category. Between 1986 and 1995, homicide arrests of juveniles increased 89.9% while the corresponding arrest rate for adults actually declined by 0.3%. In short, within the past decade, the juvenile component of all violent crimes expanded, the juvenile rate of growth far outstripped the corresponding increases for adults, and juveniles murdered people at unprecedented rates.

Two additional aspects of youth crime and violence in the period beginning in the mid-1980s have special relevance for understanding subsequent changes in juvenile court waiver and sentencing legislation in the 1990s. Differences in arrest rates for violent crimes by juveniles of different races and the unique role of guns in the dramatic surge in homicides in the late 1980s account for most of the changes in patterns of youth crime and violence in the past decade (Feld, 1999). The intersection of race, guns, and homicide fanned the public and political "panic" that, in turn, led to the recent "get-tough" reformulation of juvenile justice waiver and sentencing policies.

Police arrest black youths for a disproportionate amount of all violent offenses. In recent years police arrested black juveniles for all violent offenses at a rate about five times greater than that of white youths, and for homicide at a rate more than seven times that of white youths. In a special section on "Juveniles and Violence" in *Crime in the United States: 1991*, the FBI reported that between 1980 and 1990, the homicide arrest rate for black juveniles increased about three times as quickly as that of white juveniles (145% versus 48%) and police arrested blacks for murder at a rate 7.5 times greater than whites (FBI, 1992).

Alfred Blumstein (1995; Blumstein and Cork, 1996) analyzed these changing patterns of age- and race-specific homicide rates and attributed the dramatic increase in youth homicides to the crack cocaine drug industry that emerged in large cities during the mid-to late 1980s. Drug distribution attracted youths because juveniles faced lower risks of severe penalties than do adults and especially young urban, black males who lacked alternative economic opportunities. The ready availability of guns abets the prevalence of lethal violence because those involved in illegal markets cannot resolve their disputes through formal mechanisms (Reiss and Roth, 1993). Although guns constitute a "tool of the trade" in the drug industry, their proliferation and diffusion within the wider youth population for self-defense and status also has contributed to the escalation of homicides (Blumstein and Cork, 1996). The increased use of guns to commit murders accounted for virtually all of the increase in the homicide rate for youths in the past decade (Snyder, Sickmund, and Poe-Yamagata, 1997). As we look at all of these complex crime patterns over the past decade or two, murders with guns committed by young black males constitute the primary significant change in youth crime. Although homicide and lethal violence are very serious criminal policy problems, this extremely narrow segment of the overall youth crime phenomenon, which otherwise remained relatively stable, has driven the entire public and political debate to "get tough."

b. The Juvenile Court Waiver Conundrum: Treatment vs. Punishment, Offender vs. Offense, Future Welfare vs. Past Crime

Transfer of juvenile offenders for adult prosecution provides the conceptual and administrative nexus between the more deterministic and rehabilitative predictates of the juvenile justice process and the free will and punishment assumption of the adult criminal justice system. Older delinquents nearing the maximum age of juvenile court jurisdiction, chronic recidivists who have not responded to prior intervention and for whom successful treatment may not be feasible during the time remaining to the juvenile court, and youths charged with a very serious violent crime like rape or murder starkly pose the question of whether to prosecute and sentence a youth as a delinquent or as a criminal (Podkopacz and Feld, 1995, 1996; U.S. General Accounting Office, 1995). Politicians and the public perceive these youths as mature and sophisticated criminal offenders. Moreover, the career offenders account for a disproportionate amount of all juvenile crime. Highly visible, serious or chronic offenses evoke community outrage or fear which politicians believe only punitive adult sanctions can mollify. Laws to prosecute some youths as adults provide an important safety valve, permit the expiatory sacrifice of a few youths to quiet political and public clamor, and enable legislators to avoid otherwise irresistible pressures to lower the maximum age of juvenile court jurisdiction (Feld, 1978).

Jurisdictional waiver represents a type of *sentencing* decision. Juvenile courts traditionally assigned primary importance to rehabilitation and individualized treatment. Criminal courts accorded greater significance to the seriousness of the offense committed and attempted to proportion punishment accordingly. All of the theoretical differences between juvenile and criminal courts' sentencing philosophies become visible in transfer proceedings and in legislative policy debates. Transfer laws simultaneously attempt to resolve both fundamental crime control issues and the ambivalence embedded in our cultural construction of youth. The jurisprudential conflicts reflect many current sentencing policy debates: tensions between rehabilitation or incapacitation and retribution, between focusing on characteristics of the offender and the seriousness of the offense, between discretion and rules, and between indeterminacy and determinacy. Waiver laws attempt to reconcile the contradictory impulses engendered when the child is a criminal and the criminal is a child.

Although the technical and administrative details of states' transfer laws vary considerably, judicial waiver, legislative offense exclusion, and prosecutorial choice of forum represent the three generic legal approaches employed (Feld, 1987; Fritsch and Hemmens, 1995; Snyder and Sickmund, 1995; U.S. General Accounting Office, 1995). They emphasize a different balance of sentencing policy values, rely on different organizational actors and administrative processes, and elicit different information to determine whether to try and sentence a particular young offender as an adult or as a child.

Judicial waiver represents the most common transfer policy in virtually all states (Snyder and Sickmund, 1995; U.S. General Accounting Office, 1995). A juvenile court judge may waive juvenile court jurisdiction on a discretionary basis after conducting a hearing to determine whether a youth is "amenable to treatment" or poses a danger to public safety. These case-by-case clinical assessments reflect the traditional individualized sentencing discretion characteristic of juvenile courts.

Legislative offense exclusion frequently supplements judicial waiver provisions. This approach emphasizes the seriousness of the offense committed and reflects the retributive values of the criminal law (Feld, 1987; Snyder and Sickmund, 1995). Because legislatures create juvenile courts, they possess considerable latitude to define their jurisdiction and to exclude youths from juvenile court based on their age and the seriousness of their offenses. A number of states, for example, exclude youths 16 or older and charged with murder from juvenile court jurisdiction (Sanborn, 1996). Legislative line-drawing that sets the maximum age of juvenile court jurisdiction at 15 or 16, below the general 18 year old age of majority, results in the criminal prosecution of the largest numbers of chronological juveniles, for example, about 176,000 chronological juveniles in 1991 (Snyder and Sickmund, 1995).

About a dozen states allow prosecutors to remove some young offenders from the juvenile justice system. With this strategy, juvenile and criminal courts share concurrent jurisdiction over certain ages and offenses, typically older youths and serious crimes, and prosecutors may exercise their discretion to select either juvenile or criminal processing for such youths (McCarthy, 1994; Snyder and Sickmund, 1995). Because of the constitutional doctrine of separation of powers, courts ordinarily do not review discretionary executive decisions, and most judicial opinions characterize prosecutorial transfer as an ordinary charging decision (Feld, 1978). To the extent that a prosecutor's decision to charge a case in criminal courts divests the juvenile court of jurisdiction, prosecutorial waiver constitutes a form of offense-based decision-making like legislative offense exclusion (Thomas and Bilchik, 1985).

Each type of waiver strategy has supporters and critics. Proponents of judicial waiver endorse juvenile courts' rehabilitative philosophy and argue that individualized decisions provide an appropriate balance of flexibility and severity (Fagan, 1990; Zimring, 1991). Critics object that judges lack accurate clinical tools with which to assess amenability to treatment or to predict dangerousness and that their exercise of standardless discretion results in abuses and inequalities (Feld, 1990; Fagan and Deschenes, 1991). Proponents of offense exclusion favor "just deserts" sentencing policies, advocate sanctions based on relatively objective factors such as offense seriousness, culpability, and criminal history, and value-consistent, uniform, and equal handling of similarly situated offenders (Feld, 1981a). Critics question whether legislators can remove discretion without making the process excessively rigid and overinclusive (Zimring, 1981a, 1991). Proponents of prosecutorial waiver claim that prosecutors can act as more neutral, balanced and objective gatekeepers than either "soft" judges or "get-tough" legislators (McCarthy, 1994). Critics observe that prosecutors succumb to political pressures and symbolically posture on crime issues, exercise their discretion just as subjectively and idiosyncratically as judges, and introduce extensive geographic variability into the justice process (Bishop and Frazier, 1991).

For analytical purposes, we may characterize punishment and treatment as mutually exclusive penal goals, although in daily practice both juvenile and criminal courts often comingle the two. Punishment focuses retrospectively on the nature of the offense, whereas therapy orients prospectively on the needs of the offender. When a state *punishes*, it imposes unpleasant consequences for *past offenses*; the offender violated a legal prohibition and *deserves* the prescribed consequences (Hart, 1968; von Hirsch, 1976). By contrast, rehabilitation assumes that certain antecedent factors caused undesirable behavior, focuses on the person's psychodynamic or social circumstances, and prescribes remedial intervention to alleviate those conditions and thereby improve the offender's *future welfare* (Packer, 1968; Allen, 1981). These deterministic assumptions constitute the central tenets of positive criminology and the juvenile court's rehabilitative ideal.

Juvenile court waiver and sentencing laws and administrative practices may assign primary emphasis to characteristics of the *offender* or the seriousness of the *offense* and to *future welfare* or *past behavior*. If legislators or judges focus on the past offense when they impose sentences, then they typically employ mandatory minimum, or determinate and proportional sanctions to punish, incapacitate, or deter. In the context of waiver to criminal courts, *offense-based* criteria dominate and present offense or prior record controls prosecutors' or judges' transfer decisions. If judges focus on characteristics of the offender when they sentence, then they typically impose indeterminate and nonproportional dispositions that provide wide latitude to rehabilitate (Morris, 1974; von Hirsch, 1986). In the context of waiver decisions, judicial assessments of a youth's amenability to treatment or dangerousness reflect this flexible, discretionary sentencing policy (Feld, 1987). Judges' decisions reflect a *prediction* about an offender's likely *future* course of conduct and development.

Within the past two decades, determinate, offense-based sentencing systems increasingly have superseded indeterminate, offender-oriented sentencing regimes both for adults (Cullen and Gilbert, 1982; Tonry, 1996) and for juveniles (Feld, 1988b, 1998; Sheffer, 1995). Proponents of "just deserts" oppose indeterminate sentences because such a system vests standardless discretion in judges and correctional administrators who can neither justify empirically their differential treatment of similarly situated offenders nor demonstrate effective rehabilitation techniques or defend the inequalities and disparities that individualized sanctions produce (American Friends Service Committee, 1971; von Hirsch, 1976; Greenberg, 1977; Fogel, 1979). Because of its retributive foundation, a "just deserts" framework imposes determinate sentences based primarily on the seriousness of the offense, culpability, or past criminal conduct rather than on personal characteristics. The "just deserts" challenge to individualized sentencing practices encompasses juvenile court waiver and sentencing policies as well (Feld, 1987, 1988b, 1998).

Analyzing waiver as a sentencing decision addresses two interrelated policy issues: the bases for sentencing and waiver practices within juvenile courts and the relationship between juvenile and criminal court sentencing practices. The first implicates individualized sentencing decisions and the tension between discretion and the rule of law. The second implicates the contradictory criteria that juvenile and criminal court judges use when the former waive and the latter sentence offenders. Formulating rational and consistent social control responses to *serious* and *chronic* young offenders requires coordinated responses to youths who make the transition between the two systems. Waiver laws and policies affect two, somewhat different, albeit overlapping populations—*serious* and *chronic* young offenders. Waiver decisions affect both violent and persistent juveniles, but criminal court judges sentence violent youths and chronic offenders currently charged with property crimes significantly differently.

Judicial Waiver and Individualized Sentencing Decisions. From the juvenile court's inception, judges could deny some young offenders its protective jurisdiction and send them to criminal court (Rothman, 1980). Judicial waiver reflects juvenile courts' traditional approach to individualized sentencing and focuses on attributes of the offender to decide whether to treat a youth as a juvenile or to punish him as an adult. In *Kent v. United States*, 383 U.S. 541 (1966), the Supreme Court formalized the judicial waiver process and required juvenile courts to provide youths with some procedural protections such as assistance of counsel, access to social service investigations and other records, and written findings and conclusions that an appellate court could review. Subsequently, in *Breed v. Jones*, 421 U.S. 519 (1975), the Court applied the double jeopardy clause of the Fifth Amendment to delinquency convictions and required states to decide whether to try and sentence a youth as a juvenile or as an adult before proceeding to a trial on the merits of the charge.

Kent and *Breed* provide the formal procedural framework within which judges make waiver decisions. But the substantive bases of waiver decisions pose the principal difficulty. Until recent amendments, most states' waiver statutes allow juvenile court judges to transfer jurisdiction based on their discretionary assessment of subjective factors, such as youths' "amenability to treatment" or "dangerousness" (Feld, 1995; Snyder and Sickmund, 1995). Legislatures specify amenability criteria with varying degrees of precision and often adopt the general, contradictory list of *Kent* factors. Although some states limit waiver to felony offenses and establish some minimum age for adult prosecutions, typically 16, 15, or 14, others provide neither offense nor minimum age restrictions (Snyder and Sickmund, 1995).

In practice, judges operationalize "amenability" and "dangerousness" waiver criteria by considering three sets of variables. The first consists of a youth's age and the length of time remaining within juvenile court jurisdiction. Juvenile court judges waive older youths more readily than younger offenders (Fagan and Deschenes, 1990; Podkopacz and Feld, 1995, 1996; U.S. General Accounting Office, 1995). A youth's age in relation to the maximum dispositional jurisdiction restricts judges' sanctioning powers and provides an impetus to waive older juveniles or those whose offenses deserve a longer sentence than available in juvenile court. A youth's age may serve as a proxy for prior delinquency, since older juveniles have had a longer opportunity to acquire a prior record. Conversely, judges may view younger offenders as less blameworthy or responsible than their older and more culpable peers.

A second constellation of "amenability" factors include a youth's treatment prognosis as revealed in clinical evaluations and by prior correctional interventions. Once a juvenile exhausts the available treatment services and correctional resources, transfer becomes increasingly more likely (Podkopacz and Feld, 1995, 1996). Finally, judges pragmatically assess "dangerousness" and the threat a youth poses to others based on present offense and prior record. Dangerousness variables include the seriousness of the offense, whether the youth used a weapon, and the length of the prior record (Podkopacz and Feld, 1995, 1996). Balancing "dangerousness" factors involves a trade-off between offense seriousness and offender persistence.

As sentencing criteria, "amenability to treatment" or "dangerousness" implicates some of the most fundamental and difficult issues of penal policy and juvenile jurisprudence. A law mandating an "amenability" inquiry assumes that effective treatment programs exist for at least some serious or chronic young offenders, presumes that classification systems exist with which to differentiate among youths' treatment potentials or dangerousness, and presumes that clinicians or judges possess diagnostic tools with which to make an appropriate disposition for a particular youth. Evaluation research challenges these legislative presuppositions and raises questions whether judges or clinicians can intervene to improve the social adjustment or reduce recidivism among chronic or violent young offenders, and whether they possess the ability to identify which youths will or will not respond to treatment. Statutes that authorize judges to waive jurisdiction if a youth poses a threat to public safety require judges to predict future dangerousness even though clinicians or jurists lack the technical capacity reliably to predict low-base-rate serious criminal behavior (Monahan, 1981; Morris and Miller, 1985).

Judician waiver criteria such as "amenability to treatment" or "dangerousness" give judges broad, standardless discretion. Adding long lists of factors, such as those the Supreme Court appended in *Kent*, does not provide objective guidance to structure discretion (Twentieth Century Fund, 1978). Amorphous lists of contradictory factors reinforce judges' discretion and allow them selectively to emphasize one element or another to justify any decision.

The subjective nature of waiver decisions, the absence of effective guidelines to structure outcomes, and the lack of objective indicators or scientific tools with which to classify youths allow judges to make unequal and disparate ruling without any effective procedural or appellate limitations. Empirical studies provide compelling evidence that judges apply waiver statutes in an arbitrary, capricious, and discriminatory manner. Several nationwide, state-by-state, and intrastate analyses report enormous variations in both rates of waiver and the types of cases transferred (Hamparian *et al.*, 1982; U.S. General Accounting Office, 1995). A study of waiver decisions involving a sample of violent youths in four different jurisdictions, controlled for both offense and offender variables, and concluded that no uniform criteria guided transfer decisions (Fagan and Deschenes, 1990). Even within a single jurisdiction, judges cannot administer, interpret, or apply discretionary waiver statutes consistently from county to county or court to court (Hamparian *et al.*, 1982; Feld, 1990). Research in several states reports a contextual pattern of "justice by geography" in which where youths lived, rather than what they did, determined their juvenile or adult status (Hamparian *et al.*, 1982; Feld, 1990, 1995). In some states, for example, rural judges waive youths more readily than urban judges (Hamparian *et al.*, 1982; Feld, 1990). A study of decisions by different judges in one juvenile court reported that "the various judges within the same urban county and court applied the same law and *decided cases* of similarly-situated offenders *significantly differently*. These judicial differences influenced both the characteristics of youths waived or retained and the subsequent sentences imposed upon them as juveniles or adults" (Podkopacz and Feld, 1995:172). In addition to "justice by geography" and by judicial idiosyncrasy, a youth's race also appears to affect waiver decisions. Several studies report that judges more readily waived black youths than white youths charged with comparable offenses and prior records (Eigen, 1981a,b; Hamparian *et al.*, 1982; Fagan, Forst, and Vivona, 1987; U.S. General Accounting Office, 1995).

Legislative Exclusion and Prosecutor's Choice of Forum. Legislative waiver provides the principal conceptual alternative to judicial waiver. Some states exclude from juvenile court jurisdiction youths of certain ages charged with specified offenses or with particular prior records. Concurrent jurisdiction legislation gives to prosecutors the power to choose in which forum to try a case based on the offense charged and without justifying that decision in a judicial hearing.

Youths have challenged statutes that exclude them from juvenile court on the basis of their age and offense or that delegate to prosecutors the power to do so. They argue that "automatic adulthood" denies them the procedural safeguards required by *Kent* and constitutes an arbitrary legislative classification that violates equal protection (Feld, 1978). However, appellate courts consistently reject both these due process and equal protection challenges and uphold offense exclusion and prosecutorial waiver statutes [*United States v. Bland*, 472 F.2d 1329 (D.C. Cir. 1972); Feld, 1978]. State laws regularly classify offenders on the basis of serious and minor offenses, and as long as appellate court judges can attribute to legislators a "rational basis" to treat serious and minor offenders differently—for example, a belief that serious offenders pose a greater threat to the public, exhibit greater culpability, respond less readily to rehabilitative efforts, or interfere with the treatment of less serious offenders—they affirm the constitutional validity of the classification (Feld, 1978).

Youths have no constitutional right to a juvenile court; it exists only as a matter of legislative grace. Legislatures define their jurisdiction, powers, and purposes. What they create, they may also modify or take away. States freely set juvenile courts' maximum jurisdiction at 17, 16, or 15 years of age as a matter of state policy and without constitutional infirmity. If they define juvenile court jurisdiction to include only those persons below a jurisdictional age and whom prosecutors charge with a nonexcluded offense, then, *by statutory definition*, all others are adults for purposes of the criminal law.

States base the distinctions between treatment as a juvenile and punishment as an adult on waiver decisions or legislative lines that have no criminological significance other than their legal consequences. These jurisprudential antinomies may frustrate attempts to rationalize social control of serious and persistent young offenders. By adopting these policies, legislatures create false dichotomies and fail to acknowledge that young people mature constantly and criminal careers evolve over time. Adolescence comprises a developmental continuum; young people do not graduate from irresponsible childhood one day to responsible adulthood the next, except as a matter of law.

Moreover, the strong correlation between age and criminal activity makes the current jurisdictional bifurcation especially problematic. The rates of many kinds of criminality peak in mid- to late adolescence, exactly at the juncture between the juvenile and criminal justice systems (Blumstein, Cohen, Roth, and Visher, 1986; Farrington, 1986, 1998). Criminal careers research indicates that young offenders do not specialize in particular types of crime, that serious crime occurs within an essentially random pattern of persistent delinquent behavior, and that a small number of chronic delinquents commit many of the offenses and most of the violent crimes perpetrated by juveniles (Wolfgang, Figlio, and Sellin, 1972; Hamparian, Schuster, Dinitz, and Conrad, 1978). Serious offenders are persistent delinquents who simply add violent crimes to their repertoire of active law-breaking. Although the seriousness of a youth's initial or current offense provides little basis by which to distinguish those who will or will not recidivate, an extensive record provides the best indicator of future criminal behavior.

Waiver statutes and youth sentencing policies unsystematically attempt to differentiate between adolescent-only offenders and life-course persistent offenders, but confront an immediate and frustrating trade-off between serious and chronic offenders. For virtually all purposes, most of the significant differences among delinquents occur between those juveniles who desist after one or two delinquencies and chronic offenders, those with five or more justice system involvements. Rational sentencing policy requires integrated, consistent, and coordinated penal responses to young career offenders on both sides of the current juvenile–adult line, especially when they make the transition between the two systems. Unfortunately, the recent escalation in youth violence and homicide has focused legislative attention primarily on serious offenses rather than chronic offending, thereby fostering an over- and under-inclusive response to the problems posed by young career criminals. Waiver policies may punish severely one youth's isolated act of violence while sanctioning nominally a chronic offender's current property crime.

Despite the research on criminal careers, juvenile and criminal courts' sentencing practices often may work at cross-purposes and frustrate rather than harmonize responses as serious and chronic young offenders move between the two systems. Until the recent round of changes in waiver laws, criminal courts typically imposed longer sentences on older offenders because of their cumulative adult prior records but sentenced more leniently chronic younger offenders whose rate of criminal activity was increasing or at its peak. A number of studies examine the sentences that criminal courts imposed on judicially waived juveniles and report a "lack of fit" between juvenile waiver decisions and criminal court sentences (Feld, 1987, 1995). The "punishment gap" allows chronic and active young criminal offenders to fall between the cracks of the juvenile and criminal justice systems (Greenwood *et al.*, 1980; Hamparian *et al.*, 1982; Podkopacz and Feld, 1995, 1996).

The "punishment gap" occurs because judicial waiver decisions involve two, somewhat different but overlapping populations of young offenders, older chronic delinquents currently charged with a property crime *and* violent youths, some of whom may be persistent as well. Criminal courts respond differently to these two types of offender clusters because of the differences in the nature of their present offense. Despite the recent rise in violent youth crime, juvenile court judges continued to transfer the largest plurality of youths for property offenses (45%), rather than for crimes against the person (34%) (Snyder and Sickmund, 1995). Only in 1993 did the proportion of waived violent offenders (42%) first exceed that of property offenders (38%) (Snyder *et al.*, 1996).

The nature of the offenses for which juvenile courts transferred juveniles and their relative youthfulness affected their first criminal court sentences. Although analyses of dispositions of youths tried as adults in several jurisdictions report substantial variation in sentencing practices, a policy of leniency often prevails. Earlier studies reported that urban criminal courts incarcerated younger offenders at a lower rate than they did older offenders, youthful violent offenders received lighter sentences than did older violent offenders, and for about 2 years after becoming adults, youths benefitted from informal lenient sentencing policies in adult courts (Greendood, Abrahamse, and Zimring, 1984). A nationwide study of judicial waived youths sentenced as adults found that criminal courts subsequently fined or placed the majority (54%) of transferred juveniles on probation. Even among those confined, 40% received maximum sentences of 1 year or less and only about one-quarter (28%) received sentences of 5 years or more (Hamparian *et al.*, 1982).

More recent research reports that juvenile court judges continue to waive primarily older chronic offenders charged with a property crime like burglary rather than with a violent crime, and criminal courts subsequently fined or placed on probation most juveniles judicially transferred. Studies in several states consistently report that criminal court judges typically imposed more lenient sentences on chronic juvenile property offenders sentenced as adult first-time offenders than on comparable adults (Gillespie and Norman, 1984; Bortner, 1986; Feld, 1995). Another study compared the sentences received by youths tried as adults and those retained in juvenile court in an urban county and found that "the juvenile court sentenced youths found delinquent for non-presumptive, property offenses for terms longer than their adult counterparts" (Podkopacz and Feld, 1995:164). In short, most of the research reports that criminal court judges imprisoned judicially transferred youths at lower rates than they did adults convicted of comparable offenses and many incarcerated youths received sentences of 1 year or less, shorter sentences than juvenile court judges could impose on "deep-end" delinquents.

Recent Changes in Waiver Statutes. Within the past two decades, state legislatures have modified extensively their transfer laws. The first round of changes occurred during the 1970s in the aftermath of *Kent* and in response to the "baby-boom" upsurge in youth crime and violence. Even more extensive legislative revisions have occurred within the past decade in response to the escalation of youth homicide in the late 1980s. Legislatures use offense criteria either as a form of sentencing guidelines to limit judicial discretion, to guide prosecutorial charging decisions, or automatically to exclude certain youths from juvenile court jurisdiction. These amendments use offense criteria to integrate juvenile transfer and adult sentencing practices and to reduce the "punishment gap." Waiver laws that focus on offense seriousness and criminal history, whether obtained as a juvenile or an adult, rather than amorphous clinical considerations, better enable criminal courts to respond more consistently to chronic and violent young offenders and to maximize social control of young career offenders. The amount and scope of legislative activity and the rapidity of these changes cannot be overemphasized (Snyder and Sickmund, 1995; U.S. General Accounting Office, 1995). Since 1992, 48 of the 50 states and the District of Columbia have amended provisions of their juvenile codes, sentencing statutes, and transfer laws to target youths who commit chronic, serious, or violent crimes (Torbet *et al.*, 1996). These amendments constitute a tidal wave of law reform responding to the rise of youth violence and homicide. The overarching legislative theme is a shift from the principle of individualized justice to the principle of offense, from rehabilitation to retribution.

Although judicial waiver remains the predominant method of transfer, about three dozen states recently have amended waiver statutes to reduce their inconsistent application, to lessen intrajurisdictional disparities, and to improve the fit between waiver decisions and criminal sentencing practices (Fritsch and Hemmens, 1995; Snyder and Sickmund, 1995). Lawmakers use offense criteria as a type of sentencing guidelines to control judicial discretion, to focus on serious offenders, and to increase the numbers of youths waived. By focusing on serious crimes, often in combination with prior records, these amendments restrict judicial discretion and increase the probabilities that criminal court judges will impose significant sentences following waiver. These amendments use offense criteria to limit judicial waiver only to certain serious offenses, to identify certain offenses alone or in combination with prior record for special procedural handling, or to prescribe the dispositional consequences that follow from proof of serious offenses or prior records. Some states use offense criteria to make transfer hearings mandatory for certain offenses, or to create a presumption for transfer and shift to the youth the burden of proof to demonstrate why the juvenile court should retain jurisdiction (Feld, 1987, 1995). About 20 states have lowered from 16 to 14 or even 12 the age at which judges may transfer youths charged with serious offenses to criminal courts (Fritsch and Hemmens, 1995; Torbet *et al.*, 1996). Recent changes also shift the jurisprudential focus of waiver hearings from the offender to the offense. States have rejected "amenability to treatment" as the primary waiver criterion in favor of "public safety," defined in terms of the present offense, prior record, and youth's culpability (Feld, 1995).

Nearly two-thirds of the states now exclude some serious offenses from juvenile court jurisdiction (Snyder and Sickmund, 1995; U.S. General Accounting Office, 1995). These offense exclusion statutes typically supplement judicial waiver statutes. While some states exclude only youths charged with capital crimes, murder, or offenses punishable by life imprisonment, other exclude longer lists of offenses, or youths charged with repeat offenses. Because most excluded offense legislation targets serious violent offenses—murder, rape, kidnapping, or armed robbery—youths identified by such provisions face the prospects of substantial sentences if convicted as adults. Since 1992, nearly half the states have expanded the lists of excluded offenses, lowered the ages of eligibility for exclusion from 16 to 14 or 13 years of age, or granted prosecutors more authority to "direct file" more cases in criminal court (Fritsch and Hemmens, 1995; U.S. General Accounting Office, 1995; Torbet *et al.*, 1996). As a result, increasing numbers of younger offenders charged with serious crimes find themselves "automatically" in criminal court. However, as legislators expand lists of excluded offenses to encompass less serious crimes and lower the ages at which prosecutors may charge youths as adults, they also reduce the certainty that criminal court judges will impose significant adult sentences.

These "get-tough" policies reflect juvenile courts' more fundamental jurisprudential changes from rehabilitation to retribution. The overarching themes of these legislative amendments include a shift from individualized justice to just deserts, from offender to offense, from "amenability to treatment" to public safety, and from immature delinquent to responsible criminal. These trends reflect a fundamental cultural and legal reconceptualization of youth from innocent and dependent to responsible and autonomous. Politicians' "sound-bite" crime proposals—e.g., "adult crime, adult time"—reflect policies that provide no formal recognition of youthfulness as a mitigating factor in sentencing.

Once youths make the transition to the adult system, criminal court judges sentence them as if they are adults, impose the same sentences, send them to the same prisons, and even inflict capital punishment on them for the crimes they committed as children (Feld, 1998; *Stanford v. Kentucky*, 1989). In *Thompson v. Oklahoma* [486 U.S. 815 (1988)], the Court pondered whether a state violated the Eighth Amendment's prohibition on "cruel and unusual punishments" by executing a youth for a heinous murder he committed when he was 15 years old. The *Thompson* Court conducted a proportionality analysis to determine whether the penalty exceeded the youth's blameworthiness. A plurality of the Court concluded that "a young person is not capable of acting with the degree of culpability [as an adult] that can justify the ultimate penalty" and overturned the capital sentence [*Thompson*, 486 U.S. 823 (1988)]. The following year in *Stanford v. Kentucky* [492 U.S. 361 (1989)], a different plurality of the Court upheld the death penalty for murders committed by juveniles aged 16 or 17 years at the time of their offense. Of the 38 states and the federal government that authorize the death penalty, 21 states allow the execution of offenders for crimes committed at age 16, and an additional 4 permit their execution for crimes committed at age 17 (Streib, 1987; Snyder and Sickmund, 1995).

At the doctrinal level, the *Stanford* justices simply disagreed with those in *Thompson* who found a societal consensus against executing people for crimes committed as juveniles. As cultural and legal artifacts, *Thompson* and *Stanford* differed in their conceptions of young people. *Thompson* reflected an altruistic paternalism and proffered protective reasons to reject the death penalty for children. *Stanford*, by contrast, rejected the imagery of vulnerability, invoked the language of responsibility, endorsed an authoritarian view that young people deserved the same punishments as adults, and signaled that youthfulness carried no special legal dispensation unless a state affirmatively chose to provide it.

3. Punishing Delinquent Offenders in Juvenile Court

The jurisprudential shifts from offender to offense and from treatment to punishment that inspire changes in waiver policies increasingly affect the sentences that juvenile court judges impose on delinquent offenders as well. Progressive reformers envisioned a broader and more encompassing social welfare system for youths and did not circumscribe narrowly state power. Juvenile court's *parens patriae* ideology combined social welfare with penal social control in one institution, minimized procedural safeguards, and maximized discretion to provide flexibility in diagnosis and treatment. They focused primary attention on youths' social circumstances and accorded secondary significance either to procedural safeguards or to proof of guilt of the specific offense. More recently, however, the public impetus and political pressures to waive the most serious young offenders to criminal courts also impel juvenile courts to "get tough" and punish more severely the remaining criminal delinquents.

The assumed differences between juvenile treatment and criminal punishment provided the rationale for the Supreme Court in *McKeiver* to deny jury trials in delinquency proceedings and, more fundamentally, for states to maintain a juvenile justice system separate from the adult one (Gardner, 1982; Feld, 1997). As states' juvenile justice sentencing laws and policies increasingly "get tough," however, the always tenuous distinctions between treatment and punishment blur even further. Despite the fundamental importance of the distinctions between rehabilitation and punishment, the *McKeiver* Court did not analyze the nature of those differences. Several indicators reveal whether a juvenile court judge's disposition punishes a youth for his past offense or treats him for his future welfare. Increasingly, juvenile court legislative purpose clauses and court opinions explicitly endorse punishment as an appropriate component of juvenile sanctions. Currently, nearly half of the states use determinate or mandatory minimum sentencing provisions that base a youth's disposition on the offense she committed rather than her "real needs" to regulate at least some aspects of sentence duration, institutional commitment, or release. Empirical evaluations of juvenile courts' sentencing practices indicate that the present offense and prior record account for most of the explained variance in judges' dispositions of delinquents, and reinforce the criminal orientation of juvenile courts. Despite their penal focus, however, the individualized discretion inherent in juvenile courts' treatment ideology is often synonymous with racial discrimination. Finally, evaluations of conditions of confinement and treatment effectiveness belie any therapeutic "alternative purpose" to juvenile incarceration. In short, all of these indicators consistently reveal that treating juveniles closely resembles punishing adults. A strong, nationwide policy shift both in theory and in practice away from therapeutic dispositions toward punishment or incapacitation of young offenders characterizes sentencing practice in the contemporary juvenile court.

a. The Purpose of Juvenile Courts

Among the factors that the Supreme Court considers to determine whether seemingly punitive and coercive governmental intervention constitutes punishment or an "alternative purpose," such as treatment, is the stated legislative purpose [*Allen v. Illinois*, 478 U.S. 364 (1986); Gardner, 1982; Giardino, 1996]. Most states' juvenile codes contain a purpose clause that declares the underlying legislative rationale as an aid to courts in interpreting the statute. In the decades since *Gault* and *McKeiver*, more than one-quarter of the states have revised the statement of legislative purpose in their juvenile codes to deemphasize rehabilitation and intervention in the child's "best interest" and to assert the importance of public safety, punishment, and accountability in the juvenile justice system (Gardner, 1982; Walkover, 1984; Giardino, 1996). For example, states have redefined their juvenile courts' purposes to: "provide for the protection and safety of the public," *Cal. Welf. & Inst. Code* § 202 (West Supp. 1988); "protect society … [while] recognizing that the application of sanctions which are consistent with the seriousness of the offense is appropriate in all cases," *Fla. Stat. Ann* §39.001(2)(a) (West, 1988); "render appropriate punishment to offenders." *Haw. Rev. Stat.* § 571-1 (1993); "protect the public by enforcing the legal obligations children have to society," *Ind. Code Ann* § 31-6-1-1 (Michie 1979); "promote public safety [and] hold juvenile offenders accountable for such juvenile's behavior," *Kan Stat. Ann.* § 38-1601 (1997); and provide similar social defense objectives. Several courts recognize that these changes in purpose clauses signal basic changes in juvenile courts' philosophical directions [e.g., *In re Javier A.*,

206 Cal. Rptr. 386 (Cal. Ct. App. 1984); *In re Seven Minors*, 664 P.2d 947, 950 (Nev. 1983); *State v. Lawley*, 591 P.2d 772, 773 (Wash. 1979); *State ex rel. D.D.H. v. Dostert*, 269 S.E.2d 401 (W. Va. 1980)].

b. Juvenile Courts' Sentencing Laws and Judicial Sentencing Practices

Sentencing statutes and judicial practices provide another indicator of whether juvenile courts punish or treat delinquents. Originally, juvenile courts imposed indeterminate and nonproportional sentences to achieve the child's "best interests" (Mack, 1909; Rothman, 1980). More recently, however, many states' juvenile court sentencing laws increasingly emphasize punishment (Feld, 1988b; Sheffer, 1995; Torbet *et al.*, 1996). About half (22) the states use some type of "just deserts" determinate or mandatory minimum offense-based criteria to guide judicial sentencing discretion (Sheffer, 1995). Washington State adopted sentencing guidelines to impose presumptive, determinate, and proportional sentences on delinquents based on a juvenile's age, seriousness of the offense, and prior record [*Wash. Rev. Code Am.* § 13.40.010(2) (West Suppl 1988)]. Mandatory minimum sentencing provisions in many states typically use age and offense criteria to define serious offenders and to prescribe minimum lengths of sentences or youths' levels of security (Sheffer, 1995; Torbet *et al.*, 1996). While states' nomenclatures differ, these "therapeutic" mandatory minimum sentencing laws typically apply to "violent and repeat offenders," "mandatory sentence offenders," "aggravated juvenile offenders," "habitual offenders," "serious juvenile offenders," or "designated felons" [e.g., *Ala. Code* § 12-15-71.1 (1990); *Colo. Rev. Stat.* § 19-1-103 (1993); Sheffer, 1995]. These laws identify violent and persistent offenders over whom juvenile courts do not waive jurisdiction either because of their youthfulness or lesser culpability or complicity. More recent legislative amendments add youths whom prosecutors charge with crimes involving firearms or those who commit violent or drug crimes on school grounds to those eligible for "special" mandatory sentences [e.g., *Ark. Code Ann.* § 9-27-330(c) (Michie, 1989)]. The rate at which states amend their juvenile sentencing laws appears to have accelerated. "Since 1992, 15 States and the District of Columbia have added or modified statutes that provide for a mandatory minimum period of incarceration of juveniles committing certain violent or other serious crimes" (Torbet *et al.*, 1996:14). Similarly, many states' departments of corrections have administratively adopted security classification and release guidelines that use offense criteria to specify proportional or mandatory minimum terms of institutional confinement (Forst and Blomquist, 1991; Guarino-Ghezzi and Loughran, 1996). All of these *de jure* sentencing provisions—determinate and mandatory minimum laws, and correctional and parole release guidelines—share the common feature of offense-based dispositions that explicitly link the length of time delinquents serve to the seriousness of the crime they committed, rather than to their "real needs." They represent different methods to regulate judicial discretion and to relate the duration and intensity of a youth's sentence to the offense and prior record. These provisions use principles of proportionality and determinacy to rationalize sentencing decisions, to increase the penal bite of juvenile sanctions, and to allow legislators symbolically to demonstrate their toughness.

Juvenile court judges decide what to do with a child, in part, by reference to statutory mandates. But, practical bureaucratic considerations and paternalistic assumptions about children influence their discretionary decisions as well (Matza, 1964; Cicourel, 1968; Emerson, 1969; Bortner, 1982). In turn, the exercise of broad judicial discretion raises concerns about the discriminatory impact of "individualized justice" (Dannefer and Schutt, 1982;

McCarthy and Smith, 1986; Fagan, Slaughter, and Hartstone, 1987; Krisberg, Fishman, Eisikovits, Guttman, and Joe, 1987; Pope and Feyerherm, 1990a,b).

Despite sometimes discrepant findings, two general conclusions emerge clearly from the research evaluating juvenile court sentencing practices. First, the Principle of Offense—present offense and prior record—accounts for virtually all of the variance in juvenile court sentences that can be explained. Every methodologically rigorous study of juvenile court sentencing practices reports that judges focus primarily on the seriousness of the present offense and prior record when they impose sentences; these legal and offense variables typically explain about 25 to 30% of the variance in sentencing (Clarke and Koch, 1980; McCarthy and Smith, 1986; Fagan *et al.*, 1987a; Bishop and Frazier, 1988, 1996). In short, juvenile court judges attend to the same primary sentencing factors as do criminal court judges. While youths' chronic or serious offending may indicate greater "treatment needs," courts necessarily respond to control their criminal behavior regardless of their ability to change it.

Practical administrative and bureaucratic considerations impel judges to give primacy to offense factors when they sentence juveniles. Organizational desire to avoid public exposure, unfavorable political and media attention, and "fear of scandal" constrain judges to impose more restrictive sentences on more serious offenders (Matza, 1964; Cicourel, 1968; Emerson, 1969). By sentencing serious juvenile offenders more formally and restrictively, judges can deflect unfavorable retrospective scrutiny and political criticism. Moreover, complex organizations that pursue multiple goals develop bureaucratic strategies to simplify individualized assessments; and the present offense and prior record provide a routine basis to rationalize decisions.

The second consistent finding from juvenile court sentencing research is that, after controlling for the present offense and prior record, individualized sentencing discretion is often synonymous with racial discrimination (McCarthy and Smith, 1986; Krisberg *et al.*, 1987; Pope and Feyerherm, 1990a,b). A review of earlier juvenile court sentencing studies found "clear and consistent evidence of a racial differential operating at each decision level. Moreover, the differentials operate continuously over various decision levels to produce a substantial accumulative racial differential which transforms a more or less heterogeneous racial arrest population into a homogeneous institutionalized black population" (Liska and Tausig, 1979:205). A review of juvenile justice sentencing research two decades later reached the same conclusion. "[R]acial discrimination appears most widespread—minorities (and youth in predominantly minority jurisdictions) are more likely to be detained and receive out-of-home placements than whites regardless of 'legal' considerations. Because processing in the juvenile justice system is deeply implicated in the construction of a criminal (or 'prior') record, experiences as a juvenile serve as a major predictor of future processing" (Sampson and Lauritsen, 1997:362). While some of the differences in minority youths' overrepresentation in the juvenile justice system reflect real differences in rates of offending by race (Wolfgang *et al.*, 1972; Hindelang, 1978; FBI, 1996), multivariate research that controls for the seriousness of the present offense, prior record, and other legal variables would account for those differentials.

In 1988, Congress amended the Juvenile Justice and Delinquency Prevention Act to require states receiving federal funds to assure equitable treatment on the basis, *inter alia*, of race, and to assess the sources of minority overrepresentation in juvenile detection facilities and institutions [42 U.S.C. § 5633(a)(16) (1993 Supp.)]. In response to this JJDP ACT mandate, a number of states examined and found racial disparities in their juvenile justice systems (Bishop and Frazier, 1988, 1996; Pope and Feyerherm, 1992; Krisberg and Austin, 1993; Kempf-Leonard, Pope, and Feyerherm, 1995). A review of these evaluation studies reported that, after controlling for offense variables, minority youths were overrepresented in secure detection facilities in 41 of 42 states and in all 13 states that analyzed other phases of juvenile justice decision-making and institutional confinement (Pope, 1994).

Discretionary decisions at various states of the justice process amplify racial disparities as minority youths proceed through the system and produce more severe dispositions than for comparable white youths. The research emphasizes the importance of analyzing juvenile justice decision-making as a multistage process rather than focusing solely on the final dispositional decision. For example, dramatic increases in referral rates of minority youths to juvenile courts in 17 states resulted in corresponding increases in detection and institutional placement (McGarrell, 1993). Juvenile courts detain black youths at higher rates than they do white youths charged with similar offenses, and detained youths typically receive more severe sentences than those at liberty (Bortner and Reed, 1985; Frazier and Cochran, 1986; Krisberg and Austin, 1993).

Most recent studies confirm that minority youths receive more severe dispositions than do white youths even after controlling for relevant legal variables (Krisberg and Austin, 1993). While offense criteria affect initial screening, detention, and charging decisions, as cases progress through the adjudicatory process, youths' race affects their dispositions and minority youths receive more severe sentences. Research in Florida controlled for legal and process variables and found that a juvenile's race directly affected decisions at several stages (Bishop and Frazier, 1988). More recent analyses of Florida data reinforce these findings. "While the magnitude of the race effect varies from stage to stage, there is a consistent pattern of unequal treatment. Nonwhite youths referred for delinquent acts are more likely than comparable white youths to be recommended for petition to court, to be held in pre-adjudicatory detection, to be formally processed in juvenile court, and to receive the most formal or the most restrictive judicial dispositions" (Bishop and Frazier, 1996:405–406).

A comprehensive review of the juvenile sentencing literature concluded that most studies found racial disparities in juvenile justice administration and that cumulative decisions by court personnel heightened these disparities as youths moved through the system (Pope and Feyerherm, 1990a,b). Two-thirds of the studies reviewed showed either direct or indirect evidence of discrimination against minority youths. A national study of incarceration trends reported incarcerations rates for minority youths three to four times greater than those of white juveniles (Krisberg *et al.*, 1987). Moreover, judges sentenced most minority youths to public secure facilities and committed more white youths to private facilities. By 1991, juvenile courts confined less than one-third (31%) of non-Hispanic white juveniles in public long-term facilities; minority youths comprised more two-thirds (69%) of confined youths (Snyder and Sickmund, 1995). Juvenile courts committed black juveniles at a rate nearly five times higher than that of white youths, and blacks comprised 49% of all youths in institutions (Snyder and Sickmund, 1995).

Juvenile courts, as extensions of criminal courts, give primacy to offense factors when they sentence youths. To the extent that *parens patriae* ideology legitimates individualization and differential processing, it also exposes "disadvantaged" youths to the prospects of more extensive state intervention. According to juvenile court's treatment ideology, judges' discretionary decisions *should* disproportionally affect minority youths. The Progressives intended judges to focus on youths' social circumstances rather than simply their offenses, and designed juvenile court policies to discriminate between "our" children and "other people's children."

In a society characterized by great inequality, those meet "in need" are also those most "at risk" for juvenile court intervention. Of course, if states provided exclusively benign and effective treatment services to youths in institutions, then this might mute some of the concerns about racial disparities or socioeconomic inequalities.

c. Conditions of Juvenile Confinement and Treatment Effectiveness

Examining the correctional facilities to which judges sentence young offenders provides another indicator of the increasing punitiveness of juvenile courts. The Court in *Gault* belatedly recognized the longstanding contradictions between rehabilitative rhetoric and punitive reality; conditions of confinement motivated the Court to insist on minimal procedural safeguards for juveniles. Historical studies of the juvenile court's institutional precursor, the House of Refuge (Hawes, 1971; Rothman, 1971; Mennel, 1973; Sutton, 1988), and of the early Progressive training schools provide dismal accounts of institutions that failed to rehabilitate and were scarcely distinguishable from adult penal facilities (Schlossman, 1977; Rothman, 1980).

Contemporary evaluations of juvenile institutions reveal a continuing gap between rehabilitative rhetoric and punitive reality (Bartollas, Miller, and Dinitz, 1976; Feld, 1977, 1981b; Lerner, 1986). Research in Massachusetts described violent and punitive institutions in which staff physically abused inmates and were frequently powerless to prevent inmate violence and predation (Feld, 1977, 1981b). A study in Ohio described a similarly violent and oppressive institutional environment for the "rehabilitation" of young delinquents (Bartollas *et al.*, 1976). Studies in other jurisdictions report staff and inmate violence, physical abuse, and degrading make-work (Guggenheim, 1978; Lerner, 1986). The daily reality for juveniles confined in many "treatment" facilities is one of violence, predatory behavior, and punitive incarceration.

A recent study, *Conditions of Confinement: Juvenile Detention and Corrections Facilities*, reported endemic institutional overcrowding nationwide (Parent *et al.*, 1994). In 1991, almost half (44%) of all long-term public institutions operated above their design capacity, as did more than three-quarters (79%) of the largest facilities, those housing more than 350 inmates (Snyder and Sickmund, 1995). Nearly two-thirds (62%) of all delinquent inmates resided in overcrowded facilities. As states sentenced more youths to juvenile institutions, they increased their prisonlike character, relied more extensively on fences and walls to maintain perimeter security, and used surveillance equipment to provide internal security (Snyder and Sickmund, 1995). Nearly half (46%) of the training schools consisted of medium or maximum security facilities with perimeter fences, locked internal security, or both (Parent *et al.*, 1994).

Coinciding with these post-*Gault* evaluation studies, lawsuits challenged conditions of confinement in juvenile correctional facilities and alleged that they denied inmates their Fourteenth Amendment due process "right to treatment" or violated the Eighth Amendment's prohibition on "cruel and unusual punishment." When a state incarcerates a person for purpose of treatment or rehabilitation, due process requires that conditions of confinement bear some reasonable relationship to the purpose for which the state commits the individual [*Youngberg v. Romeo*, 457 U.S. 307 (1982)]. Because *McKeiver* and juvenile courts' "rehabilitative" theory reject punishment for crimes, delinquents have a "due process interest in freedom from unnecessary bodily restraint which entitled them to closer scrutiny of their conditions of confinement than that accorded convicted criminal" [*Santana v. Collazo*, 714

F.2d 1172 (1983)]. Juvenile institutions combine elements of mental health and *parens patriae* ideology with the ordinary criminal justice system. But, if "treatment" differs from "punishment," then juvenile corrections must do something more than simply confine criminals.

These "right to treatment," "cruel and unusual punishment," and "conditions of confinement" cases also provide an impartial judicial view of the reality of juvenile corrections. Judicial opinions and investigative reports from around the country report routine staff beatings of inmates, the use of drugs for social control purposes, extensive reliance on solitary confinement, and a virtual absence of meaningful rehabilitative programs (Holland Mlyniec, 1995). During the 1970s and 1980s, courts attempted to define the nature of juvenile "treatment" that justified fewer procedural safeguards. More recent litigation attempted to define constitutionally adequate minimum conditions of confinement without prescribing any affirmative obligations to provide treatment. Quite apart from their legal theories, however, these cases provide an independent assessment of conditions in juvenile institutions. Court opinions report that staff routinely beat inmates with a "fraternity paddle," injected them with psychotropic drugs for social control purposes, and deprived them of minimally adequate care and individualized treatment [*Nelson v. Heyne*, 355 F. Supp. 451 (N.D. Ind. 1972), 491 F.2d 352 (7th Cir. 1974)]. Other judges found inmates confined in dark, cold, dungeonlike cells in their underwear, routinely locked in solitary confinement, and subjected to a variety of punitive practices [*Inmates of Boys' Training School v. Affleck* 346 F. Supp. 1354 (D.R.I. 1972)]. Decisions in Texas found numerous instances of physical brutality and abuse, including hazing by staff and inmates, staff-administered beatings and tear-gassing, homosexual assaults, excessive use of solitary confinement, repetitive and degrading make-work, and minimal clinical services [*Morales v. Turman*, 383 F. Supp. 53 (E.D. Tex. 1974), *rev'd on other grounds* 535 F.2d 864 (5th Cir. 1976)]. One juvenile correctional system confined youths in padded cells with no windows or furnishings and only flush holes for toilets, and denied inmates access to all services, programs, or reading materials except a Bible [*Morgan v. Sproat*, 432 F. Supp. 1130 (S.D. Miss. 1977)]. Another court found inmates locked in solitary confinement, beaten and sprayed with mace by staff, required to scrub floors with a toothbrush, and subjected to punitive practices such as standing and sitting for prolonged periods without changing position [*State v. Werner*, 161 W. Va. 192, 242 S.E.2d 907 (1978)]. One judge found that the conditions of juvenile pretrial detainees who were held in an adult jail were deliberately punitive and worse than those experienced by adult convicts [*D.B. v. Tewksbury*, 545 F. Supp. 896 (D.B. Oreg. 1982)]. Reports of abusive practices in the press and in other opinions describe youths shackled spread-eagled to their bed frames, locked in isolation for "mouthing off" or swearing and restrained with handcuffs, leather straps, or leg irons [Krisberg, Lisky, and Austin, 1986; *Alexander S. v. Boyd*, 876 F. Supp. 773 (D.S.C. 1995)]. Nearly two-thirds (65%) of all delinquents confined in training schools reside in facilities subject to a court order or consent decree governing conditions of confinement and the adequacy of the "treatment" programs (Parent *et al.*, 1994).

The recent changes in juvenile court sentencing laws exacerbate institutional overcrowding. Violent inmate subcultures emerge as a function of security arrangements; the more staff impose authoritarian controls to facilitate security, the higher the levels of covert inmate violence within the subculture (Bartollas *et al.*, 1976; Feld, 1977, 1981b). Juveniles sentenced to long terms under "get-tough" legislation represent the most serious and chronic offenders, yet facilities designed to handle them often suffer from limited physical mobility, inadequate program resources and staff, and intense interaction among the most problematic youths in the system. The result is a situation that can easily produce a juvenile correctional "warehouse" with all of the worse characteristics of adult penal incarceration.

Juvenile courts' "treatment model" assumes that social or psychological factors cause delinquent behavior, that individualized sentences should be based on assessments of treatment needs, that release should occur when corrections officials determine that the juvenile has improved, and that successful treatment will reduce recidivism. Evaluations of the effectiveness of juvenile rehabilitation programs on recidivism rates provide scant support for the conclusion that juveniles confined in institutions are being treated rather than punished (Lab and Whitehead, 1988; Whitehead and Lab, 1989). Martinson's (1974:25) generally negative observation that "with few and isolated exceptions, the rehabilitative efforts that have been reported so far have had no appreciable affect on recidivism," challenged the fundamental premise of therapeutic dispositions and the juvenile court. More recent evaluations of the impact of correctional programs on recidivism counsel skepticism about the availability of programs that consistently or systematically rehabilitate adult or serious juvenile offenders (Greenberg, 1977; Sechrest, White, and Brown, 1979; Whitehead and Lab, 1989). A report by the National Academy of Science's panel on "Research on Rehabilitation Techniques" concluded that "the current research literature provides no basis for positive recommendations about techniques to rehabilitate criminal offenders. The literature does afford occasional hints of intervention that may have promise, but to recommend widespread implementation of those measures would be irresponsible. Many of them would probably be wasteful, and some would do more harm than good in the long run" (Sechrest *et al.*, 1979:102). A meta-analysis of juvenile correctional treatment evaluations appearing in the professional literature between 1975 and 1984 and meeting certain methodological criteria concluded that "the results are far from encouraging for rehabilitation proponents" (Lab and Whitehead, 1988:77).

Many researchers strenuously resist the general conclusion that "nothing works" in juvenile or adult corrections, although they have not persuasively refuted the contention (Melton, 1989). Several researchers offer literature reviews, meta-analyses, or program descriptions that stress that some types of intervention may have positive effects on selected clients under certain conditions (Gendreau and Ross, 1979, 1987; Greenwood and Zimring, 1985; Garrett, 1985; Izzo and Ross, 1990; Roberts and Camasso, 1991; Palmer, 1991). However, even optimistic assessments of the rehabilitation of "rehabilitation" conclude only that "several methods seem promising, but none have been shown to usually produce major reductions [in recidivism] when applied broadly to typical composite samples of offenders" (Palmer, 1991:340). The most recent, comprehensive meta-analysis of 200 studies of interventions with serious juvenile offenders reported that "the average intervention effect for these studies was positive, statistically significant, and equivalent to a recidivism reduction of about 6 percentage points, for example, from 50% to 44%" (Lipsey and Wilson, 1998:330).

Several factors account for the inability to demonstrate consistent, effective, and positive juvenile correctional outcomes. Many treatment evaluations lack methodological rigor (Sechrest *et al.*, 1979). Others may use insufficiently sensitive outcome measures (Fagan, 1990). Many treatment programs lack a theoretical rationale or consistent intervention strategies based on that rationale. Some evaluation studies fail to assess whether the program staff actually implemented the prescribed treatment with integrity (Gendreau and Ross, 1987). Finally, even if viable rehabilitative strategies exist, clinicians may lack techniques with which to classify offenders for appropriate forms of intervention to maximize their "responsivity." "[S]ome form of classification for treatment is necessary ... [and] efforts to date have been too little grounded in theory, too simplistic, and too much focused on individual, personal characteristics of offenders.... At the root of classification problems is the lack of any dependable means of treatment or intervention for offenders, again whether for juveniles or adults" (Sechrest, 1987:317). Thus, the inability to demonstrate consistent treatment effects may reflect either methodological flaws, poorly conceived or implemented programs, an inability to accurately match subjects with programs, or the absence of viable methods to successfully treat serious or chronic young offenders.

Some "model" programs "do work" for some offenders under appropriate conditions. Research evidence indicates several elements of correctional programs that can assure more humane conditions of confinement and contribute to youths' future well-being. But the theoretical possibility of effective treatment for some youths does not justify the punitive reality experienced by most delinquents. Unfortunately, most states do not elect to provide these programs or services to delinquents generally. Rather, they incarcerate most juveniles in euphemistically sanitized youth prisons. Even if model programs can reduce recidivism rates, public officials appear unwilling to provide such treatment services when they confront fiscal constraints, budget deficits, and competition from other, more politically potent interest groups. Organizational imperatives to achieve "economies of scale" mandate confining ever larger numbers of youths and thereby preclude the possibility of matching offenders with appropriate treatment programs. If either consistently favorable outcomes or universal access remain far from certain, then it seems difficult to justify confining most youths with fewer procedural safeguards than those provided to adult offenders. If correctional administrators do not provide effective services in responsive environment, then do any practical differences exist between treatment and punishment?

E. CRIMINAL AND SOCIAL JUSTICE FOR YOUNG OFFENDERS

More than three decades after *Gault*, juvenile courts continue to deflect, coopt, ignore, or accommodate constitutional and legislative reforms with minimal institutional change. Despite the juvenile court's transformation from a welfare agency into a scaled-down criminal court, it remains essentially unreformed. Juvenile courts punish rather than treat young offenders, but use a procedural regime under which no adult would consent to be tried.

The individualized justice of a "rehabilitative" juvenile court is necessarily lawless. The juvenile court's welfare *idea* assumes that youths are especially amenable to treatment and grants judges broad discretion to individualize dispositions. Because an individualized assessment of each child's "real needs" dictates the nature of the intervention, every case is unique. Decisional rules or objective criteria cannot constrain clinical insights. But if neither practical, scientific, nor clinical bases exist by which judges can classify for or prescribe and administer effective treatment, then the exercise of "sound discretion" is simply a euphemism for idiosyncratic judicial subjectivity. At the least, judges will sanction youths differently based on extraneous personal or social characteristics for which they are not responsible, such as gender, geography, class, or race. At the worst, if juvenile courts effectively punish, then judges impose haphazard, unequal, and discriminatory sentences on similarly situated offenders without any effective legal recourse.

Juvenile courts predicate their procedural informality on the assumption that they provide benign and effective treatment. The continuing absence or cooptation of defense counsel in many jurisdictions reduces the likelihood that courts will adhere to existing legal mandates. The closed, informal, and confidential nature of delinquency proceedings reduces the visibility and accountability of the justice process and precludes external legal checks on coercive interventions.

The fundamental shortcoming of the juvenile court's welfare *idea* reflects a failure of conception and not *simply* a century-long failure of implementation. The juvenile court's creators envisioned a social service agency in a judicial setting, and attempted to fuse its welfare mission with the power of state coercion. Combining social welfare and penal social control functions in one agency ensures that juvenile courts do both badly. Providing for child welfare represents a societal responsibility rather than a judicial one. Juvenile courts lack control over the resources necessary to meet child welfare needs exactly because of the social class and racial characteristics of their clients, and the public's fear of "other people's children." In practice, juvenile courts almost inevitably subordinate welfare concerns to crime control considerations.

If we formulated child welfare program *ab initio*, would we choose a juvenile court as the most appropriate agency through which to deliver social services, and would we make criminality a condition precedent to the receipt of services? If we would not initially choose a court to deliver social services, then does the fact of a youth's criminality confer on it any special competency as a welfare agency? Many young people who do not commit crimes desperately need social services, and many youths who commit crimes do not require or will not respond to social services. In short, criminality represents an inaccurate and haphazard criterion on which to allocate social services. Because our society denies adequate help and assistance to meet the social welfare needs of all young people, juvenile courts' treatment ideology serves primarily to legitimate judicial coercion of some youths *because of their criminality*.

The attempt to *combine social welfare* and *criminal social control* in one agency constitutes the *fundamental flaw* of the juvenile court. The juvenile court subordinates social welfare concerns to criminal social control functions because of its inherently penal focus. Legislatures do not define juvenile courts' jurisdiction on the basis of characteristics of children for which they are not responsible and for which effective intervention could improve their lives. For example, juvenile court law does not define eligibility for welfare services or create an enforceable right or entitlement based on young peoples' lack of access to quality education, lack of adequate housing or nutrition, unmet health needs, or impoverished families—*none of which are their fault*. In all of these instances, children bear the burdens of their parents' circumstances literally as innocent bystanders. Instead, states' juvenile codes define juvenile court jurisdiction based on a youth committing a crime, a prerequisite that detracts from a compassionate response. Unlike disadvantaged social conditions that are not their fault, criminal behavior represents the one characteristic for which adolescent offenders do bear at least partial responsibility. In short, juvenile courts define eligibility for services on the basis of the feature least likely to elicit sympathy and compassion, and ignore the social structural conditions or personal circumstances more likely to evoke a greater desire to help. Rather, juvenile courts' defining characteristic strengthens public antipathy to "other people's children" by emphasizing primarily that they are law violators. The recent "criminological triage" policies that stress punishment, accountability, and personal responsibility further reinforce juvenile courts' penal foundations and reduce the legitimacy of youths' claims to humanitarian assistance.

The "real" reasons states brings youths to juvenile court is because they committed crimes, not because they need social services. Accordingly, states should uncouple social welfare from social control, try all offenders in one integrated criminal justice system, and make appropriate substantive and procedural modifications to accommodate the youthfulness of some defendants. Substantive justice requires a rationale to sentence younger offenders differently, and *more leniently*, than older defendants, a formal recognition of *youthfulness as a mitigating factor*. Procedural justice requires providing youths with *full procedural parity* with adult defendants and *additional safeguards* to account for the disadvantage of youth in the justice system. These substantive and procedural modifications can avoid the "worst of both worlds," provide youths with protections functionally equivalent to those accorded adults, and do justice in sentencing.

A proposal to abolish juvenile courts constitutes neither an unqualified endorsement of punishment nor a primitive throw-back to earlier centuries' vision of children as miniature adults. Rather, it honestly acknowledges that juvenile courts currently engage in criminal social control, asserts that younger offenders in a criminal justice system *deserve* less severe penalties for their misdeeds than do more mature offenders *simply because they are young*, and addresses many problems created by trying to maintain binary, dichotomous, and contradictory criminal justice systems based on an arbitrary age classification of a youth as a child or as an adult (Feld, 1997).

Formulating a sentencing policy when the child is a criminal and the criminal is a kid entails two tasks. First, a youth sentencing policy requires a rationale to sentence younger offenders *differently*, and *more leniently*, that adult offenders. Explicitly punishing younger offenders rests on the premise that adolescents possess sufficient moral reasoning, cognitive capacity, and volitional control to hold them partially responsible for their behavior, albeit not to the same degree as adults. Developmental psychological research, jurisprudence, and criminal sentencing policy provide rationale for why young offenders deserve less severe consequences for their misdeeds than do older offenders, and justify formal recognition of youthfulness as a mitigating factor. Second, a youth sentencing policy requires a practical administrative mechanism to implement youthfulness as a mitigating factor in sentencing—a "youth discount" for reduced responsibility.

The idea of deserved punishment entails censure and condemnation for making blameworthy choices, and imposes sanctions proportional to the seriousness of a crime (von Hirsch, 1976, 1993). Two elements—harm and culpability—define the seriousness of a crime. A perpetrator's age has relatively little bearing on assessments of harm—the nature of the injury inflicted, risk created, or value taken. But, evaluations of *seriousness* also entail the quality of the actor's *choice* to engage in the criminal conduct that produced the harm. Youthfulness is a very important factor with respect to the culpability of a criminal actor because it directly affects the quality of choices. Responsibility for choices hinges on cognitive and volitional competence. Youths differ socially, physically, and psychologically from more mature adults: They have not yet fully internalized moral norms, developed sufficient empathic identification with others, acquired adequate moral comprehension, or had sufficient opportunity to develop the ability to restrain their actions. They possess neither the rationality—cognitive capacity—nor the self-control—volitional capacity—to equate their criminal responsibility fully with that of adults. In short, their immaturity affects the quality of their judgments in ways that are relevant to criminal sentencing policy. Ultimately, a youth sentencing policy should enable young offenders to survive the mistakes of adolescence with their life chances intact.

Certain characteristic developmental differences distinguish the quality of decisions that young people make from those of adults, and justify a somewhat more protective stance when states sentence younger offenders. Psychosocial "maturity," judgment, and "temperance" provide conceptual prisms through which to view adolescents' decision-making competencies and to assess the quality of their choices (Scott, 1992; Cauffman and Steinberg, 1995; Scott, Reppucci, and Woolard, 1995; Steinberg and Cauffman, 1996; Scott and Grisso, 1997). Adolescents and adults differ in the quality of judgment and self-control they exercise because of relative differences in breadth of experience, short-term versus long-term temporal perspectives, attitudes toward risk, impulsivity, and the importance they attack to peer influences. These developmentally unique attributes affect youths' degree of criminal responsibility.

Young people are more impulsive, exercise less self-control, fail adequately to calculate long-term consequences, and engage in more risky behavior than do adults. Adolescents may estimate the magnitude or probability of risks, may use a shorter time frame, or focus on opportunities for gains rather than possibilities of losses differently than adults (Furby and Beyth-Marom, 1992). Young people may discount the negative value of future consequences because they have more difficulty than adults in integrating a future consequence into their more limited experiential baseline. Adolescents' judgments may differ from adults because of their disposition toward sensation-seeking, impulsivity related to hormonal or physiological changes, and mood volatility (Cauffman and Steinberg, 1995; Steinberg and Cauffman, 1996). Adolescents respond to peer group influences more readily than do adults because of the crucial role that peer relationships play in identity formation (Zimring, 1981a; Scott, 1992). Most adolescent crime occurs in a group context, and having delinquent friends precedes an adolescent's own criminal involvement. Group-offending places normally law-abiding youth at greater risk of involvement and reduces their ability publicly to withdraw. Because of the social context of adolescent crime, young people require time, experience, and opportunities to develop the capacity for autonomous judgments and to resist peer influence.

Developmental processes affect adolescents' quality of judgment and self-control, directly influence their degree of criminal responsibility and deserved punishment, and justify a different criminal sentencing policy. While young offenders possess sufficient understanding and culpability to hold them accountable for their acts, their crimes are less blameworthy than adults' because of reduced culpability and limited appreciation of consequences *and* because their life circumstances understandably limited their capacity to learn to make fully responsible choices.

When youths offend, the families, schools, and communities that socialize them bear some responsibility for the failures of those socializing institutions. Human beings depend on others to nurture them and to enable them to develop and exercise the moral capacity for constructive behavior. The capacity for self-control and self-direction is not simply a matter of moral luck or good fortune, but a socially constructed developmental process that provides young people with the opportunity to develop a moral character. Community structures affect social conditions and the contexts within which adolescents grow and interact with peers. Unlike presumptively mobile adults, juveniles lack the means or ability to escape from their criminogenic environments because of their dependency.

Negotiating the developmental tasks of adolescence requires a "learner's permit"—a social moratorium—that gives youths the opportunity to make choices and to learn to be responsible but without suffering fully the long-term consequences of their mistakes (Zimring, 1982). The ability to make responsible choices is a learned behavior, and the dependent status of youth systematically deprives them of chances to learn to be responsible. Young peoples' socially constructed life situation understandably limits their capacity to develop self-control, restricts their opportunities to learn and exercise responsibility, and supports a partial reduction of criminal responsibility. A youth sentencing policy would entail both shorter sentence durations and a higher offense-seriousness threshold before a state incarcerates youths than for older offenders.

The binary distinctions between children and adults that provide the bases for states' legal age of majority and the jurisprudential foundation of the juvenile court ignore the reality that adolescents develop along a continuum, and create an unfortunate either–or forced choice in sentencing. By contrast, shorter sentences for reduced responsibility represent a more modest and readily attainable reason to treat young offenders differently than adults than the rehabilitative justifications advanced by Progressive "child-savers." Protecting young people from the full penal consequences of their poor decisions reflects a policy to preserve their life chances for the future when they presumably will make more mature and responsible choices. Such a policy both holds young offenders accountable for their acts because they possess sufficient culpability, and yet mitigates the severity of consequences because their choices entail less blame than those of adults.

Sentencing policy that integrates youthfulness, reduced culpability, and restricted opportunities to learn self-control with penal principles of proportionality would provide younger offenders with categorical fractional reductions of adult sentences. If adolescents as a class characteristically make poorer choices than adults, then sentencing policies should protect young people from the full penal consequences of their bad decisions. Because youthfulness constitutes a universal form of "reduced culpability" or "diminished responsibility," states should treat it categorically as a mitigating factor, without regard to nuances of individual developmental differences. Youth development is a highly variable process, and chronological age is a crude, imprecise measure of criminal maturity and the opportunity to develop the capacity for self-control. Despite the variability of adolescence, however, a categorical "youth discount" that uses age as a conclusive proxy for reduced culpability and shorter sentences remains preferable to any individualized inquiry into the criminal responsibility of each young offender. Developmental psychology does not possess reliable clinical indicators of moral development that equate readily with criminal responsibility and accountability. For young criminal actors who are responsible, to some degree, clinical testimony to precisely tailor sanctions to culpability is not worth the burden or diversion of resources that the effort would entail. Because youthful mitigated criminal responsibility is a legal concept, no psychiatric analogue exists to which clinical testimony would correspond. Rather, a youth discount categorically recognizes that criminal choices by young people differ to some degree qualitatively from those of adults and constitute a form of partial responsibility without any additional clinical indicators.

This categorical approach would take the form of an explicit "youth discount" at sentencing, a sliding scale of criminal responsibility. A 14-year-old offender might receive, for example, 25 to 33% of the adult penalty, a 16-year-old defendant, 50 to 66%, and an 18-year-old adult, the full penalty as presently occurs (Feld, 1997). The "deeper discounts" for younger offenders correspond to the developmental continuum and their more limited opportunities to learn to be responsible and to exercise self-control. Because reduced culpability provides the rationale for youthful mitigation, younger adolescents bear less responsibility and deserve proportionally shorter sentences than older youths. With the passage of time, age, and opportunities to develop the capacity for self-control, social tolerance of criminal deviance and claims for youthful mitigation decline. Discounted sentences that preserve younger offenders' life chances require that the maximum sentences they receive remain very substantially lower than those imposed on adults. Capital sentences and draconian mandatory minimum sentences, for example, life without parole, have no place in sentencing presumptively less-blameworthy adolescents. Because of the rapidity of adolescent development and the life-course disruptive consequences of incarceration, the rationale for a "youth discount" also supports requiring a higher in/out threshold of offense seriousness and culpability as a prerequisite for imprisonment.

Only states whose criminal sentencing laws provide realistic, humane, and determinate sentences that enable a judge actually to determine "real-time" sentences can readily implement a proposal for explicit fractional reductions of youths' sentences. One can only know the value of a "youth discount" in a sentencing system in which courts know in advance the standard or "going rate" for adults. In many jurisdictions, implementing a "youth discount" would require significant modification of the current sentencing laws including presumptive sentencing guidelines with strong upper limits on punishment severity, elimination of all mandatory minimum sentences, and some structured judicial discretion to mitigate penalties based on individual circumstances. Attempts to apply idiosyncratically "youth discounts" within the flawed indeterminate or mandatory-minimum sentencing regimes that currently prevail in many jurisdictions run the risk simply of reproducing all of their existing inequalities and injustices.

A graduated age-culpability sentencing scheme in an integrated criminal justice system avoids the inconsistencies associated with the binary either-juvenile-or-adult drama currently played out in judicial waiver proceedings and in prosecutorial charging decisions and introduces proportionality to the sentences imposed on the many youths currently tried as adults. It also avoids the "punishment gap" when youths make the transition from one justice system to the other, and ensures similar consequences for similarly situated offenders. Adolescence and criminal careers develop along a continuum; the current bifurcation between the two justice systems confounds efforts to respond consistently to young career offenders. A sliding scale of criminal sentences based on an offender's age-as-a-proxy-for-culpability accomplishes simply and directly what the various "blended jurisdiction" statutes attempt to achieve indirectly (Feld, 1995). A formal policy of youthfulness as a mitigating factor avoids the undesirable forced choice between either inflicting undeservedly harsh penalties on less culpable actors or doing nothing about the manifestly guilty.

As integrated justice system also allows for integrated record-keeping, and enables officials to identify and respond to career offenders more readily than the current jurisdictional bifurcation permits. Even adolescent "career offenders" *deserve* enhanced sentences based on an extensive record of prior offending. But, an integrated justice system does not require integrated prisons. The question of "how long" differs from questions of "where" and "what." States should maintain age-segregated youth correctional facilities both to protect younger offenders from adults, and to protect geriatric prisoners from younger inmates. Virtually all young offenders will return to society and the state should provide them with resources for self-improvement because of its basic responsibility to its citizens and its own self-interest. A sentencing and correctional policy must offer youths "room to reform" and provide opportunities and resources to facilitate young offenders' constructive use of their time.

Finally, affirming partial responsibility for youth constitutes a virtue. The idea of personal responsibility and accountability for behavior provides an important cultural counterweight to a popular culture that endorses the idea that everyone is a victim, that all behavior is determined, and that no one is responsible. The juvenile court elevated determinism over free will, characterized delinquents as victims rather than perpetrators, and subjected them to an indeterminate quasi-civil commitment process. The juvenile court's treatment ideology denied youths' personal responsibility, reduced offenders' duty to exercise self-control, and eroded their obligations to change. If there is any silver lining in the current cloud of "get-tough" policies, it is the affirmation of responsibility. A culture that values autonomous individuals must emphasize both freedom and responsibility. A criminal law that bases sentences on blameworthiness and responsibility must recognize the physical, psychological, and socially constructed differences between youths and adults. Affirming responsibility forces politicians to be honest when the kid is a criminal and the criminal is a kid. The real reason states bring young offenders to juvenile courts is not to deliver social services, but because they committed a crime.

A proposal to abolish the juvenile court represents an effort to uncouple social welfare and social control policies. On the one hand, such an endeavor would provoke a reexamination of criminal justice strategies toward younger offenders. On the other hand, such a strategy would enable public policies to address directly the "real needs" of all children regardless of their criminality. Social structural forces, political economic arrangements, and legal policies affect the social conditions of young people. A century ago, Progressive reformers had to choose between initiating structural social reforms that would ameliorate criminogenic forces or ministering to the individuals damaged by those adverse social conditions. Driven by class and ethnic antagonisms, they ignored the social structural implications of their delinquency theories and chose instead to "save children" and, incidentally, to preserve their own power and privilege (Platt, 1977; Rothman, 1980).

A century later, we face the same choice between "rehabilitating" damaged individuals and initiating social structural changes. In making this choice, the juvenile court welfare *idea* may constitute an obstacle to child welfare reform. The *existence* of the juvenile court provides an alibi to avoid fundamental improvement. Conservatives can deprecate it as a welfare system, albeit one that "coddles" criminals, while liberals can bemoan its lack of resources and inadequate options. A society that cares for the welfare of its children does so directly by supporting families, communities, schools, and social institutions that nurture all young people, and not by cynically incarcerating its most disadvantaged children and pretending that it is "for their own good." Providing for child welfare is ultimately a societal responsibility. It is unrealistic to expect juvenile courts or any other legal institutions to ameliorate the social ills that affect young people or to significantly reduce youth crime.

The social order significantly determines young people's access to opportunities and the lives they may fashion for themselves as adults. A society committed to equality of opportunity must adopt policies to assure that all children, regardless of their parents' socioeconomic circumstances, have at least a fair start and a meaningful chance to succeed. Current public policies contribute to the social isolation of many youths, the desperate poverty of one child in five, and the high rates of criminality that prevail among young people in general and urban black males in particular (Lindsey, 1994; Wilson, 1996). Public policies can modify the social order, improve the present circumstances of young people, and better facilitate their successful transition to responsible and competent adulthood.

If states frame child welfare policies in terms of child welfare rather than crime control, then the possibilities for positive interventions for young people expand dramatically. For example, a public health approach to youth crime and violence that identified their social, environmental, community structural, and ecological correlates such as concentrated poverty, school test-scores, availability of handguns or shots-fired, or the commercialization of violence would suggest wholly different intervention strategies than simply incarcerating minority youths. Youth violence occurs as part of a social ecological structure in areas of concentrated poverty, high teenage pregnancy, and welfare dependency. Such social indicators could identify census tracts or even zip codes for community organizing, economic development, and preventive and remedial intervention.

Poverty constitutes the biggest single risk factor for the welfare of young people (National Research Council, 1993). Family income directly affects the quality of children's lives and their social opportunities in myriad ways. It determines, for example, the quality of their housing, neighborhoods, schools, health care, nutrition, and personal safety. Children in poverty experience malnutrition, inadequate clothing, substandard housing, lack of access to health care, deficient schools, and dangerous, crime-ridden streets and neighborhoods (National Commission on Children, 1991). Children in an affluent society consigned to live in prolonged poverty suffer from a form of chronic abuse. Eliminating this pervasive, undifferentiated child abuse requires far more extensive social resources and economic reforms than any juvenile justice or child welfare system possibly can muster.

The social and community structural determinants of youth crime and violence also suggest several future directions for a child welfare policy freed from the constraints of a juvenile court. Because poverty constitutes the biggest single risk factor for youth development, public policies must address directly child poverty to facilitate youths' transition to adulthood. Because minority children disproportionately bear the brunt of economic inequality, universal child welfare policies will especially enhance their life chances (Wilson, 1987; Edelman, 1987). Because the sharp increase in homicides caused by firearms provided most of the political impetus to transform the juvenile court into a scaled-down criminal court and to "crack down" on youth crime, public policies must address directly the prevalence of guns among the young.

Three aspects of youth crime and violence suggest future social welfare policy directions regardless of their immediate impact on recidivism. First, it is imperative to provide a hopeful future for all young people. As a result of structural and economic changes since the 1980s, the ability of families to raise children, to prepare them for the transition to adulthood, and to provide them with a more promising future has declined. Many social indicators of the status of young people—poverty, homelessness, violent victimization, and crime—are negative and some of those adverse trends are accelerating. Without realistic hope for their future, young people fall into despair, nihilism, and violence. Second, the disproportionate overrepresentation of minority youths in the juvenile justice system makes imperative the pursuit of racial and social justice. A generation ago, the National Advisory Commission on Civil Disorders (1968:1), the Kerner Commission, warned that the United States was "moving toward two societies, one black, one white—separate and unequal." The Kerner Commission predicted that to continue present policies was "to make permanent the division of our country into two societies; one, largely Negro and poor, located in the central cities; the other, predominantly white and affluent, located in the suburbs." Today, we reap the bitter harvest of racial segregation, concentrated poverty, urban social disintegration, and youth violence sown by social policies and public neglect a generation ago (Wilson, 1987; Massey and Denton, 1993). Third, youth violence has become increasingly lethal as the proliferation of handguns transforms adolescent altercations into homicidal encounters. Only public policies that reduce and reverse the proliferation of guns among the youth population will stem the carnage.

While politicians may be unwilling to invest scarce social resources in young "criminals," particularly those of other colors or cultures, a demographic shift and an aging population give all of us a stake in young people and encourage us to invest in their human capital for their and our own future well-being and to maintain an intergenerational compact. Social welfare and legal policies to provide all young people with a hopeful future, to reduce racial and social inequality, and to reduce access to and use of firearms require a public and political commitment to the welfare of children that extends far beyond the resources or competencies of any juvenile justice system.

REFERENCES

Abramovitch, R., Higgins-Biss, K. L., and Biss, S. R. (1993). Young Persons' Comprehension of Waivers in Criminal Proceedings. *Canadian Journal of Criminology*, *35*, 309–322.

Aday, D. P., Jr. (1986). Court Structure, Defense Attorney Use, and Juvenile Court Decisions. *Sociological Quarterly*, *27*, 107–119.

Ainsworth, J. E. (1991). Re-imaging Childhood and Re-constructing the Legal Order: The Case for Abolishing the Juvenile Court. *North Carolina Law Review*, *69*, 1083–1133.
Allen, F. A. (1964). Legal Values and the Rehabilitative Ideal. In *The Borderland of the Criminal Law: Essays in Law and Criminology*. Chicago: University of Chicago Press.
Allen, F. (1981). *Decline of the Rehabilitative Ideal*. New Haven, CT: Yale University Press.
Allinson, R. (Ed.). (1983). *Status Offenders and the Juvenile Justice System*. Hackensack, NJ: National Council on Crime and Delinquency.
American Bar Association, Institute of Judicial Administration. (1982). *Juvenile Justice Standards Relating to Noncriminal Misbehavior*. Cambridge, MA: Ballinger.
American Bar Association. (1995). *A Call For Justice: An Assessment of Access to Counsel and Quality of Representation in Delinquency Proceedings*. Washington, DC: ABA Juvenile Justice Center.
American Friends Service Committee. (1971). *Struggle for Justice*. New York: Hill & Wang.
Andrews, R. H., and Cohn, A. H. (1974). Ungovernability: The Unjustifiable Jurisdiction. *Yale Law Journal*, *83*, 1383–1409.
Arthur, L. G. (1977). Status Offenders Need a Court of Last Resort. *Boston University Law Review*, *57*, 631–644.
Bartollas, C., Miller, S. J., and Dinitz, S. (1976). *Juvenile Victimization: The Institutional Paradox*. New York: Wiley.
Beckett, K. (1997). *Making Crime Pay: Law and Order in Contemporary American Politics*. London: Oxford University Press.
Bernard, T. J. (1992). *The Cycle of Juvenile Justice*. London: Oxford University Press.
Bishop, D. M., and Frazier, C. S. (1988). The Influence of Race in Juvenile Justice Processing. *Journal of Research in Crime and Delinquency*, *25*, 242–263.
Bishop, D. M., and Frazier, C. S. (1991). Transfer of Juveniles to Criminal Court: A Case Study and Analysis of Prosecutorial Waiver. *Notre Dame Journal of Law, Ethics and Public Policy*, *5*, 281–302.
Bishop, D. M., and Frazier, C. S. (1992). Gender Bias in Juvenile Justice Processing: Implications of the JJDP Act. *Journal of Criminal Law and Criminology*, *82*, 1162–1186.
Bishop, D. M., and Frazier, C. S. (1996). Race Effects in Juvenile Justice Decision-Making: Findings of a Statewide Analysis. *Journal of Criminal Law and Criminology*, *86*, 392–413.
Blumstein, A. (1995). Youth Violence, Guns, and the Illicit-Drug Industry. *Journal of Criminal Law and Criminology*, *86*, 10–36.
Blumstein, A., and Cork, D. (1996). Linking Gun Availability to Youth Gun Violence. *Law and Contemporary Problems*, *59*, 5–24.
Blumstein, A., Cohen, J., Roth, J. A., and Visher, C. A. (Eds.). (1986). *Criminal Careers and "Career Criminals."* Washington, DC: National Academy Press.
Bortner, M. A. (1982). *Inside a Juvenile Court*. New York: New York University Press.
Bortner, M. A. (1986). Traditional Rhetoric, Organizational Realities: Remand of Juveniles to Adult Court. *Crime and Delinquency*, *32*, 53–73.
Bortner, M. A., and Reed, W. L. (1985). The Preeminence of Process: An Example of Refocused Justice Research. *Social Science Quarterly*, *66*, 413–425.
Cauffman, E., and Steinberg, L. (1995). The Cognitive and Affective Influences on Adolescent Decision-Making. *Temple Law Review*, *68*, 1763–1789.
Chesney-Lind, M. (1988). Girls and Status Offenses: Is Juvenile Justice Still Sexist? *Criminal Justice Abstracts*, *20*, 144–165.
Cicourel, A. V. (1968). *The Social Organization of Juvenile Justice*. New York: Wiley.
Clarke, S. H., and Koch, G. G. (1980). Juvenile Court: Therapy or Crime Control, and Do Lawyers Make a Difference? *Law and Society Review*, *14*, 263–208.
Costello, J. C., and Worthington, N. L. (1981). Incarcerating Status Offenders: Attempts to Circumvent the Juvenile Justice and Delinquency Prevention Act. *Harvard Civil Rights–Civil Liberties Law Review*, *16*, 41–81.
Cremin, L. (1961). *The Transformation of the School: Progressivism in American Education, 1876–1957*. New York: Vintage Books.
Cullen, F. T., and Gilbert, K. E. (1982). *Reaffirming Rehabilitation*. Cincinnati, OH: Anderson.
Dannefer, D., and Schutt, R. (1982). Race and Juvenile Justice Processing in Court and Police Agencies. *American Journal of Sociology*, *87*, 1113–1132.
Decker, S. H. (1985). A Systematic Analysis of Diversion: Net Widening and Beyond. *Journal of Criminal Justice*, *13*, 206–216.
Degler, C. (1980). *At Odds: Women and the Family in America from the Revolution to the Present*. London: Oxford University Press.
Edelman, M. W. (1987). *Families in Peril: An Agenda for Social Change*. Cambridge, MA: Harvard University Press.

Eigen, J. (1981a). The Determinants and Impact of Jurisdictional Transfer in Philadelphia. In J. Hall, D. Hamparian, J. Pettibone, and J. White (Eds.), *Readings in Public Policy*. Columbus, OH: Academy for Contemporary Problems.

Eigen, J. (1981b). Punishing Youth Homicide Offenders in Philadelphia. *Journal of Criminal Law and Criminology, 72*, 1072–1093.

Emerson, R. M. (1969). *Judging Delinquents: Context and Process in Juvenile Court*. Chicago: Aldine.

Empey, L. T. (1973). Juvenile Justice Reform: Diversion, Due Process, and Dinstitutionalization. In L. E. Ohlin (Ed.), *Prisoners in America* (pp. 13–48). Englewood Cliffs, NJ: Prentice–Hall.

Fagan, J. (1990). Social and Legal Policy Dimensions of Violent Juvenile Crime. *Criminal Justice and Behavior, 17*, 93–133.

Fagan, J., and Deschenes, E. P. (1990). Determinates of Judicial Waiver Decisions for Violent Juvenile Offenders. *Journal of Criminal Law and Criminology, 81*, 314–347.

Fagan, J., Slaughter, E., and Hartstone, E. (1987a). Blind Justice? The Impact of Race on the Juvenile Justice Process. *Crime and Delinquency, 33*, 224–258.

Fagan, J., Forst, M., and Vivona, S. (1987b). Racial Determinants of the Judicial Transfer Decision: Prosecuting Violent Youth in Criminal Court. *Crime and Delinquency, 33*, 259–286.

Farrington, D. P. (1986). Age and Crime. In M. Tonry and N. Morris (Eds.), *Crime & Justice: An Annual Review* (Vol. 7, pp. 189–250). Chicago: University of Chicago Press.

Farrington, D. P. (1998). Predictors, Causes, and Correlates of Youth Violence. In M. Tonry and M. H. Moore (Eds.), *Crime and Justice: A Review of Research* (Vol. 24, pp. 421–476). Chicago: University of Chicago Press.

Federal Bureau of Investigation. (1992). *Crime in the United States 1991 Uniform Crime Reports*. Washington, DC: U.S. Government Printing Office.

Federal Bureau of Investigation. (1996). *Crime in the United States 1995 Uniform Crime Reports*. Washington, DC: U.S. Government Printing Office.

Feld, B. C. (1977). *Neutralizing Inmate Violence: Juvenile Offenders in Institutions*. Cambridge, MA: Ballinger.

Feld, B. C. (1978). Reference of Juvenile Offenders for Adult Prosecution: The Legislative Alternative to Asking Unanswerable Questions. *Minnesota Law Review, 62*, 515–618.

Feld, B. C. (1981a). Juvenile Court Legislative Reform and the Serious Young Offender: Dismantling the "Rehabilitative Ideal." *Minnesota Law Review, 69*, 141–242.

Feld, B. C. (1981b). A Comparative Analysis of Organizational Structure and Inmate Subcultures in Institutions for Juvenile Offenders. *Crime and Delinquency, 27*, 336–363.

Feld, B. C. (1984). Criminalizing Juvenile Justice: Rules of Procedure for Juvenile Court. *Minnesota Law Review, 69*, 141–276.

Feld, B. C. (1987). Juvenile Court Meets the Principle of Offense: Legislative Changes in Juvenile Waiver Statutes. *Journal of Criminal Law and Criminology, 78*, 471–533.

Feld, B. C. (1988a). *In re Gault* Revisited: A Cross-State Comparison of the Right to Counsel in Juvenile Court. *Crime and Delinquency, 34*, 393–424.

Feld, B. C. (1988b). Juvenile Court Meets the Principle of Offense: Punishment, Treatment, and the Difference it Makes. *Boston University Law Review, 68*, 821–915.

Feld, B. C. (1989). The Right to Counsel in Juvenile Court: An Empirical Study of When Lawyers Appear and the Difference They Make. *Journal of Criminal Law and Criminology, 79*, 1185–1346.

Feld, B. C. (1990). Bad Law Makes Hard Cases: Reflections on Teen-Aged Axe-Murderers, Judicial Activism, and Legislative Default. *Journal of Law and Inequality, 8*, 1–101.

Feld, B. C. (1991). Justice by Geography: Urban, Suburban, and Rural Variations in Juvenile Justice Administration. *Journal of Criminal Law and Criminology, 82*, 156–210.

Feld, B. C. (1993a). Criminalizing the American Juvenile Court. *Crime and Justice, 17*, 197–280.

Feld, B. C. (1993b). *Justice for Children: The Right to Counsel and the Juvenile Court*. Boston: Northeastern University Press.

Feld, B. C. (1995). Violent Youth and Public Policy: A Case-Study of Juvenile Justice Law Reform. *Minnesota Law Review, 79*, 965–1128.

Feld, B. C. (1997). Abolish the Juvenile Court: Youthfulness, Criminal Responsibility, and Sentencing Policy. *Journal of Criminal Law and Criminology, 88*, 68–136.

Feld, B. C. (1998). Juvenile and Criminal Justice Systems' Responses to Youth Violence. In M. Tonry and M. Moore (Eds.), *Crime and Justice: An Annual Review* (Vol. 24, pp. 189–262). Chicago: University of Chicago Press.

Feld, B. C. (1999). *Bad Kids: Race and the Transformation of the Juvenile Court*. London: Oxford University Press.

Ferster, E. Z., and Courtless, T. F. (1972). Predispositional Data, Role of Counsel and Decisions in a Juvenile Court. *Law and Society Review, 7*, 195–222.

Forst, M., and Blomquist, M.-E. (1991). Cracking Down on Juveniles: The Changing Ideology of Youth Corrections. *Notre Dame Journal of Law, Ethics and Public Policy, 5*, 323–375.

Fogel, D. (1979). *We are the Living Proof: The Justice Model for Corrections*. 2nd ed. Cincinnati, OH: Anderson.

Fox, S. J. (1970a). Juvenile Justice Reform: An Historical Perspective. *Stanford Law Review, 22*, 1187–1239.

Fox, S. J. (1970b). Responsibility in the Juvenile Court. *William & Mary Law Review, 11*, 659–684.

Frazier, C. E., and Cochran, J. K. (1986). Detention of Juveniles. Its Effects on Subsequent Juvenile Court Processing Decisions. *Youth and Society, 17*, 286–305.

Fritsch, E., and Hemmens, C. (1995). Juvenile Waiver in the United States 1979–1995: A Comparison and Analysis of State Waiver Statutes. *Juvenile and Family Court Judges Journal, 46*, 17–5.

Furby, L., and Beyth-Marom, R. (1992). Risk Taking in Adolescence: A Decision-Making Perspective. *Developmental Review, 12*, 1–44.

Gardner, M. L. (1982). Punishment and Juvenile Justice: A Conceptual Framework for Assessing Constitutional Rights of Youthful Offenders. *Vanderbilt Law Review, 35*, 791–847.

Gardner, M. (1987). Punitive Juvenile Justice: Some Observations on a Recent Trend. *International Journal of Law and Psychiatry, 10*, 129–151.

Garrett, C. J. (1985). Effects of Residential Treatment on Adjudicated Delinquents: A Meta-Analysis. *Journal of Research in Crime and Delinquency, 22*, 287–308.

Gendreau, P., and Ross, B. (1979). Effective Correctional Treatment: Bibliotherapy for Cynics. *Crime and Delinquency, 25*, 463–489.

Gendreau, P., and Ross, B. (1987). Revivification of Rehabilitation: Evidence from the 1980s. *Justice Quarterly, 4*, 349–407.

Giardino, L. F. (1996). Statutory Rhetoric: The Reality Behind Juvenile Justice Policies in America. *Journal of Law and Policy, 5*, 223–242.

Gillespie, L. K., and Norman, M. D. (1984). Does Certification Mean Prison: Some Preliminary Findings from Utah. *Juvenile and Family Court Journal, 35*, 23–34.

Graham, F. (1970). *The Self-Inflicted Wound*. New York: Free Press.

Greenberg, D. (1977). *Corrections and Punishment*. Beverly Hills, CA: Sage.

Greenwood, P., and Zimring, F. (1985). *One More Chance: The Pursuit of Promising Intervention Strategies for Chronic Juvenile Offenders*. Santa Monica, CA: Rand.

Greenwood, P., Petersilia, J., and Zimring, F. (1980). *Age, Crime, and Sanctions: The Transition from Juvenile to Adult Court*. Santa Monica, CA: Rand.

Greenwood, P., Lipson, A., Abrahamse, A., and Zimring, F. (1983). *Youth Crime and Juvenile Justice in California*. Santa Monica, CA: Rand.

Greenwood, P., Abrahamse, A., and Zimring, F. (1984). *Factors Affecting Sentence Severity for Young Adult Offenders*. Santa Monica, CA: Rand.

Grisso, T. (1980). Juveniles' Capacities to Waive Miranda Rights: An Empirical Analysis. *California Law Review, 68*, 1134–1166.

Grisso, T. (1981). *Juveniles' Waiver of Rights*. New York: Plenum Press.

Guarino-Ghezzi, S., and Loughran, E. J. (1996). *Balancing Juvenile Justice*. New Brunswick, NJ: Transaction Books.

Guggenheim, M. (1978). A Call to Abolish the Juvenile Justice System. *Children's Rights Reporter, 2*, 7–19.

Hagan, J., and Leon, J. (1977). Rediscovering Delinquency: Social History, Political Ideology and the Sociology of Law. *American Sociological Review, 42*, 587–598.

Hamparian, D., Schuster, R., Dinitz, S., and Conrad, J. (1978). *The Violent Few: A Study of Dangerous Juvenile Offenders*. Lexington, MA: Lexington Books.

Hamparian, D., Estep, L., Muntean, S., Priestino, R., Swisher, R., Wallace, P., and White, J. (1982). *Youth in Adult Courts: Between Two Worlds*. Washington, DC: OJJDP.

Handler, J. F. (1965). The Juvenile Court and the Adversary System: Problems of Function and Form. *Wisconsin Law Review, 1965*, 7–51.

Handler, J. F., and Zatz, J. (Eds.). (1982). *Neither Angels Nor Thieves: Studies in Deinstitutionalization of Status Offender*. Washington, DC: National Academy Press.

Hart, H. L. A. (1968). *Punishment and Responsibility*. London: Oxford University Press.

Hasenfeld, Y., and Cheung, P. P. (1985). The Juvenile Court as a People-Processing Organization: A Political Economy Perspective. *American Journal of Sociology, 90*, 801–824.

Hawes, J. (1971). *Children in Urban Society: Juvenile Delinquency in Nineteenth-Century America*. London: Oxford University Press.

Hawes, J., and Hiner, N. (Eds.). (1985). *American Childhood: A Research Guide and Historical Handbook*. Westport, CT: Greenwood Press.

Higham, J. (1988). *Strangers in the Land: Patterns of American Nativism 1860–1925* (2nd ed.). New Brunswick, NJ: Rutgers University Press.

Hindelang, M. (1978). Race and Involvement in Common Law Personal Crimes. *American Sociological Review, 43*, 93–109.

Hofstadter, R. (1955). *The Age of Reform: From Bryan to F.D.R.* New York: Knopf.

Holland, P., and Mlyniec, W. (1995). Whatever Happened to the Right to Treatment?: The Modern Quest for a Historical Promise. *Temple Law Review, 68*, 1791–1835.

Izzo, R. L., and Ross, R. R. (1990). Meta-Analysis of Rehabilitation Programs for Juvenile Delinquents. *Criminal Justice and Behavior, 17*, 134–142.

Kalven, H., and Zeisel, H. (1966). *The American Jury.* Chicago: University of Chicago Press.

Katz, A., and Teitelbaum, L. (1978). PINS Jurisdiction, the Vagueness Doctrine and the Rule of Law. *Indiana Law Journal, 53*, 1–34.

Kempf, K. L., Decker, S. H., and Bing, R. L. (1990). *An Analysis of Apparent Disparities in the Handling of Black Youth Within Missouri's Juvenile Justice Systems.* St. Louis: University of Missouri Department of Administration of Justice.

Kempf-Leonard, K., Pope, C., and Feyerherm, W. (1995). *Minorities in Juvenile Justice.* Thousand Oaks, CA: Sage.

Kett, J. F. (1977). *Rites of Passage: Adolescence in America 1790 to the Present.* New York: Basic Books.

Klein, M. W. (1979). Deinstitutionalization and Diversion of Juvenile Offenders: A Litany of Impediments. In M. Tonry and N. Morris (Eds.), *Crime and Justice: An Annual Review*, Vol. 1, pp. 145–201).

Knitzer, J., and Sobie, M. (1984). *Law Guardians in New York State: A Study of the Legal Representation of Children.* New York: New York State Bar Association.

Krisberg, B., and Austin, J. (1993). *Reinvesting Juvenile Justice.* Thousand Oaks, CA: Sage.

Krisberg, B., and Schwartz, I. (1983). Rethinking Juvenile Justice. *Crime and Delinquency, 29*, 333–364.

Krisberg, B., Lisky, P., and Austin, J. (1986). The Watershed of Juvenile Justice Reform. *Crime and Delinquency, 32*, 5–38.

Krisberg, B., Fishman, G., Eisikovits, Z., Guttman, E., and Joe, K. (1987). The Incarceration of Minority Youth. *Crime and Delinquency, 33*, 173–205.

Lab, S. P., and Whitehead, T. (1988). An Analysis of Juvenile Correctional Treatment. *Crime and Delinquency, 34*, 60–83.

Lasch, C. (1977). *Haven in a Heartless World: The Family Besieged.* New York: Basic Books.

Lefstein, N., Stapleton, V., and Teitelbaum, L. (1969). In Search of Juvenile Justice: *Gault* and Its Implementation. *Law and Society Review, 3*, 491–562.

Lemann, N. (1992). *The Promised Land: The Great Black Migration and How It Changed America.* New York: Vintage Books.

Lerman, P. (1982). *Deinstitutionalization and the Welfare State.* New Brunswick, NJ: Rutgers University Press.

Lerman, P. (1984). Child Welfare, the Private Sector, and Community-Based Corrections. *Crime and Delinquency, 30*, 5–38.

Lerner, S. (1986). *Bodily Harm.* Bolinas, CA: Common Knowledge Press.

Lindsey, D. (1994). *The Welfare of Children.* London: Oxford University Press.

Lipsey, M. W., and Wilson, D. B. (1998). Effective Intervention for Serious Juvenile Offenders. In R. Leober and D. P. Farrington (Eds.), *Serious and Violent Juvenile Offenders: Risk Factors and Successful Interventions* (pp. 313–345). Thousand Oaks, CA: Sage.

Liska, A. E., and Tausig, M. (1979). Theoretical Interpretations of Social Class and Racial Differentials in Legal Decision-Making for Juveniles. *Sociological Quarterly, 20*, 197–207.

Mack, J. W. (1909). The Juvenile Court. *Harvard Law Review, 23*, 104–122.

Martinson, R. (1974). What Works? Questions and Answers About Prison Reform. *The Public Interest, 35*, 22–54.

Massey, D. S., and Denton, N. (1993). *American Apartheid: Segregation and the Making of the Underclass.* Cambridge, MA: Harvard University Press.

Matza, D. (1964). *Delinquency and Drift.* New York: Wiley.

McCarthy, B., and Smith, B. L. (1986). The Conceptualization of Discrimination in the Juvenile Justice Process: The Impact of Administrative Factors and Screening Decisions of Juvenile Court Dispositions. *Criminology, 24*, 41–64.

McCarthy, F. B. (1977a). The Role of the Concept of Responsibility in Juvenile Delinquency Proceedings. *University of Michigan Journal of Law Reform, 10*, 181–219.

McCarthy, F. B. (1977b). Should Juvenile Delinquency Be Abolished? *Crime and Delinquency, 23*, 196–203.

McCarthy, F.B. (1981). Pre-Adjudicatory Rights in Juvenile Court: An Historical and Constitutional Analysis. *University of Pittsburgh Law Review, 42*, 457–514.

McCarthy, F. B. (1994). The Serious Offender and Juvenile Court Reform: The Case for Prosecutorial Waiver of Juvenile Court Jurisdiction. *St. Louis University Law Journal*, *38*, 629–671.

Mahoney, A. R., and Fenster, C. (1982). Female Delinquents in a Suburban Court. In N. H. Rafter and E. A. Stank (Eds.), *Judge, Lawyer, Victim, Thief: Women, Gender Roles & Criminal Justice*. Boston: Northeastern University Press.

Melton, G. B. (1989). Taking *Gault* Seriously: Toward a New Juvenile Court. *Nebraska Law Review*, *68*, 146–181.

Mennel, R. (1973). *Thorns and Thistles: Juvenile Delinquents in the United States 1825–1940*. Hanover, NH: University Press of New England.

Monahan, J. (1981). *The Clinical Prediction of Violent Behavior*. Rockville, MD: U.S. Department of Health and Human Services.

Morris, N. (1974). *The Future of Imprisonment*. Chicago: University of Chicago Press.

Morris, N., and Miller, M. (1985). Predictions of Dangerousness. In M. Tonry and N. Morris (Eds.), *Crime and Justice: A Review of Research* (Vol. 6, pp. 1–50). Chicago: University of Chicago Press.

Murray, J. P. (1983). *Status Offenders: A Sourcebook*. Boys Town, NB: Boys Town Center.

National Advisory Commission on Civil Disorders. (1968). *Report*. Washington, DC: U.S. Government Printing Office.

National Commission on Children (1991). *Beyond Rhetoric: A New American Agenda for Children and Families*. Washington, DC: U.S. Government Printing Office.

National Council on Crime and Delinquency. (1975). Jurisdiction over Status Offenses Should be Removed from the Juvenile Court: A Policy State. *Crime and Delinquency*, *21*, 97–99.

National Research Council, (1993). *Losing Generations: Adolescents in High-Risk Settings*. Washington, DC: National Academy Press.

Note. (1966). Juvenile Delinquents, the Police, State Courts, and Individualized Justice. *Harvard Law Review*, *79*, 775–810.

Packer, H. L. (1968). *The Limits of the Criminal Sanction*. Stanford, CA: Stanford University Press.

Palmer, T. (1991). The Effectiveness of Intervention: Recent Trends and Current Issues. *Crime and Delinquency*, *37*, 330–350.

Parent, D. G., Lieter, V., Kennedy, S., Livens, L., Wentworth, D., and Wilcox, S. (1994). *Conditions of Confinement: Juvenile Detention and Corrections Facilities*. Washington, DC: Office of Juvenile Justice and Delinquency Prevention.

Platt, A. (1977). *The Child Savers* (2nd ed.). Chicago: University of Chicago Press.

Podkopacz, M. R., and Feld, B. C. (1995). Judicial Waiver Policy and Practice: Persistence, Seriousness, and Race. *Journal of Law and Inequality*, *14*, 101–208.

Podkopacz, M., and Feld, B. C. (1996). The End of the Line: An Empirical Study of Judicial Waiver. *Journal of Criminal Law and Criminology*, *86*, 449–492.

Polk, K. (1984). Juvenile Diversion: A Look at the Record. *Crime and Delinquency*, *30*, 648–659.

Pope, C. E. (1994, December). Racial Disparities in Juvenile Justice System. *Overcrowded Times*, *5*, 1.

Pope, C. E., and Feyerherm, W. H. (1990a). Minority Status and Juvenile Justice Processing: An Assessment of the Research Literature (Part I). *Criminal Justice Abstracts*, *22*, 327–335.

Pope, C. E. (1990b). Minority Status and Juvenile Justice Processing: An Assessment of the Research Literature (Part II). *Criminal Justice Abstracts*, *22*, 527–542.

Pope, C. E. (1992). *Minorities and the Juvenile Justice System*. Washington, DC: Office of Juvenile Justice and Delinquency Prevention.

Postman, N. (1994). *The Disappearance of Childhood*. New York: Vintage Books.

President's Commission on Law Enforcement and Administration of Justice. (1967a). *The Challenge of Crime in a Free Society*. Washington, DC: U.S. Government Printing Office.

President's Commission on Law Enforcement and Administration of Justice. (1967b). *Task Force Report: Juvenile Delinquency and Youth Crime*. Washington, DC: U.S. Government Printing Office.

Reiss, A. J., Jr., and Roth, J. A. (Eds.). (1993). *Understanding and Preventing Violence*. Washington, DC: National Academy Press.

Roberts, A. R., and Camasso, M. J. (1991). The Effects of Juvenile Offender Treatment Programs on Recidivism: A Meta-Analysis of 46 Studies. *Notre Dame Journal of Law, Ethics and Public Policy*, *5*, 421–442.

Rosenberg, I. M. (1980). The Constitutional Rights of Children Charged with Crime: Proposal for a Return to the Not So Distant Past. *University of California Los Angeles Law Review*, *27*, 656–721.

Rosenberg, I. M. (1983). Juvenile Status Offender Statutes—New Perspectives on an Old Problem. *University of California Davis Law Review*, *16*, 283–323.

Rosenberg, I. M. and Rosenberg, Y. L. (1976). The Legacy of the Stubborn and Rebellious Son. *Michigan Law Review*, *74*, 1097–1165.

Rothman, D. J. (1971). *The Discovery of the Asylum*. Boston: Little, Brown.
Rothman, D. J. (1978). The State as Parent: Social Policy in the Progressive Era. In W. G., I. Glasser, S. Marcus, and D. Rothman (Eds.), *Doing Good: The Limits of Benevolence* (pp. 67–96). New York: Panetheon Books.
Rothman, D. J. (1980). *Conscience and Convenience*. Boston: Little, Brown.
Rubin, H. T. (1985). *Juvenile Justice: Policy, Practice, and Law* (2nd ed.). New York: Random House.
Ryerson, E. (1978). *The Best-laid Plans: America's Juvenile Court Experiment*. New York: Hill & Wang.
Sampson, R. J., and Laub, J. H. (1993). Structural Variations in Juvenile Court Processing: Inequality, the Underclass, and Social Control. *Law and Society Review, 27*, 285–311.
Sanborn, J. B., Jr. (1996). Policies Regarding the Prosecution of Juvenile Murderers: Which System and Who Should Decide? *Law and Policy, 18*, 151–178.
Schlossman, S. (1977). *Love and the American Delinquent*. Chicago: University of Chicago Press.
Schlossman, S., and Wallach, S. (1978). The Crime of Precocious Sexuality: Female Juvenile Delinquency in the Progressive Era. *Harvard Educational Review, 48*, 65–94.
Schneider, A. L. (1984). Deinstitutionalization of Status Offenders: The Impact on Recidivism and Secure Confinement. *Criminal Justice Abstracts, 16*, 410–432.
Schwartz, I. M. (1989a). *In Justice for Juveniles: Rethinking the Best Interests of the Child*. Lexington, MA: Lexington Books.
Schwartz, I. M. (1989b). Hospitalization of Adolescents for Psychiatric and Substance Abuse Treatment. *Journal of Adolescent Health Care, 10*, 1–6.
Schwartz, I. M., Jackson-Beeck, M., and Anderson, R. (1984). The Hidden System of Juvenile Control. *Crime and Delinquency, 30*, 371–385.
Scott, E. S. (1992). Judgment and Reasoning in Adolescent Decisionmaking. *Villanova Law Review, 37*, 1607–1669.
Scott, E. S., and Grisso, T. (1998). The Evolution of Adolescence: A Developmental Perspective on Juvenile Justice Reform. *Journal of Criminal Law and Criminology, 88*, 137–189.
Scott, E. S., Reppucci, N. D., and Woolard, J. L. (1995). Evaluating Adolescent Decision Making in Legal Contexts. *Law and Human Behavior, 19*, 221–224.
Sechrest, L. B. (1987). Classification for Treatment. In M. Tonry and N. Morris (Eds.), *Crime and Justice: An Annual Review* (Vol. 9). Chicago: University of Chicago Press.
Sechrest, L. B., White, S. O., and Brown, E. D. (1979). *The Rehabilitation of Criminal Offenders* (pp. 293–322). Washington, DC: National Academy of Sciences.
Shaughnessy, P. L. (1979). The Right to a Jury Under the Juvenile Justice Act of 1977. *Gonzaga Law Review, 14*, 401–421.
Sheffer, J. P. (1995). Serious and Habitual Juvenile Offender Statutes: Reconciling Punishment and Rehabilitation within the Juvenile Justice System. *Vanderbilt Law Review, 48*, 479–506.
Smith, E. M. (1992). In a Child's Best Interest: Juvenile Status Offenders Deserve Procedural Due Process. *Law and Inequality, 10*, 253–284.
Snyder, H. N. (1997). *Juvenile Arrests 1996*. Washington, DC: Office of Juvenile Justice and Delinquency Prevention.
Snyder, H. N., Sickmund, M. (1995). *Juvenile Offenders and Victims: A National Report*. Washington, DC: Office of Juvenile Justice and Delinquency Prevention.
Snyder, H. N., Sickmund, M., and Poe-Yamagata, E. (1997). *Juvenile Offenders and Victims: 1996 Update on Violence*. Washington, DC: Office of Juvenile Justice and Delinquency Prevention, National Center for Juvenile Justice.
Stapleton, W. V., and Teitelbaum, L. E. (1972). *In Defense of Youth: A Study of the Role of Counsel in American Juvenile Courts*. New York: Rusell Sage Foundation.
Stapleton, W. V., Aday, D. P., Jr., and Ito, J. A. (1982). An Empirical Typology of American Metropolitan Juvenile Courts. *American Journal of Sociology, 88*, 549–564.
Steinberg, L., and Cauffman, E. (1996). Maturity of Judgment in Adolescence: Psychosocial Factors in Adolescent Decision Making. *Law and Human Behavior, 20*, 249–272.
Streib, V. L. (1987). *Death Penalty for Juveniles*. Bloomington: Indiana University Press.
Sussman, A. (1977). Sex-Based Discrimination and the PINS Jurisdiction. In L. H. Teitelbaum and A. R. Gough (Eds.), *Beyond Control: Status Offenders in the Juvenile Court* (pp. 101–139). Cambridge, MA: Ballinger.
Sutton, J. R. (1988). *Stubborn Children: Controlling Delinquency in the United States*. Berkeley: University of California Press.
Teitelbaum, L. E., and Gough, A. R. (Eds.). (1977). *Beyond Control: Status Offenders in the Juvenile Court*. Cambridge, MA: Ballinger.
Thomas, C. W., and Bilchik, S. (1985). Prosecuting Juveniles in Criminal Courts: A Legal and Empirical Analysis. *Journal of Criminal Law and Criminology, 76*, 439–479.

Tiffin, S. (1982). *In Whose Best Interest? Child Welfare Reform in the Progressive Era*. Westport, CT: Greenwood Press.

Tonry, M. (1995). *Malign Neglect: Race, Crime, and Punishment in America*. London: Oxford University Press.

Torbet, P., Gable, R., Hurst, H., IV, Montgomery, I., Szymanski, L., and Thomas, D. (1996). *State Responses to Serious and Violent Juvenile Crime: Research Report*. Washington, DC: Office of Juvenile Justice and Delinquency Prevention, National Center for Juvenile Justice.

Trattner, W. (1970). *Crusade for the Children: A History of the National Child Labor Committee and Child Labor Reform in New York State*. Chicago: Quadrangle Books.

Twentieth Century Fund Task Force on Sentencing Policy Toward Young Offenders (1978). *Confronting Youth Crime*. New York: Holmes & Meier.

United States General Accounting Office. (1995). *Juvenile Justice: Juveniles Processed in Criminal Court and Case Dispositions*. Washington, DC: General Accounting Office.

von Hirsch, A. (1976). *Doing Justice*. New York: Hill & Wang.

von Hirsch, A. (1986). *Past vs. Future Crimes*. New Brunswick, NJ: Rutgers University Press.

von Hirsch, A. (1993). *Censure and Sanctions*. London: Oxford University Press.

Walkover, A. (1984). The Infancy Defense in the New Juvenile Court. *University of California Los Angeles Law Review*, *31*, 503–562.

Walter, J. D., and Ostrander, S. A. (1982). An Observational Study of a Juvenile Court. *Juvenile and Family Court Journal*, *33*, 53–69.

Weissman, J. C. (1983). Toward an Integrated Theory of Delinquency Responsibility. *Denver Law Journal*, *60*, 485–518.

Weithorn, L. A. (1988). Mental Hospitalization of Troublesome Youth: An Analysis of Skyrocketing Admission Rates. *Stanford Law Review*, *40*, 773–838.

Whitehead, J. T., and Lab, S. P. (1989). A Meta-Analysis of Juvenile Correctional Treatment. *Journal of Research on Crime and Delinquency*, *26*, 276–295.

Wiebe, R. H. (1967). *The Search for Order 1877– 1920*. New York: Hill & Wang.

Wilson, W. J. (1987). *The Truly Disadvantaged*. Chicago: University of Chicago Press.

Wilson, W. J. (1996). *When Work Disappears: The World of the New Urban Poor*. New York: Knopf.

Wolfgang, M., Figlio, R., and Sellin, T. (1972). *Delinquency in a Birth Cohort*. Chicago: University of Chicago Press.

Zimring, F. (1981a). Notes Toward a Jurisprudence of Waiver. In J. C. Hall, D. M. Hamparian, J. M. Pettibone, and J. L. White (Eds.), *Readings in Public Policy*. Columbus, OH: Academy for Contemporary Problems.

Zimring, F. (1981b). Kids, Groups and Crime: Some Implications of a Well-Known Secret. *Journal of Criminal Law and Criminology*, *72*, 867–902.

Zimring, F. (1982). *The Changing Legal World of Adolescence*. New York: Free Press.

Zimring, F. (1991). The Treatment of Hard Cases in American Juvenile Justice: In Defense of Discretionary Waiver. *Notre Dame Journal of Law, Ethics and Public Policy*, *5*, 267–280.

7

Legal Institutions in Civil Disputes

Regulatory and Administrative Agencies

Robert M. Howard and John T. Scholz

Our traditional notion of justice for individual litigants in civil disputes is premised on an adversarial process tried before an impartial arbiter. That is, each party to a dispute presents his or her side of the story, usually with the aid of a skilled advocate, in front of a disinterested fact-finder and interpreter of the law. In the jury system, the jury decides factual matters and the judge interprets the law, although in other parts of our legal system both roles can be performed by the same individual. The critical aspect of the adversarial model is that factual matters and legal interpretations are made dispassionately by an authority uninvolved in the issues, based on the facts presented to it by the parties involved. In the Madisonian view of government based on separation of powers, this dispassionate role is given to the judicial branch of government, the branch that in theory is not actively involved in the formation or implementation of policy.

With the complexity of modern life, however, has come a significant expansion of regulatory and administrative agencies, a branch of government perhaps not contemplated by the Founders. They have been called a "headless, fourth branch of government,"[1] a branch that blurs distinctions between legislative, executive, and judicial functions (Rosenbloom, 1983:21–22). As the Supreme Court stated, "there is no doubt that the development of the administrative agency in response to modern legislative and administrative need has placed a severe strain on the separation-of-powers principle in its pristine formulation" (*Buckley v. Valeo*, 1976:280–281). In the modern world, citizens come into conflict not only with other citizens, but increasingly with administrative agencies. Thus, when an individual citizen has a dispute with an administrative or regulatory agency, she is confronting as an adversary the agency with whom she has a dispute. The issue is decided not by an impartial arbiter, but by the very same agency—at least until the citizen exhausts her administrative remedies within the

Robert Howard • Department of Political Science, Georgia State University, Atlanta, Georgia 30303. John Scholz • Department of Political Science, State University of New York at Stony Brook, Stony Brook, New York 11794.

Handbook of Justice Research in Law, edited by Sanders and Hamilton. Kluwer Academic / Plenum Publishers, New York, 2000.

agency. This, of course, is the exact opposite of the justice one expects from the adversarial model.

In this chapter we will examine how agencies attempt to ensure that principles of justice prevail when agencies interact with citizens. We consider what is meant by justice for agencies, individual citizens, the citizenry as a whole, and for citizens and agencies involved in civil disputes.

A. AGENCY JUSTICE AS THE MINIMIZATION OF ERRORS

In the United States, citizens and their government have a social contract within which the government sets policies as determined by elected officials within the boundaries of the Constitution, and citizens are expected to obey those policies. These policies redefine the rights and duties of all citizens, bestowing certain benefits or rights for some citizens while imposing certain obligations or duties on others. Federal, state, and local agencies implement these policies by defining the rights and duties in concrete situations, and thus directly determine which citizens are affected by the policies.

In a just society, elected officials pass laws reflecting the will of the people and agencies allocate and distribute the rights and duties consistent with the policies of the elected officials. Agency justice, then, consists of the proper implementation of just policies supported by the citizenry and enacted into legislation by the elected officials. Injustice occurs when an agency makes a mistake in interpreting just policies.

Agency justice often proves elusive even when the policies themselves are just. Translating policy goals in an informationally complex world into just actions and behaviors is a hard and difficult task. Even intense training, well-established interpretations, and adequate information can leave the most-skilled bureaucrat unprepared for new situations.

Perhaps the most critical problem is the constant balancing between the rights and duties of the populace as a whole—the common good—and the rights and duties of the individual citizen. Public policies, even those dealing with individual rights and obligations, are justified in terms of the common good. At the same time there is a longstanding notion of respect for individual rights even when the exercise of such rights is adverse to the good of the commons. Every time a citizen applies for some governmental benefit, or potentially confronts the power of the state enforcing some duty, the street-level bureaucrat must balance these two competing considerations.

Citizens can compound this difficulty by exploiting the agency's procedures in order to gain undeserved benefits or illegally avoid duties. Citizens generally know more about their own situation than the agency does, and can use this information asymmetry to their advantage. Since the opportunism of individuals works against the public good, an agency must design procedures to guard against the problems arising from information asymmetries and opportunism. In this chapter, we refer to agencies that are primarily involved in distributing benefits and rights as *administrative* and agencies that enforce duties as *regulatory*. Administrative agencies must design procedures to prevent opportunistic citizens from claiming undeserved benefits, while regulatory agencies need procedures to prevent them from shirking duties. We will also use the term *citizen* to emphasize our focus on justice for individuals, even though agencies, particularly regulatory agencies, affect entities other than the individual.

Thus, government agencies confront problems of a technical, philosophical, and incentive-related nature. The bureaucrat has to interpret complex and potentially ambiguous legislation, gather sufficient information to evaluate the consequences of alternative interpretations, establish appropriate procedures that minimize opportunism, and make timely determinations potentially involving large numbers of citizens, and must do this within a limited budget allocation. A mistake in denying a right, or improperly enforcing an obligation where none exists, harms the individual. We will call these errors of excessive *stringency*. A mistake in granting a right where none exists, or in failing to enforce an obligation that does exist, harms the common good. We will call these errors of excessive *leniency*.

For example, an official in an administrative agency reviewing one of several hundred Medicaid applications on her desk must decide if Medicaid covers the applicant within the meaning of the statutes and regulations. The reviewer must in some way balance the common good versus the individual's right to Medicaid, while dealing with an information asymmetry vis-à-vis the applicant, and make a decision within a relatively short period of time. Excessive stringency would lead to denying a true claim, while excessive leniency would lead to paying a false claim. Similarly, in a regulatory agency, a tax examiner with 100 returns to audit within a limited time must determine if the individual is telling the truth on her return, and decide how rigorously to investigate this particular taxpayer. The examiner would be excessively stringent if a qualifying deduction were disallowed, and excessively lenient if an erroneous deduction passed through.

Justice is best served when agencies correctly categorize all cases and avoid both leniency and stringency. Unfortunately, absolute justice in the sense of avoiding all error is an unattainable goal. Even when laws are unambiguous, as we shall discuss in the next section, justice involves striking the appropriate balance between stringency and leniency for the particular circumstances of the agency.

How is the appropriate balance determined in a particular case? When an individual feels wronged by the agency's decision, what standards of justice can be applied? The adversarial model of civil disputes is not directly relevant, since one of the parties involved—the agency—decides both factual and legal interpretations, at least until matters are appealed to the courts.

We argue that agency justice depends on agency procedures, and that appropriate procedures depend on the relative problems caused by stringency and leniency in implementing a given policy. The legislation to be implemented is an attempt to define some vision or idea of substantive justice. Citizens should pay income tax based on specifically defined ability to pay, and should have access to public health services based on a particular definition of need. Agencies must develop an administrative system to provide rights and enforce duties consonant with the vision of substantive justice. Agencies must develop rules, regulations, and procedures to minimize the impact of errors in terms of the vision of substantive justice as determined by society's policymaking institutions. Minimization of errors through the development of agency procedures will not only fulfill a normative goal of substantive justice, but also should have the added benefit of increasing compliance. Designing a system that reduces errors can ensure that the citizen accepts the outcome as fair. Fairness leads to compliance, as we will discuss later.

In the next two sections we consider the causes and consequences of agency errors. We begin with the simpler case when laws are unambiguous, and then consider the case when laws are ambiguous and based on conflicting visions of substantive justice.

1. Agency Errors under Unambiguous Law

The ideal of autonomous law is founded on clear statutes capable of supporting "the rule of laws, not of men." There is no room for the individual vagaries, biases, and whims of administrators, since a law either applies to an individual, or it does not. In practice, of course, it is difficult to draft a clear, precise statutory definition of rights and duties that decision makers can decide unambiguously in all likely circumstances with information available to the agency. This ideal, however, of unambiguous law provides a good starting point for our discussion of the causes and consequences of agency errors.

2. Medicaid and the Errors of Administrative Agencies

Let us begin with an administrative agency that provides benefits. Medicaid is designed to be a payer of last resort for medical needs of indigent individuals who have neither insurance nor assets to pay their own medical bills. Federal law establishes general guidelines for eligibility, and each state within those guidelines is able to establish its own income and resource limits.[2] Further, each state has its own agency to administer the Medicaid program, and its own application forms.

Imagine two different applicants for Medicaid, Carrie and Lucy (for clear law examples, we will use a name starting with a "C" for the cheating, ineligible applicant, and an "L" name for a legitimate applicant). Let us assume that Carrie and Lucy are senior citizens who are currently residing in nursing homes, or in the Medicaid parlance, in long-term care facilities. When Carrie and Lucy entered the nursing home, each filled out an application and listed assets of $75,000 in cash accounts. After staying in the nursing home and privately paying for 7 months, they, or their representative (usually an adult child), inform the nursing home that their assets will be used up in a few more months,[3] and that each needs to apply for Medicaid. The home's social worker meets with Carrie and with Lucy to go over the requirements for Medicaid, including the need for proof of income, assets, birth date, and state of residence. The worker would then give each an application, and the name and number of a representative from the local Department of Social Services (DSS) office.

Carrie and Lucy then call and schedule an appointment, and each brings the required documents on the scheduled day. By the eligibility rules, Carrie and Lucy can have no more than $3000 in cash or liquid assets, a burial fund of $1500, and an income of $50 per month. The application includes this information. What Carrie does not put down is that she has $100,000 in savings bonds, purchased by her over many years, payable to her and her son. She has just given these to her son. By Medicaid rules, this is a transfer of assets that would make Carrie ineligible for many months.[4]

Lucy has no such hidden asset, and is legitimately eligible. She has, however, mistakenly listed on her application a joint account of $50,000 that she holds with her daughter, and which her daughter entirely funded. Since her daughter funded the money, it is not includable as an asset of Lucy.

Thus, the agency has two individuals, one of whom is actually eligible, but appears ineligible, and the other who appears eligible, but is actually ineligible. In this case justice requires awarding Medicaid to Lucy, but not to Carrie. What does the agency do to avoid both errors?

3. Income Tax and the Errors of Regulatory Agencies

A similar problem emerges for regulatory agencies in the enforcement of duties. Take for example the requirement to pay taxes on income earned from employment.[5] Taxpayers must report all such income on some version of the 1040 Federal Tax Return regardless of whether they earn the income by working for someone as an employee, or as a self-employed individual.

Suppose there are two taxpayers, Chuck and Lester, who work for a local business. In addition, each has a small moonlighting venture as self-employed house painters. Tax is due on the income earned from both jobs. In January, their respective employers give each a W-2 Wage and Tax Statement. The form lists the annual wages paid and the federal, state, city (if any), social security and Medicaid taxes withheld and forwarded to the respective government agencies charged with collecting tax revenue. On the federal level, the Internal Revenue Service is responsible for the collection of tax revenue, and given vast enforcement powers in connection with that responsibility.

Chuck and Lester dutifully attach their W-2 to their tax return and list the wages paid to them on their return. At the same time, each is responsible for reporting his self-employment income on the Schedule C form for business income, and inclusion of his net income in the appropriate 1040 section. Chuck, however, has earned \$20,000 in cash from his painting business, but has reported only \$10,000 of this on his tax return. Chuck also reported \$1000 of expenses as deductions, listing a net taxable income of \$9000. Lester earned \$10,000 and reported all of the income on his Schedule C form, and in the proper line on his return. Lester, however, also purchased several expensive items for his painting business in the same year, and appropriately and legitimately listed these items as deductions on his tax return. The effect of the deductions was to reduce Lester's taxable income to \$5000.

Both taxpayers reported the same gross income, but Lester has taken a larger deduction. Lester, however, has paid the right tax, while Chuck should pay additional tax, interest, and penalty. Here justice requires that the IRS audit Chuck and require him to pay more, while the IRS should not audit Lester. What does the IRS do to avoid error?

Thus, for both regulatory and administrative agencies, the standard of justice seems straightforward as long as the law is unambiguous. Problems emerge only in making correct classifications. Either the applicants met the income requirements, or they do not. If they do, they are potentially eligible for Medicaid. If they do not, they are ineligible. Either the law has been complied with, and income and deductions have properly been reported, or the law has not been complied with, and income and deductions have inappropriately been reported.

4. Sources of Errors When Laws Are Clear

There are several reasons why the task of properly applying clear law is so hard, and thus why errors occur even when the assignment of rights and duties is reasonably clear. The DSS representative confronts two improperly filled out applications: one due to an honest error, the other due to intentional misrepresentation. The tax examiner confronts a similar dilemma. Chuck appears to report the proper income and deductions, although the return contains an intentional underreporting of income. Lester does report accurately, but appears to be claiming an unusually large deduction. Information asymmetries, limited time and money resources, and the delicate balancing of stringency and leniency make the decision more complex and more difficult than one would initially imagine given the clear law.

5. Technical Causes of Errors

The sources of errors can be assigned to one of two different categories, technical and opportunism. While opportunism is a problem in any legal system, technical problems have become a major concern of administrative justice in twentieth century. These are problems caused by size, training, motivation, and coordination of the activities in large administrative and regulatory agencies.

First, recently hired bureaucrats often lack proper training to perform the agency's tasks and make the initial street-level determinations of rights and duties. Citizens make mistakes on required forms by including irrelevant data or excluding pertinent information, or even knowingly submit false information. Poorly trained or novice bureaucrats can misread applications and income tax returns, and lack the motivation to correct such errors. Thus, the DSS examiner might lack the background training to spot Lucy's error, or to detect Carrie's misrepresentation. The tax examiner might not have acquired the experience to know that start-up businesses have large expenses, or what to look for to ascertain if self-employed individuals are hiding income.

Errors can also occur as a result of technological complexity. The sheer number of forms to be processed can overwhelm human efforts to cope and deal with them in any coherent manner. The IRS, for example, processes over one billion forms submitted by taxpayers each year (Internal Revenue Service, 1990:4). To handle this volume and complexity, agencies standardize the processing of applications and returns, and divide the implementation and enforcement task into several specialized tasks (Diver, 1980:257). Specialization enables bureaucrats to better understand their limited task, and to process necessary forms more efficiently and quickly.

On the other hand, specialization can lead to difficulty in detecting and correcting errors. Specialized units become more concerned with fulfilling their task quotas than with the overall task of the agency, which no single individual may understand in any detail. Specialization limits the ability of managers trained to correct certain errors to consider other issues of greater importance to substantive justice as envisioned in the policy. Thus, the DSS bureaucrat might be trained to detect Carrie's misrepresentations but have no training or procedures that might help in correcting Lucy's honest mistake.

Problems that don't quite fit into one or the other specialized tasks are ignored. The IRS, for example, has found it most efficient to separate the tasks of processing tax returns, auditing them, adjusting the amounts due after audits or amended filings, and collecting taxes that are due. Individual taxpayers can get caught in conflicts between different units. For example, when a taxpayer submits a payment without the proper taxpayer identification number, collections might seize her checking account for the tax due. At the same time, the taxpayer is trying to straighten out the amount due with the adjustments branch. Conversely, if forms are lost or delayed beyond the statute of limitations while being transferred from audit to collections, a tax and penalty imposed by the auditor may go uncollected. When millions of forms are handled each year, even a very low error rate means that thousands of errors will occur each year.

Technological advances can make certain tasks and efforts easier by enhancing analytic and data processing capabilities. For example, the IRS uses complex statistical analyses of special audits to determine a "DIF" score that can be calculated for each tax return. The higher the DIF score, the more likely that an audit of that return will find improper reporting by the taxpayer. Auditors can thus focus their efforts on returns with higher scores, increasing their chance of catching tax cheats. However, the ability to use new and emerging computer and data technology demands new and improved skills, and this of course requires additional training. Furthermore, the actions of technical specialists need to be coordinated with experienced field agents to make new technologies minimize the potential for error. Thus, the computers cross-checking Chuck's and Lester's 1940's and W-2's, or Carrie's and Lucy's Medicaid applications can make mistakes and find discrepancies even where none exist. They are likely, for example, to find Lester's accurate return when looking for patterns of discrepan cies. Experience is needed to determine what and where errors have been made in advanced technologies. Even where the computer has properly done its job, skill, experience, and training are needed to properly read the computer-generated analyses.

Skill levels and agency turnover further compound training problems. Given the difference between public and private sector pay, government agencies have difficulty attracting skilled employees in areas with low unemployment. Furthermore, they lose many competent employees to higher-paying private sector law and accounting positions, leaving less competent or less experienced bureaucrats to do tasks of ever-increasing difficulty (Burnham, 1989; Quirk, 1981). IRS-trained employees often have high-paying, prestigious law and accounting positions open to them. The problem appears most acute for regulatory agencies, but the private sector often seeks trained and skillful advocates from administrative agencies as well.

Finally, agencies have limited resources. Mistakes and errors slip through because the agencies lack the personnel and equipment to check every bit of information they must process, or cross-check such information with other agency bureaucrats. Agency managers and the street-level bureaucrats under their auspices daily make decisions about which kinds of errors to focus their limited resources or correcting. In practice this frequently means a choice between stringency and leniency for a given task, frequently with the consequence that different applicants receive different treatment.

6. Opportunism, Voluntary Compliance, and Agency Errors

All of the above errors are compounded and magnified because opportunistic citizens are tempted to take advantage of agency procedures to enhance their individual well-being at the expense of the common good. Thus, agency procedures must not only avoid errors due to honest mistakes by citizens or bureaucrats, but also must be robust against possible strategies by opportunistic citizens (and bureaucrats, which will be considered later) designed to exploit agency procedures.

a. The Case for Stringency

Opportunism suggests that agencies should err on the side of stringency. Catch the fraudulent applicants and tax cheaters, punish them, and the bulk of the population will then comply. This is the concept of deterrence. My neighbor cheated on his taxes and was caught. Since the IRS discovered his cheating, he had to pay additional tax, penalties, and interest. He would have been better off if he did not cheat. Since he was caught, I could get caught if I cheat, therefore I will not cheat. Thus, deterrence promotes the common good as it discourages cheating.

If all citizens were opportunistic, however, the costs of maintaining an enforcement system capable of detecting and deterring all noncompliance would be prohibitive. In a world of limited agency resources, it is impossible to verify every bit of information that an agency has before it. Thus, the public is asked to voluntarily comply with the process. The DSS expects Medicaid applicants to provide truthful, verifiable information on their applications. Although a fraudulent applicant faces severe civil and criminal penalties, the resources problem again produces a need for voluntary truthfulness.

Even voluntary compliance depends on stringent enforcement aimed at "bad apples" in the population. Chester Bowles observed after his experience as head of the Office of Price Administration during World War II that 20% of the population are basically honest and automatically comply with any regulation. The opportunistic Carries and Chucks of the world will always attempt to evade, but only make up 5% of the population. The remaining 75% will go along with the regulation, like Lester and Lucy, but only as long as the agency makes a credible attempt to catch and punish the Carries and Chucks.[6] To control opportunism of this large middle group of citizens who are neither angels nor thieves, stringent enforcement is required against the Carries and Chucks.

Excessive stringency could lead to a loss of the Medicaid benefit to both Carrie and Lucy. After they filled out their application, the examiner will interview Carrie and Lucy,[7] and attempt to verify the income sources, and also attempt to ascertain additional sources of income not listed on the application. If the DSS focuses on the elimination of fraud and abuse, it may opt for excessive stringency. It orders an investigation of Carrie and determines that Carrie had purchased these bonds at her local bank. Applying the formula, Carrie is ineligible for Medicaid funding for several additional months.[8] This is a just result. Since stringency seeks the elimination of fraud and abuse, a cursory examination of Lucy's application will unfortunately result in a quick denial of Medicaid benefits based on the erroneously reported savings. This is an unjust result.

For the IRS, excessive stringency could increase the tax obligation for both Chuck and Lester. A stringent audit program could root out Chuck's unreported income, which is a just result. However, an IRS emphasis on detecting cheating could hurt Lester, since business expenses of $5000 on $10,000 of income may appear excessive. In addition to the emotional and financial cost of an audit, Lester could have to pay additional tax, penalty, and interest if he failed to keep adequate records, or received inadequate legal or accounting advice. This is injustice.

b. The Case for Leniency

As the examples illustrate, procedures that effectively control opportunism may be overly intrusive when applied to honest citizens. Audits are necessary for finding tax evaders, but it is impossible to avoid auditing honest taxpayers. Audit techniques that minimize the psychic and preparation cost imposed on audited honest taxpayers are also likely to reduce the effectiveness of an audit in detecting evasion. For example, specifying exactly what tax items are to be reviewed during an audit and limiting the documentation required of the taxpayer would reduce the cost for honest taxpayers. This would, however, also deprive the auditor of "fishing expeditions" in other tax matters that appear questionable during the audit. Allowing auditors to demand unrestricted access to all of Chuck's financial documents would increase the agency's ability to detect and punish opportunistic taxpayers. Requiring, however, Lester to produce all documents would impose excessive costs on an honest taxpayer. Stringent enforcement techniques mistakenly used on the Lucys and Lesters may destroy their willingness to voluntarily comply with the law.

Leniency is not without its problems. A DSS examiner concerned with ensuring that no eligible beneficiaries are denied their benefits could quickly discover Lucy's error, and correct her erroneous listing of assets. The same examiner is unlikely to discover Carrie's omitted bonds. Hence, Carrie qualifies for Medicaid, even though it is unjust. Similarly, a tax examiner who is willing to give the benefit of the doubt to Lester is also unlikely to probe with sufficient tenacity to uncover Chuck's unreported income.

In short, avoiding leniency when dealing with the bad apples may be as important as avoiding excessive stringency when dealing with the large middle group who voluntarily comply. If the agencies do not discover and discourage cheating, then scarce resources are squandered, and the large middle group might lose its incentive to comply.

Thus, agencies must use their limited resources to foster as much voluntary compliance as possible, finding the appropriate balance of stringency and leniency that can maximize justice as perceived by those who voluntarily comply. Excessive stringency by an agency leads to a coercive, harsh government, undermining substantive justice defined in the law. Excessive leniency leads to a weak government unable to protect the public good from opportunistic shirkers.

The agency's choice between leniency and stringency becomes even more difficult when we consider the implementation of ambiguous laws that do not provide clear and easy definitions of rights and duties. The next section examines these added complications.

7. Added Complications: Errors under Ambiguous Law

The statutory language of law is rarely clear enough to provide unambiguous interpretations over all relevant situations. Even when they are unambiguous, the rights and duties the define may conflict with other established rights and duties. Whether by happenstance, poor draftsmanship, or design, words and phrases mean very different things to different individuals. In short, law, by design or otherwise, is often ambiguous.

Ambiguity can arise from several different circumstances. They include complexity of the subject matter, diversity or heterogeneity of the population, change from the circumstances that led to the original policy, conflicts between lawmakers and agencies, and conflicts between agencies.

The more complex the policy and the more heterogeneous the target population, the more difficult it is to foresee all potential conflicts and to enact laws or rules that will be clearly defined in every situation. A nationwide program providing a broad set of benefits, such as Medicaid, will inevitably end up complex and confusing. How does one define the truly needy? What should the program pay for, and how much? What income or assets do you examine and include of the spouse of a potential recipient, or of the adult children?

Similarly, a nationwide revenue code will inevitably be complicated, given the complexity of the economy that it must deal with. What constitutes income? Do you distinguish between earned and unearned income? What tax rate should apply to the income of children or other dependents? What deductions should the government allow? What are legitimate business expenses?[9] Any change in the tax code will both positively and negatively affect significant numbers of individuals. Minute alterations in language could make or break a business. Questions such as these are frequently left to be worked out during the implementation process, where adjustments are easier to make as more detailed information becomes available.

A second reason for ambiguity is unforeseen change of circumstances over time. When Congress established Medicaid, the enactors viewed the program as a payer of last resort for those too poor to afford medical care. Few in 1965 could have foreseen that long-term care could by 1995 impoverish all but extremely wealthy individuals, and could become a primary cause of the crisis of funding Medicaid.[10] In 1995, with an expanding elderly population, and with nursing home costs exceeding $8000 per month in some areas, Medicaid applicants have increasingly been middle-class individuals who have divested themselves of their wealth over time in order to qualify for Medicaid. Thus, a program designed to cover the basic medical needs of the very poor, instead became an entitlement program and a way for middle-class senior citizens to transfer wealth to the next generation and have the government pick up the tab for their medical care.

Consider how changes in the economy affect the use of home offices, and hence the definition of home office as a legitimate business expense.[11] The IRS at times has argued for a restrictive definition, and at other times has allowed a more relaxed view of a home office.[12] When most Americans commuted to an office, the IRS viewed expenses claimed for the home office as a common tax dodge used by commuters to claim improper expenditures for normal home expenses such as power, phone, and depreciation. Hence, the restrictive interpretation. With working mothers, new communication technologies, and corporate attempts to cut central office expenditures and get workers closer to the field, greater numbers of citizens work at home at least part of the time, thereby justifying a more liberal definition of the home office. With the expected evolution of telecommuting, taxpayers and the IRS will continue to argue over the meaning of home office.

Conflict over legislative goals provides a third source for ambiguity. Compromise lies at the heart of the legislative process, and vague legislative language enables coalitions to pass legislation that might not pass if all details were filled in. Furthermore, opponents may attempt to add language that intentionally weakens the ability of the agency to enforce the law.[13] In addition, conflict can also exist between agencies implementing different laws that affect the same individual or company. For example, OSHA might mandate certain safety regulations that conflict with the EPA's environmental safeguards or with the FDA's health regulations for processing foods.

To more clearly understand the problems ambiguity causes for both bureaucrat and citizen, we will consider two examples. The administrative agency example concerns Social Security Disability, and the regulatory agency example concerns a home office deduction taken by a taxpayer. In both examples, there is no clear policy, and error can occur despite the best training and most skilled bureaucrats reviewing the matters.

a. Ambiguity in Social Security Disability

Suppose Angela ("A" names shall mean ambiguity), a 48-year-old single woman, suffered an injury that damaged her hip to the extent that sitting for extended periods of time became painful. She has to stand or lie down to relieve the pain and pressure. Prior to the injury, Angela supported herself as a secretary in a small law office, working there for 20 years. Her duties consisted of answering the phone, greeting clients, and typing letters and other material. While there she used what is now an outdated word processing system. It is the only system she knows, and she does not consider herself computer literate. Angela injured herself at home, and the injury was due to her own negligence, so neither worker's compensation nor any personal injury recovery is available. In her employer's opinion, Angela cannot now adequately perform her duties.

Angela has no other means of support. Family cannot help her, and her savings are too meager to sustain her for any period of time. While her employer is kindly, she cannot afford to retain Angela on her payroll, hence she has informed Angela that she will terminate her employment in one month.

Angela then travels to the local office of the Health and Human Services Department and applies for Social Security Disability (42 U.S.C. Secs. 401–433, pp. 1381–1383c) through the Social Security Administration.[14] The Act provides for income support, and eventually, some medical benefits. The Act defines a person to have a disability:

> only if his physical or mental impairment or impairments are of such a severity that he is not only unable to perform his previous work but cannot, considering his age, education and

> work experience, engage in any other kind of substantial work which exists in the national economy, regardless of whether such work exists in the immediate area in which he lives, or whether a specific job vacancy exists for him, or whether he would be hired if he applied for work. (42 U.S.C. Sec. 423(d)(2))

The act defines work as that which exists in the national economy in significant numbers. It also provides for referral to appropriate vocational rehabilitation services. The problem for applicants, lawyers, SSA workers, judges, and legislators is, what does that mean? Is Angela disabled under the meaning of the above-cited act? Can she take another law job with a larger firm more able to absorb the delays due to her injury? Could she obtain another job, given her age, training, skill level, and experience?

If Angela can obtain other work, then granting her disability benefits would constitute a leniency. If, however, because of her disability, age, and limited experience, she could not obtain other work, then denying her disability would constitute excessive stringency.

b. Ambiguity in Home Office Expenses

Andrew is a certified public accountant who prepares individual tax returns. His main office lies several miles from his home in another county. Being a smart accountant and to maximize his business opportunities, Andrew also has a home office, upstairs in a spare room. In the room he has a computer that he uses to do his tax returns, and copy and fax machines. On the computer he finds it convenient to access the Internet through a popular online service. He uses it to access statute, and tax code books. He finds it less expensive than ordering lots of books, and he picks up many good tips and ideas from other accountants on an accountant chat line.

Andrew, being a good accountant, is scrupulous about keeping his home office separate from the rest of his house. He tries to keep his children from the room, and closes the door when he is at his main office. Accordingly, Andrew deducts home office expenditures as a business expense on his tax return. He deducts a portion of his telephone and other utility bills as business expenses, and depreciates a portion of his house as it relates to his business. He also depreciates the furniture and equipment used in the room, including the computer, fax and copy machines.

Despite Andrew's scrupulous attempts, however, he and his family use the room for other purposes. When guests come, they use the room as a guest room. Sometimes Andrew or his wife read there because it is quieter than the rest of the house. The children, with their father's permission, use the computer to access the Internet and play a few computer games when their father is not using the computer. Andrew's wife and children often use the copy and fax machines.

The Internal Revenue Service audits Andrew, and the examiner challenges the deduction of the home office expenses. Does the examiner disallow the entire deduction because Andrew does not use the room 100% as a home office? Does he allow the entire deduction because of an arguably substantial use? Does he disallow part and allow part? If the latter, what is allowed, and what is disallowed? At stake for Andrew, in addition to the home office deductions, are several thousands of dollars of travel expenses he has deducted as travel between his home office and his main office. The examiner is also challenging those as nondeductible commuting expenses.

The statute itself does not resolve the rights and duties in either example. Stringent enforcement disallowing the deduction favors the common good, while leniency favors the individual's perception of his tax obligation. In such situations, justice depends not on the individual decision, but on the procedures the agency adapts to resolve problems of ambiguity and to minimize the errors in applying the resolution to the diversity of relevant cases.

B. JUSTICE AS PROCEDURE

1. Controlling Errors and Their Consequences

The greater the ambiguity in a legislated policy, the more important are the administrative procedures that are used to resolve ambiguity in a manner consistent with the vision of substantive justice. How well these procedures bring about the vision of substantive justice provides one standard of procedural justice. But there is a competing standard of procedural justice that emphasizes a more universal standard for procedures to guarantee "due process" for all citizens who interact with agencies. The historical development of administrative procedures provides a useful context for comparing these somewhat different views of justice in administrative settings.

2. Historical Development of Formal Procedures: Case-by-Case Adjudication in Early Bureaucracy

In the early part of this century, administrative and regulatory agencies in the United States clarified ambiguity primarily on a case-by-case basis (Strauss, Rakoff, Schotland, and Farina, 1995:256). This tradition of deciding policy through adjudication dates from early Anglo-Saxon legal history. In twelfth-century England, judges (often the wealthy local landowner) developed laws and rules by the process of deciding individual matters in front of crude tribunals. Each adjudicated ruling became the basis for deciding factually similar matters. This is the basis for common or judge-made law. Legislative statutes as the basis of law developed only after Parliament rose in power. Thus, for several centuries, rules and laws were developed through an adjudicated procedure and defined by some law giver.

This common law tradition carried over into the early legal institutions in the United States (Friedman, 1973). For example, two old English concepts defining inheritance rights of husbands and wives, dower and curtesy, survived in many states into the 1930s (Friedman, 1973:375). Early congresses and state legislatures were part-time positions passing relatively little legislation, and the bureaucracy was small and manageable. Most U.S. lawyers still carried around their worn leather copies of Blackstone's *Commentaries* (Friedman, 1973:16), and judges making common law defined the bulk of rules and responsibilities for the citizenry (Friedman, 1973:98).

The small bureaucracy consisted of such far-flung agencies as the Postal Service and the Bureau of Indian Affairs. Communication with the central office was costly and time consuming. The agent in charge of each outpost, usually staffed by no more than a few individuals, would decide matters on the spot, and then communicate the results to Washington (Miller, 1992:19). The affected clientele was small, and usually knowledgeable about the issues and thus competent to present their case before the local agency officials.

The growth of the welfare state out of the New Deal and the central planning required during World War II to fight a two-front global effort significantly expanded the size of the bureaucracy and its impact on citizens. Waves of immigration continued to increase the heterogeneous character of the nation, and government decisions increasingly affected citizens with little knowledge of the issues or problems. The national economy became increasingly integrated and specialized. Decisions on complex problems in one state could have major ramifications across the country. The vast expansion of administrative agencies in the twentieth century meant an expansion of their power and impact on every aspect of life in United States.

a. The Demand for Formal Procedures and the APA Movement

The increasing size and scope of governmental power increased the concern with the potential problem of arbitrariness in using case-by-case adjudication to interpret law and rules. In order to safeguard impacted citizens from arbitrary and biased use of administrative power, the need to impose at least some level of standardization on procedures used by agency officials became increasingly evident (*Wong Yang Sung v. McGrath*, 1950). In response, an influential group of legal theorists known as the legal realists developed the concept of formalism.

The development of a formal set of common rules, laws, and regulations to govern the behavior of all federal agencies was viewed as a great advance over the chaotic system of case-by-case adjudication in which every agency developed its own procedures and precedents. In many instances such procedures were not codified. Only experienced private parties had any familiarity with them.

In addition, case-by-case adjudication was inefficient in dealing with large numbers of similar cases. Potential litigants could not be sure of precedent, and thus the citizen often had to cope with the agency with little or no guidance. Adjudication took a great deal of time. It often left the litigants emotionally drained and financially exhausted.

Case-by-case adjudication also raises concerns of fairness (*Dixon v. Love*, 1977). Even a developed legal system leaves the litigants open to the whims and vagaries of the presiding judge. This is so despite the claims of the first dean of the Harvard Law School, Christopher Langdell. Langdell and others argued that trained judges could, in some scientific manner, apply the proper precedent to the case before them.[15] Such training would then eliminate the individual biases of the judge. The legal realism movement led by Llewellyn and others effectively demolished the notion of independent judges applying and using the case law evenly and without bias to the matters before them. Following on the seminal ideas of Justice Holmes, the legal realism movement argued against the idea that judges could dispassionately use cold scientific logic to apply the right case and matching fact pattern to all cases or controversy before them.

In response to these concerns, Llewellyn and his group spearheaded the Restatement of Laws movement. This movement attempted to codify and statutorily define human conduct, thereby avoiding the vagaries and biases of judges using the case law method of adjudication. While the legal realism movement was codifying and changing the law as made by judges, the Administrative Procedures Act (APA) movement was "judicializing" administrative activities in the process of inventing administrative law. The concern behind the APA movement was not the biases of judges, but the need to control bureaucratic opportunism. The growing agency power brought about by the New Deal and World War II also meant growing power held by unelected, and in many cases, unaccountable officials. The APA provided the means to limit the problems of corruption and of overzealous bureaucrats.

Efforts to formalize administrative procedures began as early as 1929, and eventually resulted in the McCarran–Sumners bill, introduced in 1945, which became the Administrative Procedures Act of 1946.[16] The enactment and use of the *Federal Register*, and the Code of Federal Regulations further strengthened the formalism of administrative justice.

The APA imposed consistent adjudication procedures to ensure due process in agency proceedings. Its greatest innovation, however, was the introduction of administrative rule-making procedures that agencies could use to specify the agency's interpretation of laws. Kenneth C. Davis, the administrative law scholar quoted most often by judges (Carter and Harrington, 1990:269), has called these rule-making procedures and the resultant codified body of rules "one of the great inventions of modern government" (Davis, 1973:243). Through their texts, treatises, and law review articles on the APA, Davis and others promulgated, interpreted, and promoted formalized rule-making and adjudication procedures for generations of law students, lawyers, judges, and scholars.

Although the APA restricted agencies to specific procedures, these very restrictions legitimized the increased role that agencies began to play in the policy process. Formalized rules reduced what appeared to be the arbitrary exercise of bureaucratic power. Agency rule-making activities significantly increased in the 1970s and 1980s. As Shapiro noted, the APA represented an "almost total victory for the liberal New Dealers ... Congress' delegation of vast lawmaking power to the agencies was acknowledged and legitimized. Rule making was to be quasi-legislative, not quasi judicial" (Shapiro, 1986:452–454).

b. APA Procedures

The APA distinguishes between rulemaking and adjudication. Rule making is the process for formulating policy for the future by promulgating, amending, or repealing a rule that provides the agency's official interpretation of the statutes it implements and enforces. Adjudication is the process for the formulation of an order that applies to a specific case. The APA further distinguishes between formal and informal rule making and adjudication. Formal hearings are proceedings that are required to be on the record, which is available to the public and provides a basis for appeals of agency decisions to the courts. Informal procedures are intended for minor issues where the costs and delays associated with formal procedures are not justified by the stakes in the decision. For Davis, the purpose of formal and informal procedures is to ensure that the agency clarifies ambiguities in the law through legitimate rule making proceedings, and applies the laws uniformly through legitimate adjudicative proceedings.[17]

c. Rule Making

The process of issuing formal rules depends on the type of rule. The most important and familiar is the legislative rule. The legislative rule has the "force and effect of law" (*Chrysler Corp. v. Brown*, 1979:302). The issuance of such a rule is usually preceded by a public procedure of notice and comment. The Food and Drug Administration (FDA), for example, uses this procedure in issuing rules. The Code of Federal Regulations codifies the rules from all federal agencies. Woe to any lawyer who does not become thoroughly familiar with regulations issued by and pertinent to any agency before representing a client. Many state agencies follow similar procedures. In applying the Medicaid law, codified in Mckinney's Social Service Law sections 367 *et seq.*, the New York DSS has promulgated myriad interpreting rules and regulations that can be found in the New York Code of Rules and Regulations (see 18 N.Y.C.R.R.).

Informal rule making procedures are a misnomer, in that they are still subject to significant legal controls. Agencies generally issue complex and complete rules and procedures to guide bureaucrats and citizens in these informal processes. Informal procedures are still bound by the due process clause of the United States Constitution and subject to judicial review. Of course, a reviewing court may find it difficult to determine what errors, if any, the agency has committed when informal hearings produce only minimal records.

An example of informal rule making is provided by the advisory opinions issued by the IRS. The IRS issues two categories of written advice: unpublished private letter rulings issued by branch offices, and published revenue rulings approved by the Commissioner. Private letter rulings pertain only to the specific taxpayer, and do not change agency policy. Revenue rulings represent agency policy, and the public may rely on them. Both processes are informal because there are no open hearings that produce a public record of what led to the rule. Private letter rulings are far more numerous than published revenue rulings. In 1990, for example, the IRS issued 129 private letter rulings and 49 revenue rulings, compared to only 35 formal regulations (Internal Revenue Service, 1990).

Adjudication. Formal adjudication is required to decide the disposition of a given case when the relevant statute specifies an evidentiary hearing. The formal process provides the same kinds of guarantees of due process involved in court trials. Formal adjudication is an adversary process that includes proper notice, pleadings, discovery, presentation and evaluation of evidence, examination and cross-examination, proposed findings of fact and conclusions of law, and a decision by an administrative law judge who is independent of the agency. An immigration hearing provides an example of a formal adjudication.

Informal adjudications can include all of the above, but the proceedings will be off the record. The hearings officer can use less formal evidentiary rules with concomitant savings in time and expense. Of course, less formal litigation and evidentiary rules also mean admission of potentially poor evidence and misjudgments on the application of law. Preliminary Medicaid hearings are an example of an informal adjudication.

d. Purposive Law Critiques of Formal Procedures

Although standardized rule-making and adjudication procedures advanced the effort to resolve ambiguity in legislation in a just way, the attempt to cubbyhole each situation into a box governed by a specified formal rule produced a different set of problems for agencies and a different concern about justice. In addition, the savings of time and money and efficiency can also be illusory.[18] Scholarly efforts in recent years have focused on the problems that have developed as agencies greatly increased the use of rules and rule-making procedures. In particular, scholars have focused on procedures that appear to produce results at odds with the purpose and image of substantive justice in the legislation being implemented.

Nonet and Selznick argued that the concept of "autonomous law" as envisioned by APA advocates is inappropriate for the active role played by government and law in complex modern societies (Nonet and Selznick, 1978:53–58). Procedural justice alone will not produce substantive justice. They developed the concept of "responsive law" that required agencies and courts to be responsive to the consequences of decisions for substantive justice, not just to the procedures used to reach the decisions. The point of procedural fairness is to ensure a substantively just outcome. Mere legal formalism does not lead automatically to substantive fairness.

In addition, compliance with law often depends not just on substantive justice, but also on perceptions of fair treatment. In the long run just outcomes are a normative and necessary goal. For each particular citizen confronting agency power, however, a fair procedure, regardless of the outcome, can lead to acceptance of the result. As Tyler notes, the citizenry is more likely to accept an adverse outcome as long as the perception exists that the procedure itself is fair. Legal formalism is often not perceived as fair (Tyler, 1990).

In essence, Nonet and Selznick argue for agency administrators to keep the policy goals in mind in assessing individual cases and in making policy decisions. Even the best procedures implemented by the most public-minded officials are going to produce unanticipated and undesirable results. The postbureaucratic agency requires procedures that "facilitate(s) process and build(s) a spirit of self correction into the governmental process." A properly working appeals process not only finds errors, but also corrects the errors that occur when previous agency interpretations are found to produce outcomes inconsistent with substantive justice.

Drawing on his experience as an attorney in the Office of Emergency Preparedness (OEP) and the Cost of Living Council (CLC) that implemented and enforced the 1971 wage and price freeze, Kagan (1978) posited four different modes of rule application and rule making. An agency could either emphasize or deemphasize adherence to rules, and emphasize or deemphasize the realization of legislative goals. A deemphasis of rules leads to unauthorized discretion, the primary concern of the APA movement. A deemphasis of goals leads to legalism (Nonet and Selznick's excessive formalism), and a deemphasis of both rules and ends leads to retreatism. The preferred mode of judicialism requires that an agency be concerned with both adherence to rules and the realization of legislative goals.

Kagan's description of the appeals process at OEP illustrates how an agency can use new cases to correct and refine previous decisions. For most cases, the question is whether the agency applied appropriate precedents to the factual circumstances of the case—as in the initial discussion of Carrie, Lucy, Chuck, and Lester. When the precedents appear to undermine the goal of controlling inflation, however, the case generally presents a new problem not anticipated in previous decisions. As in the case of Angela and Andrew, the critical issue is what precedent should the agency set for this and all similar cases. The decision requires knowledge about the likely consequences of alternative decisions, and a judgment about the appropriateness of each consequence given the legislative goal and view of substantive justice.

Consider the ambiguity encountered in the case of Andrew's home office expense. Ideally, the judicial mode would extend substantive justice by generating a precedent that enabled most of the new work force to claim the deduction but successfully discriminated against false claims of home office use. More frequently the agency must choose between less than satisfactory alternatives. Option "a" will result in just claims by perhaps 90% of the eligible taxpayers but allow unjust claims by 10%, while option "b" will eliminate all unjust claims but result in just claims by less than 75% of eligible taxpayers. The concepts of "responsive law" and "judicial mode" point out the critical importance of this difficult question, but do not provide a simple answer for how the responsible authority is to make the decision. Even in the rare event of consensus on the likely consequences of either choice, problems remain. How should the decision maker weigh the injustice for individuals wrongly deprived of the deduction, against the injustice for the collective wrongly deprived of the tax owed by opportunists falsely claiming the office expense?

Lempert and Sanders suggest that the complex answer is based on a procedure from a typology developed by Trubek called *logical formal rationality* (Lempert and Sanders, 1986:10). This is not the rigid formal procedures of the APA, but an interpretation of procedure that is responsive to issues of substantive justice. Instead of relying on a benevolent dictator, oracle, religious teachings, natural law, or other mystic source of appropriate decision criteria, logical formal rationality is firmly grounded in the procedures of the legal system as they exist at a particular historic period. These institutions provide the context and constraints in which an authority considers the consequences of a decision for substantive justice.

Their argument is based on Rawls's conjecture about fairness. Although individuals will differ on the fairness of a given decision because of their different social positions, they are more likely to agree on the fairness of a decision procedure to be applied in contexts where they could be either plaintiff or defendant. In other words, Andrew's judgment about fairness in the IRS case is clouded because of the specific impact it will have on his current position. This bias would be less a problem in determining what procedure the IRS should follow in other ambiguous cases, as long as Andrew is unclear about whether he will be involved as an individual denied a benefit or as a general taxpayer concerned with minimizing the evasion of others. The veil of ignorance about individual consequences is more likely to produce a consensus on procedures to make decisions.

This moving consensus is the basis for the "logical formal rationality" of agency decisions. It does not lead to a rigid formalism in following existing procedures, since existing procedures may not be in equilibrium with the moving consensus at any point in time. Procedural justice, in following this consensus, thus defines and determines substantive justice.[19] Agency procedures will best serve substantive justice by minimizing the errors most repugnant to the moving consensus.

Mashaw's (1983) study of the Social Security Administration (SSA) emphasizes the role of organizational design in determining substantive justice when consensual principles are applied to administrative agencies. Mashaw develops three different models of administrative adjudication—professional treatment, moral judgment, and bureaucratic rationality—that are based on different consensual principles.

The professional treatment model provides a client-oriented approach in which professionals treat clients according to shared professional knowledge and standards. There is little reliance on rigid rules and formal regulations, and more reliance on the professional judgment about what is in the client's best interest. The moral judgment model provides a courtlike conflict-resolution approach in which conflicts between the agency and citizen are decided by an independent judge, based on an adversarial procedure. Formal regulations as interpreted by the independent judge provide the legal basis for each decision. The bureaucratic rationality model provides a consistent implementation of policy by the designated agency. A bureaucrat applies the agency's precisely defined written rules and regulations to each claim submitted by the citizen to determine eligibility. Eligibility is determined on the basis of officially sanctioned information, and no consequences of a decision are relevant to the decision.

Mashaw argues that each model has its strengths and weaknesses that are appropriate for different circumstances. The bureaucratic rationality model, for example, avoids injustices from inconsistent and capricious decisions of bureaucrats when the law is clear, but will suffer substantive injustices associated with excess formalism when the law is ambiguous. The professional treatment model may provide more substantive justice because of the professional concern with outcomes, but at the cost of more inconsistent treatment.

Mashaw traces the problem of administrative injustice in the SSA not to any one model, but rather to the misapplication of different models to parts of the same administrative process. The SSA is designed around the bureaucratic rationality model for processing of applications. The appeals process for dissatisfied applicants, however, is then based on the moral judgment model. In this process, an administrative law judge's independent interpretation of ambiguous aspects of the law reflects a different set of concerns than those of the agency rendering decisions. The conflict between the policy views of the agency and the administrative law judge results in cases being overturned unless the agency reverts to a rigid formalism in which strict adherence to formal rules and regulations dominates the substantive concern for policy goals. For Mashaw, the solution is to structure the dispute process so that the initial decision makers have appropriate incentives and resources. This will produce decisions that are substantively just as well as rationally consistent, rather than attempting to gain substantive justice through the appeals process. The process presumably would be similar to that employed by Kagan and his cohorts while working for the OEP and CLC.

In sum, the argument against undue reliance on formal procedures of rule making and adjudication focuses on the inefficiencies and ineffectiveness that arise if procedures become reified at the expense of perceptions of fairness and the substantive justice envisioned in legitimate policy initiatives. The argument is not against the codification of procedures necessary in the organizational context of modern administrative agencies, but against the insistence on the use of procedures in situations where they increase rather than decrease agency errors, and hence diminish substantive justice. A just agency is one that has institutionalized procedures that can constantly monitor and adjust the balance between stringency and leniency. Existing administrative procedures lie between the unbridled discretion feared by the APA movement and the excessive formalism critiqued by more recent scholars. In the next section we turn from theory to practice as we describe in greater detail the typical procedures involved in the processing of cases and their role in preventing or correcting errors.

3. Examples of Administrative Procedures that Balance Stringency and Leniency

Let us return to the examples of our claimants, Carrie, Lucy, Chuck, Lester, Angela, and Andrew, to follow the administrative procedures typically involved in deciding benefits and duties. For Carrie and Lucy, the citizen takes first initiative by filling out an application for Medicaid. It is up to the citizen to know that she can apply. Relying initially on the citizen could cause injustice if eligible citizens did not know enough to apply. In the case of Medicaid, however, the nursing homes and other actors in the health care system that rely on Medicaid payments have both the knowledge and the incentive to instruct qualifying citizens once they are already in the system.

The first act by the agency is to review the application in a personal interview. The applicant can appear herself or can have another individual represent her. The examiner reviews the information, checks the applicable Rules and Regulations, and renders a judgment as to whether or not to grant Medicaid. This reliance on formal rules is a process that resembles Mashaw's bureaucratic rationality model.

In our first example, Carrie is incorrectly awarded Medicaid and Lucy is improperly denied Medicaid because of errors on the application form. Since the DSS awarded Carrie Medicaid, she obviously will not appeal the decision. Errors caused by opportunistic applicants are particularly difficult to uncover without extensive investigative work. If insufficient initial investigation did not discover Carrie's misrepresentation, only a yearly review or revealing information from outside the agency might correct the original error.

Lucy will receive a letter of denial. On the denial letter, there is a box for Lucy to check protesting the denial.[20] She has 60 days from receipt of the denial letter in which to protest. The protest requests a fair hearing in front of an independent administrative law judge (ALJ). Lucy will generally receive notice some 2 months after her request, with the fair hearing scheduled for 2 to 3 weeks after the date of information letter. It is virtually costless to protest a denial, and unless one chooses to retain an attorney, will remain almost cost free.

This process is an example of a quasi-formal adjudication process that resembles Mashaw's moral judgment model. The DSS will send a representative and the case file containing all of the relevant documents. Lucy can have representatives, witnesses, and an attorney.[21] The process is quasi-formal in an evidentiary and personal sense. Hearsay, unproved copies of documents, professional letters without foundation, and other evidence that would be excluded in a trial are all permissible as evidence. In addition, the ALJ and the DSS representative usually try to make Lucy feel at ease.[22] As stated before, the DSS often will not have an attorney there to represent it. There also is an effort by the ALJ to play an active role in discovering the truth, rather than just act as a passive referee.[23]

The formality comes because the process is adversarial, with the DSS arguing for the denial, and Lucy and her representative arguing for inclusion in the program. There is no guarantee that Lucy's error will be corrected. The outcome will depend on the effectiveness of her advocate or the ALJ in discovering and sufficiently documenting that Lucy should not have included her daughter's account on the application. The problem with the quasi-formal proceeding is that attorneys could provide effective representation, but they cost money that many applicants don't have. Since Lucy's problem is unambiguous, the chances are reasonable that it will be corrected.

If the decision is against her, Lucy's remedies are court proceedings either in federal district court or in state court. Both are time consuming and expensive, but afford all of the procedural safeguards and guarantees of court proceedings.[24] If the claimant still is not satisfied with the result, she can appeal to a state or federal appellate court, where that court will review the record of the lower tribunals to determine if an error was made at either stage. If errors were made in the proceedings, then Lucy can have an opportunity to resubmit her case at the level where the error was made.

Lucy's problem would be greater if her case were ambiguous, as in Angela's case with SSA. The operating procedures of field examiners may not allow them the flexibility of giving disability to Angela even if there is a strong case in terms of substantive justice. Angela's appeal of the SSA decision has one advantage that is unavailable to Lucy. Attorney fees are set by a schedule awarded by the ALJ (similar to workers' compensation hearings). As a consequence, citizens adversely affected by routine SSA decisions are more likely to be represented by experienced attorneys, enhancing the likelihood that even ambiguous cases are more likely to be resolved in accordance with substantive justice.

The IRS enforcement of duty, like the DSS provision of benefits, begins when the citizen "voluntarily" submits the tax return. Of course, the IRS has several programs to find delinquent taxpayers who fail to file, but the predominant work of the agency is in processing and examining the tax returns filed by taxpayers. With over 200 million returns to process, the IRS relies on computer scrutiny of most returns. Programs based on these computer reviews as well as on other information are used to select less than 1% of all returns to audit.

The errors of leniency and stringency for the IRS depend initially on how well the audit-selection programs detect errors. If Chuck is not audited, his underreporting of income will go undiscovered unless someone (perhaps an angry business partner, or soon-to-be divorced spouse) reports him to the IRS, or he is audited in the future on a related matter.[25]

If the IRS audits Lester, he will have to document his deductions. One can characterize the audit as an informal adjudication based on adversarial proceeding, with the IRS acting as prosecutor and judge. The IRS may request Lester to submit his documents by mail, or it may require him to bring them into the local IRS office. There he will have a direct meeting with the tax examiner or agent. In the most intensive audits, a revenue agent may come to Lester's home or office for a more thorough review of Lester's files. He can, of course, have an attorney or accountant represent him, but privilege will only extend to the relationship with his attorney. During this audit procedure, informal negotiations may ensue between Lester and the IRS agent and the agent's supervisor in an attempt to reach some settlement satisfactory to both the IRS and Lester.

Circumstances of a given case will influence the kind of error the IRS is likely to make. Lester bears the burden of providing sufficient proof of the expenses he claims. If Chuck were audited, on the other hand, the IRS would bear the burden of proving that he had more income than he reported. Unreported income is difficult to document, particularly if there are no "paper trails" like checks or bank records that could substantiate the income. The auditor could assess the tax based on indirect evidence if Chuck would agree, but such assessments are difficult to uphold in the courts.

If no agreement is reached, then Chuck or Lester can ask for an internal appeal of the examiner's assessment. An experienced official in the appeals division of the IRS will review the case and hear the taxpayer's reasons for disputing the assessment. Unlike in the case of the DSS, this internal appeal is based on the same IRS policy as the original audit. The appeals official, however, generally has a broader perspective and less production pressures to close cases than the initial auditor. The subtle differences in motivation and experience may allow this second look at the case to correct some clear errors of undue stringency.

More importantly, the internal appeals process provides the agency with an opportunity to reassess existing policies when concrete situations reveal ambiguities in existing IRS interpretations. If a sufficient pattern of ambiguity across a number of cases like Andrew's is noted at the appeals level, the IRS can initiate formal or informal procedures to clarify policy and correct the substantive injustice arising from current interpretations. The appeals division within the IRS, as the ALJs described in Mashaw, may conflict with the field office auditors on how to interpret the law in Andrew's case. However, the unified organizational structure in the IRS provides greater possibilities for resolving the conflict at a higher level of the organization, thereby avoiding the dysfunctional formalism that Mashaw analyzed in the SSA. In short, organizational structures capable of correcting errors with the least conflict are an important aspect of administrative justice.

If the IRS upholds the assessment on Lester after the appeal, the court system has developed several options. He can pay. This might be unjust, but the proceeding terminates. He can withhold payment and sue in tax court, or he can pay and sue for a refund in federal district court, or the court of claims. In either court, Lester and the IRS are adversaries in a formal adjudicatory process. How well Lester fares in court will depend on how well he can present evidence of his undocumented deductions to the court's satisfaction. His testimony, and that of other witnesses of his, of course has probative evidence. The IRS, through the U.S. Attorney's office, will have the opportunity to cross examine Lester and his witnesses.

Many taxpayers represent themselves, particularly in tax court, to save the potentially enormous expense of legal fees that can sometimes exceed the contested amount. If the contested amount is less than $10,000, then Lester can use a less formal small-claims proceeding at the tax court to keep costs low. In formal proceedings, taxpayers without legal representation are at a distinct disadvantage against the IRS's own attorneys at the tax court or U.S. Attorney's office attorneys at the federal district court.

After the federal court proceedings, the losing party, whether it is the IRS or the taxpayer, has the right to appeal to the federal appeals court.[26] Again this court, reviewing the record, will examine it to see if an error has been committed, and if so, remand it back to the tax court or the district court for additional proceedings.

C. AGENCY JUSTICE

As these examples indicate, we can look at the decision process in agencies as a sequence of decisions, with each decision-point prone to different kinds of errors. The process frequently begins with an initial action by the citizen. Citizens can make unintended mistakes due to misinformation and misunderstandings even when laws are clear, and are more likely to make mistakes when laws are complex, in conflict, or are simply ambiguous in their application to the citizen's particular circumstances. Citizens also make opportunistic errors in their favor, whether through conscious calculation or opportunistic neglect.

For most programs, citizen errors associated with undue stringency are unlikely to be corrected during a later stage in the process. That is, applicants who fail to claim benefits or deductions are unlikely to have their claims made for them. Proactive programs to find and correct these problems are unusual, although most agencies and many private organizations have some outreach programs intended to inform potential beneficiaries of their benefits and the application process.

The street-level bureaucrat examining the citizen's claim attempts to correct citizen errors, but in the process may introduce a different set of errors induced by organizational operating procedures or personal characteristics. Particular examiners may be inclined to be lenient or stringent, and the procedures developed by agencies under different political and resource pressures may be more effective at catching errors of leniency or of stringency (Bardach and Kagan, 1980). Given resource constraints and the difficulties in detecting errors, each agency faces different limitations in its ability to reduce errors. Frequently the reduction of leniency errors comes at the expense of increasing the stringency errors, as when one inadvertently denies legitimate claims in an attempt to crack down on fraud.

Errors of undue leniency by street-level examiners are least likely to be corrected elsewhere in the process. If the IRS auditor or the DSS examiner does not detect the error, few opportunists who escape a duty or receive an undeserved benefit will reappear elsewhere in the system. This "first-line defense" against fraudulent claims is therefore generally more oriented toward preventing errors of leniency, even at a cost of undue stringency.

The appeals stage of the administrative process provides a partial correction for the stringent orientation of street-level examiners, as long as the appeals process functions well. More informal procedures can correct errors of undue stringency quickly and at lower cost to aggrieved citizens and agency alike. More formal procedures cost more and take longer, but provide a more substantial record and more thorough consideration of the issues. Informal procedures are best suited for cases involving the application of clear laws, while formal procedures may be worth the additional costs for setting precedents that clarify ambiguities in the law when standard operating procedures produce substantively unjust results. Since both citizen and agency can appeal most decisions to higher levels of appeal, there is not a clear bias toward stringency or leniency in the appeals stage.

As a practical matter, courts generally defer to agency interpretations of the law and uphold agency decisions a large percentage of the time. The Supreme Court, for example, from 1953 to 1990, upheld the IRS position over 70% of the time (Epstein, Segal, Spaeth, and Walker, 1994:574). However, when the appeals process does overturn the agency's initial decision in favor of the individual, errors will generally be on the side of leniency.

While data on the error mixture at the street level are difficult to obtain, court data appear to substantiate the initial stringency and later leniency error reduction formula. For example, one author who studied the tax court noted, "statistically speaking taxpayers don't do very well at Tax Court" (MacLachlan, 1995:53). Another author states that taxpayers win only 5% of the time in tax court (Daily, 1992:106). Taxpayers fare only slightly better in district court.

An analysis of individual tax cases in the district courts from 1976 through 1994 shows that taxpayers win less than 10% of the time.[27] At the appeals court level, however, taxpayers fare better. At this level, right below the Supreme Court, the taxpayer wins over 33% of the time.[28] A similar pattern exists for social security cases. At the district court level, depending on the particular matter, the citizen wins between 16 and 43% of the time. At the appellate level the citizen wins slightly more than 50% of the time.[29]

The more aggressively the appeals process overturns initial decisions, the more likely the agency will modify procedures to produce fewer such cases. This may simply encourage agencies to process all cases "by the book," following the codified laws with little regard for substantive justice, as Mashaw described. Alternatively, the agency may respond by clarifying legal ambiguities responsible for the overturned cases, as Kagan noted. Additionally, they may improve the training and supervision of field agents and the internal procedures for initiating and processing the kinds of cases that were overturned. Unlike Mashaw's case, these agency responses are likely to reduce the overall errors produced by the system.

Whether the agency retreats into a formalistic defense or reforms its operating codes and procedures depends in part on the extent to which the decisions arising in the appeals process are generally perceived as reflecting the kind of broader consensus discussed by Lempert and Sanders, or simply a partisan view of those opposed to agency procedures. As Moe noted, the U.S. political system frequently produces legislation in which the appeals process reflects the interests of those who were not strong enough to defeat legislation, but were sufficiently strong to restrict the ability of the agency to effectively implement the policy.[30] Thus, conflict between an agency and independent review board involves a continuing political process of negotiation over the meaning of the legislation, much to the discomfort of citizens caught in the middle of conflicting interpretations of policy and the underlying image of substantive justice. This form of injustice is beyond the scope of administrative justice as we have defined it, and rests instead in the realm of injustice imposed by the political system—a more amorphous but very critical realm.

In summary, we have defined administrative justice in terms of the errors made by agencies responsible for implementing legitimate policies. Administrative agencies ensure that citizens gain their legitimate rights and benefits, while regulatory agencies ensure that citizens perform their required duties. Errors of leniency hurt the public good, and involve a failure to enforce duties or an erroneous provision of benefits to ineligible recipients. Errors of stringency hurt the individual, and involve a failure to provide a benefit to an eligible recipient or the erroneous enforcement of a duty where none exists. Both errors result in administrative injustice.

We argue that the quest for administrative justice involves a continuing search for administrative procedures that minimize the overall level of injustice caused by administrative errors in the implementation of a given law under a given set of circumstances. We know of no magic set of procedures that will guarantee administrative justice across the myriad conditions that agencies encounter in modern societies. Indeed, most procedures that reduce errors of stringency will tend to exacerbate errors of leniency, and vice versa. We favor instead the quest for procedural reforms based on analyses of current problems. Such analyses need to consider the balance of errors produced by current procedures, the error-correction potential offered by alternative administrative procedures and enforcement techniques an agency could adopt, and the acceptability of the new procedures and resultant balance of errors to the citizens most affected as well as to the wider public.

We strongly emphasize that analyses of administrative justice are not just a technical matter to be performed by trained administrators, although such analyses should be an ongoing function of every agency. Nor are they a task that democratic governance can safely relegate to the oversight activities of congressional committees or similar elected institutions, although these oversight institutions should play a key role in the process. Administrative justice ultimately involves the vision of substantive justice shared within the broader political community, and therefore needs to be an integral part of ongoing political discussions about the rights and duties of citizens in the broader political community.

In the current political climate it is easy (particularly for attorneys practicing before an agency) to accept the widespread notion that the bureaucrat is the enemy of the citizen. Bureaucrats are chastised on the one hand for being excessively stringent, particularly in poignant press accounts of aggrieved citizens. On the other, they are accused of excessive leniency in detecting fraud and in spending the public's hard-earned tax money on undeserving cases. But bureaucrats are merely a convenient political target. The real issue in need of resolution in the current debate over the rights and duties of citizens is a realistic understanding of the role that government agencies are expected to play in ensuring those rights and duties.

D. ENDNOTES

1. Horwitz (1994), quoting a phrase "in vogue during the New Deal."
2. Medicaid is established under 42 U.S.C.A. Although established by federal law, it is an unfunded program, thus each state has to pay for administering and distributing the entitlement. This has led to substantial differences across states. For example, as of this writing, a community spouse in New York could retain $66,000 in assets, and still have his or her spouse receive Medicaid, while in Connecticut, the spouse could retain only $13,000. This of course brings up additional issues of justice. Different treatment in two neighboring states could in theory encourage citizens to set up domicile in the state with the most favorable interpretation.
3. While nursing home costs vary greatly from state to state, and even within a state, assume Lucy resides in a nursing home within a major metropolitan area. There costs at such a facility can easily exceed $7000 per month.
4. In New York the formula is stated in Social Service Law §366. Generally, you divide the amount transferred by the DSS reimbursement rate to Long Term Care facilities in that area, and the applicant is ineligible for that period of time. Thus, if the DSS reimburses at $5000 per month, a transfer of $100,000 would thus make Carrie ineligible for 20 months.
5. See IRC §1(A)(I)(1) Imposition of Income Tax on Individuals.
6. Quoted in Kagan, *Regulatory Justice*, p. 75, New York: Russell Sage Foundation (1978) from Chester Bowles, *Promises to Keep*, p. 25 (1971).
7. Actually, the interview will be of the representative, often the adult child. Most nursing home applicants are either quite elderly, or infirm or both, and unable to attend these sessions.
8. The issue of fraud is not a subject of this chapter. *Black's Law Dictionary* defines fraud as deceiving with intent (p. 788). Carrie could argue this was an unintentional oversight. Carrie would now have to obtain the bonds back from her adult child. If her child refuses, arguing the transfer of bonds represented a completed gift, then Carrie is between the proverbial rock and hard place. She is not eligible for Medicaid, and the nursing home can move to evict her for lack of payment. The moral, if any, is before transferring assets to your children, make sure you can trust them completely.
9. Almost every new administration comes into office promising tax reform. Even the simple analysis above demonstrates just how difficult "reform" is, with the inherent complexity of a nationwide tax system.
10. Most standard medical insurance policies cover only "skilled" care, which is usually care of a doctor or a registered nurse. Most long-term care is considered "custodial," and thus the care given by licensed practical nurses and other therapists and nursing home workers will not be covered by medical insurance.
11. IRC §280A(c)(1)(A) defines home office generally as a principal place of business.
12. See Revenue Ruling 94-241994-1 C.B. 87 Section 280A—Business Use of Home (1994), where the IRS stated that "relative importance" and "time tests" will be used to determine the eligibility of a home for a home office deduction. Earlier rulings held that the home office had to be exclusively used for a business.
13. Moe, The Politics of Bureaucratic Structure. In P. Peterson and J. Chubb (Eds.), *Can Governments Govern?* Washington, DC: Brookings (1989).
14. A typical application process in a medium to large city can be an intimidating and tedious process. The applicant

first must go to the nearest Health and Human Services office. On entering, she would go to the front desk, then a receptionist would ask her the nature of her business. The receptionist would give her a place in line, and the appropriate form to examine and/or fill out. She would then wait her turn for an examiner to become free. The waiting area is usually a large, windowless room where she would sit on metal folding chairs with all of the other citizens waiting to do business with Health and Human Services. Finally she would be called in to some partitioned office, most often without benefit of counsel, and interviewed by the examiner.

15. Christopher Columbus Langdell, the first dean of the Harvard Law School, served in that capacity from 1870 until 1895. He is generally considered the founder of the case study method of learning the law (Gilmore, 1974). It is still the primary teaching method in law schools, and one that continues to plague generations of law students.
16. Much of this section is from Gellhorn and Levin (1990). Readers are directed to that work for a more comprehensive treatment and understanding of the APA, and Administrative Law.
17. 5 U.S.C. §§ 551, 553, 554, 556, 557. A rule is defined as the "agency statement ... designed to implement, interpret, or prescribe law or policy."
18. Gellhorn and Levin cite the FDA and the "notorious Peanut Butter" rule-making case. The weeks of testimony and hundreds of pages of transcript were used, for example, on such issues as to whether peanut butter should contain 87 or 90% peanuts.
19. Rawls (1971) argued for a system of distributive or substantive justice that would be determined by a procedure Rawls labeled a veil of ignorance. If you took a group of people and sat them around a table, and imposed a veil of ignorance around them, what system of distributive justice would they enact? By veil of ignorance, Rawls meant that each person would have no knowledge of what their riches, station in life, abilities, talents, or any other matter, would be once the world began. Given this, Rawls argued people would take a conservative approach to distributive justice. They would opt for an equal distribution of goods and resources, unless, under a Pareto optimality principle, an unequal distribution would advantage the most disadvantaged member of society.
20. The denied claimant can also request a conference. Such conferences take place on the same day as the hearing, and are attended by the claimant, the DSS decision maker, and the representatives of the claimant. This conference can be considered an informal adjudication.
21. The DSS may or may not send an attorney. In Nassau County on Long Island, the DSS practice is to send an attorney only if the claimant is represented by an attorney. Several hearings are scheduled for the same day, and are most often done on a first-come first-served basis. Unless some exceptional matter is involved, the hearings usually take no more than 45 minutes, and are often much shorter.
22. Unless the DSS has some reason to believe outright fraud is involved.
23. The hearing is often recorded on a cassette, with no sidebar conferences or off-the-record discussions allowed.
24. In general the Article 78 proceeding will be less expensive, but more time consuming than a federal court action. Federal court dockets are less crowded, and the federal judiciary much more determined in moving cases along.
25. Although there is generally a 3-year statute of limitations, there is no statute of limitations for fraud.
26. There is no right of appeal, for either side, in a small-claims tax proceeding.
27. This finding is derived from judicial statistics available at the Internet site teddy.law.cornell.edu:8090/questata.htm.
28. This finding is derived from Appeals Court Data Base compiled and collected by Donald Songer.
29. The data for the district courts and appeals courts come from the same sources as the tax cases. For particular matters at the district court level the breakdown is: for welfare cases, citizens win 27%; for Health Insurance, 17%; for Supplemental Security Income, 39%; and for Disability, 43%.
30. Moe, *op. cit.*

REFERENCES

Bardach, E., and Kagan, R. A. (1980). *Going by the Book: The Problem of Regulatory Unreasonableness*. Philadelphia, PA: Temple University Press.

Black, H. C. (1968). *Black's Law Dictionary* (4th ed.). St. Paul, MN: West Publishing.

Bowles, C. (1971). *Promises to Keep*. New York: Harper & Row.

Buckley v. Valeo, 424 U.S. 1 (1976).

Burnham, D. (1989). *A Law Unto Itself, Power, Politics and the IRS*. New York: Random House.

Carter, L. H., and Harrington, C. B. (1990). *Administrative Law and Politics: Cases and Comments* (2nd ed.). New York: Harper Collins.

Chrysler Corp. v. Brown, 441 U.S. 281 (1979).

Daily, F. W. (1992). *Stand Up to the IRS*. Berkeley, CA: Nolo Press.
Davis, K. C. (1973). *Administrative Law*. St. Paul, MN: West Publishing.
Diver, C. S. (1980). A Theory of Regulatory Enforcement. *Public Policy*, *28*, 257.
Dixon v. Love, 431 U.S. 105 (1977).
Epstein, L., Segal, J. A., Spaeth, H., and Walker, T. G. (1994). *The Supreme Court Compendium*. Washington, DC: Congressional Quarterly.
Friedman, L. M. (1973). *A History of American Law*. New York: Simon & Schuster.
Gellhorn, E., and Levin, R. M. (1990). *Administrative Law and Process in a Nutshell*. St. Paul, MN: West Publishing.
Gilmore, G. (1974). *The Death of Contract*. Columbus: Ohio University Press.
Horwitz, R. B. (1994). Judicial Review of Regulatory Decisions: The Changing Criteria. *Political Science Quarterly*, *109*, 133.
Internal Revenue Service. (1990). *Annual Report*.
Kagan, R. A. (1978). *Regulatory Justice*. New York: Russell Sage Foundation.
Kagan, R. A. (1994). Regulatory Enforcement. In D. H. Rosenbloom and R. D. Schwartz (Eds.), *Handbook of Regulation and Administrative Law*. New York: Dekker. 383–422.
Lempert, R., and Sanders, J. (1986). *An Invitation to Law and Social Science*. New York: Longman.
MacLachlan, C. (1995, September 27). The Tax Bench: A Code Apart, *The National Law Journal*, p. 1.
Mashaw, J. L. (1983). *Bureaucratic Justice: Managing Social Security Disability Claims*. New Haven, CT: Yale University Press.
Miller, G. (1992). *Managerial Dilemmas*. London: Cambridge University Press.
Moe, T. M. (1989). The Politics of Bureaucratic Structure. In P. Peterson and J. Chubb (Eds.), *Can Governments Govern?* Washington, DC: Brookings. 267–329.
Nonet, P., and Selznick, P. (1978). *Law and Society in Transition: Toward Responsive Law*. New York: Harper & Row.
Quirk, P. J. (1981). *Industry Influence in Federal Regulatory Agencies*. Princeton: Princeton University Press.
Rawls, J. (1971). *A Theory of Justice*. Cambridge, MA: Belknap Press.
Rosenbloom, D. (1983). *Public Administration & the Law: Bench v. Bureau*. New York: Dekker.
Shapiro, M. (1986). APA: Past, Present and Future. *Virginia Law Review*, *72*, 447, 452–454.
Strauss, P. L., Rakoff, T., Schotland, R. A., and Farina, C. R. (1995). *Gellhorn and Byse's Administrative Law* (9th ed.). Westbury, NY: The Foundation Press.
Tyler, T. R. (1990). *Why People Obey the Law*. New Haven, CT: Yale University Press.
Wong Yang Sung v. McGrath, 339 U.S. 33 (1950).

8

In Search of "Good" Mediation

Rhetoric, Practice, and Empiricism[1]

Deborah R. Hensler[2]

A. INTRODUCTION

The contemporary alternative dispute resolution (ADR) movement is now more than two decades old.[3] From its inception, ADR has meant different things to different people: Proponents have hailed it, variously, as a device for promoting problem solving, individual and community empowerment, and more rational allocation of scarce judicial resources (Henry, 1991; Bush and Folger, 1994; Shonholtz, 1993; Sander, 1976). Opponents have assailed it as throttling "rights-talk," promoting the hegemony of the affluent majority and creating unnecessary and costly way stations on the road to trial (Fiss, 1984; Nader, 1993).

As commonly used by legal practitioners and legal scholars, the term *ADR* encompasses a variety of dispute resolution mechanisms. Indeed, Professor Frank Sander's seminal articulation of the application of ADR to civil litigation envisioned a multidoored "dispute resolution center" (in place of the traditional courthouse) in which disputants would be directed to fact-finding, mediation, arbitration, trial, or other procedures, as appropriate to the nature of the dispute (Sander, 1976).

But at the core of the ADR movement is the promise of *mediation*: to empower disputants to resolve their disputes on their own, with the assistance of a nonauthoritative neutral. Among ADR procedures used in the contemporary U.S. legal system, it is mediation, with its rejection of neutral fact-finding and assignment of fault, that is most distinguishable from the formal bench or jury trial to which ADR is offered as an alternative. In contrast, arbitration, with its adversarial evidentiary proceedings and third-party decision making, mimics full-blown adjudication, albeit without binding itself to the substantive or procedural norms that undergird public adjudication.[4] There is a widespread perception that mediation is outpacing arbitration as a popular means of resolving legal disputes.[5]

But just *what* mediation is has been in contention, since the inception of the contemporary

Deborah R. Hensler • Stanford University Law School, Stanford, California 94305.

Handbook of Justice Research in Law, edited by Sanders and Hamilton. Kluwer Academic / Plenum Publishers, New York, 2000.

ADR movement.[6] Is it a method of facilitating disposition of legal disputes "in the shadow of the law" (Freund, 1994; Higgins and O'Connell, 1997)? Is it a means of escaping that shadow, to the (arguably) more productive avenues of problem solving (Bennett and Hermann, 1996)? Or is it not even about resolving disputes, but rather a means of empowering individuals to take control of their lives and a means of enhancing their abilities to understand the needs of others (Bush and Folger, 1994)?

If mediation of legal disputes were purely a private venture, an option for disputants who wish to avoid litigation entirely, the nature of "good" mediation might simply be a matter for debate among practitioners and scholars. But as federal and state court jurisdictions nationwide have begun requiring civil litigants to attempt to resolve their disputes through mediation before allowing them to exercise their trial rights,[7] contention over what mediation is—and is not—has become more than theoretical. If courts mandate mediation, then, some argue, the courts have a responsibility to articulate quality standards for the mediation programs to which litigants are referred (Center for Dispute Settlement and the Institute for Judicial Administration, undated). Others would go further than the articulation of standards, to requiring mediator training consistent with those standards, certifying to serve as mediators only those who have demonstrated competence and providing procedures for sanctioning mediators who violate standards.[8]

Articulated sharply and implemented strictly, standards can become vehicles for establishing certain models of mediation. Of course, standard setting and certification, justified on the ground of satisfying courts' responsibility to protect litigants' rights to fair process, also have the consequence of excluding some from the practice of mediation, while privileging others. Not surprisingly, as a private market for mediation services has developed, the nature of standards has become a subject of controversy.

A recent study by the RAND Institute for Civil Justice raised the controversy over what mediation *is* and *ought to be* a notch higher. RAND's study of court-connected mediation programs was conducted as a part of a larger study of the Civil Justice Reform Act (CJRA),[9] itself a controversial attempt to reform federal court management of civil cases. RAND's finding that mediation (and another form of ADR, termed *early neutral evaluation*) had little statistically significant effect on the efficiency of civil case processing (measured in terms of time to disposition and public and private transaction costs) was met with a storm of criticism from the ADR community, particularly the adherents of mediation.[10] The criticism was remarkably intense.[11] Although commentators had different perspectives of RAND's findings, the common thread running through their critiques was that RAND had not studied "exemplary" programs and that, if they had, the results would have shown salutary effects of mediation (Plapinger, 1997; Jaffe and Stamato, 1997; Feliciano, 1997).

In this chapter, I discuss the debate over "good" mediation and explore what we know about the effects of implementing different mediation paradigms for resolving civil legal disputes. Section B reviews the scholarly and practitioner commentary on the meaning of mediation. Section C reviews the recent empirical literature on mediation practice. Section D assesses the evidentiary basis for claims that different forms of mediation have different consequences. Section E presents previously unpublished analyses of the RAND study data, undertaken in response to the controversy over that study. Section F brings together the rhetorical, practitioner, and empirical strands of the paper's discussion, and considers how procedural and distributive justice research might help explain the divergence between goals of the mediation movement and its outcomes to date.

My discussion throughout focuses on the mediation of civil legal disputes over money damages—such as tort and contract cases—in trial courts of general jurisdiction, not including family law cases and/or small-claims cases. Although the use of mediation in family law cases has created its own set of controversies, they are separable from the larger debate about "good" mediation, and the community of practitioners, legal scholars, and empirical researchers involved in that debate are separate from (although somewhat overlapping with) those involved in the larger debate.[12] Similarly, research on small-claims courts and small-claims mediation constitutes a separate area of scholarship.

B. RHETORIC

At first blush, it would appear that there is considerable scholarly and practical consensus about the definition of mediation. Numerous textbooks define mediation as a process in which a neutral third party is invited into a dispute resolution process by the disputants, to assist them in reaching a resolution of their dispute (see, e.g., Goldberg, Sander, and Rogers, 1992:3; Riskin and Westbrook, 1987:4; Murray, Rau, and Sherman, 1996:4). But as the use of mediation for resolving civil lawsuits has spread, the distinction between mediation and other forms of ADR has eroded. The voluntary basis for the process has been brought into question by court mandates (Bennett and Hermann, 1996). Mediators are variously exhorted to assist disputants by telling them how to settle their dispute, by helping them identify the interests that underlie their dispute but *not* suggesting an outcome, or by doing neither of these and instead helping disputants toward a better understanding of themselves and each other.

The rhetorical debate over mediation reflects, in part, different notions on the nature of legal disputes and different theories of negotiation. On one side of the debate are those who view civil legal disputes as primarily distributive: controversies over who will get the biggest piece of the metaphorical pie. In this view, most legal disputes are chiefly, if not wholly, about money. Parties to these disputes initiate litigation with widely divergent views of how much they would gain or lose if the case were to reach trial verdict, and the process of negotiation involves them—or more usually, their lawyer-agents—making sequential concessions until they converge on an agreeable monetary transfer. Rational negotiators estimate how the case would be decided at trial, and then discount the expected value of the case by the costs of proceeding to trial and the risk of misestimating the trial outcome, to reach an acceptable settlement amount—hence the phrase "bargaining in the shadow of the law."[13] The role of a mediator is to help parties reach this convergence. Neutral mediators can play an important role in helping the parties exchange information about the strengths and weakness of their legal and factual claims (see, e.g., Ayres and Nalebuff, forthcoming). They can also help the parties overcome communicative and cognitive obstacles to negotiation (including individuals' tendencies to overestimate the strength of their own positions and to discount the value of their opponents' concessions),[14] by offering a neutral assessment of the monetary value of the case. Because of its focus on assessing the value of the legal dispute, this form of mediation is often termed *evaluative*.

An important feature of this perspective on negotiation and mediation is its tendency to privilege lawyers over clients (because the former have more experience in valuing cases than the latter), and neutral third parties with experience in the litigation process (who are likely to be lawyers themselves) over third parties whose expertise is more process-oriented (whose training may be in other areas, such as psychology). Disputants' involvement in the resolution process is viewed as beneficial (if at all) primarily because their permission is necessary to settle the dispute, and secondarily, because their exposure to the mediator may influence their own assessments of the case's monetary value and, hence, their willingness to approve a settlement.

On the other side of the debate over the proper meaning of mediation are those who view legal disputes as multifaceted interest-based conflicts. According to this view, instead of staking out opposing positions and then moving toward a value between these, parties should focus on identifying the different interests that underlie their dispute and on attempting to shape a mutually beneficial resolution—a so-called "win–win" solution. Rather than narrowing the issues in the case to a consideration of monetary value, parties may be advised to put more issues on the table, so as to create more opportunities for trade-offs.[15] The role of the mediator, from this perspective, is to help parties focus on their interests, rather than on their bargaining positions, and to assist them in generating options for resolving their dispute that will maximize joint gains. An effective mediator facilitates this value-creating process, rather than pressing parties to put a compromise dollar value on their dispute; hence, this process is often called *facilitative mediation.*[16]

The interest-based theory of negotiation leads legal disputants out of the shadow of the law, into the realm of problem solving. "What occurred in the past is not the central focus of mediation," says one representative text. "Attempts to fix blame for past behavior can create obstacles to otherwise acceptable solutions" (Leeson and Johnston, 1992). Determining liability—a central question for law—seems to play little role in this form of dispute resolution.

The facilitative perspective on mediation tends to place more weight on the parties' roles in dispute resolution (by comparison with the evaluative), since it is the parties who should best understand the nature of the problem that led to the dispute. Lawyers' specialized expertise is also less relevant to reaching a resolution. "The mediators are not there to make a decision, nor to say who is right and who is wrong," says another practice-oriented text. "The mediators are there to promote the *disputants'* [italics added] use of constructive problem-solving skills" (Bennett and Hermann, 1996:7; Alfini, 1991). Indeed, some mediation processes modeled on this theory exclude lawyers from the process altogether. Similarly, it is less important that facilitative mediators (by comparison with evaluative mediators) have legal expertise or experience valuing legal cases and (arguably) more important that they have good "process" skills.[17]

Although pragmatists might suggest that many disputes have both distributive and nondistributive aspects (Freund, 1994) and hence, effective mediators might combine evaluative and facilitative skills,[18] this notion is contested by some scholars and practitioners. When Professor Leonard Riskin proposed an analytic grid for sorting different types of mediation according to the role of the mediator (evaluative versus facilitative) and how narrowly or broadly the dispute is defined[19] his ideas were greeted with a storm of criticism.[20] A representative critique averred: "Evaluative mediation is an oxymoron," and argued that mediation is, by definition, facilitative (Kovach and Love, 1996). In a more extensive analysis, Professor Joshua Stulberg also rejected Riskin's analysis, arguing that accepting the full range of mediative practices implied by Riskin's grid would lead to untenable consequences, most notably an inability to assess mediator quality by any other factor than whether the dispute settled (Riskin, 1997). Mediators who adopt the evaluative practices attributed to some by Professor Riskin would, according to Stulberg, veer quickly into an adjudicatory role (and hence outside of the realm of mediation). But, Professor Stulberg also wrote, facilitative mediators who focused on process to the extent of ignoring substance would be ineffective, as would mediators who required disputants to leave all tendencies to view disputes as distributive at the mediation room door (Riskin, 1997).

A recent series of electronic mail messages among subscribers to a popular dispute resolution "listserv" conveys some of the flavor of practitioner debate about "good mediation." The first two messages appeared at the close of a debate about the morality of the then-recently announced tentative tobacco litigation settlement.

> To be really practical, durable solutions must look to the longest term and the biggest picture possible in the situation. This includes the interdependent interests of all those affected directly and indirectly. It's too bad that short-term expediency tends to dictate many (most?) agreements. Short-sighted agreements that ignore the interests of affected others inevitably contain the seeds of future conflicts.... What responsibility do mediators have to encourage parties to see and care about the big picture?[21]

In response another subscriber wrote:

> An acknowledgment that—irrespective of motivation—the outcome of mediation, and probably of other forms of ADR, is the adoption or restoration of a positive, life-affirming relationship, would be extremely useful. While some may argue that this approach is not relevant where the disputants are strangers and have no previous relationship, or have a relationship which is antagonistic, I suggest that even under these circumstances, there are compelling reasons to find common ground.[22]

A month later, discussion on the listserv had moved on to debate about evaluative versus facilitative mediation:

> Those of you are just becoming mediators might as well get an early dose of the rhetoric in the field. This debate continues to grow.... In the ranks of judges and litigators, there are those who think that a highly evaluative (structured settlement conference model) approach is the only alternative. Because there is a lack of exposure to the other models of mediation (through Riskin's spectrum to the highly facilitative) these folks generally view mediation as the province of the normal cast of characters in the judicial (settlement conference) world, to wit, judges and litigators.... It is important that all of us in the field at least recognize where others are coming from in their points of view, whether we agree or not.[23]

The battle was quickly joined. Noting that he had received a call the day before from "an 'attorney mediator' (read 'lawyer')," regarding a mediation training seminar, another subscriber wrote:

> He questioned my "ethics" for not properly protecting the "legal rights" of employees who participate in problem-solving discussions that employ non-adversarial communication methods.
>
> My explanation that "managerial mediation is just a way to have a business meeting about a business problem" and that it is used simply to help people get along better in the workplace was met only with a disapproving grunt. Learning that I've been doing/teaching/training workplace mediation for over twenty years didn't seem to diminish his concerns.[24]

In response, another subscriber wrote:

> While you are not pleased with addressing the issue of the employees "legal rights," it is a very valid concern.... How many people will accept that such "managerial mediation is just a way to have a business meeting about a business problem." If that opens a party to providing discoverable information, or worse admissible evidence, against the interests of any of the parties, they absolutely need to know and understand the severe risks they are

> undertaking.... If the "business mediator" is not even competent enough to recognize the issues, how can they help the parties make an informed, empowered decision?[25]

Subsequently, the author of the first message wrote (apologizing for generalizing about attorney mediators):

> Unfortunately, my experience has indeed been that every attorney-mediator I have encountered takes what I regard as an unnecessarily and counter-productively legalistic, adversarial, rule-bound, rights-oriented approach to dispute resolution. My occupational niche is mediation of relatively simple interpersonal workplace conflicts (often of the "personality clash" genre).... In my area of practice, it is essential to keep the focus on interest-reconciliation, not letting parties frame it as a rights context.[26]

Although this exchange evolved into a discussion over attorney versus nonattorney mediators, it is instructive to note that both correspondents are talking about the same sort of dispute, i.e., a dispute arising in the workplace. What distinguishes their views are the way they frame the dispute and their belief about how best to resolve it. As the exchange continued, another subscriber struggled to sum up the underlying issues:

> Are we trying to include too much in the role of mediation? Are we laying too much responsibility on the mediator in the matter or content of the dispute? My experience indicates that it is quite helpful to me as a mediator to have knowledge of the subject field in which the parties are disputing but it does not allow me to impose my knowledge on the parties or to pose as an expert. My job is facilitating their decision-making and when special information can do this and I have that information I can make it available to them.... What I'm trying to say here is that we may be calling something mediation which is not that. We may be confused as to just what the mediation process can and cannot do. We may be utterly confused about who should mediate, and we may be more confused than that about the nature of human struggle and dispute and where the various dispute resolution processes are best used.[27]

A day later he added more positively:

> I keep asking for a functional definition of mediation because that is where we start. As a mediator I perceive my role as a facilitator of decision-making by two or more persons who have been unable to make [a] joint decision about issues over which they differ.... I see mediation as a significant and beautiful process that stands alone in the dispute resolution spectrum of alternatives, and ... demands of the mediator a magnificent discipline in controlling self bias, personal agenda, and other predispositions that would contaminate the true facilitative process. (Keltner, 1997)

What accounts for the intensity of the rhetorical debate about what constitutes "good" mediation?[28] First, there is the ideological fervor that has accompanied the ADR movement. Social movements gain some of their momentum from the emotional attachment of their followers to the movement's core beliefs. Because ADR has been promoted, in part, on the grounds of its transformative potential, ADR paradigms that more closely mimic conventional legal dispute resolution procedures may be rejected in favor of less conventional paradigms. Evaluative mediation, framed as helping legal disputants negotiate in the shadow of the law, has more in common with traditional judicial settlement conferences[29] than with attempts to empower disputants and to enhance their understandings of themselves and each other. In contrast, facilitative mediation, with its emphasis on disputants' preferences and capacities, espouses more revolutionary goals.

Second, the debate over "good" mediation signals an emerging power struggle between lawyers and nonlawyers, including other professionals, such as psychologists, and laypersons, over who will control the new dispute resolution processes that are being incorporated into the legal system. If evaluative mediation achieves the dominant position, lawyers, with their superior knowledge of the bases for valuing legal disputes, will be in a better position than nonlawyers to sell their services to civil disputants. As the legal profession has moved from rejection to indifference to embrace of the ADR movement, the competition between lawyers and nonlawyers for mediation "business" has increased.[30]

Competition between lawyer and nonlawyer mediators lies close to the surface of practitioners' debate over "good" mediation. "I'm wondering," wrote one subscriber to the dispute resolution listserv,

> if it is realistic to hope that mental health professionals might gain and maintain a secure place in the mediation industry as it matures. I wonder if attorneys are going to take 90 to 99 percent of the for-fee mediations, leaving the crumbs and volunteer mediations to people of other professional origins.

Replied another subscriber:

> I'm just back from a trip and am blessed with a number of postings on topics that have long been issues for me. I find the DISPUTES [sic] forming between Mediators who are also lawyers (please, let's rub out the term Attorney mediators. Which are you and which are you first?) with mediators who are of the variety of backgrounds represented by our industry a very sad commentary on our burgeoning profession.[31]

After much electronic mail had been exchanged on the subject, another offered:

> The legal background of an attorney—including knowledge of procedure, statutes, and case law—is invaluable in mediation. Right or wrong, this is a situation where you are attempting to get to a legal resolution even though it often doesn't feel like a legal problem to the parties.[32]

To which yet another replied:

> That is your opinion and it is not shared by many proficient, successful mediators in the field.[33]

Third, not only are mediators competing with each other in the private ADR market, but mediation programs may also be competing for public resources. An interesting aspect of the evolution of ADR in the legal system has been the apparent dependence of ADR professionals and programs on the court system for referral business.[34] Wrote an attorney-mediator to the dispute resolution listserv:

> Mediation is actually a great deal more than mediating court-annexed conflicts—but, at the same time, the good, for-pay, mediation almost all fit within that realm (excluding labor and other mediation that involve very few of us).... The explosion of "for fee" mediation was driven by attorney-mediators (especially groups like [he names several national for-profit mediation providers] soliciting other attorneys for mediation. A non-attorney needs to confront breaking into a different socialization group (attorneys) who are gatekeepers.[35]

Private ADR organizations have collaborated with public agencies in promoting the use of ADR for civil legal disputes.[36] By prodding courts to choose particular forms of ADR, such as mediation, and by shaping the nature of court-connected mediation programs, ADR organizations may consciously or unconsciously shape the market for ADR services.

Finally, the rhetorical debate over "good" mediation implicates a broader debate over the power of women, minorities, and other historically disadvantaged groups in the legal system. Feminist legal scholars and critical race theorists have been in the forefront of academic criticism of the courts' embrace of the ADR movement. Although their critique is multi-faceted, their primary concern is whether less powerful groups can effectively claim rights and remedies that they have been accorded by law when the resolution of their disputes depends on their own (rather than agents') negotiating skills and styles, and when these skills have been shaped by cultures in which they are assigned to subordinate roles.

To an important extent, this critique centers on those features of mediation and ADR that are central to the facilitative paradigm. In her widely cited critique of the consequences of mediation for women, Professor Tina Grillo characterized the process as "reject[ing] an objectivist approach to conflict resolution, and promis[ing] to consider disputes in terms of relationships and responsibility" (1991:1548). She argued that mediation requires "[women] to speak in a setting they have not chosen and often imposes a rigid orthodoxy as to how they should speak, make decisions, and be," and that because women have a more "relational" sense of self, they are disadvantaged in a process in which they "may feel compelled to maintain [their] connection with the other [disputant], even to [their] own detriment."[37]

Professor Richard Delgado, another leading critic of the ADR movement, and his colleagues argue more broadly that informal processes, such as mediation, "tend to foster prejudiced behavior" (1985:1375) and are therefore potentially harmful to the socially disadvantaged, especially racial and ethnic minority groups.[38] In adversarial courtroom proceedings, Professor Delgado and colleagues argue,

> [e]quality of status, or something approaching it, is preserved—each party is represented by an attorney and has a prescribed time and manner for speaking, putting on evidence, and questioning the other side. Equally important, formal adjudication avoids the unstructured, intimate interactions that, according to social scientists, foster prejudice. The rules of procedure maintain distance between the parties. Counsel for the parties do not address one another, but present the issue to the trier of fact. The rules preserve the formality of the setting by dictating in detail how this confrontation is to be conducted. (1985:1388)

In other words, for Delgado and his colleagues, the model dispute resolution procedure is the antithesis of facilitative mediation.

Generally absent from the practitioner and scholarly debates over "good" mediation are concerns about the efficiency of dispute resolution. But these concerns loom large in the public arguments in favor of court adoption (and funding) of mediation (and other ADR).[39] Reflecting on RAND's report of its findings on court-connected mediation programs under the CJRA, U.S. District Court Judge Ann Williams, chair of the Judicial Conference's Committee on Court Administration and Case Management, said: "We were disappointed that the RAND study didn't affirm our belief that ADR reduces cost and delay" (Erickson, 1997:6). Similarly, at a meeting of state court Chief Justices focused on court-connected ADR programs and held shortly after the release of RAND's findings, Chief Judge Annice Wagner said: "For two decades, courts have looked to mediation and ADR to speed cases and save money." She then went on to express concern about the implications of RAND's findings on mediation in the federal courts, for state courts.[40] By promoting mediation as a means of reducing court work loads (for court-connected programs) and private litigation costs, supporters and providers of mediation have taken on the challenge of demonstrating that mediation—in whatever form it takes—not only enhances the quality of the dispute resolution process and its outcomes, but also achieves these outcomes faster and cheaper.

C. PRACTICE

Despite the intensity of the rhetorical debate over "good" mediation, there is little systematic empirical information about the proportion of civil legal disputes that are mediated in a facilitative, rather than evaluative fashion.[41] In this section, I review what we can learn about practice from six empirical studies of mediation. I selected these studies for comment because they include empirical data on the range of mediator practices within certain programs, collected by independent researchers. Two of the six studies are based on observational data, one relies on survey data, and the remaining four use a combination of qualitative interviews and quantitative record and survey data analysis. Five of the six studies describe court-sponsored mediation programs; the sixth is an analysis of cases handled by private ADR providers.[42]

In reviewing these studies, I looked for signs that the mediation program's philosophy and/or reports of mediators' actual behaviors were generally facilitative or evaluative. I regarded adopting an interests-based negotiation approach, assigning value to party participation, communication and relationships, and assigning value to process as well as outcomes, as indicia of facilitative mediation. I regarded adopting a distributive-oriented negotiation process, assigning priority to attorney participation and communication, and (especially) assigning priority to settlement, as indicia of evaluative mediation. Using these criteria, I interpret the findings of these leading studies as showing that the practice of mediation, at least as it applies to civil lawsuits other than family law cases, is generally evaluative.[43] When designing programs, courts are more likely to offer evaluative than facilitative mediation. When given a choice, parties (or, at least, their attorneys) frequently opt for evaluative modes of mediation.

1. The Florida Mediation Program

Florida's court-sponsored mediation program is one of the most comprehensive in the nation.[44] Beginning in the mid-1970s, Florida's limited jurisdiction courts began experimenting with mediation of minor civil disputes, and in the late 1970s, the first court-sponsored divorce mediation program was established in Ft. Lauderdale (Broward County). By the late 1980s, as a result of legislative and court action, mediation was incorporated in the trial courts of general jurisdiction. Hundreds of individuals, primarily lawyers and retired judges, have been trained and certified under the Florida rules. The original training program was developed by a group of nationally recognized mediators, including Professor Joshua Stulberg. It is one of the most intensive training programs in the nation, requiring 40 hours of formal training, observation of four mediation sessions, and conduct of four mediations under the supervision of a certified mediator (Alfini, 1991:51).

In 1990, Professor James Alfini interviewed 11 mediators and 9 attorneys who had been involved collectively in several hundred civil case mediations to determine mediation practices. He found three prevalent styles, which he termed "trashing," "bashing," and "hashing." Of the three, only "hashing" appears to bear any resemblance to facilitative mediation. "Trashers" and "bashers" differ from each other, not in their degree of attention to process and relationships rather than outcomes, but in how they go about pressing the lawyers and disputants to reach an outcome. The "trashers" focus on "tearing down" the disputants' case; the "bashers" focus on whittling away at the disputants' initial settlement offers.

Although Professor Alfini's methodology did not permit him to estimate the relative proportions of the three styles, he concluded that "if one focuses on the emerging conception of the circuit mediation process in Florida, the question [is this the end of 'good' mediation?] becomes more problematic" (Alfini, 1991:74). At recent meetings of key figures in Florida's program and interested academicians (including the author), the director of Florida's Dispute Resolution Center has expressed concern that evaluative mediation has come to dominate the state's program.

2. The Wisconsin Medical Mediation Screening Panel Program

The impetus for the Wisconsin medical malpractice program was the desire to rein in perceived excesses in medical malpractice awards. Hence, it is grounded in a quite different policy domain—that of tort reform—than Florida's program. But it is instructive to review what is known about this program, because it was labeled by policymakers as a mediation program and promoted as an ADR program.[45]

Under the Wisconsin program, plaintiffs filing medical malpractice claims are required to attempt to first mediate the dispute before a three-person court-appointed panel consisting of a physician, a lawyer, and a layperson, before the case will be permitted to proceed through litigation. During the mediation period, all discovery and other litigation-related activities are stayed.

The key feature of the Wisconsin program for the purposes of this paper is its directions to mediators, who are supposed to: "discuss the strengths and weaknesses of the case, discuss their recommended disposition or settlement figure and ascertain the 'bottom line' settlement positions of the parties." If an impasse is reached, "the mediators [are to] provide the parties with their objective evaluation of the case."[46]

Meschievitz (1991) analyzed case-level data from the Wisconsin program and observed 20 mediation sessions. Although she described mediators' styles as varied, the litigants themselves participated very little in the sessions she observed:

> Some attorneys allowed their clients to speak openly; others did not allow them to speak at all. In about one-third of the sessions [the defendants were not present]. There was no direct exchange between the claimant [plaintiff] and the respondents [doctors and/or hospital representatives] in any of the observed sessions. (1991:210)

She concluded that the program "allows for little direct party participation, results in few mediated settlements and does little to promote harmony, reciprocal understanding of party needs, or active processes for interaction and joint resolution." Tellingly, she added, "[The program] is certainly not mediation in its classic sense" (Meschievitz, 1991:212).

3. The North Carolina Mediated Settlement Conference Program

The North Carolina Mediated Settlement Conference Program was authorized by the state legislature in 1991, in response to recommendations from a committee of judges, lawyers, and others whose vision of mediation was shaped by the Florida program (Clarke, Ellen, and McCormick, 1995:3). Mediation was defined by the North Carolina legislature as "an informal process conducted by a mediator with the objective of helping parties voluntarily reach a mutually acceptable settlement of their dispute," and a mediator was defined as "a neutral person who acts to encourage and facilitate a resolution of a pending civil action [but] does not render a judgment as to the merit of the action" [Clarke *et al.*, 1995, Sec. 7A-38(a)]. Under the new state law, all civil cases were subject to the program except those involving actions for extraordinary writs, but judges had discretion to decide whether or not to order cases to mediation. Mediators were certified by the Administrative Office of the North Carolina Courts (AOC), after completing 40 hours of training. Parties could select their own mediators, but if they declined to do so, judges would appoint a mediator from the list of certified mediators. Parties split the mediators' fees. The program was initially adopted in eight jurisdictions on a pilot basis and the AOC was directed to determine whether the program made "the operation of the superior courts more efficient, less costly and more satisfying to the litigants" (Clarke *et al.*, 1995, at v). During the pilot phase, about 55% of the cases assigned to mediation were tort suits, about 20% were suits arising from contract disputes, and the remainder were a mix of other money damage claims. Most of the disputes involved amounts of $10,000 or more (Clarke *et al.*, 1995:7).

The North Carolina program has been the subject of two published evaluation studies, one describing the pilot phase of the program and evaluating its outcomes for all civil cases (Clarke *et al.*, 1995) and the other focusing exclusively on medial malpractice cases (Metzloff, Peeples, and Harris, 1997). Both of the studies included observations of actual mediation sessions, and analyzed data collected from court and other administrative records and by surveying litigants and their attorneys.

Both studies found that in the large majority of cases, there was a single mediation session lasting, on average, just a few hours. As one of the teams of researchers put it: "Whatever magic could be accomplished in the mediation had to be worked at the initial session" (Metzloff *et al.*, 1997:111). Although North Carolina's legislation requires parties (as well as their attorneys) to be present at mediation sessions, both studies found that the disputants themselves played little role in the mediations.

The team that conducted the evaluation of the pilot program observed 34 mediations. In these mediations they reported "the attorneys did most of the negotiating. Much of their communication with each other was through the mediator in separate caucuses ... rather than directly to the other side.... Litigants rarely suggest possible solutions, speak to each other, or speak to opposing counsel.... It was not uncommon for the mediator to meet with both opposing attorneys without their clients present to try to work out something without the emotional input of the litigants."[47] Some mediators were "very patient and sympathetic" but some had "no interest in letting litigants express their feelings." The researchers referred to sessions where litigants were permitted or encouraged to express themselves as "show and tell" (Clarke *et al.*, 1995:11). The clear implication is that encouraging litigants to participate in mediation has emotional value for them but is not useful in identifying their interests or crafting a resolution of their dispute.

The team that conducted the evaluation of the mediation of medical malpractice disputes likewise found that plaintiffs rarely participated in the opening session of the mediation (when mediators spoke with all of the attorneys and parties present). In caucuses with the mediator, plaintiffs had "substantial involvement" in about one-third of the cases, but were limited to answering a few questions or making a few comments in the remainder. Indeed, in about 15% of cases, plaintiffs did not participate at all in caucuses. Notwithstanding the rules requiring parties' presence, physician-defendants were sometimes absent from the mediations. When present, physicians tended to participate even less than plaintiffs, although, given their higher levels of education and professional experience, we might have expected the opposite (Metzloff *et al.*, 1997:117, 199).

Both studies of the North Carolina program describe mediator practices as more evaluative than facilitative. After an opening session in which they invite attorneys to present the facts of the dispute and ask clarification questions, mediators spend most of their time caucusing separately with each side. They shuttle between the sides with information and settlement offers, and use various tactics, including setting deadlines, to press the attorneys and their clients to reach a resolution. In their study of medical malpractice litigation, Metzloff and associates tabulated the types of strategies used by mediators in the 40 cases they observed. Thirteen of the fourteen strategies they identified involve identifying or highlighting the strengths and weaknesses of each side's case or the costs and risks associated with not resolving the case at mediation. Only one technique, "advis[ing] party how to present/ structure offer/demand," might be considered facilitative (Metzloff *et al.*, 1997:122). Summarizing what transpires in mediation sessions, the researchers said: "Lawyers talking about money is the norm" (Metzloff *et al.*, 1997:145).

In sum, when applied to "ordinary litigation" and more complex medical malpractice disputes, mediation in North Carolina implements an evaluative paradigm. As Professor Metzloff and his colleagues concluded: "The program as it has evolved is usually nothing more than a structured, traditional settlement conference conducted by a neutral third party" (1997:145).

4. The Brett *et al.* Study of ADR in the Private Sector

A recent study by Jeanne Brett and associates offers a rare example of empirical analysis of the distribution of evaluative versus facilitative mediation *outside* the courts.[48] Their study focuses on cases in which ADR services were provided by private organizations, including nonprofit and for-profit organizations. Using surveys of lawyers and litigants, the research team collected data on 449 cases.[49] Although only a quarter of the cases were referred to the ADR provider organizations by the courts,[50] the mix of cases is similar to what one would expect in a civil caseload: tort personal injury and property damage, contract, construction, and so forth (Brett, Barsness, and Goldberg, 1996:Figure 3). About 22% of the cases chose arbitration, 27% chose what Brett *et al.* denote "interests-based mediation," 39% chose interests-based mediation "with an advisory opinion," and the remainder chose a miscellany of minitrials, neutral evaluation, and so forth.[51]

Just how to interpret the distribution of ADR choices is unclear. The authors seem inclined to view the results as a popular vote in favor of mediation, based on the evidence that two-thirds of the cases chose this procedure. An alternative interpretation would be that 61% chose an evaluative procedure, with one-third of these opting for a binding evaluation (i.e., arbitration) and the majority choosing a nonbinding advisory opinion.

5. The CJRA Demonstration Programs

Under the Civil Justice Reform Act of 1990, five courts were selected by Congress to experiment with various methods for reducing cost and delay; three of these [the Northern District of California (CA(N)), Western District of Missouri (MO(W)), and Northern District of West Virginia (WVA(N))] were specifically directed to experiment with ADR, and the remaining two (the Western District of Michigan and the Northern District of Ohio) were directed to experiment with differentiated case management. [CA(N) actually mounted both types of demonstration programs, providing three demonstrations of each approach.] The Federal Judicial Center (FJC) was charged with evaluating the implementation and outcomes of the five courts (Stienstra *et al.*, 1997). In the course of its study, the FJC interviewed members of the district courts' advisory groups, court staff, and judges, and surveyed the lead attorneys in samples of cases terminated in each court in 1995–1996 (Stienstra *et al.*, 1997:iii).

One of the three courts, MO(W), mounted a randomized experiment, in which one-third of cases were ordered to ADR, another third were invited but not ordered, and the remainder were precluded from using the ADR program (so as to provide a baseline comparison group). In the other two courts, there were no comparison groups for analysis.

As reported by the FJC, all three of the ADR courts adopted programs that had at least some mandatory component and all three shared the goals of providing the parties an opportunity to meet and learn each other's views of the dispute, as well as reducing litigation time and costs. As a result, all required that parties attend the ADR sessions. And all offered mediation as one ADR option (Stienstra *et al.*, 1997:3). Based on the FJC's description of ADR sessions and analyses of attorney survey data, it appears that most ADR procedures were more evaluative than facilitative.

In two of the three districts, some or all of the attorneys and parties were able to choose which type of ADR they preferred. In CA(N), when given a choice, almost half (48%) selected early neutral evaluation (ENE) (48%), an ADR program explicitly intended to provide an evaluation of the merits of the case, as its name suggests. Another 20% chose an early settlement conference conducted by a magistrate judge; the FJC notes that case evaluation is "a likely expectation" for these conferences (Stienstra *et al.*, 1997:185). A scant 3% chose nonbinding arbitration. In all, then, close to three-quarters of those given a choice, opted for an evaluative session. About one-quarter (23%) chose mediation.[52]

Whether mediation sessions in CA(N) were facilitative, evaluative, or a mix of the two cannot be determined with confidence from the FJC report. But there are some indications that mediation was at least more facilitative than ENE sessions. The report indicates that judges were more likely to refer cases to mediation when they "require[s] facilitation," and more likely to refer cases to ENE when the case "requires evaluation or subject matter expertise" (Stienstra *et al.*, 1997:186). Attorneys' reasons for choosing a particular ADR option did not differ substantially by type of ADR procedure.[53]

In MO(W), at an initial administrative session, the ADR administrator (a member of the court staff with extensive prior litigation experience) offers to mediate the case and almost all attorneys and parties accept his offer. As a result, the FJC found that virtually all cases referred to ADR in this court are mediated by a single individual.[54]

Although the FJC report notes that "every case is handled according to its needs," the modal session that the report describes sounds more evaluative than facilitative. The sessions are held early in the litigation and party participation is mandatory. Before the session, the administrator reviews the case file and prepares background notes, although he does not require the attorneys to file statements of facts. According to the FJC, the parties are told that the purpose of the initial session is "to help them evaluate their case, understand the other side's view of it, and lay the groundwork for settlement by identifying the information they need." In a footnote, they add that the administrator "said his goal in the [session] is to make sure the parties have a realistic view of their respective cases and to settle the case as soon as is practicable" (Stienstra *et al.*, 1997:228, Fn 159). In the initial session, the administrator does much what we would expect of an evaluative civil case mediator—inviting the parties, in order, to present the facts, discussing the legal issues, and caucusing with each side to assess the strengths and weaknesses of their case and to discuss the relative costs and benefits of settling versus trial. Parties are given the opportunity to indicate that they would prefer to proceed to another form of ADR or mediation with another mediator, but most choose to continue to mediate the case with the program administrator (Stienstra *et al.*, 1997:299).

In the third demonstration court, WVA(N), the court's approach to ADR under CJRA was to expand a preexisting "settlement week" program. "Settlement weeks" have traditionally been used by courts to reduce court backlogs. Typically, attorneys volunteer to serve as "settlement judges," and assist the attorneys in settling their cases, using evaluative techniques (Hensler, 1990:352–354). In WVA(N), the program utilized attorneys trained in mediation techniques by the local law school and other continuing legal education (CLE). Cases reach settlement week conferences either voluntarily or by judicial reference.

Based on the FJC's description, it appears that mediations in this jurisdiction are largely evaluative:

> the mediator's opening remarks were generally followed by brief opening statements by the parties' attorneys, usually focusing on the strengths of their respective cases. The mediator then held a series of separate caucuses with each party, beginning with the plaintiff. At these caucuses the mediator discussed the strengths and weaknesses of the party's case, including offering his or her own opinion of what the strengths and weaknesses were (e.g., "I think one strength of your case is the damages aspect;" "the plaintiff is salt-of-the-earth—a jury will believe her from Day 1;" "you have a lot of cards in terms of the law."). The mediator generally tried to move parties quickly to generate a specific dollar figure for a settlement demand or offer that the mediator could bring to the other side. (Streustra, 1997:267)

6. The CJRA Pilot Programs

The CJRA demonstration courts were selected as exemplars of what courts might achieve with ADR and differentiated case management. In contrast, the CJRA pilot program was intended to test the consequences of the Act's requirements for a representative sample of federal district courts (Kakalik *et al.*, 1997a). Under the Act, ten courts were selected by the Judicial Conference and directed to adopt specified procedures and practices, including ADR; another ten courts, with closely matching characteristics, were selected as "control" or comparison courts and merely required to conform to the looser requirements of the Act. RAND's Institute for Civil Justice was selected by the Administrative Office of the U.S. Courts to conduct the evaluation of the CJRA's consequences (Kakalik *et al.*, 1997a:3).

While the main CJRA evaluation focused on case management, RAND conducted a supplemental study focusing on ADR. Although the main study included 20 courts (10 pilot and 10 comparison), the ADR study was limited to 6 courts whose ADR programs handled sufficient numbers of cases to permit an empirical analysis of their effects; of these, 4 courts provided voluntary or mandatory mediation and the remaining 2 courts provided ENE.[55] RAND's analysis is based on interviews with judges, court administrators, and advisory group members in each district, surveys of attorneys, litigants, and ADR providers, and reviews of court records.

Although the RAND report describes all four of the mediation programs it studied as "facilitative" (Kakalik *et al.*, 1997b), its qualitative descriptions of program operations and survey findings suggest that the programs varied substantially along the facilitative–evaluative dimension. Two courts, the Western District of Oklahoma [OK(W)] and the Southern District of Texas [TX(S)], opted for voluntary mediation. In both districts, the court certified mediators, who were selected and paid by the parties. OK(W) required 24 hours of training for certification, plus observations of two mediations plus conduct of two pro bono sessions. TX(S) required 40 hours of training for mediator certification, plus conduct of one or two pro bono sessions, plus 5 hours of retraining annually. The same organization provided much of

TABLE 1. Mediator Background Characteristics

	OK(W)	TX(S)	NY(S)	PA(E)
Median years practicing law in federal courts	17	21	23	27
Median number of federal, state, and private ADR cases/years	33	60	4	3

Source. RAND ADR Report (Table 4.5 at 33). Data from ADR provider surveys.

the training in both districts, and the training was said to be facilitatively focused.[56] The other two courts, the Southern Districts of New York [NY(S)] and the Eastern District of Pennsylvania [PA(E)], adopted mandatory mediation. In NY(S), the court developed a list of mediators, who were required to attend a 2-day training seminar, and the ADR program administrator selected the mediator, who served pro bono, for the parties. In PA(E), the court also developed a mediator list, but the requirements were based on years in practice, and no special mediation training was required. PA(E) also selected the mediators, who served pro bono, for the parties. As shown in Table 1, these varied approaches to mediator selection, produced mediator pools with considerably more ADR (i.e., process-oriented) experience in OK(W) and TX(S). As seen in Table 2, the nature of the sessions varied substantially across the courts as well. It seems unlikely that Eastern Pennsylvania's brief sessions, with parties virtually always absent, would much resemble facilitative mediation.[57]

Indeed, RAND's quantitative reports on whether case evaluation took place at the mediation session are consistent with the more qualitative indicia of the mediation paradigm that prevailed in the respective districts. Table 3 shows two measures of what happened at the mediation sessions: (1) the ADR provider's report of whether he or she offered an evaluation of the case and (2) the percentage of cases in which *any* participant surveyed (lawyer, litigant, or provider) reported such an evaluation. We might expect the first measure to be influenced at least somewhat by the prevailing norms. Judged by this measure, only OK(W) exemplifies the pure facilitative mode. The second measure presents a more ambiguous picture of the extent to which sessions are evaluative, but it shows the same pattern of differences as the first. Note that whether the mediator provided a neutral assessment of case value is but one indicator of mediation paradigm.

D. OUTCOMES

My review of the fragmentary empirical literature on mediation practices suggests that the facilitative rhetoric of mediation has had limited effect on practice in the civil litigation domain. But these data are far from comprehensive. And even if they reflect the true state of

TABLE 2. Mediation Characteristics

	OK(W)	TX(S)	NY(S)	PA(E)
% sessions with parties present	100	98	65	11
Median number of minutes, all sessions	240	510	300	90

Source. RAND ADR Report (Tables 4.4 and 4.5 at 32–33). Data from ADR provider surveys.

Table 3. Extent of Case Evaluation

	OK(W)	TX(S)	NY(S)	PA(E)
% of mediators saying they gave an evaluation of the case to each side	15	48	58	69
% of cases in which any participant reported that an evaluation was given	38	54	62	64

Source. RAND ADR Report (Table 4.4 at 32). Data from ADR provider surveys, and new analyses of RAND survey data by author.

practice in the civil litigation domain, they do not tell us what difference it makes—for disputes and disputants—whether mediators are facilitative, evaluative, or use a mix of approaches.

While we have little systematic information about the distribution of mediation practices, we know even less about the consequences of implementing different mediation paradigms.[58] The reasons are myriad, including the difficulty of conducting causal analyses (i.e., analyses that would demonstrate that a particular practice consistently leads to a particular set of outcomes),[59] the difficulty of measuring outcomes, and the lack of research infrastructure, including funding, for civil justice research.[60]

In this section, I review the findings of the studies previously discussed in Section B, seeking empirical evidence of differential effects of implementing facilitative versus evaluative mediation paradigms. Because the Florida, Wisconsin, and North Carolina data indicate that those programs are largely evaluative and do not provide outcomes data that are linked to mediator styles, the discussion is limited to the Brett *et al.* study, and the FJC and RAND studies of mediation under the Civil Justice Reform Act. I focus on effects that have been discussed by scholars, practitioners, and court ADR enthusiasts that the empiricists have studied: resolution rates, transaction costs, effects on party relationships, and process and outcome evaluations. To date, the limited empirical research that has been conducted on the outcomes of mediation has focused on the effects of mediating cases, compared to not mediating them. I review that evidence. But, based on the information reviewed previously, I argue that some programs are more facilitative (evaluative) than others, and also look for differences in effects between these.

1. ADR in the Private Sector (Brett *et al.*, 1996)

Brett *et al.* compared the results of mediating cases versus arbitrating them. They found that mediation was significantly (in both the substantive and statistical sense of the word) less expensive than arbitration (measured by litigation costs and lawyer and client hours), and that the time from beginning to end of the procedure was significantly shorter for mediation than for arbitration. They also found that individual participants in mediation were significantly more likely to be satisfied with the process and outcome of the procedure compared with arbitration participants, and that the former were significantly more likely to think the process had improved the relationship between the parties. When an advisory opinion was offered, mediation was somewhat more likely to lead to settlement (81%) than when there was no case evaluation (74%), but these differences were not statistically significant. And interestingly, the rate of settlement at the mediation conference was the same for both paradigms.[61]

2. The CJRA Demonstration Programs

The FJC study of the three CJRA demonstration districts found that a majority of the attorneys they surveyed, in all three districts, thought that ADR reduced time to disposition and substantially reduced litigation costs. A majority thought that ADR served to resolve all or part of their legal dispute. A majority also thought that ADR allowed clients to be more involved in the resolution of their cases than they otherwise would have been and improved communication between the sides (Stienstra *et al.*, 1997:16–22).

The FJC warns that readers should be cautious in interpreting these data. Because they were unable to construct comparison groups against which to measure the outcomes of mediated cases in two of the three courts, the FJC's findings for these courts rely exclusively on attorneys' self-reports of time and cost savings, and effects on settlement. In all courts, attorneys' assessments of whether ADR achieved efficiency gains are correlated with their reports of whether or not the case settled as a result of ADR: Attorneys whose cases are reported as settled are much more likely to report time and cost savings. In CA(N), attorneys' assessments of efficiency gains are also correlated with the method of referral, with attorneys who selected the particular type of ADR used more likely to report savings (Stienstra *et al.*, 1997:16–22). Other studies have found that attorneys' subjective evaluations of cost savings due to ADR are frequently not confirmed by objective comparison of costs for cases referred and not referred to ADR (Kakalik *et al.*, 1997a:12).

In MO(W), however, the FJC's findings are based on experimental data, and therefore can be more confidently interpreted as demonstrating the effects of mediation. Cases ordered to mediation had a median time to disposition that was about 30% less than cases that were precluded from going to ADR (the "control group"). Cases referred to mediation were somewhat more likely to settle than cases that were not referred, and the latter were more likely to terminate in a trial or other judgment. In later reports, the FJC intends to present objective cost analyses for the Western District of Missouri.

My review of the FJC study (see Section C) suggested that CA(N)'s mediation program may have been more facilitative than the programs in MO(W), and particularly, WVA(N). Table 4 compares attorneys' assessment of the ways in which mediation was helpful, or not helpful, across the three programs. Because FJC used somewhat different questions and question wording in the three different courts, not all responses are directly comparable. Some questions were only asked in one or two courts. Drawing from the published data and an additional tabulation for the CA(N) mediation program, which FJC analyst Donna Stienstra graciously shared with me, I have grouped the responses to different questionnaire items by whether they seem to refer mainly to distributional aspects of mediation, mainly to interest-based and relational aspects, or mainly to other process aspects. (Note that these categorizations are my own, and may not accord with the FJC's interpretation of the data.)

Judging by these data, all three programs seem to have had a mix of facilitative and evaluative characteristics. In all programs, there appears to have been some effort to both increase attorneys' and parties' understanding of the other side's position, and to move parties away from these positions. Across all three programs, a majority of the attorneys surveyed thought that mediation was helpful in encouraging more client participation in dispute resolution and increasing communication. In one of the two courts in which the question was asked, the responses suggest that interest-based negotiation took place and was perceived by many to be helpful; in the other there is little evidence of such discussion. [In CA(N), more than two-thirds said such exploration took place and was at least somewhat helpful; in WVA(N), more than

Table 4. Proportion of Attorneys Saying Mediation Was "Very" or "Somewhat" Helpful in Various Ways: CJRA Demonstration Court

	CA(N) %	MO(W) %	WVA(N) %
Settlement-oriented			
Moving the parties toward settlement	71	—	64
Distribution-oriented			
Clarifying or narrowing monetary differences	65	—	—
Clarifying or narrowing liability issues	43	—	—
Clarifying or narrowing the issues	—	—	39
Encouraging the parties to be more realistic about their respective positions	66	77	64
Allowing me to identify strengths and weaknesses of the other side's case	47	—	40
Allowing me to better understand and evaluate the other side's position	—	68	—
Allowing me to identify the strengths and weaknesses of my client's case	46	65	38
Providing an opportunity to evaluate the other side's attorney	—	63	—
Providing a neutral evaluation of the case	45	—	43
Interests-oriented			
Allowing the parties to explore solutions that would not be likely through trial and motions	48	—	28
Moving the parties toward stipulations and/or eliminating issues from case	23	—	14
Relational			
Allowing the clients to become more involved in the resolution of the case	54	72	57
Improving communication between the different sides in this case	49	55	58
Preserving a relationship between the parties	18	—	22
Improving relations between the parties	—	42	—
Process-oriented			
Giving parties an opportunity to tell their story	63	—	56
Other			
Assisting with organizing pretrial process	3	—	15
Encouraging early discovery	—	38	—

Note. CA(N) and WVA(N) attorneys were asked to rate various factors as "very helpful, somewhat helpful, slightly helpful, or of no help as all." MO(W) attorneys were asked if each factor was "helpful, detrimental, or had no effect." The questionnaires used in the three courts varied somewhat. The table groups similar items together.
Source. FJC Study (Tables 95 and 108 at 249 and 278) and additional data tabulations provided to the author by Donna Stienstra, senior author of the FJC Report. I am grateful to Ms. Stienstra for sharing these data.

40% said mediation was "of no help at all" in this regard.] In both courts in which the question was asked, less than one-quarter of attorneys thought that mediation helped to preserve the relationship between the parties. [In CA(N), about a third said mediation was "of no help at all" in preserving a relationship between the parties, and one-quarter said that issue was not applicable to their case. Of those who thought it relevant, about one-quarter said it was helpful. In MO(W), the FJC asked a more general question about "improving relations," as opposed to preserving a relationship, and 40% reported that mediation was helpful in this regard.]

3. The CJRA Pilot Courts

RAND conducted analyses of differences *within* each of the four CJRA pilot courts that referred substantial numbers of cases to mediation, comparing cases referred to mediation and cases that were not referred. In the two mandatory mediation courts, NY(S) and PA(E), cases were randomly assigned to mediation or the control (no mediation) condition. In the two voluntary mediation courts, TX(S) and OK(W), RAND constructed comparison groups of cases whose characteristics were "matched" to those of the cases that had volunteered for mediation.

To measure time to disposition and certain aspects of case outcome (e.g., whether the case ended in settlement or judgment), RAND relied on court records that had been incorporated into the database for RAND's main CJRA evaluation. To measure litigation costs, RAND relied on attorneys' (and to a limited extent, litigants') reports of actual time spent working on the sampled cases, and on their reports of legal expenses that were billed. RAND also asked attorneys to report the amount of monetary settlements and any other nonmonetary agreements. By using experimental and quasiexperimental designs and more objective measures of time, costs, and outcomes, RAND was able to enhance the validity of its study findings, beyond that of studies that lack such designs and measures.

Based on its *within*-district analyses, RAND concluded that mediation, as implemented in these four districts, had no consistent statistically significant effect on time to disposition, litigation costs, lawyers' satisfaction with the litigation process, or lawyers' perceptions of fairness. RAND found that cases referred to mediation in TX(S) were significantly slower to terminate and required more lawyer time than cases not referred, but suggested that this was a result of more-difficult-to-settle cases opting for or being referred to mediation in that district. RAND found that in three of the four mediation courts, cases referred to mediation were less likely to terminate by dispositive judgment than cases not referred, and it found in all four courts that cases referred to mediation were more likely than cases not referred to terminate with money changing hands. In three of the four districts, RAND found that litigants in cases referred to mediation were more satisfied, on average, with the litigation process than litigants whose cases were not referred.

RAND's charge was to determine whether mediation, as implemented in the CJRA courts, had significant effects on the outcomes of interest to Congress, not to examine the effects of differences in mediation approach. As a result, and because there were myriad differences among the mediation programs and also differences among the courts in other factors that might affect civil case processing, RAND presented district-by-district findings, and, for the most part, did not attempt to draw any inferences about differences among districts.

In the next section, I present some further analyses of the RAND data, focusing on differences between facilitative and evaluative mediation. I caution readers that there may be multiple explanations of any differences I find and that the sample sizes for these analyses are often very small. Thus, these analyses should be treated as exploratory only and the results as suggestive, rather than conclusive.

E. NEW ANALYSES OF THE RAND ADR DATA

In Section C.5, I argued that although RAND termed all of the CJRA pilot mediation programs "facilitative," the qualitative and quantitative data RAND collected suggest that the dominant paradigms of the four programs differed, such that they can be arrayed across a continuum from facilitative to evaluative as follows:

OK(W) TX(S) NY(S) PS(E)

More facilitative ——— More evaluative

By comparing outcomes across these courts, we might be able to learn something about what difference it makes whether the dominant mediation paradigm in a particular jurisdiction is facilitative or evaluative.

It is important to note initially that the four pilot mediation programs differed in other regards as well. As shown in Table 5, two of the programs referred cases to mediation about 3 months after filing, and the other two referred cases about 8–9 months after filing.

The average elapsed time from referral to mediation also varied from about 1 month, to 2 months, to 6 months. Any difference in the average time to resolve a mediated case across these courts would more likely be related to these differences in program design, than to the nature of the mediation process. (Note, however, that these features of program timing do not seem to be linked to mediation paradigm.)

Similarly, the public and private costs of mediation varied across the courts, as fees were charged to parties in the voluntary courts, but not the mandatory mediation courts, and some courts invested substantially more personnel and other resources in administering their programs than others. Differences in the cost of mediation to parties would reflect the absence or presence of a fee. The decision to provide mediation free to parties appears to be linked to the decision to require parties to engage in it, rather than to offer it on a voluntary basis. That latter decision *is*, arguably, linked to mediation paradigm, as it is generally those whose mediation perspective is transformative or facilitative who are most opposed to mandating it.

Finally, differences in the level of public resources invested in a mediation program may also have effects on program outcomes that are distinct from the effects of the dominant mediation paradigm, although decisions about resources might also be linked to decision makers' views on what "good" mediation is.[62] The variety of program design features, to my mind, controvert the notion that the pilot courts are somehow aberrational; like court-annexed programs that I and RAND and other colleagues have studied over more than a decade, they share certain central features and differ with regard to many others. PA(E)'s program, which has been widely criticized as nonconformist (and which has been modified since RAND's study), strikes me as not surprising for a district that has had long and successful experience with an early referral, streamlined nonbinding court-annexed arbitration program.[63] Although seemingly designed for evaluation, it seems little different to me in that regard from the WVA(N) demonstration program studied by the FJC.

The pilot courts' mediation programs not only differed with regards to program design factors other than mediation paradigm, the characteristics of the cases reaching mediation hearings also differed, probably in part because of these program design differences.[64] As

TABLE 5. Profile of CJRA Pilot Mediation Programs

	OK(W)	TX(S)	NY(S)	PA(E)
Basis for referral	Vol.	Vol.	Mand.	Mand.
Median time from filing to ADR referral (days)	99	232	271	90
Median time from ADR referral to mediation session(s) (days)	61	78	182	30
Written information from lawyers submitted in advance?	97	95	96	23
Pleadings and other court materials reviewed in advance?	77	23	55	97
Median time in mediation (hours)	4	8	5	1.5
Average mediator fee per case (split by parties)	$660	$1800	$0	$0
Public costs for court administration/case referred	$490	$170	$410	$130

Source. RAND ADR Report (Tables 4.1, 4.2, 4.4, 4.5, 4.11 at 30–39).

TABLE 6. Caseload Characteristics, CJRA Pilot Mediation Programs (Mediated Cases Only)

	OK(W) (%)	TX(S) (%)	NY(S) (%)	PA(E) (%)
*Case type****				
Tort	47	22	26	37
Contract	21	28	40	18
Other	32	50	34	45
N (of cases with information)	*121*	*111*	*107*	*130*
*Parties***				
Two	60	37	50	48
More than two	40	63	50	52
N (of cases with information)	*121*	*111*	*107*	*130*
Stakes				
Less than $500,000	71	60	62	78
$500,000+	29	40	38	22
N (of cases with information)	*89*	*88*	*72*	*94*
*Complexity****				
High	10	22	8	8
Medium	63	49	48	44
Low	26	30	44	49
N (of cases with information)	*114*	*105*	*98*	*105*
*Difficulty in party relations**				
High	15	23	15	18
Medium	21	36	34	24
Low	63	41	52	57
N (of cases with information)	*112*	*105*	*95*	*103*

Note. Chi-square tests of significance for differences across courts: *** = $p < 0.001$, ** = $p < 0.01$, * = $p < 0.05$.
Source. RAND ADR database. The case-level variables shown here were constructed by RAND from a mix of court records and judge and attorney survey data.

shown in Table 6, OK(W)'s program was more likely than other programs to mediate torts, and TX(S) and PA(E) were more likely than other programs to mediate cases other than torts and contracts. TX(S)'s mediated cases were particularly likely to involve more than two parties, and TX(S) and OK(W) were both more likely to mediate cases viewed by lawyers and judges as complex. TX(S)'s mediated cases were particularly likely to involve parties whose relationships were viewed by the attorneys or judge as problematic.[65] In TX(S) and NY(S), cases reaching hearing included a higher proportion of high-monetary-stakes disputes, compared to OK(W) or PA(E). (The latter differences are not quite large enough to be statistically significant.) Additional tabulations, not presented here, indicate that TX(S) also has a higher proportion of cases reaching hearing that were removed from state court (another likely indicator of contentiousness among the parties), relative to the other courts.

Differences in the effects of mediation culture might be obscured by these differences in case mix across mediation.

Keeping in mind these differences in program and caseload characteristics, I now turn to the question: Is there any evidence of differences in dispute resolution outcomes related to whether the dominant mediation paradigm is facilitative or evaluative? I examine four sets of outcomes: efficiency (Table 7), case outcome evaluations (Table 8), relational outcomes (Table 9), and process evaluations (Table 10).

1. Efficiency

Comparing cases referred to mediation and comparable cases *not* referred within each court, RAND found no statistically significant differences in the most commonly used measures of ADR's effects on efficiency, average time to disposition, or lawyer hours spent on cases. (Recall that RAND used record data and lawyer reports of actual hours, not lawyers' subjective assessments of time and cost savings.) But, Table 7 shows that the rate of settlement attributed to mediation[66] was substantially lower in PA(E), the apparently most evaluative program, compared to the other three districts. But the rate of settlement attributed to mediation was higher in NY(S) than in OK(W) or TX(S), the apparently more facilitative.

How likely is it that the difference in settlement success across programs is explained by differences in mediation paradigm culture rather than other differences in program features and case mix? Recall that while PA(E) refers cases to mediation very early in the litigation process (a factor that some argue militates against settlement), OK(W) refers cases almost as early, and its settlement rate is substantially higher than PA(E)'s. And PA(E)'s case mix does not contain a high proportion of complex cases or cases with difficult party relationships, which might be especially difficult to settle, relative to the other courts. Moreover, additional analyses, controlling for case type and complexity (not presented here), find the same pattern of settlement rates across courts, for high- and low-complexity cases, and for cases where party relationships were and were not reported as problematic.

Table 7 shows that attorneys' *subjective* evaluations of the effects of mediation on time to disposition and costs also vary significantly across courts. PA(E) lawyers are least likely to attribute time and cost savings to mediation. Additional analyses, not shown here, indicate that among those cases where mediation was reported to have settled the case, there is far less difference in attorneys' assessments of time and cost savings across the courts, suggesting that it is the perceived success of a program in settling cases (or lack thereof) that is linked to

TABLE 7. Efficiency-Related Outcomes, CJRA Pilot Mediation Programs (Mediated Cases Only)

	OK(W) (%)	TX(S) (%)	NY(S) (%)	PA(E) (%)
*Did the case settle as a result of mediation?****				
Yes	59	60	73	24
No	41	40	27	76
N (of cases with information)	*121*	*111*	*107*	*130*
*What effect did mediation have on time to disposition?****				
Decreased	63	59	56	25
No effect	30	30	26	64
Increased	7	11	18	11
N (of lawyers responding)	*106*	*107*	*70*	*74*
*What effect did mediation have on costs?****				
Decreased	60	51	54	22
No effect	22	18	23	53
Increased	18	31	23	24
N (of lawyers responding)	*115*	*112*	*76*	*78*

Note. Chi-square tests of significance: *** = $p < 0.001$, ** = $p < 0.01$, * = $p < 0.05$.
Source. RAND CJRA-ADR database.

assessments of time and cost savings, rather than the dominant mediation paradigm. While this may seem logical, it merits further comment: RAND's experimental analysis suggests that cases referred to mediation do not, in fact, resolve themselves more quickly or with less expense, compared to cases that are not referred. Hence, it seems likely that the subjective assessment reported here reflects a cognitive bias. When cases settle at or quite closely connected with the mediation session, lawyers *believe* that there has been a gain in efficiency, probably because they compare their time and expense to the likely costs of trial, rather than looking to the cost of settlement without mediation as their benchmark.

2. Case Outcomes

RAND found that, within three of the four pilot courts, cases referred to mediation were more likely than comparable nonreferred cases to result in a monetary transfer (rather than other pretrial disposition). RAND found no statistically significant differences between cases referred to mediation and nonreferred cases in the average size of monetary outcomes (Kakalik *et al.*, 1997b:40–41).

Table 8 displays attorneys' views of the fairness of mediation outcomes and how satisfactory they were for their clients. The distributions of attorneys' assessments across the four programs are roughly the same, and we see the same patterns when we examine different subsets of cases, including those said to be more complex and those said to have more problematic party relationships. Moreover, when we examine the subset of attorneys whose cases are reported to have settled as a result of mediation—where we would most expect to see qualitative differences in outcomes linked to the mediation process—we also find no consistent pattern of differences in assessments of outcome fairness or outcome satisfaction across districts. Judging by these data, differences in mediation paradigm do not appear to have strong consequences for attorneys' evaluations of outcomes. (Note that litigants' outcome assessments might differ; we do not analyze those data here, because the sample sizes are very small.)

TABLE 8. Case Outcome Evaluations, CJRA Pilot Mediation Programs (Mediated Cases Only)

	OK(W) (%)	TX(S) (%)	NY(S) (%)	PA(E) (%)
How satisfied were you with the outcome for your party(ies)? (N.S.)				
Very satisfied	43	41	37	44
Somewhat satisfied	34	33	33	27
Neutral or dissatisfied	24	26	29	28
N (of lawyers responding)	*133*	*130*	*82*	*110*
How fair ... was the outcome for your party(ies)? (N.S.)				
Very fair	50	48	48	51
Somewhat fair	38	39	30	25
Unfair	12	13	22	24
N (of lawyers responding)	*116*	*109*	*75*	*61*

Note. Chi-square tests of significance: *** = $p < 0.001$, ** = $p < 0.01$, * = $p < 0.05$., N.S., not significant.
Source. RAND CJRA-ADR database.

TABLE 9. Relational Outcomes, CJRA Pilot Mediation Programs (Mediated Cases Only)

	OK(W) (%)	TX(S) (%)	NY(S) (%)	PA(E) (%)
Was mediation ... helpful in improving relations between the parties? (N.S.)				
Helpful	29	34	22	27
Not	71	66	78	73
N (of lawyers responding)	*118*	*115*	*75*	*76*
Difference between lawyers' assessments of relationship difficulties at the beginning and end of case (N.S.)				
Decreased	10	13	18	11
No effect	84	78	76	79
Increased	6	10	6	10
N (of lawyers responding)	*132*	*133*	*85*	*115*

Note. Chi-square tests of significance for differences: *** = $p < 0.001$, ** = $p < 0.01$, * = $p < 0.05$., N.S., not significant.
Source. RAND CJRA-ADR database.

3. Relational Outcomes

Different mediation paradigms might product the same overall assessments of outcomes, and nonetheless lead to different assessments of mediation's effects on relationships between the parties. But, as shown in Table 9, attorneys' assessments of the effect of mediation on parties' relationships do not differ much across these programs.[67] Moreover, these patterns are replicated among high-complexity cases and among cases with more problematic party relationships, where practitioners have suggested we might find more of an impact of mediation paradigm. (Note again that litigants' assessments might differ.)

4. Process Evaluations

Previous research on court-connected ADR programs has found that litigants whose cases are arbitrated (in nonbinding programs) give higher fairness ratings to the litigation process than those whose cases are settled, by bilateral negotiation or with the assistance of a settlement judge (Lind *et al.*, 1989). Because of its greater focus on party participation and party expression, we might expect that litigants whose cases were mediated in a facilitative program would give higher fairness ratings to that process than those whose cases were mediated in an evaluative program. Table 10 presents *attorneys'* assessments of the fairness of mediation and how satisfactory it was to their clients. Although attorneys' views may not accurately reflect their clients', their views of process are nonetheless worth examining.

As Table 10 shows, attorneys' fairness assessments are not very different across the four programs, but there are statistically significant differences in attorneys' assessments of how satisfactory mediation was for their clients. OK(W)'s program garners the highest ratings of satisfaction, and PA(E)'s the least.

How likely is it that differences in process satisfaction reflect greater satisfaction with facilitative mediation? Recall that OK(W) and TX(S) are both voluntary programs, and both are judged more satisfactory, overall, than the two mandatory programs, suggesting that this

Table 10. Process Evaluations, CJRA Pilot Mediation Programs (Mediated Cases Only)

	OK(W) (%)	TX(S) (%)	NY(S) (%)	PA(E) (%)
How fair ... was mediation for your party(ies)? (N.S.)				
Very fair	70	59	59	59
Somewhat fair	24	33	28	36
Unfair	6	7	13	5
N (of lawyers responding)	*116*	*109*	*75*	*61*
*How satisfied were you with mediation for your party(ies)?***				
Very satisfied	53	40	46	33
Somewhat satisfied	26	28	13	21
Neutral or dissatisfied	21	32	42	46
N (of lawyers responding)	*120*	*116*	*77*	*70*

Note. Chi-square tests of significance for differences: *** = $p < 0.001$, ** = $p < 0.01$, * = $p < 0.05$., N.S., not significant.
Source. RAND CJRA-ADR database.

factor might partially explain the differences observed. Perhaps more importantly, additional analyses show that among attorneys whose cases are reported to have been settled as a result of mediation, satisfaction with the mediation process is far more similar across the four programs. In other words, differences in *attorneys'* process satisfaction are more likely linked to whether the process led to a settlement, than to whether the dominant mediation paradigm was facilitative or evaluative. [Research on litigants' assessments of their litigation experience indicates that they perform separate evaluations of process and outcome and may give contrasting ratings to the two, depending on how they view the quality of the process (Lind *et al.*, 1989).]

5. Paradigm or Behavior?

My additional analyses of RAND data find few clear differences across the four CJRA pilot mediation programs. Moreover, those differences that I do find appear to reflect differences in the programs' success at settling cases, and the relationship between that outcome and whether the dominant mediation paradigm is facilitative or evaluative is ambiguous.

Although I have argued that the programs can be arrayed along a continuum from facilitative to evaluative, I earlier presented data (see Table 3) indicating that among mediated cases *within* each of the programs, there are some in which the third-party neutral is reported to have offered a personal assessment of the cases' value, and others in which none of the actors report this taking place. Perhaps these differences within programs blur the distinctions that I have suggested are present among programs in the dominant mediation paradigm.

Table 11 presents data relevant to exploring this possibility. For each of the variables discussed above, Table 11 shows the difference in results for cases in which evaluation, reportedly, did and did not take place. Note that the sample sizes are extremely small. Although I report statistical tests of significance, readers should focus their attention on the numerical patterns, as differences observed in these data might not reach statistical significance because of the small size of the samples.

Keeping in mind that the samples for this analysis are very small, there are few if any

Table 11. Dispute Resolution Outcomes, CJRA Pilot Mediation Programs, by Whether Neutral Evaluated the Case (Mediated Cases Only)

	OK(W)		TX(S)		NY(S)		PA(E)	
	No %	Yes %	No %	Yes %	No %	Yes %	No %	Yes %
Did the case settle as a result of mediation?								
Yes	47	85	76	54	72	72	29	28
No	53	15***	24	46*	28	28	71	72
N (of cases with information)	*66*	*40*	*45*	*52*	*36*	*58*	*28*	*50*
How satisfied were you with the outcome for your party(ies)?								
Very satisfied	37	47	41	41	44	33	39	55
Somewhat satisfied	41	26	36	31	22	38	35	21
Neutral or dissatisfied	23	26	23	28	34	28	26	22
N (of lawyers responding)	*65*	*62*	*52*	*67*	*22*	*59*	*31*	*56*
How fair was the outcome ... for your party(ies)?								
Very fair	44	56	53	45	55	43	60	55
Less than very fair	56	44	47	55	45	57	40	45
N (of lawyers responding)	*65*	*58*	*50*	*65*	*22*	*57*	*30*	*53*
Was mediation ... helpful or detrimental in improving relations between the parties?								
Helpful	29	27	35	33	20	22	15	34
No effect or detrimental	71	73	65	67	80	78	85	65
N (of lawyers responding)	*58*	*59*	*49*	*64*	*20*	*55*	*26*	*49*
Differential between lawyers' assessments of relationship difficulties at the beginning and end of case								
Decreased	12	7	12	14	11	20	3	9
No effect								
Increased	2	9	14	6	9	5	6	11
N (of lawyers responding)	*64*	*61*	*52*	*70*	*24*	*58*	*34*	*56*
How fair ... was mediation for your party(ies)?								
Very fair	72	68	66	55	59	58	60	61
Less than very fair	28	32	34	45	41	42	40	39
N (of lawyers responding)	*59*	*58*	*40*	*59*	*21*	*53*	*15*	*44*
How satisfied were you with mediation for your party(ies)?								
Very satisfied	53	54	51	32*	43	47	43	27
Somewhat satisfied	26	26	17	34	17	10	4	27
Neutral or dissatisfied	21	20	32	34	39	43	52	41
N (of lawyers responding)	*61*	*60*	*48*	*65*	*51*	*55*	*21*	*47*

Note. Chi-square tests of significance for differences within courts: *** = $p < 0.001$, ** = $p < 0.01$, * = $p < 0.05$. Other differences not significant.
Source. RAND CJRA-ADR database.

observable patterns in these data. A higher proportion of cases in OK(W) settled when mediators did not offer evaluations than when they did, but in TX(S) the opposite pattern prevails, and in the two other programs there is no discernible difference at all in settlement rates by whether the case was evaluated or not. Attorneys seem somewhat more satisfied with the outcome in OK(W) and in PA(E) when mediators evaluate cases than when they don't. The difference is large in PA(E)—where attorneys probably expected mediators to evaluate cases—but the sample size there is extremely small. There is no general pattern with regard to perceptions of outcome fairness. Nor are there discernible differences within most of the programs, by whether the case was evaluated or not, with regard to perceived effects of mediation on party relationships, or perceptions of process fairness. In TX(S) attorneys seem more satisfied with mediation overall when mediators did not offer evaluations than when they did. Recall with regard to PA(E) data that many cases were not resolved at mediation, whether or not the mediator offered a case evaluation.

In sum, these data do not provide any additional support for the general notion that nonevaluative (facilitative) mediation has better—or different—consequences, other than the possible greater effectiveness of evaluative mediation at settling cases.

Because of the small sample sizes, as well as possible selection bias into modes of mediation [e.g., because certain attorneys, with certain types of cases might seek evaluation (facilitation) or some mediators might selectively use different approaches], these data do not demonstrate that there are no differences in the outcomes of facilitative versus evaluative mediation. But they do not strengthen the empirical case for such differences.

F. CONCLUSION

Since the inception of the current era of ADR, theorists have debated the virtues of different mediation goals and strategies. Recent debate on civil legal dispute resolution has focused on facilitative versus evaluative mediation paradigms. Anecdotal and systematic observational data on mediation practices have identified differences in mediators' goals and approaches, but there is little systematic information on the relative prevalence of different mediation paradigms in the civil legal environment. Moreover, there has been little empirical analysis of the consequences of implementing different paradigms for civil disputes and disputants.

The accumulation of empirical information about the relationships between mediation practice and outcomes has been complicated by the variety of settings in which dispute resolution takes place, as well as the variety of disputes that have been the subject of mediation within settings. Because mediation often takes place outside of public dispute resolution fora and because one of its defining features is privacy, access to parties and records is constrained. Moreover, because mediation programs are often adopted after great debate and investment of financial and political resources, program administrators and practitioners are often unenthusiastic about mounting true experiments, which require assigning cases randomly to mediation and nonmediation conditions. In the court context, concerns about due process may also impede experimentation.

Data on the use of mediation for civil disputes that are resolved outside of court are hard to come by, but what little data there are suggest that the proportion of cases assigned to mediation is a small but growing fraction of the total civil dispute universe. Increasing numbers of courts have adopted mediation programs in recent years, but the limited available information suggests that usage by civil litigants is low, particularly when courts leave it to clients (or their attorneys) to volunteer for mediation, rather than requiring it.

When mediation moves into the court system, the debate over appropriate paradigms becomes part of a larger debate about the need for and ways of achieving reductions in court delay and public and private litigation costs. Mediation rhetoric expands to include efficiency claims, as well as claims concerning the quality of mediation outcomes, including long-term effects on disputants' relationships, and effects on disputants' abilities to understand and deal with difficulties that arise in their relationships with others. Often efficiency claims and evaluative paradigms dominate.

Recent experiments with mediation of civil disputes undertaken under the CJRA have produced mixed results. As analysts have found in studies of other ADR programs, most attorneys who participate in mediation as advocates or neutrals are positive about their experiences, and many of them are enthusiastic. Few suggest that programs should be abandoned. But the evidence to support either efficiency claims or claims of improved quality of outcomes and relationships is thin.

Some CJRA programs did not incorporate features that would permit strong inferences about the effects of mediation. Researchers analyzing those programs must rely on the reports of those whose cases were referred to the program, an inadequate basis for assessing program consequences. For those programs that incorporated experimental designs that permit stronger inferences about consequences, researchers have found no evidence that cases referred to mediation had different outcomes than cases that were not referred.

Criticisms of these unwelcome findings have centered around the character of the mediation programs studied, especially whether they were facilitative or evaluative. Because the research was not designed to systematically assess the consequences of different mediation paradigms, the data that address this issue are suggestive, rather than conclusive. Reviewing previous observational studies, analyses of CJRA mediation programs conducted by the Federal Judicial Center and RAND, and results of additional analyses that I have conducted, I conclude:

- Legal practitioners, including judges and attorneys, generally prefer evaluative mediation paradigms for resolving civil disputes. This preference likely reflects the belief that most civil legal disputes are wholly or mostly distributive in nature, and a general disinterest or disinclination for broader party (client) participation in dispute resolution.
- To date, there is no evidence that introducing ADR, including mediation, into the litigation process *after a suit is filed*, will consistently result in lower transaction costs and shorter time to disposition, compared to settling cases without third-party involvement. Nor is there evidence that facilitative mediation is more likely than evaluative mediation to produce such results, or that the converse is true. Where court-connected mediation programs result in shorter time to disposition, the explanation appears to lie in the combination of early referral times and high settlement rates. Just how early is *too* early to achieve high settlement rates is unclear from the available data.
- Available data do not provide evidence that facilitative mediation has more positive effects than evaluative mediation on party relationships, or on disputants' own abilities to manage their disputes and to understand themselves and others.

The evidence on the final point is thin, because empirical analysts have not, to date, done a good job of characterizing pre- and postdispute relations among the parties or determining whether mediation is truly facilitative, rather than evaluative.[68] In part, this failure on the part of empiricists may result from a weakness in the theoretical literature concerning types of disputes and disputing relationships. Without a stronger theoretical framework for distinguishing types of disputes and dispute resolution paradigms, empirical analysts are left with inadequate tools for testing claims that particular types of paradigms are more or less effective for particular types of disputes. On a more practical note, empirical research on the effects of mediation on disputants themselves is impeded by the difficulty of locating disputants (as opposed to their attorneys) from court records, by attorneys' unwillingness to provide access to their clients, and by ADR providers and some disputants' desires to maintain the privacy that mediation offers as one of its prime features.

As discussed elsewhere in this volume, procedural justice researchers have found that individual disputants separately evaluate procedure and outcomes and that satisfaction with dispute resolution is related to both (Tyler and Lind, this volume). Experimental and field study data suggest different explanations for individuals' procedural justice evaluations, including preferences for control over process, opportunities for "voice," and perceptions that one has been treated with dignity. Recently, Lind has proposed that individuals may use fairness perceptions as a "heuristic" for judging the likelihood of obtaining a fair outcome and, hence, deciding whether to comply with the outcome of dispute resolution.

What factors determine individuals' perceptions of the fairness of mediation processes and whether and how such perceptions are related to mediation paradigm are currently unknown. In their contribution to this volume, Tyler and Lind discuss the "discourse and consensus" theories of procedural justice, which hold that disputants can reach common norms about outcome fairness by communicating their views and needs. Tyler and Lind suggest that the increasing popularity of mediation in the United States may derive from its application of discourse theory. But, as I have shown, mediation *in practice*, at least as applied to civil money disputes, may provide little opportunity for disputants to engage in discourse and consensus processes. If mediation is promoted to parties as facilitative or transformative, offering opportunities for participation, communication, and consensus building, but is experienced as simply another form of hard bargaining, under the control of lawyers and other experts, individuals may feel that the process has been falsely represented and respond negatively. Conversely, if early judgments of procedural fairness have a persistent effect on ultimate judgments, as Lind suggests, then the initial phase of evaluative mediation—with its call for opening presentations and appeal to parties to find common ground—may overwhelm the later reality of distributive bargaining between the lawyers, to produce enthusiastic individual assessments of mediation fairness.

Evaluative mediators focus on obtaining a negotiated outcome of a legal dispute within the "shadow of the law." Such outcomes are usually distributive in nature, as are the outcomes delivered by adjudication. Facilitative mediators focus on helping parties obtain solutions to problems that maximize joint gains. Such outcomes are likely to include a mix of money and other agreements that could not be imposed by a judge. Distributive justice research, reviewed in a separate chapter of this volume, teaches us that individuals' preferences for different dispute outcomes are shaped by situational factors, which in turn are mediated by attributions (Hegtvedt and Cook, this volume). In some circumstances, disputants might prefer the sharp "win–lose" outcome produced by evaluative mediation and adjudication; in others, the same disputants might prefer an outcome that maximizes relational gains, which is more likely to result from facilitative mediation. But mediation practitioners generally seem to espouse one or another of these perspectives, rather than seeking to identify parties' preferences for particular sorts of outcomes.

Contemporary ADR enthusiasts espouse facilitative and transformative models of mediation for the resolution of civil legal disputes. Research suggesting that mediation may have little effect on the costs of dispute resolution or time to disposition has been met with arguments that researchers have not looked at "good" mediation programs, and have not measured the right outcomes of instituting mediation in the legal arena. But the available empirical evidence suggests that mediation in practice is generally evaluative, offering little opportunity for individuals to engage in discourse or participate in shaping outcomes, and that outcomes are largely distributive. Although public policy has shifted sharply away from adjudication of legal disputes and toward negotiation, problem solving, and mediation, we know little about how individuals assess the procedural fairness and distributive justice of these forms of dispute resolution, what expectations they bring to these processes, and what their procedural preferences might be if they better understood the nature of what is being offered to them. Before we can decide what "good" mediation is, we need to know more about what mediation is doing and to and for whom.

G. ENDNOTES

1. I would like to acknowledge James Alfini's article, entitled "Trashing, Bashing, and Hashing It Out: Is This the End of 'Good Mediation'?" (Alfini, 1991), as the inspiration for this title. Professor Alfini, in turn, credits mediator Albie Davis as the source of the "good mediation" rubric.
2. Judge John W. Ford, Professor of Dispute Resolution, Stanford Law School and Senior Fellow, RAND Institute for Civil Justice. I am grateful to RAND colleague Nicholas M. Pace for assistance with data analysis. Support for this project was provided in part by the Hewlett Foundation Conflict Resolution Theory Development Center program.
3. Although much of the literature on ADR is present-focused, several commentators have noted that ADR is scarcely a new phenomenon. Carrington (1996) (comparing current motivations for ADR, in part, to those of the Puritan era in the United States); Schuyler (1995), "Coercive Harmony: An Anthropologist and a Former Federal Judge Debate the Purpose of Mandatory ADR (quoting Laura Nader, comparing ADR movement to efforts by fifteenth-century colonial power to "pacify natives").
4. For example, arbitration proceedings usually are guided by relaxed rules of evidence, permitting decisions to be made "on the papers," without the necessity of calling fact witnesses. Discovery may be subject to decision by the arbitrator. An arbitration clause may specify that the substantive law of a given jurisdiction may apply. But some arbitration programs apply substantive norms derived from industry custom. See Bernstein (1992).
5. The American Arbitration Association (AAA), whose name used to signal its devotion to a particular method of alternative dispute resolution, recently adopted a mediation program and changed the name of its house publication from *The Arbitration Journal* to the *Dispute Resolution Journal* to demonstrate its interest in alternatives to arbitration. Some observers have attributed the AAA's actions as a response to competition from newer ADR organizations, such as the Center for Public Resources, which promote mediation.

   An increase in court adoption of mediation programs and abandonment of arbitration have been alleged in discussions at recent judicial and bar conferences. A recent sourcebook on alternative dispute resolution in the federal courts, jointly published by the Federal Judicial Center and the Center for Public Resources, asserts: "Mediation has emerged as the primary ADR process in the federal district courts." The sourcebook notes that "(Non-binding) Arbitration is the second most frequently authorized ADR program, but falls well short of mediation in the number of courts that have implemented it." A footnote points out that Congress has limited adoption of arbitration to 20 federal district courts. No such limitation pertains to court mediation programs. See Plapinger and Stienstra (1996:6). In their study of three ADR demonstration programs, undertaken under the Civil Justice Reform Act of 1990 (CJRA), the Federal Judicial Center found evidence of growth in court-connected mediation programs and decline in nonbinding court-annexed arbitration. See Stienstra *et al.* (1997).

   Because there are no comprehensive statistics on cases that use alternative dispute resolution mechanisms in the private sector, the relative popularity of arbitration and mediation are currently unknown. A recent RAND Institute for Civil Justice study of the private ADR market in Los Angeles County found that 58% of disputes processed by private ADR providers were arbitrated, 22% were mediated, and the remainder were handled with a mix of "private judging" and what the authors termed "voluntary settlement conferences." See Rolph *et al.* (1994). A survey of 528 Fortune 1000 corporations conducted in 1996 by the Cornell/PERC Institute on Conflict Resolution found that 78% reported having used arbitration and 87% reported having used mediation. More than 60% said they generally included mediation clauses in contracts, while 82% said they included arbitration clauses. See Donzhue and Deinhardt (1997).
6. The multiplicity of meanings of mediation has often been noted. See, e.g., McEwen and Maiman (1984).
7. On the spread of court-mandated ADR, see, e.g., Katz (1993), Menkel-Meadow (1991), Resnik (1995), Sherman (1993).
8. See, e.g., Society for Professionals in Dispute Resolution (undated). The state of Florida, which has one of the most comprehensive mediation statutes in the country, provides, by court rule, for training and certification of

mediators. The Florida Supreme Court publishes a list of certified circuit court (trial court of general jurisdiction) mediators, and has appointed a Mediation Training Review Board, charged with enforcing standards. See Dispute Resolution Center (1995), Florida Dispute Resolution Center (1996).

9. The Civil Justice Reform Act of 1990 required all federal district courts to adopt plans for reducing "congestion and delay" on their civil calendars. Initially, the supporters of the legislation, led by Senator Joseph Biden, then-Chair of the U.S. Senate Judiciary Committee, intended to require courts to adopt specific programs and practices, including alternative dispute resolution, as mechanisms to reduce cost and delay. As a result of a legislative compromise, the final bill did not specify the content of most courts' plans. But 10 districts, denoted as "pilot courts," were required to adopt specific plan provisions for experimental study purposes. Another 10 courts, with similar characteristics to those of the pilot courts, were required to participate in the study as "controls," but were left free to design their own plans for delay and cost reduction. The RAND Institute for Civil Justice was selected by the Administrative Office of the U.S. Courts to conduct the congressionally mandated research evaluation. See Kakalik *et al.* (1997a). The Court Administration and Case Management Committee of the Judicial Conference of the United States, which oversaw the study, asked RAND to undertake a special evaluation of the district courts' ADR efforts. The results of the ADR evaluation are described in Kakalik *et al.* (1997b).
10. In response to the controversy, the ABA Section of Dispute Resolution devoted its entire summer issue to commentary on the RAND Report. See the RAND Report and Federal Court ADR Dispute Resolution Magazine 3(4) (1997). The ABA Section of Litigation also covered the controversy. See *Litig. News* (1997:4–5).
11. See Reuben (1997). While committee deliberations were ongoing, a statement urging public policymakers not to rely on RAND's findings in making decisions on whether to provide continuing financial support for federal court mediation was issued under the aegis of the Center for Public Resources Judicial Project. See "Views on RAND's CJRA Report: Concerns and Recommendations" (1997). An editorial by CPR project director Elizabeth Plapinger, questioning the validity of the study's findings, appeared in the *National Law Journal.* See Plapinger (1997:B18). On the local level, a federal district court committee that had commissioned an evaluation of its mediation program that reached conclusions similar to RAND's was pressed by private providers of mediation not to release its findings (confidential conversation with a member of the local district court CJRA advisory committee). The author attended an academic colloquium on ADR during this period at which RAND's report on the CJRA evaluation was hissed by an audience including eminent judges, practitioners, and ADR scholars.
12. I also do not attempt to review the descriptive or analytic literature on small-claims court mediation, or on community justice centers. Neither of these domains is centrally implicated in the current debate about "good mediation."
13. Mnookin and Korhnhauser (1979). This model of negotiation underlies the prevailing law and economics model of legal dispute resolution. See, e.g., Cooter and Rubinfeld (1989), Danzon and Lillard (1983), Priest and Klein (1984), Shavell (1982). Surveys of civil litigants and individuals' narratives of their experiences in litigation suggest, in contrast, that many legal disputants have nonmonetary interests and goals. See, e.g., Hensler (1998). Procedural justice theory and empirical research indicate that civil litigants care about the nature of the dispute resolution process as well as its outcomes, and that civil litigants' satisfaction with the legal system is a function of their perceptions of process and outcomes. See, e.g., Lind and Tyler (1988), Lind *et al.* (1990). Social scientists who have studied negotiations of minor civil disputes and family law cases have also noted that the shadow of the law may play less of a role in determining outcomes than some legal analysts anticipate. See, e.g., Erlanger, Chambliss, and Melli (1987), Vidmar (1985).
14. On cognitive and social psychological influences on dispute resolution, see Kahneman and Tversky (1995) and Ross (1995).
15. The classic popular articulation of this negotiation theory is Fisher and Uhry (1981).
16. My description of theoretical constructs informing scholarly debate on conflict resolution is incomplete. Other perspective includes, e.g., rights-based and power-based disputing and dispute resolution. I focus here on the evaluative versus facilitative distinction because it has attracted the most recent attention among those concerned with civil legal disputing.
17. Some mediation practitioners and scholars who reject the evaluative mediation paradigm give even more weight to process values, arguing that the measure of mediation's effectiveness is not whether the dispute is resolved, but rather whether the disputants enhance their understanding of their own and other disputants' needs and their ability to manage their lives. See Bush and Folger (1994c). Although this "transformative" view of mediation does not appear to have made great inroads into mediation practice as it applies to civil legal disputes, the language of "empowerment" and "understanding" is an important strand in the discourse in favor of facilitative mediation. See Riskin (1997).
18. The early social science literature on mediation is replete with analytic typologies for sorting mediator styles and tactics. See, e.g., Kolb (1983) (distinguishing "orchestrators" and "deal-makers" among labor mediators);

Kressel and Pruitt (1983:188–195) [proposing a two-dimensional grid for sorting mediators by their degree of assertiveness and the distribution of their "interventions" into "reflexive" (self-referential), "contextual" (relational), and "substantive" (outcome-oriented) categories]; Shapiro, Drieghe, and Brett (1983:109) (finding labor mediators' styles can be distinguished as "deal making" versus "shuttle diplomacy," and that most mediators adopt styles tailored for the dispute at hand).

19. Riskin (1996). An earlier version of Professor Riskin's analysis was published as "Mediator Orientations, Strategies, and Techniques" (1994). Concerning the narrowness or broadness of dispute definitions, recall that broadening the dispute is one technique recommended by facilitative mediators.
20. Professor Riskin himself lightheartedly reviewed the criticism of his critique in a poem, "Mediation Quandaries" (1997).
21. Morris, whose email is "included" in a message from Ginger McCarthy (Altdisres@aol.com), "Re: Morality," July 22, 1997.
22. McCarthy (Altdisres@aol.com), "Re: Morality," July 22, 1997.
23. Rosenthal (rjr@trgnational.com), "re: non-attorney mediators," August 21, 1997.
24. Dana (mti@mediationworks.com), "re: non-attorney mediators," August 22, 1997, on dispute-res@listserv.law.cornell.edu. Note that this comment implicates not only contested paradigms for dispute resolution but also the issue of competition between lawyer and nonlawyer mediators, discussed further below.
25. Faulkner (natnladr@onramp.net), "re: non-attorney mediators," August 22, 1997, on dispute-res@listserv.law.cornell.edu. Mr. Faulkner identifies himself as an "attorney-mediator."
26. Dana (mti@mediationworks.com), "re: non-attorney mediators," August 23, 1997, on dispute-res@listserv.law.cornell.edu. Mr. Dana's comments further indicate that he is not an attorney.
27. Keltner (keltnerj@ucs.orst.edu), "re: attorney-mediators," August 25, 1997, on dispute-res@listserv.law.cornell.edu.
28. For an interesting discussion of disputes among dispute resolution practitioners, see Kobach (1996:410–412).
29. For some empirical information on judicial settlement strategies, see Wall and Rude (1985). Provine (1986) describes variations in judicial settlement strategies, drawing primarily on anecdotal data. Galanter (1985) describes the apparent increase in judicial enthusiasm for settlement, referring to contemporary judicial management literature. See also Rosenthal (1997).
30. Perhaps the best example of the power struggle between nonlawyer and lawyer mediators has taken place in Florida, since its adoption, by statute, of mandatory mediation for civil damage suits. Under the original Florida Supreme Court rules, non-family law civil suits brought in Florida's trial courts of general jurisdiction could only be mediated by experienced lawyers or retired judges; later amendments to the Florida rules provide for narrow exceptions to this requirement. The Florida requirements led to a nationwide controversy within the mediation practitioner community. According to Professor Alfini, they also "spawned" a "mediation industry populated by experienced trial lawyers and retired judges" (Alfini, 1991).

    Of federal district courts that adopted mediation programs under the Civil Justice Reform Act, only 10 explicitly provide for nonattorney mediators (Plapinger and Stienstra, 1992:Table 4).

    In contrast to civil case mediation, in most jurisdictions, divorce mediation has long been the province of nonlawyer mediators. Therapists and other mental health professionals account for close to 80% of privately employed divorce mediators and about 90% of publicly employed mediators. See Milne and Folberg (1988) (citing a survey by the Divorce Mediation Research Project). In some courts, lawyer-mediators are limited to dealing with financial matters, with custody and visitation issues assigned to mental health professionals. Lawyer-mediators are drawn primarily from domestic relations law. Divorce mediators distinguish between "therapeutic" and "structured" approaches to mediation, the first typically the province of the mental health professional and the second, the province of the lawyer (Milne and Folberg, 1988:14–15). The distinction is similar (albeit not identical) to the evaluative–facilitative distinction as defined in the broader debate over mediation paradigms.
31. Hastings (tinamediate@mindspring.com), "Re: non-attorney mediators," August 20, 1997, on dispute-res@listserv.law.cornell. edu. Ms. Hastings identifies herself as a "Mediator (full time)."
32. Bruce (medarb@gdi.net), "Re: non-attorney mediators," August 24, 1997, on dispute-res@listserv.law.cornell.edu.
33. Rosenthal (rjr@TRGnational.com), "non-attorney mediators," August 23, 1997.
34. The San Francisco Community Boards program, for example, "found only a limited market for its services" in the neighborhoods that it served. See DuBow and McEwen (1993). Unlike other neighborhood justice centers founded in the same era that turned to the criminal courts for referrals [see, e.g., Felstiner and Williams (1980)], SFCB depended on residents to come to its offices with their disputes.

    A RAND study of the private market for dispute resolution services in Los Angeles County estimated that in 1993 private providers attracted roughly 5% of civil damage disputes in that jurisdiction (Rolph, 1994),

Studies of court-annexed nonbinding arbitration have generally found that the percentage of cases in voluntary programs is substantially lower than the percentage of cases in court-mandated programs (Rauma and Krafka, 1994).

35. Marsh (ethesis@aol.com), "re: mental health professionals," August 16, 1997.

36. For example, the nonprofit, privately funded Center for Public Resources, which promotes the use of ADR especially for business disputes, collaborated with the Federal Judicial Center, the publicly funded research and judicial education arm of the federal judiciary, on a sourcebook for judges and lawyers. See Plapinger and Stienstra (1992) (described as "a joint project" of the two organizations). CPR earlier cosponsored along with the Federal Judicial Center, the American Bar Association Litigation Section, and the Harvard Law School a National ADR Institute for Federal Judges (November 12–13, 1993, Harvard Law School).

    The American Arbitration Association, acting on the recommendation of a special mass tort task force, is assembling and training panels of neutrals to assist judges in resolving mass tort claims. See Feinberg (1997).

37. Grillo (1991:1550). Drawing on observational data from their study of family mediation in the United Kingdom, David Greatbatch and Robert Dingwall argue that mediators "regularly" use a "selective facilitation" strategy to shape the outcomes of disputes (Greatbatch and Dingwall, 1989:617).

38. Delgado *et al.* (1985:1375). LaFree and Rack (1996) find limited empirical support for the proposition that minority group members and women are disadvantaged by mediation.

39. For an example of efficiency claims for mediation in the small-claims court context, see Raitt *et al.* (1993) ("Numerous factors have led to the development of mediation programs in small claims courts.... First, there are the cost savings for the courts themselves" at 61.) For a review of empirical findings on the efficiency outcomes of mediation, see Kressel and Pruitt (1985) and Kakalik *et al.* (1997b:9–13).

40. Annual Conference of State Court Chief Justices, "Townhall Meeting on ADR," July 30, 1997, Cleveland, Ohio. The author was in the audience and noted Chief Justice Wagner's remarks.

41. There are, however, numerous articles and monographs describing and distinguishing mediator styles, some of which are highly qualitative and a smaller number of which are empirically based. For an example of the former directed to practitioners, see Honeyman (1988). For examples of the latter, see Kolb (1983) and Silbey and Merry (1986).

42. I limit my review to mediation of civil damage suits in trial courts of general jurisdiction. For a discussion of mediation practices in domestic violence cases, including a review of the empirical literature, see Fischer, Vidmar, and Ellis (1993). Fischer *et al.* argue that the ideology of mediation, including its conflict mitigating goal, future orientation, participatory norms, and practices, including caucuses and drafting agreements, are inappropriate for domestic violence cases.

    For discussions and analyses of small-claims mediation, see, e.g., McEwen and Maiman (1984), Vidmar (1984), and Goerdt (1992). Summarizing small-claims court mediation practices, Vidmar writes: "[T]he process cannot be described as 'deep' mediation since few attempts are made at conciliation or at the exploration of non-legal issues that might underlie the dispute ... attempts by either party to stray beyond the legal case at hand are usually cut short. There is frequent discussion of how the case will probably be decided at trial. The hearings are not, however, totally legalistic. The referee may attempt to cajole the parties to 'split the difference' " (1984:523).

43. This conclusion is supported by anecdotal data shared by participants at recent conferences that I have attended: Virtually without exception, these mediator-participants bemoan what they perceive to be the dominance of the evaluative model in court-connected mediation.

44. This history is drawn from Alfini (1991:50–59).

45. This discussion of Wisconsin's medical mediation program is drawn from Meschievitz (1991).

46. Office of the State Courts (1989), quoted in Meschievitz (1991) at Fn 33.

47. Clarke *et al.* (1995:10). However, in one session, the client took charge of the mediation, ignoring his attorney—who is described as having been retained just a few days before the mediation.

48. Brett, Barsness, and Goldberg (1996). Brett *et al.* also provide empirical data on the outcomes of mediation.

49. The response rate to the individual surveys was a disappointing 16%. But because questionnaires were sent to all of the litigants and attorneys involved, the case-level response rate was 50%. The analysis is based on case-level data constructed from the individual questionnaires. The report does not include any discussion of nonresponse bias (Brett *et al.*, 1996:9–10).

50. Another quarter were required to use ADR by a contractual provision. The remainder of the cases reached the provider through various voluntary channels (Brett *et al.*, 1996:Figure 5).

51. Brett *et al.* (1996:Figure 4). When ADR was required by contract, arbitration was usually the procedure specified. When parties volunteered for ADR or were referred by the court, they usually chose mediation (Brett *et al.*, 1996:14).

52. Stienstra *et al.* (1997:Table 64, p. 185). The FJC researchers were only able to ascertain the ADR choice for 961 of

the total 2555 cases who were permitted to select their own ADR option. The FJC indicates that most of the remaining cases probably did not participate in any ADR program. The percentages in the text are my calculations, based on the raw frequency distribution for the 961 cases.

53. Stienstra *et al.* (1997:188). The FJC report is a bit ambiguous on this point. In a brief paragraph discussing variations from the general pattern, the only finding that is reported that is specific to mediation (rather than to the combination of all ADR procedures in that court) is that attorneys whose cases were mediated (either by choice or by judicial reference) were more likely than other attorneys to select as a very or somewhat important factor the facilitatively oriented statement: "The ADR process would permit more flexibility in finding a solution than the regular litigation process would." Eighty percent of those whose cases were mediated ranked this factor as important, compared to 74% overall.
54. Stienstra *et al.* (1997:22). Note that if parties choose to select a different neutral, they must pay market rates for that person's services. The court recruited and trained 75 neutrals for this purpose (Stienstra *et al.*, 1997:225). Participation in some form of ADR is mandatory, except for those cases excluded for purposes of the randomized experiment.
55. All 20 courts provided for voluntary or mandatory ADR, including mediation. In 14 of these courts, mediation programs handled less than 1% of the civil caseload, during the study period. In 4 courts, mediation programs handled between 1 and 5% of the caseload; in another 2 courts, mediation programs handled more than 5% of civil cases (Kakalik *et al.*, 1997b:Table 2.1, p. 14). Some criticism of RAND's study has suggested that RAND selection criteria were somehow biased against finding "good mediation" (Feliciano, 1997). In fact, the courts included in RAND's study represent about one-third of the federal district court caseload and judgeships and comprise a statistically representative sample of regional, size, and caseload differences within the federal court system (Kakalik *et al.*, 1997a:7–22). Other critics question the wisdom of RAND's limiting its study to programs with substantial caseloads. See, e.g., Erickson (1991). RAND's threshold requirement seems quite modest, however. And, however effective they might be in resolving the cases that they handle, programs that deal with less than 150 cases annually cannot have a large impact on most courts' caseloads. Some critics also question RAND's decision to limit its ADR research to mediation and ENE (Erickson, 1991). However, as RAND explains, court-annexed arbitration has been extensively studied over the past two decades, and other court-connected ADR programs have caseloads that are even smaller than those of the mediation and ENE programs RAND studied.
56. Discussion with RAND analysts.
57. According to RAND analysts who conducted interviews in PA(E), the primary purpose of that district's mediation program was to obtain an early settlement. If settlement could not be achieved, the district felt that the program could serve an important secondary purpose of narrowing the issues in dispute and focusing discovery on these. Hence, mediation in PA(E) seemed to have aspects of ENE, as implemented in other districts. (Additional information provided by RAND analysts.)
58. Galanter and Cahill (1994) review the empirical literature on outcomes of court-connected mediation, focusing on judicial settlement conferences. Referring to claims that settlement might produce more "normative richness" and "inventiveness" (which they find in what I have termed the facilitative mediation literature), they say that they have not found any attempts to "verify [such claims] by systematic observation" (1994:1372–1377).
59. For a discussion of the uses of experimental designs for determining the effects of changes in court procedures and practices, see Federal Judicial Center (1981).
60. For a discussion of the challenges of conducting civil justice research without a sound infrastructure and financial base, see Galanter, Garth, Hensler, and Zemans (1994) and Hensler (1994).
61. Brett *et al.* (1996:16–18). Brett *et al.* present data suggesting that these results are not solely a function of self-selection of cases into the different ADR processes (1996:18–19). With the exception of resolution rates, Brett *et al.* do not report differences in outcomes for interests-based mediation and mediation with an advisory opinion.
62. It should be noted that, in aggregate terms, NY(S) spent the most on its mediation program, about $200,000 annually, while the other three courts all spent between $50,000 and $70,000. The pattern of differences in per case costs reflects not only the differences in total expenditures but also the size of the program caseloads. OK(W)'s costs are high because it had the smallest annual number of referrals. In the aggregate, it spent only a couple of thousand dollars more than PA(E), but the latter program's caseload was about three and one-half times the size of OK(W) (Kakalik *et al.*, 1997b:Table 4.11, at 39).
63. For a discussion of variations in court-annexed arbitration programs, see Hensler (1990b), "Court-Ordered Arbitration: An Alternative View."
64. Note that not all cases assigned to mediation actually reach hearing. For purposes of the analyses reported here, I examine cases reaching hearing only. RAND included cases referred to mediation but not heard in its analysis, since referrals may affect settlement patterns. Hearing rates range from 82% in OK(W) to 88% in PA(E) (Kakalik *et al.*, 1997b:Table 4,3 p. 32).

65. RAND reports, based on its interviews, that TX(S) judges encouraged cases that they viewed as particularly difficult to settle to volunteer for mediation, while OK(W) judges encouraged all cases to volunteer (Kakalik *et al.*, 1997b:30–31).
66. The settlement measure was constructed based on a combination of record data on time to disposition and survey reports (conversations with RAND CJRA staff).
67. The difference in difficulty of relationship measure was constructed by comparing a questionnaire item asking attorneys to rate party relationships at the beginning of and end of the case.
68. Pruitt *et al.* (1993) offer a nice exception to this rule, showing how a carefully nuanced conceptual scheme, accompanied by a detailed measurement scheme, may lead to disconfirmation of some of our assumptions about mediation's effects, as well as confirmation of others.

REFERENCES

Alfini, J. (1991). Trashing, Bashing, and Hashing It Out: Is This the End of "Good Mediation"? *Florida State University Law Review, 19,* 1947.

Annual Conference of State Court Chief Justices. (1997, July 30). Townhall Meeting on ADR, Cleveland, OH.

Ayres, I., and Nalebuff, B. (1997). Common Knowledge as a Barrier to Negotiation. *UCLA Law Review, 44,* 1631.

Bennett, M., and Hermann, M. (1996). *The Art of Mediation.* Notre Dame, IN: National Institute for Trial Advocacy.

Bernstein, L. (1992). Opting Out of the Legal System: Extralegal Contractual Relations in the Diamond Industry. *Journal of Legal Studies, 15,* 485.

Brett, J., Barsness, Z., and Goldberg, S. (1996). *ADR in the Private Sector.* San Francisco: Jossey–Bass.

Bruce. (1997, August 24). (medarb@gdi.net), "Re: non-attorney mediators," on dispute-res@listserv.law.cornell.edu.

Bush, R. B., and Folger, J. (1994). *The Promise of Mediation.* San Francisco: Jossey–Bass.

Carrington, P. (1996). ADR and Future Adjudication: A Primer on Dispute Resolution. *Review of Litigation,* p. 485.

Center for Dispute Settlement and the Institute for Judicial Administration. (undated). National Standards for Court-Connected Mediation Programs.

Clarke, S., Ellen, E., and McCormick, K. (1995). *Court-Ordered Civil Case Mediation in North Carolina: An Evaluation of Its Effects.* University of North Carolina Institute of Government, Chapel Hill.

Cooter, R., and Rubinfeld, D. (1989). Economic Analysis of Legal Disputes and Their Resolution. *Journal of Economic Litigation, 27,* 1067.

Dana, D. (1997, August 22). (mti@mediationworks.com), "re: non-attorney mediators."

Dana, D. (1997, August 23). (mti@mediationworks.com), "re: non-attorney mediators" on dispute-res@listserv.law.cornell.edu. Mr. Dana's comments further indicate that he is not an attorney.

Danzon, P., and Lillard, L. (1983). Settlement Out of Court: The Disposition of Medical Malpractice Claims. *Journal of Legal Studies, 12,* 345.

Delgado, R., Donn, C., Brown, P., Lee, H., and Hubbert, D. (1985). Fairness and Formality: Minimizing the Risk of Prejudice in Alternative Dispute Resolution. *Wisconsin Law Review, 1985,* 1359.

Dispute Resolution Center. (1995). *Florida Mediation/Arbitration Programs: A Compendium.* Tallahassee, Florida.

Donzhue, T., and Deinhardt, B. (1997). Survey: ADR Use Increasing. *Alternatives to High Cost Litigation, 15*(5), 66.

DuBow, F., and McEwen, C. (1976). Community Boards: An Analytic Profile. In S. Merry and N. Milner (Eds.), *The Possibility of Popular Justice.* Ann Arbor: University of Michigan Press.

Erickson, W. (1997). The RAND Report: Concerns and Future Choices. *ADR Currents, 2*(3), 6.

Erlanger, H., Chambliss, E., and Melli, M. (1987). Participation and Flexibility in Informal Processes: Cautions from the Divorce Context. *Law & Society Review, 21,* 585.

Faulkner, R. (1997, August 22). (natnladr@onramp.net), "re: non-attorney mediators," on dispute-res@listserv.law.cornell.edu.

Federal Judicial Center. (1981). *Experimentation in the Law: Report of the Federal Judicial Center Advisory Committee on Experimentation in the Law.* Washington, DC: Author.

Feinberg, K. (1997). The Role of ADR in Mass Torts. *ADR Currents, 2*(3), 5.

Feliciano, J. C. (1997). Welcoming Scrutiny of ADR. *Dispute Resolution Magazine, 3*(4), 2.

Felstiner, W., and Williams, L. (1980). *Community Mediation in Dorchester, Massachusetts.* Washington, DC: U.S. Department of Justice, National Institute of Justice.

Fischer, K., Vidmar, N., and Ellis, R. (1993). The Culture of Battering and the Role of Mediation in Domestic Violence Cases. *SMU Law Review, 46,* 2117.

Fisher, R., and Uhry, W. (1981). *Getting to Yes.* New York: Penguin.

Fiss, O. (1984). Against Settlement. *Yale Law Journal, 93*, 1073.

Florida Dispute Resolution Center. (1996). *The Resolution Report, 11*(1).

Freund, J. (1994). *The Neutral Negotiator: Why and How Mediation Can Work to Resolve Dollar Disputes.* Englewood Cliffs, NJ: Prentice–Hall Law & Business.

Galanter, M. (1985). A Settlement Judge, Not a Trial Judge: Judicial Mediation in the United States. *Journal of Law & Society, 12*, 1.

Galanter, M., and Cahill, M. (1994). Most Cases Settle: Judicial Promotion and Regulation of Settlements. *Stanford Law Review, 46*, 1339.

Galanter, M., Garth, B., Hensler, D., and Zemans, F. (1994). How to Improve Civil Justice Policy. *Judicature, 77.*

Goerdt, J. (1992). *Small Claims and Traffic Courts.* Williamsburg, VA: National Center for State Courts, Washington, DC: State Justice Institute.

Goldberg, S. B., Sander, F., and Rogers, N. (1992). *Dispute Resolution: Negotiation, Mediation and Other Processes* (2nd ed.). Boston: Little, Brown.

Greatbatch, D., and Dingwall, R. (1989). Selective Facilitation: Some Preliminary Observations on a Strategy Used by Divorce Mediators. *Law & Society Review, 23*, 613.

Grillo, T. (1991). The Mediation Alternative: Process Dangers for Women. *Yale Law Journal, 100*, 1545.

Hastings, T. (1997, August 20). (tinamediate@mindspring.com), "Re: non-attorney mediators," on dispute-res@listserv.law.cornell.edu. Ms. Hastings identifies herself as a "Mediator (full time)."

Henry, J. (1991, July 22). Built-In Protection Against Litigation Blues. *Wall Street Journal.*

Hensler, D. (1990a). Court-Annexed ADR. In J. Wilkinson (Ed.), Donovan, Leisure, Newton, and Irvine, *ADR Practice Book* (pp. 352–354). New York: Wiley Law Publications.

Hensler, D. (1990b). Court-Ordered Arbitration: An Alternative View. *University of Chicago Legal Forum*, p. 399.

Hensler, D. (1994, Fall). Why We Don't Know More About the Civil Justice System—And What We Could Do About It. *USC Law.*

Hensler, D. (1998). The Real World of Tort Litigation. In A. Sarat, M. Constable, D. Engel, V. Hans, and S. Lawrence (Eds.), *Everyday Practices and Trouble Cases*, Evanston, IL: Northwestern University Press.

Higgins, G., and O'Connell, W. (1997, March 24). Mediation, Arbitration Square Off. *National Law Journal*, p. B18.

Honeyman, C. (1988). Five Elements of Mediation. *Negotiation Journal, 4*, 149.

Jaffe, S., and Stamato, L. (1997). No Short Cuts to Justice. *Alternatives to High Cost Litigation, 15*(5), 67.

Kahneman, D., and Tversky, A. (1995). Conflict Resolution: A Cognitive Perspective. In K. Arrow, R. Mnookin, L. Ross, A. Tversky, and R. Wilson (Eds.), *Barriers to Conflict Resolution.* New York: Norton.

Kakalik, J., Donsworth, T., Hill, L., McCaffrey, D., Oshiro, M., Pace, N., and Vaiana, M. (1997a). *Just, Speedy and Inexpensive? An Evaluation of Judicial Case Management Under the Civil Justice Reform Act.* Santa Monica, CA: RAND.

Kakalik, J., Donsworth, T., Hill, L., McCaffrey, D., Oshiro, M., Pace, N., and Vaiana, M. (1997b). *An Evaluation of Mediation and Early Neutral Evaluation Under the Civil Justice Reform Act.* Santa Monica, CA: RAND.

Katz, L. (1993). Compulsory Dispute Resolution and Volunteerism: Two-Headed Monster or Two Sides of the Coin? *Journal of Dispute Resolution, 1993*, 1.

Keltner, J. (1997, August 25). (keltnerj@ucs.orst.edu), "re: attorney-mediators," on dispute-res@listserv.law.cornell.edu.

Kolb, D. (1983). *The Mediators.* Cambridge, MA: MIT Press.

Kovach, K. (1996). Mediation for Mediators? If You Talk the Talk, You Better Walk the Walk: An Examination of How Dispute Resolvers Resolve Disputes. *Ohio State Journal of Dispute Resolution, 11*, 403.

Kovach, K., and Love, L. (1996). Evaluative Mediation is an Oxymoron. *Alternatives to High Cost Litigation, 14*, 31.

Kressel, K., and Pruitt, D. (1985). Themes in the Mediation of Social Conflict. *Journal of Social Issues, 1985*, 179.

LaFree, G., and Rack, C. (1996). The Effects of Participants' Ethnicity and Gender on Monetary Outcomes in Mediated and Adjudicated Civil Cases. *Law & Society Review, 30*, 767.

Leeson, S., and Johnston, B. (1992). *Ending It: Dispute Resolution in America.* Cincinnati, OH: Anderson Publication.

Lind, E. A., and Tyler, T. (1988). *The Social Psychology of Procedural Justice.* New York: Plenum Press.

Lind, E. A., MacCoun, R., Ebener, P. A., Felstiner, W. L. F., Hensler, D. R., Resnick, J., and Tyler, T. R. (1989). *The Perception of Justice: Tort Litigants' Views of Trials, Court-Annexed Arbitration, and Judicial Settlement Conferences.* Santa Monica, CA: RAND.

Lind, E A., MacCoun, R., Ebener, P. A., Felstiner, W. L. F., Hensler, D. R., Resnick, J., and Tyler, T. R. (1990). In the Eye of the Beholder: Tort Litigants' Evaluations of Their Experiences in the Civil Justice System. *Law & Society Review, 24*, 953.

Marsh, S. (1997, August 16). (ethesis@aol.com), "re: mental health professionals."

McCarthy, G. (1997, July 22). (Altdisres@aol.com), "Re: Morality."

McEwen, C., and Maiman, R. (1984). Mediation in Small Claims Court: Achieving Compliance Through Consent. *Law & Society Review*, *18*, 1.

Menkel-Meadow, C. (1991). Pursuing Settlement in an Adversary Culture: A Tale of Innovation Co-Opted or the Law of ADR. *Florida State Law Review*, *19*, 1.

Meschievitz, C. (1991). Mediation and Medical Malpractice: Problems with Definition and Implementation. *Law & Contemporary Problems*, *54*, 195.

Metzloff, T., Peeples, R., and Harris, C. (1997). Empirical Perspectives on Mediation and Malpractice. *Law & Contemporary Problems*, *60*, 101.

Milne, A., and Folberg, J. (1988). The Theory and Practice of Divorce Mediation: An Overview. In J. Folberg and A. Milne, *Divorce Mediation: Theory and Practice*. San Francisco: Jossey–Bass.

Mnookin, R., and Korhnhauser, L. (1979). Bargaining in the Shadow of the Law: The Case of Divorce. *Yale Law Journal*, *88*, 950.

Morris, C. (1997, July 22). Whose email is "included" in a message from Ginger McCarthy (Altdisres@aol.com), "Re: Morality."

Murray, J., Rau, A., and Sherman, E. (1996). *Process of Dispute Resolution: The Role of Lawyers* (2nd ed.). New York: Foundation Press.

Nader, L. (1993). Controlling Processes in the Practice of Law: Hierarchy and Pacification in the Movement to Re-Form Dispute Ideology. *Ohio State Journal of Dispute Resolution*, *9*, 1.

Office of the State Courts. (1989). Status Report on the Medical Mediation Panel System in Wisconsin. Quoted in Meschievitz (1991) at Fn 33. *Law & Contemporary Problems*, *54*, 195.

Plapinger, E. (1997, March 24). RAND Study of Civil Justice Reform Act Sparks Debate. *National Law Journal*, p. B18.

Plapinger, E., and Stienstra, D. (1996). *ADR and Settlement in the Federal District Courts: A Sourcebook for Judges and Lawyers*. Washington, DC: Federal Judicial Center.

Priest, G., and Klein, B. (1984). The Selection of Disputes for Litigation. *Journal of Legal Studies*, *13*, 1.

Provine, M. (1986). *Settlement Strategies for Federal District Judges*. Washington, DC: Federal Judicial Center.

Pruitt, D., Pierce, R. S., McGillicuddy, N. B., Welton, G. L., and Castrianno, L. M. (1993). Long-Term Success in Mediation. *Law & Human Behavior*, *17*, 313.

Raitt, S., Folberg, J., Rosenberg, J., and Barnett, R. (1993). The Use of Mediation in Small Claims Court. *Ohio State Journal of Dispute Resolution*, *9*, 55.

Rauma, D., and Krafka, C. (1994). *Voluntary Arbitration in Eight Federal District Courts: An Evaluation*. Washington, DC: Federal Judicial Center.

Resnik, J. (1995). Many Doors? Closing Doors? Alternative Dispute Resolution and Adjudication. *Ohio State Journal of Dispute Resolution*, *10*, 212.

Reuben, R. (1997). Perspectives on the RAND Report: The Dialogue Continues. *Dispute Resolution Magazine*, *3*(4), 3.

Riskin, L. (1994). Mediator Orientations, Strategies, and Techniques. *Alternatives to High Cost Litigation*.

Riskin, L. (1996). Understanding Mediators' Orientations, Strategies, and Techniques: A Grid for the Perplexed. *Harvard Negotiation Law Review*, *1*, 7.

Riskin, L. (1997). Mediation Quandaries. *Florida State Law Review*, *24*, 1007.

Riskin, L., and Westbrook, J. (1997). *Dispute Resolution and Lawyers*. West/Wadsworth.

Rolph, E., Muller, E., and Peterson, L. (1994). *Escaping the Courthouse: Private Alternative Dispute Resolution in Los Angeles*. Santa Monica, CA: RAND.

Rosenthal, R. (1997, August 21). (rjr@trgnational.com), "re: non-attorney mediators."

Rosenthal, R. (1997, August 23). (rjr@trgnational.com), "re: non-attorney mediators."

Ross, L. (1995). Reactive Devaluation in Negotiation and Conflict Resolution, in K. Arrow, R. Mnookin, L. Ross, A. Tversky, and R. Wilson (Eds.), *Barriers to Conflict Resolution*. New York: Norton.

Sander, F. (1976). Varieties of Dispute Processing. *F.R.D.*, *70*, 79.

Schuyler, N. (1995). Coercive Harmony: An Anthropologist and a Former Federal Judge Debate the Purpose of Mandatory ADR. *California Law*, *5*, 37.

Shapiro, D., Drieghe, R., and Brett, J. (1983). Mediator Behavior and the Outcome of Mediation. *Journal of Social Issues*, *41*, 101.

Shavell, S. (1982). Suit, Settlement and Trial: A Theoretical Analysis under Alternative Methods for the Allocation of Legal Costs. *Journal of Legal Studies*, *11*, 55.

Sherman, E. F. (1993). Court-Mandated Alternative Dispute Resolution: What Form of Participation Should Be Required? *SMU Law Review*, *46*, 2079.

Shonhotz, R. (1993). Justice from Another Perspective: The Ideology and Developmental History of the Community

Boards Program. In S. Merry and N. Milner (Eds.), *The Possibility of Popular Justice*, University of Michigan Press, Ann Arbor.

Silbey, S., and Merry, S. (1986). Mediator Settlement Strategies. *Law & Policy*, *8*, 7.

Society for Professionals in Dispute Resolution (SPIDR). (undated). *Qualifying Dispute Resolution Practitioners: Guideline for Court-Connected Programs*. San Francisco: Jossey–Bass.

Stienstra, D., *et al.* (1997). *Report of the Judicial Conference Committee on Court Administration and Case Management: A Study of the Five Demonstration Programs Established under the Civil Justice Reform Act of 1990*.

Stulberg, J. (1997). Facilitative versus Evaluative Mediator Orientations: Piercing the "Grid" Lock. *Florida State University Law Review*, *24*, 985.

Vidmar, N. (1984). The Small Claims Court: A Reconceptualization of Disputes and an Empirical Investigation. *Law Society Review*, *18*, 515.

Vidmar, N. (1985). An Assessment of Mediation in a Small Claims Court. *Journal of Social Issues*, *41*, 127.

Views on RAND's CJRA Report: Concerns and Recommendations. (1997). *Alternatives to High Cost Litigation*, *15*(5), 67.

Wall, J., and Rude, D. (1985). Judicial Mediation: Techniques, Strategies and Situational Effects. *Journal of Social Issues*, *41*, 47.

9

Wage Justice for Women

Markets, Firms, and the Law Governing Gender Differences in Pay

Robert L. Nelson and William P. Bridges

A. INTRODUCTION

Wage inequality between men and women remains one of the most pressing justice concerns in the United States. Despite the passage of the Equal Pay Act of 1963, which mandated equal pay when men and women do the same job, and the broader prohibition of gender-based employment discrimination in the Civil Rights Act of 1964 (as amended in 1972), women continue to earn only three-quarters of men's pay. Women's groups still list pay equity as a leading legislative goal; and several pay equity proposals are pending in Congress (see *New York Times*, 1997:B10; *Chicago Sun-Times*, 1998:1–2). Yet there also is no consensus in legal, policy, or academic circles that the pay gap is unjust. Analysts recognize that a significant portion of the wage gap resides between different jobs that are held predominantly by men or by women. Although such between-job wage differentials have been attacked by proponents of comparable worth, most economists characterize these differences as the product of noninvidious, market forces.

Indeed, the question of the legality, if not the justness, of wage differences between predominantly male and predominantly female jobs was directly tested in a series of lawsuits litigated in the 1980s. In *County of Washington v. Gunther*, 452 U.S. 161 (1981), a bitterly divided Supreme Court ruled in favor of a more expansive interpretation of Title VII by holding that the law against pay discrimination could reach cases involving male and female workers occupying different jobs. The abstract opening provided by *Gunther* was quickly shut, however. When federal courts confronted broader claims of pay discrimination against jobs

---

Robert L. Nelson • Department of Sociology, Northwestern University, Evanston, Illinois 60208. William P. Bridges • Department of Sociology, University of Illinois at Chicago, Chicago, Illinois 60607.

Handbook of Justice Research in Law, edited by Sanders and Hamilton. Kluwer Academic / Plenum Publishers, New York, 2000.

held predominantly by women, they invoked the market explanation. Judge Kennedy's words in the pivotal decision in the *AFSCME* case offered a sweeping rejection of a theory of discrimination based on comparable worth. "Neither law nor logic deems the free market a suspect enterprise" (*American Federation of State, County, and Municipal Employees v. State of Washington*, 1985). While the struggle for pay equity continued in scattered legislative and collective bargaining arenas (see McCann, 1994), the market view of between-job wage differences clearly had triumphed in the courts.

In this essay we examine the market-based explanation of gender-based wage differences embraced by the courts and consider the implications of this judicial position for wage justice in the United States. After presenting the legal background, we review the empirical literature on between-job, male–female wage differences. We propose a new "organizational" conception of the sources of male–female pay differences, in which we argue that wage differences between jobs held predominantly by men and those held predominantly by women largely reflect organizational processes rather than market processes. Moreover, these organizational processes unfairly disadvantage female workers, for they create wage differences that are not linked to genuine differences in productivity or measured value. Our findings stand in stark contrast to the pronouncements of federal courts in cases involving allegations of between-job wage discrimination. We argue that the federal courts have contributed to the cultural triumph of the market view by offering empirical interpretations that go beyond the data in the cases before them. In this sense, we suggest the courts have "legalized" a fundamental aspect of gender-based wage inequality in U.S. society.

Our argument rests on an effort to test the empirical claims of the market-based interpretation in the very arena in which it has had its most direct consequences, namely, litigation involving claims of sex-based pay discrimination.[1] We have analyzed four cases and four employing organizations. Two cases involve public organizations—the State of Washington personnel system and the nonprofessional staff of the University of Iowa. Two cases involve private organizations—Sears, Roebuck & Co. and a bank we refer to by the pseudonym of Coastal Bank.[2] In three cases the plaintiffs lost based on the court's conclusions concerning market and efficiency explanations of observed wage differentials. In the one case in which the plaintiffs prevailed, there was no explicit attention to between-job pay differences and the settlement reached in the wake of the judgment did nothing to realign the organization's pay system.

In both public- and private-sector organizations, we find that gender inequality cannot be adequately explained by market forces or efficiency reasons. These patterns require a rethinking of the relationship between law, markets, and gender inequality in organizations. Contrary to the dominant interpretation in economics, the law, and in these organizations themselves, employing organizations bear considerable responsibility for the fact that men and women are paid less for work requiring similar effort, training, and skill. The results thus suggest the need for a new theoretical focus on the organizational dimensions of gender inequality, particularly on the processes through which organizations mediate market wages. Our findings also call for reopening policy debates on pay equity. If male–female wage differences are not the product of market forces or efficiency principles, how should these be dealt with through regulation or antidiscrimination law? Finally, our research has implications for theories about the relationship between law and gender inequality in U.S. society. We will argue that the courts have "legalized" gender inequality. By giving authoritative approval to the market justification for between-job earnings differences, they have played a distinct role in the social construction of markets and female earnings. The law not only has granted legal protection to a given set of institutional pay practices, it has itself been a powerful source of a gendered view of markets and unequal pay.

B. THE LEGAL TREATMENT OF GENDER-BASED WAGE DISCRIMINATION

1. The Legal Background: The Equal Pay Act, Title VII, and *Gunther*

The two principal federal laws against gender-based wage discrimination are the Equal Pay Act of 1963 [29 U.S.C. Sec. 206(d)(1990)] and Title VII of the Civil Rights Act of 1964 (42 U.S.C. Secs. 2000e-1 to 2000e-17, 1982). The Equal Pay Act prohibits employers from paying male and female employees differently for "equal work on the jobs the performance of which requires equal skill, effort, and responsibility, and which are performed under similar working conditions, except where such payment is made pursuant to (i) a seniority system; (ii) a merit system; (iii) a system which measures earnings by quantity or quality of production; or (iv) a differential based on any other factor other than sex." The Equal Pay Act contains something close to a strict liability standard. If a female employee establishes a wage differential for the same job that does not fall within one of the four exceptions, that is sufficient to win. The employee is not required to prove the employer's intent to discriminate based on gender.

The main limitation of the Equal Pay Act with respect to gender-based wage differences is the equal work requirement. While the courts interpret the Act to reach "substantially similar jobs," even though they may have different job titles, it only applies to contexts where men and women work in the same jobs. Given the high levels of sex segregation by job in the U.S. economy, the Act has a limited purview. As recently as 1991, 53% of either working women or working men would have to change jobs to produce a fully integrated U.S. labor force (Reskin and Padavic, 1994:54). Thus, a large portion of the gender gap in earnings appears to reside in differences between traditionally female jobs and traditionally male jobs, rather than in the earnings differences of men and women doing the same job.

Title VII of the Civil Rights Act of 1964 is not so limited on its fact. It contains a blanket prohibition against discrimination in compensation because of an individual's sex, race, religion, or national origin (42 U.S.C. §20003-2). Title VII's broad wage discrimination rule is limited by the so-called Bennett Amendment, which sought to clarify the relationship between Title VII and the Equal Pay Act. The Bennett Amendment excuses sex-based wage differentials "if such differentiation is authorized by the provisions of section 206(d) of title 29 [i.e., The Equal Pay Act]" [42 U.S.C. 20003-20(h)]. The language of the Bennett Amendment is ambiguous. Did it import only the affirmative defenses to Equal Pay Act claims into Title VII? Or did it also import the equal work requirement? Until the Supreme Court's decision in *County of Washington v. Gunther*, 452 U.S. 161 (1981), there was considerable division among the lower courts on this question.

The County of Washington paid its prison matrons (all females) only 70% as much as it paid its prison guards (all males). The guards and matrons did much the same work. And the County's job evaluation study assigned the matron position 95% as many job evaluation points as the guard position. When the matrons sued under Title VII, the district court dismissed the case, in large part due to its interpretation of the Bennett Amendment. Both the Ninth Circuit Court of Appeals and the Supreme Court disagreed. By a 5-to-4 majority, the Supreme Court held that Title VII's wage discrimination provisions could extend beyond those of the Equal Pay Act. The Court specifically refused to endorse "the controversial concept of comparable worth" (452 U.S. 161, p. 166), but ruled that an employer could be liable for discrimination in how it paid two different jobs, one held by men, one by women. Over the strenuous objections of the dissent, the majority in *Gunther* read the Bennett Amendment as bringing only the affirmative defenses to the Equal Pay Act into Title VII, while leaving the equal work requirement out.

Gunther was a doctrinal turning point for wage discrimination claims under Title VII. It meant that employers could be liable for between-job pay disparities if plaintiffs established that they resulted from gender-based discrimination. Although *Gunther* was a weak precedent, in the sense that the opinion commanded a bare majority of the Court and was coupled with a vigorous, often-cited dissent by Justice Rehnquist, it reaffirmed the purposive nature of Title VII's antidiscrimination principles. At a minimum, egregious forms of pay discrimination against women would not be tolerated just because male and female workers held different jobs. But how far would the courts go to redress between-job pay disparities? What would they recognize as evidence of employer discrimination in these cases?

2. The Post-*Gunther* Cases: The Demise of Comparable Worth and the Adoption of the Market Explanation

After *Gunther*, a series of cases were filed, all against public-sector employers, that used comparable worth theories of pay discrimination. By "comparable worth" we mean that the plaintiffs primarily relied on job evaluation studies in making their claims of between-job pay discrimination. The lawsuits also typically included other allegations of intentional discrimination, such as job segregation, refusals to hire and promote female employees for various jobs, and discriminatory pay practices within job categories. But these allegations assumed a relatively minor role in the lawsuits; the plaintiffs' key allegation concerned pay differentials between predominantly male and predominantly female jobs, after controlling for job evaluation points.

Before we describe the judicial treatment of comparable worth claims, some background on Title VII theories of discrimination is necessary. The Supreme Court has formulated two broad theories of employment discrimination under Title VII: disparate treatment and disparate impact (generally see Sullivan, Zimmer, and Richards, 1988, Vol. 1, pp. 38–46). Disparate treatment involves instances in which employers treat some people less favorably than others because of their race, color, religion, sex, or national origin. "Proof of discriminatory motive is critical although it can ... be inferred from the mere fact of differences in treatment" (*International Bd. of Teamsters v. United States*, 335 h. 15). Systemic disparate treatment cases focus on either formal policies that discriminate among various groups or practices that use race or gender to discriminate despite the employer's denial that such factors are used. Plaintiffs may establish a prima facie case of discrimination employing either statistical evidence of disparate treatment or anecdotal evidence or some combination of both. The burden of proof then shifts to the employer to rebut the evidence of discrimination by disputing the showing of a disparity or showing valid, nondiscriminatory reasons for the disparity in employment outcomes.

Disparate impact cases involve employment practices that appear neutral on their face, but results in different employment outcomes for different groups. Proof of discriminatory intent is not required. A plaintiff makes out a prima facie case by showing the disparate impact of an employer practice on a protected group. The employer must then respond by challenging the showing of a disparity, by claiming that the disparity results from a practice that is excepted from Title VII (such as a bona fide seniority system), or by demonstrating that the practice is justified by business necessity. Disparate impact theories potentially have broad application because they do not require proof of discriminatory intent.[3]

The first post-*Gunther* comparable worth case to reach a decision at trial was *AFSCME v. State of Washington*. It was the only trial court victory for the plaintiffs among all comparable worth cases, and it too was overruled by the Court of Appeals. The trial court opinion held in favor of the plaintiffs on both disparate treatment and disparate impact theories of Title VII liability.

District Court Judge Tanner was persuaded that the plaintiffs had made out a prima facie case of a disparate impact theory because: "Several comparable worth studies, since 1974, found a 20% disparity in salary between predominantly male and predominantly female jobs which require an equivalent or lesser composite of skill, effort, responsibility, and working conditions as reflected by an equal number of job evaluation points" (578 F. Supp. 863). He also found that the State had not produced evidence of a legitimate, overriding business justification for such differentials. The judge found evidence of the discriminatory intent required to make out a disparate treatment case in part based on the fact that state officials had publicly acknowledged the meaning of the job evaluation studies and yet were continuing the present wage system (578 F. Supp. 863).

Judge Tanner's formulation, if it had prevailed, would have given plaintiffs very powerful tools to challenge employer wage systems in which job evaluation studies had revealed unexplained wage differences: (1) It would treat the unexplained, gender-based wage differences in job evaluation studies as valid evidence of disparate impact. Employers would then have to justify their wage-setting policies based on business justifications. (2) Failure to act on job evaluation results showing unexplained gender differences would be construed as intentional discrimination. Such a doctrine would have turned lead into gold for classes of female workers. Job evaluation studies consistently yield an unexplained gender gap in pay. (An "unexplained wage gap" is the gap between average male and female earnings after controlling statistically for other factors that may affect the wages of workers.) Under Judge Tanner's approach, this gap would be transformed into evidence of discrimination to which employers would have to respond.

No other court has embraced the kind of "pure" comparable worth theory Judge Tanner adopted in the *AFSCME* case, however. The Court of Appeals directly rejected those principles most clearly associated with comparable worth. First, it rejected the application of a disparate impact theory to the State of Washington's "practice of taking prevailing market rates into account in setting wages" (*AFSCME v. State of Washington*, 1985:1405). According to the court, disparate impact analysis was to be limited to cases challenging "a specific, clearly delineated employment practice applied at a single point in the job selection process" (*id.* at 1405). Citing another Ninth Circuit case, the court ruled that "the decision to base compensation on the competitive market, rather than on a theory of comparable worth, involves the assessment of a number of complex factors not easily ascertainable, an assessment too multifaceted to be appropriate for disparate impact analysis. *Spaulding v. University of Washington*, 740 F.2d 686 (9th Cir. 1984)" (*AFSCME v. State of Washington*, 1985:1406). The complexity of the practices at issue were to be controlled by a disparate treatment theory.

Second, the court dismissed the notion that job evaluation studies and comparable worth statistics by themselves would be enough to establish the requisite proof of discriminatory intent (*AFSCME v. State of Washington*, 1985:1407). Third, it rejected the contention that having commissioned the job evaluation study, the State of Washington was required to implement the study. The court reasoned that employers should be able to treat job evaluation as one diagnostic tool among others. If employers were bound by law to incorporate such studies, it would simply discourage employers from engaging in such analysis.

In addition to rejecting the "pure" comparable worth theory of the plaintiffs, the Ninth Circuit indicated that it was not otherwise persuaded by the evidence that the State of Washington had intentionally discriminated against workers in predominately female jobs.

Historical patterns of sex segregation of jobs were not enough to support such an inference. And the court singled out the fact that none of the named plaintiffs testified regarding specific incidents of discrimination (*AFSCME v. State of Washington*, 1985:1408).

Much of the appellate court's opinion in *AFSCME* can be read as a specific response to the district court's comparable worth theory, that is, refusing to find liability solely based on job evaluation results or for attempting to follow market rates. Yet at several points the language of the opinion takes for granted that the gender differentials resulted from the state following a market rate system.[4]

After the defeat in *AFSCME*, plaintiffs went to lengths to distance themselves from the label "comparable worth" in their complaints and briefs, and sought instead to demonstrate intentional discrimination on the part of public pay systems. Judges often were not sympathetic. They applied the term to the plaintiffs' cases, despite the plaintiffs' protestations (see, e.g., *Spaulding v. University of Washington*, 1984:710; *American Nurses' Association v. State of Illinois*, 1985; *International Union, UAW v. State of Michigan*, 1987). In case after case, the courts ruled against the plaintiffs' claims of between-job pay discrimination. While each opinion varied somewhat, depending on the specific context and the evidence presented, the unifying theme in the judicial analysis was that the market, not the employing organization, produced the gender differences in pay (see, e.g., *Briggs v. City of Madison*, 1982; *Spaulding v. University of Washington*, 1984; *California State Employees' Association v. State of California*, 1987; *International U.A.W. v. State of Michigan*, 1987; *AFSCME v. County of Nassau*, 1992). Emblematic of the economic perspective within the judiciary is a passage from an opinion by Judge Richard Posner, a leading figure in the law and economics movement within legal scholarship, writing here as a court of appeals judge.

> Economists have conducted studies which show that virtually the entire difference in the average hourly wage of men and women, including that due to the fact that men and women tend to be concentrated in different types of jobs, can be explained by the fact that most women take time out of the labor force in order to take care of their children. As a result they tend to invest less in their "human capital" (earning capacity); since part of any wage is a return on human capital, they tend therefore to be found in jobs that pay less. (*American Nurses' Association v. State of Illinois*, 1986)

Posner is no ordinary judge, of course. Indeed, this quotation comes from a decision in which Posner reversed a lower court ruling against women in a wage discrimination case. Posner and his panel ruled that the women must be given a chance to prove their contention, as unusual as it may seem. Yet Posner offered just a somewhat more erudite statement of the world-view that comes through in the opinions on between-job wage claims.

What is certain for Posner and other judges in cases raising complaints about wage differences between jobs held predominantly by men compared to those held predominantly by women, we find empirically questionable. After briefly reviewing the empirical literature on between-job wage differences, we present results from our own case studies within organizations.

C. WHAT EXPLAINS THE WAGE GAP?

Characterizing wage determination in the United States as *decentralized* is a bit like describing pebbles on a beach as "nonsquare"—the descriptor is accurate, but ignores great variation in the subject. The complexity that results when pay decisions are made in thousands of different local contexts can be a source of clarification as well as confusion for the social analyst.[5] The underlying premise of our argument is that wage levels are the outcome of the interaction of distinct social forces, which can be grouped, at least initially, into three main categories: market, organization, and culture. Because these basic forces are spread unevenly over the terrain of the U.S. employment system, comparison of wage setting across different contexts is a revealing exercise. In more centralized systems, it can be quite difficult to see how these forces operate or interact when they are congealed in a unitary decision process. For example, market supply and demand pressures do not go out of existence when a national wage structure is put in place, but their operation may be both transformed and rendered less visible compared to some wage setting arenas in a decentralized milieu.

In the next section we consider theories of between-job wage inequality in which market forces play a central role. Our discussion begins with conventional market models that deemphasize employment discrimination and other invidious labor market processes. We then turn to an examination of what can be called "tainted" market models that allow for the introduction of various discriminatory distortions into the market process, but which at the same time rely on market mechanisms as a proximate cause of between-job wage differences.

1. Market Theories of Between-Job Wage Differences

a. Conventional Models

In explaining between-job gender differences in pay, market-based theories rely on the same fundamental principles that they use to explain wage differences in general. On the demand side, individual employers each confront a marginal revenue product schedule for their output and are willing to pay different labor inputs—people to different jobs or occupations—differing amounts depending on their contribution to that revenue product. The market aggregates these various preferences into a marketwide demand schedule for each kind of labor. For example, if public preferences shift toward taking more exercise under the tutelage of aerobic instructors and personal trainers, the demand curves for these occupations will, other things equal, move to the right as health clubs and other facilities shift their production more in this direction. On the supply side, individual decisions also weigh heavily as workers, of various types, gauge the advantages and disadvantages of various bundles of work activities (occupations), and decide how much money they would need to work a given amount in a given job. If more individuals, of any type, find a given bundle of activities more attractive—or at least less onerous—the supply curve to that occupation will shift to the right as well. The wage rate for a given occupation will be determined by the intersection of these curves, and will, when the system works smoothly, mostly reflect the relative preferences of consumers and workers.[6]

An integral element of this theory is that at any given time, both those interested in buying labor, employers, and those selling it, employees, will confront market prices for occupations as a fixed reality. Whatever discretion they exercise in the short run will be directed toward questions of quantity. Thus, employing organizations are portrayed as price takers, and our hypothetical health club will decide how many hours they can schedule of aerobics instruction at a given wage rate, but will have little individual influence on the going rate for employees in this occupation.

Applying these principles to the explanation of differing wage rates for predominantly male and female types of work appears to be a straightforward endeavor. Perhaps the most essential modification necessary is to account for the existence of occupations that depart so dramatically from a balanced mix of male and female workers. Aside from the possibility of employer discrimination, an issue we will address shortly, the concentration of women in some jobs and men in others could be based on choice—a preposition that market theories endorse. There are at least two plausible accounts of how men and women make different occupational choices.

First, the duties and performances involved in the work of some occupations might be more attractive to women and less attractive to men (or vice versa). For example, more women than men may be drawn to lines of work that require one to give care to or to nurture others. For our purposes, there is no need to debate whether this attraction results from biological causes or from the way in which most boys and girls are socialized by parents and schools. In either case, to the extent that there is a "problem" to be solved in this area, it is hard to envision how it is a problem that devolves onto employers to rectify.

Second, the organization of work typical of an occupation, but not its intrinsic duties, might be better suited to the other social roles occupied more frequently by women. The best known hypothesis of this sort is the "skill depreciation–career interruption" conjecture put forward by Solomon Polachek (1981) and others. The basic idea is that in some occupations one's skills atrophy at a faster rate during periods of inactivity or withdrawal from the labor force. At the same time, the working population is thought to be segmented into two groups that have very different chances of interrupting their careers to pursue other activities, specifically, child bearing and child rearing. If so, it would be logical to expect women to gravitate toward those occupations in which the penalty for episodic departures from the labor force was relatively small (Polachek, 1981). As logically compelling as such a link might seem, support for it has been quite scarce in the empirical literature. Marini cites several studies that among other things show that: (1) "women in predominately female occupations do not experience lower wage depreciation than women in predominately male occupations" (see England, 1982, 1984); (2) "women with continuous labor force participation are no less likely to be in predominately female occupations than are women who have experienced labor force interruptions" (see England, 1982; Corcoran, Duncan, and Ponza, 1984); and (3) "women's anticipated labor force participation in adolescence and early adulthood has no significant effect on the sex type of the occupation in which they are later employed" (see Lehrer and Stokes, 1985).

In sum, the pure market-based theory of between-job wage differences of men and women rests ultimately on a hybrid account that draws on both economic and noneconomic reasoning. Occupations are paid what the market will bear based on supply and demand, but the most convincing account of why men and women choose different occupations involves some combination of presumed innate inclination and the powerful shaping influence of differential socialization. However, once the door is opened to the influence of socialization and cultural factors generally, it becomes difficult to argue that they do not also influence the "market process" itself. Thus, we now turn our attention to a second group of theories that we identify as "tainted market models."

b. Tainted Market Models

This variant of the market approach raises the possibility that between-job, male–female earnings differences result in part from marketwide tendencies to discriminate against women. Tainted market models share the assumption that supply and demand forces are still important in wage determination and continue, for the most part, to see individual employers as "price takers." Or, stated differently, one would find unexplained "pay gaps" between those working in predominantly male and female jobs even among nondiscriminatory employers. These theories contend, however, that there are external, invidious factors that intervene in the market process to the detriment of those working in predominantly female jobs.

Crowding theory is one explanation of this type. The essence of this model is that there is persistent discrimination against women that prevents or strongly discourages them from entering traditionally male jobs. As a result, women are restricted to a limited subject of jobs in which the market has too many job-seekers chasing too few offers, i.e., it is "overcrowded," and wage rates decline as the labor supply curve shifts to the right (Bergmann, 1974; England, 1992:72; Sorensen, 1994:38). Although there are other variants of the crowding idea, in this particular version it is not necessary to assume that there are any preexisting wage differences between "male" and "female" jobs. Discrimination in hiring and job assignment is sufficient to produce the observed results of depressed female sector wages.

Nonetheless, there are some difficult issues that this theory raises. First, it is necessary to explain why the net flow of women out of male jobs that is produced by discrimination is not counterbalanced by an influx of male "refugees" from the depressed wages that appear in the "nondiscriminatory" sector. This counterflow of male workers would be in the interests of "male sector" employers who would confront a looser labor market and lower wage rates. If it did occur, it would also tend to reestablish higher wage rates in the female sector that these males were deserting. In a similar vein, Baron, Mittman, and Newman (1991:156) note that "men were no less concentrated in male-dominated jobs than were women in female-dominated jobs." In reply, it might be argued that the jobs that women are excluded from also contain entry barriers against other workers as well—as in the construction trades, for example—that would prevent such countermovements from taking place. But once this argument is made, one can no longer presume that the wage rates of the two types of jobs would be equal in the absence of gender discrimination, and a different model is called for.[7]

Killingsworth (1985:89–91) does offer a model that combines discrimination against women in hiring with preexisting wage differences between various occupations (although in his model the preexisting wage differences are due to normal, and justifiable, economic forces such as differences in productivity and/or differences in nonpecuniary aspects of the jobs in question, and are not monopoly rents that arise from other kids of barriers to entry). His model holds that employers of labor in high-wage occupations prefer to hire men and will pay them a wage premium and will try to avoid hiring women. Or, if they cannot avoid women completely, they will not pay them the wage premium. The end result is that (1) high-paying occupations now overrepresent men and vice versa; (2) the original wage difference between the two types of occupations, i.e., the economically rational part, is widened; and (3) there is a within-occupation wage difference in the high-paying sector that favors males.

It is curious that Killingsworth adds the stipulation that women are paid lower wages when they are hired into male sector jobs. A widening of the between-job wage difference would occur even without this added measure of invidious treatment. Furthermore, it raises two additional problems to be explained. The first, and perhaps lesser of the two (although the only one Killingsworth addresses), is the argument that normal competitive forces should lead rational employers to undercut the within-job wage differences by bidding up the price of the services of the equally productive, but undervalued, female workers. The second is that this kind of discrimination flies directly in the face of the least controversial and longest-standing piece of antidiscriminatory federal legislation, the 1963 Equal Pay Act. (If the theoretical problem is to account for a residual within-occupation difference, an alternative, and more plausible, explanation would involve examining the possibility that women in high-wage occupations are more likely than men to work for low-wage firms.) A modified discrimination model, one without Equal Pay Act violations, can be offered, however. Under this model, employers do prefer to hire males in high-wage occupations, do systematically exclude women from such positions, but do pay the few female exceptions who are hired the same wage premiums.

It is worth pausing briefly to examine the implications this model has for the kind of wage discrimination that would appear in conventional statistical analyses. Under this model, male occupations and female occupations would be observed to earn different wages even if the qualifications of incumbents (e.g., education, training, experience) were taken into account. However, once *job* and *occupational* characteristics were taken into consideration, whether these were productivity related or "rent" related, the wage difference between predominantly male and female occupations should disappear. That is, the primary mechanism in this model is a differential access or hiring mechanism. If the hiring discrimination nut were to be cracked, there would be no need for any additional steps to be taken to redress the "between-job" differences between men and women.

2. Cultural Models of Between-Job Wage Differences

Not surprisingly, comparable worth advocates feel the need to offer an alternative account of the source of between-job, male–female pay differences. That is, only if the sex composition of jobs itself is implicated as a direct cause of reduced earnings is a remedy required that goes beyond ensuring equal opportunity in the hiring/job placement process. Some advocates adopt a variation on the theme of tainted markets that adds a broader array of factors that taint the market. First, and most central to the explanation, is the idea of cultural devaluation. Not only women as a gender, but most things feminine, including female skills, traits, and tasks, are undervalued by society and male decision-makers. Second, there is the proposition that this devaluation insinuates itself into the wage determination process by affecting the kinds of judgments that are made in the job evaluation schemes found among major employers. England, a leading proponent of this viewpoint—which she sees as cultural capital theory applied to gender—makes these arguments explicitly:

> Feminist critics of current job evaluation practices charge that the choice of factors and weights is biased in favor of men.... The contention is that the skills or tasks that typify female jobs will receive lower positive or even negative returns (weights) in comparison to skills and tasks typical to men's jobs. (1992:104–105)

Among the female task traits that are alleged to be devalued in this way are verbal skills, small-motor manual dexterity, and facility in "nurturant" human interaction.

A third point, although one that is more implicit than explicit in this approach, is that the diminished wages that accompany cultural devaluation become a marketwide phenomenon. Thus, the position that defendant organizations in pay equality litigation often adopt, what we have labeled the "market defense," is held by comparable worth theorists to be no defense at all. This is the fundamental contribution that follows from arguing that the discrimination in question flows from cultural sources. As elements of a cultural system, the beliefs involved can be seen both as pervasive and as unconsciously held. Because they are socialized into these belief systems as children, adult decision makers of either gender may put them into play without even realizing that they are doing so. From this point of view, it is logically consistent to assert simultaneously that employers are price takers and that the market is "wrong." The market wage only seems untainted, and might appear so even to a female employer, because it is based on beliefs that everyone takes for granted.

If one accepts this portrait of the labor market, the case for comparable worth takes on renewed luster, at least initially. If the market is populated by cultural automata, little remediation can be expected from the forces of competition. Moreover, by increasing wage rates for jobs that are predominantly female, comparable worth mandates kill two birds with one stone. In the short run, they diminish the wage gap between women and men, and in the long run, they lead to a recalibration of the cultural yardsticks that measure female work unfairly. The assumed logic here is that if "librarians make as much as fire hydrant inspectors, they must be doing something that is pretty important" (see Sunstein, 1991; England, 1992:118).

Before moving on, however, it is appropriate to ask whether the premise of this argument is as plausible as it seems at first glance. First, not every employment sector is dominated by organizations that use job evaluation systems and pay matrices. In some sectors, it may be quite reasonable to assume that wage rates are influenced by "derived" demand, that is, the amount that each type of work contributes to the value of the final product. Under these circumstances, there will be a powerful incentive for an employer who is spending too little on workers in predominantly female jobs to increase the rate of pay and hire more productive individuals up to the point at which the marginal increase in pay matches the marginal increase in contribution to the final product. In situations in which an occupational market is composed of both kinds of employers, that is, those subject to competitive forces and those relatively immune from them, it is reasonable to ask whether the market-driven segment might set the terms for the administered pay segment, as well as vice versa. After all, market surveys are a routine part of the salary setting process in almost all bureaucratic pay systems. In short, the cultural capital version of the tainted market theory shares with its more orthodox counterpart a tendency to make global assumptions about aspects of market functioning that might better be addressed through attention to market contexts per se.

The cultural bias theory flies in the face of federal court rulings that have consistently refused to hold individual employers liable for gender differences in pay that result from their paying market-determined wage rates. Underlying the courts' reasoning are neoclassical economic principles, tenets that would require that *all* of the market difference in rates be removed before a comparable worth claim could be supported. Thus, the battle lines are drawn in a debate over market functioning. Unfortunately, the debate has taken a somewhat abstract and philosophical turn. For their part, the neoclassically minded assert that cultural bias, like other forms of taste discrimination, is costly in markets and will tend to be driven out by the forces of competition. In the terms of rational choice theory, maintenance of gender bias in pay among a group of employers is a "collective" good that requires some unidentified mechanism that restrains individual employers from acting in their own self-interest, which in this case would be to hire away high-quality female workers from their competitors by paying them fairly. To this argument, cultural bias theorists have responded that there are other considerations that would allow such a bias to persist. [One possibility is monopsony, that is, lack of effective competition among employers or employer control of a labor market; another is that the wage difference might be the result of male employers' altruistic bias in favor of male workers. On monopsony, see Madden (1973); on male altruism, see England (1992).]

This debate has not proven fruitful, primarily because the etiological issues are only thinly buried beneath the surface of assertion and counterassertion. A better starting point, in our view, is to recognize the existence of both pervasive cultural bias and competitive markets, but to challenge the causal primacy of either influence. With this background in mind, we now address some structural features of the labor market that require us to pay more explicit attention to the organizational context in which between-job wage differences are found.

D. A NEW VIEW: THE ORGANIZATIONAL INEQUALITY APPROACH

1. Organizations and Labor Markets

There are two related aspects of the growth in size of employing organizations that have tempered the influence of competitive labor market conditions on the nature of employment relationships. The first has been the spread of the so-called internal labor market, and the second the emergence and proliferation of bureaucratic personnel systems. [Other studies refer to this second element in various terms: Burawoy (1979) describes the rise of the "internal state," Edwards (1979) and Baron, Devereaux-Jennings, and Dobbin (1988) discuss the spread of "bureaucratic control systems," while Bridges and Villemez (1994) investigate the nature of "bureaucratic personnel management."] From the point of view of organizational influences on wage determination and possible discrimination, both patterns embody a similar logic. Each represents the institutionalization of nonmarket, organizational influences that tend to interfere with pure market determination of wage rates, and in this sense, increase managerial discretion. Precisely because both represent *institutionalized* systems, however, managerial discretion is not unlimited and is, in fact, channeled in predictable ways by these practices. Together we refer to these institutions as the administered labor system.

a. Internal Labor Markets

Among the most important developments that affect the legal resolution of wage disparities between men and women is the creation of internal labor markets (ILMs). In the context of our analysis, the definition of an ILM is crucial. Following Kerr (1954), some scholars take a broad view that recognizes almost all closed or restricted labor markets as "internal" and include craft labor markets under the same general rubric as firm-specific employment systems. Because we are interested in developing an organizational theory of gender inequality, we must necessarily adopt a narrower definition. An employer that hired only from craft (internal) labor markets and paid the "going rate" in all instances would seem to be in an ideal position to justify any resulting gender wage disparities as both a genuine business exigency and a reasonable response to market forces. Organizational intermediation would not play a role in such a wage system. Thus, the internal labor markets of interest here are those that some have called "firm internal labor markets" (see Althauser and Kalleberg, 1981).

Although definitions vary, a central element in most representations of firm internal labor markets is the recognition of two classes of job. The first are idiosyncratic and are defined only in terms of a division of labor which is specific to a given enterprise or employer; the second are those that are standardized and defined with reference to an external occupational system (see Williamson, 1975; Bridges and Villemez, 1991). Partially overlapping this distinction is another that distinguishes between jobs that employers fill from within the firm and those that are filled by hiring from the external market. In practice, these two dimensions tend to converge, but, for a variety of reasons, employers may choose to establish promotion sequences and "job clusters" that protect the standardized jobs as well as the idiosyncratic ones. When such systems are well institutionalized, with hiring restricted to certain "ports of entry" and labor allocation determined by administrative rules, an internal labor market can be said to exist (Gitelman, 1966; Doeringer, 1967; Doeringer and Piore, 1971; Althauser and Kalleberg, 1981; Finlay, 1983; Jacoby, 1984; Pfeffer and Cohen, 1984; Osterman, 1984; Baron, Davis-Blake, and Bielby, 1986; Althauser, 1989; Bridges and Villemez, 1991, 1994).

The existence of internal labor markets has important implications for the legal analysis of between-job wage disparities. If the competitive market is operative only in establishing wage rates for entry-level jobs, much of the invidious effect of occupational gender segregation will lie sheltered from the competitive discipline of the market. Trieman and Hartmann (1981) recognize these tendencies explicitly:

> Only for entry-level jobs are wage rates strongly influenced by the competitive forces of supply and demand. The major supply for the jobs higher on the ladder are those workers already in the firm, and the only effective demand for those particular workers is that of their current employers. Some of the jobs have few, if any analogues in the external labor market and no established market wage rates; rather it is the employer, and possibly workers, who determine appropriate wage rates for the jobs. (p. 47)

Nevertheless, the role of ILMs in sustaining between-job gender disparities in pay has been given only passing attention. One of the most comprehensive treatments of pay equity to date, Paula England's *Comparable Worth* devotes only a few scant paragraphs to the topic, essentially arguing that the major importance of ILMs is to retard any closing of the pay gap that might be achieved through open and discrimination-free market competition (1992:282). Sorensen offers a stronger argument linking internal labor markets to between-job gender differences in pay under the rubric of an "institutional model of discrimination." Her rendition of this linkage is that internal markets are the cause of pay equity violations:

> firms with internal labor markets are more likely to discriminate than other firms. Since they use occupations as their unit of decision to establish pay and promotional opportunities, individuals within these occupations are treated similarly. Hence, it is to the firm's advantage to make sure that workers within each job are as similar as possible. (1994:47)

While ILMs might conceivably take the form of parallel, but unequal, job ladders for men and women (and on occasion have taken this form), there is nothing inherent in the construction of ILMs to require racial, ethnic, gender, or class-origin homogeneity in their staffing. To the contrary, ILMs closely resemble the promotion hierarchies that are one of the essential features of the Weberian model of rational bureaucracies, and by analogy, might be expected to operate on universalistic and achieved criteria rather than particularistic and ascriptive ones.

Our belief about the role that ILMs play in between-job gender inequality lies somewhere between these two positions. In contrast to England, we want to emphasize that ILMs have some bearing on the *origin* of gender differences in pay. But unlike Sorensen, we would not argue that ILMs *require* such inequality. Instead, ILMs are a critical feature of many organizations that allow them to maintain invidious pay differences in the face of countervailing pressures that might otherwise tend to reduce such differences. This role of ILMs is particularly significant when taken in conjunction with other elements of bureaucratic personnel management.

There is also evidence that ILMs have become a widespread feature of the organizational landscape in the twentieth century. Baron, Dobbin, and Devereaux-Jennings provide data on the diffusion of "promotion and transfer systems" between 1927 and 1935. Their sample is drawn from National Industrial Conference Board files, and is somewhat skewed in favor of larger establishments. Across all industries, and among firms with more than 250 employees, these systems were found in 24% of establishments in 1927 and in 17% in 1935 (Baron *et al.*,

1986b:357). By 1980, Bridges and Villemez found that among a random sample of Chicago employees 49% of workers were employed in jobs that their employers reported as being part of promotion ladders—regardless of the size of the employing organization (Bridges and Villemez, 1994:62). Data from the General Social Survey for 1989, a representative national sample, show patterns that are consistent with these trends. In that survey, employers reported that they used formal procedures to promote employees in 49% of the jobs studied—either to a higher level within the current job or to an entirely higher level job classification (Kalleberg and Van Buren, 1996).[8] In short, although some authors have suggested that ILMs may have been waning in recent years (Pfeffer and Baron, 1988; Abraham, 1990), systematic evidence of their demise has not yet appeared.

b. Bureaucratic Personnel Systems

Modern personnel administration with its embedded notions of due process and industrial justice is empirically related to, but analytically distinct from, the establishments of ILMs. Observers of these systems have long recognized the implications that rule-ordered, internal "states" have for the experience of industrial work as a system of social control (Selznick, 1969; Burawoy, 1979; Halaby, 1986). Equally important, but perhaps not as widely appreciated, is the influence that modern personnel practices have had on the determination of wages in large, contemporary organizations. However, some like Baron *et al.* (1986b) have recognized this connection. In discussing the spread of modern personnel practices during the 1940s, they make the following observation about a 1947 job evaluation plan in the steel industry:

> Labor viewed the new system as consistent with their aim of eradicating capricious wage differentials, while steel companies saw the chance of systematizing and streamlining employment practices. (p. 372)

The thrust of our argument is that rationally designed compensation schemes, involving job evaluation and, in some instances, external wage surveys, need to be considered as integral elements of quasi-legal governance systems that arise in some large bureaucratic work organizations. Considerable data exist showing that structured pay plans or compensation schemes are a widespread feature of U.S. corporate and organizational life. In a 1976 survey of corporations in six industries (consumer goods manufacturing, industrial goods manufacturing, banking, insurance, public utilities, and retail trade), the Conference Board elicited information on the use of job evaluation for various types of positions. Among nonexempt salaried workers (largely lower-level office and clerical personnel), the percentage of firms using job evaluation ranged from 50% in retail trade to 88% in banking. In each of these industries the system used in well over half of the cases was formalized "point factor" technique (Weeks, 1976:46). (Perhaps the most famous of these is the Hay system developed by the Hay consulting firm.) In their historical study, Baron *et al.* (1986b) report that among companies with more than 250 employees, the percentage of those companies doing job evaluation increased from 18% in 1935 to 61% in 1946.

Compensation schemes, just like systematic grievance procedures, lead to a structure in which "normative beliefs establish a prescriptive baseline that workers use to grade the employer's exercise of authority, and thereby set their level of attachment" (Halaby, 1986:635). That is to say, personnel systems grounded in rational-legal norms provide an important legitimating function for contemporary management. Thus, employees come to expect fairness and due process in the allocation of rewards as well as punishments in these settings. In short, it is no accident that employers frequently depart from strict adherence to a price (wage) schedule set by supply and demand in the external market; it is a structural exigency of organizational life.

It would be a mistake, however, to describe these systems as if they completely ignored the market. To the contrary, as has been recognized for many years, "scientifically" based compensation systems purport to follow the market by incorporating information on prevailing rates in an area for what are sometimes referred to as "key" or "driver" jobs (Hildebrand, 1963; Dunlop, 1957). Two points are of immediate importance.

The first is that even if one assumes real market determination of the wage rates for these "key" jobs, the linkage of other wage rates to these key rates must of necessity involve the exercise of managerial discretion. This is true because there are a host of competing principles that must be taken into account in maintaining internal equity: honoring the "natural" social comparisons that employees make to those around them (see Gartrell, 1982); maintaining wage differentials that are large enough to encourage labor supply from "feeder" to "receiver" jobs, and providing wage differentials that are not too far out of line with differences in skill, effort, training, and responsibility.

The second point is that it is never entirely clear whether wage rates in the "key" jobs are established through actual market testing and individual bargaining with prospective workers (and prospective quitters), or whether the wage surveys that are carried out for such positions are merely a way of justifying decisions that have already been made. Thus, a key issue in any assessment of gender inequality in organizations that employ "scientific" compensation schemes is how wage surveys are conducted and utilized.

To conclude this section, we observe that contemporary managerial practice in both profit- and non-profit-making organizations frequently collides with the dictum that economic efficiency requires these organizations to act as mere price takers in the market for labor. Considerations related to both the "internal labor markets" and "bureaucratic personnel systems" suggest that managers in large formal organizations are often able to exercise considerable discretion in establishing wage rates for various kinds of jobs. While compensation schemes that incorporate data from external wage surveys can be described as "market sensitive," they can hardly be characterized as market determined, and involve multiple layers of discretionary judgments. What remains to be seen, however, is whether this discretionary power is used systematically to the detriment of those who work in predominantly female job classifications. Thus, a key question for empirical study is, "under what circumstances in the system of personnel relations does the necessary combination of discretionary opportunity and discriminatory motive arise to produce invidious between-job wage discrimination?" Weiler (1986), in perhaps the most comprehensive treatment of comparable worth to date, offers a diagnosis that is in much the same spirit:

> As illustrated by *Lemons*, real world labor markets leave a good deal of leeway for countless managerial judgements about how to classify, value, and pay certain jobs in comparison to others. The exercise of such discretion makes possible, although not inevitable, the exercise of sex discrimination.... This is not to deny that real competition obtains in different labor and product markets, which does place definite economic constraints upon the ability of firms to engage in discriminatory employment practices, not only in this new area of comparable worth, but also in the area long governed by title VII and the Equal Pay Act. But the issue of whether sex discrimination has a sufficiently depressive effect upon the wages paid for female work, thus warranting a public policy response, is a matter to be resolved only by detailed empirical investigation and not by a priori judgements about what a "market" must entail. (pp. 1762–1763)

2. Organizational Models

The foregoing suggests the need to develop more comprehensive theories of how the interactions of organizations with markets affects gender inequality in pay. As a beginning step in this endeavor, we offer two alternative models of this interaction. These models are the administered efficiency model, and an organizational inequality model that emphasizes two dimensions of organizational life as significant sources of gender inequality: (1) organizational or bureaucratic politics and (2) the organizational reproduction of cultural advantage.

a. The Administered Efficiency Model

The administered efficiency model is characteristic of those branches of economics that recognize that organizational influences might alter pure market determination of wage rates. For example, "efficiency-wage theorists" have argued that organizational effectiveness might be enhanced if some workers are paid more than their marginal products (Akerlof, 1984). More relevant to present concerns are an earlier generation of institutional economists who addressed the problem of systematic differences among wage rates within firms (Dunlop, 1957; Livernash, 1957).

The most sophisticated statement on the issue remains that provided by Hildebrand, who worried that "the notion of a range of indeterminacy [in organizational wage rates] can be pushed too far, at the cost of losing all the economics of wage determination" (1963:297). We can use Hildebrand's analysis to identify the key elements of the administered efficiency model: First is a tight linkage between the development of an internal job structure and an internal wage structure. Conceptually, these are different aspects of a firm's internal makeup, and it is likely that some factors that exert a major influence on the job structure (e.g., technology) exert only a minor or indirect influence on the wage structure. Without the existence of a "firm-specific" division of labor, however, wage rates would be set almost completely by external supply and demand. Second, the pay structure is anchored to the external labor market through the establishment of "key jobs," positions that are closely tied to similar jobs in the outside market. Of crucial importance is the fact that wage determination in the key jobs is assumed to proceed through the simple mechanism of supply and demand.[9] While wage surveys are both feasible and frequently used for jobs of this type, these formal methods can be regarded as a means of convenience, and identical results, with perhaps longer time lags, could be accomplished by a process of trial and error in making wage offers to prospective applicants and quitters.

The third, and final, aspect of the administered efficiency model concerns the nature of the wage relationships it identifies between "key" and "nonkey" jobs. Although almost all statements in the "institutionalist" paradigm leave room for the operation of factors such as custom and equity, these influences are never regarded as fully legitimate and the prime consideration in establishing within job-cluster differentials is the efficient allocation of labor among jobs differing in their contribution to economic output. Although never analyzed with complete precision, there are two assumptions about what efficiency means in organizational practice.

The first is that rate differentials are tied to differences in labor productivity associated with differences in skill, effort, or responsibility. The second is the principle of homogeneity of interest within management and labor and their opposition to one another. Workers, particularly when organized, are seen as creatures of habit favoring the maintenance of the status quo in relative wage rates. Management, by contrast, is unequivocally on the side of efficiency, preferring change over stasis when confronted with altered conditions requiring changing organizational solutions to the problem of efficiency.

Again, Hildebrand's treatment is revealing.

> Even without unionism, the key job and its associated cluster are natural units from which the design of the internal wage structure must proceed. Where management is free to act alone, it usually will rank its jobs by effort and skill, tying dependent job rates to key rates.... Second, they [internal wage differentials] should furnish adequate incentives for high worker efficiency throughout the organization. In purport, job evaluation seeks to achieve these objectives in systematic fashion—if you wish, by substituting technical standards and uniform procedures for the results that otherwise would be provided by an effectively competitive labor market, if one were available. (pp. 288, 290)

The administered efficiency model is silent on the question of whether the external labor market is tainted with sex discrimination, leading to the invidious undervaluation of women's work. Because the model portrays the internal wage structure as mirroring the effects of supply and demand in the external market, it would not be inconsistent with the model to find gender-based wage differentials inside organizations similar in size to those found in the outside world. The model implies, however, that the internal wage structure would not exacerbate such gender differences: To the extent rate differentials in the internal system are not directly linked to the external market, the model suggests they will be determined by differences in skill, effort, responsibility, and working conditions.

Although the administered efficiency approach does bring organizational considerations to bear on our understanding of the wage determination process, it ignores many of the normative, cultural, and institutional forces operating in work organizations. Specifically, its portrayal of organization management as a unitary and efficiency-seeking group fails to capture important forces that are rooted in the quasi-legal systems that govern work rules, employee discipline, pay, and other personnel matters in large bureaucracies (Selznick, 1969). Sometimes labeled "internal states" (Burawoy, 1979), these governance mechanisms create an arena in which normative and political considerations exert substantial influence over wage policies. Thus, the types of compensation schemes we analyze in this chapter do not exist in isolation from other elements of these governance systems, and employees come to expect fairness in the allocation of both rewards and punishments in these settings, e.g., internal equity (Halaby, 1986:635). Furthermore, the centralization of pay decisions in a well-defined organizational subunit creates a focal point for the expression of competing claims on the size and distribution of the payroll budget.

b. The Organizational Inequality Model

Bureaucratic Politics and Pay Determination. Our theory of organizational inequality more explicitly incorporates these normative and political dimensions and considers their consequences for gender-based wage inequality. We will refer to one important set of these factors under the rubric of "bureaucratic politics." The key insight of this approach is that noneconomic influences on pay levels are neither random nor minor deviations from market- or productivity-based considerations, but are systematically linked to the interests of organizational constituencies and are important sources of wage differences. The idea of bureaucratic politics is quite consistent with principles set forth in the literature on "power in organizations." The interest of organizational power theorists in explaining budget allocations directly parallels our concern with understanding salary determination (in fact, in many public sector contexts, salaries are the major portion of the budget). Both bureaucratic politics and organizational power theories question the assumption of homogeneous goals within organizations (see, e.g., Pondy, 1970; Pfeffer, 1981). Furthermore, both theories recognize that outcomes reflect the level of resources, broadly defined, available to different groups and constituencies within organizations (Perrow, 1970; Fligstein, 1987).

From our standpoint, the bureaucratic politics dimension of pay determination is perhaps best seen as a special case of organizational power theory in which several points are emphasized. First, power is not only lodged in formally defined organizational subunits, such as corporate functional groups or academic departments (Pfeffer and Moore, 1980; Miner, 1987), but also in other actors who are influential participants in salary setting. For example, the main actors in many large organizations would include staff officials within personnel departments, line officials in various departments, senior management, employee unions, and other activist groups. Second, we emphasize the significance of bureaucratic rules as opposed to bureaucratic subunits. Rules governing salary determination are important not only as an object of bureaucratic political struggle (Pondy, 1970), but also because they literally create some of the participants in the system, they specify the issues on which various groups can claim to have a legitimate interest, and they determine the kinds of political resources that can be brought to bear on the decision-making process. For example, in the public sector, some states allow union representation, but do not permit collective bargaining over wage rates. In other states, labor relations rules may permit both. We expect that the latter will exhibit different constellations of political influence than the former. Third, we emphasize the nature of the decision-making principles that govern the system (such as the prevailing rate standard, or the organization's market "positioning" wage policy) and how these formal principles are translated into organizational practice (e.g., through the implementation of a wage survey).

The bureaucratic politics perspective has different implications about the sources of between-job gender inequality than does the administered efficiency model. Rather than viewing gender differentials as the organizationally internalized product of market or efficiency considerations, the bureaucratic politics model provides more room for the operation of other organizational factors that produce between-job gender inequality. For example, in this model "internal equity" is not simply a free-floating subjective value, but is a principle that in some contexts is institutionalized in the practices and beliefs of the bureaucrats who administer the organization's pay system. Likewise concern for external legitimacy becomes a tool that can be wielded by various employee interest groups intent on rewiring an organization's compensation circuit boards. In yet other situations, the combination of parochial organizational climate with traditions of sponsorship and patronage produces a system of personal politics that can have dramatic implications for the shape of reward systems. What each of these considerations have in common, though, is that they suggest that the imbalance of political resources between the incumbents of predominantly male and predominantly female jobs can, in various organizational contexts, generate economic inequality between men and women.

The Organizational Reproduction of Male Cultural Advantage. The second organizational dimension of between-job inequality we consider is the organizational reproduction of cultural (i.e., male) advantage. Like some versions of the tainted market model, it is based on the premise that women occupy a cultural position that devalues their economic contributions.[10] It differs from them, however, in asserting that the general cultural disparagement of things feminine has its most pronounced influence on pay disparities in *interaction with the culture and structure of employing organizations*. In other words, a presumed deficit in cultural capital is not a handicap that uniformly diminishes the rates of pay associated with women or with jobs that have "feminine" traits. Instead, it will diminish their rewards differentially depending on other normative and structural aspects of the organization's environment.

There are some scattered precedents in the sociological and popular literature for looking at organizational employment patterns as reproductive of communally based status differences. In some instances the explicit emphasis is on the work organization as a nearly passive receptacle for status patterns found in the local community. Thus, Mack (1954) describes how a Midwestern industrial concern maintains an internal labor force that is completely segregated by ethnicity in the same manner as the local community.[11] Dalton's (1959) depiction of another Midwestern site contains a compelling portrait of how for the last several decades an internal spoils system has operated in favor of members of the local Masonic order at the expense of Catholics.

> if we drop the Catholics from our calculation, because as a group they considered themselves to be ineligible, we see that nearly 80 percent of the eligible managers were Masons. This is a highly significant difference and suggests, with the other data, that Masonic membership was usually an unofficial requirement for getting up—and for remaining there. (p. 191)

Although one might see this as an example of how internal status patterns directly replicate external ones, other considerations temper this conclusion. First, Dalton alludes to a much earlier era at the factory when a reverse pattern of dominance existed, i.e., Catholics were on top, and second, although Dalton studied three other industrial and commercial sites in the same locale, he makes no mention of the Masonic–Catholic status split in those institutions.[12] Significantly, he does mention several instances in which mobility-oriented employees put aside their preexisting reluctance and affiliated with the Masonic order in a highly calculative manner. In other words, the institutionalization of a communally based status characteristics inside the factor produced a kind of feedback loop in which the significance of the external split is reinforced.

There have been several studies of organizational gender inequality that are broadly consistent with our concept of the organizational reproduction of male cultural advantage. Ruth Milkman's study of job segregation by sex in the twentieth century automobile industry and electrical industry is relevant to this discussion in two major aspects (Milkman, 1987). First, her research demonstrates that gender-related patterns in job assignment and wage levels were quite variable across different employment contexts. She gives primary emphasis to variability between the two industries themselves, particularly their different histories and technologies. Because work in the electrical industry was controlled through piece rates rather than high-speed assembly lines, and was also in general somewhat "lighter," the electrical industry employed a much higher proportion of women than automobile manufacturing. At the same time, even though both industries practiced widespread job segregation and explicitly recognized "men's" and "women's" jobs, gender boundaries were less rigid in the electrical industry (1987:30–31). Milkman also provides numerous accounts of variability in gender employment patterns at the plant level within industries. Unfortunately, while noting the importance of this variability, Milkman fails to offer much explanation of it, and instead presents it as an argument for the arbitrariness of gender segregation in general.

The second major contribution that Milkman makes is to recognize the influence of the wider culture on gender employment patterns in particular factories. Management in each industry was not driven by a simple calculus of short-run profit maximization, which, for example, would have led them to engage in widespread substitution of female for male labor during the Great Depression. Equally important is her appreciation of the way industrial organization mediates elements of the broader culture that are brought into the production sphere. She describes "idioms" of sex typing—the specific ideological constructions that are used to explain and justify gender segregation somewhat differently in different industries.

> In the manufacturing sector, sex-typing speaks a different language, rooted not in women's family role, but in their real or imagined physical characteristics and capacities. No one pretends that being nurturant or knowing how to make a good cup of coffee are important qualities for factory jobs. Here the idiom centers on such qualities as manual dexterity, attention to detail, ability to tolerate monotony, and, above all, women's relative lack of physical strength. (1987:15–16)

Milkman's analysis deals primarily with job assignment rather than pay determination. But the argument is readily extended to pay determination in organizations. This is the explicit focus of a set of studies carried out by comparable worth scholar-activist Ronnie Steinberg (Steinberg, 1992; Steinberg and Walter, 1992; Steinberg and Jacobs, 1994). In her account, the primary organizational loci in which male cultural advantages have become congealed are the various job evaluation and pay systems adopted by employers in the last 50 years. Included here are the well-known Hay Point Factor System, but also other systems such as the SKEW (Stevenson, Kellogg, Ernst, and Whinney) plan. The central criticism of these systems is not that they explicitly reward job complexity, but that they implicitly define job complexity as an attribute that corresponds to level in a bureaucratic or supervisory hierarchy. In defining complexity in this way, other kinds of job complexity that are more likely to be found in lower-level positions go unrecognized and unrewarded. Since women and predominantly female jobs are less likely to be located anywhere except at the bottom or first level of authority in organizations, these systems inevitably shortchange them. A second fault Steinberg detects in most job evaluation and pay plans is that they promote inertia in the relative pay levels of different jobs. Given that many systems have been in place since the early 1950s, a time when pay differences between men and women even in the same job were accepted, utilizing a system that perpetuates this pattern is obviously discriminatory.

E. SELECTED FINDINGS

Do differing rates of pay in predominantly male and predominantly female jobs result from individual employers "following the market"? To answer this question, we conducted extensive case studies in four organizations where litigation over sex discrimination had left a rich record of documents and trial evidence. Because final dispositions had been reached in most of the selected cases, we were also able to interview key participants in these contests. The organizations themselves were a mix of public bureaucracies and private sector firms. On the public sector side, in-depth investigations were undertaken of the University of Northern Iowa (UNI), the respondent in *Dhristensen v. Iowa* (1977), and of the entire personnel system of the State of Washington, the defendant in *AFSCME v. State of Washington* (1985). The private sector firms that were scrutinized were Sears Roebuck, the subject of the well-known *EEOC v. Sears* case (1988), and a bank that we identify only by the pseudonym of Coastal Bank, which was the defendant organization in another discrimination case from the mid-1980s.

The public–private distinction is widely thought to be crucial to labor–management relations in organizations generally and wage administration in particular. First, management in public sector organizations is not driven by profit motives. There is some speculation, therefore, that public sector management may be able to indulge discriminatory preferences without facing the same kinds of economic costs that private management does. Indeed, Sorensen's (1994) analysis of census data suggests that the male–female earnings gap is larger in the public sector than in private industry. Second, public sector organizations tend to have more rigid pay systems, whereby wages are more strictly determined by job grade and rank within grade, than in the private sector, in which there is more managerial discretion in setting wage levels, at least within grade. Thus, a larger proportion of gender inequality in public sector pay systems may reside in differences between jobs rather than in differences between males and females. Third, public pay systems may have a more explicitly political character than private wage systems. Not only is the pay of state workers an item in the state budget, and thus open to scrutiny and debate, but the pay of workers and job categories is often a matter of public record. It is possible for one group of workers to learn what other workers are paid. Such information is closely guarded in private firms, perhaps in part to prevent comparisons and contention among workers.

The public–private distinction also tracks a very significant difference in pay discrimination litigation. With minor exceptions, comparable worth litigation, comparable worth legislation, and collectively bargained pay equity adjustments have been confined to the public sector.

The four organizations each exhibited significant gender-based pay differences, even after statistical adjustments were made for a variety of human capital characteristics such as education and seniority. These male–female wage gaps were largely the product of between-job wage differences among all state workers in Washington, among nonprofessional workers at UNI, and among lower-level, nonofficers at Coastal Bank. However, within-job pay differences figured more prominently in the Sears case and among the officer corps at Coastal. These variations in the locus of pay differences across organizational contexts imply the difficulty of mounting an adequate theory of organizational inequality without attending to organizational variation itself.

Most of these organizations engaged in activities that could be construed as consistent with market determination of pay rates. Surveys were conducted of pay rates among other employers, wage increases were implemented in response to increases in turnover, and hiring problems for occupations embedded in "tight" labor markets occasionally resulted in temporary increases in pay rates. Nevertheless the case studies strikingly demonstrate how large organizations mediate between the price of labor in the labor market and the wage schedules within organizations. Of central importance is the presence within each organization of a bureaucratic personnel system and a cadre of personnel officials who actively managed employment relations and promulgated and applied rules about pay practices.

These personnel bureaucracies did not simply attempt to incorporate market pricing into their organizations, but instead pursued a course of technocratic pragmatism with respect to wages. On some occasions pay bureaucrats and outside consultants openly rejected the market as a basis for setting wages, because it would have made wage administration too chaotic and uncertain. Pay officials in the State of Washington disregarded market rates by "averaging" the salary survey rates for several jobs to create a single, internal wage benchmark. Coastal Bank followed a common approach in large organizations: they surveyed the market primarily to determine how large an across-the-board increase to grant each year. In numerous ways, we found that these organizations were only loosely following the market.

1. The small proportion of jobs whose salaries were actually compared to external market rates. In all four organizations, the primary method employed to measure the market was a salary survey, done either by an outside consultant or by their own

personnel department. The surveys generated salary data on only a small fraction of the jobs in the organization, leaving considerable discretion to personnel officials about how to use the survey results. In the State of Washington case, we found that unexplained gender inequality was higher among jobs that were not used as market benchmarks than in jobs that were.

2. The arbitrariness of salary survey methods. We found that how a salary survey was actually conducted could be crucial to its results. Interested parties could influence such important decisions as what jobs to survey, what data to reject as inaccurate, and what situations called for the collection of additional data to correct results from earlier rounds of data gathering. In the State of Washington salary survey, agency officials and representatives of the state employees union had access to the survey process at every stage. The survey was transparently political in some respects. Officials consulted agency heads and employee groups about whether to use an in-state survey, an out-of-state survey, how to write job descriptions, and so on. In one instance, in response to agency pressure, survey officials dropped small employers from the survey results to produce a significantly higher "market" rate.
3. Arbitrariness in choosing appropriate market data for comparisons. We found in Coastal Bank that the "market rate" for a job varies substantially depending on what segment of the market is chosen for comparison. Wages would be calibrated differently, for example, if New York banks were chosen rather than banks in other cities. A striking example of the malleability of these comparisons was presented in the trial court opinion in *Christensen*. The judge demonstrated the wage gap between market pay rates for male and female jobs by selecting the highest paid male occupation in one community and the lowest paid female occupation in another community. The comparison was misleading. It ignored the variation in wage rates across communities for predominantly male and predominantly female jobs. And it gave an exaggerated impression of the wage gap for most male and female jobs.
4. The preservation of traditional wage differences among organizational positions. Similar to Rosenbaum's (1984) findings on the continuity of between-job wage patterns after the revision of a formal pay system, we found that personnel officers often openly resisted altering the relative pay rates of jobs. UNI refused to follow their own consultant's recommendation to put certain "male" and "female" jobs in the same job category. In the State of Washington wage survey, results largely maintained historical pay patterns. Despite a wide-ranging set of job evaluations, relatively few Coastal Bank jobs were targeted for special treatment because they were overpaid or underpaid. It appeared that the job evaluations, done largely by incumbent Coastal management, reproduced the existing job and pay hierarchy.
5. Managerial discretion to set pay levels. In the private sector firms we find that managers have substantial discretion about how to pay the employees under their own immediate supervision. Pre-1970's Sears presents an extreme case of decentralized pay authority. Store managers and other division heads apparently could strike their own deals with employees already in the organization to assemble their own managerial teams. As a result, the outside pay consultants found that pay levels varied widely and, overall, were well above what other comparable employers were paying. In the Coastal Bank case, supervisors could recognize "potential" as well as "performance" in establishing pay rates for their subordinates. An internal compensation committee's decision about the overall pay increase in the bank set the bounds on how an increase could be awarded without special justification. Within these bounds, however, managers could make their own judgments about what was an appropriate case.

These practices would have less significance if we found that the organizations continuously responded to market forces in other ways. However, there was little evidence of this. Turnover and retention data were rarely used to assess the adequacy of existing salary structures. There was an almost total absence of documented instances in which organizations had to adjust pay levels to get and keep workers. Although Coastal Bank was forced to raise the pay levels for computer programmers, after a few years they merged the technical jobs back into the regular pay schedule. More importantly, market exceptions were made in a highly particularistic manner. UNI, the State of Washington, and Coastal Bank all created exceptions for certain jobs from the regular salary structure. The jobs excepted were stereotypically male—craft workers at UNI and in Washington State; blue-collar workers in Coastal. In UNI and Washington, the decision to grant the exceptions was transparently political as they were concessions to organized labor's insistence that government pay "prevailing" (i.e., unionized) wage rates. These sorts of "market" exceptions stand in sharp contrast to the decisions on granting nurses an exception to the scheduled wage rates. It was not until turnover in state nursing positions had reached almost 50% that personnel officials approved ad hoc pay rate increases for nurses. In sum, in these organizations there are very few manifestations of universalistic, gender-neutral interactions between market forces and pay decision.

1. Evidence of Organizational Sources of Gender Inequality in Pay

At this point, the effect of organizational processes and interests on gender inequality in pay has been established mostly by indirection. That is, we have found evidence of the role of market forces to be so weak that considerable room is left for some other set of influences, a factor "X" if you will. But what documentation is there that this factor X is indeed organizationally situated?

First, a variety of organizational process data reveal that several aspects of organizational pay practices directly contribute to gender inequality. The most active participants in debates about wage surveys and job evaluations are male—male workers, male union representatives, and male managers. For example, at UNI, male administrators were fearful of the response of male physical plant workers to proposals to change the starting wages for some positions, but enjoyed paternalistic control over female clerical workers. As a result, they refused to adopt revisions in the pay scheme that would have tended to close the gender gap.

Many of the principles that Sears fostered in its pay and promotion system tended to disadvantage women or left male managerial discretion relatively unchecked. The axiom that "to get ahead you had to move" clearly put female employees at a disadvantage for promotions and relocation pay raises. Significantly, Sears's outside consultants advised a change in the policy of permanent pay raises based on relocations on the very ground of its inefficiency, contradicting a possible rational, sex-neutral justification of the practice.

At Coastal Bank, until the 1960s management had maintained separate personnel systems for men and women; had referred to its officer recruitment and training program as the "College Men's" program; and had systematically diverted female college graduates into lower-level managerial and even clerical positions. The top group of profit-sharing officers were all male, and our informants suggested that the basis for selection and promotion of individuals into some of the top positions was the nature of their social connections, even past athletic prowess.

These and other findings establish the link between organizational pay practices and gender inequality. The mechanisms that generate inequality to a certain extent are unique for each organization. The character and magnitude of wage differences are not the same across each organization. But in each case, we find significant unexplained wage differences between male and female jobs whose roots can be traced to organizational practices.

F. CONCLUSION

The most obvious implication of our results is to call into question the dominant discourse's explanation for between-job gender inequality in pay in large organizations. While we expect the relative influence of market and organizational processes to vary across market and organizational contexts, social scientists, courts, and policymakers should not uncritically assume that between-job wage differences are a simple reflection of market processes. Indeed, it is ironic that one of the leading criticisms of comparable worth as a policy is the subjective character of the job evaluation procedures on which it relies. We have established that supposedly market-based wage-setting systems in organizations also are subject to manipulation and reconstruction.

Yet we are not advocates of comparable worth as the best solution to the problem of between-job gender discrimination in pay. One of the implications of our results is that simply changing the formal aspects of a pay system, without changing its political configuration, is not likely to be effective. Some jurisdictions that experimented with comparable worth systems discovered that while the gender gap in wages narrowed temporarily in response to equity pay raises, the gains were quickly recaptured by other participants in the pay system, such as union members, supervisors, and professional groups. Given the practical and political difficulties posed by comparable worth, we favor other approaches that are not inherently opposed to market values and may in fact try to incorporate them more fairly and accurately. These include more intensive scrutiny of between-job wage differences under Title VII that would expand and revise on present notions of intentional discrimination, the promulgation of a set of "best practices" models of pay determination that eliminate some of the mechanisms that predictably yield unjustified male–female wage differences, and possibly, mandates for employers to conduct pay equity studies of their firms.

One of the puzzles our analysis presents is why the federal courts opened the door to between-job discrimination cases in *Gunther*, but then in effect closed the door on such cases by adopting the conventional market-based explanation for the wage differences at issue. One can think of several possible answers: (1) There is the conventional doctrinal explanation: the courts applied the law to the facts and concluded that the plaintiffs had not made out their case. (2) There is a standard judicial politics explanation: the political costs to the courts of invalidating the pay systems of large employers were too high, even if the judges thought the plaintiffs had valid claims. (3) There is the radical judicial politics explanation: the courts cynically created a mythical right of redress in order to relieve the strains of injustice in society, but then refused to honor those claims in practice. Although these are not mutually exclusive explanations, we do not find them persuasive. While it is true that the plaintiffs occasionally bungled the presentation of their theories and evidence in these cases, it is clear from the in-depth case studies and the reading of the other opinions that the courts typically went well beyond merely stating that the plaintiffs had failed to carry their burden of proof. With a few exceptions, the opinions offered sweeping pronouncements that market forces and efficiency considerations explained the wage differences between male and female jobs. To be sure, the opinions do occasionally refer to the fact that a finding for the plaintiffs would raise difficult issues of how to design an appropriate remedy, but such statements usually go hand in hand with statements that the wage determination process is better left to market forces and the business judgments of employers.

The more radical formulation—that courts are participating in the creation of mythical rights—cannot be tested directly, but also does not seem to fit. The *Gunther* case that opened up the possibility of using Title VII for between-job discrimination was a bitterly contested, 5-to-4 decision that resolved conflicting interpretations by several lower courts. The *Gunther*-majority was unwilling to interpret Title VII in a fashion that would countenance blatant forms of intentional pay discrimination just because the workers involved held different jobs. We are more inclined to read *Gunther* as evidence of the normative appeal of the antidiscrimination principle than as a merely symbolic gesture toward gender equality.

Thus, we come down in favor of an ideological explanation of these cases. That is, the courts saw the evidence present in these cases through the lens of the dominant discourse on between-job gender inequality. The certainty of this vision is revealed in the texts of these opinions, such as we quoted from Justice Kennedy and Judge Posner, where judges consistently invoked the market as the explanation for the wage differences at issue, despite often powerful evidence to the contrary in the record. This is an instance of what Kim Scheppele (1987) refers to as perceptual fault lines—the courts in these cases would acknowledge the antidiscrimination principle articulated by *Gunther*, but were largely unwilling to question the dominant explanation of "the facts" before them. Schultz and Pettersen (1992) mount a similar argument to explain the higher success rates of African-American plaintiffs than female plaintiffs in Title VII sex segregation cases. The lack of interest defense by employers resonated with judges' world-views on gender roles, but they did not have such a cultural script for why African-Americans would choose different jobs than whites.

The courts' decisions had both a practical and ideological effect. The practical effect was to block efforts of women to use the law as a mechanism for redressing wage inequality. The decisions' ideological effects also are local and global. The message within the organizations where defendants won in court was that the law had validated the status quo. The opinions also affect the broader discourse about gender inequality. In a sense the courts gave authority to the very ideology on which the opinions rested. Many economists would applaud the promarket pronouncements of the courts. Other observers who are not intimately involved in problems of gender inequality may tend to equate the certainty of judicial opinion with the certainty of the market explanation. We suspect that this is what lies behind the question we almost always get from colleagues with whom we are discussing this project: "Isn't that a dead issue now?"

We see the courts engaged in legitimation and denial. The *Gunther* decision declared that the law would respond to glaring instances of inequality, even if there were some question about the formal correctness of such an interpretation of the law. In light of that declaration of jurisdiction, the courts then consistently refused to find instances of pay inequality worthy of judicial intervention. In this two-step move, the courts simultaneously legitimated the law as an institution and denied that there were problems with the pay practices of employers. The courts effectively legalized a fundamental aspect of gender inequality.

The failed effort to define some kinds of between-job pay differences as discrimination is an illustration of how the law's capacity to "construct social reality" (Comaroff, 1994) can dampen, as well as encourage, resistance to inequality. The post-*Gunther* cases reconfirmed the ideology of the market as the source of gender inequality in pay. The cases did not "unravel the workings of power" or lead to a "reconstruction of received realities"—as Comaroff suggests law can do. Rather, these cases reinforced the social constructions of the existing gender order in organizations.

It is not necessary to end on a completely gloomy note. There is nothing inherent or unchangeable in the stance of the courts. If expert opinion on these matters changes, the courts too might reconsider the issue. Of course, economics retains its dominant position within the body of social science consulted by the courts, at least on questions of wage inequality. While many economists show little inclination to reexamine the issues we have raised, Williamson (1975) and others have begun to argue for new conceptions of the boundary between markets and firms that may lead to new economic models of wage determination of organizations. Part of the problem until now is that the debate about the male–female wage gap has been polarized in ways that have impoverished both our understanding of the phenomenon and the range of possible responses through law and regulatory policy. The assertion by comparable worth advocates that the market is the problem has left undeveloped alternative sociological conceptions of the sources of wage inequality. If sociologists construct programs of empirical research that better articulate the relationship between organizations, markets, and wages, they may produce more powerful explanations of pay determination than orthodox economists and comparable worth advocates have thus far. This in turn may break the current stalemate in academic circles. This ferment may in turn change the legal and regulatory climate.

Such intellectual change requires a measure of power. The law currently gives employers the right to control access to the kinds of data that are required to rigorously examine organizational pay practices. Until such data are made available, social scientists, policymakers, and the courts will not be able to make informed judgments.

G. ENDNOTES

1. This chapter draws heavily from our book manuscript, Nelson and Bridges (1999).
2. The case citations are *AFSCME v. State of Washington*, 1985; *Christensen v. State of Iowa*, 1977; and *EEOC v. Sears, Roebuck & Co.*, 1988. We cannot disclose the case citation for the Coastal Bank case.
3. In *Wards Cove Packing Co. v. Atonio*, 1989, the Supreme Court significantly narrowed the doctrine by holding that only certain kinds of comparisons would be considered relevant to the questions of discrimination. The Civil Rights Act of 1991 legislatively reversed *Wards Cove*, mandating that the law on disparate impact was to be returned to what existed prior to the *Wards Cove* decision. The comparable worth cases we review here were decided before *Wards Cove*. Therefore, the precedents should not be affected by that case or the Civil Rights Act of 1991.
4. See, e.g., *AFSCME v. State of Washington* (1985:1406): "A compensation system that is responsive to supply and demand and other market forces is not the type of specific, clearly delineated employment policy contemplated by *Dothard* and *Griggs*; such a compensation system, the result of a complex of market forces, does not constitute a single practice that suffices to support a claim under disparate impact theory."
5. The term *local* is used here to mean the opposite of global, and is not meant to imply a widespread tendency toward geographic particularization. The fact that the U.S. federal government imposes a unified wage structure on its employees is, thus, a confirmation of local determination, not a refutation of it. (This is true because the federal government's practice is but one of many ways in which pay scales are set.)
6. We should add that the demand for workers also depends on the technology that relates occupational performances to the output produces by each firm.
7. We are deferring discussion of whether this, or any other type of market "taint," would be eroded by competitive market pressures over the long run. These are important issues but they appear with regard to almost all kinds of discrimination, not just for the simple crowding model.
8. These percentages are based on the 727 CORE and the 727 GSS jobs that were studied by the General Social Survey researchers. We excluded from these recalculations data on the matching sample of managers, because they would have tended to add an upward bias to these estimates.
9. "The labor market exerts its main force upon internal wage rates through 'market-oriented' jobs, that is, jobs that are fairly uniform in duties and vocational requirements as among firms in the local area.... Such jobs will be particularly sensitive to the market, which manifests itself through the number and quality of new applicants and through the voluntary quit rate" (Hildebrand, 1963:274–275). "Thus, they [market-oriented jobs] represent one kind of key job, with a key rate in the structure. They do so because the work is comparable, the employers compete for this kind of labor, and mobility is greater among such workers. Accordingly, the rate for a market-oriented key job must be adequate to hold the quantity of labor sought, in the numbers desired" (Hildebrand, 1963:276).

10. In many contexts, however, the economic devaluation of women does not necessarily consign them to a ubiquitous dishonorable status. To the contrary, economic disparagement can often be combined with rather inflated notions of female virtue and honor.
11. The factory is a railroad repair shop in which the Italians work at the lighter, less intensive patchwork jobs, and the Swedes and Finns specialize in the heavier complete rebuilding of badly damaged cars. Interestingly, this division of labor is supported by a set of opposed cultural representations that allow each group to see the work of the other as consistent with a derogatory group stereotype. For example, the Italians regard the heavy rebuilding work as well-suited to the alleged stolid and slow-witted nature of the Swedes.
12. It is difficult to discern whether this silence is due to a lack of comprehensive data on the other sites or the absence of the structural split.

REFERENCES

Abraham, K. G. (1990). Restructuring the Employment Relationship: The Growth of Market Mediated Work Arrangements. In K. G. Abraham and R. McKensie (Eds.), *New Developments in the Labor Market: Toward a New Institutional Paradigm*. Cambridge, MA: MIT Press. 85–120.

Akerlof, G. (1984). Gift Exchange and Efficiency-Wage Theory: Four Views. *American Economic Review*, *74* (May), 79–83.

Althauser, R. P. (1989). Internal Labor Markets. In W. R. Scott and J. Blake (Eds.), *Annual Review of Sociology* (Vol. 15). Palo Alto, CA: Annual Reviews. 143–161.

Althauser, R. P., and Kalleberg, A. (1981). Firms, Occupations, and the Structure of Labor Markets: A Conceptual Analysis. In I. Berg (Ed.), *Sociological Perspectives on Labor Markets*. New York: Academic Press. 119–149.

Baron, J., Davis-Blake, N., and Bielby, W. T. (1986a). The Structure of Opportunity: How Promotion Ladders Vary within and among Organizations. *Administrative Science Quarterly*, *31*, 248–273.

Baron, J. N., Dobbin, F. R., and Devereaux-Jennings, P. (1986b). War and Peace: The Evolution of Modern Personnel Administration in U.S. Industry. *American Journal of Sociology*, *92*, 350–383.

Baron, J. N., Devereaux-Jennings, P., and Dobbin, F. R. (1988). Mission Control? The Development of Personnel Systems in U.S. Industry. *American Sociological Review*, *53*, 497–514.

Baron, J. N., Mittman, B., and Newman, A. (1991). Targets of Opportunity: Organizational and Environmental Determinants of Gender Integration within the California Civil Service, 1979–1985. *American Journal of Sociology*, *96*, 1362–1401.

Bergmann, B. R. (1974). Occupational Segregation, Wages, and Profits when Employers Discriminate by Race or Sex. *Eastern Economic Journal*, *1*, 103–110.

Bridges, W. P., and Villemez, W. J. (1991). Employment Relations and the Labor Market: Integrating Institutional and Market Perspectives. *American Sociological Review*, *56*, 748–764.

Bridges, W. P., and Villemez, W. J. (1994). *The Employment Relationship: Causes and Consequences of Modern Personnel Administration*. New York: Plenum Press.

Burawoy, M. (1979). *Manufacturing Consent*. Chicago: University of Chicago Press.

Chicago Sun-Times. (1998, June 10). Women's Wages Rise. pp. 1–2.

Comaroff, J. L. (1994). Foreword. In M. Lazarus-Black and S. F. Hirsch (Eds.), *Contested States: Law, Hegemony, and Resistance*. London: Routledge. ix–xiii.

Corcoran, M., Duncan, G. J., and Ponza, M. (1984). Work Experience, Job Segregation, and Wages. In B. F. Reskin (Ed.), *Sex Segregation in the Workplace: Trends, Explanations, Remedies*. Washington, DC: National Academy Press. 171–191.

Dalton, M. (1959). *Men Who Manage*. New York: John Wiley and Sons.

Doeringer, P. (1967). Determinants of the Structure of Industrial Type Internal Labor Markets. *Industrial and Labor Relations Review*, *20* (Jan.), 206–220.

Doeringer, P., and Piore, M. (1971). *Internal Labor Markets and Manpower Analysts*. Lexington, MA: Heath.

Dunlop, J. T. (1957). The Task of Contemporary Wage Theory. In G. Tayler and F. Pierson (Eds.), *New Concepts in Wage Determination*. New York: McGraw–Hill.

Edwards, R. (1979). *Contested Terrain*. New York: Basic Books.

England, P. (1982). The Failure of Human Capital Theory to Explain Occupational Sex Segregation. *Journal of Human Resources*, *17*, 358–369.

England, P. (1984). Wage Appreciation and Depreciation: A Test of Neoclassical Economic Explanations of Occupational Sex Segregation. *Social Forces*, *62*, 726–749.

England, P. (1992). *Comparable Worth: Theories and Evidence.* New York: Aldine de Gruyter.
Finlay, W. (1983). One Occupation, Two Labor Markets: The Case of Longshore Crane Operators. *American Sociological Review, 48*, 306–315.
Fligstein, N. (1987). The Intraorganizational Power Struggle: Rise of Financial Personnel to Top Leadership in Large Corporations, 1919–1979. *American Sociological Review, 52*, 44–58.
Gartrell, C. D. (1982). On the Visibility of Wage Referents. *Canadian Journal of Sociology, 7*, 117–143.
Gitelman, H. M. (1966). Occupational Mobility within the Firm. *Industrial and Labor Relations Review, 20* (Oct.), 50–65.
Halaby, C. (1986). Worker Attachment and Workplace Authority. *American Sociological Review, 51*, 634–649.
Hildebrand, G. (1963). External Influences and the Determination of the Internal Wage Structure. In J. L. Meij (Ed.), *Internal Wage Structures.* Amsterdam: North-Holland.
Jacoby, S. (1984). The Development of Internal Labor Markets in American Manufacturing Firms. In P. Osterman (Ed.), *Internal Labor Markets.* Cambridge, MA: MIT Press. 23–69.
Kalleberg, A. L., and Van Buren, M. (1996). Is Bigger Better? Explaining the Relationship between Organization Size and Job Rewards. *American Sociological Review, 61*, 47–66.
Kerr, C. (1954). The Balkanization of Labor Markets. In *Labor Mobility and Economic Opportunity.* New York: Wiley. 92–110.
Killingsworth, M. (1985). The Economics of Comparable Worth: Analytical, Empirical, and Policy Questions. In H. Hartmann (Ed.), *Comparable Worth: New Directions for Research.* Washington, DC: National Academy Press. 86–115.
Lehrer, E. L., and Stokes, H. H. (1985). Determinants of the Female Occupational Distribution: A Log-Linear Analysis. *Review of Economics and Statistics, 67*, 395–404.
Livernash, E. R. (1957). The Internal Wage Structure. In G. Taylor and F. Pierson (Eds.), *New Concepts in Wage Determination.* New York: McGraw–Hill. 142–145.
Mack, R. (1954). Ecological Patterns in an Industrial Shop. *Social Forces, 32*, 351–356.
Madden, J. F. (1973). *The Economics of Sex Discrimination.* Lexington, MA: Lexington Books.
McCann, M. (1994). *Rights at Work: Pay Equity Reform and the Politics of Legal Mobilization.* Chicago: University of Chicago Press.
Milkman, R. (1987). *Gender at Work: The Dynamics of Job Segregation by Sex during World War II.* Urbana: University of Illinois Press.
Miner, A. (1987). Idiosyncratic Jobs in Formalized Organizations. *Administrative Science Quarterly, 32*, 327–351.
Nelson, R. L., and Bridges, W. P. (1999). *Legalizing Gender Inequality.* New York: Cambridge University Press.
New York Times. (1997, September 21). Wage Disparities for Men and Women Persist, p. B10.
Osterman, P. (1984). Introduction: The Nature and Importance of Internal Labor Markets. In P. Osterman (Ed.), *Internal Labor Markets.* Cambridge, MA: MIT Press. 1–22.
Perrow, C. (1970). Departmental Power and Perspective in Industrial Firms. In M. Zald (Ed.), *Power in Organizations.* Nashville, TN: Vanderbilt University Press. 59–89.
Pfeffer, J. (1981). *Power in Organizations.* Marshfield, MA: Pittman.
Pfeffer, J., and Baron, J. (1988). Taking the Workers Back Out: Recent Trends in the Structuring of Employment. In B. M. Staw and L. L. Cummings (Eds.), *Research in Organizational Behavior.* Greenwich, CT: JAI Press. 257–303.
Pfeffer, J., and Cohen, Y. (1984). Determinants of Internal Labor Markets in Organization. *Administrative Science Quarterly, 29*, 550–572.
Pfeffer, J., and Moore, W. (1980). Power in University Budgeting: A Replication and Extension. *Administrative Science Quarterly, 25*, 637–653.
Polachek, S. (1981). Occupational Self-Selection: A Human Capital Approach to Sex Differences in Occupational Structure. *Review of Economics and Statistics, 63*, 60–69.
Pondy, L. R. (1970). Toward a Theory of Internal Resource-Allocation. In M. Zald (Ed.), *Power in Organizations.* Nashville, TN: Vanderbilt University Press. 270–311.
Reskin, B., and Padavic, I. (1994). *Women and Men at Work.* Thousand Oaks, CA: Pine Forge Press.
Rosenbaum, J. (1984). *Career Mobility in a Corporate Hierarchy.* New York: Academic Press.
Scheppele, K. L. (1987). The Re-Vision of Rape Law. *University of Chicago Law Review, 54*, 1095–1116.
Schultz, V., and Pettersen, S. (1992). Race, Gender, Work, and Choice: An Empirical Study of the Lack of Interest Defense in Title VII Cases Challenging Job Segregation. *University of Chicago Law Review, 59*, 1073–1181.
Selznick, P. (1969). *Law, Society, and Industrial Justice.* New York: Russell Sage Foundation.
Sorensen, E. (1994). *Comparable Worth: Is It a Worthy Policy?* Princeton, NJ: Princeton University Press.
Steinberg, R. J. (1992). Gender on the Agenda: Male Advantage in Organizations. *Contemporary Sociology, 21*, 576–581.

Steinberg, R. J., and Jacobs, J. A. (1994). Pay Equity in Nonprofit Organizations: Making Women's Work Visible. In T. Odendahl and M. O'Neill (Eds.), *Women and Power in the Nonprofit Sector*. San Francisco: Jossey–Bass. 79–120.

Steinberg, R., and Walter, W. L. (1992). *Making Women's Work Visible, the Case of Nursing: First Steps in the Design of a Gender-Neutral Job Comparison System*. Paper presented at the Third Women's Policy Research Conference. Institute for Women's Policy Research, Washington, DC.

Sullivan, C. A., Zimmer, M. J., and Richards, R. F. (1988). *Employment Discrimination* (2nd ed.). Boston: Little, Brown.

Sunstein, C. R. (1991). Why Markets Don't Stop Discrimination. *Social Philosophy & Politics*, *8*, 22–37.

Treiman, D. J., and Hartmann, H. S. (1981). *Women, Work, and Wages: Equal Pay Jobs of Equal Worth*. Washington, DC: National Academy Press.

Weeks, D. A. (1976). Compensating Employees: Lessons of the 1970's. *Report 707*. New York: Conference Board.

Weiler, P. (1986). The Wages of Sex: The Uses and Limits of Comparable Worth. *Harvard Law Review*, *99*, 1728–1807.

Williamson, O. (1975). *Markets and Hierarchies*. New York: Free Press.

IV

Law and Culture

10

Gender, Law, and Justice

Jill McCorkel, Frederika E. Schmitt, and Valerie P. Hans

A. INTRODUCTION

One of the liveliest, most productive, and most controversial issues in contemporary sociolegal scholarship is the relationship of gender and law. No comprehensive handbook on law and social science would be complete without a chapter reflecting the tremendous theoretical and research advances that scholars have made over the last several decades in understanding this relationship.

The chapter begins with an in-depth examination of feminist theories of law. Feminist legal theorizing emerged as a significant strand of jurisprudence during the heyday of the contemporary women's movement in the early 1970s. Early feminist critiques focused on gender-specific laws that meted out different privileges and punishments according to gender, and on a variety of institutional practices that discriminated on the basis of sex. Feminist jurisprudence was preoccupied by "sameness," in that justice meant men and women should receive equal treatment under the law. An equal treatment approach was appealing on a number of levels, particularly since it held the liberal promise of readily rectifying social inequality. At the same time, it tended to ignore other differences in the life experiences of women and men that complicated the application of equal treatment.

Throughout the 1980s, feminist legal theory was polarized by ideas about difference. It became increasingly apparent that justice for women could not be achieved solely through equal application of the law. Indeed, the fact that men and women are not similarly situated within institutions and social relationships renders liberal strategies at best ineffective, and at worst harmful. The sameness/difference debate, reviewed in detail below, proved quite fertile in giving rise to a number of different strands of feminist legal theorizing, including radical feminism, difference feminism, and critical feminism. At the forefront of contemporary debate lies the challenges posed by postmodernist analyses of gender and discourse, and the distinctly

Jill McCorkel • Department of Sociology, Northern Illinois University, De Kalb, Illinois 60115. Frederika E. Schmitt • Department of Sociology and Anthropology, Millersville University, Millersville, Pennsylvania 17551. Valerie P. Hans • Department of Psychology, University of Delaware, Wilmington, Delaware 19802.

Handbook of Justice Research in Law, edited by Sanders and Hamilton. Kluwer Academic / Plenum Publishers, New York, 2000.

sociological "gendered institutions" approach which investigates the extent to which gender is embedded in the institutional practices and structures of the legal system. Throughout, the chapter shows links between theoretical ideas and research traditions in feminist scholarship. Contrasting these different theoretical traditions is quite useful in that each is characterized by distinctive ideas regarding the nature of gender inequality and how best to achieve justice for women through law.

After describing the traditions of feminist legal thought, the chapter takes an empirical turn. We look at "law in action," that is, how the justice system operates with female victims, offenders, and other participants in the court process. We focus particularly on violence against women, including three issues that have generated substantial bodies of research: rape, domestic violence, and sexual harassment. We address the charge that feminist scholars have been so concerned with female victimization that they have glorified women's status as "victims." The chapter concludes with an assessment of several unresolved issues in feminist scholarship on law and legal institutions.

B. THEORIZING LAW AND JUSTICE: TOWARD A FEMINIST JURISPRUDENCE

Jurisprudence, broadly conceptualized, is a theory of the relationship between law and social life. It serves as the scaffolding on which law as an institution and practice can be located and understood. Jurisprudence guides the development of law and provides the baseline from which that development is critiqued and restructured. Implicit in this theory of what the law should be and how it should serve its constituents—that is, how best to achieve justice—are a series of assumptions about social structure, social relations, and human nature. Feminist theories of the law can be distinguished from other jurisprudential endeavors according to the content of these assumptions.

At the center of feminist critique is the contention that law is not gender neutral. Indeed, feminist theories argue that gender influences the development and interpretation of the law, how (and to whom) the law is applied, and the organization and practice of law (Becker, Bowman, and Torrey, 1994; Bender, 1988). Embedded in feminist legal theorizing, then, is the contention that gender matters. Accounting for the influence of gender on social structure, social relations, and human nature distinguishes feminist theorizing from traditional legal liberalism and from other critical approaches that fail to acknowledge gender as a prime source of social inequality.

It would be a mistake, however, to suggest that a unified feminist jurisprudence exists. It is more accurate to refer to feminist legal *theories*. Just as feminism makes different assumptions about human nature and social life when compared to other theories of jurisprudence, feminist theorists themselves differ in their assumptions about law and social life and in the remedies they propose to rectify gender-based inequalities.

1. Liberal Feminism: The Struggle for Equal Treatment

Liberal feminism has its origins in such early works as Mary Wollstonecraft's (1792/1975) *A Vindication of the Rights of Women*, John Stuart Mill's (1869/1970) "The Subjection of Women," and Harriet Taylor Mill's (1851/1970) "Enfranchisement of Women." Each of these early philosophers suggested that women's degraded social status is the result of legal and social obstacles that inhibit their capacity to participate fully in economic and public life. By eradicating legal and other barriers, gender equality is possible. Like traditional liberal theorists, liberal feminists assume that it is in the state's best interest to maximize individual freedom by allowing all individuals the capacity to pursue their own goals. The function of law is to ensure that individuals have an equal opportunity to pursue their goals and to allow other individuals to pursue theirs, regulating behavior so that individuals do not infringe on each other.

Liberal feminists share these assumptions, but maintain a focus on gender relations—that men and women are not treated equally by the law, which in turn produces differences in political, social, and economic opportunities. As such, liberal feminists do not criticize the structure or epistemology of the Western legal tradition, but instead demand that this tradition remain true to its own tenets. If all individuals are the same under the eyes of the law, then there should be no discrimination on the basis of sex (Eisenstein, 1982).

In the wake of gains established during Civil Rights era legislation, feminist scholars during the 1970s worked to promote women's rights and status. The Equal Protection Clause of the Fourteenth Amendment became an important strategy for securing gender equality. In a series of cases applying the Equal Protection Clause, the U.S. Supreme Court established different levels of scrutiny for differential treatment of individuals (see Goldstein, 1994). Specifically, the Court held that differential treatment must bear a rational relation to the legitimate government purpose. A "strict" standard of scrutiny is used for characteristics beyond individual control, such as race or ethnicity. Under strict scrutiny, the state must demonstrate that differential treatment is necessary to achieve a compelling governmental purpose in order that such treatment pass constitutional muster. The U.S. Supreme Court has refused to apply the strict scrutiny standard for assessing differential treatment on the basis of gender, but the Court has established an "intermediate" standard of scrutiny with which to judge laws that differentiate on the basis of gender. Under this standard, a gender-based classification must bear a substantial relationship to an important governmental purpose. Formally, this standard is weaker than the strict scrutiny standard but warrants more review than the rational basis test used for most other types of classifications.

During the 1970s, attorneys used the existence of the intermediate scrutiny standard to challenge the constitutionality of a number of administrative and statutory classifications that differentiated on the basis of sex. Sex-specific classifications took any number of forms, including setting the number of hours women could work a day, limiting the amount of weight women could be required to lift in their jobs, restricting jury duty and military service, and preventing women from holding certain jobs. *Reed v. Reed*, decided by the Supreme Court in 1971, officially broke the Court's prior policy of routinely upholding gender-specific laws. The *Reed* case involved an Idaho statute stating that when two individuals are equally qualified to administer an estate (in terms of their relationship to the decedent), a man should receive preference over a woman. Idaho justified the classification by asserting that men have more experience with business affairs and, therefore, would be more efficient in administering the estate. The Court invalidated the statute on the basis that the classification violated the Equal Protection Clause.

The intermediate scrutiny standard has served to limit governmental reliance on stereotyped assumptions about men's and women's natures, abilities, or characteristics as the basis for differential treatment of women and men who are similarly situated (see, e.g., *Frontiero v. Richardson*, 1983; *Craig v. Boren*, 1976). Indeed, recent decisions by the U.S. Supreme Court suggest that a majority of the Justices are strongly committed to equal treatment principles regarding gender. Even longstanding practices of differential treatment (e.g., state-supported, male-only schools such as the Citadel and Virginia Military Institute) have been overturned in recent years. Few state and federal laws that currently discriminate on the basis of sex are likely to survive constitutional scrutiny [see, e.g., Goldstein and Stech's (1995) analysis of trends in the Supreme Court's treatment of gender equity cases]. Furthermore, the notion of equal treatment is immensely popular with the public. Indeed, affirmative action practices that are seen as providing special consideration for disadvantaged groups (including women) are increasingly attacked as violating the basic normal of equal treatment.

A liberal emphasis on equality has generated a prodigious amount of scholarly research on the legal system's treatment of women compared to men. For example, in the area of criminal law numerous studies have contrasted the rates at which men and women are arrested and convicted for criminal conduct (see, e.g., the reviews in Belknap, 1996; Price and Sokoloff, 1995), and there is ongoing research and debate about the extent to which women receive more lenient criminal sentences (Chesney-Lind, 1995; Daly, 1994; McCorkel, 1996). Many studies of the impact of gender on the processing of defendants has discovered that the law is differentially applied to women and men, and disparate treatment is the result (Adler, 1975; Heilbrun and Heilbrun, 1986; Simon and Landis, 1991). However, there is sharp disagreement about whether women receive more lenient or more severe treatment than men in the criminal justice system.

The leniency model argues that women, regardless of race or class, receive preferential treatment within the criminal justice system. In its original formulation, the leniency model was based on the assumption that female offenders receive preferential treatment because the predominantly male army of police, lawyers, and judges they confronted exhibited chivalrous and paternalistic behavior in their social interactions with women (Adler, 1975; Pollak, 1950; Smart, 1977). This point was later reformulated to suggest that institutional actors (of either sex) working within the criminal justice system treat men and women differently because of gender role distinctions. Advocates of the leniency model have found empirical support for their position in nearly every area of the criminal justice system. Comprehensive arrest statistics such as the Uniform Crime Reports demonstrate that men are far more likely to be arrested for criminal offenses than women. While most leniency theorists would not dispute the fact that men commit more crime than women, they do suggest that women commit much more crime than is reflected in arrest statistics (Box and Hale, 1984; Smith and Visher, 1981). Some scholars have used the low female arrest rate to argue that police are more likely to treat women leniently by not arresting them, while others contend that women are able to get away with more crime than men because police view them as less capable criminals (Box and Hale, 1984; Krohn, Curry, and Nelson-Kilger, 1983; Steffensmeir, 1980).

Lenient treatment of women appears to be present in other parts of the criminal justice system as well. Studies of prosecutorial discretion, for example, find that women are more likely than men to have their cases dismissed (Pope, 1976; Spohn, Gruhl, and Welch, 1987). A number of quantitative analyses have found that, after controlling for legally relevant variables, women appear to receive preferential treatment in sentencing outcomes (Daly, 1989; Moulds, 1980; Simon and Landis, 1991; Steffensmeir, Kramer, and Streifel, 1993).

Conversely, the severity model is based on the contention that women, like other oppressed social groups, are treated punitively by the criminal justice system. Proponents of the severity model argue that female offenders receive harsher treatment in the criminal justice system because they have not only violated conventional norms of behavior by engaging in a crime, but they have also overstepped the acceptable range of behavior for women in this society (Feinman, 1994; Temin, 1980; Chesney-Lind, 1997). The earliest studies in this tradition sought to expose how women were doubly punished as criminals and as deviant women. A number of studies, for example, have demonstrated that, far from being chivalrous and lenient, a significant portion of police response toward women is quite severe. Studies of police encounters and family courts found that girls charged with status offenses and sexual and morals offenses are far more likely than boys to be treated harshly (Rosenbaum and Chesney-Lind, 1994; Chesney-Lind, 1977; Datesman and Scarpitti, 1980). Further, proponents of the severity model argue that although men may be sentenced to longer periods of incarceration, women actually serve a larger portion of their sentence in prison (see Simon and Landis, 1991) and, as inmates, are subject to harsher conditions of confinement and have access to fewer resources (Chesney-Lind, 1995; Baskin, Sommers, Tessler, and Stendman, 1989; Morash, Haarr, and Rucker, 1994).

In addition to the substantial amount of work on whether women receive equal treatment in the criminal justice system, other scholars have compared how women fare compared to men in the civil justice system. Early research by Nagel and Weitzman (1972), based on automobile accident cases from the 1960s, found some disparities in civil damage awards to male and female plaintiffs. In cases with comparable injuries, men's awards were higher than the average, while women's were lower. Goodman, Loftus, Miller, and Greene (1991) reported on archival data from the state of Washington during the 1980s on wrongful death lawsuits for male and female decedents. Although lawsuits brought on behalf of female decedents were more likely to succeed, the awards were substantially lower. They conducted two follow-up juror simulation studies that systematically varied whether a civil case requested damages for a male or a female decedent but held all other facts of the case constant. In both studies, awards were higher for the male decedent, reflecting the mock jurors' assumptions of the higher lost income of the man compared to the woman who had died. This research focused on wrongful death lawsuits, often brought by the surviving spouses. Hence, the results suggest that female spouses who bring such lawsuits would benefit by the legal rule that highlights lost income as a prime feature of compensatory damages. However, in other personal injury cases that allow jurors to consider a female plaintiff's lost wages, the fact that on average female workers earn less than male workers will disadvantage them. The important point is that the law reflects inequality in the labor market through its rules regarding compensatory damages. Other studies have examined the experiences of female litigants in bankruptcy filings (Driscoll, 1994) and immigration hearings (Root and Tejani, 1994).

Comparative work has contrasted men's and women's experiences in law school (Guinier *et al.*, 1994), as law clerks (D.C. Circuit Task Force on Gender, Race, and Ethnic Bias, 1995:IVA-23–26), as attorneys (Hagan and Kay, 1995), as expert witnesses (Walters, 1994), and as judges (Ninth Circuit Task Gender Bias Task Force, 1993). Gender bias task forces in many states (New Jersey Supreme Court Task Force, 1984, 1986) and in several federal circuits (see, e.g., Ninth Circuit Gender Bias Task Force, 1993; D.C. Circuit Task Force, 1995) have documented numerous differences in the experiences of men and women in the legal system and have called for reforms to ensure more equal treatment. Thus, a considerable amount of scholarly work comparing men's and women's experiences, and many reform efforts, have been driven by a strong belief in the value of equal treatment of men and women in the legal system. Even those who do not subscribe to all of the theoretical underpinnings of liberal feminist jurisprudence acknowledge the value of employing comparative analysis of men and women in the law (see, e.g., Jackson, 1994).

2. The Limits of an Equal Treatment Approach

Liberal feminism left intact the assumptions classic liberalism made regarding human nature and social relations. For liberal feminists, justice lay in ensuring that certain values—

autonomy, self-determination, equality—were upheld by the law for both women and men. Their struggle was to secure, for women, the rights that men (particularly those from privileged classes) had always enjoyed. According to this strategy, equality for women could be achieved by eliminating gender distinctions in the law. As viable as this approach was in rendering certain egregious forms of sex discrimination unconstitutional, it has become the subject of serious critique.

During the 1980s, it was increasingly clear that pursuing a gender-neutral, rights-based strategy was inherently limiting. Indeed, in their effort to promote gender neutrality, many scholars began to recognize that "neutral" law was not always synonymous with equal justice (Binion, 1993). In particular, the pursuit of equal treatment has deleterious effects in those contexts where men and women are not similarly situated, such as in rape, pregnancy, the family, and the labor market (Scales, 1986).

The critique that emerged in response to the failures of an equal treatment approach attacked the strategy on two fronts. First, laws and policies that are gender neutral in content are not necessarily gender neutral in practice (Golden, 1991; Rhode, 1990; Littleton, 1987). Second, the emphasis on sameness obscures the fact that women and men are not similarly situated (West, 1988; Dworkin, 1981). Gender-neutral law treats women as if they are men, even though women occupy different positions in the labor market, earn comparatively less, have greater family ties and demands, are the subjects of sexual objectification, and occupy few positions of political power (Williams, 1989).

One example of the limitations of the equal treatment approach may be found in Lenore Weitzman's research on the impact of divorce law changes in California (Weitzman, 1985; see also Jacob, 1988). In 1970, California became the first state in the nation to ratify a no-fault divorce law. Before the change, under California's traditional fault-based system, the party not at fault in the divorce (usually the wife) received more than half of the community property. Although ostensibly justified because the wife was the "innocent" party, the practice was in part justified because it tended to soften the economic hardship of the divorce for women, who earned less money and usually retained custody of the children from the marriage. But after no-fault divorce was introduced in 1970, courts were instructed to divide assets equally between the husband and the wife, with very few exceptions. Weitzman's before-and-after study revealed that the equal treatment approach of no-fault divorce worsened women's situations. After the change, wives were less likely to be awarded the family home and household furnishings, increasing forced sales of the home and disruption in the lives of minor children. Long-term comparisons of the financial state of divorced husbands and wives showed that several years after the divorce, the husband's financial situation had improved while the wife's had declined. Reanalysis of the Weitzman data showed that the income drop was not as extreme as originally reported (Peterson, 1996a,b; Weitzman, 1996). However, the study remains a striking illustration that the application of equal treatment to parties who are not similarly situated can result in significant inequities.

An equal treatment approach also fails to deal appropriately with the unique condition of pregnancy. In the 1974 case of *Gedulidig v. Aiello*, for example, the Supreme Court ruled that an insurance firm that refused to pay benefits for disabilities arising from pregnancy (even though it covered certain disabilities unique to men) did not violate the equal protection clause because there was no evidence of gender discrimination. According to the Court, classifications involving pregnancy do not necessarily constitute gender discrimination since the distinction revolves around persons who are pregnant and those who are not pregnant. An apparently gender-neutral standard is challenged by the fact that only women are capable of being pregnant, and thus only women are subject to the restriction on benefits.

Scholars who critiqued the equal treatment approach came to be identified as difference feminists, in recognition of their emphasis on the limitations of equal treatment and their insistence on physical, cultural, and social differences between men and women (Goldstein, 1992). Within this school of thought, two distinct strands can be identified: radical feminists and different voice feminists. Radical and difference feminists possess distinct assumptions regarding the source of gender difference, and they propose divergent solutions to gender inequities. The next two sections detail the contributions of these scholars.

3. Radical Feminist Critiques

Radical feminism emerged as an immediate response to what its proponents viewed as the reformism of liberal feminists. In radical feminist thought, the state is not a potential source of equality, but the vehicle through which patriarchy realizes its power through the oppression of women (MacKinnon, 1989; Millett, 1970). Thus, a strategy that relies on the state and the legal system to correct gender inequalities is self-defeating. The state may grant women access to certain pockets of activity, but it will always work to prevent their full inclusion.

Radical feminists have focused particular attention on laws targeting pornography, abortion, sexual harassment, rape, and domestic violence, attempting to show that these laws promote male oppression of women. Dworkin (1981, 1993), for example, argues that the Court's handling of obscenity laws and the First Amendment demonstrates the state's continued interest in protecting and promoting pornography. For Dworkin, pornography in all of its various forms provides both material and ideological bases for men's domination of women. In her analysis, pornography serves to "crush a whole class of people through violence and subjugation, and sex is the vehicle that does the crushing. … Pornography, unlike obscenity, is a discrete, identifiable system of sexual exploitation that hurts women as a class by creating inequality and abuse" (Dworkin, 1993:453). In the radical feminist view, legal distinctions between obscene and protected speech are little more than public squabbles among men over morality. Obscenity law does not serve women's interests by banning the dehumanization or subordination of women, it only prescribes which forms of these portrayals are acceptable.

Radical feminists see women as victims of patriarchal subjugation (Firestone, 1970; Rich, 1974), a social domination that is rooted in physical domination. Men's control over women is exercised through violence and control of social institutions. As a theory of law, radical feminists suggest that justice can only emerge with the dissolution of the modern liberal state and the replacement of legal liberalism, both of which are inextricably linked to patriarchal power.

4. Difference Feminists

Difference feminists suggest that the unequal character of gender relations is a product primarily of limited social roles available to women and the experiences that are unique to women as a group (Chodorow, 1978; Gilligan, 1982). Gender equity cannot be achieved by reforming the liberal state (as proposed by liberal feminism) or in seeking its dissolution (as with radical feminists). Rather, equality can only occur through a restructuring of the legal order through the inclusion of women's voice. Within the broad range of legal scholarship categorized as difference feminism, the different voice paradigm has enjoyed considerably more support and scholarly attention than radical feminism, even when the latter perspective was at its peak.

The idea that women might bring a different voice to law dates to the early part of the century, when the notion of separate spheres for men (public) and women (private) prevailed. In "A Jury of Her Peers," written in 1917 before U.S. women had the right to vote, Susan Glaspell (1987) provides a compelling fictional account of Minnie Wright, suspected of strangling her husband while he was sleeping. Minnie is in jail, and the sheriff and the county attorney (both men) bring their wives along with them to Minnie's house while the men look for evidence that might implicate the wife. The men explore the house and the barn, leaving the women in the kitchen, their separate sphere. Here, by looking at small details, the women discover much that tells them of the difficulty and dreariness of Minnie's life with her husband, and the motive for her killing. The men return empty-handed from their search for hard, cold evidence. But the women keep their private sphere evidence a secret, becoming the jury of peers that judges Minnie not guilty.

Reflecting some of the same ideas, Carol Gilligan's significant work, *In a Different Voice: Psychological Theory and Women's Development*, was published in 1982. It was crucial to the development of different voice theory because it generated an alternative account of moral development. In her work, Gilligan suggests that prominent psychological theories of moral development (particularly ideas advanced by Kohlberg) are, in fact, theories of male moral development that exclude and undervalue the moral reasoning of women. Her research concentrated on examining the ways in which males and females reasoned about both real-life and hypothetical moral dilemmas.

Perhaps the best-known example is Gilligan's comparison of the moral reasoning of two children, Jake and Amy, in response to Kohlberg's famous "Heinz" dilemma. Heinz's wife is dying of cancer. The drug that could save her is prohibitively expensive, and the druggist who has the drug available insists on the full price. Heinz steals the drug. The question for the subjects is: Should Heinz have stolen the drug? Though similarly situated in terms of age, intelligence, and social class, Jake and Amy evaluate and reason about the Heinz dilemma in different ways. Jake concludes that Heinz should definitely have stolen the drug, explaining that the wife's right to live trumps the druggist's right to make a profit from his merchandise. Thus, Jake arrives at his solution through the application of logic and moral reasoning (what Gilligan refers to as the ethic of rights or logic of justice). Amy, on the other hand, is not sure that Heinz should have stolen the drug. She presses for other possibilities—couldn't the druggist and Heinz have worked out some sort of payment schedule?—and observes that if Heinz is arrested he will not be able to be helpful to his wife. Thus, Amy responds to the dilemma according to considerations of communication and reciprocity in relationships (referred to as an ethic of care). Within Kohlberg's hierarchical model of moral development, children are designated as morally mature when their reasoning is structured according to logical deduction and is guided by established legal principles and dominant normative codes. Amy's response (to the extent that it can even be scored within this model) is considered immature, evidence of a lower level of moral development.

Gilligan challenges the soundness of Kohlberg's model by suggesting that men and women follow different trajectories of moral development, leading to different paradigms of moral reasoning. The fact that Amy's response to the Heinz dilemma is just as complex and considerate as Jake's shows that Kohlberg's model obscures alternative modes of moral reasoning. Gilligan concludes that gender-patterned differences in socialization and life experience may produce different frameworks for moral reasoning among men and women. In essence, women may have a different, rather than underdeveloped, maladjusted, or inadequate, voice relative to men. Gilligan's different voice theory is important, not simply because of its contributions to psychology, but because it suggests that legal norms based on men's moral reasoning systematically exclude the moral voice of women. It has been highly influential in the world of jurisprudence, frequently cited in the law reviews and occupying a central place in feminist legal theory. A Lexis search of law review citations to Gilligan between January 1, 1989 and January 1, 1995 revealed that 357 law review articles had cited Gilligan's work. By way of contrast, Roscoe Pound, John Stuart Mill, and H.L.A. Hart were cited 441, 507, and 539 times, respectively, during the same period, showing that Gilligan is not far off the mark of these traditional and highly influential legal theorists (Turnier, Conover, and Lowery, 1996).

Feminist legal scholars sympathetic to Gilligan's work have taken up two dominant themes raised by the discovery of women's different voice. First, Gilligan's work provides empirical support for the contention that to the degree law and legal institutions reflect one specific style of reasoning they are not gender neutral, but instead reflect fundamentally masculine normative codes and moral paradigms. Second, in demonstrating the complexity of women's moral reasoning, Gilligan provides support for an alternate model of legal reasoning and structure.

Radical feminists were among the first legal scholars to suggest that law and legal institutions were inherently male and served to advance men's interests. In suggesting that law was an instrument of patriarchy, however, radical feminists were limited in their capacity to substantiate this contention through empirical scholarship. Proponents of radical feminism contend that the law is an instrument of men's power because men control law and legal institutions. The argument falters on a tautology: The law is male because men are in control, and men are in control because of the maleness of the law. Male power implies male voice and male voice implies male power. With the advance of Gilligan, however, feminist legal scholars had a locus of empirical investigation—moral development.

Links between men's moral reasoning and legal rules have been explored both theoretically and empirically. Robin West (1988), a disciple of Gilligan, suggests that modern legal theory—both liberal and critical approaches—is grounded in a distinctively masculinist separation thesis. According to West, both liberal and critical legal theories assume that it is the subjective awareness of separation—the distinction between the individual and the social—that gives rise to human consciousness and distinguishes humans from animals. Men's separation from a maternal figure marks the earliest stages of their consciousness and, in turn, is reflected in modern legal theory. Liberal philosophy, with its emphasis on maximizing individual interests and minimizing individual responsibilities to the community, embodies men's sense of individuation from the social. From the perspective of women's lives, the separation thesis makes little sense. West points out that by virtue of their biology (particularly menstruation, heterosexual intercourse, pregnancy, and breast-feeding), women are inextricably linked to the social world.

West contends that the separation thesis is neither an intrinsic nor a desirable element in legal epistemology. Legal liberalism, with its emphasis on separation, is not a theory of law and human interaction, but a theory of law and male interaction. The problem for feminist jurists, according to West, is how to resolve the disjuncture between a philosophy of law that fails to adequately conceptualize the content and character of women's lives.

In suggesting that women's moral frame differs from men's, Gilligan's work provided difference scholars with a model of what a feminist jurisprudence might look like. In particular, difference feminists suggested that gender equity could be achieved through the valuation of women's differences and the incorporation of women's moral voice in the framework of legal theory and practice (see, e.g., Littleton, 1987). Menkel-Meadow (1985) has used the different voice model to speculate that masculine traits like competition, hierarchy, and aggression that characterize the advocacy-adversarial model will be tempered by the entrance of women into the legal profession. Menkel-Meadow, citing Gilligan, hypothesizes that the ethic of care that characterizes women's moral framework means that female lawyers are more likely to prefer cooperation to competition and mediation to adversarial opposition. As women gain increased access to influential positions in the legal profession, it is likely that legal practice will change and that the abstract application of legal principles to cases will be abandoned in favor of context-specific solutions to legal dilemmas.

Bender's (1988) examination of tort law demonstrates how the inclusion of women's moral reasoning would transform features like the reasonableness standard of care. Traditionally, the courts judged the defendant's exercise of caution and reason according to whether a reasonable man would have acted in a similar manner. Although the phrase "reasonable man" has largely been replaced by references to the "reasonable person," the standard continues to reflect men's concerns and expectations. Bender argues that a feminist model of tort would replace the reasonable person standard with a specification of social relationship—responsible neighbor or social acquaintance. Further, feminist tort law would articulate responsibility over rights, interconnectedness over individuality. As Bender notes, the reasonable person standard would then be replaced by a duty of care designed to promote "acting responsibly towards others to avoid harm, with a concern about the human consequences of our acts or failures to act" (Bender, 1988:34).

While the different voice model has led feminist scholars to the crucial insight that law is a reflection of men's interests rather than a reservoir of neutrality and objectivity, the model is weakened by a number of handicaps. First, Gilligan's influential research has been widely criticized. One major source of concern involves the small size and other limitations of her research samples. Gilligan's work has been particularly criticized because she concentrated on white and relatively affluent women at the expense of more heterogeneous samples. Other research that she conducted and described in her book examined moral reasoning about women's decisions to have abortions, a moral dilemma that may have highlighted concerns about relationships. The major contrast in Gilligan's book was between women and men, but differences in moral reasoning may be the product of other factors not assessed in the research. There is a danger of artificially universalizing the experience of all men and all women, when black women and white women, for example, may have dramatically distinctive lives (Kline, 1989; Roach Anleu, 1992).

Scholars have expressed concern that a different voice model contributes to a grossly exaggerated dichotomy of moral reasoning: Masculine reasoning is deductive, objective, and abstract, while feminine reasoning is inductive, subjective, and contextualized. This polarization of difference could lead scholars to focus on stereotypically male and adversarial aspects of the adversary system while obscuring the degree to which the adversary system is characterized by negotiation and accommodation (Blumberg, 1967; Eisenstein and Jacob, 1977; Kritzer, 1991). If negotiation is a stereotypically feminine preference, how do scholars explain the pervasiveness of negotiation and out-of-court settlements in our presently male-dominated legal system?

In addition to theoretical concerns, the empirical research testing whether or not women speak in a distinctive voice has yielded mixed results (Menkel-Meadow, 1996). A survey of 61 studies using the Kohlberg paradigm to examine sex differences in moral reasoning found no consistent differences attributable to gender through adolescence. Adult scores differed in several studies. However, further analysis found that women in these studies tended to have less education than men. Once the level of education was controlled, no significant differences in moral reasoning remained (Turnier *et al.*, 1996).

The different voice analysis suggests that male and female judges might well reason about their cases in distinctive ways. Sue Davis put the different voice hypothesis to the test in several studies of the appellate opinions of male and female judges, but found no consistent support for a distinctive style of legal reasoning (Davis, 1993, 1993–1994). In particular, female judges did not seem more likely than male judges to reflect an ethic of care in their legal opinions. Davis and her colleagues (Davis, Haire, and Songer, 1993) found that female circuit court judges were more likely than their male counterparts to favor the plaintiff in employment discrimination cases, and to support the criminal defendant in search and seizure cases. Once the party of the appointing president was controlled for, however, the only difference that persisted was that female judges appointed by a Democratic president were more likely than their male brethren to vote for the employment discrimination claimant. As the authors point out, women's greater support for these plaintiffs could be due to identification with members of a subordinate group rather than the result of a distinctive brand of moral reasoning (Davis *et al.*, 1993). As Supreme Court Justice Ruth Bader Ginsberg observed:

> In working as a lawyer, law teacher, and now judge, I have discerned no distinctively male or female styles of thinking or writing. And I agree with Minnesota Supreme Court Justice Jeanne Coyne, who said, when asked whether women judges decide cases differently because they are women: "A wise old man and a wise old woman reach the same conclusion." (1996:1654)

Davis has advanced a number of reasons why female and male judges may sound more similar than different (see Davis, 1993; Davis *et al.*, 1993). First, Gilligan's theory may be wrong. Second, it may not apply to federal judges chosen after a highly political selection process wherein a president nominates those candidates most likely to espouse compatible views. Third, analyses of voting behavior or appellate opinions may not be adequate vehicles for detecting a different voice. Fourth, the highly masculine nature of law and the legal system may mute a tendency toward a feminine voice in the law, particularly for the women now serving on the bench who typically went to law school and practiced law in an era when feminist jurisprudence was just beginning to emerge.

Despite the ambiguous conclusions of the empirical work on differences in moral/legal reasoning, research that we detail below shows striking and consistent differences between women and men in their perceptions of the justice system and their judgments about rape, domestic violence, and sexual harassment. Whether one subscribes to the tenets of difference feminism or not, thoughtful scholars must acknowledge the persistent differences in the views that men and women hold about law and justice. We must also note the tremendous heuristic value of Gilligan's work in stimulating research and theory in feminist jurisprudence.

5. Critical Feminism: Difference as Subjugation Rather Than a Cause for Celebration

Critical feminist legal theory is concerned with weaknesses present in both sameness and difference approaches. Radical feminism laid the groundwork for critical feminism. Like radical feminists, critical feminists regard the state as a men's preserve and are not sanguine about legal action as a resource for attaining gender equality (Rifkin, 1980). Gender-neutral laws and the denial of gender difference cannot eradicate gender inequality because they obscure the extent to which men and women are differently situated and they mask the legal and institutional bases of men's power (MacKinnon, 1989).

According to critical feminists, women's different voice is a product of their subordination. In discovering this voice, difference feminists reproduce the very ideology that justifies men's power and women's subjugation. The division between critical and difference feminism was crystallized in an exchange between Gilligan and MacKinnon during a 1984 "conversation" at the Buffalo School of Law. Gilligan argued that the goal of feminist jurisprudence should be to revalue and incorporate Amy's voice in mainstream legal and political discourse. MacKinnon retorted that the goal of critical feminism was to have Amy achieve a new voice, one that "would articulate what she cannot now because his foot is on her throat" (Williams, 1989). In this view, difference feminism tends to legitimize the practice of sexual stereotyping (Baer, 1991). Although the valuation of supposedly feminine characteristics holds the promise of broadening male-centered norms and standards of behavior, the more likely event is the use of such categories to justify unequal treatment and protect male power.

The fear that celebration of women's difference would ultimately produce backlash in the form of sex-stereotyping and unequal treatment was realized in the 1986 case of *EEOC v. Sears, Roebuck & Co.* In this case, the EEOC claimed that Sears discriminated against women by failing to hire them for high-paying commission sales positions. The district court in this case asked the EEOC not only to demonstrate statistical disparities, but also to show that men and women had equal interest in the commission sales jobs. Sears embraced the rhetoric advanced by difference feminists and used it to suggest that women preferred domestic responsibilities to career demands, and a supportive work environment over a competitive one. The scholar Rosalind Rosenberg testified that women are humane and nurturing, more relationship-oriented, more concerned about a job's impact on their families, and less competitive than men (Offer of Proof Concerning the Testimony of Dr. Rosalind Rosenberg, 1986). The capacity of Sears to mobilize experts to testify to the veracity of gender-based stereotypes worked to override both the testimony of individual women who reported that they desired commission sales positions, and the testimony of Alice Kessler-Harris, who argued that the supposed preferences of female workers were primarily a reflection of their opportunities (Written Testimony of Alice Kessler-Harris, 1986). The trial judge concluded that the EEOC had not proven its case against Sears (see Cooper, 1986; *EEOC v. Sears, Roebuck & Co.*, 1986).

The use of gender stereotypes against women is precisely what critical feminists would have predicted. For critical feminists, the locus of investigation is social structure and the source of difference is access to power. Critical feminism represents a radical reshaping of Marxist theory in that the structure of gender relations, rather than class relations, is at its center. Yet, like Marxists, critical legal feminists remain committed to theorizing about the social-structural bases of inequality. It is the structure of male domination with all its material manifestations (e.g., gender-based job segregation, wage inequality, rape, sexual harassment, pornography) that generates the ideology of masculine and feminine (MacKinnon, 1989; Rhode, 1990). The power of patriarchy lies, in part, in its capacity to make power imbalances appear natural.

Further, critical feminists charge difference feminism with essentialism. Despite Gilligan's (1982) protestations to the contrary, her work and the legal scholarship that have followed in its wake imply (and in some cases explicitly announce) that different types of moral reasoning are an *inherent* part of men's and women's natures. When differences are essentialized, the model of male power becomes a static one (Roach Anleu, 1992). The difference model cannot explain how masculine moralities achieved dominance through codification into law, nor can it prescribe a viable means for introducing feminine moralities into the law. Critical feminism, with its Marxist roots, is interested in explicating the engine that drives historical change. Locating differences in individual natures, as opposed to individual and institutional practices, makes theorizing change virtually impossible. Yet it is clear that changes in the power configuration of gender relations have occurred through time. Critical feminists suggest that as long as men retain control of dominant social institutions and justify this control by referencing allegedly natural differences between the sexes, it is unlikely that the structure and practice of masculine law will change (MacKinnon, 1989).

Law appears to be the neutral, objective arbiter of justice and equality. Part of the strategy of disrobing patriarchy involves showing how legal liberalism makes male dominance invisible and legitimate through its adoption of men's self-interested standpoint and enforcement of it as the status quo (MacKinnon, 1989). For critical feminists, there is no disinterested, objective standpoint (Smith, 1987). Rather, the strategy for overcoming women's subjugation lies in using women's standpoint to critique the existing legal system.

Critical feminists avoid some of the pitfalls encountered by difference feminists in that they recognize that women emerge from a plurality of experiences and social locations. Despite these differences, there is a baseline from which to pursue justice for women. This baseline involves women's common experience as objects available for consumption by the male gaze and the eroticization of this objectification (as evidenced, for example, by the overwhelming use and manipulation of women's bodies in both pornography and mainstream advertising) (MacKinnon, 1989). Justice can be pursued through the shared standpoint of objectification, exclusion, and subordination. Gender inequality is better thought about as domination and subordination than sameness and difference. For MacKinnon (1989) and Rhode (1990), the central means by which to challenge unjust laws and institutional practices is not through an investigation of whether the sexes are similarly situated, but on whether the recognition of gender difference is likely to reproduce gender inequality. This strategy discards the all-or-nothing debate occurring between sameness and difference advocates by presupposing specific, local, historical moments in the relationship between men and women (see Connell, 1989).

Research emerging from the critical feminist legal tradition has emphasized the extent to which certain laws and legal practices perpetuate gender inequality. Indeed, MacKinnon (1989) suggests that the focus of critical feminist research must be toward an understanding of how the law is used as an instrument of male power, exposing the ways in which seemingly gender-neutral doctrines and practices activate conditions of inequality and domination.

Perhaps no work in feminist jurisprudence has been more controversial than MacKinnon's (1989) and Sworkin's (1981) coordinated attack on obscenity laws. MacKinnon (1989) argues that in reading opinions in obscenity cases, one would be falsely led to believe that the controversy surrounding pornography is a debate over sexual practices and morality. But, that belief would obscure the degree to which the very existence of pornography reinforces women's subordination. It fails to acknowledge that it is men who are the predominant producers and consumers of pornographic materials, and it is women who are the primary objects represented and manipulated as the stuff of men's sexual fantasies. In MacKinnon's view, the legal question should not be whether certain kinds of pornography are offensive but whether pornography harms women.

A substantial amount of research on the impact of pornography has been conducted over a span of 25 years, stimulated by questions that MacKinnon and others have raised about its potential harmful effects (for a review, see Donnerstein, Linz, and Penrod, 1987). Although that research is too complex and voluminous to describe in detail here, a number of experimental studies have documented the negative effects of viewing violent pornography. The violent quality of the pornography is key; few effects are found for exposure to nonviolent pornography.

Several studies have found that men exposed to violent pornographic material become more likely to espouse rape myths and to find interpersonal violence acceptable. In some studies, men who watched violent, sexually explicit images or films were more likely to engage in aggressive behavior toward women in laboratory settings (Donnerstein *et al.*, 1987; Linz, Penrod, and Donnerstein, 1987; Malamuth and Briere, 1986; Malamuth and Check, 1981). In one of the few experimental studies to examine the impact of pornography on women, Krafka and her colleagues (Krafka, Linz, Donnerstein, and Penrod, 1997) observed partial confirmation that violent pornography could negatively affect women as well. Women who had viewed violent, sexually explicit films on four successive days rated the films as less degrading to women by the fourth day. Furthermore, women who viewed mildly sexually explicit but graphically violent films (so-called slasher films) became less sensitive to a rape victim in a subsequent study, downgrading the severity of her injuries; however, there was little evidence from the study that exposure to pornography encouraged women to see themselves as victims. Compared to a control group, women who had watched different types of pornography experienced no overall differences in their level of self-esteem, satisfaction with their body images, or rape myth acceptance.

Their contention that pornography harms women led MacKinnon and Dworkin to fashion a model antipornography ordinance, which was adopted in Minneapolis and Indianapolis, but subsequently vetoed in the first city and overturned by court order in the second (*American Booksellers Association v. Hudnut*, 1985). The highly controversial ordinance defined pornography as the graphic, sexually explicit subordination of women, and made producing and distributing pornography a violation of women's civil rights. Women who could demonstrate harm from pornography could sue for money damages. Thus, the civil rights ordinance diverged significantly from the traditional way of controlling pornography through obscenity laws. The ordinance generated a tremendous amount of debate within the feminist community. Feminists disagreed about the extent to which pornography actually harmed women, and about the danger that the ordinance could be used to suppress sexually explicit feminist work (Frug, 1992b). Although the ordinance was controversial and ultimately declared unconstitutional, it illustrated how feminist legal scholars can reimagine conventional approaches to law in creative ways that focus on women's experiences.

Despite the disapproval that critical feminists have voiced against difference feminists, a number of scholars have begun questioning the degree to which MacKinnon, Rhode, and other critical scholars have really abandoned the difference divide in feminist legal scholarship. Roach Anleu (1992), for example, suggests that while MacKinnon verbally acknowledges the multiplicity of oppressions and privileges that cross-cut the category "woman," she continues to rely on the assumption that objectification can be similarly experienced across these compelling social divides. Indeed, in seeking to funnel women's experiences into a singular critique, MacKinnon embraces the very strategy she decries—difference. The ultimate difference embraced by critical feminism is victimization. The standpoint that serves as the basis for reordering the social structure and unifying women is the distinction that women by virtue of their gender are victimized and men are not. The inability of feminist jurists to abandon the difference divide begs the question, what difference does difference make?

6. Postmodernist Legal Feminism: What Difference Does Difference Make?

Postmodernist legal feminism, while still in its infancy, has begun to develop alternative critiques of the legal order. Postmodernists are interested in understanding why feminist legal theories have patterned themselves so consistently around the notion of difference (Frug,

1992a). Indeed, postmodernism contends that, despite their protestations to the contrary, feminist legal scholars are not outside the discourses they critique. These scholars contribute to the very phenomenon they reject—the conflation of gender with inequality, sex with domination.

Postmodernist theorizing is broadly concerned with the production and dissemination of knowledge claims and how power configurations are embedded and advanced through claims to truth and knowledge (Seidman and Wagner, 1991; Nicholson, 1990; Foucault, 1980). It is, in its simplest form, an internal critique of modernity. Central to modern thought is a belief in the centrality of the human subject and the contention that law and the state are the primary vessels of power. Postmodernism discards both of these core assumptions. Foucault (1977) rejects the notion of a prediscursive self. There is no self, no experience, no individual without discourse. Power and knowledge configurations in particular historical moments mark and define discrete selves. Discursive forms give rise to a separation thesis of sorts in that they make us believe that we are individuals, that we are differentiable from each other and from the social.

Foucault (1979, 1980) disputes the notion that power is negative and emergent from the state. Modernity is characterized in part by its obsession with detailing and criticizing the capacity of the state through its laws to repress individual behavior. In focusing on law, repression, and the state, traditional scholars mistakenly conflate power with repression, but, for Foucault, power is productive and creative. Legal theory distorts our understanding of power because it assumes the centrality of the law. For Foucault, norms rather than laws are critical; knowledge and science, rather than the state, are the source of power. Power does not act on human subjects, it gives rise to them.

Following from this view, feminist legal scholarship could be seen as reifying male dominance because it locates the primary source of male power in the law and thereby obscures the multiple, fragmented, and productive sources of gender inequality. Indeed, postmodernists argue that belief in the sexed body and the binary gender categories of men and women are both a product and reproduction of power relations. In this view, the categorization mystifies the processes and motives through which science, religion, and other powerful sources have produced gender as a category that differentiates humans from one another. Talking about men and women as natural categories of being interferes with our ability to recognize that gender is socially constructed.

Butler (1990), for example, challenges the idea that the body has a materiality—a beingness—prior to culture. For Butler, it is not enough for critical feminism to critique assumptions regarding "natural" feminine and masculine traits; critical feminists must critique, more broadly, the notion that there are men and women if they are ever to understand the source of gender inequality. To the extent that feminist work (even work that is critical of male power) is invested in the category of woman and in the female subject, it will never adequately counteract gender relations.

Frug's (1992a) important work, *Postmodern Legal Feminism*, is heavily influenced by currents in social theory articulated by Foucault and Butler. Frug is critical of Foucault's minimization of the law, arguing that while law may not be a central force in any given power/knowledge regime, it still constructs certain basic truths about the female body. Through harassment laws, stalking laws, laws regulating women's sexuality, policies regarding discrimination, the law constructs the category of women. Embodied in each of these policies are images of victimized, sexualized, and maternal women. At the site where law marks the body, the categories of women and men are constructed (this is similarly the case for adults and children, people of color and whites, citizens and aliens). Frug sends feminist jurisprudence in an entirely different direction. Instead of using the category of difference to criticize domination, feminist scholars must undermine the concept of gender by avoiding a conception of gender that constructs men and women as distinct and coherent beings. Because domination is embedded in these separate categories, justice can only be achieved when these categories are eliminated.

In eschewing gender categories, postmodernist feminist scholars have been critical of traditional empirical scholarship that presumes categories of women and men. Instead, postmodernists favor the practice of deconstruction, that is, demonstrating how certain social or linguistic truths that we take for granted are not in themselves signifiers of social reality, but are instances of the capacity of one social group to impose its perception of social reality on others and to elevate this perception to the level of truth or science or law (Derrida, 1978).

Postmodernist legal scholars are particularly interested in exposing how women and men are constructed by the law, and how laws reproduce gender relations. For example, Frug (1992a:53) deconstructs a contracts casebook, finding that women are presented infrequently, and when they are presented, they tend to be portrayed in stereotypical and unflattering ways. In undertaking this analysis, Frug aims to demonstrate not that women receive unfair treatment (that might have been the aim of an equal treatment scholar) but rather that the category woman is consistently associated with negative, marginalized, and oppressive images. Her analysis is intended to demonstrate the underlying patterns in the use of gender categories, and to illuminate how readers' conceptions of themselves as men and women are implicated in and influenced by the process of learning contract law.

Postmodernist analysis is attractive to many feminist scholars, who tend to share the presumptions that gender is socially constructed and who likewise tend to be skeptical about the claims of science and law (Andersen, 1997). Yet, the complete elimination of gender as a category poses serious difficulties for a social science enterprise (see Daly, 1997, for a discussion of the tension between the real world and discourse). In addition, whether postmodernist feminist scholarship will create change in women's legal and social position is open to question. In his Law & Society Association Presidential address, Joel Handler took issue with postmodernism generally, arguing that "without a positive theory of institutions, postmodernism cannot come to grips with institutionally based power" (Handler, 1992:724). Other scholars point out that the postmodernist tendency to deconstruct and to prefer the individual, the unique, and the indeterminate make it difficult to observe commonalities of experience that are essential to scientific analysis of social structure and to collaborative efforts for social change (Andersen, 1997; Calvita and Seron, 1992). Calavita and Seron urge us to "harness the postmodernists' insights without succumbing to the potential for nihilism that underlies their approach and impedes the recognition of collective interests" (1992:771, emphasis deleted).

7. Gendered Institutions: Exploring the Embeddedness of Gender Inequality

A final set of theoretical ideas that we wish to discuss in this review is recent work on the gendered nature of institutions, including institutions of law and justice. Some of the ideas presented earlier, especially those of the critical feminists, in combination with sociological work on organizations, have led a number of feminist sociologists to consider whether gender is a feature of institutions, rather than an attribute of individuals. Acker (1990:141) uses the term *gendered institutions* to refer to the nature of the processes, images, discourses, and arrangements of power throughout an institution. Major institutional settings—law, religion, politics, military, and the economy—are gendered in the sense that they have historically operated to exclude or minimize women's participation, are currently dominated by men, and are symbolically organized through the epistemological standpoint of men (Steinberg, 1992). In other words, the institutions themselves take on characteristics of gender, helping us to see that gender is more than an individual attribute, as liberal feminism and difference theories imply.

Research examining the gendered character of institutions reveals that ideologies regarding gender difference and patterned social arrangements are deeply embedded in the social landscape. Variation that occurs within interpersonal and local contexts may not stir change in longstanding institutional orders. Gender is produced at the interactional level and amplified in such institutional arenas as the family, the economy, and the state (Lorber, 1994; Andersen, 1997; Connell, 1987). Research that examines religious (Davidman, 1991), familial (Thorne and Yalom, 1992), and workplace (Reskin and Roos, 1990; Milkman, 1986) organizations reveals the overwhelmingly gendered character of daily interaction, ideological frameworks, and relational arrangements. Research such as Acker's (1989) on the infiltration of gender into definitions and conceptions of job skill demonstrates that the elimination of gender inequality will involve considerably more than the eradication of sexist stereotypes and overtly discriminatory policies.

Although it has yet to be widely applied to studies of law and the justice system, the concept of gendered institutions holds considerable promise in accounting for the influence of gender on such institutional practices as sentencing, prosecution of sex crimes, and child custody. Further, a gendered institutions model could help to explain why women who gain ascendence in male-dominated institutional contexts do not uniformly exhibit such stereotypically feminine characteristics as empathy, nurturance, and cooperation. In viewing gender not as an attribute held by an individual, but as a performance demanded by an institution, it is clear that male-dominated institutions remain characteristically masculine long after women have entered the ranks. It is not the influx of women that will change how the law is organized and practiced, but the structure and ideology persistent in the legal institution itself. In this way, institutions are more than individuals; they are entities that are responsive to, but not at the whim of, the individuals who constitute them. This framework adds several layers of complexity to how to conceptualize and investigate the influence of gender on social life. In so doing, it has called into question the narrow and restrictive frameworks role theorists use to conceptualize gender inequality and casts doubt on the effectiveness of both liberal and difference feminist agendas. At the same time, however, the gendered institutions approach provides a powerful framework for theorizing and researching gender and the law.

McCorkel (1996) recently applied the gendered institutions paradigm to inform the debate over the treatment of women offenders in the criminal justice system between proponents of the leniency and the severity models discussed earlier. The leniency/severity debate received considerable attention from the 1970s through the 1980s. In general, research suggests that relative to men, women are less likely to receive prison sentences and, when they do, are sentenced to shorter periods of incarceration. There is, however, considerable variation with respect to the treatment women receive. White, middle-class women fare far better in the system than African-American, Latina, and poor women, and evidence suggests that familied women are granted leniency relative to those women who do not have dependent children (McCorkel, 1996; Daly, 1994, 1989). Unfortunately, most of the work emerging from the leniency/severity debate fails to examine race and class differences, and with its reliance on statistical analyses of case outcomes, is unable to analyze the contexts in which differential treatment occurs and the intersections of race, class, and gender (McCorkel, 1996).

Anomalies emerging from the leniency/severity debate become explicable when one analyzes the criminal justice system as a gendered institution. Viewing the criminal justice system as a gendered institution involves investigating how certain images of men and women become embedded in the organization of the institution and the effects such images have on those who are processed in them. Historical studies of sentencing practices, for example, demonstrate how changing relations between men and women and notions of acceptable femininity are enacted as institutional policies and procedures (Boritch, 1992).

Similarly, contemporary studies of the organizational structure of men's and women's correctional facilities demonstrate the gendered character of these institutions. Differences in institutional structure, techniques of control, and in the content and availability of educational/vocational programming in men's and women's institutions suggest that gender fundamentally informs the practice and ideology of punishment. Silberman's research (1995, 1996) demonstrates that men's prisons exist largely to punish behavior that is thought to be a natural product of the male character. Institutional goals are focused on teaching the inmate to channel his aggressive behavior into legitimate economic channels; indeed, even rehabilitative responses are directed toward his reintegration into the economic sphere of social relations. On the other hand, the institutional goal for female inmates involves reintegrating them into domestic roles and relations that are traditionally subject to familial control (Simon and Landis, 1991; Feinman, 1979, 1994; see also Haney, 1996).

Viewing the criminal justice system as a gendered institution allows us to make sense out of previous contradictions. The treatment of female defendants, for example, varies historically in accordance with ideologies of femininity and masculinity and women's access to various forms of social power. Treatment of women also varies according to race and class considerations. Numerous studies report that white, middle-class women receive preferential treatment while extremely harsh forms of punishment are reserved for poor, African-American, and Latina women (see Arnold, 1992; Spohn *et al.*, 1987; Visher, 1983).

Looking at the legal profession as a gendered institution also helps to explain the reports of the severe difficulties that female lawyers encounter in becoming fully accepted and integrated within the profession. Arguably, the most dramatic change in law over the last several decades has been a striking increase in the number of women in the legal profession (Babcock, 1988; Menkel-Meadow, 1989). In 1960, in the United States, there were only 7543 women lawyers, constituting just 3% of the total number of lawyers. But 30 years later, in 1991, that number had jumped to 159,377, 20% of the total (Bureau of the Census, 1995). An even sharper contrast may be found in law school degrees. In 1967, just 4% of law degrees went to women, but in the 1990s, it is typical to find that between 40 and 50% of entering law school classes are women. It is primarily white women who are benefiting from the major expansion of women into law schools and the legal profession. Members of ethnic and racial minorities continue to be drastically underrepresented (Price and Sokoloff, 1995). Nevertheless, many women today are involved in the formal legal arena; they investigate, file charges, prosecute, defend, judge, and serve on juries in great numbers.

This trend is of great interest to gender theorists. How has the increasing representation of women in a traditionally male-dominated field affected the profession? Will women change the law, or will the law change women (Menkel-Meadow, 1989)? Scholars supportive of Gilligan's ideas of differing moralities might expect that women would bring distinct qualities to the content and practice of law. Those who see law as a gendered institution would predict substantial resistance and slow change. It is too soon to tell, and there is some evidence that women have made some major inroads (the proliferation of gender bias task forces is a clear example). There is ample evidence, however, of the legal profession's resistance to change as a result of the influx of women. Guinier and her colleagues at the University of Pennsylvania Law School titled their report of the experiences of female law students "Becoming Gentleman ..." to convey the disjuncture the women felt between themselves and what they perceived as the predominantly male atmosphere of the law school (Guinier *et al.*, 1994). Even though female and male law students had equivalent LSAT scores and college grades, women reported serious difficulty operating in the competitive atmosphere and responding to classroom discussions organized around the Socratic method. Studies of female lawyers indicate that a significant number are frequently questioned in legal settings about whether or not they are lawyers (D.C. Circuit Task Force on Gender, Race, and Ethnic Bias, 1995). To many observers, women do not seem to fit their preexisting image of a lawyer. Female lawyers report being interrupted more frequently than male lawyers as they speak in the courtroom (Ninth Circuit Gender Bias Task Force, 1993; D.C. Circuit Task Force on Gender, Race, and Ethnic Bias, 1995), leading them to wonder whether their contributions are accorded the same weight. Female lawyers also report significant problems with sexual harassment, and indicate that the structure of the law practice makes it difficult to combine family and a legal career. Indeed, studies have shown that female lawyers are much less likely to have children than their male colleagues (D.C. Circuit Task Force on Gender, Race, and Ethnic Bias, 1995). Law firms that have accommodated women by providing pregnancy leaves and part-time law practice options have improved the situation for some female lawyers, but it is often at the cost of the woman's advancement in her job. All of these findings suggest that the legal profession's gendered nature is resistant to change.

Schmitt (1998) used the gendered institutions framework in her examination of the relevance of gender for decision making by prosecutors in sexual assault cases. Her initial research questions were grounded in a sex differences perspective and asked if female prosecutors charged their cases differently from their male colleagues. Schmitt ultimately concluded, however, that it was necessary to move beyond the individual comparison of men versus women to consider gender's impact at the institutional level.

Acker's (1990) theory of gendered institutions is most useful in explaining her findings. Using this theory as a framework for analysis, Schmitt (1998) discovered that the men and women of the rape unit made charging decisions in similar ways and yet experienced their jobs quite differently. Even though overall there were no strong differences in the factors that male and female prosecutors considered in bringing rape charges, there were subtle gender differences in their charging decisions that pointed to the female prosecutors' attempts to treat rape victims more responsively. Additionally, as predicted by gendered institutions theory, the prosecutors developed personas that were appropriately gendered for the legal institution in which they work.

The female and male prosecutors engaged in three gendered personas: the aggressive trial attorney, the empathetic legal counselor, and the detached officer of the court. Although the women and men all agreed that their job required them to enact each of these three personas to do their job effectively, they each found some of these roles a stretch. The women most frequently expressed frustration concerning the aggressive trial attorney persona, while the men complained that acting empathetically was not something that came "naturally" to them.

This analysis illustrates a major theme of gendered institutions, namely, that gender is best understood as a performance demanded by the institution. Seeing gender at the institutional level provides a critical insight that helps to explain why simply adding women is not enough to create substantial change in how the law is practiced.

Of course, the gendered institutions paradigm as it relates to law and the justice system is in need of further development and empirical investigation, but it shows considerable promise.

The gendered institutions approach can provide a more comprehensive and rigorous understanding of how gender structures the organization of the legal and criminal justice systems, as well as unpacking the interaction between the individual and the system itself.

C. LAW IN ACTION: LEGAL TREATMENT OF VIOLENCE AGAINST WOMEN

The preceding review and assessment of feminist jurisprudence reports the ongoing theoretical debate about how best to conceptualize and achieve justice for women in law. However, it does not tell the whole story of the field. The discussion thus far might lead readers to conclude falsely that the field is preoccupied with and predominantly driven by theory. To the contrary, for the last three decades a substantial amount of the scholarship and social action relating to women and law has been strongly problem-focused.

In this problem-oriented research, one set of issues has stood out. Feminist researchers and activists have been deeply concerned about violence against women. Starting in the 1970s, feminist analyses of law served to focus attention on how the law treated women who were victims of male physical violence. A focus on violence was in part stimulated by theorizing about the sources and consequences of power differences between men and women, but it was also fueled by evidence suggesting that women were more likely than ever to be sexually assaulted. According to police statistics, the decade between 1965 and 1975 saw a doubling of reported rapes in the United States. In 1965, the rate of reported rapes was 23 per 100,000 women; by 1975 the figure jumped to 51 per 100,000 women. This enormous increase gained the attention of activists and scholars and raised the level of fear of crime among the public. Thus, rape was the first crime against women to receive concerted attention. Empirical study of domestic violence and the problem of battered women soon followed. Finally, increasing numbers of women in the work force created newly visible concerns about sexual harassment in the workplace. We look at the empirical work in each of these three areas in turn, with the goal of illustrating how such scholarship contributed to legal reforms to promote justice for women. The work also confirms insights of different theoretical perspectives.

In each of the areas, issues that were initially identified by feminist legal theorists are apparent. First, the "law on the books," the legal codes and rules that describe criminal behavior, often reflects a male perspective. One of the key insights of feminist jurisprudence is that gender is a factor in determining what constitutes a crime, in defining who is a criminal, and in labeling which individuals are "true" victims, and thus deserving of our sympathy. Whether it is sexual assault, domestic violence, or sexual harassment in the workplace, many women who are victimized have had no voice and no recourse in the legal arena. Second, no matter when the official rules, the law in practice often serves to disadvantage female victims of male aggression, so that even violence against women that is proscribed by law still goes unpunished. Third, efforts to reform law and practice in these three areas show some gains but substantial resistance.

Research on violence against women is significant for those scholars arguing for equal treatment, because as we will show, crimes of violence against women (especially those committed by acquaintances and family members) are at times not treated as seriously as crimes of violence against men. Furthermore, the pervasive nature of sexual harassment creates significant problems for women's equal opportunity in the workplace. Laws regarding violence against women also speak to radical and critical feminists who argue that the structure of law is inherently patriarchal, and more concerned about men's power and privilege than about injuries to women. Scholars who espouse a gendered institutions analysis also find the research significant, because it tends to show the difficulties in the processing of offenses against women in a gendered, predominantly masculine environment. Postmodernist feminists can use some of this research to analyze the assumptions regarding victimization, power, violence, and justice that structure various sets of discourses on rape, domestic violence, and sexual harassment.

1. Rape

Beginning in the 1970s, activists in the women's movement provided a societal analysis of rape (Brownmiller, 1975; Pride, 1981) and drew from their analysis concrete recommendations for action and social change (Harvey, 1985). Early research discovered that rape was widespread but often not reported. Scholars analyzed the content of rape laws, concluding that traditional rape law was not created to protect women from sexual assault but to solidify men's right to subordinate and possess women as sexual objects (Brownmiller, 1975; Griffin, 1971) and to protect male property (MacKinnon, 1983; Dworkin, 1981). Empirical study of rape case processing by the criminal justice system indicated that it was highly unfavorable to women who had been raped. Feminist scholars and activists then joined forces with police, prosecutors, and lawmakers to effect significant law reform.

One of the continuing empirical puzzles that has perplexed scholars is the actual frequency of the crime of rape. Sexual assaults are presumed to be underreported due to a variety of factors, including a victim's fear of social stigma, actual and presumed police hostility to rape victims, lack of social support, and an inhospitable legal system. Even official sources differ in their estimates of rape rates. Before 1992, the federal surveys of crime victimization asked only general questions about sexual victimization; a redesigned survey starting in 1992 specifically asked respondents about whether they had experienced different types of sexual assaults (Bachman and Saltzman, 1995). In 1997, the Uniform Crime Reports (UCR) figures based on official police reports set the rape rate, which includes attempts, at 35.9/100,000; the National Crime Victimization Survey (NCVS), relying on victims' self-reports, gave the rate of 90/100,000 for the same year. In 1997, the NCVS reported rates of 50/100,000 completed rapes and 50/100,000 other sexual assaults. Even using the most conservative figures, it is clear that sexual violence against women is a major social problem.

Socially disadvantaged women are most vulnerable to rape. Divorced and separated women are much more likely to be raped compared to married women, and for all women the rape rate is highest for those with incomes under $10,000 a year. The picture for racial and ethnic minorities is mixed. Some studies have shown that black women are more likely to be raped than white women, but they are also less likely to report their rapes to the police and to have their cases result in convictions (McCahill, Meyer, and Fischman, 1979; Collins, 1990). Overall, these patterns tend to support the assertion of a number of feminist legal scholars that violence against women is linked to women's economic and political powerlessness.

Comparisons of rape rates across nations that show wide disparities also indicate that high rates of sexual violence are related to cultural attitudes, the power relationship between men and women, the social and economic status of women relative to men, and the amount of other forms of violence in the society (Sanday, 1973; Scully, 1990). Understanding and reducing rape cannot be accomplished by focusing only on individuals who commit or are victimized by rape. It is necessary to consider the cultural, societal, and institutional structures that form the context for the crime and its punishment.

a. Criminal Justice Processing of Rape Cases

Starting in the 1970s, activists in the women's movement articulated the physical and emotional trauma of rape victims and denounced the extent to which their trauma was often ignored, or worse, exacerbated by medical personnel, police officers, and participants in the justice system (Harvey, 1985). Early research on police processing of rape complaints gave much cause for concern (Sales, Baum, and Shore, 1984). Police tended to identify rape complaints as unfounded, that is, as not constituting a crime, at a much higher rate than other citizen complaints. Two national studies dating to the 1970s found that in most police departments the rate of marking cases unfounded was dramatically higher for rape than for other complaints, and that rape victims were expected to meet a higher standard of conduct than the law required (Battelle Human Affairs Research Center, 1975; Brodyaga, Gates, Singer, Tucker, and White, 1975). Even if the police decided to define a complaint as founded, the chances were low that the offender would be arrested, tried, and convicted of rape.

In examining the treatment of rape complaints by police and prosecutors, many scholars (Estrich, 1987; Griffin, 1971; Hall, 1983; Williams, 1984) found support for the argument that the response of the criminal justice system is predicated on misleading stereotypes about rape and rape victims and that the most serious dispositions are reserved for "real rapes" involving "genuine victims" (Spohn and Horney, 1992). Police officers' judgments of the strength of a complaint were linked to the characteristics of the victim and her relationship to the offender as well as the extent to which a rape case is aggravated by additional violence or multiple perpetrators (Holmstrom and Burgess, 1978; Rose and Randall, 1982). The police investigated reports of rape by a stranger much more thoroughly than reports of rape by an acquaintance (McCahill *et al.*, 1979) and were more likely to dismiss reports of rape by an acquaintance (Kerstetter, 1990). A prosecutor's decision to file charges was also influenced by the relationship between the victim and the offender (Battelle Memorial Institute, 1975; Loh, 1980; Williams, 1978), and the likelihood that the defendant will be convicted (Battelle Human Affairs Research Center, 1975) or incarcerated (McCahill *et al.*, 1979). Juries, too, appeared to differentiate between what Kalven and Zeisel (1966) called "simple" and "aggravated" rapes. A simple rape is characterized by a single assailant, who may be known to the victim, and no additional violence above and beyond the rape. An aggravated rape may include multiple assailants, additional violence, and the rapist is unknown to the victim. In criminal jury trials from the 1950s, Kalven and Zeisel (1966) found that judges disagreed at a very high rate with juries in simple rape cases. It seemed to appear to the jurors that although the accused may have done something wrong, it did not deserve the opprobrium of the label of rape.

Men and women have consistently different views of the crime of rape, a consistent finding across a wide array of studies (Barnett and Feild, 1977; Bridges and McGrail, 1989; Calhoun, Selby, and Warring, 1976; Feild, 1978; Feldman-Summers and Lindner, 1976; Gilmartin-Zena, 1983; Hans and Vidmar, 1986). This led scholars to suspect that these views made it more difficult for rape victims to be treated justly and fairly in the male-dominated criminal justice system.

b. The Male Bias of Traditional Rape Laws

Although some of the problems experienced by rape victims were the result of maltreatment by police or prosecutors, feminist scholars identified the legal rules regarding rape cases as a prime source of difficulty. Radical and other feminist legal scholars argued that traditional rape law was premised on the definition of women as the property of men. These laws governed women's sexuality and protected male rights to possess women as sexual objects (Edwards, 1981; Field, 1983). The traditional definition of rape only included occurrences of penile–vaginal penetration, excluded men as possible victims, and exempted spouses from prosecution on the assumption that when a woman married she was invariably sexually available to her husband.

An extremely powerful weapon was the legal rule that evidence of the victim's prior sexual history was admissible to impugn her character and therefore her testimony. The defendant's ability to present information about the victim's past life and other sexual relationships reduced a prosecutor's ability to obtain convictions in rape cases. Researchers have shown that decision makers are influenced by victim behaviors, such as hitchhiking or drinking (Bohmer, 1974; Kalven and Zeisel, 1966; LaFree, 1981; McCahill *et al.*, 1979; Nelson and Amir, 1975); by the victim's age, race, occupation, and education (McCahill *et al.*, 1979), and by the victim's reputation (Amir, 1971; Feild and Biene, 1980; Feldman-Summers and Linder, 1976; Hans and Vidmar, 1986; Holmstrom and Burgess, 1978; McCahill *et al.*, 1979).

Furthermore, the law both reflected and reinforced the public's doubts about the seriousness of rape and the truthfulness of women's claims of rape. Corroboration instructions, in which jurors were exhorted to look for evidence that corroborated or was consistent with a victim's testimony, were used in rape cases, suggesting that uncorroborated testimony was unreliable (Hans and Brooks, 1977). Special cautionary instructions were given to juries to explain that rape was a charge that was easily made but difficult for the defendant to disprove, even if innocent. Legal scholars, feminists, and social scientists pointed out the problematic assumptions underlying these special procedures, which were rarely invoked in other cases.

Feminist scholars criticized traditional rape laws that spotlighted the character and behavior of the *victim* instead of shedding light on the behavior of the offender. Traditional rape laws both undermined the status of victims and made the prosecution of rape more difficult. The laws came to be seen as partially responsible for the low rates of reporting, arrest, prosecution, and conviction for rape. Images of women as immoral and dishonest were combined with conceptions of women as the property of males, producing a wide range of prejudicial justice system practices in the handling of rape cases (Field, 1983; Robin, 1977; Tong, 1984).

c. *Rape Law Reform*

Rape law reform occupied a prime place on the feminist agenda during the 1970s and 1980s. Some feminist scholars were pessimistic about whether law reform could bring substantial change to the position of women. Yet, despite some doubts about the promise of law reform, many feminists saw it as a worthwhile venture on both instrumental and symbolic grounds (Freeman, 1975; Marsh, Geist, and Caplan, 1982). The contemporary feminist movement can be given credit for a number of legal reforms in the treatment of violence against women (Freeman, 1975; Rose, 1977; Tierney, 1982), most recently in the Violence Against Women Act of 1994. They promoted changes in the definition of rape and the evidentiary rules that would embody in law the notion that rape is a crime of violence.

Those advocating for law reform predicted that improved treatment of victims by criminal justice officials, especially the police, would lead to increased reporting. Reformers argued that their changes to the rape law would remove barriers to effective prosecution and would make arrest, prosecution, and conviction more likely in these cases (Marsh *et al.*, 1982). In short, reformers hoped that statutory changes would reduce both the doubts of criminal justice officials toward the claims of rape victims and their reliance on extralegal considerations in decision making.

By the mid-1980s nearly all states had enacted some type of rape reform legislation. The most common changes included redefining rape and replacing the single crime of rape with a series of graded offenses defined by the presence or absence of aggravating conditions; rape shield laws, which restricted evidence of the victim's prior sexual history; eliminating the requirement that the victim physically resist her attacker; and disposing of the requirement that the victim's testimony be corroborated (Spohn and Horney, 1992).

The reforms symbolized a change in the legal conception of women. Under the traditional rape laws women were seen as inferior beings defined by family roles and men's ownership. Ideally, the reforms meant a movement toward a view of women as responsible, autonomous persons who possess the right to personal, sexual, and bodily self-determination (Schwendinger and Schwendinger, 1983).

d. The Impact of Rape Law Reform

At present all states have reformed rape laws on their books, but how do these laws work in practice? Whether or not legal reform can substantially improve justice for women, of course, is a bone of contention among different schools of feminist jurisprudence, with some theorists highly skeptical of the value of incremental legal change (Smart, 1989). In addition, many sociolegal scholars point to the problems of determining the impact of specific laws (for a review of relevant case studies, see Macauley, Friedman, and Stookey, 1995). Nevertheless, a major feminist project has been to assess the impact of rape reform laws. The aim of legal changes was to increase the rate of rape reporting and to increase rape case convictions, so several studies have focused on these outcome measures. Other studies have analyzed how the rape case processing has been altered by reform efforts, and whether the experience for rape victims was less traumatic.

Interviews with criminal justice personnel, as well as with rape crisis center workers, suggest that officials' attitudes toward rape victims have improved and that, on average, victims now experience less trauma during the criminal justice process (Marsh *et al.*, 1982; Spohn and Horney, 1991). The question remains whether this improved treatment is because of rape law reform or some other factor such as general attitude change, or political pressure on the legal system to improve the treatment of rape victims (e.g., Brodyaga *et al.*, 1975; Holmes, 1980; Martin and Powell, 1994).

In a comprehensive study of rape law reform in six jurisdictions, Spohn and Horney (1991, 1992; Horney and Spohn, 1991) found that in one of the six jurisdictions, Michigan, which had enacted strong reforms, the reforms had discernible impact, increasing reporting and indictments. There was also an increase in the ratio of indictments to reports, suggesting that prosecutors were more inclined to file charges in what previously might have been considered marginal cases. Alternatively, the greater willingness to prosecute could be linked to the fact that after rape law reform, the definitions of sexual misconduct were much clearer than the old definition of rape. Spohn and Horney concluded that in Michigan, women raped in simple as opposed to aggravated cases were more likely to report their crimes to the police after the reform, and that police and prosecutors after the reforms had apparently begun to consider those cases more legitimate (Spohn and Horney, 1996). In one other jurisdiction that Spohn and Horney studied, Texas, there was also an increase in rape reports, but contrary to expectations, a *decline* in the indictment ratio (Spohn and Horney, 1992). There was no clear impact of the law in the other four jurisdictions. Two other studies that focused on specific states also found modest effects of rape law reform. Marsh *et al.* (1982) analyzed the Michigan reforms, finding increases in reported rapes as well as increases in arrests and convictions on the original charge of rape. Loh (1980) studied the impact of rape law reform in the Seattle area, finding that prosecutors did not change their charging decisions following Washington's rape law reform. After law reform, even though the overall conviction rate did not change, rape cases were more likely to result in convictions for rape than for lesser included offenses.

The modest impact of rape law reform suggests that many criminal justice officials continue to operate on the basis of traditional assumptions and that they do not always comply with the statutes (Bienen, 1980; Frohman, 1991; Marsh *et al.*, 1982; Spohn and Horney, 1992). Decisions regarding sexual assault cases are still open to a great deal of discretion, and the reforms do not necessarily affect prosecutors' units or the courtroom workgroup. LaFree (1989) has shown that information about the woman's sexual history is often disclosed in the process of a rape trial. Another limitation is that rape shield laws pertain only to trial proceedings, but most cases are handled informally through plea bargaining (Caringella-MacDonald, 1984). Despite reformers' efforts to institute a feminist perspective and create rape law reflective of the experiences of victims and women, the law continues to define rape from a male perspective, that of the accused's possession of criminal intent (MacKinnon, 1983).

Two studies by Bachman and her colleagues pain a more positive picture of the impact of changes in rape case processing (Bachman and Paternoster, 1993; Bachman and Smith, 1992). In contrast to several other studies, Bachman examined changes in rape cases over a broad period of time, from the 1970s to the late 1980s (Bachman and Smith, 1992) and early 1990s (Bachman and Paternoster, 1993). The studies contrasted changes over time in rape cases with the control crime of robbery (Bachman and Smith, 1992) or both robbery and assault (Bachman and Paternoster, 1993). These analyses showed a number of small but important changes over time in rape cases compared to the control cases. For example, national victimization survey data indicated that the number of women who reported their rapes to the police increased about 10% from the early 1970s to the early 1990s (Bachman and Paternoster, 1993). Official police reports of rape increased by about the same amount during the time period. Arrested rapists were more likely to be sent to prison, and, significantly, there was an increase in the percentage of acquaintance rapists who were imprisoned (Bachman and Paternoster, 1993). In another analysis, conviction rates for rape increased over and above the rates of conviction for robbery in three states (Bachman and Smith, 1992). Thus, both sets of statistical analyses by Bachman and her colleagues showed some important and positive changes in the processing of rape cases over two decades. Of course, it is difficult to link the changes exclusively to rape law reform, because other factors such as general change in attitudes toward the crime of rape shifted during these decades.

Ironically, the mixed success of rape law reform on rape case processing provides something for everyone. Those who believe in the possibility of reform can point to small, specific improvements in some jurisdictions, while the pessimists can argue that overall the changes in rape case processing were neither overwhelming nor universal. Some sociolegal scholars suggest that meaningful change in rape law is most likely to be accomplished when law reform efforts are informed by assessments of their social and political context, since these will constrain or enhance the implementation of legal change (Frohman and Mertz, 1994). Spohn and Horney (1991) furthermore argue that the symbolic message of rape law reform may be even more important than any immediate instrumental changes. The law not only sets rules and issues sanctions for violation of rules but also educates people by providing information about issues and confers legitimacy on new social norms (Kidder, 1983). For instance, men may not accept the feminist definition of rape, but they may be aware that the law defines a wide array of behaviors as sexual assault and that women may be more likely to define certain sexual actions as intolerable and to be more motivated to report them as crimes (see Bachman, Paternoster, and Ward, 1992; Orcutt and Faison, 1988). Over time, then, one would expect rape law reform to enhance the deterrent value of the law. Bachman's studies of change over two decades are consistent with this expectation. Thus, rape law reform as one component of social change may have broader impact than current assessments suggest.

2. Domestic Violence

A second major focus of inquiry among feminist scholars has been domestic violence, that is, violence occurring between members of a household. This can be abuse between intimate partners/spouses, violence enacted by parents toward children, and incest or sexual violence perpetrated by family members. Most attention thus far has been devoted to wife beating or women battered by their male partners (but, for an alternative account see Robson, 1995). This form of violence is particularly salient to feminist scholars because it deals with the patriarchal institution of the family and vividly presents the negative consequences of power differences between men and women.

A person is more likely to be assaulted by a family member than by a stranger. Indeed, family violence experts argue that the family is one of society's most violent institutions (Gelles and Straus, 1988). In their national survey of family violence, Straus, Gelles, and Steinmetz (1980) found that almost two million Americans had at some time faced a husband or wife wielding a knife or a gun and slightly more than two million had been beaten up by his or her spouse. These experts consider these figures to be an underestimate of the problem and believe that the more realistic rate of violence in American families is probably roughly double what their figures reveal (Straus *et al.*, 1980). Critics point out that a closer look at the violence committed by women against intimates reveals that it is less injurious, nonthreatening, and most often done in self-defense.

Contemporary scholarship has detailed the profound economic and social disadvantages of many women who are in violent relationships and the difficulties of removing themselves from those relationships (Dutton, 1988; Martin, 1976; Miller and Barberet, 1995). The fewer social and economic resources the woman has, the less likely she will be able to seek outside intervention or to leave her husband. Indeed, women with an annual family income under $10,000 are more likely to report having experienced violence by an intimate than those with higher incomes (Bachman and Saltzman, 1995). However, according to one recent study, violence against women perpetrated by intimates seems to be comparable across racial and ethnic boundaries. Black and white women and Hispanic and non-Hispanic women sustained about the same amount of violence by intimate partners (Bachman and Saltzman, 1995).

Family violence is often seen as a private problem unsuitable for the legal system. In a parallel to acquaintance rape cases, violence between intimates is frequently defined as belonging in the private sphere. Indeed, many instances of family violence remain firmly within that sphere. One major challenge presented by domestic violence cases is that many women do not report the violence to outsiders. Often, they remain with the men who beat them until the violence escalates unacceptably. If the case comes to the attention of the police or justice system, either because the man's violence is finally observed or reported, or because she strikes back and harms him, becoming a criminal defendant herself, the results are often unsatisfactory.

There are costs to taking domestic abuse outside the private sphere. Seeking outside help is often a mixed experience for battered women. Prior to the late 1970s, police were reluctant to respond to complaints of wife beating, in part because they regarded it as a family matter and in part because of a reported high incidence of police injuries and fatalities during domestic disturbance calls. In 1981, the Minneapolis Police Department began an experiment to determine whether police arrest or other responses, such as advice giving and being ordered off the premises, were more effective in reducing their incidence. The experiment clearly demonstrated the superior deterrent effect of arrest (Sherman and Berk, 1984). Within a 6-month period, 19% of the arrested suspects had committed another assault or other crime against the woman who made the original complaint. That was significantly lower than the 37% of the advised suspects and the 33% of the suspects ordered off the premises. The initial success of the early experiment, though, was not matched by replication studies (Dunford, Huizinga, and Elliott, 1990; Sherman *et al.*, 1991; Sherman and Smith, 1992; Pate and Hamilton, 1992; Berk, Campbell, Klap, and Western, 1992). In these later studies, there were few overall differences between arrested and nonarrested men. Although in line with the earlier study, arrested men who were employed tended to decrease their postarrest battering, men who were unemployed and arrested for domestic violence actually *increased* their postarrest battering, compared to similarly situated men who had not been arrested. This pattern suggests that employed men who have a higher stake in conformity and in the community can sometimes be deterred from deviance through the negative labeling event of arrest. However, men with a lower stake in conformity, such as unemployed men, do not respond in the same manner to the attempt at deviance labeling through arrest (Sherman and Smith, 1992; for further analysis, see Frohman and Mertz, 1994).

Domestic violence cases do not fare well in the criminal justice system, with dismissal of charges and lenient penalties the rule rather than the exception. (For an interesting cross-cultural comparison of the situation of battered women in the United States and Spain, see Miller and Barberet, 1995.) Many feminist scholars trace the leniency to a longstanding historical pattern, in which a man's prerogative to beat his wife was acknowledged, even sanctioned, by the criminal law. For many years, a criminal identity did not attach to men who beat their spouses. Only the outer boundaries of this behavior—fatal beatings—were policed. Thus, for many years, domestic violence was not typically considered a crime of the public sphere, the husband was not labeled a criminal, and the wife's victimization was usually not acknowledged. Feminist legal scholars have contested these historical traditions. Indeed, radical feminists have argued that the legal system's inadequate response to domestic violence was a means by which all men kept all women subordinate (Moran and Bart, 1993).

Women who struck back at their batterers also found an unsympathetic audience in the courtroom. Legal personnel and jurors often focused on the woman, asking why she did not leave the abusive situation. Studies uncovered strong and consistent gender differences in the perception of domestic violence, with men holding more negative attitudes toward battered women and women more disapproving of intimate violence (Schuller and Vidmar, 1992; see also Miller and Simpson, 1991, who document differences in men's and women's perceptions of and reactions to violence in dating relationships). The gender differences were considered significant because critical decision-makers, including police, prosecutors, and judges, were likely to be male.

Beginning in the late 1970s in the case of *Ibn-Tamas v. U.S.* (1979), advocates began offering courtroom testimony on behalf of battered women who killed their husbands. Their testimony was designed to support self-defense claims or to reduce murder charges to lesser included offenses. A battered woman claiming self-defense in the killing of her batterer often faced insurmountable problems. To prevail in a self-defense claim, the defendant must have a reasonable fear of danger and a reasonable belief in its immediacy. The first problem for battered women who killed their abusers was that many of them killed while the husband was inattentive or even asleep, making it difficult to argue that they were in immediate danger. Second, the degree of force used in self-defense is required to be no more than necessary to protect oneself. Thus, a slap should be met with another slap, not a gunshot. Yet the equal force rule assumes that the participants in a fight are roughly equal in terms of physical strength, an assumption usually not met in domestic violence. Third, in some instances, someone claiming self-defense must show that there were no avenues of retreat. Many battered women, however, may perceive no opportunities to escape and no alternatives to violence.

Psychologist Lenore Walker pioneered the use of expert testimony in battered women trials (see Walker, 1979, 1984, 1989). She aimed to provide judges and jurors with an alternative to the popular conceptions of domestic violence. On the witness stand she described her own conception of a cyclical theory of battering, the phenomenon of learned helplessness, and other social and psychological factors to help explain why battered women have a continual sense of fear, a narrowing of perceived alternatives, and great difficulty leaving battering relationships. Schuller (1992; see also Schuller and Vidmar, 1992) has demonstrated in a series of studies that such testimony can indeed lead to interpretations of domestic violence that are more favorable to the woman and that increase the chance of greater leniency in the courtroom. For example, in two mock jury experiments, she presented information about a homicide trial in which the woman killed her abusive husband. Some subjects received expert testimony about the battered woman syndrome, while others heard no such testimony. The subjects' verdicts and jury discussions were influenced by the expert testimony in a manner favorable to the female defendant (Schuller, 1992).

After showing some initial reluctance, the courts have generally supported defense requests to include expert testimony pertaining to battered woman syndrome (see, e.g., *New Jersey v. Kelly*, 1984; *Dunn v. Roberts*, 1992; and the discussion on pp. 410–420 in Monahan and Walker, 1994). An appellate court has affirmed a prosecutor's use of battered woman syndrome evidence (*Arcoren v. U.S.*, 1991), and similar to several other states, the California Evidence Code contains a specific provision permitting the use of battered woman syndrome (Monahan and Walker, 1994).

However, the use of battered woman syndrome has been sharply criticized, particularly by feminist scholars. Schneider (1986) was among the first to suggest that the focus on a woman's psychological deficiencies, and on her passivity and seeming irrationality, had several negative consequences. In the specific case at hand, it might tend to lessen the decision maker's belief in the reasonableness of the woman's actions. Schuller's (1992) study provides some suggestive trends: She found that mock jurors who heard expert evidence about the battered woman syndrome tended to believe that she had less control over her actions, and a number spontaneously argued that she should have pleaded temporary insanity. Although these impressions supported a more lenient court outcome for the battered woman, they also imply that jurors formed views of the battered woman as a helpless victim. Whether expert testimony does create strong impressions of the battered woman as irrational and damaged deserves more investigation (Schuller, 1992). Ammons (1995) raises another problem in the use of the battered woman syndrome for battered black women. She argues that the image of the "classic" battered woman as weak and passive is at odds with racial stereotypes of black women. Thus, expert testimony on the battered woman syndrome is seriously deficient if it does not deal with the potentially misleading impact of racial stereotypes in such cases.

There is a broader potential impact of the use of battered woman syndrome. The use of an argument that some women are so afflicted by a syndrome that they cannot behave rationally in the face of danger tends to reinforce traditional gender stereotypes (Schneider, 1986). Coughlin (1994) points out that the defense assumes that women suffer a lack of capacity for rational self-control that is distinctively different from that of men. This limitation of women raises the specter of additional state control over women under certain circumstances. Coughlin argues forcefully that the practice of excusing women with a syndrome shows the incompleteness of the criminal law's theory of responsibility. In her view, currently the law can accommodate women's life experiences only by judging women to be different from—and decidedly inferior to—the model human actor.

3. Sexual Harassment

Sexual harassment became a strong focus of attention among feminist scholars in the 1980s. It bears some relationship to rape and domestic violence in that it is an issue where women are the prime targets of men's aggression. Yet, rather than the physical violence that typifies rape and serious domestic disputes, sexual harassment also deals with verbal assaults and job-related consequences in the workplace. The problem of sexual harassment catapulted to national attention when law professor Anita Hill claimed that Supreme Court nominee Clarence Thomas had sexually harassed her when he was her supervisor at the Equal Employment Opportunity Commission. Although Thomas was eventually confirmed, the hearings about sexual harassment galvanized debate about race, gender, and workplace equity (Morrison, 1992; Scheppele, 1994). And there is continuing controversy over sexual harassment, with the Tailhook and Aberdeen scandals in the U.S. military and the Paula Jones sexual harassment lawsuit against President Clinton, which ended in a settlement between the parties.

Although the behavior has existed historically, the term *sexual harassment* was not used until the 1970s when Catherine MacKinnon brought it to public attention (MacKinnon, 1979). As she observes, the development of a specific legal claim for sexual harassment was the first time, historically, that women rather than men took the lead in crafting a law pertaining to women's injuries (MacKinnon, 1987). She believes that this is a highly significant fact, because in contrast to male-defined laws about women's victimizations, sexual harassment laws require a decision maker to take account of the perspective of the victim.

There is little consensus about exactly how to define sexual harassment, but it is typically considered to include quid pro quo sexual harassment (in which a reward or punishment is promised in exchange for sex), as well as repeated and unwanted sexist or sexual remarks, requests, and touches (Fitzgerald, 1990). Public surveys and academic research show that quid pro quo sexual harassment is viewed by both women and men as a clear instance of sexual harassment (Fitzgerald *et al.*, 1988; Fitzgerald and Ormerod, 1991; Gutek, 1985, 1992; Konrad and Gutek, 1986; Padgitt and Padgitt, 1986). For example, Konrad and Gutek (1986) reported that 94% of men and 98% of the women in their sample agreed that "being asked to have sexual relations with the understanding that it would hurt your job situation if you refused or help if you accepted" was definitely sexual harassment. There is more disagreement, sometimes substantial, between men and women about whether other sexual invitations, innuendoes, and jokes constitute sexual harassment. Women are more likely than men to perceive particular social-sexual behavior at work as sexual harassment (Fitzgerald and Ormerod, 1991; Gutek, 1985; Gutek, Morash, and Cohen, 1983; Padgitt and Padgitt, 1986; United States Merit Systems Protection Board, 1981).

Like the crimes of rape and domestic violence, estimates of the incidence of sexual harassment vary widely. Researchers agree that it affects a vast number of working women and students (Fitzgerald *et al.*, 1988; Gruber, 1990; Gutek, 1985; Lafontaine and Tredeau, 1986;

United States Merit Systems Protection Board, 1981). According to one survey conducted in 1988 of over 20,000 federal employees, 42% of the female workers said that they had experienced at least one episode of sexual harassment on the job during the previous 2 years (Brownmiller and Alexander, 1992). Research has shown that men tend to be the perpetrators and women the targets of sexual harassment. Sexual harassment occurs frequently in hierarchical organizations and where men predominate numerically (Konrad and Gutek, 1986). Most victims of sexual harassment do not file official complaints (MacKinnon, 1987).

Sexual harassment is now considered by the courts as a form of gender discrimination. Early cases brought claims of sexual harassment under Title VII of the Civil Rights Act of 1964, under the reasoning that when women lost their jobs for resisting sexual advances, they had been subject to employment discrimination on the basis of their sex. These early cases lost in the district courts, with judges often concluding that the situations amounted to personal dysfunctions and did not constitute employment discrimination. In a pattern reminiscent of rape and battered woman cases, district court judges and company lawyers often focused on the possible contributory role of the plaintiff in sexual harassment claims (MacKinnon, 1987). However, several appellate courts overturned these rulings, the Equal Employment Opportunity Commission issued guidelines asserting that harassment on the basis of sex was a violation of Title VII, and the U.S. Supreme Court declared it to be so in the case of *Meritor Savings Bank, FSB v. Vinson* (1986). Most importantly, the *Meritor* case held that whether or not sexual misconduct is linked to the provision of job benefits (as in quid pro quo cases), the creation of a hostile work environment through unwelcome sexual advances and sexual conduct can constitute a legally actionable case of sexual harassment under Title VII.

However, defining the boundaries of legally permissible, sexually oriented conduct in work environments has proven to be a challenge for the courts. In *Rabidue v. Osceola Refining Co.* (1986), for example, the Sixth Circuit found that a plaintiff who had documented that a fellow employee had regularly directed obscene comments at her and other women workers, and that other men in the company displayed pictures of nude women in work areas, did not make the case that these features resulted in a working environment that was intimidating, hostile, or offensive. In a more expansive reading of sexual harassment law, the U.S. Supreme Court ruled in *Harris v. Forklift Systems, Inc.* (1993) that a woman suing her boss for sexual harassment does not have to prove that she has suffered severe psychological injury from the alleged offense. The Supreme Court simply defined sexual harassment as any conduct that makes the workplace environment so hostile or abusive to a reasonable person that the victim finds it harder to perform her job. Harris had spent 6 years trying to convince judges that she was sexually harassed in violation of federal law, citing offensive conduct that included her boss asking her to the local Holiday Inn to negotiate her raise, asking her and other women to retrieve coins from his pants pockets, and commenting to her that she was a "dumb-ass woman." But, the lower court judges found that Hardy's conduct was not severe enough to seriously affect Harris's psychological well-being. The Supreme Court disagreed, arguing that federal law "comes into play before the harassing conduct leads to a nervous breakdown."

An interesting development in sexual harassment cases is that some circuits have now concluded that decision makers should adopt a "reasonable woman" standard, rather than a reasonable man or a reasonable person, in assessing plaintiff behavior and claims. In a California sexual harassment case, the Ninth Circuit stated:

> We adopt the perspective of a reasonable woman primarily because we believe that a sex-blind reasonable person standard tends to be male-biased and tends to systematically ignore the experiences of women. The reasonable woman standard does not establish a higher

> level of protection for woman than men. Instead, a gender-conscious examination of sexual harassment enables women to participate in the workplace on an equal footing with men. (*Ellison v. Brady*, 1991)

Several other circuits have followed suit. The use of the reasonable woman test raises interesting questions about the role of gender in a legal standard. Given the consistent differences between men and women in their evaluations of sexual harassment, and the male bias of the law, it might seem to be a refreshing and corrective element. The reasonable woman test has been roundly criticized, however, for being too broad, failing to recognize the many differences among women, and providing an overly generalized view of the reasonable woman. It is also criticized for its narrow focus on sex to the exclusion of other significant social characteristics such as race and class that interact powerfully with gender (Dobbin, Gatowski, Stewart, and Ross, 1996). Thus, its use raises concerns about the reliance on misleading stereotypes of women's behavior. Furthermore, in at least one juror simulation experiment, changing the legal standard from reasonable person to reasonable woman produced no differences in the outcomes of the cases (Wiener, Watts, Goldkamp, and Gasper, 1995).

D. STUDYING VIOLENCE AGAINST WOMEN: DOES IT LEAD TO VICTIM FEMINISM?

A good deal of feminist scholarship, both theoretically driven and practice-oriented, has explored women's victimization. Although that work has resulted in much greater knowledge about violence against women, and has produced some improvement in the legal system's treatment of women, the scrutiny of women's victimization by scholars and activists has come in for some serious criticism. The feminist focus on violence against women has been denounced as creating victim feminism. Women come to see themselves primarily through the lens of their victimization, with the result that their very identity is bound up in being a victim. Thus, the movement to bring more attention to crimes of violence against women has allegedly produced a cult of the victim. A woman who thinks of herself as a victim is not likely to feel a sense of agency, of herself as powerful and confident, the critics charge. Wolf (1993) argues that victim feminism has slowed women's progress, impeded their self-knowledge, and been responsible for inconsistent, negative, and regressive thinking that alienates women and men.

A similar critique was delivered at the 1994 D.C. Circuit Judicial Conference meeting devoted to a discussion of the findings of the D.C. Circuit's Task Force project on gender, race, and ethnic bias. The Task Force's Special Committee on Gender, in its preliminary report, had found that the D.C. Circuit had made considerable progress toward equal treatment of female attorneys, but also reported some instances in which female attorneys were at a disadvantage compared to their male counterparts. The Task Force developed a set of recommendations to promote gender equity. Criticizing these recommendations, a representative of the conservative Independent Women's Forum argued:

> I am very fearful that this heightened sensitivity—if that is what is called for—once obtained by the judiciary in the D.C. Circuit will lead to stereotyping, or even worse, patronizing conduct, which will operate from the premise that I am weak, incapable of defending myself, and unequal due to my gender ... I am here to tell you, as a woman and practicing lawyer in these courts, that is the worst thing you could do to me. It will demean me before my clients and my peers, and will undermine the hard-fought confidence that I

> have developed in myself and that other women have strived so hard to attain. (Independent Women's Forum, 1994)

The media's fascination with feminism's so-called victim problem both reflects and distorts struggles with feminist legal theory and practice. One of feminism's strengths has been its ability to reveal barriers to women's full and equal participation in society. But feminist efforts to expose the pervasiveness of restraints on women's lives sometimes appear to contradict feminist visions of women as self-determining agents capable of creatively shaping the world (McCluskey, 1997). Many feminists have emphasized women's experiences as victims of male violence and of male sexual abuse in part in an attempt to demonstrate that those harms are serious problems deserving of legal protection. At the same time, feminists themselves have expressed concerns about how the legal system can be used to recognize and redress these previously hidden injuries to women without contributing to old stories that cast women as inevitably damaged and vulnerable to male control (Schneider, 1986).

The conflicting identities of victim and agent have spurred McCluskey (1997) to ask: "How can we name and challenge the ways in which many women are victims of gender-related harms without denying that most (if not all) women also share in a complex reality of power, pleasure and privilege?" McCluskey's thesis is that we can learn how to better respond to this apparent "victim/agent" dilemma by looking at another side of the story—at media representations of some who claim to be victims of feminism. Narratives from both feminist victims and those who feel victimized by feminism demonstrate that telling stories of suffering is an act of power as well as a confession of powerlessness. Though the preexisting social and political context influences whether a narrator's stories of harm are interpreted as heroic or victimizing, those victim stories can also contribute to reshaping the narrator's authority and the broader political context in which the narratives are interpreted. Stories of victimization may have limited value for ending oppression not because they make the oppressed seem too dependent and lacking in agency, but because they may make oppression seem too individualized. Feminists should strive to use expressions of personal harm not simply as individual catharsis but to question and change the institutions in which harm is interpreted.

E. CONCLUSION

Since coming of age, feminist jurisprudence has stimulated a prodigious amount of research and scholarly writing. Although most of the debates among feminist legal theorists have been productive, some scholars have questioned whether those arguing from a divergent perspective can offer anything to the study of gender and the law. Like many other feminist scholars (see, e.g., Andersen, 1997; Daly, 1997; Jackson, 1994), we favor an eclectic, big tent approach, drawing on a range of theoretical positions and methodological approaches to generate and test ideas about how to promote justice for women in the legal system. Perhaps the biggest challenge to the social science study of women and law has come from postmodernism. Postmodernist questioning has illuminated the problematic nature of gender categories and gendered assumptions that undergird law and legal institutions. Although we believe it is a serious mistake to abandon empirical study of the treatment of women in law and the legal system, the dialogue between postmodernists and social scientists leads us to be more careful and reflective in our employment of the categories of woman and man.

There is promising work to be done on a variety of fronts. Several pressing matters could help to inform the debate over feminist jurisprudential theories. The dramatic changes in the representative of women in the legal profession and the justice system provide a living laboratory within which theories about women's distinctive voice, gendered institutions, and the immutability of patriarchy can be tested. Here, work on organizational change and the inclusion of women into male-dominated occupations can offer some insights (see Andersen, 1987; Daly, 1995). In business and other domains, as long as women remain a minority there is a tendency to "add women and stir," that is, to accommodate women by slight modifications in the organizational structure. As women become more numerous, they develop the potential for creating more fundamental change.

In the field of criminology, for instance, the increasing presence of female scholars has led to identifiable changes in the underlying assumptions and topics of research, and the field's sensitivity to issues relating to women (Daly, 1995). Although women today remain a numerical minority in the legal profession, the law school professorate, and the judiciary, as women begin to achieve parity with men they may help to envision and create a decidedly different legal world. Whether or not one subscribes to the different voice school of thought, the fact that men and women differ systematically in their attitudes toward certain legal wrongs, including rape, domestic violence, and sexual harassment, suggests that a legal system arranged and populated by women will reflect their distinct perspectives.

At the beginning of the 1970s, rape was a word rarely spoken. Women who were victims of their husbands' physical abuse were often silent. Sexual harassment was not even a recognized term, but no longer are these issues the exclusive province of academic feminists. Today, violence against women commands widespread public and political attention. In a speech given the day that the Violence Against Women Act became law, its chief sponsor, Delaware Senator Joseph Biden, echoed themes that were first voiced in the feminist literature of the 1970s (Biden, 1994). In particular, he argued strongly that violence against women, including sexual assault and domestic violence, deserved to be taken very seriously as a social problem.

In part, increased attention to crimes of violence against women is part of a larger trend toward societal punitiveness toward crime and longer prison terms for criminal offenders; and the Act contains numerous provisions to strengthen law enforcement and prosecution for assaults against women. But it also insists as a condition of funding that states pay for forensic medical services for victims of sexual assault; and it provides funds for victim services for battered women. It is clearly the most far-reaching law passed in the United States pertaining to crimes of violence against women. One of the interesting questions that bears systematic examination is the extent to which a large and no doubt unwieldy law such as this one can create significant change and bring justice to women who have been victimized. Here, as with the reception to sexual harassment laws, the impact of the Violence Against Women Act and its initiatives will constitute an experiment in the possibility of progressive feminist legal change.

A continuing challenge is to articulate, through theory and research, whether and how a feminist jurisprudence and feminist-inspired legal order might differ from the existing legal world. Our brief survey shows that feminist legal theorists envision distinctive alternative arrangements. Liberal feminists continue to push for legal equality for men and women, while difference feminists advocate a new legal order based on an ethic of care. Radical and critical scholars argue for dismantling the liberal state and abandoning gender categories to achieve justice for women. Changes in the presence of women in law and in the laws affecting women will provide new theoretical and empirical insights into these and other approaches to feminist justice.

ACKNOWLEDGMENTS. We benefitted tremendously from the reviews and comments of Margaret Andersen, Kathy Daly, Leslie Goldstein, Susan Miller, and Joe Sanders. A fellowship in the Center for Advanced Study at the University of Delaware facilitated Valerie Hans's work on this chapter.

REFERENCES

Acker, J. (1989). *Doing Comparable Worth*. Philadelphia: Temple University Press.

Acker, J. (1990). Hierarchies, Jobs, Bodies: A Theory of Gendered Organizations. *Gender & Society, 4*, 139–155.

Adler, F. (1975). *Sisters in Crime*. New York: McGraw–Hill.

American Booksellers Association v. Hudnut, 771 F.2d 323 (7th Cir. 1985), aff'd mem., 475 U.S. 1001 (1986).

Amir, M. (1971). *Patterns in Forcible Rape*. Chicago: University of Chicago Press.

Ammons, L. L. (1995). Mules, Madonnas, Babies, Bathwater, Racial Imagery and Stereotypes: The African-American Woman and the Battered Woman Syndrome. *Wisconsin Law Review, 1995*, 1003–1080.

Andersen, M. L. (1987). Changing the Curriculum in Higher Education. *Signs, 12*, 222–254.

Andersen, M. L. (1997). *Thinking about Women: Sociological Perspectives on Sex and Gender* (4th ed.). Boston: Allyn & Bacon.

Arcoren v. United States, 929 F.2d 1235 (8th Cir. 1991).

Arnold, R. (1992). Processes of Victimization and Criminalization of Black Women. *Social Justice, 17*, 153–164.

Babcock, B. A. (1988). Clara Shortridge Foltz: First Woman. *Arizona Law Review, 30*, 673–717.

Bachman, R., and Paternoster, R. (1993). A Contemporary Look at the Effects of Rape Law Reform: How Far Have We Really Come? *Journal of Criminal Law and Criminology, 84*, 554–574.

Bachman, R., and Saltzman, L. E. (1995, August). *Violence against Women: Estimates from the Redesigned Survey* (Bureau of Justice Statistics Special Report). Washington, DC: U.S. Department of Justice, Office of Justice Programs.

Bachman, R., and Smith, P. (1992). The Adjudication of Rape since Reforms: Examining the Probability of Conviction and Incarceration at the National and Three State Levels. *Criminal Justice Policy Review, 6*, 342–358.

Bachman, R., Paternoster, R., and Ward, S. (1992). The Rationality of Sex Offending: Testing a Deterrence/Rational Choice Conception of Sexual Assault. *Law & Society Review, 26*, 343–372.

Baer, J. A. (1991). Nasty Law or Nice Ladies? Jurisprudence, Feminism, and Gender Difference. *Women & Politics, 11*, 1–31.

Barnett, N., and Feild, H. (1977). Sex Differences in University Students' Attitudes toward Rape. *Journal of College Student Personnel, 2*, 93–96.

Baskin, D. R., Sommers, I., Tessler, R., and Steadman, H. J. (1989). Role Incongruence and Gender Variation in the Provision of Prison Mental Health Services. *Journal of Health and Social Behavior, 30*, 305–314.

Battelle Human Affairs Research Center. (1975). *Forcible Rape: A National Survey of the Response by Police*. Unpublished report, Law and Justice Center, Seattle, WA.

Becker, M., Bowman, C. G., and Torrey, M. (1994). *Feminist Jurisprudence: Taking Women Seriously*. St. Paul, MN: West Publishing Co.

Belknap, J. (1996). *The Invisible Woman: Gender, Crime, and Justice*. Belmont, CA: Wadsworth.

Bender, L. (1988). A Lawyer's Primer on Feminist Theory and Tort. *Journal of Legal Education, 28*, 3–37.

Berk, R., Campbell, A., Klap, R., and Western, B. (1992). The Deterrent Effect of Arrest in Incidents of Domestic Violence: A Bayesian Analysis of Four Field Experiments. *American Sociological Review, 57*, 698–709.

Bienen, L. (1980). Rape III—National Developments in Rape Reform Legislation. *Women's Rights Law Reporter, 6*, 170–213.

Binion, G. (1993). The Nature of Feminist Jurisprudence. *Judicature, 77*, 140–143.

Blumberg, A. S. (1967). The Practice of Law as Confidence Game: Organizational Cooptation of a Profession. *Law & Society Review, 1*, 15–39.

Bohmer, C. (1974). Judicial attitudes toward rape victims. *Judicature, 57*, 303–307.

Boritch, H. (1992). Gender and Criminal Court Outcomes: An Historical Analysis. *Criminology, 30*, 293–325.

Box, S., and Hale, C. (1984). Liberation/Emancipation, Economic Margins or Less Chivalry. *Criminology, 22*, 473–497.

Bridges, J. S., and McGrail, C. A. (1989). Attributions of Responsibility for Date and Stranger Rape. *Sex Roles, 21*, 273–286.

Brodyaga, L., Gates, M., Singer, S. Tucker, M., and White, R. (1975). *Rape and Its Victims: A Report for Citizens, Health Facilities and Criminal Justice Agencies*. Washington, DC: National Institute of Law Enforcement and Criminal Justice.

Brownmiller, S. (1975). *Against Our Will: Men, Women, and Rape*. New York: Simon & Schuster.
Brownmiller, S., and Alexander, D. (1992, January/February). How We Got Here: From Carmita Wood to Anita Hill. *Ms.*, pp. 70–71.
Butler, J. (1990). *Gender Trouble: Feminism and the Subversion of Identity*. London: Routledge.
Calavita, K., and Seron, C. (1992). Postmodernism and Protest: Recovering the Sociological Imagination. *Law & Society Review*, *26*, 765–771.
Calhoun, L. G., Selby, J. W., and Warring, L. J. (1976). Social Perception of the Victim's Causal Role in Rape: An Exploratory Examination of Four Factors. *Human Relations*, *29*, 517–526.
Caringella-MacDonald, S. (1984). Sexual Assault Prosecution: An Examination of Model Rape Legislation in Michigan. *Women and Politics*, *4*, 65–82.
Chesney-Lind, M. (1977). Judicial Paternalism and the Female Status Offender. *Crime and Delinquency*, *23*, 121–130.
Chesney-Lind, M. (1995). Rethinking Women's Imprisonment: A Critical Examination of Trends in Female Incarceration. In B. R. Price and N. J. Sokoloff (Eds.), *The Criminal Justice System and Women: Offenders, Victims, and Workers* (2nd ed., pp. 105–117). New York: McGraw–Hill.
Chodorow, N. (1978). *The Reproduction of Mothering*. Berkeley: University of California Press.
Cockburn, C. (1991). *In the Way of Women: Men's Resistance to Sex Equality in Organizations*. Ithaca, NY: ILR Press.
Collins, P. H. (1990). *Black Feminist Thought: Knowledge, Consciousness, and the Politics of Empowerment*. Boston: Unwin Hyman.
Connell, R. W. (1987). *Gender and Power*. Stanford: Stanford University Press.
Cooper, S. E. (1986). Women's History Goes to Trial: EEOC v Sears, Roebuck, and Company: Introduction to the Documents. *Signs*, *11*, 751–756.
Coughlin, A. M. (1994). Excusing Women. *California Law Review*, *82*, 1–93.
Daly, K. (1989). Neither Conflict nor Labelling nor Paternalism Will Suffice: Race, Ethnicity, Gender, and Family in Criminal Court Decisions. *Crime and Delinquency*, *35*, 136–168.
Daly, K. (1994). *Gender, Crime, and Punishment*. New Haven, CT: Yale University Press.
Daly, K. (1995). Looking Back, Looking Forward: The Promise of Feminist Transformation. In B. R. Price and N. J. Sokoloff (Eds.), *The Criminal Justice System and Women: Offenders, Victims, and Workers* (2nd ed., pp. 443–457). New York: McGraw–Hill.
Daly, K. (1997). Different Ways of Conceptualizing Sex/Gender in Feminist Theory and Their Implications for Criminology. *Theoretical Criminology*, *1*, 25–51.
Datesman, S. K., and Scarpitti, F. R. (1980). Unequal Protection for Males and Females in Juvenile Court. In S. Datesman and F. Scarpitti (Eds.), *Women, Crime, and Justice*. Lincoln: Oxford University Press.
Davidman, L. (1991). *Tradition in a Rootless World*. Los Angeles: University of California Press.
Davis, S. (1993). The Voice of Sandra Day O'Connor. *Judicature*, *77*, 134–139.
Davis, S. (1993–1994). Do Women Judges Speak "In a Different Voice?" Carol Gilligan, Feminist Legal Theory, and the Ninth Circuit. *Wisconsin Women's Law Journal*, *7–8*, 143–173.
D.C. Circuit Task Force on Gender, Race, and Ethnic Bias. (1995). *The Gender, Race, and Ethnic Bias Task Force Project in the D.C. Circuit* (2 vols.). [Report of the Special Committee on Gender reprinted in *Georgetown University Law Review*.]
Derrida, J. (1978). *Spurs: Nietzsche's Styles*. Chicago: University of Chicago Press.
Dobbin, S. A., Gatowski, S. I., Stewart, M. W., and Ross, J. A. (1996). *Reasonableness and Gender in the Law: Moving beyond the Reasonable Person and Reasonable Woman Standards*. Unpublished manuscript, University of Nevada, Reno. [Earlier version of the paper presented at LSA, Glasgow, 1996.]
Donnerstein, E., Linz, D., and Penrod, S. (1987). *The Question of Pornography: Research Findings and Policy Implications*. New York: Free Press.
Driscoll, S. (1994). Consumer Bankruptcy and Gender. *Georgetown Law Journal*, *83*, 525–557.
Dunford, F., Huizinga, D., and Elliott, D. (1990). The Role of Arrest in Domestic Assault: The Omaha Police Experiment. *Criminology*, *28*, 183–206.
Dunn v. Roberts, 963 F.2d 308 (10th Cir. 1992)
Dutton, D. (1988). *The Domestic Assault of Women: Psychological and Criminal Justice Perspectives*. Boston: Allyn & Bacon.
Dworkin, A. (1981). *Pornography: Men Possessing Women*. New York: Putnam.
Dworkin, A. (1993). Living in Terror, Pain: Being a Battered Wife. In P. Bart and E. G. Moran (Eds.), *Violence against Women: The Bloody Footprints* (pp. 443–460). Thousand Oaks, CA: Sage.
Edwards, S. (1981). *Female Sexuality and the Law*. Oxford: Martin Robertson.
EEOC v. Sears, Roebuck & Company, 628 F. Supp. 1264, aff'd, 839 F.2d 302 (7th Cir. 1988).
Eisenstein, J., and Jacob, H. (1977). *Felony Justice: An Organizational Analysis of Criminal Courts*. Boston: Little, Brown.

Eisenstein, Z. R. (1982). The Sexual Politics of the New Right: Understanding the "Crisis" of Liberalism for the 1980s. *Signs*, *7*, 567–588.
Ellison v. Brady, 924 F.2d 872 (9th Cir. 1991).
Estrich, S. (1987). *Real Rape*. Cambridge, MA: Harvard University Press.
Feild, H. (1978). Attitudes toward Rape: A Comparative Analysis of Police, Rapists, Crisis Counselors, and Citizens. *Journal of Personality and Social Psychology*, *36*, 156–179.
Feild, H., and Bienen, L. (1980). *Jurors and Rape: A Study in Psychology and Law*. Lexington, MA: Lexington Books.
Feinman, C. (1979). Sex Role Stereotypes and Justice for Women. *Crime and Delinquency*, *25*, 87–94.
Feinman, C. (1994). *Women in the Criminal Justice System*. New York: Praeger.
Feldman-Summers, S., and Lindner, K. (1976). Perceptions of Victims and Defendants in Criminal Assault Cases. *Criminal Justice & Behavior*, *3*, 135–150.
Field, M. (1983). Rape: Legal Aspects. In S. Kadish (Ed.), *Encyclopedia of Crime and Justice* (Vol. 4). New York: Free Press. 1356–1364.
Firestone, S. (1970). *The Dialectic of Sex*. New York: Bantam Books.
Fitzgerald, L. (1990). Sexual Harassment: The Definition and Measurement of a Construct. In M. A. Paludi (Ed.), *Ivory Power: Sexual Harassment on Campus*. Albany: State University of New York Press.
Fitzgeraid, L., and Ormerod, A. (1991). Perceptions of Sexual Harassment: The Influence of Gender and Academic Context. *Psychology of Women Quarterly*, *15*, 281–294.
Fitzgerald, L., Shullman, S., Bailey, N., Richards, M., Swecker, J., Gold, Y., Ormerod, M., and Weitzman, L. (1988). Incidence and Dimensions of Sexual Harassment in Academia and the Workplace. *Journal of Vocational Behavior*, *32*, 152– 175.
Foucault, M. (1977). Nietzsche, Genealogy, History. In D. F. Bouchad and S. Simon (Eds.), *Language, Counter-Memory, Practice*. Ithaca, NY: Cornell University Press. 130–152.
Foucault, M. (1979). *Discipline and Punish*. New York: Vintage Books.
Foucault, M. (1980). *Power/Knowledge*. New York: Pantheon Books.
Freeman, J. (1975). *The Politics of Women's Liberation*. New York: David McKay.
Frohman, L. (1991). Discrediting Victims' Allegations of Sexual Assault: Prosecutorial Accounts of Case Rejection. *Social Problems*, *38*, 213–226.
Frohman, L., and Mertz, E. (1994). Legal Reform and Social Construction: Violence, Gender, and the Law. *Law & Social Inquiry*, *19*, 829–851.
Frug, M. J. (1992a). *Postmodern Legal Feminism*. London: Routledge.
Frug, M. J. (1992b). *Women and the Law*. Westbury, NY: Foundation Press.
Geduldig v. Aiello, 417 U.S. 484 (1974).
Gelles, R., and Straus, M. (1988). *Intimate Violence: The Causes and Consequences of Abuse in the American Family*. New York: Simon & Schuster.
Gilligan, C. (1982). *In a Different Voice: Psychological Theory and Women's Development*. Cambridge, MA: Harvard University Press.
Gilmartin-Zena, P. (1983). Attribution Theory and Rape Victim Responsibility. *Deviant Behavior*, *4*, 357–374.
Ginsberg, R. B. (1996). Foreword [Report of the Special Committee on Gender to the Gender, Race, and Ethnic Bias Task Force Project in the D.C. Circuit]. *Georgetown Law Journal*, *84*, 1651–1655.
Glaspell, S. (1987). *Plays by Susan Glaspell*. Edited by and with an Introduction by C. W. E. Bigsby. New York: Cambridge University Press.
Golden, M. R. (1991). When Pregnancy Discrimination is Gender Discrimination: The Constitutionality of Excluding Pregnant Women from Drug Treatment Programs. *New York University Law Review*, *66*, 1832–1880.
Goldstein, L. F. (1992). *Feminist Jurisprudence: The Difference Debate*. Savage, MD: Rowman & Littlefield.
Goldstein, L. F. (1994). *Contemporary Cases in Women's Rights*. Madison: University of Wisconsin Press.
Goldstein, L. F., and Stech, D. (1995). Explaining Transformations in Supreme Court Policy. *Judicature*, *79*, 80–85.
Goodman, J., Loftus, E. F., Miller, M., and Greene, E. (1991). Money, Sex, and Death: Gender Bias in Wrongful Death Damage Awards. *Law & Society Review*, *25*, 263–285.
Griffin, S. (1971). Rape: The All-American Crime. *Ramparts*, *10*, 26–35.
Gruber, J. (1990). Methodological Problems and Policy Implications in Sexual Harassment Research. *Population Research and Review*, *9*, 235–254.
Guinier, L., Fine, M., and Balin, J., with Bartow, A., and Stachel, D. L. (1994). Becoming Gentlemen: Women's Experiences at One Ivy League Law School. *University of Pennsylvania Law Review*, *143*, 1–110.
Gutek, B. A. (1985). *Sex and the Workplace: The Impact of Sexual Behavior and Harassment on Women, Men and Organizations*. San Francisco: Jossey–Bass.

Gutek, B. A. (1992). Understanding Sexual Harassments at Work. *Notre Dame Journal of Law, Ethics and Public Policy, 6*, 335–358.

Cutek, B. A., Morash, B., and Cohen, A. G. (1983). Interpreting Social-Sexual Behavior in a Work Setting. *Journal of Vocational Behavior, 20*, 30–48.

Hagan, J., and Kay, F. (1995). *Gender in Practice: A Study of Lawyers' Lives*. London: Oxford University Press.

Hall, J. D. (1983). The Mind that Burns in Each Body: Women, Rape and Racial Violence. In A. Snitow, C. Stansell, and S. Thompson (Eds.), *Powers of Desire: The Politics of Sexuality* (pp. 328–349). New York: Monthly Review Press.

Handler, J. F. (1992). Postmodernism, Protest, and the New Social Movements. *Law & Society Review, 26*, 697–731.

Haney, L. (1996). Homeboys, Babies, and Men in Suits: The State and the Reproduction of Male Dominance. *American Sociological Review, 61*, 759–778.

Hans, V. P.., and Brooks, N. (1977). Effects of Corroboration Instructions in a Rape Case on Experimental Juries. *Osgoode Hall Law Journal, 15*, 701–716.

Hans, V. P., and Vidmar, N. (1986). *Judging the Jury*. New York: Plenum Press.

Harris v. Forklift Systems, Inc., 114 S. Ct. 367 (1993).

Harvey, M. (1985). *Exemplary Rape Crisis Programs: A Cross-Site Analysis and Case Studies*. National Center for the Prevention and Control of Rape. Washington, DC: U.S. Government Printing Office.

Heilbrun, A., and Heilbrun, M. (1986). The Treatment of Women within the Criminal Justice System. *Psychology of Women Quarterly, 10*, 240–251.

Holmes, K. (1980). Justice for Whom? Rape Victims Assess the Legal–Judicial System. *Free Inquiry in Creative Sociology, 8*, 126–130.

Holmstrom, L., and Burgess, A. (1978). *The Victim of Rape: Institutional Reactions*. New York: Wiley–Interscience.

Horney, J., and Spohn, C. (1991). Rape Laws and Instrumental Change in Six Urban Jurisdictions. *Law & Society Review, 25*, 117–153.

Ibn-Tamas v. United States, 407 A.2d 626 (1979).

Independent Women's Forum. (1994). Comments on Preliminary Report of the Special Committee on Gender. *D.C. Circuit Task Force on Gender, Race, and Ethnic Bias*. Washington, DC: U.S. Government Printing Office. p. 211.

Jackson, V. C. (1994). Empiricism, Gender, and Legal Pedagogy: An Experiment in a Federal Courts Seminar at Georgetown University Law Center. *Georgetown Law Journal, 83*, 461–524.

Jacob, H. (1988). *Silent Revolution: The Transformation of Divorce Law in the United States*. Chicago: University of Chicago Press.

Kalven, H., Jr., and Seizel, H. (1966). *The American Jury*. Boston: Little, Brown.

Kerstetter, W. (1990). Gateway to Justice: Police and Prosecutorial Response to Sexual Assaults against Women. *The Journal of Criminal Law and Criminology, 81*, 267–313.

Kidder, R. (1983). *Connecting Law and Society: An Introduction to Research and Theory*. Englewood Cliffs, NJ: Prentice–Hall.

Kline, M. (1989). Race, Racism, and Feminist Legal Theory. *Harvard Women's Law Journal, 150*, 115–150.

Konrad, A. M., and Gutek, B. (1986). Impact of Work Experience on Attitudes toward Sexual Harassment. *Administrative Science Quarterly, 31*, 422–438.

Krafka, C., Linz, D., Donnerstein, E., and Penrod, S. D. (1997). Women's Reactions to Sexually Aggressive Mass Media Depictions. *Violence Against Women, 3*, 149–181.

Kritzer, H. M. (1991). *Let's Make a Deal: Understanding the Negotiation Process in Ordinary Litigation*. Madison: University of Wisconsin Press.

Krohn, M., Curry, J., and Nelson-Kilger, S. (1983). Is Chivalry Dead? *Criminology, 21*, 417–437.

Lafontaine, E., and Tredeau, L. (1986). The Frequency, Source and Correlates of Sexual Harassment among Women in Traditional Male Occupations. *Sex Roles, 15*, 433–442.

LaFree, G. D. (1981). Official Reactions to Social Problems: Police Decisions in Sexual Assault Cases. *Social Problems, 28*, 582–594.

LaFree, G. D. (1989). *Rape and Criminal Justice: The Social Construction of Sexual Assault*. Belmont, CA: Wadsworth.

Linz, D., Penrod, S. D., and Donnerstein, E. (1987). The Attorney General's Commission on Pornography: The Gaps between "Findings" and Facts. *American Bar Foundation Research Journal, 1987*, 713–736.

Littleton, C. A. (1987). Reconstructing Sexual Equality. *California Law Review, 75*, 1279–1337.

Loh, W. D. (1980). The Impact of Common Law and Reform Rape Statutes on Prosecution: An Empirical Study. *Washington Law Review, 55*, 543–652.

Lorber, J. (1994). *Paradoxes of Gender*. New Haven, CT: Yale University Press.

Macauley, S., Friedman, L. M., and Stookey, J. (Eds.). (1995). *Law and Society: Readings on the Social Studies of Law*. New York: Norton.
MacKinnon, C. (1979). *Sexual Harassment of Working Women: A Case of Sex Discrimination*. New Haven, CT: Yale University Press.
MacKinnon, C. (1983). Feminism, Marxism, Method, and the State: Toward Feminist Jurisprudence. *Signs, 8*, 635–658.
MacKinnon, C. (1987). *Feminism Unmodified*. Cambridge, MA: Harvard University Press.
MacKinnon, C. (1989). *Toward a Feminist Theory of the State*. Cambridge, MA: Harvard University Press.
Malamuth, N. M., and Briere, J. (1986). Sexual Violence in the Media: Indirect Effects on Aggression against Women. *Journal of Social Issues, 42*, 75–92.
Malamuth, N. M., and Check, J. V. P. (1981). The Effects of Mass Media Exposure on Acceptance of Violence against Women: A Field Experiment. *Journal of Research in Personality, 15*, 436–446.
Marsh, J., Geist, A., and Caplan, N. (1982). *Rape and the Limits of Law Reform*. Boston: Auburn House.
Martin, D. (1976). *Battered Wives*. San Francisco: Glide Publications.
Martin, P. Y., and Powell, R. M. (1994). Accounting for the "Second Assault": Legal Organizations' Framing of Rape Victims. *Law & Social Inquiry, 19*, 853–890.
McCahill, T., Meyer, L., and Fischman, A. (1979). *The Aftermath of Rape*. Lexington, MA: Lexington Books.
McCluskey, M. (1997). Fear of Feminism: Media Stories of Feminist Victims and Victims of Feminism on College Campuses. In M. Fineman and M. McCluskey (Eds.), *Feminism, Media and the Law*. London: Oxford University Press. 57–71.
McCorkel, J. (1996). Justice, Gender, and Incarceration: An Analysis of the Leniency and Severity Debate. In J. A. Inciardi (Ed.), *Examining the Justice Process* (pp. 157–176). New York: Harcourt Brace.
Menkel-Meadow, C. (1985). Portia in a Difference Voice: Speculations on a Women's Lawyering Process. *Berkeley Women's Law Journal, 1*, 39–63.
Menkel-Meadow, C. (1989). Feminization of the Legal Profession: The Comparative Sociology of Women Lawyers. In R. L. Abel and P. S. C. Lewis (Eds.), *Lawyers in Society: Comparative Theories* (Vol. 3). Berkeley: University of California Press. 196–238.
Menkel-Meadow, C. (1996). What's Gender Got to Do With It? The Politics and Morality of an Ethic of Care [Review of J. C. Tronto, *Moral Boundaries: A Political Argument for an Ethic of Care*]. *New York University Review of Law and Social Change, 22*, 265–293.
Meritor Savings Bank, FSB v. Vinson, 477 U.S. 57 (1986).
Milkman, R. (1987). *Gender at Work*. Chicago: University of Illinois Press.
Mill, H. T. (1970). Enfranchisement of Women. In A. S. Rossi (Ed.), *Essays on Sex Equality* (pp. 89–122). Chicago: University of Chicago Press. (Original work published 1851).
Mill, J. S. (1970). The Subjection of Women. In A. S. Rossi (Ed.), *Essays on Sex Equality* (pp. 123–242). Chicago: University of Chicago Press. (Original work published 1869).
Miller, S. L., and Barberet, R. (1995). A Cross-Cultural Comparison of Social Reform: The Growing Pains of the Battered Women's Movements in Washington, D.C., and Madrid, Spain. *Law & Social Inquiry, 19*, 923–966.
Miller, S. L., and Simpson, S. S. (1991). Courtship Violence and Social Control: Does Gender Matter? *Law & Society Review, 25*, 335–365.
Millett, K. (1970). *Sexual Politics*. Garden City, NY: Doubleday.
Monahan, J., and Walker, L. (1994). *Social Science in Law: Cases and Materials* (3rd ed.). Westbury, NY: Foundation Press.
Moran, E. G., and Bart, P. (1993). *Violence against Women: The Bloody Footprints*. Thousand Oaks, CA: Sage.
Morash, M., Haarr, R., and Rucker, L. (1994). A Comparison of Programming for Women and Men in U.S. Prisons in the 1980s. *Crime and Delinquency, 40*, 197–221.
Morrison, T. (ed.). (1992). *Race-ing Justice, En-Gendering Power: Essays on Anita Hill, Clarence Thomas, and the Construction of Social Reality*. New York: Pantheon.
Moulds, E. (1980). Chivalry and Paternalism: Disparities of Treatment in the Criminal Justice System. In S. Datesman and F. Scarpitti (Eds.), *Women, Crime, and Justice*. London: Oxford University Press. 31–54.
Nagel, S., and Weitzman, L. J. (1972). Sex and the Unbiased Jury. *Judicature, 56*, 108.
Nelson, S, and Amir, M. (1975). The Hitch-Hike Victim of Rape: A Research Report. In I. Drapkin and E. Viano (Eds.), *Victimology: A New Focus* (pp. 47–58). Lexington, MA: Lexington Books.
New Jersey Supreme Court Task Force on Women in the Courts. (1984). First Year Report of the New Jersey Supreme Court Task Force on Women in the Courts. Reprinted in *Women's Rights Law Reporter*. Vol. 9. 129.
New Jersey v. Kelly, 97 N.J. 178, 478 A.2d 364 (1984).
Nicholson, L. J. (1990). *Feminism/Postmodernism*. London: Routledge.

Ninth Circuit Gender Bias Task Force. (1993). *The Effects of Gender in the Federal Courts: Final Report of the Ninth Circuit Gender Bias Task Force*, reprinted in *Southern California Law Review*, *67*, 745–1106.
Offer of Proof Concerning the Testimony of Dr. Rosalind Rosenberg. (1986). *Signs*, *11*, 757–766.
Orcutt, J., and Faison, R. (1988). Sex-Role Attitude Change and Reporting of Rape Victimization, 1973–1985. *Sociological Quarterly*, *29*, 589–604.
Padgitt, S. C., and Padgitt, J. S. (1986). Cognitive Structure of Sexual Harassment: Implications for University Policy. *Journal of College Student Personnel*, *27*, 34–49.
Pate, A., and Hamilton, E. (1992). Formal and Informal Deterrents to Domestic Violence: The Dade County Spousal Assault Experiment. *American Sociological Review*, *57*, 691–697.
Peterson, R. R. (1996a). A Re-Evaluation of the Economic Consequences of Divorce. *American Sociological Review*, *61*, 528–536.
Peterson, R. R. (1996b). Statistical Errors, Faulty Conclusions, Misguided Policy: Reply to Weitzman. *American Sociological Review*, *61*, 539–540.
Pollak, O. (1950). *The Criminality of Women*. Philadelphia: Temple University Press.
Pope, C. (1976). The Influence of Social and Legal Factors on Sentencing Dispositions: A Preliminary Analysis of Offender-Based Transaction Statistics. *Journal of Criminal Justice*, *4*, 203–221.
Price, B. R., and Sokoloff, N. J. (1995). *The Criminal Justice System and Women: Offenders, Victims, and Workers* (2nd ed.). New York: McGraw–Hill.
Pride, A. (1981). To Respectability and Back: A Ten Year View of the Anti-Rape Movement. In F. Delacoste and F. Newman (Eds.), *Fight Back: Feminist Resistance to Male Violence*. San Francisco: Cleis Press. 114–118.
Rabidue v. Osceola Refining Col., 805 F.2d 611 (6th Cir. 1986), cert. denied, 481 U.S. 1041 (1987).
Rafter, N. H., and Stanko, E. (1982). *Judge, Lawyer, Victim, Thief*. Chicago: Northeastern University Press.
Reed v. Reed, 404 U.S. 71 (1971).
Reskin, B., and Roos, P. (1990). *Job Queues, Gender Queues*. Philadelphia: Temple University Press.
Rhode, D. L. (1990). Feminist Critical Theories. *Stanford Law Review*, *42*, 617–638.
Rich, A. (1974). *Of Woman Born: Motherhood as Experience and Institution*. New York: Pantheon Books.
Rifkin, J. (1980). Toward a Theory of Law and Patriarchy. *Harvard Women's Law Journal*, *3*, 83–108.
Roach Anleu, S. L. (1992). Critiquing the Law: Themes and Dilemmas in Anglo-American Feminist Legal Theory. *Journal of Law and Society*, *19*, 423–439.
Robin, G. (1977). Forcible Rape: Institutionalized Sexism in the Criminal Justice System. *Crime and Delinquency*, *23*, 136–153.
Robson, R. (1995). Violence against Lesbians. In B. R. Price and N. J. Sokoloff (Eds.), *The Criminal Justice System and Women: Offenders, Victims, and Workers* (2nd ed., pp. 312–320). New York: McGraw–Hill.
Root, N. A., and Tejani, S. A. (1994). Undocumented: The Roles of Women in Immigration Law. *Georgetown Law Journal*, *83*, 605–634.
Rose, V. M. (1977). Rape as a Social Problem: A By-Product of the Feminist Movement. *Social Problems*, *25*, 75–89.
Rose, V. M., and Randall, S. (1982). The Impact of Investigator Perceptions of Victim Legitimacy on the Processing of Rape/Sexual Assault Cases. *Symbolic Interaction*, *5*, 23–36.
Rosenbaum, J., and Chesney-Lind, M. (1994). Appearance and Delinquency: A Research Note. *Crime & Delinquency*, *40*, 250–261.
Sales, E., Baum, M., and Shore, B. (1984). Victim Readjustment Following Assault. *Journal of Social Issues*, *40*, 117–136.
Sanday, P. (1973). Toward a Theory of the Status of Women. *American Anthropology*, *75*, 1682–1700.
Scales, A. (1986). The Emergence of Feminist Jurisprudence: An Essay. *Yale Law Journal*, *95*, 1373–1403.
Scheppele, K. L. (1994). Manners of Imagining the Real. *Law & Social Inquiry*, *19*, 995–1022.
Schmitt, R. E. (1998). *What Difference Do Women Make? Prosecutorial Decision Making in Sexual Assault Cases*. Unpublished doctoral dissertation, University of Delaware.
Schneider, E. M. (1986). Describing and Changing Woman's Self-Defense Work and the Problem of Expert Testimony on Battering. *Women's Rights Law Reporter*, *9*, 195–222.
Schuller, R. A. (1992). The Impact of Battered Woman Syndrome Evidence on Jury Decision Processes. *Law & Human Behavior*, *16*, 597–620.
Schuller, R. A., and Vidmar, N. (1992). Battered Woman Syndrome Evidence in the Courtroom: A Review of the Literature. *Law & Human Behavior*, *16*, 273–291.
Schwendinger, J., and Schwendinger, H. (1983). *Rape and Inequality*. Thousand Oaks, CA: Sage.
Scully, D. (1990). *Understanding Sexual Violence: A Study of Convicted Rapists*. Boston: Unwin Hyman.
Seidman, S., and Wagner, D. (1991). *Postmodernism and Social Theory*. Oxford: Blackwell.
Sherman, L. W., and Berk, R. A. (1984). The Specific Deterrent Effects of Arrest for Domestic Assault. *American Sociological Review*, *49*, 261–272.

Sherman, L., and Smith, D. (1992). Crime, Punishment, and Stake in Conformity: Legal and Informal Control of Domestic Violence. *American Sociological Review, 57*, 680–690.

Sherman, L. W., Schmidt, J. D., Rogan, D. P., Gartin, P. R., Cohn, E. G., Collins, D. J., and Bacich, A. R. (1991). From Initial Deterrence to Longterm Escalation: Short Custody Arrest for Poverty Ghetto Domestic Violence. *Criminology, 29*, 821–850.

Silberman, M. (1995). *A World of Violence: Corrections in America*. Belmont, CA: Wadsworth.

Silberman, M. (1996, August 16). *New Institutionalism and the Social Control of Prison Life: Patriarchy and the Legal Rights of Incarcerated Women*. Paper presented at the annual meetings of the American Sociological Association, New York City.

Simon, R. J., and Landis, J. (1991). *The Crimes Women Commit and the Punishments They Receive*. Lexington, MA: Lexington Books.

Smart, C. (1977). *Women, Crime and Criminology: A Feminist Critique*. London: Routledge & Kegan Paul.

Smart, C. (1989). *Feminism and the Power of Law*. London: Routledge.

Smith, D. (1987). *The Everyday World as Problematic*. Boston: Northeastern University Press.

Smith, D., and Visher, C. (1981). Street-Level Justice: Situational Determinants of Police Arrest Decision. *Social Problems, 29*, 167–177.

Smith, P. (Ed.). (1993). *Feminist Jurisprudence*. London: Oxford University Press.

Spohn, C, and Horney, J. (1991). "The Law's the Law, but Fair Is Fair." Rape Shield Laws and Officials' Assessment of Sexual History Evidence. *Criminology, 29*, 137–160.

Spohn, C., and Horney, J. (1992). *Rape Law Reform: A Grassroots Revolution and Its Impact*. New York: Plenum Press.

Spohn, C., and Horney, J. (1996). The Impact of Rape Law Reform on the Processing of Simple and Aggravated Rape Cases. *Journal of Criminal Law & Criminology, 86*, 861–884.

Spohn, C., Gruhl, J., and Welch, S. (1987). The Impact of Ethnicity and Gender of Defendants on the Decision to Reject or Dismiss Felony Charges. *Criminology, 25*, 175–191.

Steffensmeir, D. (1980). Assessing the Impact of the Women's Movement on Sex-Based Differences in the Handling of Adult Criminal Defendants. *Crime and Delinquency, 26*, 344–357.

Steffensmeir, D., Kramer, J., and Steifel, C. (1993). Gender and Imprisonment Decisions. *Criminology, 31*, 411–446.

Steinberg, R. J. (1992). Gendered Instructions. *Work and Occupations, 19*, 387–423.

Straus, M., Gelles, R., and Steinmetz, S. (1980). *Behind Closed Doors: Violence in the American Family*. Garden City, NY: Doubleday.

Temin, C. E. (1980). Discriminatory Sentencing of Female Offenders: The Argument for ERA in a Nutshell. In S. Datesman and F. Scarpitti (Eds.), *Women, Crime and Justice*. London: Oxford University Press. 144–187.

Thorne, B., and Yalom, M. (Eds.). (1992). *Rethinking the Family*. Boston: Northeastern University Press.

Tierney, K. (1982). The Battered Women Movement and the Creation of the Wife Beating Problem. *Social Problems, 29*, 207–220.

Tong, R. (1984). *Women, Sex, and the Law*. Totowa, NJ: Rowman & Allanheld.

Turnier, W. J., Conover, P. J., and Lowery, D. (1996). Redistributive Justice and Cultural Feminism. *American University Law Review, 45*.

United States Merit Systems Protection Board. (1981). *Sexual Harassment in the Workplace: Is It a Problem?* Washington, D.C.: U.S. Government Printing Office.

U.S. Bureau of Census. (1995). *Subjects Reports: Occupational Characteristics*. Washington, D.C.: U.S. Government Printing Office.

Visher, C. (1983). Gender, Police Arrest Decisions, and Notions of Chivalry. *Criminology, 21*, 5–28.

Walker, L. E. (1979). *The Battered Woman*. New York: Harper & Row.

Walker, L. E. (1984). *The Battered Woman Syndrome*. Berlin: Springer.

Walker, L. E. (1989). *Terrifying Love: Why Battered Women Kill and How Society Responds*. New York: Harper & Row.

Walters, A. P. (1994). Gender and the Role of Expert Witnesses in the Federal Courts. *Georgetown Law Journal, 83*, 635–664.

Weitzman, L. J. (1985). *The Divorce Revolution: The Unexpected Social and Economic Consequences for Women and Children in America*. New York: Free Press.

Weitzman, L. J. (1996). The Economic Consequences of Divorce Are Still Unequal: Comment on Peterson. *American Sociological Review, 61*, 537–538.

West, R. (1988). Jurisprudence and Gender. *The University of Chicago Law Review, 55*, 1–72.

Wiener, R. L., Watts, B. A., Goldkamp, K. H., and Gasper, C. (1995). Social Analytic Investigation of Hostile Work Environments: A Test of the Reasonable Woman Standard. *Law & Human Behavior, 19*, 263–281.

Williams, J. C. (1989). Deconstructing Gender. *Michigan Law Review*, *87*, 797–845.
Williams, K. (1978). *The Prosecution of Sexual Assaults*. Washington, D.C.: Institute for Law and Social research.
Williams, L. (1984). The Classic Rape: When Do Victims Report? *Social Problems*, *31*, 459–467.
Wolf, N. (1993). *Fire with Fire: The New Female Power and How It Will Change the 21st Century*. New York: Random House.
Wolfgang, M., and Riedel, M. (1973). Race, Judicial Discretion, and the Death Penalty. *Annals of the American Academy of Political and Social Science*, *407*, 249–261.
Wollstonecraft, M. (1975). *A Vindication of the Rights of Women*. New York: Norton. (Original work published 1792.)
Written Testimony of Alice Kessler-Harris. (1986). *Signs*, *11*, 767–779.

11

Justice Through the Lens of Culture and Ethnicity

Kwok Leung and Michael W. Morris

A. INTRODUCTION

In Western iconography, Justice is blindfolded and holds aloft a balance scale. The blindfold represents impartiality—because Justice cannot see the people before her, her decisions will not be prejudiced by their appearance. The scale represents the use of publicly accepted principles—all can see as Justice weighs the punishment to the crime. Several doubts about the correspondence between this ideal and the reality of how justice is administered in nations and other organizations surface when justice is considered in relation to cultural and ethnic differences. Most familiar, but *not* the emphasis of this chapter, is the objection that Justice wears no blindfold: Justice administrators not only see but take into account ethnicity and culture.[1] This chapter focuses on an objection to the notion of universally accepted principles that is signified by Justice's scale. There is increasing doubt that principles of justice, like the principles of physics that govern a scale, are recognized by people everywhere. That is, some claim that what we see when we see justice depends on the lens of one's culture or ethnicity. Such differences in perceptions of justice create a deep difficulty for a society or organization that aspires to provide "justice for all," because even if partiality is purged from the system it will be impossible to deliver decisions that all of the people perceive as just.

In a long tradition, philosophers from Aristotle to Rawls have studied *objective* principles of justice. That is, they have endeavored to identify principles of social conduct that are just according to external logical standards. In a much shorter tradition, social psychologists have studied *subjective* principles of justice. That is, psychologists have addressed the question of what principles determine people's perception of a social situation as just or unjust. This work has produced complex models of the psychological processes that lead one to perceive fairness in a particular way of distributing scarce resources, or of making a socially important decision,

Kwok Leung • Department of Management, City University of Hong Kong, Hong Kong, China. Michael W. Morris • Graduate School of Business, Stanford University, Stanford, California 94305.

Handbook of Justice Research in Law, edited by Sanders and Hamilton. Kluwer Academic / Plenum Publishers, New York, 2000.

or of sanctioning a person who harms another (see chapters in this volume by Hegtvedt and Cook, Tyler and Lind, and Vidmar). These models are supported by an abundance of empirical studies of justice perceptions that use experimental or survey methods. Yet a weakness of psychological research on justice is that almost all studies have been conducted in the United States and a few other Western societies. Moreover, most classic studies of justice perceptions have focused on university populations and hence have not sampled the full cultural diversity of people within those societies. In recent years, there has been a surge in studies of justice perceptions in a wider range of cultural settings, some of which have replicated findings of classic studies, and some of which have produced results that differ in predicted or unpredicted ways. This chapter attempts to review and integrate what has been learned about the influence of culture and ethnicity on justice perceptions with an eye toward the question of whether the ideal of justice based on universally accepted principles makes sense in a multicultural society and across different cultural groups.

We introduce the subject by considering the problems and benefits of research that makes cross-cultural comparisons. We first analyze why this topic benefits from cross-cultural comparative research. We also contend that cultural differences in justice perceptions have taken on an increased practical importance in recent decades because of increasing intercultural interaction. The introduction closes with a clarification of two different approaches to understanding culture—"etic" and "emic" analyses. The review continues with a consideration of the scope of justice concerns from a cross-cultural perspective, and then examines in turn the cross-cultural work on the three primary facets of the psychology of justice: perceptions of fair outcomes ("distributive justice"), perceptions of fair processes ("procedural justice"), and perceptions of fair sanctions for transgressions ("retributive justice"). We end with a discussion of the special difficulties encountered in conflicts between ethnicities and cultures.

B. WHY STUDY JUSTICE ACROSS CULTURES?

1. Theoretical Development

Popular discourse about cultural differences in psychological processes consists largely of polemics between adherents of universalism and relativism. Universalists assert that, except in superficial respects, people think the same way wherever you go. Relativists respond that psychological tendencies differ dramatically, perhaps incommensurably. Researchers of justice perceptions across cultures tend to take a position in between these two extreme poles. For the most part, they have tried to identify limited cultural differences within more general patterns of cross-cultural similarity. Justice is one of many areas in psychology that has seen a groundswell of recent cross-cultural studies. Comparative studies have contributed substantially to the advancement of theories of justice perception, a claim that cannot be made about all areas of cross-cultural psychology. It is worth analyzing the conditions under which cross-cultural comparisons are scientifically useful in order to understand what has been learned from comparative studies of the psychology of justice.

When are cultural comparisons meaningful? Our position is that comparative studies are most likely to bring about theoretical advances with regard to a process in which systematic cultural differences occur, but they are against a broader background of cultural invariance (Campbell, 1964). If cross-cultural research uncovers few cross-cultural differences, universality can be claimed, and further cross-cultural comparisons are unlikely to shed much light on the psychological mechanisms involved. On the other hand, when one finds that the approach of people in different cultures to an issue differs dramatically, one might question whether the psychological processes involved can be meaningfully compared. When a central phenomenon in one culture, for example the Western syndrome of romantic love, is not recognizable in another culture (such as Japan; Kitayama, 1995), cross-cultural comparisons may be meaningless and are unlikely to contribute to an understanding of the psychological processes involved. Proverbially, we learn little by comparing apples to oranges.[2]

Some scholars have questioned whether there is enough universality in conceptions of justice across cultures to warrant meaningful cross-cultural comparisons. Arguments of this sort are often prompted by observations of differences in how concepts are lexicalized in different languages. Kidder (1986) questioned the universality of justice concerns based on the observation that the English word *justice* does not easily translate into Japanese; it does not correspond to a frequently occurring word and no corresponding word carries the same set of connotations. Underlying this argument is some version of the Whorf (1956) hypothesis that one's thoughts are directly shaped by the categories of one's language. The strong version of this hypothesis is disconfirmed by everyday episodes of cross-cultural understanding. For example, it is difficult to translate the Chinese word *renao* (which denotes hot and noisy and connotes liveliness and joy) into English. Yet when *renao* was used by the first author of this chapter to praise a Hong Kong dim sum restaurant to the second author, the construct was recognized as referring to a busy ambience also prized albeit not lexicalized in New York.

While the accessibility of constructs varies across cultures, this difference does not seem to be driven primarily by language. In domains such as color, the categories drawn by one's language seem to have no influence on the mental concepts used to perceive and recall stimuli (Heider, 1972). Likewise, the words used to talk about justice differ more than the concepts used to perceive and think about justice (Sugahara and Huo, 1994). In sum, perceptions of justice are enough alike across cultures to permit comparison and enough different to make the comparisons interesting.

2. Increasing Practical Importance

It is increasingly the case that social organizations of all kinds comprise people who identify with and adhere to different cultures. At the level of nations, the image of a melting pot that culturally assimilates immigrants has been replaced by the image of a multicultural mosaic. Migration patterns have rapidly changed the ethnic composition of once relatively homogenous regions. Eastern Europeans now abound in many Western European countries. In the United States, migrations have brought an increasing influence of Hispanic cultures in the Southwest and of Asian cultures on the West Coast. Americans of European ethnic identification are forecasted to be outnumbered by minority group members soon. Both in the United States and worldwide, there is a clear trend toward a resurgence rather than waning of ethnic identification. Business organizations have also become more multicultural through the globalization of businesses. Multinational corporations, such as Citicorp, Philips, and Sony, maintain coordination by continually transplanting managers from one country to another. Noncommercial organizations and groups are being affected in similar ways by the changes in communication and transportation technologies that have brought the globalization of business organizations. Because of these changes, cultural differences in justice perceptions that may have once been primarily of academic interest are increasingly relevant to the practical problem of administering justice in organizations and nations.

A second reason for the increasing practical importance of understanding culture and justice perceptions is the growing need for multinational solutions to many of the Earth's problems. Although the benefits of technological advances have not always been shared worldwide, possible burdens created by side effects of industrialization and urbanization will be felt everywhere. Such conjectured problems as global warming, ozone depletion, and deforestation are a few obvious examples. An increasing reliance on multinational efforts to political and economic problems can also be seen. The war waged against Iraq involved many nations, and so has the peacekeeping mission in Bosnia. The summit of the seven industrialized nations influences stock markets and currency exchange rates worldwide. Trade talks among America, Japan, and the Eurocommunity have become major economic events because of their importance to the world economy. Again, a better understanding of culture is crucial to effective international cooperation. In a world of increasing contact among cultures and ethnicities, even small differences in perceptions of justice may have large consequences.

C. BASIC CONCEPTUAL ISSUES

1. A Functional Analysis of Justice Norms

Many scholars have argued that rules of justice become established as social norms in order to reduce conflict over the allocation of resources in a group. As such, some norms of justice should be recognizable in any culture with organized social groups. Some theorists have emphasized that societies have to allocate resources in a way that rewards outstanding contributions yet does not sacrifice group cohesion, and have proposed that basic principles of justice evolve to serve this function (e.g., Campbell, 1975; Cook and Messick, 1983; Mikula, 1980). A slightly different view has accompanied the relational model of justice proposed by Lind and Tyler (Lind, 1994; Lind and Tyler, 1988; Tyler and Lind, 1992, this volume). In a recent theoretical statement, Lind (1994) suggested that people are confronted with a fundamental dilemma about how much to submit to a group. This dilemma is based on the notion that people are motivated to identify with a group as well as to maintain a self-identity, and very often these two goals involve trade-offs. People are in a constant struggle between these two opposing forces, and a stable social system must have evolved some solutions to this dilemma. Lind (1994) argued that the most efficient solution to this problem is the use of justice principles. "By specifying power-limiting rules about how people should be treated, how decisions should be made, and how outcomes are to be allocated, rules of justice limit the potential for exploitation and allow people to invest their identity and effort in the group with confidence that they will not be badly used by the group" (p. 30).

A functional view leads to the expectation that basic principles of justice will be shared as norms in every society wherever the organized sharing of resources has extended beyond the family to larger communities such as the village. At this point, it is useful to distinguish between abstract principles of justice and the specific beliefs that people apply to link abstract principles to particular social situations. Abstract principles of justice, such as the equity rule that outcomes should be proportional to inputs, should be present in all communities. An equity norm may govern the social status conferred onto individuals, say, in every village in Asia. However, even if the equity principle is shared across villages, the more specific beliefs that determine how the principle applies may vary from one village to the next. That is, people in one village may believe that the relevant contribution is the number of years one has lived in the village, whereas people in another village may believe that the relevant contribution is

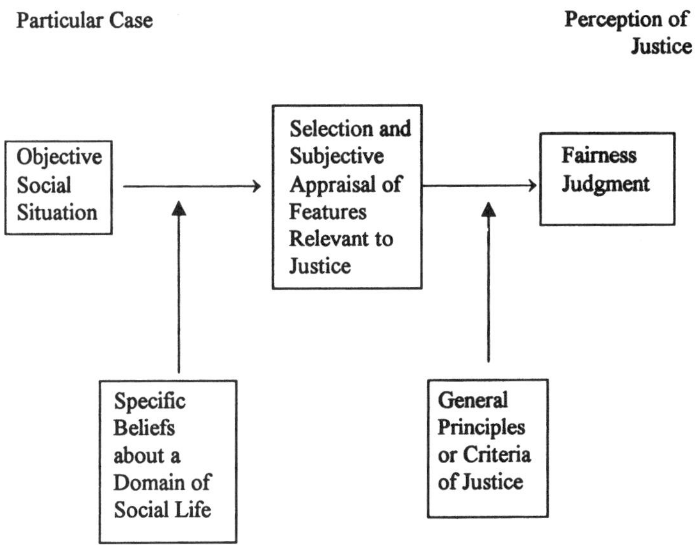

Figure 1. A general two-stage framework for justice perception

one's productivity at work. Figure 1 presents a general framework for justice perception that distinguishes the roles of specific beliefs and general principles.[3] A functional view of justice perception predicts that general principles will be shared across villages (the second half of the process) but not necessarily that specific beliefs will be shared across villages (the first half of the process).

What are the factors that determine the domain-specific beliefs used to appraise social situations for features relevant to justice concerns? Returning to the example of status allocation in villages, it is important to social functioning that beliefs about this matter be shared *within* the village as a local norm, so status competition is channeled into constructive contributions rather than erupting into open conflict. And across villages, in a traditional era when villages were largely independent, differences in local norms about which contributions entitle one to most status would not interfere with social functioning. Only emigrants from one village to the next would be troubled by these differences, and they would be expected to adopt the local norms. From a functional view, one would expect not similarity but differences *across* villages because norms would evolve to reward the contribution most needed in the local ecological conditions.

One may ask whether this picture has changed in the modern era of the "global village." In recent decades, there has been increased interaction and interdependence across the lines of traditional villages, ethnicities, and cultures. Many scholars have marshaled evidence that a global convergence of social norms is under way, especially in private sector organizations (e.g., Biggart and Hamilton, 1992). However, others have pointed to reactions against the global village in the form of renewed adherence to traditional norms (Barber, 1995). Whether or not the global village has brought a decline in the variation of justice beliefs, it has certainly brought an increase in the problems stemming from differences in justice perceptions. Whereas traditionally local variation in justice beliefs would create problems of misperceived injustices only for immigrants, today the practical problems that stem from different rules of justice are manifold.

2. Views of Culture: External (Etic) and Internal (Emic)

How do researchers define culture and conceptualize its impact on psychological processes? Many definitions of culture have been used in anthropology and psychology (Berry, Poortinga, Segall, and Dasen, 1992:Chapter 7). A definition proposed by Kroeber (1952) encompasses both objective patterns (public behaviors and artifacts) and subjective patterns (cognitive, conative, and affective tendencies): "Culture consists of patterns, explicit and implicit, of and for behavior acquired and transmitted by symbols, constituting the distinctive achievements of human groups, including their embodiments in artifacts; the essential core of culture consists of traditional (i.e., historically derived and selected) ideas and especially their attached values" (p. 118). Psychologists have been primarily concerned with subjective culture, which is investigated at the level of cognitive structures that represent beliefs and values. These structures are assumed to be widespread among the members of a group and to guide the interpretation of experience in a particular domain.

In current research on subjective culture by psychologists, two approaches can be distinguished. The camp of researchers engaged in "cross-cultural psychology" attempt to describe these knowledge structures from the point of view of an objective outsider (an "etic" view), whereas the camp who call their project "cultural psychology" attempt to describe these structures from the perspective of a cultural insider (an "emic" view). Cross-cultural psychologists study behavior across a number of cultures and try to develop universally valid models of human behavior (e.g., Triandis, 1980; Berry *et al.*, 1992:Chapter 1). In these models, culture is represented in terms of constructs developed by the researcher to describe the range of cultures under consideration (e.g., Berry, 1969, 1989; Hui and Triandis, 1985; Leung and Bond, 1989; Triandis, 1978). A common strategy is to decompose culture into a set of dimensions and use these dimensions to explain a variety of cultural differences (Van de Vijver and Leung, 1997). For instance, one of the most influential constructs in etic analysis has been the dimension of individualism–collectivism (Hofstede, 1980; Triandis, 1989). Briefly put, individualism refers to a tendency to put a stronger emphasis on one's personal interest and goals, whereas collectivism refers to a stronger emphasis on the interests and goals of one's in-group members. Another dimension is power distance, which refers to the acceptance of hierarchy in a society. Some societies accord relatively more privilege and deference to those at the top of organizations. In short, the cross-cultural method tends to employ the most general set of etic constructs to explain cultural differences in psychological phenomena. These constructs may be incorporated into existing models as moderators or mediators of relationships between other variables. Hofstede (1980:Chapter 1) and Triandis (1983) have provided a list of cultural dimensions that are commonly used in the cross-cultural approach.

The approach of cultural psychology is characterized by a greater emphasis on the concerns and methods of anthropology. One manifesto charged the field with studying "the way cultural traditions and social practices regulate, express, transform, and permute the human psyche, resulting in less psychic unity for humankind than in ethnic divergences in mind, self, and emotions" (Shweder, 1990:1). There is more focus on modeling the distinctive features of a psychological process in a given culture than the goal of capturing differences between cultures in a general model. This approach often involves uncovering the indigenous psychological constructs that shape the thoughts of people in a culture—the lay theories, systems of meaning, implicit beliefs, or ethnopsychologies. In other words, researchers build models from constructs that are relatively close to the experience of the people described. One reason for the focus on "emic" constructs is a suspicion that attempts to take an objective, external vantage point lead to "pseudo-etic" constructs that are highly influenced by the researcher's culture. Another reason is interest in intersubjective understanding and a concomitant adoption of an interpretative or hermeneutic paradigm rather than an empiricist, positivist paradigm (see Habermas, 1971). But the most important reason from our perspective is the belief that an empirical understanding of cultural effects on psychological processes requires attention to specific beliefs (the first link shown in Figure 1) as well as general principles (the second link) and that these specific beliefs are often better understood in terms of emic constructs. A case in point is the research on moral reasoning across culture by Shweder, Mahapatra, and Miller (1987). They observed some general principles that govern the moral reasoning of adults and children in both the United States and India; however, to understand moral judgments about particular cases in each culture, it was necessary to understand the more specific belief systems that shaped their reasoning:

> At some abstract level,... there are "deep" universals of all moral codes. The rub, and the irony, is that if one merely focuses upon the abstract principles underlying a judgment about a particular case, then the principles so abstracted do not make it possible to predict informants' judgments about particular cases.... If we are to understand our informants' moral judgments about particular cases we are going to have to understand the culture-specific aspects of their moral codes, and we are going to have to understand the way those culture-specific aspects interact with the more universal aspects to produce a moral judgment. (p. 97)

3. The Scope of Justice

A premise of this review is that justice is a universal human concern. This does not imply, however, that people extend their justice concerns universally to fellow humans. Nor does it imply that there is universality in the place that justice concerns hold within the larger realm of moral thoughts and feelings.

a. Who Is Included?

A notable tendency in people's perceptions of injustice is their insensitivity toward the plight of certain kinds of people. Some other persons are seen as deserving the same justice as oneself, and some groups as deserving no justice whatsoever. As Deutsch (1985) argued, "Justice is not involved in relations with others—such as "heathens," "inferior races," "heretics," "perverts"—who are perceived to be outside one's potential moral community" (p. 36). People do not extend their justice concerns universally but do so within certain boundaries. According to Opotow (1990), "moral exclusion occurs when individuals or groups are perceived as outside the boundary in which moral values, rules, and considerations of fairness apply" (p. 1). This tends to occur under two conditions. First, when there is intense conflict between two sides, the other side is likely to be subject to moral exclusion. Second, if the other party is seen as unconnected to oneself, moral exclusion is likely to occur.

To discuss the impact of culture on moral exclusion and inclusion, it is useful to posit several moral boundaries that can be thought of as concentric circles. The least inclusive social boundary is what social scientists call the *in-group*. The in-group generally consists of an individual's closest friends and immediate family, his or her kith and kin. Different principles of justice are followed with in-group members than with outsiders. For instance, we see it as just to allocate resources to in-group members in proportion to need whereas with outsiders we see it as just to allocate in proportion to contributions. Two kinds of cultural differences in the psychology of the in-group can be noted. First, the size and shape of the in-group boundary vary. It has been argued that in-groups in individualistic societies are larger (Wheeler, Reis, and Bond, 1989) and include a higher proportion of friends rather than family (Bellah, Madsen, Sullivan, Swidler, and Tipton, 1985; Hsu, 1953). Second, the importance attached to the in-group boundary varies. A great deal of research has investigated whether etic constructs such as the individualism–collectivism value dimension affect the weight placed on the in-group boundary. Another approach is to study a society in which in-groups and out-groups are dramatically distinguished, such as China, and investigate emic constructs, such as the relationship-specific imperatives of Confucian ethics, that might underlie the distinction.

A wider boundary is that which separates other humans who are entitled to justice from those who are not. This boundary, which is Opotow's focus, tends to run along social categories based on ascribed characteristics such as ethnicity, culture, and race. Many writers have used concepts similar to moral exclusion in explaining the atrocities that one group can inflict on other groups, such as in the Holocaust (Bar-Tal, 1990), or the unfair treatment of native peoples by European settlers (Berry and Wells, 1994). The victimized group is often categorized as socially undesirable, dehumanized, and delegitimized, and excluded from moral considerations. Some theorists argue that a primary mechanism by which the dominant group in a society oppresses a despised out-group is the "justice system" (Sidaneous, 1991).

Finally, there are boundaries that extend beyond the human realm that delimit the extension of more diffuse moral concerns. In Asian cultures greatly influenced by Buddhist ideals, there is a tradition of concern for living things other than humans. In Western cultures rooted in the Judeo-Christian heritage, a stronger moral boundary has been drawn between human beings and other living things. However, the traditional pattern of this cultural difference has been mitigated or perhaps even reversed by countervailing force of the environmentalist movement. A shifting of this moral boundary has the goal of "green" scholarship (e.g., deep ecology, the Gaia hypotheses) and activism (e.g., preservation of old forests, liberation of laboratory animals). Many environmental dilemmas facing political decision makers turn on the question of justice for nonhuman animals and for future generations of humans (see Bazerman, Wade-Bensoni, and Benzoni, 1995). Cross-cultural studies of the animal rights issue (e.g., Bowd and Shapiro, 1993) have found that people in Japan are less concerned about the overexploitation and cruelty toward animals than Americans or Germans (Kellert, 1993). We know of no research on the etic or emic constructs that underlie cultural differences in the extension of justice concerns to animals.

b. The Moral Basis of Justice

Appeals to abstract principles of justice are one of many ways to respond to moral dilemmas. The tradition of research on moral reasoning developed by Kohlberg (1981) investigated how people respond to dilemmas that put norms of justice in conflict with other social norms, such as interpersonal reciprocity and conformity to social conventions. Drawing on Piaget's theory of cognitive development, Kohlberg proposed that moral reasoning develops in stages: from an early focus on social convention, to interpersonal responsibilities, and eventually (for some individuals) to abstract principles of justice. Gilligan (1982) criticized this unidirectional stage theory based on the findings that few women arrive at the stage of applying justice principles to moral dilemmas. She proposed that there are two distinct "voices" or systems of thought and feeling in moral reasoning, one based on abstract justice principles and one based on interpersonal responsibilities. Justice principles are universalistic and rational, whereas interpersonal responsibilities are particularistic and affect based.

Gilligan's objection to a universal, unidirectional stage theory has been supported by subsequent research; however, her emphasis on gender as the primary moderator of moral reasoning modality has been questioned. For instance, Miller and her colleagues have revealed strong principles in moral reasoning between Americans and Hindu Indians, but weak or nonexistent gender differences. Specifically, research in the United States has shown that interpersonal responsibilities are often seen as personal decisions rather than moral issues (e.g., Higgins, Power, and Kohlberg, 1984). In contrast, cross-cultural research with Indian subjects has shown that interpersonal obligations are seen as moral issues (Miller, Bersoff, and Harwood, 1990; Miller and Luthar, 1989; Shweder *et al.*, 1987). Miller and Bersoff (1992) have studied how American and Indian students reacted to a situation in which justice was in conflict with interpersonal responsibilities. They found that compared with Americans, Indians were more likely to yield to interpersonal responsibilities than to justice concerns. When asked to justify their choices, Americans mentioned fairness and rights more frequently, whereas Indians mentioned role-related obligations and nonresponsiveness to others' need more. Consistent with this finding, the Japanese, another group that emphasizes the interdependent self, also gave more weight to role obligations in judgments of responsibility than did Americans (Hamilton and Sanders, 1983; Hagiwara, 1992).

In light of these empirical results, Miller (1994) argued that both the approaches of Kohlberg and Gilligan have not sufficiently considered the role of culture. She draws on the notion that many Western psychological models implicitly assume an independent as contrasted with interdependent self-concept (Markus and Kitayama, 1991; Triandis, 1989). Thus, the U.S. moral code is explained in terms of the central notion of Western liberalism that individual autonomy is more fundamental and more natural than social obligations. From this premise, a moral concern with general justice principles that limit infringements on the liberty of other persons follows as a necessary derivation, whereas a moral concern with specific role-based obligations to other persons does not. In contrast, the Hindu Indian moral code is explained in terms of the notion of *dharma*, which denotes both moral duty and inherent character (Kakar, 1978; Marriott, 1990). It is assumed that one's *dharma* depends on his or her social role and the situations one enters and that following social role expectations in a given situation is the means to realize one's true nature. From this premise, it follows that moral concerns will extend to a broad set of role-based interpersonal obligations. In sum, Miller and her colleagues clearly show that the moral basis of justice principles varies across cultures.

D. THREE FACETS OF JUSTICE

Three major forms of justice perception are distinguished in the literature: distributive, procedural, and retributive justice. In this section, we review the evidence about the impact of culture and ethnicity on each of these justice perceptions.

1. Distributive Justice: Perceptions of Fair Outcomes

The problem of judging the fairness of distribution depends largely on three issues. First, one judges to whom to compare oneself because social comparison processes are central to judgment of distributive justice (e.g., Adams, 1965). Second, one has to judge what inputs and rewards are relevant (Komorita and Leung, 1985). Third, one must decide what allocation rules should be used. A number of allocation rules are possible, and the following four are most common:

- *Equity rule*—outcomes should be directly proportional to contributions across individuals.
- *Equality rule*—everyone's outcome should be identical.
- *Need rule*—outcomes should be directly proportional to needs across individuals.
- *Generosity rule*—one's own outcome should not exceed others.

Etic Analyses

a. With Whom Do People Compare Themselves?

Theories of distributive justice have drawn on what is known about social comparison processes to answer the question of with whom do people make equity comparisons (e.g., Adams, 1963). Early theories, guided by Festinger's (1954) theory of social comparison, described reference groups as individuals with similar attributes or in a similar situation as the actor. A classic study in this vein is that of Stouffer and his associates, which found that African-American soldiers in the northern United States were less satisfied than those in the South because they compared themselves primarily to civilian African-Americans who were better off in the North than the South (Stouffer, Suchman, DeVinney, Star, and Williams, 1949; Stouffer, Lunsdaine, Williams, Smith, Janis, Star, and Cottrell, 1949). Although we know of no empirical evidence, it seems plausible that this general tendency to make basic fairness comparisons within social groups marked by ascribed characteristics such as race, gender, ethnicity, class, and so forth would be stronger in collectivist than individualist cultures.

The status-value approach to distributive justice forwarded by Berger, Zelditch, Anderson, and Cohen (1972) differs in that it focuses on comparisons to generalized others and to nonsimilar referent groups. To simplify the discussion, let's assume that there are two groups and that one, the dominant group, has a higher socioeconomic status than the other, the subordinate group. An example of this situation would be European- and African-Americans in the United States. When members of the subordinate group evaluate the fairness of their outcomes, equity theory suggests that they will compare themselves to similar others. The status-value approach suggests that they will also compare themselves to the dominant group. Because the dominant group is generally better off than the subordinate group, this social comparison process will result in a sense of injustice, regardless of the specific characteristics of the inputs and outcomes of individual minority members. It seems likely that the tendency to make comparisons to the dominant group and perceive injustice as a result will be stronger among groups with low power distance (or egalitarian) values rather than high power distance (or hierarchical) values. The latter values give legitimacy to inequalities of power and privilege, including in some cases the greater power of the dominant social group.

The perceptions of legitimacy that affect justice perceptions are also moderated by historical factors. For instance, in a review of the reactions to the internment of Japanese Americans during the Second World War, Nagata (1990) concluded that Nisei (second generation) Japanese-Americans reacted less negatively to the internment than did Sansei (third generation) Japanese-Americans. One reason for this difference is that the Sansei grew up in the civil rights era and were more conscious of civil rights of citizens. As a result they were more likely to see the internment as highly illegitimate. In a study of joint ventures in China, Leung, Smith, Wang, and Sun (1996) found that Chinese employees did not compare their salary with expatriate employees, despite the fact that the salaries of expatriates are many times higher than those of locals. Inequitable distribution of resources to groups is not always seen as illegitimate.

b. What Counts as an Input in the Calculation of Reward?

The concept of input is crucial for distributive norms that prescribe an unequal allocation of resources among individuals. For these norms, the choice of input is pivotal to the outcome of the distribution. People may agree on what distributive norms should be used, but they may hold very different views as to what constitutes a legitimate input (Komorita and Leung, 1985). This issue is especially important from a cross-cultural perspective, because the legitimacy of inputs may vary across cultures. Komorita (1984) has made a distinction between task-relevant and task-irrelevant inputs. Task-relevant inputs refer to attributes that are directly related to performance, such as time spent on task. Task-irrelevant inputs refer to attributes that bear no direct relationship to performance, such as seniority. It is possible that the perceived relationship between various forms of inputs and performance may be subject to the influence of culture, and the influence is probably stronger for task-irrelevant inputs. Several cultural dimensions that may affect this link are discussed below.

Individualism–Collectivism. As described before, in collectivist societies, attachment and loyalty to in-groups are emphasized. Thus, seniority becomes important because a long tenure can be interpreted as an indication of a person's commitment and loyalty to a group. Evidence for this argument comes from the extensive literature on Japanese management. The basic observation is that seniority is a more important factor in determining compensations in Japanese than in American organizations (e.g., Ouchi and Jaeger, 1978).

Power Distance. In high power distance societies, relatively more privilege and deference are accorded to those at the top of organizations, and explicitly hierarchical relationships are more likely to be accepted. It follows that status and position are more likely to carry weight and be regarded as a legitimate input in resource allocation in high power distance societies (see Mendonca and Kanungo, 1994, for a similar discussion). Unfortunately, this proposition has not been directly tested.

Other Etic Constructs. Parsons and Shils (1951) have contrasted cultures in their relative emphasis on ascribed versus achieved attributes of persons. Ascribed characteristics are usually acquired by birth and include such variables as race and social class, whereas achieved characteristics are those earned by an individual's actions. In their analysis, China and India were regarded as ascription-oriented, whereas the United States is achievement-oriented. To the best of our knowledge, this dimension has not been employed in empirical work in distributive justice. However, one can hypothesize that task-irrelevant inputs such as social class and gender are more likely to be used as legitimate inputs in ascription-oriented than in achievement-oriented societies.

One way of studying different patterns of social cognition is to search for basic underlying assumptions about human nature (see Wrightsman, 1992). One of these, the assumption of human malleability, refers to the belief that the personality, ability, and performance of a person can change over time (Chen and Uttal, 1988). Although this assumption has not been studied cross-culturally, there is reason to believe that cultures differ in belief in human malleability. Stevenson and his colleagues have conducted extensive research on the academic achievement of American, Japanese, and Chinese students (e.g., Stevenson *et al.*, 1990). One basic finding is that compared to Americans, Chinese and Japanese regarded effort as more important than ability in determining academic performance. In other words, Chinese and Japanese are more likely to endorse the view that one can achieve better academic results by working harder. This may indicate that Chinese and Japanese regard the intellectual and personality traits related to academic achievement as more malleable than Americans. Such differences in malleability beliefs should affect how inputs are weighted in a fair distribution of academic rewards. It is well-documented that both actual performance as well as effort are regarded as a legitimate basis for reward in educational settings (e.g., Weiner and Kukla, 1970). In light of the work of Stevenson *et al.* (1990), more weight may be placed on effort as an input for resource allocation in cultures where there is a stronger assumption of malleability, such as China and Japan. In other words, cross-cultural differences in the belief in human malleability may be related to the differential emphasis on effort as a legitimate input across cultures, a hypothesis that should be evaluated in future work.

c. How Is an Allocation Rule Selected?

A number of cross-cultural studies have been undertaken to find out how culture may influence the preference for allocation norms (for reviews, see Leung, 1988, 1997; James, 1993). Individualism–collectivism has been the dominant theoretical framework used for interpreting the evidence. This tradition began with the research of Leung and Bond (1984), which tested the hypothesis that the group membership of the recipient should markedly affect the choice of allocation rules in collectivist cultures. Collectivists should adopt a generosity rule with in-group members that would give them a bigger share. That is, collectivists would use the equality rule when their own input or contribution is high, and use the equity rule when their own input is low. With out-group members, however, collectivists should act like individualists and use the equity rule. Leung and Bond (1984) have obtained results in support of this complicated relationship between collectivism and distributive behavior. See Leung (1997) for a review of other supporting evidence.

However, Leung (1997) has noted that the individualism–collectivism framework fails to account for several findings. In a study of the allocation behavior of Indonesian and American subjects, Marin (1985) found that both cultural groups preferred equity over equality regardless of the relationship between the allocator and the recipients (strangers, friends, or relatives). Kim, Park, and Suzuki (1990) compared the allocation behavior of Korean, Japanese, and American subjects. Results indicated that Korean subjects followed the equality rule more closely than Japanese and American subjects, and there was no difference between the allocation pattern of American and Japanese subjects. In an earlier study, however, Leung and Iwawaki (1988) found that there was no cultural difference among Japanese, Korean, and American subjects in allocation behavior. It seems difficult to reconcile the results of Leung and Iwawaki (1988) and Kim *et al.* (1990).

The most disturbing result for the individualism–collectivism framework comes from a study by Hui, Triandis, and Yee (1991), who compared the distributive behavior of Chinese and American subjects. A special feature of this study is that individualism–collectivism was measured and used as a covariate. An analysis of covariance shows that the tendency for Chinese subjects to follow the generosity rule was not adequately explained by collectivism. Hui *et al.* (1991) concluded that the individualism–collectivism framework may be too global to explain and predict specific allocation behaviors.

In light of these difficulties, Leung (1997) proposed a more general framework, the contextual model, to account for the empirical evidence available. This model, which is based on a goal-directed view of allocation behavior (e.g., Deutsch, 1975; Leung and Park, 1986), assumes that culture interacts with a number of situational variables to determine the allocation rule used. In other words, individualists and collectivists may respond to the contextual factors underlying an allocation differently, leading to differences in their allocation behavior. Interactional goals are hypothesized to be the immediate antecedent of allocation preferences. Three major interactional goals have been identified that are central to allocation decisions: productivity, interpersonal harmony, and well-being of recipients (Deutsch, 1975).

Two situational variables are proposed to interact with culture to affect the allocation rule adopted. First, based on the individualism–collectivism framework, the relationship between the allocators and the recipients may affect the choice of the interactional goal. If the allocators and the recipients have an in-group relationship, collectivists are more likely to pursue the goal of harmony enhancement and employ a harmony enhancing allocation rule, such as the equality rule or the generosity rule. If the allocators and the recipients are not closely related, like individualists, collectivists will pursue the productivity goal and employ the equity norm (Leung and Bond, 1984).

The second situational variable is the role assumed by the allocator, and at least two roles are relevant to our discussion. The first is a dual role, in which the allocator is also a recipient. In the second role, the allocator is given the responsibility to allocate a group reward, and does not receive any share of the reward. This role is typical of supervisors and managers in a work setting. It is proposed that collectivists who are placed in the allocator/recipient dual role will be influenced by the harmony enhancing goal and show a stronger preference for either the equality rule or the generosity rule (e.g., Leung and Bond, 1984; Hui *et al.*, 1991). In contrast, when collectivists are placed in the supervisory role, the harmony enhancing goal should be less salient than the productivity goal. The selection of the allocation rule should be more affected by the expectation the allocator has for the work group rather than his/her personal relationship with the recipients. This reasoning suggests that in this situation, collectivists should behave like individualists and prefer the equity rule to enhance productivity. In fact, two studies show that collectivists actually adhered to the equity norm more closely than did Americans. Marin (1985) asked subjects to allocate a reward for two recipients and found that Indonesian subjects showed a stronger preference for equity than American subjects regardless of the relationship between the allocator and the recipients. Chen (1995) asked subjects to role-play the president of a company and allocate several rewards for the employees of the company. His results revealed that Chinese subjects showed a stronger preference for equity than did American subjects.

Situational variables may sometimes override the effects of culture through their impact on the salience of interactional goals. For instance, Murphy-Berman, Berman, Singh, Pacharui, and Kumar (1984) and Berman, Murphy-Berman, and Singh (1985) both found that the need norm was followed more closely by Indians than by Americans. Leung (1988) suggested that because resources are scarce in India, the protection of the well-being of the recipients is a more salient goal than the maintenance of harmonious relationships. Thus, despite the collectivistic tendency of Indians, the need norm is more salient than the equality norm. In sum, it is hypothesized that allocators will attempt to follow an allocation norm based on an interactional goal that is regarded as most appropriate for the situation.

Emic Analyses

Not much work has been done on culture-specific constructs that channel the thoughts of persons making decisions about the allocation of resources. This gap in our knowledge is suboptimal as emic work is able to shed light on specific allocation processes within a culture. Nevertheless, the research that has taken this perspective nicely complements the work based on universal, etic constructs. To our knowledge, there is no compelling evidence for the use of indigenous allocation rules other than those identified before, such as equity, equality, need, generosity, and so forth. However, one way in which emic analyses have been instructive is in understanding the goals that mediate the selection of these rules. Another way is in understanding the individual attributes that are counted as contributions when an equity rule is applied.

As described before, Leung (1997) proposed the contextual model to integrate the complex pattern of the selection of allocation rules observed in Chinese and other Confucian-influenced societies. In his approach, interpersonal harmony occupies a central role. In the Confucian world-view, interpersonal harmony represents one of the most important goals pursued in social interactions (e.g., Bond and Hwang, 1986; Gabrenya and Hwang, 1996). A number of indigenous concepts are related to interpersonal harmony in Chinese social life. For instance, Chinese are very concerned with *guanxi* (interpersonal networks), and consider the maintenance and development of guanxi with others as a major goal in social interactions (King, 1991). *Renqin* is another key concept in Chinese social life, which provides guidance to behaviors that promote interpersonal harmony (Gabrenya and Hwang, 1996).

Leung (1997) proposed that two motives that are related to harmony need to be distinguished, *disintegration avoidance* and *harmony enhancement*. In disintegration avoidance, the motive is to maintain the relationship at an acceptable level, and effort will be made to avoid the disintegration of the relationship. Many of the traditional thoughts about harmony in China are actually concerned with disintegration avoidance. Such popular sayings as "Forbearance for one moment may save trouble for a hundred days" and "Noble minds do not remember past annoyances" are good examples (Chen, 1973). In harmony enhancement, however, the motive is to improve the social relationship, and effort will be made to do so. "Befriend a thousand, be enemy to none" and "Better remove enmity than contract it" are popular sayings that clearly reflect this orientation (Chen, 1973).

The above emic analysis of Chinese concepts will be likely to illuminate aspects of the psychology of justice in other collectivist societies. It is possible that in collectivist societies, with potential in-group members or members or a peripheral in-group, disintegration avoidance would be the primary goal, and equality will generally be favored. This prediction is in line with the finding that collectivists preferred equality over equity in interactions with a fellow student (see the review by James, 1993). With close friends, collectivists will regard harmony enhancement as the primary goal and hence prefer the generosity rule (Leung and Bond, 1984). Finally, as argued before, with out-group members, both collectivists and individualists would use the equity rule. Their preference for equity is driven by the perception of efficiency and productivity as salient goals in these situations. In sum, disintegration avoidance is hypothesized to be associated with equality, harmony enhancement with generosity, and efficiency with equity.

When an equity rule is applied, the question of what counts as a contribution arises. One interesting difference across cultures is the extent to which an individuals' relationships are recognized as a resource that the individual contributes. Given the evidence that a relationship to a resource allocator brings one a more favorable outcome in collectivist societies, it is not surprising that people cultivate social ties and regard them as an asset. Some insight about the kinds of relations that are valuable and hence recognized as inputs in particular societies comes from studies of the indigenous constructs used to think about these relationships, such as guanxi. A person is expected to receive preferential treatment from another person if there is good guanxi between them. Such preferential treatment may be regarded as favoritism in the West, but may be regarded as legitimate among Chinese. Guanxi is often established by prior exchanges but it differs from more universal norms of reciprocity in that the exchange tends to be more distant in time; it can be a favor done long ago, even a favor done by a family member in previous generations. Also the relationship created by the exchange is likely to be multiplex, not purely instrumental. A person's guanxi is a contribution to the group because it determines the person's social "face," *mianzi*, and hence the person's social credit rating (Hu, 1944; Hsu, 1971; Earley, 1995). In many Latin cultures, there are similar constructs about forms of interpersonal relations that are valuable and count among a person's resources, but the form of valuable relation differs. In Spain, an important resource that members bring to a group are *conocidos*, acquaintances on whom they can call for a favor to handle problems that the group encounters (J. Fernándex-Dols, personal communication, 1996). In Mexico, importance is placed on the closer and more restricted relations known as *compadres*, persons to whom one is connected as a godfather or as a godfather to a family member (J. Garcia, personal communication, 1995). To predict whether a person's relationships will be regarded as a contribution in a particular concrete case, it is helpful to know the culture- specific constructs that guide thinking about which relationships are resources.

Summary

Cultural influences on the perception of distributive justice can be illustrated in terms of the two-stage model presented before (see Figure 1). When perceivers consider a particular case of resource allocation in a group, there is first a stage in which they code certain features of that situation as relevant to the problem of just allocation. That is, they construe certain persons or groups as appropriate comparison referents and construe certain of their actions or properties as contributions to be taken into account. We have argued that some differences in this initial appraisal process can be accounted for in terms of etic constructs, such as collectivism and power distance, yet other differences can only be understood in terms of emic constructs, such as the norms governing interpersonal relations. The second stage of distributive justice judgment involves the application of a general principle to determine the appropriate distribution of rewards. There is considerable evidence that the selection of these rules depends on etic cultural constructs in interaction with contextual variables. In particular, the equity rule, so central to the psychology of distributive justice for individualists, is replaced by the equity, need, or generosity rules for collectivists.

2. Procedural Justice: Perception of Fair Process

Thibaut and Walker (1975) introduced the psychology of procedural justice, which refers to the perceived fairness of the procedure that an authority or a group uses to decide how resources are allocated. Thibaut and Walker demonstrated convincingly that people's reactions to an outcome are not solely a matter of how resources are distributed in the final outcome but also of the process used to arrive at this allocation decision. Subsequent work has shown that perceptions of fair process are related both to formal properties of the decision procedure and to the treatment received from the persons who enact the procedures. This latter concern is often distinguished as interactional justice (Bies and Moag, 1986; Tyler and Bies, 1990).

Two theoretical perspectives have been advanced to explain why people care about the process of decision making about social resources. The first wave of research by Thibaut,

Walker, and colleagues demonstrated that justice perceptions are driven by perceptions that a procedure offers control over the process to the people who are affected. For example, people prefer conflict resolution procedures that allow the disputants control over the issues considered, such as adversary adjudication procedure or a mediation procedure; they tend not to prefer procedures in which a third party controls the agenda, such as inquisitorial adjudication procedure. Subsequent work found that an opportunity to express one's views is a particularly important determinant of the assessment of a procedure as fair (Folger, 1977). Another aspect of the process that affects people's judgments of its fairness is its capacity to reduce animosity (Lissak and Sheppard, 1983). Leventhal (1980) has provided a fuller list of criteria that people use to evaluate the fairness of a procedure. We state two principles of procedural justice perception that are most relevant to our discussion as follows:

- *Process control*—the extent to which disputants can influence and control the process by which the dispute is resolved and communicate their views freely during the process
- *Animosity reduction*—the extent to which the procedure can reduce the animosity between disputants

A question raised about these principles is whether these process concerns are ends for people or whether they are merely the means to the end of favorable outcomes over the long term. The second wave of research argues that people are concerned with fair process, not for instrumental reasons, but because of what it symbolizes about their relationship to the decision-making authorities and the group they represent. The group-value model of procedural justice (Lind and Tyler, 1988) is based on the notion that people are concerned about their standing in a group and infer their status from the treatment they receive from the group in the procedures used to allocate social benefits and burdens. Relational factors refer to issues surrounding the interaction between decision makers and the recipients. Several important relational concerns have been identified by Tyler (1990), which we can summarize as follows:

- *Neutrality*—whether the authority acts in an unbiased manner
- *Dignity*—whether the authority treats individuals with dignity and respect
- *Trust*—whether the authority considers the views of individuals and attempts to act fairly

Recent studies supporting the group-value model have found that these relational concerns have a stronger impact on fairness perception than instrumental concerns (Tyler and Lind, 1992; Tyler, 1994).

Etic Analyses

Cross-cultural research on procedural and interactional justice is quite limited, but the available evidence suggests that the same general principles determine people's perception across culture. First, the available cross-cultural evidence suggests that the content of procedural and interactional justice is largely similar across cultures. The relation between perceived process control granted by a procedure and the perceived fairness of the procedure that Thibaut and Walker identified has been replicated in many countries other than the United States, including Britain, France, Germany (Lind, Erickson, Friedland, and Dickenberger, 1978), Hong Kong (Leung, 1987), Japan, and Spain (Leung, Au, Fernández-Dols, and Iwawaki, 1992). The properties of one's personal interaction with a decision maker that drive one's fairness perception have been studied in Hong Kong and China, with results supporting the validity of these constructs outside of the United States (Leung and Chiu, 1993; Leung and Li, 1990; Leung *et al.*, 1996). In other words, these studies showed that procedural and interactional justice seemed to be defined in a similar way across the several cultures studied.

Second, the consequences of perceived procedural and interactional justice also seem to be similar across cultures. For instance, perception of procedural and interactional justice is related to the perception of outcomes and decision makers in the United States (Lind and Tyler, 1988; Tyler and Bies, 1990). Leung and his colleagues have documented similar effects with Chinese subjects from Hong Kong and China (Leung and Li, 1990; Leung *et al.*, 1993, 1996).

There is increasing evidence that the group-value model of procedural justice also holds across cultural lines. In a study of ethnic groups in the United States, Lind, Huo, and Tyler (1994) studied the preferences for different conflict resolution procedures of African, Hispanic, Asian, and European Americans. For all four groups, procedural fairness was found to be a more important predictor than perceived favorability of the outcome in predicting procedural preference and the affect experienced during the disputing process. Likewise, in a study in Japan, Sugawara and Huo (1994) found that relational issues were rated as more important than instrumental issues in determining preferences for conflict resolution procedures. In a comparative analysis of data from American, German, and Hong Kong Chinese students, Lind (1994) found that perception of procedural aspects determined overall fairness judgments more than did perceptions of outcome favorability. Within the set of procedural elements studied, relational factors generally showed a stronger effect than perceived process control for all three cultural groups, which suggests that fair process is defined in largely the same way across cultures. Lind, Tyler, and Huo (1997) reported that the impact of voice, the opportunity to express one's views, on procedural justice judgments was mediated by relational variables, and this pattern is similar across the United States, Germany, Hong Kong, and Japan.

Results also suggest generality in the consequences of perceptions of fair process: Willingness to use a conflict resolution procedure was a function of its perceived fairness for all three cultural groups. Despite the consistent support for cultural universality of some general principles of procedural justice, researchers have also observed consistent cultural differences related to broad dimensions of national culture, as follows.

a. Collectivism

As with distributive justice, the cultural dimension most often linked to procedural justice has been individualism–collectivism. Thibaut and Walker (1975, 1978) found that people prefer conflict resolution procedures that grant disputants process control, but place the decision in the hands of an impartial third party (outcome control). The most common example embodying these two characteristics is the adversary adjudication system used in English-speaking countries. Lind *et al.* (1978) further found that adversary adjudication was most preferred even in France and Germany, in which adversary adjudication was not used as a legal procedure. This finding is interpreted as providing strong support to the theory of Thibaut and Walker.

Anthropologists, however, have consistently reported findings that deviate from the results of Thibaut and Walker (1975, 1978). Nader and Todd (1978) and Gulliver (1979) argued that in societies in which interpersonal relationships are stable and ongoing, procedures that allow for compromises, such as mediation and negotiation, are preferred. For instance, mediation is strongly preferred in Japan (Kawashima, 1963) and China (Doo, 1973). In light of these results, Leung (1987) argued that the preference for adversary procedure is stronger in individualist than in collectivist societies. All of the evidence in support of the theory of Thibaut and Walker (1975) was obtained in individualist societies, whereas the contradictory anthropological findings were obtained in collectivist societies. In a study of Chinese and Americans, Leung (1987) found that Chinese preferred mediation and negotiation to a larger extent than did Americans, and that the reason for their stronger preference for these procedures was the perception that these two procedures were more likely to lead to animosity reduction. The cultural difference in procedural preference was not explainable in terms of cultural difference placed on the value of harmony enhancement. This pattern of results was replicated by Leung *et al.* (1992) with participants from Spain, Japan, the Netherlands, and Canada. Morris, Leung, and Sethi (1995) replicated this pattern of results again with Chinese and Americans.

Bierbrauer (1994) took a different angle on the question of how cultural collectivism may relate to perceptions of the fairness of procedures. He compared relatively individualistic German citizens with relatively collectivist Kurdish and Lebanese asylum seekers in their preferences for dispute resolution procedures. Consistent with previous findings (Leung, 1987), Kurds and Lebanese were less willing to use state law to resolve a conflict with family members or acquaintances than were Germans. In fact, Bierbrauer (1994) found that Kurds and Lebanese accepted the norms of religion and tradition as more legitimate, and state law as less legitimate, for conflict resolution than did Germans. This set of findings suggests that individualism–collectivism affects the extent to which a legal procedure is regarded as fair and legitimate. Furthermore, in line with the individualism–collectivism framework, which suggests that norms have a bigger impact on collectivists than individualists (Triandis, 1995), Bierbrauer (1992) also found that Kurds and Lebanese reported a higher level of both shame and guilt if they violated state laws, traditional norms, or religious norms. For both cultural groups, collectivism was correlated with the level of shame and guilt experienced after violation of norms or rules.

Unlike in past studies, however, there was strong evidence for differences in the goals of dispute resolution, not simply perceptions of the characteristics of different procedures. When evaluating different procedures, Kurds and Lebanese regarded restoring harmony as a more important goal and following legal rules as a less important goal than did Germans. It is interesting to consider the characteristics of the groups that Bierbrauer surveyed, which are quite different from groups included in other cross-cultural studies reviewed before. One reason that several studies have compared people in the United States and Hong Kong is that their legal systems are fairly similar (based on the English tradition) while their social values differ. However, in the study by Bierbrauer, subjects were asked to respond to each question in light of what their behavior would be at home in Turkey or Lebanon, not what their behavior would be in Germany. Bierbrauer was specifically interested in legal culture, so he selected countries with vastly different legal institutions. Very different procedures, such as following traditions, were studied. Another factor that must be considered when interpreting the goals, preferences, and reactions of Kurds and Lebanese that Bierbrauer reports is that they were asylum seekers, which may have given them reasons to avoid entangling themselves in legal proceedings that are independent of their general preferences. Further work is needed to clarify the relationship between individualism–collectivism and perceived fairness and legitimacy of conflict resolution procedures.

b. Power Distance

The evidence about procedural justice perceptions and the power distance dimension of culture seems to be more straightforward. As one recent review concluded, "cultures that inculcate an acceptance of power differences lead individuals to expect, take for granted and, therefore, not get angry about, injustices (James, 1993:23). Gudykunst and Ting-Toomey (1988) analyzed the data on anger and justice from seven European countries reported by Babad and Wallbott (1986) and Wallbott and Scherer (1986). They found a strong correlation between the anger expressed in reaction to injustice and power distance (Hofstede, 1980). The higher the power distance of a society, the less that perception of unjust treatment triggers a reaction of anger. In higher power distance cultures, people's acceptance of unequal social prerogatives gives them a tolerance of unfair treatment. In contrast, in lower power distance societies, people's rejection of inequality makes them less tolerant of unfair treatment received. This reasoning is able to explain why more anger is expressed about injustice in low power distance societies.

While the conclusion of Gudykunst and Ting-Toomey (1988) is concerned with general feelings of justice and is based on indirect evidence, Bond, Wan, Leung, and Giacalone (1985) studied interactional justice and provided direct evidence to support this argument. Compared to American subjects, Chinese subjects were more willing to accept insulting remarks from a high-status in-group person. However, no difference was found when the insult came from a low-status individual. In an even more direct test, Leung, Morris, and Su (1998) put American and Chinese subjects in the role of an employee whose suggestion was criticized by a manager in a manner that did not recognize the employee's standing and hence violates a requirement of the relational model of procedural justice; that is, the manager interrupted, failed to listen closely, and was dismissive toward the employee. The manager was either someone of essentially equal level in the organization or someone substantially more senior. Consistent with previous studies, these researchers found that compared to Americans, Chinese perceived a senior manager's actions as less unjust and were less negative about the superior. A final piece of evidence comes from a study that measured the relative contribution of relational and instrumental concerns to people's judgment that an authority's actions to resolve a conflict were just. Tyler, Lind, and Huo (1995) found that relational concerns are more important to people low in power distance orientation than to those high in power distance orientation.

In high power distance societies, the intervention of a high-status third party in a dispute should be regarded as more legitimate. In line with this argument, court litigants look to the judge to provide facts about the case and ultimate justice in high power countries like Hong Kong and Japan, whereas American litigants are more inclined to rely on their own efforts to argue for their case (Benjamin, 1975; Leung and Lind, 1986; Tanabe, 1963). In a culture-level study of 23 national groups, Smith, Peterson, Leung, and Dugan (1998) found that in countries with a low power distance, subjects were more likely to rely on their own training and experiences, their peers, their subordinates, but less likely to rely on their boss, to resolve a dispute within their work group. Tse, Francis, and Walls (1994) found that compared to Canadian executives, executives from China were more likely to consult their superior in a conflict. Finally, Graham, Mintu, and Rodgers (1994) found that in high power distance societies, bargainers are more sensitive to bargaining roles (buyer or seller), which signals the power differential between the bargainers.

Emic Approaches to Culture and Procedural Justice

Although a fairly good understanding of procedural justice perceptions is offered by culture-general models, there are some remaining anomalies that call for emic analyses. For instance, although we have presented abundant evidence that people in high power distance cultures such as Hong Kong accept inconsiderate treatment from an authority that would raise the hackles of someone from a low power distance culture such as the United States, at the same time there is anecdotal as well as systematic evidence that people in Hong Kong are more sensitive to mistreatment in some ways. Advice books for Westerners who will become managers in Chinese societies traffic in examples of supervisory behavior that would constitute nothing more than "playful ribbing" in the United States but that would cause a Chinese employee to "lose face." Some insight about how Chinese can be, at the same time, more accepting and yet more sensitive to unfair treatment comes from the study of Leung *et al.* (1998). These researchers argued that Chinese recipients of inconsiderate treatment would understand this behavior in terms of the prerogatives of the supervisor's role and hence would be less inclined than Americans to attribute the behavior to the supervisor's personality or to respond by reacting negatively toward the supervisor. Yet, drawing on emic analyses of Chinese organizational behavior, these researchers argued that Chinese employees relate to powerful supervisors according to a norm derived from filial piety (they exchange loyalty and deference for regard and protection) and read their status in how they are treated by powerful supervisors (not in feedback that comes through bureaucratic channels). From this analysis, these researchers were able to predict that Chinese employees who suffered from treatment that lacked recognition of their standing would be more inclined to react by reducing their altruistic or entrepreneurial behavior in the organization.

In addition to accounting for anomalous findings, there is another more basic purpose for emic analyses of perception of fair process. Current models of procedural justice allow us to predict fairness perceptions once we know how a situation has been appraised in terms of instrumental criteria such as process control and relational criteria such as recognition of standing. However, these are very abstract properties at a considerable interpretive distance from any particular objective characteristics of a decision-making process. One reason for the cross-cultural convergence in procedural justice research may be that the survey items used to capture these constructs are pitched at an abstract level (e.g., Lind *et al.*, 1977). It is well-known that cross-cultural equivalence is more likely to the extent that constructs are defined at a highly abstract level (e.g., Van de Vijver and Leung, 1997).

The degree of control and standing offered in a particular social situation are abstract properties that are not self-evident. Emic analyses may be required to understand the specific beliefs that are used in a particular culture to infer these abstract properties from concrete aspects of the objective situation. For instance, an objective behavior that corresponds to recognition of standing in the United States, such as not interrupting, may not have the same relation to the abstract construct for people in every culture. Graham (1985) showed that the average number of times that negotiators explicitly disagree with each other has been measured at 18 per hour in the United States, at 11 in Japan, yet at over 150 in Brazil. Norms regarding "conversational overlaps" also differ: Brazilians talk while the negotiation partner is speaking three times as much as Americans. It seems that in every culture, there is a range of tolerable conversational overlap, and compliance with this norm is relied on as a cue to status recognition. It is also possible that while interruption signals one's standing in the United States, other behaviors are more diagnostic of the authorities' recognition of one's status in Japan and Brazil. Understanding conversational norms that are specific to cultures and even ethnic subcultures (Tannen, 1990, 1994) is necessary to predict when an interruption will be appraised as a sign of disrespect.

Emic analyses may also point to constructs that have not been considered in current research on procedural justice. Sinha (1987) has presented an account of *ahimsa*, a technique of conflict resolution advocated by Gandhi against the British Colonial regime. Ahimsa involves a very different conceptualization of procedural justice, and conventional constructs, such as process control, seem peripheral to this procedure. Ahimsa originates from Buddhism, Jainism, Hinduism, and Sanskrit, and the Indian traditions, and is based on the refusal to do harm, and a related concept, Satyagraha which refers to a force born of truth and love. Ahimsa involves two basic principles, maha-karuna (great compassion) and maha-prajna (great wisdom). It is assumed that the strong emotional attachment and love toward all beings and the perception that all beings are equal would prevent people from harming other beings. Guided by these two principles, an Indian may proceed with three steps of conflict resolution. The first step involves persuading the other disputing party through reasoning. If that fails, he or she may persuade the other party through self-suffering, intended to arouse a feeling of guilt in the opponent and/or put the opponent in a morally wrong situation for inflicting harm on a "helpless" and nonviolent individual. If these two steps fail, nonviolent coercion such as noncooperation, civil disobedience, boycott, and fast may be adopted. These strategies are based on a fundamental assumption that "violence cannot stop violence," and that it is only through peace that violence can be stopped.

The ahimsa technique seems to involve the principle that a procedure is just if it brings a greater moral self-awareness to the parties involved. Although many conflict resolution procedures in the West also gain legitimacy from their capacity to arouse moral emotions, this issue has not been included in mainstream research on the attributes that lead a procedure to be perceived as fair. Once again, the study of an emic construct may lead us to a new etic construct and expand the assumptions in current research programs.

Summary

Cultural influences on procedural justice perceptions appear less dramatic than those on distributive justice, but cultural effects in the two stages of the process can once again be distinguished (see Figure 1). When perceivers consider a particular case of a decision-making process, there is first a stage in which they code certain features of the procedure and the person's behavior as relevant to justice judgments. That is, they might appraise a particular aspect of the formal structure as process control, or aspect of the decision maker's judgment as indicative of status recognition. We assert that research is lacking with regard to how this initial appraisal process differs across cultures. Analysis in terms of emic constructs, such as conversational norms, is needed. The second stage of the process involves the application of general principles to determine one's perception of fair process. Although this stage of the process appears to be quite general across cultures, there is some evidence that the application of these principles is moderated by collectivism and consistent evidence that it is moderated by power distance.

3. Retributive Justice: Perception of Fair Sanctions

The facets of justice that we have discussed thus far occur in the context of decision making about the allocation of rights and resources in a social group. Since decisions about resources and procedures are ripe occasions for conflict, groups and societies minimize the negotiation of these decisions by creating rules that guide and restrict behavior. Some rules are formal laws; others are merely informal norms. Importantly, these social rules provide an individual with a sense of justice and a basis for confidently engaging in social interactions only so long as the individual believes that others follow the rules. The third facet of justice—retributive justice—arises when one individual observes another's act that breaks a rule and causes a harm. The observer first judges whether the other is responsible for the act and then judges whether punishment is deserved. These punishments are enacted by the justice system in case of violations of formal laws, or by interpersonal means such as ostracism in the case of violations of informal norms. In both cases, there seems to be a similar set of principles guiding thoughts about the appropriateness of sanctions. There have been fewer empirical psychological studies of retributive than distributive or procedural justice, but the tradition of legal and philosophical scholarship on this issue is longer than for other forms of justice. The concepts involved in retributive justice underlie questions that continually confront and reconfront a society, such as questions about the fairness of punishments for individuals involved in a crime (Hogan and Emler, 1981) and, at a more collective level, about the legitimacy of a group's act of civil disobedience or revolution (Martin, Scully, and Levitt, 1990).

A judgment about the fairness of a punishment rests on a chain of inferences about the actor, the context of the act, and the severity of its consequences. As with distributive and procedural justice judgments, it can be conceived in terms of two general stages. In the initial stage, the outcome is appraised with regard to its severity and the extent of the actor's responsibility. In the second stage, a principle is applied to determine the sanction that the actor deserves. Models of the first stage are rooted in Heider's (1958) model of attribution of responsibility, which integrated psychological observations with distinctions from previous scholarship on legal and moral responsibility. Empirical studies have proved useful in highlighting ways in which the psychology of retributive justice departs from the normative models laid out by scholars of ethics or jurisprudence. For example, subjects attribute more responsibility to an actor for an accident when its consequences are severe than minor, apparently reflecting the attributor's greater need to lay blame for a severe outcome (Walster, 1966).

Other researchers have refined the description of the stages that Heider outlined. Models by Shaver (1985) and by Shultz and colleagues (Shultz and Schleifer, 1983; Shultz, Schleider, and Altman, 1981) propose that observers of an act with negative consequences engage in a stepwise attribution process. First, an analysis of the actor's causal relation to the negative outcome is performed. Was the actor the only cause of this outcome or were there other contributing factors that mitigate the actor's responsibility for the outcome? Next the observer appraises the extent to which the act was intentional. Cues to the actor's intent are the actor's pattern of behavior before the act, apparent state of mind during the act, and behavior after the outcome (Miller and Vidmar, 1981). The degree of causality and intentionality perceived determines the degree of responsibility attributed to the actor. There is evidence for sufficient universality in the process of responsibility judgment that cultural differences can be meaningfully compared. In the most extensive comparative study, Hamilton and Sanders (1983) found that the same kind of factors relevant to severity, causality, and intentionality govern responsibility judgment in the United States and in Japan, although (as we shall see below) cultures differ in the emphasis accorded to these factors. Moreover, at least with regard to major crimes, there is evidence that perception of the relative seriousness of offenses is similar across a variety of cultures (Evans and Scott, 1984).

Once an actor is perceived to be responsible for the harmful violation of a social rule, it has to be decided what constitutes a fair punishment. A few general principles seem to channel judgments about the fairness of punishment:

- *Retribution* involves making the actor suffer to compensate the victims whose suffering he or she caused.

- *Incapacitation* involves removing the individual from the group to preclude him or her from breaking the rule again.
- *Deterrence* involves punishing the actor in order to teach a lesson, to increase his or her perception of the costs of this act. General deterrence is the sanctioning of one offender as an example to others.
- *Rehabilitation* aims to change the actor, but through a process that transforms the individual's inner values and goals rather than merely his or her perceptions of the costs of the act.
- *Restoration* involves attempting directly to repair the social relationship between the actor and the victim. Two elements are restitution, which attempts to restore the victim's condition, and apology, which attempts to restore the actor's appearance as an acceptor of the rule.

As with the first, this second stage of retributive justice seems to be recognizably similar across cultures. The studies of Hamilton and Sanders (1992) have found parallel relationships in the United States and Japan between attributions of responsibility and decisions to punish. And although the overall prevalence of appeals to each principle differ between Americans and Japanese, a similar set of principles seems to be drawn on, and the same factors (such as whether the actor is a stranger or not) moderate the selection of principles. In the following, we turn to cultural differences observed in this study and others that can be interpreted in terms of the etic and emic cultural constructs that affect the psychology of retributive justice.

Etic Analyses

a. Individualism–Collectivism

The most discussed cultural construct with regard to retributive justice has been individualism–collectivism.[4] Different components of individualism and collectivism may be most relevant to particular stages of retributive justice judgments. A component of the cultural syndrome of individualism is the belief that persons are autonomous and not constrained in their behavior by the social context (Lukes, 1973). Evidence that there is less emphasis on individual autonomy in collectivist cultures comes from ethnographic reports that the stories told to explain behavior make less reference to internal traits and intentions (Hsu, 1971; Selby, 1975) and from comparative studies of everyday explanation that have tallied the prevalence of trait versus situational references (Miller, 1984). Morris and Peng (1994) presented evidence for differences between the United States and China in implicit theories of social behavior. In the United States, a theory centered on the autonomous person channels attributions to an individual actor's internal, stable properties. In China, a theory centered on situations and groups directs attributions to the actor's embeddedness in constraining social groups. In the case of social behavior, where the causal relationships are self-evident or where attributors are motivated to analyze the information carefully, these theories would have little impact. But in cases where the information about causation is ambiguous or complex, or where the attributor's attention is sharply limited, these theories would affect the details that are attended to at first and which carries the most weight in the attribution of causality.

Given that responsibility is assigned based on principles of causality and intentionality, one might expect that responsibility assignment diverges across cultures in its responsiveness to certain kinds of information. A clear case for this can be seen in the results of Hamilton and

Sanders (1992), who surveyed American and Japanese responses to vignettes about wrongdoings in an array of everyday situations and varied factors related to the actor and the social context. As for the actor, his or her state of mind during the act as well as past pattern of behavior were varied. As for the social context, the presence of other persons in the chain of events surrounding the act and the presence of role obligations were varied. Across conditions, Americans perceived the acts to be more purposive or reflective of the actor's enduring intentions than did Japanese. Also, strikingly, Americans' responsibility attributions were roughly twice as sensitive to manipulations of information about the actor. This sensitivity extended to indirect cues to intentionality, such as the past pattern of behavior. Japanese were more sensitive to the actor's social role and to the influence of other parties in the social context. In a similar vein, Na and Loftus (1998) reported that American law experts and college students were more likely to attribute criminal behavior to personality traits, drug abuse, and family problems, whereas Korean law experts and college students were more likely to attribute criminal behavior to situational and societal factors. This attributional difference probably explained why the Korean respondents showed more favorable attitudes toward lenient treatment of criminals than did their American counterparts.

Results from Hamilton and Sanders's research program suggest that the second stage of retributive justice—decisions about punishment—may also be affected by the individualism–collectivism dimension. Hamilton and Sanders (1988) argued Japanese have a stronger belief in society's obligation to guide the individual to a mature state of conformity to social norms. Hence, an individual's transgression of a social norm or law is seen as reflecting a failure of society to socialize and guide the individual property. Accordingly, their goal in punishing a transgression should be to redress this inadequate socialization. This was seen in Japanese respondents' decisions about sanctions for wrongdoers and the rationales favored. With regard to how to punish a responsible wrongdoer, "Japanese respondents were more likely to choose sanctions that restore the relationship between actor and victim and that provide restitution for the victim … Americans were more likely to suggest sanctions to isolate the individual" (p. 183) When asked to endorse rationales for punishment corresponding to the major principles of retributive justice, "Rationales for punishment were also examined. Americans were more favorably disposed than Japanese to retribution, incapacitation, and general deterrence as rationals … Japanese were more favorably disposed to specific deterrence, rehabilitation, and restitution." In sum, Japanese respondents favored sanctions that "reintegrate the wrongdoer and restore relationships" whereas Americans favored sanctions that isolated the wrongdoer and thus prevented reexpression of his or her antisocial disposition.[5]

b. Power Distance

Other researchers have investigated how the difference between egalitarian and hierarchical value systems affects retributive justice. In particular, people with different power distance orientations were found to differ in beliefs about the rights of authorities and in responses to injustices committed by them (Gudykunst and Ting-Toomey, 1988). A hierarchical value orientation has been linked to acceptance of injustice behavior by persons in power (James, 1993) and to the willingness to tolerate inequality in the distribution of resources (Scase, 1974). However, a different view of the matter is presented in the Hamilton and Sanders (1995) studies. They hypothesized that Japanese respondents would be more sensitive to the obligations implied by an actor's authority role and hence hold a powerful person to a higher standard. Some of their results are consistent with this hypothesis. In general, Japanese assigned less responsibility to an actor in a group than an actor alone but this was not the case when the actor held an authority role in the group. This pattern of results suggests that the impact of power distance on retributive justice may differ from that on procedural and distributive, an interesting topic for future research.

c. *Other Dimensions*

One puzzle is how culture may be related to the affective content of responses to injustice. Studies have found, for example, that anger in response to injustice varies substantially across European countries (Babad and Wallbott, 1986; Wallbott and Scherer, 1986). Although little researched by psychologists, a general cultural dimension is the extent to which honor is linked to the way one responds to interpersonal affronts. It has been argued that Mediterranean and Latin cultures are characterized by a culture of honor that prescribes that men respond with violence to affronts on self or family (e.g., Peristiany, 1965). Evidence suggests that in conditions where laws are not externally enforced and resources are vulnerable, this pattern develops. The southern United States is marked by these conditions and the spirals of escalating violence that result. According to a historian of that region:

> In the absence of any strong sense of order as unity, hierarchy, or social peace, backsettlers shared an idea of order as a system of retributive justice. The prevailing principle was *lex talionis*, the rule of retaliation. It held that a good man must seek to do right in the world, but when wrong was done to him, he must punish the wrongdoer himself by an act of retribution that restored order and justice to the world. (Fischer, 1989)

A series of comparative studies by Cohen (1996) documented that a southern culture of honor is codified in social and legal institutions. Cohen and Nisbett (1993) demonstrated that Northerners and Southerners differ in a specific set of social attitudes about appropriate responses to interpersonal threat. In a series of compelling experiments, evidence was obtained that northern and southern white male students at the same university reacted differently to an ambiguous insult (Cohen, Nisbett, Bowdle, and Schwarz, 1996). The North–South difference in aggression was observed in behaviors toward the offender, in semantic associations after the incident, and even in physiological measures of hormonal indicators of aggression. As the U.S. public increasingly loses faith in the justice system, one might expect a culture of honor to expand as citizens need to personally enact justice. One sign of this is the trend of increasingly lenient jury verdicts for violent crimes committed in self-defense or in acts of vigilante retribution (Robinson and Darley, 1995). Although norms about honor are present in many collectivist, hierarchical cultures, there is reason to believe that honor is not merely part of collectivism or power distance. One of many examples of divergence is that Chinese culture, which is high in collectivism and power distance, is suffused with a value on responding to a conflict by controlling one's response to it rather than by lashing out in violence (for a review, see Leung and Fan, 1996).

Another dimension likely to be relevant is the belief in the malleability of personal dispositions. It is straightforward that this belief should be associated with endorsement of certain rationalizations for punishment. That is, those who do not believe that personality is malleable will likely be less invested in the goal of rehabilitation and more in the goal of incapacitation. An informal comparison of adherents of left-wing versus right-wing political positions in many societies supports this hypothesis. Consistent with this argument, Epstein (1986) has compared the reformatory education organizations for juvenile offenders in Taiwan, China, and Hong Kong and concluded that reformatory institutes in Taiwan and China are similar in their emphasis on indoctrination and political education during the process of institutionalization. One may argue that this orientation reflects an underlying assumption that offenders can be changed through a vigorous program of "reeducation." In contrast, because of British influence, such institutes in Hong Kong rely more on rewards and incentives, and less on indoctrination and reeducation, to channel the offenders back to a normal pattern of life.

Emic Analyses

Researchers have noted several indigenous constructs about rule-breaking and sanctions that seem to play a central role in the psychology of retributive justice in collectivistic societies. The belief systems in societies that have been highly shaped by Confucian social values are centered on a norm of interpersonal harmony. At first glance, the presence of a harmony norm might seem to reduce retributive tendencies. Yet Lebra (1984) argues the opposite case with regard to the concept of *wa* (group harmony) in Japanese culture. It is the final Chinese character taught to all school children and figures in a key proverb used to socialize children about conforming to social norms "*Deru kui wa utateru*" ("the protruding stake is hammered down"). Lebra argues that harmony concerns make Japanese more likely to sanction others for violations of informal rules:

> If the Japanese place more value, as I believe they do, upon social interdependence, cooperation, solidarity, or harmony than, say, the Americans, they are more likely to interfere with one another's actions. The norm of harmony may be precisely what makes people more aware of conflicts with others, conflicts between their self-interest and obligations, and so forth.... The cultural value of harmony may intensify, instead of mitigate, conflict. (1984:56)

Lebra's (1984) argument is consistent with the results of Yamagishi (1988a), who found that in the absence of a sanctioning system, Japanese actually showed a lower level of trust and commitment toward other group members than did Americans. Compared with Americans, Japanese were more likely to exit a group that lacked a monitoring and sanctioning system (Yamagishi, 1988b). Thus, despite the emphasis on harmony by Japanese, they rely on sanctioning more than do Americans to maintain the proper functioning of a group.

This analysis points out a more general area of likely cultural variation in retributive justice perceptions and responses. Although cultures seem similar in their judgments of the severity of major violations of formalized rules (crimes), they may vary sharply in the degree to which deviation from informal social rules is regarded as severe enough to evoke thoughts about the fairness of a sanctioning response. For instance, an argument about when an actor will be absolved for a wrongdoing has been forwarded by Miller and colleagues in their research on the duty-based ethics of Hindu Indians. Miller and Luthar (1989) examined responses to an actor who in a dilemma between acting in line with social rules (e.g., laws) or role obligations chose the latter. Indians were more likely than Americans to absolve these actors from a sanction. In another study, Bersoff and Miller (1993) found that compared to American subjects, Indian subjects were more likely to absolve justice breaches that were due to immaturity or emotional duress (fear or anger). Miller and her colleagues argued that Indians view others as embedded in the situation and construe responsibility in terms of right action in the situation, *dharma*.

Retribution may take many different forms, and different cultures may have different emic beliefs about forms of retribution. For instance, in the Chinese tradition, *bao* is an emic concept of retribution (e.g., Hsu, 1971; Yang, 1957). Chinese believe that bao may not necessarily occur to the harmdoer, but may occur to his or her relatives and offspring, and even to his or her next avatar after reincarnation (e.g., Chiu, 1991). In indigenous Hawaiian culture, illness and injury are sometimes regarded as caused by retribution (Ito, 1982).

In some cultures, retribution may not be a salient issue. For instance, Hindu Indians believe that it is by fate or *karma* (Hines, Garcia-Preto, McGoldrick, Almedia, and Weltman, 1992) that people are reincarnated into a member of a particular social caste. Therefore, even harmful behavior by another may be accepted as predestined. Since karma can only be changed through death and rebirth, tolerance, sacrifice, even suffering may be more acceptable responses to wrongdoing. In sum, certain belief systems may reduce the centrality of retribution.

Summary

The cultural influences on retributive justice judgments can be summarized in terms of the two stages laid out in Figure 1. When a particular case of a harmful, rule-violating behavior is observed, there is first a stage in which the attribution of causality, intentionality, and responsibility to the person is decided. There is clear evidence that aspects of individualism affect causal attribution to personal dispositions, affect the ascription of intentionality, and affect the strength of the link between these inferences and the attribution of responsibility.

The second stage is applying a principle to determine how to sanction the person responsible for the wrongdoing. There is some evidence that the power distance dimension influences the principles applied to reasons about wrongdoing by authorities. The principle applied in responding to interpersonal affronts seems to differ between cultures that are high and low in concern for honor. A variety of culture-specific constructs also influence the rules applied to responding to violations of justice. Some are beliefs in retribution in the afterlife or in future generations. These beliefs steer people away from a need for retribution in their own life.

4. Justice Issues in Relations between Ethnic or Cultural Groups

Interethnic and intercultural contact has become commonplace, but not all such contact is cooperative and harmonious. Bloodshed and confrontation among ethnic groups often make news headlines. Although many factors shape the course of intergroup contact, justice issues are often central to many intercultural conflicts. In the following, we examine a few factors that may cause difficulties in intercultural interaction.

a. Ethnocentric Fairness Bias

Many studies have examined the processes underlying intergroup contact, and in-group favoritism is one of the most robust findings. People tend to favor their in-group and derogate the out-groups (e.g., Tajfel, 1982), and this bias is also documented in resource allocation. A number of studies have found that people show a tendency to allocate a larger share of a reward to in-group members than to out-group members (e.g., Tajfel, 1978; Mg, 1984). People also tend to regard their in-group as morally superior and more trustworthy than out-groups (Brewer, 1986). According to social identity theory, this in-group bias reflects people's tendency to promote a positive, group-based social identity (Tajfel and Turner, 1979).

Messick, Bloom, Boldizar, and Samuelson (1985) found that people recalled more fair acts and fewer unfair acts that they performed than those performed by others. Messick *et al.* (1985) labeled this phenomenon the *egocentric fairness bias*. The results on in-group favoritism suggest that interethnic and intercultural contact is vulnerable to an *ethnocentric fairness bias*. People are likely to perceive that the actions of their in-group are fairer than the actions of the out-group. Some support of this argument comes from a study comparing the "just world" belief of British and white South African students (Furnham, 1985). South African students showed a stronger belief in the just world, and Furnham (1985) argued that this difference can be interpreted as a mechanism for whites in South Africa to justify the negative treatment of the victims of apartheid.

b. Similarity Bias

It is well known that people are attracted to others who are similar to themselves (Byrne, 1971). In resource allocation across cultural lines, it is possible that a similar bias is in operation. People may regard the allocation of a larger reward to out-group members who are more similar to themselves as fair. In a multicultural situation, this reasoning suggests that the dominant group may reward members of subordinate groups who are more similar to themselves. Leong (1996) reported two studies in the United States, both of which lend support to this hypothesis. Both studies are concerned with the occupational outcomes of Asian-Americans. In the first study, it was found that more acculturated subjects reported a higher level of job satisfaction. Acculturation here refers to the adoption of the values and practices of the mainstream American culture. The second study found that Asian-Americans who were more acculturated were given higher performance ratings by their supervisors. These two sets of results suggest that members of minority groups who are more acculturated and hence more similar to their superiors, who are from the majority group, are likely to enjoy better job outcomes.

c. Clash of Conversational Styles

Research has shown that interactive styles vary drastically across cultures. During an intercultural contact, misunderstanding arising from different interactive style may lead to a feeling of interactional injustice. One may interpret a behavior of the other interactant as rude and condescending from one's cultural standpoint, and as a result may feel unpleasant and even annoyed. However, this behavior may be perfectly acceptable from the other person's cultural standpoint (for a review, see Gudykunst and Bond, 1997). For instance, it is well documented that African- and European-Americans have different conversational norms (e.g., Waters, 1992). Eye contact usually indicates paying attention for European-Americans, whereas for some urban African-Americans, lack of eye contact does not signal a lack of attention if the conversants know each other well (Asante and Davis, 1985). If a European-American talks to an African-American and notices that she is not making eye contact, the European-American may ask the African American whether she is listening. The African-American may feel that the question is rude and uncalled for. Similarly, Tannen (1990) illustrates how differences between New Yorkers and Californians in the frequency of interruptions can lead to conflict and misperception of intent.

d. The Redress of Past Injustice

Intergroup conflict is a common phenomenon, and in situations where one group has historically inflicted severe loss or atrocities on another group, the redress of past injustice becomes a salient issue in the interaction between members from these groups. For instance, in many parts of the world, such as Canada and New Zealand, native peoples have been displaced by European settlers, who have become the dominant group. The native group typically suffers from economic hardship and is in constant negotiation with the dominant group about ways to redress the injustice imposed on them earlier. Severe disagreements and stalemates are common in these negotiations, but very little research has examined such processes from a justice perspective. We believe that this is a major area that should be tackled in future work.

E. CONCLUSION

Our review of the literature suggests that differences between cultures and perceptions of justice can be accounted for in terms of both culture-general (etic) constructs that are abstracted from psychological experiences and in terms of culture-specific (emic) constructs that come from the experience of the people described. One purpose of this chapter has been to bridge the discussion of these two approaches to culture to assess the distinctive contributions that these two approaches have made to justice theories. Our review has revealed an interesting pattern that etic constructs tend to be related to the more abstract latter stages of justice judgment. Emic constructs are more strongly related to the more concrete initial stages. This observation suggests that a researcher's choice of how to analyze culture may direct him or her to different research problems. However, it is well-known that analyses of emic constructs often provide the first step in the development of etic constructs (Van de Vijver and Leung, 1997). What is explicit and articulated in one culture may be implicit and unrecognized in another. For example, studies of the psychology of karma in Hindu Indian society may lead to a better understanding of fatalistic reasoning that helps one better assess the less marked versions of it that predominate in other societies, such as the just world hypothesis. A number of emic constructs that bear on justice have been reviewed, and we believe that many of these constructs have the potential to be developed into etic constructs and become core constructs in general theories of justice.

Another purpose of this review has been to assess the prospects for intercultural understanding on issues of justice. Although we have focused on differences in this review, it is important to note that effects of culture on justice perception under some situations may not be large. General models of distributive, procedural, and retributive justice seem to account fairly well for the perceptions of justice that have been observed in different cultures. Thus, general models of justice perception may potentially play the role of a conceptual bridge for intercultural understanding. However, our review also suggests that cultural diversity seems to occur in the appraisals of a situation that come before inferences about justice per se and in the weights given to criteria used in the judgmental process. It is crucial that these differences be explicitly acknowledged in order to guarantee an effective intercultural contact.

ACKNOWLEDGMENTS. We would like to thank Dave Kenny, Lee Hamilton, and Jim Wall for their insightful comments on earlier drafts of this paper.

F. ENDNOTES

1. For instance, African-Americans were more likely to be incarcerated than European-Americans (Spohn, Gruhl, and Welch, 1982).
2. To an anthropologist interested in the role of this psychological process in a larger cultural system, the absence of romantic love might be telling and might motivate further comparison. But to a psychologist interested in workings of the process, comparative studies would be of relatively little probative value.

3. This appraisal framework is similar to that in theories of emotion and culture (Ellsworth, 1996). An analogy can be drawn to the methodological stance of cross-cultural researchers who favor using different sorts of measures in each culture to tap the same etic constructs (e.g., Berry, 1989; Davision, Jaccard, Triandis, Morales, and Diaz-Guerrero, 1976; Triandis and Marin, 1983).
4. Lest this review give the impression that most variation across cultures in justice perceptions can be reduced to a single value dimension, two qualifications are in order. First, there are some historical reasons why this dimension has received the most research attention, such as that the United States emerged at the extreme individualist end of the dimension in Hofstede's (1980) analysis of national culture and that reliable scales for individualism–collectivism have been developed and disseminated by Triandis and colleagues (e.g., Triandis, McCusker, and Hui, 1990). Second, there is increasing recognition that individualism–collectivism comprises a number of intertwined but distinct cultural dimensions (Kashima *et al.*, 1995; Triandis, 1995).
5. We have interpreted the Hamilton and Sanders findings in terms of a slight cultural variation in the psychology of retributive justice. Another interpretation is that both Americans and Japanese have two modes of thinking about responsibility and punishment, one that is reserved for acts in the context of high-solidarity relationships and one for acts in the context of strangers, and that Japanese use the former mode more of the time because acts in their culture are more likely to be in the context of high-solidarity ties. Studies of interpersonal networks among employees in individualist and collectivist cultures support the notion that in collectivist societies there is a greater distribution of strong, multiplex ties (Morris and Podolny, 1996).

   The distinction between these two proximal explanations for the effect of the general individualism–collectivism dimension could be tested by unconfounding the culture of the respondent and the culture of the actor described in the vignette. If Japanese respondents asked about rule-breakers in Detroit endorsed incapacitation rather than rehabilitation, for example, then we might question whether their psychology of retribution really differs.

REFERENCES

Adams, J. S. (1963). Toward an Understanding of Inequity. *Journal of Abnormal and Social Psychology, 67,* 422–436.

Adams, J. S. (1965). Inequity in Social Exchange. In L. Berkowitz (Ed.), *Advances in Experimental Social Psychology* (pp. 267–299). New York: Academic Press.

Asante, M., and Davis, A. (1985). Black and White Communication: Analyzing Work Place Encounters. *Journal of Black Studies, 16,* 77–93.

Babad, E. Y., and Wallbott, H. G. (1986). The Effects of Social Factors on Emotional Reactions. In K. S. Scherer, H. G. Wallbott, and A. B. Summerfield (Eds.), *Experiencing Emotion: A Cross-Cultural Study* (pp. 154–172). London: Cambridge University Press.

Barber, B. R. (1995). *Jihad vs. McWorld.* New York: Times Books.

Bar-Tao, R. (1990). Causes and Consequences of Delegitimization: Models of Conflict and Ethnocentrism. *Journal of Social Issues, 46,* 65–82.

Bazerman, M. H., Wde-Bensoni, K. A., and Benzoni, F. J. (1995). *Environmental Degradation: Exploring the Rift between Environmentally Benign Attitudes and Environmentally Destructive Behaviors.* Unpublished manuscript, Kellogg Graduate School of Management, Northwestern University.

Bellah, R. N., Madsen, R., Sullivan, W. M., Swidler, A., and Tipton, S. (1985). *Habits of the Heart: Individualism and Commitment in American Life.* Berkeley: University of California Press.

Benjamin, R. W. (1975). Images of Conflict Resolution and Social Control: American and Japanese Attitudes to the Adversary System. *Journal of Conflict Resolution, 19,* 123–137.

Berger, J., Zelditch, M., Anderson, B., and Cohen, B. P. (1972). Structural Aspects of Distributive Justice: A Status-Value Formulation. In J. Berger, M. Zelditch, and B. Anderson (Eds.), *Sociological Theories in Progress* (Vol. 2, pp. 119–246). Boston: Houghton Mifflin.

Berman, J. J., Murphy-Berman, V., and Singh, P. (1985). Cross-Cultural Similarities and Differences in Perception of Fairness. *Journal of Cross-Cultural Psychology, 16,* 55–67.

Berry, J. W. (1969). On Cross-Cultural Comparability. *International Journal of Psychology, 4,* 119–128.

Berry, J. W. (1989). Imposed Etics–Emics–Derived Etics: The Operationalization of a Compelling Idea. *International Journal of Psychology, 24,* 721–735.

Berry, J. W., and Wells, M. (1994). Attitudes toward Aboriginal Peoples and Aboriginal Self-Government in Canada. In J. H. Hylton (Ed.), *Aboriginal Self-Government in Canada.* Saskatchewan, Canada: Purich Publishing. 215–232.

Berry, J. W., Poortinga, Y. H., Segall, M. H., and Dasen, P. R. (1992). *Cross-Cultural Psychology.* London: Cambridge University Press.

Bersoff, D. M., and Miller, J. G. (1993). Culture, Context, and the Development of Moral Accountability Judgments. *Developmental Psychology*, *29*, 664–676.

Bierbrauer, G. (1992). Reactions to Violation of Normative Standards: A Cross-Cultural Analysis of Shame and Guilt. *International Journal of Psychology*, *27*, 181–194.

Bierbrauer, G. (1994). Toward an Understanding of Legal Culture: Variations in Individualism and Collectivism between Kurds, Lebanese, and Germans. *Law and Society Review*, *28*, 243–264.

Bies, R. J., and Moag, J. S. (1986). Interactional Justice: Communication Criteria of Fairness. In R. J. Lewicki, B. H. Sheppard, and M. H. Bazerman (Eds.), *Research on Negotiation in Organizations* (pp. 43–55). Greenwich, CT: JAI Press.

Biggart, N. W., and Hamilton, G. G. (1992). On the Limits of a Firm-Based Theory to Explain Business Networks: The Western Bias of Neoclassical Economics. In N. Nohria and R. G. Eccles (Eds.), *Networks and Organizations* (pp. 471–490). Boston, MA: Harvard University Business School Press.

Bond, M. H., and Hwang, K. K. (1986). The Social Psychology of Chinese People. In M. H. Bond (Ed.), *The Psychology of the Chinese People* (pp. 213–266). London: Oxford University Press.

Bond, M. H., Wan, K. C., Leung, K., and Giacalone, R. (1985). How Are Responses to Verbal Insults Related to Cultural Collectivism and Power Distance? *Journal of Cross-Cultural Psychology*, *16*, 111–127.

Bowd, A. D., and Shapiro, K. J. (1993). The Case against Laboratory Animal Research in Psychology. *Journal of Social Issues*, *49*, 133–142.

Brewer, M. B. (1986). The Role of Ethnocentrism in Intergroup Conflict. In S. Worchel and W. G. Austin (Eds.), *Psychology of Intergroup Conflict* (pp. 88–102). Chicago: Nelson–Hall.

Byrne, D. (1971). *The Attraction Paradigm*. New York: Academic Press.

Campbell, D. T. (1964). Distinguishing Differences of Perception from Failures of Communication in Cross-Cultural Studies. In F. S. C. Northrop and H. H. Livington (Eds.), *Cross-Cultural Understanding: Epistemology in Anthropology* (pp. 308–336). New York: Harper & Row.

Campbell, D. T. (1975). On the Conflicts between Biological and Social Evolution and between Psychology and the Moral Tradition. *American Psychologist*, *30*, 1103–1126.

Chen, C. C. (1995). New Trends in Rewards Allocation Preferences: A Sino–U.S. Comparison. *Academy of Management Journal*, *38*, 408–428.

Chen, C. S., and Uttal, D. H. (1988). Cultural Values, Parents' Beliefs, and Children's Achievement in the United States and China. *Human Development*, *31*, 351–358.

Chen, J. T. S. (1973). *1001 Chinese Sayings*. Hong Kong: Chung Chi College, Chinese University of Hong Kong.

Chiu, C. Y. (1991). Responses to Injustice in Popular Chinese Sayings among Hong Kong Chinese Students. *Journal of Social Psychology*, *131*, 655–665.

Cohen, D. (1996). Law, Social Policy, and Violence: The Impact of Regional Cultures. *Journal of Personality and Social Psychology*, *70*, 961–978.

Cohen, D., and Nisbett, R. E. (1993). Self-Protection and the Culture of Honor: Explaining Southern Homicide. *Personality and Social Psychology Bulletin*, *20*, 551–567.

Cohen, D., Nisbett, R. E., Bowdle, B. F., and Schwarz, N. (1996). Insult, Aggression, and the Southern Culture of Honor: An "Experimental Ethnography." *Journal of Personality and Social Psychology*, *70*, 945–960.

Cook, K. S., and Messick, D. M. (1983). Psychological and Sociological Perspectives on Distributive Justice: Convergent, Divergent, and Parallel Lines. In D. M. Messick and K. S. Cook (Eds.), *Equity Theory: Psychological and Sociological Perspectives* (pp. 1–12). New York: Praeger.

Davision, A. R., Jaccard, J. J., Triandis, H. C., Morales, M. L., and Diaz-Guerrero, R. L. (1976). Cross-Cultural Model Testing: Toward a Solution to the Etic–Emic Dilemma. *International Journal of Psychology*, *11*, 1–14.

Deutsch, M. (1975). Equity, Equality, and Need: What Determines Which Value Will Be Used as the basis of Distributive Justice? *Journal of Social Issues*, *31*, 137–149.

Deutsch, M. (1985). *Distributive Justice*. New Haven: Yale University Press.

Doo, L. (1973). Dispute Settlement in Chinese-American Communities. *American Journal of Comparative Law*, *21*, 627–663.

Early, P. C. (1995). *The Faces of Culture*. Workshop on Culture and Conflicts. Graduate School of Business, Stanford University.

Ellsworth, P. (1996). *Culture and Appraisal Models of Emotion*. Paper presented at the McArthur Conference on Cultural Psychology, Center for Advanced Study in Behavioral Science.

Epstein, I. I. (1986). Reformatory Education in Chinese Society. *International Journal of Offender Therapy and Comparative Criminology*, *30*, 87–100.

Evans, S. S., and Scott, J. E. (1984). The Seriousness of Crime Cross-Culturally. *Criminology*, *22*, 39–59.

Festinger, L. (1954). A Theory of Social Comparison Processes. *Human Relations*, *7*, 117–140.

Fischer, D. H. (1989). *Albion's Seed: Four British Folkways in America*. London: Oxford University Press.

Folger, R. (1977). Distributive and Procedural Justice: Combined Impact of "Voice" and Improvement on Experienced Inequity. *Journal of Personality and Social Psychology, 35*, 108–119.

Furnham, A. (1985). Just World Beliefs in an Unjust Society: A Cross-Cultural Comparison. *European Journal of Social Psychology, 15*, 363–366.

Gabrenya, W. K., and Hwang, K. K. (1996). Chinese Social Interaction: Harmony and Hierarchy on the Good Earth. In M. H. Bond (Ed.), *Handbook of Chinese Psychology* (pp. 309–321). London: Oxford University Press.

Gilligan, C. (1982). *In a Different Voice: Psychological Theory and Women's Development*. Cambridge, MA: Harvard University Press.

Graham, J. (1985). The Influence of Culture on Business Negotiations. *Journal of International Business Studies, 16*, 81–96.

Graham, J. L., Mintu, A. T., and Rodgers, W. (1994). Explorations of Negotiation Behaviors in Ten Foreign Cultures Using a Model Developed in the United States. *Management Science, 40*, 72–95.

Gudykunst, W. B., and Bond, M. H. (1997). Intergroup Relations across Cultures. In J. W. Berry, M. H. Segall, and C. Kagitcibasi (Eds.), *Handbook of Cross-Cultural Psychology* (pp. 119–162). Boston: Allyn & Bacon.

Gudykunst, W. G., and Ting-Toomey, S. (1988). Culture and Affective Communication. *American Behavioral Scientist, 31*, 384–400.

Gulliver, P. H. (1979). *Disputes and Negotiations: A Cross-Cultural Perspective*. New York: Academic Press.

Habermas, J. (1971). *Knowledge and Human Interests*. Boston: Beacon Press.

Hagiwara, S. (1992). The Concept of Responsibility and Determinants of Responsibility Judgment in the Japanese Context. *International Journal of Psychology, 27*, 143–156.

Hamilton, V. L., and Sanders, J. (1983). Universals in Judging Wrongdoing: Japanese and Americans Compared. *American Sociological Review, 48*, 199–211.

Hamilton, V. L., and Sanders, J. (1988). Punishment and the Individual in the United States and Japan. *Law and Society Review, 22*, 301–328.

Hamilton, V. L., and Sanders, J. (1992). *Everyday Justice: Responsibility and the Individual in Japan and the United States*. New Haven: Yale University Press.

Hamilton, V. L., and Sanders, J. (1995). Crimes of Obedience and Conformity in Corporate Settings: Surveys of Americans, Russians, and Japanese. *Journal of Social Issues, 51*, 67–88.

Heider, E. R. (1972). Universals in Color Naming and Memory. *Journal of Experimental Psychology, 93*, 10–20.

Heider, F. (1958). *The Psychology of Interpersonal Relations*. New York: Wiley.

Higgins, A., Power, C., and Kohlberg, L. (1984). The Relationship of Moral Atmosphere to Judgments of Responsibility. In W. M. Kurtines and J. L. Gewirtz (Eds.), *Morality, Moral Behavior and Moral Development* (pp. 74–106). New York: Wiley.

Hines, P. M., Garcia-Preto, N., McGoldrick, M., Almeida, R., and Weltman, S. (1992). Intergenerational Relationships across Cultures. *Families in Society, 73*(6), 323–338.

Hofstede, G. (1980). *Culture's Consequences: International Differences in Work-Related Values*. Thousand Oaks, CA: Sage.

Hogan, R., and Emler, N. P. (1981). Retributive Justice. In M. J. Lerner and S. C. Lerner (Eds.), *The Justice Motive in Social Behavior*. New York: Academic Press. 125–143.

Hsu, F. L. K. (1953). *Americans and Chinese: Two Ways of Life*. New York: Abelard–Schuman.

Hsu, F. L. K. (1971). Eros, Affect, and *Pao*. In F. L. K. Hsu (Ed.), *Kinship and Culture* (pp. 439–475). Chicago: Aldine.

Hu, H. C. (1944). The Chinese Concepts of Face. *American Anthropologist, 46*, 45–64.

Hui, C. H., and Triandis, H. C. (1985). Measurement in Cross-Cultural Psychology: A Review and Comparison of Strategies. *Journal of Cross-Cultural Psychology, 16*, 131–152.

Hui, C. H., Triandis, H. C., and Yee, C. (1991). Cultural Differences in Reward Allocation: Is Collectivism the Explanation? *British Journal of Social Psychology, 30*, 145–157.

Ito, K. L. (1982). Illness as Retribution: A Cultural Form of Self Analysis among Urban Hawaiian Women. *Culture, Medicine, and Psychiatry, 6*(4), 385–403.

James, K. (1993). The Social Context of Organizational Justice: Cultural, Intergroup, and Structural Effects on Justice Behaviors and Perceptions. In R. Cropanzano (Ed.), *Justice in the Workplace* (pp. 21–50). Hillsdale, NJ: Erlbaum.

Kakar, S. (1978). *The Inner World: A Psychoanalytic Study of Childhood and Society in India*. London: Oxford University Press.

Kashima, Y., Yamaguchi, S., Kim, U., Choi, S. C., Gelfand, M., and Yuki, M. (1995). Culture, Gender, and Self: A Perspective from Individualism–Collectivism Research. *Journal of Personality and Social Psychology, 69*, 925–937.

Kawashima, T. (1963). Dispute Resolution in Contemporary Japan. In A. T. von Mehren (Ed.), *Law in Japan: The Legal Order in a Changing Society* (pp. 41–72). Cambridge, MA: Harvard University Press.

Kellert, S. R. (1993). Attitudes, Knowledge, and Behavior toward Wildlife among the Industrial Superpowers: United States, Japan, and Germany. *Journal of Social Issues, 49*, 53–70.

Kidder, L. H. (1986, July). *There Is No Word for "Fair"—Notes from Japan.* Paper presented at the International Conference on Social Justice in Human Relations, Leiden University, Netherlands.

Kim, K. I., Park, H. J., and Suzuki, N. (1990). Reward Allocations in the United States, Japan, and Korea: A Comparison of Individualistic and Collectivistic Cultures. *Academy of Management Journal, 33*, 188–198.

King, A. Y. C. (1991). Kuan-hsi and Network Building: A Sociological Interpretation. *Daedalus, 120*, 63–84.

Kitayama, S. (1995). *Remarks on Culture and Emotion.* Workshop on Culture and Conflicts, Graduate School of Business, Standard University.

Kohlberg, L. (1981). *The Philosophy of Moral Development: Moral Stages and the Idea of Justice.* New York: Harper & Row.

Komorita, S. S. (1984). Coalition Bargaining. In L. Berkowitz (Ed.), *Advances in Experimental Social Psychology* (Vol. 18, pp. 185–206). New York: Academic Press.

Komorita, S. S., and Leung, K. (1985). Toward a Synthesis of Power and Justice in Reward Allocation. In E. J. Lawler (Ed.), *Advances in Group Processes* (Vol. 2, pp. 169–196). Greenwich, CT: JAI Press.

Kroeber, A. L., and Kluckhohn, C. (1952). *Culture: A Critical Review of Concepts and Definitions.* Cambridge, MA: Peabody Museum.

Lebra, T. (1984). Nonconfrontational Strategies for Management of Interpersonal Conflicts. In E. S. Krauss, T. P. Rohlen, and P. G. Steinhoff (Eds.), *Conflict in Japan* (pp. 41–60). Honolulu: University of Hawaii Press.

Leong, F. T. L. (1996). *Acculturation and Asian Values in the United States.* Paper presented at the Conference on Global Organizations. Hong Kong University of Science and Technology, Hong Kong.

Leung, K. (1987). Some Determinants of Reactions to Procedural Models for Conflict Resolution: A Cross-National Study. *Journal of Personality and Social Psychology, 53*, 898–908.

Leung, K. (1988). Theoretical Advances in Justice Behavior: Some Cross-Cultural Input. In M. H. Bond (Ed.), *The Cross-Cultural Challenge to Social Psychology* (pp. 218–229). Thousand Oaks, CA: Sage.

Leung, K. (1997). Negotiation and Reward Allocations across Cultures. In P. C. Earley and M. Erez (Eds.), *New Perspectives on International Industrial/Organizational Psychology* (pp. 640–675). San Francisco: Jossey–Bass.

Leung, K., and Bond, M. H. (1984). The Impact of Cultural Collectivism on Reward Allocation. *Journal of Personality and Social Psychology, 47*, 793–804.

Leung, K., and Bond, M. H. (1989). On the Empirical Identification of Dimensions for Cross-Cultural Comparison. *Journal of Cross-Cultural Psychology, 20*, 133–151.

Leung, K., and Fan, R. M. (1996). Adolescent Delinquent Behavior in Chinese Societies. In S. Lau (Ed.), *Growing Up the Chinese Way* (pp. 237–264). Hong Kong: Chinese University Press.

Leung, K., and Iwawaki, S. (1988). Cultural Collectivism and Distributive Behavior: A Cross-National Study. *Journal of Cross-Cultural Psychology, 19*, 35–49.

Leung, K., and Li, W. K. (1990). Psychological Mechanisms of Process Control Effects. *Journal of Applied Psychology, 75*, 613–620.

Leung, K., and Lind, E. A. (1986). Procedure and Culture: Effects of Culture, Gender, and Investigator Status on Procedural Preferences. *Journal of Personality and Social Psychology, 50*, 1134–1140.

Leung, K., and Park, H. J. (1986). Effects of Interactional Goal on Choice of Allocation Rules: A Cross-Cultural Study. *Organizational Behavior and Human Decision Processes, 37*, 111–120.

Leung, K., Au, Y. F., Fernández-Dols, J. M., and Iwawaki, S. (1992). Preferences for Methods of Conflict Processing in Two Collectivist Cultures. *International Journal of Psychology, 27*, 195–209.

Leung, K., Chiu, W. H., and Au, Y. F. (1993). Sympathy and Support for Industrial Actions: A Justice Analysis. *Journal of Applied Psychology, 78*, 781–787.

Leung, K., Smith, P. B., Wang, Z. M., and Sun, H. F. (1996). Job Satisfaction in Joint Venture Hotels in China: An Organizational Justice Analysis. *Journal of International Business Studies, 27*, 947–962.

Leung, K., Morris, M. A., and Su, S. K. (1998). *When Criticism is Not Constructive? The Role of Fairness Perceptions and Dispositional Attributions in Employee Acceptance of Supervisory Feedback.* Manuscript submitted for publication.

Lind, E. A. (1994). Procedural Justice and Culture: Evidence for Ubiquitous Process Concerns. *Zeitschrift für Rechtssoziologie, 15*, 24–36.

Lind, E. A., and Tyler, T. R. (1988). *The Social Psychology of Procedural Justice.* New York: Plenum Press.

Lind, E. A., Tyler, T. R., and Huo, Y. J. (1977). Procedural Context and Culture: Variation in the Antecedents of Procedural Justice Judgments. *Journal of Personality and Social Psychology, 73*, 767–780.

Lind, E. A., Erickson, B. E., Friedland, N., and Dickenberger, M. (1978). Reactions to Procedural Models for Adjudicative Conflict Resolution: A Cross-National Study. *Journal of Conflict Resolution, 2*, 318–341.

Lind, E. A., Huo, Y. J., and Tyler, T. R. (1994). … And Justice for All: Ethnicity, Gender, and Preferences for Dispute Resolution Procedures. *Law and Human Behavior, 18*, 269–290.

Lissak, R. I., and Sheppard, B. H. (1993). Beyond Fairness: The Criterion Problem in Research on Dispute Intervention. *Journal of Applied Social Psychology, 13*, 45–65.

Lukes, S. (1973). *Individualism*. Oxford: Blackwell.

Marin, G. (1985). The Preference for Equity When Judging the Attractiveness and Fairness of an Allocator: The Role of Familiarity and Culture. *Journal of Social Psychology, 125*, 543–549.

Markus, H., and Kitayama, S. (1991). Culture and Self. *Psychological Review, 98*, 224–253.

Marriott, M. (1990). *India through Hindu Categories*. Thousand Oaks, CA: Sage.

Martin, J., Scully, M., and Levitt, B. (1990). Injustice and the Legitimation of Revolution: Damming the Past, Excusing the Present and Neglecting the Future. *Journal of Personality and Social Psychology, 59*, 281–290.

Mendonca, M., and Kanungo, R. N. (1994). Motivation through Effective Reward Management in Developing Countries. In R. N. Kanungo and M. Mendonca (Eds.), *Work Motivation: Models for Developing Countries* (pp. 49–83). Thousand Oaks, CA: Sage.

Messick, D. M., Bloom, S., Boldizar, J. P., and Samuelson, C. D. (1985). Why Are We Fairer Than Others. *Journal of Experimental Social Psychology, 21*, 480–500.

Mikula, G. (1980). Introduction: Main Issues in the Psychological Research on Justice. In G. Mikula (Ed.), *Justice and Social Interaction* (pp. 13–24). Berlin: Springer-Verlag.

Miller, D. T., and Vidmar, N. (1981). The Social Psychology of Punishment Reactions. In M. J. Lerner and S. C. Lerner (Eds.), *The Justice Motive in Social Behavior* (pp. 145–172). New York: Plenum Press.

Miller, J. G. (1984). Culture and the Development of Everyday Social Explanation. *Journal of Personality and Social Psychology, 46*, 961–978.

Miller, J. G. (1994). Cultural Diversity in the Morality of Caring: Individually-Oriented versus Duty-Based Interpersonal Moral Codes. *Cross-Cultural Research, 28*, 3–39.

Miller, J. G., and Bersoff, D. M. (1992). Culture and Moral Judgment: How Are Conflicts between Justice and Friendship Resolved? *Journal of Personality and Social Psychology, 62*, 541–554.

Miller, J. G., and Luthar, S. (1989). Issues of Interpersonal Responsibility and Accountability: A Comparison of Indians' and Americans' Moral Judgments. *Social Cognition, 3*, 237–261.

Miller, J. G., Bersoff, D. M., and Harwood, R. L. (1990). Perceptions of Social Responsibilities in India and in the United States: Moral Imperatives or Personal Decisions? *Journal of Personality and Social Psychology, 58*, 33–47.

Morris, M. W., and Peng, K. (1994). Culture and Cause: American and Chinese Attributions for Social and Physical Events. *Journal of Personality and Social Psychology, 67*, 949–971.

Morris, M. W., and Podolny, J. M. (1996). *National Culture and the Structure of Employee Networks*. Unpublished manuscript, Stanford Graduate School of Business.

Morris, M. W., Leung, K., and Sethi, S. (1998). *Person Perception in the Heat of Conflict: Perceptions of Opponents' Traits and Conflict Resolution Choices in Two Cultures*. Manuscript submitted for publication.

Murphy-Berman, V., Berman, J. J., Singh, P., Pacharui, A., and Kumar, P. (1984). Factors Affecting Allocation to Needy and Meritorious Recipients: A Cross-Cultural Comparison. *Journal of Personality and Social Psychology, 46*, 1267–1272.

Na, E. Y., and Loftus, E. F. (in press). Attitudes towards Law and Prisoners, Conservative Authoritarianism, Attribution, and Internal–External Locus of Control: Korean and American Law Students and Undergraduates. *Journal of Cross-Cultural Psychology, 29*, 595–615.

Nader, L., and Todd, H. F. (1978). *The Disputing Process: Law in Ten Societies*. New York: Columbia University Press.

Nagata, D. K. (1990). The Japanese-American Internment: Perceptions of Moral Community, Fairness, and Redress. *Journal of Social Issues, 46*, 133–146.

Ng, S. H. (1984). Equity and Social Categorization Effects on Intergroup Allocations of Reward. *British Journal of Social Psychology, 23*, 165–172.

Opotow, S. (1990). Moral Exclusion and Injustice: An Introduction. *Journal of Social Issues, 46*, 1–20.

Ouchi, W. G., and Jaeger, A. M. (1978). Type Z Organization: Stability in the Midst of Mobility. *Academy of Management Review, 3*, 305–314.

Parsons, T., and Shils, E. A. (1951). *Toward a General Theory of Action*. Cambridge, MA: Harvard University Press.

Peristiany, J. G. (Ed.). (1965). *Honour and Shame: The Values of Mediterranean Society*. London: Weidenfeld & Nicolson.

Robinson, P. H., and Darley, J. M. (1995). *Justice, Liability, and Blame: Community Views and the Criminal Law*. San Francisco: Westview Press.

Scase, R. (1974). Relative Deprivation: A Comparison of English and Swedish Manual Workers. In D. Wedderburn (Ed.), *Poverty, Inequality, and Class Structure* (pp. 197–216). London: Cambridge University Press.

Selby, H. A. (1975). Semantics and Causality in the Study of Deviance. In M. Sanches and B. Blount (Eds.), *Sociocultural Dimensions of Language Use* (pp. 11–24). New York: Academic Press.

Shaver, K. G. (1985). *The Attribution of Blame*. Berlin: Springer-Verlag.

Shultz, T. R., and Schleider, M. (1983). Toward a Refinement of Attribution Concepts. In J. Jaspars, F. D. Fincham, and M. Hewstone (Eds.), *Attribution Theory and Research: Conceptual, Developmental and Social Dimensions* (pp. 37–62). New York: Academic Press.

Shultz, T. R., Schleider, M., and Altman, I. (1981). Judgments of Causation, Responsibility, and Punishment in Cases of Harm-Doing. *Canadian Journal of Behavioral Science, 13*, 238–253.

Shweder, R. A. (1990). Cultural Psychology—What Is It? In J. W. Stigler, R. A. Shweder, and G. Herdt (Eds.), *Cultural Psychology: Essays on Comparative Human Development* (pp. 1–43). London: Cambridge University Press.

Shweder, R. A., Mahapatra, M., and Miller, J. G. (1987). Cultural and Moral Development in India and the United States. In J. Kagan and S. Lamb (Eds.), *The Emergence of Morality in Young Children* (pp. 1–89). Chicago: University of Chicago Press.

Sidaneous, J. (1991). *Collective Representations and Social Dominance*. Paper presented at the Russell Sage Conference on Collective Representations, Ann Arbor, MI.

Sinha, D. (1987). *Ahimsa as Conflict Resolution Technique and Instrument of Peace: A Psychological Appraisal*. Paper presented at the seminar on Peace and Conflict Resolution in the World Community, India.

Smith, P. B., Peterson, M. F., Leung, K., and Dugan, S. (1998). Individualism–Collectivism, Power Distance, and Handling of Disagreement: A Cross-National Study. *International Journal of Intercultural Relations, 22*, 351–367.

Spohn, C., Gruhl, J., and Welch, S. (1982). The Effect of Race on Sentencing: A Reexamination of an Unsettled Question. *Law and Society Review, 16*, 71–88.

Stevenson, H. W., Lee, S. Y., Chen, C. S., Stigler, J. W., Hsu, C. C., and Kitamura, S. (1990). Contexts of Achievement: A Study of American, Chinese, and Japanese Children. *Monographs of the Society for Research in Child Development, 55*(1–2, Serial No. 221).

Stouffer, S. A., Suchman, E. A., DeVinney, L. C., Star, S. A., and Williams, R. M., Jr. (1949a). *The American Soldier: Adjustment during Army Life* (Vol. I). Princeton, NJ: Princeton University Press.

Stouffer, S. A., Lunsdaine, A. A., Williams, R. M., Smith, M. B., Janis, I. L., Star, S. A., and Cottrell, L. J. (1949b). *The American Soldier: Combat and Its Aftermath* (Vol. II). Princeton, NJ: Princeton University Press.

Sugahara, I., and Huo, Y. J. (1994). Disputes in Japan: A Cross-Cultural Test of the Procedural Justice Model. *Social Justice Research, 7*, 129–144.

Tajfel, H. (1978). *Differentiation between Social Groups: Studies in the Social Psychology of Intergroup Relations*. New York: Academic Press.

Tajfel, H. (1982). Social Psychology of Intergroup Relations. *Annual Review of Psychology, 33*, 1–39.

Tajfel, H., and Turner, J. C. (1979). An Integrative Theory of Intergroup Conflict. In W. G. Austin and S. Worchel (Eds.), *The Social Psychology of Intergroup Relations* (pp. 33–47). Belmont, CA: Wadsworth.

Tanabe, K. (1963). The Process of Litigation: An Experiment with the Adversary System. In A. T. von Mehren (Ed.), *Law in Japan: The Legal Order in a Changing Society* (pp. 73–110). Cambridge, MA: Harvard University Press.

Tannen, D. (1990). *You Just Don't Understand: Women and Men in Conversation*. New York: Morrow.

Tannen, D. (1994). *Talking from 9 to 5*. New York: Morrow.

Thibaut, J., and Walker, L. (1975). *Procedural Justice: A Psychological Analysis*. Hillsdale, NJ: Erlbaum.

Thibaut, J., and Walker, L. (1978). A Theory of Procedure. *California Law Review, 66*, 541–566.

Triandis, H. C. (1978). Some Universals of Social Behavior. *Personality and Social Psychology Bulletin, 4*, 1–16.

Triandis, H. C. (1980). Values, Attitudes, and Interpersonal Behavior. In H. E. Howe and M. M. Page (Eds.), *Nebraska Symposium on Motivation, 1979* (pp. 195–260). Lincoln: University of Nebraska Press.

Triandis, H. C. (1983). Dimensions of Cultural variation as Parameters of Organizational Theories. *International Studies of Management and Organization, 12*, 139–169.

Triandis, H. C. (1989). Self and Social Behavior in Differing Cultural Contexts. *Psychological Review, 96*, 269–289.

Triandis, H. C. (1995). *Individualism and Collectivism*. Boulder, CO: Westview Press.

Triandis, H. C., and Marin, G. (1983). Etic plus Emic versus Pseudoetic: A Test of a Basic Assumption of Contemporary Cross-Cultural Psychology. *Journal of Cross-Cultural Psychology, 14*, 489–500.

Triandis, H. C., McCusker, C., and Hui, C. H. (1990). Multimethod Probes of Individualism and Collectivism. *Journal of Personality and Social Psychology, 59*, 1006–1020.

Tse, D. K., Francis, J., and Walls, J. (1994). Cultural Differences in Conducting Intra- and Inter-Cultural Negotiations: A Sino-Canadian Comparison. *Journal of International Business Studies, 25*, 537–555.

Tyler, T. R. (1990). *Why People Follow the Law: Procedural Justice, Legitimacy, and Compliance*. New Haven, CT: Yale University Press.

Tyler, T. R. (1994). Psychological Models of the Justice Models. *Journal of Personality and Social Psychology, 67*, 850–863.

Tyler, T. R., and Bies, R. J. (1990). Beyond Formal Procedures: The Interpersonal Context of Procedural Justice. In J. S. Carroll (Ed.), *Applied Social Psychology and Organizational Settings* (pp. 77–98). Hillsdale, NJ: Erlbaum.

Tyler, T. R., and Lind, E. A. (1992). A Relational Model of Authority in Groups. In M. Zanna (Ed.), *Advances in Experimental Social Psychology* (pp. 115–191). New York: Academic Press.

Tyler, T. R., and Lind, E. A. (2000). Procedural Justice. In J. Sanders and V. L. Hamilton (Eds.), *Handbook of Justice Research in Law*. New York: Plenum Press.

Tyler, T. R., Lind, E. A., and Huo, Y. J. (1995). *Culture, Ethnicity, and Authority: Social Categorization and Social Orientation Effects on the Psychology of Legitimacy*. Unpublished manuscript, University of California, Berkeley.

Van de Vijver, F., and Leung, K. (1997). *Methods and Data Analysis for Cross-Cultural Research*. Thousand Oaks, CA: Sage.

Wallbott, H. G., and Scherer, K. R. (1986). The Antecedents of Emotional Experiences. In K. S. Scherer, H. G. Wallbott, and A. B. Summerfield (Eds.), *Experiencing Emotion: A Cross-Cultural Study* (pp. 69–83). London: Cambridge University Press.

Walster, E. (1966). Assignment of Responsibility for an Accident. *Journal of Personality and Social Psychology, 3*, 73–79.

Waters, H. (1992). Race, Culture, and Interpersonal Conflict. *International Journal of Intercultural Relations, 16*, 437–454.

Weiner, B., and Kukla, A. (1970). An Attributional Analysis of Achievement Motivation. *Journal of Personality and Social Psychology, 15*, 1–20.

Wheeler, L. Reis, H. T., and Bond, M. H. (1989). Collectivism–Individualism in Everyday Life: The Middle Kingdom and the Melting Pot. *Journal of Personality and Social Psychology, 57*, 79–86.

Whorf, B. (1956). *Language, Thought, and Reality*. Cambridge, MA: MIT Press.

Wrightsman, L. S. (1992). *Assumptions about Human Nature*. Thousand Oaks, CA: Sage.

Yamagishi, T. (1988a). The Provision of a Sanctioning System in the United States and Japan. *Social Psychology Quarterly, 51*, 265–271.

Yamagishi, T. (1988b). Exit from the Group as an Individualistic Solution to the Free Rider Problem in the United States and Japan. *Journal of Experimental Social Psychology, 24*, 530–542.

Yang, L. S. (1957). The Concept of *Pao* as a Basis for Social Relations in China. In J. K. Fairbank (Ed.), *Chinese Thought and Institutions* (pp. 291–309). Chicago: University of Chicago Press.

Index